Russia's Penal Colony in the Far East

Russia's Penal Colony in the Far East

A Translation of Vlas Doroshevich's "Sakhalin"

Translated and annotated by
ANDREW A. GENTES

ANTHEM PRESS
LONDON · NEW YORK · DELHI

Anthem Press
An imprint of Wimbledon Publishing Company
www.anthempress.com

This edition first published in UK and USA 2011
by ANTHEM PRESS
75-76 Blackfriars Road, London SE1 8HA, UK
or PO Box 9779, London SW19 7ZG, UK
and
244 Madison Ave. #116, New York, NY 10016, USA

Copyright © Andrew A. Gentes 2011

The author asserts the moral right to be identified as the author of this work.

All rights reserved. Without limiting the rights under copyright reserved above,
no part of this publication may be reproduced, stored or introduced into
a retrieval system, or transmitted, in any form or by any means
(electronic, mechanical, photocopying, recording or otherwise),
without the prior written permission of both the copyright
owner and the above publisher of this book.

British Library Cataloguing in Publication Data
A catalogue record for this book is available from the British Library.

Library of Congress Cataloging in Publication Data
The Library of Congress has cataloged the hardcover edition as follows:
Doroshevich, V. M. (Vlas Mikhailovich), 1864–1922.
 [Sakhalin. English]
Russia's penal colony in the Far East/a translation of Vlas Doroshevich's "Sakhalin";
translated and annotated by Andrew A. Gentes.
 p. cm.
 ISBN-13: 978-1-84331-309-0 (hardcover : alk. paper)
 ISBN-10: 1-84331-309-X (hardcover : alk. paper) 1. Prisons—Russia
(Federation)—Sakhalin (Sakhalinskaia oblast')—History. 2. Forced labor—Russia
(Federation)—Sakhalin (Sakhalinskaia oblast')—History. 3. Sakhalin
(Sakhalinskaia oblast', Russia)—Description and travel. I. Gentes,
Andrew Armand, 1964- II. Title.
 HV9715.15.Z8S25313 2009
 365'.34—dc22
 2009020259

ISBN-13: 978 0 85728 391 7 (Pbk)
ISBN-10: 0 85728 391 X (Pbk)

This title is also available as an eBook.

*Dedicated to my former students at
Norco State Prison, California,
and to E.M.D.,
my teacher of hard knocks*

TABLE OF CONTENTS

List of Illustrations   xi
Acknowledgements   xiii
Introduction   xv

Part One

1	Portraits of Sakhalin	3
2	First Impressions	10
3	The Infirmary	13
4	The *Katorga* Cemetery	19
5	A Day in Prison	22
6	The Chains Prison	30
7	The Free Prison	34
8	Workshops	35
9	"Aid Station"	37
10	The Women's Prison	39
11	The Isolators	40
12	"Reformed"	42
13	Two Odessans	43
14	The Murderers (A Married Couple)	48
15	Grebeniuk and His Homestead	51
16	Paklin (From My Notebook)	56
17	Settlements (The Exile-Settlers)	61
18	The Female Cohabitant	63
19	The Male Cohabitant	66
20	Those Who've Voluntarily Followed	68

21	The Homeowners	70
22	Reztsov	72
23	Freemen on Sakhalin	74
24	The *Katorga* Theater	85
25	*Katorga* Actors	92
26	The *Brodiaga* Sokolsky	95
27	Crimes in Korsakovsk District	98
28	Departure	100
29	Real *Katorga*	103
30	The Capital of Sakhalin	109
31	Aleksandrovsk Post	113
32	Sentenced to Penal Labor…	118
33	Who Runs *Katorga*?	130
34	Prison Wardens	147
35	The Death Penalty	152
36	Executioners	165
37	Corporal Punishments	174
38	*Katorga*'s Ways	183
39	Matvey's Trouble	196
40	The Indefinitely-Sentenced Probationer Glovatsky	198
41	*Katorga* Types	203
42	Initiation into the Penal Laborers	216
43	Educated Persons in *Katorga*	222
44	Talma on Sakhalin	228
45	The Card Game	232
46	*Katorga*'s Laws	236
47	The Language of *Katorga*	241
48	*Katorga* Songs	247
49	*Katorga* and Religion	253
50	Sectarians on Sakhalin Island	259
51	Criminals and Crimes	266
52	Criminals and Justice (From Observations on Sakhalin)	277
53	*Katorga* Labors of a Konovalova	280

54	The Most Unfortunate of Women	284
55	Voluntary Followers	287
56	Natives of Sakhalin Island	299

Part Two

1	Golden Hand	309
2	Poluliakhov	315
3	A Famous Moscow Murderer	332
4	The Specialist	341
5	Cannibals	349
6	The Penal Laborer Baroness Heimbrück	359
7	Landsberg	366
8	The Grandfather of Russian *Katorga*	373
9	The Apostate	379
10	*Katorga*'s Aristocrat	382
11	The Plebeian	388
12	The Parricide	391
13	Shkandyba	395
14	Hired Murderers	400
15	The Suicide	407
16	The Frenzied	410
17	The Educated Man	413
18	Poet-Murderers (In the Form of a Preface)	416
19	Mentally Ill Criminals	437
20	Sakhalin's Monte Carlo (The *Katorga* Almshouse in Derbinsk Settlement)	444

Notes	455
Bibliography	475
Glossary	479

LIST OF ILLUSTRATIONS

Fig. 1:	V. M. Doroshevich	xv
Fig. 2:	Map of Sakhalin	xxxi
Fig. 3:	Prisoners aboard a steamer	4
Fig. 4:	Sakhalin coastline	5
Fig. 5:	Waterfall in northern Sakhalin	6
Fig. 6:	Giliak children	7
Fig. 7:	Korsakovsk Post	12
Fig. 8:	Shackling a prisoner	33
Fig. 9:	Sick ward in Aleksandrovsk Post	38
Fig. 10:	Group of prisoners	51
Fig. 11:	Bridge in the *taiga*	60
Fig. 12:	A settlement	63
Fig. 13:	Cohabitant	66
Fig. 14:	A shackled prisoner	92
Fig. 15:	Prisoner	94
Fig. 16:	Prisoner	97
Fig. 17:	Prisoner	99
Fig. 18:	Prisoner	102
Fig. 19:	Jetty, Aleksandrovsk Post	104
Fig. 20:	Aleksandrovsk Post	113
Fig. 21:	Aleksandrovsk Prison	126
Fig. 22:	A mining "cut"	130
Fig. 23:	A Sakhalin mine	136
Fig. 24:	A "wheelbarrow man"	146
Fig. 25:	Dué Post	152
Fig. 26:	Logging crew	165
Fig. 27:	Komlev	172
Fig. 28:	Prisoner	183
Fig. 29:	Drs R. A. Pogaevsky, L. V. Poddubsky and N. S. Lobas (left to right)	203
Fig. 30:	Prisoner	305

Fig. 31:	Sofia Bloeffstein	314
Fig. 32:	Poluliakhov	321
Fig. 33:	Ivan Kazeev	329
Fig. 34:	Nikolay Viktorov	340
Fig. 35:	The Onor trail	350
Fig. 36:	Vasilev	355
Fig. 37:	Gubar	357
Fig. 38:	K. Kh. Landsberg and his wife	372
Fig. 39:	M. V. Sokolov	378
Fig. 40:	Pazulsky	387
Fig. 41:	Prisoner	399
Fig. 42:	Prisoner	409
Fig. 43:	Residents of Derbinsk almshouse	448

ACKNOWLEDGEMENTS

This translation has been many years in the making, and so it is with pleasure that I may now thank some of those who helped me along the way. Sharyl Corrado, Steven Marks, Eva-Maria Stolberg, Alan Wood, Vic Mote, Sarah Babcock, Tom Gleason, Patricia Herlihy, Matt Tan, Lyndall Morgan, John McNair, Larry Duffy and many others, including several of my students, expressed their interest and so encouraged me to complete it. I wish to thank Tej P. S. Sood, Paolo Cabrelli, Alex Beecroft and Anthem Press for recognizing its importance and helping me improve it; S. V. Bukchin for his own scholarship, which helped considerably, and for alerting me to problems with new editions of Doroshevich, so that I instead acquired the original 1903 edition; Lonna Thiem for proofreading the typescript on short notice and in record time; and especially Nadia Golenkova who, with occasional emergency calls to her father, helped translate particularly arcane passages. I alone remain responsible for any mistakes.

AAG
Brisbane
March 2009

Fig. 1: V. M. Doroshevich

INTRODUCTION

On First Impressions and Lasting Choices

"The first impression is always the strongest," writes Doroshevich of his initial view of Sakhalin island, and this well-worn adage is also appropriate here, for this translation introduces Doroshevich to English-language readers.[1] Despite having been imperial Russia's most famous and successful journalist; having changed Russian journalism with his feuilleton-style; having been read by every segment of society and lauded by such literati as L. N. Tolstoi, A. P. Chekhov, V. G. Korolenko, A. M. Gor'kii and V. V. Stasov; and despite his Sakhalin feuilletons' renewed popularity in post-Communist Russia, Doroshevich remains largely unknown to non-Russian readers. A pity, for he deserves wider recognition.

Vlas Mikhailovich Doroshevich was born 5 January 1865 (old style) to Aleksandra Ivanovna Sokolova (1836–1914), of the wealthy and titled Denis'ev clan of Riazan´ Province. Details concerning Vlas's father are vague, but he appears to have been an unsuccessful writer who died shortly before his son's birth. Aleksandra was educated at the prestigious Smol´nyi Institute, but was disinherited by her parents for having married beneath her social status. Struggling, and with two other children, Aleksandra took her son when he was six months old to Moscow and gave him to a childless woman and her husband, one Mikhail Doroshevich, with a note pinned to the infant's blouse requesting he be called Blez (Blaise) in honor of the French philosopher Blaise Pascal. The couple took the boy in but Russianized his name as Vlasii, or Vlas, for short. Ten years later, Aleksandra reclaimed her son through a legal procedure that Doroshevich later characterized as depriving him of his personal rights.

Vlas's mother endowed him with what one contemporary observed was her "murderous sarcasm" and—most importantly—an interest in journalism. Aleksandra had begun writing for the *Moscow Times* (*Moskovskie vedomosti*) and other newspapers in 1868, and eventually earned a modest reputation such that her memoirs were serialized in the *Historical News* (*Istoricheskii vestnik*) shortly before her death. Remarkable for being a woman in a business dominated to this day by men, she invested Vlas with a similar sense of ambition; and despite considerable tension between the two, his success as a journalist, fiction-writer and essayist must have exceeded her expectations. Yet it was Vlas's rebelliousness that was sooner evident. When he was sixteen years old he withdrew from *gimnaziia*[2]—where he had stayed long enough to become familiar with Russia's literary canon and conversant in French and English—because, as he later said, he could not stomach the "Pharisees" who ran the place. He soon left home as well. To speak anachronistically, Doroshevich tuned in and dropped out so as "to go to the people"—a notion then still popular among young Russians and one that recalled the "Going to the People" movement of 1874, when thousands of students poured into the countryside in a fit of romantic solidarity with the peasantry, or *narod*, who they imagined embodied Russia's heart and soul. But peasants proved suspicious of these students' well-intentioned efforts to bring them modern education and medicine, and ended up turning many in to the police. In contrast to these utopian proselytizers, young Vlas became a common laborer as well as a dockyard worker. The repeated invocation in his feuilletons of the phrase "to the people" thus serves as a double-edged commentary on both his youthful experiences and the sanctimoniousness of many a social worker. All the same, it is to his credit that his stint as a manual laborer was brief, for he soon found work as a proof-reader and actor. The latter job helps explain his writer's interest in theater and theater criticism,[3] an interest captured in this book in his wonderful description of the Easter spectacular staged by Sakhalin's convicts.

Doroshevich's big break came at the age of seventeen, when his writing attracted the attention of N. I. Pastukhov, publisher and editor of the *Moscow Flyer* (*Moskovskii listok*). From this point on he earned his living as a writer. During the 1880s, as the newspaper business took off thanks to growing literacy and a rapidly expanding urban population, Doroshevich honed his style, creating "a new language"[4] that "changed news coverage in Russia during the two decades before the 1917 revolution."[5] By turns satirical and serious, he was similar to the muck-raking journalists then becoming popular in the United States and who exposed the venality, corruption and absurdities of everyday life. He wrote for other serials, including *Entertainment* (*Razvlechenie*), *Alarm Clock* (*Budil'nik*) and the *Petersburg Gazette* (*Peterburgskaia gazeta*). In autumn 1893, Doroshevich moved to Odessa to become a reporter for the *Odessa Flyer* (*Odesskii listok*), which had been founded in 1880 and enjoyed a circulation of some 10 000 thanks to its coverage of local and national affairs, critical reviews and articles on economics and politics. Multi-ethnic Odessa (as of 1892 one of the empire's largest cities, with a population of 340 000[6]), nestled along the Black Sea and renowned for its criminality, corruption and public scandals, offered considerable material for a writer like Doroshevich. It also boasted a vibrant artistic culture, and so in between his wry accounts of human folly he managed to celebrate its theater and other gems.

In 1897, Doroshevich visited Sakhalin as part of a larger overseas assignment that included the United States (about which he wrote several articles). He had already gained foreign experience thanks to an earlier assignment to Western Europe, and it was there, in France, that Doroshevich had been impressed by the Parisian "feuilletons—brief essays, familiar in tone and catholic in subject."[7] He began imitating this style—a style, it must be said, that was not to every reader's liking. Poet and literary critic Zinaida Hippius sniffed that his appeal to "the unsophisticated provincial" was no substitute for literary talent. Doroshevich's very popularity therefore cast doubt on him. A rival editor called him "the basest of men," and poet Aleksandr Blok labeled him an "untalented scoundrel."[8]

In 1899, he became principal correspondent for *Russia* (*Rossiia*), a short-lived affair that led, in 1902, to *The Russian Word* (*Russkoe slovo*), for which he served as editor until 1918. As Doroshevich's fame grew along with his Sakhalin feuilletons' serialization in *Russian Wealth* (*Russkoe bogatstvo*), *God's World* (*Mir bozhii*) and other journals, and after their publication in book-form, he set about recounting his world travels and, in 1905, began publishing a multi-volume collection of all his feuilletons that was, however, not a commercial success. Doroshevich also made a name for himself as a short-story writer, novelist and commentator on religious topics, penning such titles as *In the Promised Land (Palestine)* (*V zemle obetovanoi [Palestina]*) (1900), *Mu-shan: A Chinese*

Novel (*Mu-sian: Kitaiskii roman*) (1901) and *Legends and Stories of the East* (*Legendy i skazki Vostoka*) (1902). However, his collected Sakhalin feuilletons remained his most popular book.⁹ Doroshevich—perhaps in part because of his outcast status among intellectuals, though despite a love of the high life that included a motorcar, trips to Monte Carlo and failed marriages to two actresses—welcomed both the Romanovs' demise and the Bolsheviks' rise. His last published feuilleton was directed against the royals; and after his death in Petrograd (soon to be renamed Leningrad) on 22 February 1922, he was buried next to the grave of Vera Zasulich, a terrorist and failed assassin of a tsarist official.

Before turning to the feuilletons that make up this book, a few words first need to be said about Sakhalin and the Siberian exile system. The Russian autocracy began forcibly transferring subjects across the Urals in 1590, with 1593 marking Siberian exile's first use as a punitive punishment. From the outset, however, exile's utilitarian function greatly outweighed its penal role, and the small numbers exiled prior to 1649 comprised mostly Polish and Latvian war prisoners assigned to military service. Exiles' numbers greatly increased following the 1649 Law Code (*Ulozhenie*), which largely replaced capital punishment with flogging or mutilation and banishment to Siberia. Those who survived the one-to-two-year march in chains to Eniseisk, Krasnoiarsk, Ilimsk or Okhotsk—with nostrils ripped out, noses, ears or hands cut off, backs shredded by the knout, or faces and bodies branded by an equivalent of the mark of Cain—were generally tasked with becoming state peasants whose job it was to supply both the Cossacks engaged in stringing up, burning, raping or otherwise coercing natives into handing over their fur caches, and the state servitors who processed and delivered these sable, fox and mink furs to the Kremlin. But for all the state's many efforts to transform criminals and other societal deviants into productive peasants, this was largely an exercise in futility. That Russia's leaders never abandoned this effort says much about a political system which, by definition, preyed upon and condemned to premature death a sizeable proportion of subjects. Between 1807 and 1917 over 1 000 000 people were forcibly removed to Siberia, including a quarter-million children. Not all died prematurely or even necessarily suffered worse than if they had never been exiled; and it is important to add that over half were exiled by their own village communes through administrative procedures bypassing the judiciary. Nonetheless, as of the fin-de-siècle, the 300-year-old festering sore of Siberian exile was giving tsarism an anachronistic stench that Doroshevich and others found intolerable.

Apposite the exile system was Russia's penal labor regime known as *katorga*, created in 1696 by Peter the Great for the purpose of building his Black Sea fleet. *Katorga* sites throughout the empire became destinations for thousands of men and women, often sentenced for the most minor infractions. Penal laborers (*katorzhane*) built navy yards along the Baltic Sea, allowed the emperor to realize his so called "window on the West," and constructed fortifications against the Swedes in the north and the Kazakhs in the south. Beginning in 1767, Catherine the Great assigned most penal laborers to the Nerchinsk Mining Command, whose mines and smelteries spider-webbed throughout Transbaikalia and served as *katorga*'s epicenter until the 1880s. Conditions were such that "Nerchinsk *katorga*" became a metonym in contemporary folk songs for torture and suffering.[10]

For several reasons, not least the exhaustion of Transbaikalia's silver and lead deposits, *katorga* became during the 1860s more a boondoggle than a boon for the autocracy, its prisons dilapidated and understaffed and its prisoners escaping in droves to join Siberia's enormous and often violent vagabond (*brodiaga*) population. Similar to the homeless in England and the United States at that time, Siberian *brodiagi* drew the attention of both authorities and social commentators such as S. V. Maksimov and N. M. Iadrintsev, who alternately heroized and denigrated them. Whether discussing those "on the run" (*v begakh*) or already incarcerated, Doroshevich in his Sakhalin feuilletons built upon this *brodiaga*-literature and, as such, contributed to the construction of an "other" against which his readers could favorably compare themselves.

Nerchinsk *katorga*'s decline compelled the government to search for an alternate location for its 14 000 penal laborers, and in 1868, the Imperial Cabinet, Ministry of Internal Affairs and Main Administration of Eastern Siberia initiated plans to transform Sakhalin into a penal colony. Eastern Siberia's willful governor-general N. N. Murav´ev had first asserted Russian sovereignty over the island a decade earlier; but official annexation came only when contesting power Japan agreed to the 1875 St Petersburg Treaty, which opened the way for what some envisaged would be a Russian version of Australia. Plans were launched to assign penal laborers to the navy's mines at Dué Post (Duiskii post) and, once their labor sentences ended, to use them as exile-settlers (*ssyl´no-poselentsy*) to build and populate settlements that would "russify" and secure the island against foreign powers. Petersburg had by 1875 already shipped several hundred male and female convicts to Sakhalin, though because coal deposits were failing to meet expectations only about half were laboring in Dué while the rest were assigned nearby to a so-called "model farm." Convicts and guards alike lived in dreadful conditions, occupying hastily-constructed barracks and subsisting on cabbage and salt pork. The colony stagnated for several years due to administrative problems stemming from the 1881 assassination of Alexander II and frequent leadership changes at the interior ministry. Nonetheless, during the period 1879–83 500 prisoners a year were deported to Sakhalin, and twice this number during 1884–85. As of 1884, when a *katorga* administration was at last officially established on Sakhalin, 4 000 exiles were there; and by 1897, the year Doroshevich visited, some 22 000 were there. On the eve of the 1905 Japanese invasion that put an end to the colony, Sakhalin's non-indigenous population totaled 35 000, the vast majority of which consisted of exiles and their families.[11] Sakhalin was one of the largest penal colonies ever established, and bears similarities to those established in New South Wales, French Guiana, New Caledonia, Bermuda, Malacca, and Mauritius.

Despite Petersburg's dream of reinvigorating *katorga*, Sakhalin replicated the problems at Nerchinsk and other sites to become an even greater burden on the treasury. Island administrators routinely violated convicts' already meager legal protections, constantly flogged them using either the birch rod or *plet´* (similar to the cat-o'-nine-tails), and hanged a number of men. Hangings had subsided by 1897, though Doroshevich did witness several floggings. But it was the entire *mise en scène*, he writes, and "the sight of doleful, forced laborers [which] showed that I had traveled back fifty years, that what surrounded me was nothing less than serfdom." This impression strengthened over time:

> The same forced labor, the same people with no rights whatsoever, the degrading punishments, the same pre-Reform regime,[12] the endless bureaucratic red tape, the same appraisal of a person as "living inventory," the same ordering around of a person "per discretion," the same cohabitating through contract marriages as under peasant law (based not on desire or attraction but according to directive, such is the convict so viewed like a peasant)—all of serfdom's old "accouterments," the compulsory "mincing and shuffling"—it all created an utter illusion of that "bygone era."

As this passage suggests, Sakhalin's military administration and distance from the capital allowed the colony to exist in a time-warp, where terror propped up a system that reduced prisoners to sub-humans.

So why did Doroshevich want to visit this degrading hell-hole? First, his youthful rebelliousness and penchant for rooting out corruption and hypocrisy must be considered as factors. Nearly all prisoners sentenced to Sakhalin were pooled together from throughout the empire and quarantined in Odessa before departing aboard Volunteer Fleet steamers, and so Odessa always had a number of convicts who could be seen marching through the streets in chains. Yet local newspapers ignored them and their fate, probably for fear of invoking government wrath. That is, until the *Odessa Flyer*'s star reporter boarded the prison steamer *Iaroslavl´* so as to report back from the mysterious "dead island" (*mertvyi ostrov*).

"Dead island," evoking as it does Fedor Dostoevskii's *Notes from a Dead House*,[13] points to another reason for Doroshevich's interest in Sakhalin.

Fragments of Dostoevskii's pivotal work had first appeared in the journal *Russian World* (*Russkii mir*) in 1860–61, with the full text serialized by *Time* (*Vremia*) in 1861–62 and a separate volume appearing in 1862. The first major work to even acknowledge Siberian exiles' existence, *Dead House* inaugurated the literary canon on Siberian exile and, as such, is lauded several times by Doroshevich. Its influence is particularly evident in his feuilleton "*Katorga* Theater," an homage to Dostoevskii's marvelous description of the Christmas spectacular his fellow prisoners performed in the Omsk fortress. Doroshevich may also have been influenced by another semi-autobiographical prison memoir, *In the World of the Outcasts: Notes of a Former Penal Laborer*, written by the political exile P. F. Iakubovich using the pseudonym "L. Mel'shin" and first serialized by *Russian Wealth* in 1895–98. Doroshevich was possibly familiar as well with several important studies of Siberian exile published before his journey, and with American explorer George Kennan's articles and two-volume *Siberia and the Exile System*.[14]

But more than any other work, Anton Chekhov's *Sakhalin Island* (*Ostrov Sakhalin*) influenced Doroshevich's decision to visit the island. Chekhov's own visit of 1890 is much more famous, principally because of his greater literary renown, though *Sakhalin Island* (first serialized by *Russian Thought* [*Russkaia mysl'*] in 1893–94) is perhaps his least-known work. Scholars debate the reasons for his journey (which unlike Doroshevich he made overland) largely because Chekhov himself seems not to have been entirely sure why he wanted to go. Letters only reveal that he was dissatisfied with his work to that point and felt a need to contribute something "useful" to society. To make his account more veracious, Chekhov eliminated almost all qualitative language and, through a compensatory and considerable amount of quantifiable data, ended up producing a quirky sociological analysis of the penal colony. He even compiled a census that accounted for nearly every exile and consists of some 10 000 standardized questionnaires now archived in Moscow's Russian State Library.[15] His monograph (which he incidentally unsuccessfully defended as his doctoral dissertation) is by turns informative, interesting and, unfortunately, rather dry. It does contain instances of classic Chekhovian understatement and wit, but only the chapter "Egor's Story" matches his best writing.

Doroshevich admired Chekhov but thought he could write a better book. In a eulogy penned shortly after the writer's death he delivered his opinion of *Sakhalin Island*:

> The abundance of statistical figures, actually hindering the artistry of the Chekhovian *Sakhalin*, resulted, in all probability, from Chekhov's desire to show that he was *serious, serious, serious*. ...

Such a writer as Tolstoi says of the Chekhovian *Sakhalin*:
"*Sakhalin* was poorly written!"
We are obliged to agree with this critique.[16]

This along with other factors pushed him to make his own visit to what had by then become—thanks in no small part to Chekhov—the most diabolical place in the empire. "Sakhalin was an important boundary-line for Doroshevich," writes S. V. Bukchin,[17] for despite having enjoyed considerable success as a journalist, he felt like Chekhov that he was selling his talents too cheaply and wanted to contribute a work of social import. By following Chekhov's lead, Doroshevich was trying to ascend to a higher literary stratum.

A final reason for Doroshevich's decision to visit Sakhalin is indicated by a book he published two years after his Sakhalin feuilletons first appeared in book-form. *How I Got to Sakhalin* is a sardonic account of how, thanks to the embarrassment Chekhov had already caused the government, Doroshevich had to negotiate a series of bureaucratic hurdles to reach his goal. As it was, the Main Prison Administration allowed him to depart aboard the *Iaroslavl'* on 20 February 1897 without formally granting him permission to actually debark on Sakhalin. It also ordered him not to speak to any of the several hundred prisoners aboard the steamer. Captain and crew begrudgingly tolerated their unwanted passenger: "Two powers struggled with each other. On one side there was order and discipline. On the other there was the correspondent, everywhere, like a nasty smell, a bacillus, a scoundrel, a microbe, the penetrating correspondent."[18] Fortunately, during the journey the crew relaxed to the extent that Doroshevich was allowed to read letters the prisoners were sending home from the port of Aden. In his feuilleton "Voluntary Followers" he quotes liberally from these letters, providing a fascinating glimpse into underclass spousal relations at that time. But the ever intrepid reporter was not content with this. Ignoring orders, he snuck around after dark to eavesdrop on and eventually speak with convicts. "The topics for discussion were most various," he writes. "Everything was touched on, as should be when you want to know a person. We talked about prison arrangements, prison news, their former lives, about crimes, God, justice, punishment." His account of these first conversations reveals a paternal compassion not dissimilar from that expressed by Dostoevskii in both *Dead House*'s conclusion and letters he wrote soon after leaving prison.[19] "I often encountered such original, powerful, audacious worldviews," writes Doroshevich, "views such as would not seem could enter a simple person's head especially. You happened to learn about such sufferings, about such misfortunes, as would never present themselves to you."[20]

On 5 April, after a journey that included the Suez Canal, Horn of Africa and brief stops in Ceylon and Japan, the *Iaroslavl'* arrived at Vladivostok. Doroshevich's comment that this was the Orthodox calendar's Palm Saturday suggests the importance he attributed to his mission. Despite the daily *Vladivostok* announcing the arrival of an "outstanding, professional and well-traveled journalist" and kindly adding, "We wish Vlas Doroshevich complete success in his undertaking to study the dead island,"[21] the reporter had little more than faith to get him the rest of the way to Sakhalin. Local officials told him that only the Priamur Territory's governor-general, Sergei Mikhailovich Dukhovskoi,[22] could grant permission to visit the island, and so at first Doroshevich planned to take the train to his headquarters in Khabarovsk, several hundred miles north along the Amur River, to lodge a personal appeal. But one of the river's tributaries flooded and washed out both tracks and telegraph line; and then Doroshevich learned that even if he could reach Khabarovsk, this would not matter, because Dukhovskoi was leaving on a tour of Kamchatka. With Vladivostok's regional governor in Japan for a medical procedure, a now desperate Doroshevich approached the vice-governor, who did little more than grumble and roll a cigarette during the entire interview. Like some *Catch-22* character, Doroshevich found himself reeling at the bureaucratic *formal'nost'* he was encountering: "[T]here opened up a corner of such a bestial, monstrous and improbable 'world of miracles' as should have been impossible for me to fall into. Sakhalin now became not a mania—it became my illness."[23] Indeed, this "illness" led him to concoct the following plan:

> If everything fell through, I would leave my belongings with passport and money at the Volunteer Fleet agency for later pickup. I would then go to the first city I found in Ussuri Territory and, having dressed shabbily, present myself to the police.
> "I'm a *brodiaga*, origins forgotten."
> I'd be arrested, tried and, as was normal, sentenced to a year-and-a-half of *katorga* labor on Sakhalin.[24]

Doroshevich guessed that no more than eight months would pass before officials learned his identity as a *brodiaga-nepomniashchii* (a vagabond who refused to identify himself) was false, by which time he would have gathered all the information he needed to write about Sakhalin *katorga*. Apocryphal or not, this story suggests the lengths he was willing to go to reach what increasingly seemed a forbidden island defended by all the subterfuge bureaucrats could manage, yet made all the more intriguing because of this:

> I repeat: all life, all interests for me merged into one. Sakhalin! Sakhalin hid all of life from me. For me, nothing existed outside of Sakhalin. I'd lie down, get up, talk, eat thinking of only one thing—Sakhalin.[25]

The obsessive or mad can be strangely convincing, and so perhaps this explains how Doroshevich managed to be aboard the *Iaroslavl'* when it left Vladivostok for Korsakovsk Post, the first of two stops on Sakhalin. He had not yet received permission from Dukhovskoi; but with the governor-general incommunicado somewhere in Kamchatka, neither had Doroshevich been explicitly denied permission to travel. No subordinate was willing to risk a decision the governor-general might later reverse, and so Doroshevich, by now incapable of imagining any destination other than Sakhalin, simply wormed his way through the chinks in the armor. He also seems to have found sympathy among officials who believed he would publicize their plights, too. During the brief trip across the Tatar Straits Doroshevich met several officials returning from furlough; none was happy to be returning to Sakhalin, and one told him, "It's an accursed life. Understand that I had a kind of derangement of the mind. Yes! A proper derangement. I'm telling you, I fancied myself a horse. I'd stamp my feet and demand hay."[26]

On 16 April, the *Iaroslavl'* dropped anchor within sight of Korsakovsk's lighthouse, which also happened to be the site of the prison graveyard. The contrast between light and dark figures prominently in Doroshevich's book, and when applying this dichotomy to people he often finds light among the exiles but dark among the officials. At anchor, the steamer was visited by a group of Korsakovsk officials. "It was they who held my 'fate' in their hands," recalls Doroshevich.

> After ten minutes I entered the wardroom. It could have been imagined I'd landed in the wings during a production of *The Inspector*. The actors, seeming to be Gogolesque personages, were drinking vodka, eating appetizers and smacking their lips. There was noisy uproar and laughter.
>
> ...To a man, they were coarse. Marvellously coarse. Coarse not in the raw and exposed sense. But a terrible spiritual coarseness showed through these individuals' features.[27]

However, these Gogolesque personages did not prevent Doroshevich going ashore and visiting Korsakovsk. Indeed, the local warden allowed him to visit the prison whenever he wanted.

Doroshevich's account does not make clear how long he spent in Korskovsk, but his stay was sufficient for him to be feted by local officials and to learn much. While there, he met two of his most valuable informants. One was a young *brodiaga*, identified only as Sokol'skii, who proved a useful source on prison life and who figures in several feuilletons. Doroshevich does not say why Sokol'skii became a *brodiaga-nepomniashchii*, but notes that he had been a Moscow university student in his former life, all of which suggests Sokol'skii was a radical who disguised his identity to avoid harsher punishment. Far less winsome is the administrator Vladimir Nikolaevich Bestuzhev, who filled Doroshevich in on the exile settlements' corrupt management—ironically, mostly at his own hands. "But I didn't trust a single word of Bestuzhev or Sokol'skii without verification," adds Doroshevich, who also accepted unctuous petty officials' dinner invitations to learn more of Korsakovsk's secrets.[28]

It was nevertheless general knowledge that "real *katorga*" was not to be found in Korsakovsk, but rather to the north in Aleksandrovsk Post, headquarters of Vladimir Dmitrievich Merkazin, Sakhalin's military governor. With the *Iaroslavl'* scheduled to depart soon for Aleksandrovsk, Doroshevich managed to send a telegram to Merkazin asking permission for a visit he had already commenced. Like his counterparts on the mainland, Merkazin replied that only Dukhovskoi could grant such permission, but added that Dukhovskoi would be stopping in Korsakovsk during his return from Kamchatka, albeit not until after the *Iaroslavl'* was scheduled to leave. Doroshevich planned to wait for Dukhovskoi, but writes that his presence sent Korsakovsk's commander into a panic for fear that he would be punished for having allowed Doroshevich to land in the first place. And then there was Bestuzhev—"a Hercules, his hauberked chest covered with orders and medals"—who paid Doroshevich a visit the night before the *Iaroslavl'* was to leave and warned him against publishing what he had told him. "The finale of *The Inspector* was warming up," quips Doroshevich, and so, like a holy fool pilgriming to the Promised Land, he boarded the *Iaroslavl'* for Aleksandrovsk.

Upon arriving, he was at first allowed ashore only to tour the dockyards. But it was here, in the rancid eating-houses (*kharchevni*) lining the wharf, that he met seventy-year-old prostitutes, one of the several floggers he describes in "The Executioners," and the feral and punch-drunk Sashka-the-Bear; though at this point the officials there avoided him like the plague. Doroshevich eventually made the acquaintance of Nikolai Stepanovich Lobas, a medical doctor much loved by his convict-patients and who turned out to be, like him, one of the few "humanitarians" on Sakhalin. It was apparently thanks to this doctor's intercession that, when Dukhovskoi finally responded to the attempts to contact him, he granted Doroshevich unfettered access to every individual and institution there. Doroshevich enjoyed a level of access surpassing even that given Chekhov. Even taking into account Lobas's influence, Dukhovskoi's leniency is nevertheless rather difficult to explain. Dukhovskoi's sympathy for the plight of Siberia's exiles is on record, and so perhaps he thought Doroshevich could communicate the truth of the matter to Petersburg in a way that he, in his official capacity, could not. Alternatively, Dukhovskoi may have been trying to use the reporter for his own ends in the back-stabbing world of tsarist politics. Finally, he may not have cared one way or the other, but simply found it easier to let Doroshevich stay where he had already dared go.

Whatever the case, *How I Got to Sakhalin* (which Doroshevich called a "preface" to his Sakhalin feuilletons) not only explains his efforts to get there, but further suggests his motivations for going in the first place. In a somewhat rhapsodic conclusion, he writes:

> I've considered this necessary to write so as to tell the public what for our brother journalist, deprived of all rights, happens to constitute the truth. I dedicate this preface to my brothers, the journalists, not of course as a boast:
> "Look, I've done well! I was opposed, but I succeeded!"
> I've written this simply because the story of a journalist's mishaps is more familiar and understandable to them than other things. I've written this in order to tell them:
> "Friends! Don't complain about opposition! Be grateful for it! Often, when we are opposed, we become only stronger because of this. This opposition is often only a token of our independence."
> In concluding this preface, I consider it necessary to express a deep recognition for all who "opposed" my going to Sakhalin. Thanks only to this did I avoid a great misfortune—seeing through someone else's eyes.
> I was not shown—I saw.
> I was not shown what was convenient. But I saw what needed to be seen. And thanks only to this was I able to write a book in which there were a thousand defects but all told a singular virtue: The truth.
> This I can surely say.[29]

Sakhalin's officials unswervingly followed Dukhovskoi's order, striving to outdo each other by hosting the (now even more) "obviously important journalist." Doroshevich learned so much from these contacts that his reportage on former prison warden A. S. Fel'dman earned him a lawsuit for slander, though Fel'dman's charges were eventually dismissed. In addition to officials, the murderers Poluliakhov and Pazul'skii, like Sokol'skii earlier, proved to be valuable contacts and informants, introducing Doroshevich to numerous prisoners and guaranteeing his protection. Pazul'skii even wrote a letter of recommendation so that he could safely visit prisons in the settlements of Rykovsk and Onor. Doroshevich confesses that he gave away a lot of money in return for information, but avoided "tossing it around… so as not to lose *katorga*'s respect."[30] Journalistic ethics were certainly not what they are supposed to be today, but like any good reporter Doroshevich tried to corroborate what he was told.

Within weeks after arriving on the island Doroshevich began telegraphing his feuilletons to the *Odessa Flyer*, which ran them on a weekly basis between August 1897 and March 1898, after which they appeared less frequently. Doroshevich later signed a contract with publisher A. V. Amfiteatrov to publish his Sakhalin feuilletons in *Russia* beginning 6 July 1899. When *Russia* folded after three years, *The Russian Word* acquired publishing rights. Aside from serialization, the collected feuilletons first appeared in a two-volume Polish translation published in Warsaw in 1901. The first Russian edition came out in 1903 under two imprints: I. D. Shchukin and I. D. Sytin. By 1907 a fourth edition had come out. For obvious reasons the book was not published in the Soviet Union, though an émigré publication was produced in Paris in 1935. The several editions published since the Soviet Union's collapse attest to Doroshevich's enduring readability, though it should be noted that Zakharov's 2001 edition is bowdlerized. The translation here is from I. D. Sytin's 1903 edition. Doroshevich continued to write about Sakhalin and penal labor. For example, he contributed the introduction to a Russian-language study of French penal labor, and wrote a series on Sakhalin's small number of political exiles that appeared in *The Russian Word* in 1906.

Russian-language scholars have naturally drawn comparisons between Doroshevich's and Chekhov's accounts, though in the end the choice as to which is superior comes down to personal taste. However, it must be said that Chekhov translator Brian Reeve's comment that Doroshevich's book lacks substance and consists mostly of "pages... devoted to sensational interviews, conducted in racy slang, with the most infamous and colourful of the Sakhalin prisoners"[31] is both prudish and misleading. Whereas the feuilletons do contain many interviews and considerable slang, both reflect Doroshevich's effort to let Sakhalin's outcasts tell their stories in their own words. By comparison, Chekhov, through his reliance on statistics, does what so many social scientists are prone to do: reduce human beings to numbers. Perhaps just such a concern led Doroshevich to give flesh and blood to those who were at best abstractions for many readers. Though sensationalized by the genre of bandit stories, vagabonds and criminals were disdained as untouchables by a readership that hoped itself immune to their depredations. Doroshevich's lengthy verbatim renderings of exiles' personal stories therefore represent a Dostoevskian effort to humanize the stigmatized and to suggest that crime has social origins. Despite his frequent religious invocations, Doroshevich was aware that Sakhalin's exiles were not reducible to being simply evil men and women, but were men and women, pure and simple, who in many cases and for various reasons had committed extraordinarily evil crimes. He uses their personal histories and origins to query the sources of these crimes and arrives at both biological and cultural explanations—in other words, explanations not dissimilar from those of today's criminologists.

Doroshevich borrowed many of his analytical categories from his contemporary, Cesare Lombroso, the Italian criminologist who believed that physiognomy indicated criminal proclivity and that such proclivity was genetically transmitted. Lombroso's *Criminal Man* (*L'uomo delinquente*) was internationally popular and profoundly influential, going through five heavily revised editions between 1876 and 1897. Like Lombroso, Doroshevich discusses "criminals and religion," "tattoos," "jargon," "suicide among criminals," and so on. The inclusion in his book of head shots of so-called "prisoner types" (*arestantskie tipy*), some of which are reproduced here, replicated those used by Lombroso to typify putative criminal physiognomies. Despite such mimicry, Doroshevich abjured the statistical methodology Lombroso and other criminologists used.

Doroshevich's Sakhalin feuilletons do not constitute a chronological or even consistent narrative whole; rather, his book is like a shoebox containing a random number of hand-painted postcards. Five recurrent themes nevertheless give the collection structural integrity; but before turning to these it is essential to understand how Doroshevich uses the word *katorga*. As noted above, *katorga* was the penal labor regime established by Peter the Great. Apropos this penologico-administrative apparatus, Doroshevich is therefore able to speak of "Nerchinsk *katorga*," "Sakhalin *katorga*" and other adjectivized forms of penal labor. *Katorga* also means "penal labor" in the abstract, that is, non-institutional, sense of the word, and so Doroshevich may use "*katorga* labor" so as to make a distinction with "free labor." Finally, Doroshevich frequently uses *katorga* as a collective noun signifying prison society: "*katorga* believes this," "*katorga* does that." He sometimes rarefies it, so as to distinguish the caste of hardened professional criminals from the mass of "first-timers" and "short-termers" disdained as "the herd" (*shpanka*).

Katorga—its composition, history, stratification, mores, traditions, behavior, etc.—is therefore the first of the book's five themes. Doroshevich's description of *katorga*, from its foundation myths to its song cycles and modes of dress, reflects Russian ethnographers' efforts to understand that great "other," the *narod*, through taxonomy. Historian Cathy Frierson has shown how writers alternately romanticized peasants as noble savages and demonized them as feral beasts.[32] Doroshevich tends to assign similar roles to criminals and *brodiagi*, though he plays with these and other tropes, often ironically. For example, he describes the *brodiaga* Sokol'skii as a pure-hearted soul whose appearance on Sakhalin seems a mistake; but refers to the mass-murderer Poluliakhov as a "natural killer." But the details he subsequently provides about both belie these initial descriptions. Despite sincere efforts to understand and even sympathize with his subjects, Doroshevich could not escape being an outsider, however, even when interviewing such educated offenders as Baroness

Heimbrück or Karl Landsberg. It should therefore be emphasized that his are artistic portraits rather than factually accurate snapshots of these persons.

A second theme running through the feuilletons is autobiographical. Much more than does Chekhov, Doroshevich places himself at the center of his reportage, in a style that renders him a precursor of John Reed or even Hunter S. Thompson.[33] He frequently shares with the reader his impressions of the island and its inhabitants, and builds upon these impressions to produce (in a value-neutral sense) a *sensationalistic* account. His frequent allusions to himself and transcriptions of his own words suggest a narcissistic tendency, particularly when Doroshevich takes ample credit for coining the phrase "*Katorga* begins when it ends." That said, one cannot help but sympathize with most of his observations and feelings.

Another theme is the island itself. Doroshevich's first feuilleton, which I have re-titled "Portraits of Sakhalin,"[34] is an impressionistic account of a quasi-imaginary journey down the length of the island, which he likens to an enormous mottled monster. Throughout the feuilletons the island behaves as a character in its own right, an anthropomorphized demon who, through its control of climate and geography, visits upon inhabitants yet another degree of suffering.

Crime and the supposed "criminal nature" figure as the fourth theme. Book Two especially includes extended descriptions of the crimes that precipitated the deportations of many of Doroshevich's interviewees. Some of Doroshevich's best prose is here, particularly his bone-chilling account of the Poluliakhov killings and his memorializing of "Poet-Murderers." Doroshevich was an established crime reporter before going to Sakhalin, and so his stories of exiled murderers reflect the titillating style of tsarist Russia's boulevard press. He also gives broad license to his fictional skills here—fictionalization having generally characterized pre-revolutionary journalism. These feuilletons are therefore not the kind of *factual* accounts we expect from today's journalists. To again contrast Chekhov's account of Sakhalin: Doroshevich wanted to provide readers a *visceral* understanding and, in so doing, communicate via what were at times obvious fictional devices a knowledge that was no less truthful for its lack of empirical evidence.

This visceral understanding introduces the book's fifth and perhaps major theme, which is that despite their often inhuman (or all too-human, as Nietzsche would have put it) behavior, Sakhalin's convicts are nevertheless human beings, and that this status carries with it certain inalienable rights. At that time, this was not fully appreciated in Russia, where religion and class reinforced an elitist view that equated criminality with a venality supposedly inherent in the underclass. Doroshevich therefore goes to what modern readers may find are excessive lengths to humanize his exiles. There is no small degree of sentimentality here. Yet, by establishing and reaffirming the basic humanity of those exiled to Sakhalin, he is rejecting both the arbitrary and the systematic violation of human rights that regularly took place throughout the empire. In this regard Doroshevich was not only inspired by, but also perpetuated, a literary campaign to which Lev Tolstoi (like Dostoevskii and Chekhov earlier) contributed with his 1899 novel *Resurrection*, his searing indictment of the penal justice system. Soon after the Sakhalin feuilletons began appearing, A. P. Salomon, a former director of the Main Prison Administration, wrote a similarly scathing exposé of the penal colony for *Prison News* (*Tiuremnyi vestnik*),[35] and in 1903, the jurist N. Ia. Novombergskii published his critical history of Sakhalin.[36] Due in part to these and other publications, the government scaled back its use of exile for a time, but it never voluntarily closed the Sakhalin colony, and, following the 1905 revolution, it increased the numbers it exiled to Siberia generally.

Whether Doroshevich and others would have made a greater impact on Russia's penal development if tsarism had not collapsed is impossible to say, but with so many citizens directly or indirectly affected by tsarist penality, the Sakhalin penal colony clearly helped to discredit the old regime. The popularity of Doroshevich's Sakhalin feuilletons may even have furthered the public's renunciation of the Romanovs. But events after 1917 show that "humanitarianism"—a dirty word for Sakhalin's officials, as Doroshevich repeatedly points out—unfortunately found even less sympathy among the new ruling elite.

Note on the Translation

Doroshevich loved the Russian language, especially the many ways it was variously spoken in late imperial Russia. Like Mark Twain with American English, he recreated regional dialects and colloquialisms, with occasionally baffling results for the reader. But then, ambiguity was part of his style. Given that imperial Russia was a huge territory with many distinct regional vernaculars, I have tried to give individual voices to his characters by expropriating words and pronunciations from different parts of the Anglophone world, though principally the United States, Great Britain and Australia. Both Doroshevich and his characters rely heavily on colloquialisms to communicate. Some of these colloquialisms would make no sense to Anglophone readers, and so I have used rough English-language equivalents for these while retaining verbatim translations of those which, though unfamiliar, can nevertheless be understood. Doroshevich's staccato descriptions of people, places and things are sometimes ambiguous, or at least impressionistic. Many descriptions amount to a single word in Russian. For the

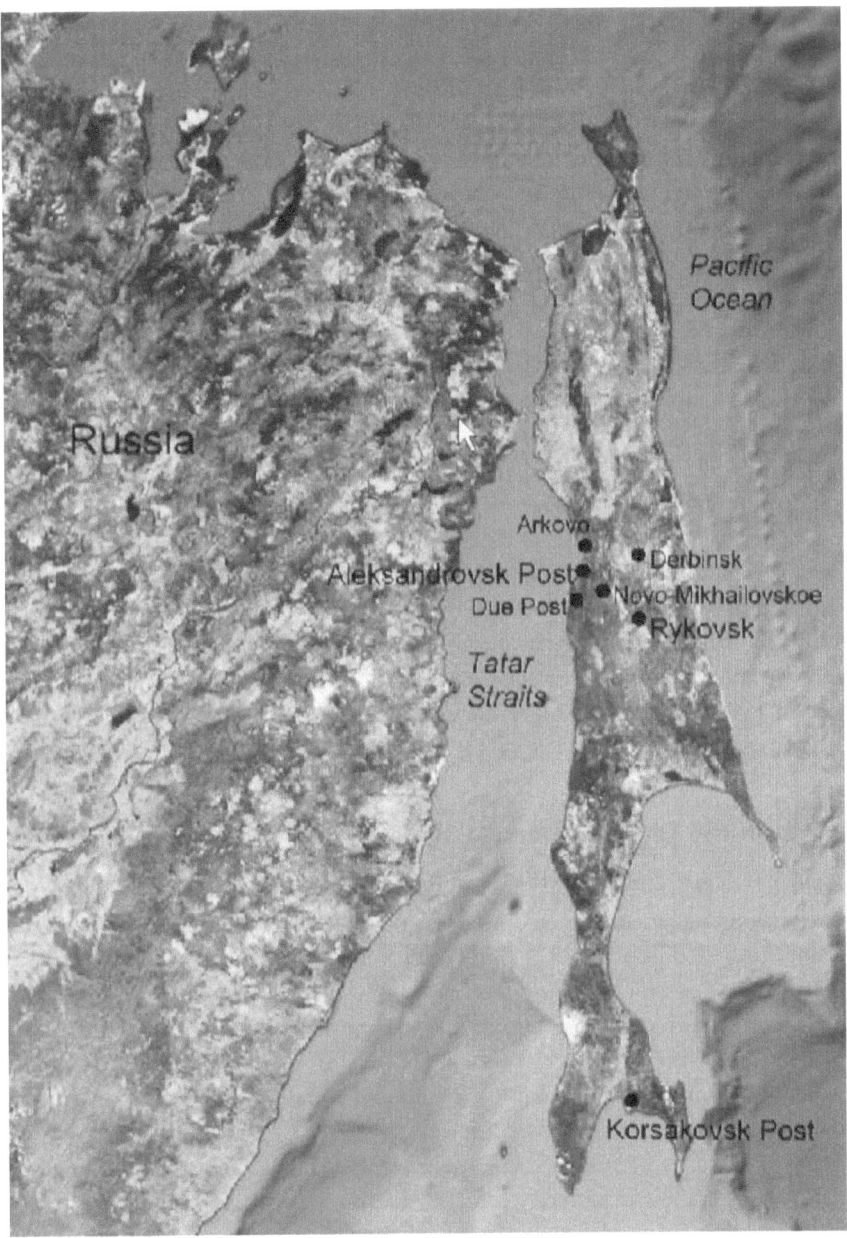

Fig. 2: Map of Sakhalin

sake of comprehensibility, I usually tried to disambiguate such passages while attempting to reproduce the spirit of the original. In a few cases where there seemed no satisfactory English equivalent, I have retained Russian words with which readers may not be familiar and which can be found in the glossary. I will use this opportunity to warn readers ahead of time about my reliance on the convict slang word *fart*. An abbreviation of *fartuna*, which means "luck" and was derived from the English "fortune," *fart* was widely used by exiles both on Sakhalin and in Siberia. The trouble I had as a translator was that Doroshevich goes into detail about this word, explaining that its verbal form (to *fart*) means "to prostitute (oneself)" and that its adverbial form (*fartovyi*) modifies people and things. In the end, I decided to forego trying to find an English substitute and to accept the consequences of using the word strictly transliterated.

Because the feuilletons originated as newspaper dispatches, they lack the polish normally associated with published writing. Here and there it was necessary to correct obvious mistakes.

Finally, I have used a modified version of the Library of Congress's transliteration system for the body of the text, but conformed strictly to the LOC in the introduction, footnotes (including those by Doroshevich) and bibliography. Occasional inconsistencies ("Nikolay," "Nikolai") will, I hope, not prove confusing. All dates correspond to the Julian calendar, in use in Russia until 1918.

Note on the Illustrations

With the exception of Doroshevich's portrait and the map of Sakhalin, the illustrations included here come from those that originally appeared in the 1903 Sytin edition (which had something of a subtitle: "with many illustrations"). Some were photographs of the island and its buildings; but most were apparently the photographs of prisoners known to have been taken by the administration for identification purposes—"mug shots," in other words. A Lombrosian notion of criminal taxonomy clearly informed the decision to illustrate the Sytin edition using these mug shots, for most (despite being of separate individuals) were simply labeled "prisoner types" (*arestantskie tipy*). Only in a few instances were individuals identified by name.

Inclusion in this translation of some of these mug shots does not in any way condone Lombrosianism. On the contrary, the intent is to give a human face to the individuals described within its pages, even if separate faces and individuals cannot be definitively matched.

Russia's Penal Colony in the Far East

Part One

1
PORTRAITS OF SAKHALIN

It was 16 April. The piercing northwest wind was cold and gusty as the steamer lolled from side to side. I stood on the top deck and watched as the bleak, inhospitable rocky shoreline, still covered in snow, came into view. This first impression was gloomy, heavy and oppressive. The island stretched out like some kind of monster, dead and awaiting disposal, with ridges covering its back.

"This is where the *Kostroma* went down," the captain told me.

I descended to the lower deck. Prisoners' faces crowded the deck's portholes as they gazed intently at the shoreline of the island where their lives would end. They gloomily muttered: "Sa*kal*in!"

"It's still winter!"

"Let me see!"

"There's nothing to see. Everything's covered in snow."

The steamer began to rock more violently. We were entering the La Perouse Straits.[1] To the left was the Krilovsky lighthouse; to the right the roiling and frothing boulders of the submerged "Calamity Rock." Straight ahead and drawing near, an ice floe. More ice floes obscured the horizon.

Here indeed was some bitter mockery: to transport people nearly around the globe, to show them a small corner of earthly paradise (magnificent blooming Ceylon), to give them "but a glance" of Singapore, that luxurious, divine, fantastic blooming garden a degree-and-a-half from the equator, to allow—near the entrance to Nagasaki—just a glimpse of Japan's magical and picturesque coast (a coastline you cannot tear your eyes away from), only to deliver them, after all this, to bleak rocky shores still covered in snow as of mid-April, to this land of blizzards, storms, fogs and ice floes—and then to say: "Thrive!"

Sakhalin…

"Water all around, but in the middle—misfortune! Sea all around, but in the middle—woe!" So the penal laborers name it.

"Island of despair. Island without freedom. A dead island!"[2] So it is called by Sakhalin officials.

Fig. 3: Prisoners aboard a steamer

The island is a prison.

If you look at a map of Asia you'll see in the upper right, stretching lengthwise along the coast, something truly resembling a monster that has opened its mouth and appears ready to gobble up Matsmai,[3] lying opposite. Its steep coal-lined cliffs, their zigzagged and broken lines revealing layers of shale, proclaim that some great event has taken place here. The monster's back is ribbed, mottled by gigantic breakers running from northeast to southwest. Not for nothing do Sakhalin's mountains actually resemble enormous, frozen breakers; and the valleys—or "notches" as they say in Siberia—seem like abysses that open between waves during a hurricane. But the hurricane is over. The monster has calmed and shudders here and there only occasionally.

This is an inhospitable island separated from the mainland by the Tatar Straits, the most tempestuous, violent, capricious and spiteful straits in the world. During a winter blizzard it is pitch dark in these straits; and in summer the storms give way to fog so thick a steamer's top-mast can hardly be seen amid the white shroud. A navigator has to travel through these straits fully dressed, snatching just fifteen minutes of sleep at a time, for calm waters can turn into violent storms in a matter of five or ten minutes. At first it's completely calm. Suddenly the rigging begins to whistle and you raise the flags, cut the anchor, and head out to sea if you don't want to be smashed to pieces on the rocks.

PORTRAITS OF SAKHALIN

Fig. 4: Sakhalin coastline

The sea here is a traitor. Yet the coast is not a sailor's friend but his enemy. One must fear both land and sea here, for Sakhalin repels and its severe, steep, rocky shores are a foil. Along the entire western shore there isn't a single road in which to harbor: the bottom is smooth and flat flagstone to which no anchor will hold you during a storm. Many steamers are buried in these straits!

Sakhalin is a severe and cold island. Since time immemorial frigid northern currents have forced their way through the Tatar Straits to lap its rocky coast. Winter here is cruel and fierce: a blizzard lasts weeks, churns up huge waterspouts, buries a house up to its roof. Here, the joyless spring resembles autumn; summer is short, cold and foggy; only the autumn is familiar. On 20 May I arrived in Onor, a distant settlement in the very center of the island, and on the 21st I awakened to a bright, fresh, beautiful winter's morning. Snow had fallen that night and a shroud 14 inches deep covered everything—roofs and ground, prison and settlement. The snow stuck around for two days, finally melting on 23 May. And that's what they call the "weather" on Sakhalin.

The monster's sinuous back is covered by thick coniferous taiga, like quills standing on end. The coast's tall, perpendicular, unscalable cliffs are zigzagged by yellow layers of clay, either smoke-colored (from bituminous shale) or white (from sandstone). In places there is the rust of iron ore. Beyond the cliffs is the taiga. Spruce and pine, exposed and completely lacking branches on their windward sides, sprout on one side only. The pine trees have lost their tops to the wind like smoke from a steamer's funnel, and like

Fig. 5: Waterfall in northern Sakhalin

smoke these great trees, missing arms, flee this terrible shore, this severe, cold, brutal sea and wind.

You clamber into the depths. There is a deathly silence. Only the crunching of wind-fallen branches underfoot. Stop, and there's no sound. No bird sings, not a peep... One is awestruck, as if in an empty church. The silence of the Sakhalin taiga—it is the stillness of a desolate abandoned cathedral beneath whose arches no whispered prayers are heard.

Deeper into this land of eternal silence. Here, there's no light; darkness surrounds you. It's as if a huge baobab were standing atop a dozen tree trunks: winds have pushed the pine-tops together, pinned boughs and needles to each other to form a single enormous carapace, a sturdy roof on which it seems you could walk! It is oppressive here. It is difficult here. Difficult even for the trees. Here, even these giants are ill, their trunks distorted by enormous diseased excrescences.

This is your picture of nature in northern Sakhalin.

Twenty-seven years ago there roamed here both bears and Giliaks—pathetic, unfortunate savages whose intelligence and morals were little better than those of their taiga compatriots. Not without reason do Giliaks believe the bear possesses the same spirit as the Giliak, that following death the bear's spirit goes to its "master," the god of the taiga, to complain to him about the

Fig. 6: Giliak children

Giliaks, but that the master judges both equally. They even believe the bear has "married a Giliak"! For these pathetic savages, this signifies the spiritual equality between them and bears. Bears and Giliaks are now scattered thinly across this land.

Sakhalin's typical settlement is a pitiful sight. Houses built "per-the-law" so as to earn the right to join the peasantry[4] are abandoned, ruined or half-destroyed. No sound here as well. Just eternal silence.

"Anyone living here?" Two or three houses turn out to be inhabited, the rest abandoned. "Well, how's life?"

"What a life! We suffer."

"What do you plant, what do you sow?"

"What grows here! A single potato, and barely just that."

They live in silence, each morose and shut up within himself, miserably hanging on until his term of settlement ends and he can join the peasantry and leave for the mainland, far, far from this gloomy land.

Neighing and crashing into each other, our trio of small, sturdy, swift Sakhalin horses leads us from hill to hill, dale to dale south through the island. The coachman shows you "this is where they killed Kazeev (one of the Artsimoviches' murderers[5])... Here, during a blizzard, the snow buried a woman and her child... I brought the doctor here the other day—they took an exile-settler down from a tree... Hanged himself... Exile-settler Lavrov was murdered here last year..."

A typical Sakhalin travel route.

The natural picture changes. The sad, northern Sakhalin pine and spruce give way to cheerful, cordial larches, themselves soon surpassed by soft, delicate, aromatic branches of conifer. Birch groves whiten some areas. The birch have yet to blossom, but after the pine forest's gloomy dark-green, the dressing of their white trunks appears so cheerful, elegant and clean. A willow, lithe and weeping, leans over a brook as if peering into its swift currents. Snow still lies in the gullies; but on hillocks warmed by sunlight the burdock is already growing luxuriantly.

The mountains become steeper, the notches broader. There are no more gorges, no gigantic clefts between the mountains but rather spacious plains. The settlements you encounter gradually improve. Trading villages are the larger, and to the question "How's life?" comes the answer: "We get by somehow or other. Only, summers are pretty short." Along the way there are oxen harnessed to a plow. In every settlement you find two, three or more prosperous householders. This is Tymovsk District, in central Sakhalin.

Further on begins the tundra or "trunda," as Sakhalinites call it. The wheels sink and barely turn in the peaty mass. The coachman dismounts and walks alongside so the horses can pull more easily. We're hardly moving; steam pours off the horses.

There's the smell of heather. An asphyxiating, heavy fragrance like the smell of cypress, it gives me a headache. The whole tundra is absolutely covered by its red bushes. Like clotted blood.

The tundra and the taiga. And still not a sound. Only a woodpecker pecks and a cuckoo coos in the distance.

Melancholy—aching, pinching, piercing the soul. Something sad hovers around me. You cannot believe that somewhere in the world there is an Italy, blue sky, warm sun, that there are songs and laughter in the world... Everything ever seen up to now seems so distant, as if on some other planet, as if it were dreamt, unreal, unfeasible.

An ocean of tundra and taiga. And in this ocean tiny little islands, pieces of solid land. Settlements were stuck on these little islands. People tried to live, to struggle, were unable to, and left. Doleful abandoned settlements from here to Onor; and further on nothing but swamps and bogs where dogsleds are needed to travel in winter and you can't get through in summer...

In this region Korsakovsk District begins, in southern Sakhalin. There's a variety of deciduous flora; the climate is comparatively mild. Living and breathing are easier here. If you look at a detailed map, all southern Sakhalin is covered in black dots—these are all settlements. You can at least stand on solid ground here. Labor is difficult but gives some reward.

Here, it is already early spring. Handsome swans stretch in a line flying north. A white border of fish eggs runs like a milky river along the coast up to a mile out to sea, mixing with the seaweed and spawning herring. Birds whistle and call one another in the taiga.

Here, at last, is life, sun and brightness.

These are your pictures of Sakhalin.

Here, the air is filled with heavy sighs. Here, a birdcall at night sounds like a moan. Here, much blood has been shed by wretches who kill each other over a penny. Here, every spot holds terrible memories. Here, everyone exhales suffering. Here, there's been much crime and trouble. Here, you have to fight for everything. Sakhalin's soil yields nothing without sweat and tears being poured into it.

Many riches hide in Sakhalin's depths. Potent strata of coal; there's oil, probably iron. It's even said there's gold. But Sakhalin jealously guards its riches, strongly grips and holds them. It blocks your way through the impenetrable taiga, buries you in its tundra bogs. A man has to make his way here with iron and fire and then, spice the soil with blood and tears and devote half his life to it so the other half might be somewhat tolerable.

This is what this island-prison is like. Nature created it in a moment of spite when what was wanted here was a prison and nothing else. It would be difficult to build better prison walls than the Tatar and La Perouse straits. True, prisoners escape across both. But is there really a prison wall in the world that cannot be over-stepped by a person with a strong enough will?

Yet nature was too cruel when it built this island prison. In clear weather walk along the repellent island's coast and see clearly across the straits the opposite shore that teases and beckons, its blue lines stretching in the distance. Realize that it's so close yet so unattainable. What torment the very weather creates!

2

FIRST IMPRESSIONS

A first impression is always the strongest, and so I'll never forget the moment when, early in the morning and unsteady from the steamer's side-to-side rocking, I walked along the jetty at Korsakovsk Post. People were schooling along the shoreline: several more steps and I would be diving into that sea, so terrifying, yet which I so excruciatingly wanted to know.

A sea of what?

From the three and a half months I spent among penal conditions two impressions are strangely impossible to forget. Two impressions that weighed down, oppressed and sat like lead on my soul. They weigh down and oppress it still.

One was the journey itself to Sakhalin. I've been unable to shut out this comparison: our steamer delivering penal laborers from Odessa seemed a huge scow, like those typically used by coastal cities to ferry garbage out to sea. And Sakhalin's posts and settlements, appearing gray along the shoreline, seemed nothing more than colossal garbage heaps. Knowing there was in the hold beneath your feet a humanity that, in the end, will rot just like you yet nonetheless remain as this "garbage," was heavy on the soul.

The second impression was simply that of Sakhalin. From my very first steps the sight of doleful forced laborers showed I had traveled back fifty years, that what surrounded me was nothing less than serfdom. As I came to know Sakhalin and as this impression lodged ever more deeply in my soul, this initial comparison became all the more valid. The same forced labor, the same people with no rights whatsoever, the degrading punishments, the same pre-Reform regime,[1] the endless bureaucratic red tape, the same appraisal of a person as "living inventory," the same ordering around of a person "per discretion," the same cohabitating through contract marriages as under peasant law (based not on desire or attraction but according to directive, such is the convict so viewed like a peasant)—all of serfdom's old "accouterments," the compulsory "mincing and shuffling"—it all created an utter illusion of that "bygone era."

And how difficult, so very difficult, it was to breathe, may you know!

Wish fulfilled: after proceeding along the jetty I found myself among a crowd of penal laborers working the shoreline. Seventy convicts dressed in prison uniforms were lowering a barge into the sea to unload a steamer. They were singing "Dubinushka,"[2] and as they sang the barge, seemingly reluctantly, began creeping away from shore. Alongside them on another barge stood the choir's leader, a disheveled, tousled, pathetic, wretched muzhik in a ragged prisoner's jacket singing "Dubinushka" in a broken, ringing tenor that betrayed his requisite versatility and cynical, preternatural resourcefulness. His cynicism had somehow not reached "the limit" but attained a sort of virtuosity.

All this clamor, of course, was meant to cause laughter. But no one was smiling. They listened indifferently, or rather, listened not at all, just sang the refrain by shouting "oooh" somewhat lazily, reluctantly, as if this, too, were a compulsory labor.

I later recovered; but this first impression of forced labor was a heavy and oppressive one.

Others were hauling a fishing net together. They pulled heavily, slowly, reluctantly; a mass of fish was writhing, jumping and quivering in the net. What wasn't there! Colossal gobies, which they don't eat here; *glosy*,[3] oblong with white bellies, which they also don't eat here; lampreys, wriggling like snakes, which they especially don't eat; and small good-for-nothing minnows, which they do eat here. The convicts all stood around the net, then two or three grabbed some of the better fish from out of the bunch with such skill it was like they were tossing stones.

Exile-settlers were greeting each other and mechanically doffing their caps along the entire seashore road from the jetty to the post. I waved my arm in answer to their greetings, and sincerely acknowledged as well those audacious fellows who didn't vouchsafe me the honor of a convict salute. Exile-settlers were wandering about like sleepy houseflies, without any apparent destination or purpose. "They say another steamer's arrived. More of the same." If there was a kind of gravity on the faces of the laborers, then here among the exile-settlers was written a terrible, oppressive, interminable boredom. A melancholy. Such is the condition when a man absolutely does not know what to do with himself, to what to apply himself, but simply watches things pass by, whether it be a large fly, a man or a dog. His eyes may follow something, then the melancholy returns to his face.

Is that a song?...

The droshky in which I was riding turned onto the post's main street and skirted a wooden stage that had been hastily knocked together for Easter celebrations. Beside it were some ragged worn-out swings. Given his cheerless face, that must have been the "entrepreneur" at the entrance. Nearby, a crowd of bored exile-settlers listened without smiles to vulgar jokes from a clown on a theater balcony, a convict in face-paint and baggy calico overalls. Onstage, a choir was wildly mewling a discordant song. Chains were clanging: a convoy of fettered prisoners was marched past the stage... We continued up the post's main street.

Fig. 7: Korsakovsk Post

My first sight of Korsakovsk made, all in all, a winning impression. Nothing seemed like "*katorga*." This was a clean little city. Administrators' neat inviting homes were laid out in two rows, as if prepared to scamper along the high hills. Highest of all ran the prison. But the prison doesn't *loom* over Korsakovsk. It's one story, not very tall, and regardless of its elevated position neither offends the eye nor dominates or commands the place. In the declivity of two ravines, along both sides of a hill and as if tumbling lazily down the slopes, are little houses. This is the exile-settlers' village. In general, there's nothing "terrible" or dismal in any of this. And so you're prepared to go into raptures over the "facilities," to proceed down Korsakovsk's main street ready to smile and say, "Yes, all this is very, very, so really very nice…"

But wait! Sakhalin is a bog, its surface covered by sparkling emerald grass. It seems a wonderful little meadow—but people take a step and fall into a deep, sucking, clinging cold quagmire. "Nice" cannot exit your mouth, for you hear chains clinking from around a corner. Harnessed to a telega, grasping its shaft, penal laborers are hauling manure. What a depressing impression these people make, performing equine labor. Your path takes you past the prison, where dark grimy windows peer from behind their grilles. Ahead is the infirmary and just across from it, the cemetery.

3
THE INFIRMARY

Later, in Aleksandrovsk and in Rykovsk District, I saw fully outfitted prison hospitals; but what a ghastly place, what a Dantesque evil pit, was this hospital in Korsakovsk Post. I came to know all Sakhalin's "prisons," but the gloomiest was Korsakovsk's infirmary.

A man covered in scabs from an unknown infection is lying side-by-side with a surgery patient. An insane Kirgiz named Naur-Sali is circling them. As with most of Sakhalin's insane, he suffers from megalomania. His is "a protest of the spirit," a "divine affliction." In sum, the disfranchised and poor fancy themselves either the rulers of nature or incalculably wealthy, or in extreme cases even wardens or guards. The Kirgiz Naur-Sali belongs to the incalculably wealthy. He possesses innumerable herds of sheep and camels, earns an inestimable income... But he's surrounded by enemies. Sakhalin's heavy, oppressive environment often produces persecution mania.

It seems that in the past, Naur-Sali's herd was attacked by a pack of wolves that crept upon them through the steppe's feather-grass. His herd was scattered and lost and he was ruined. Now fear distorts and constantly grips the face of Naur-Sali (he's an epileptic and suffers from St Vitus's dance[1]), who weaves from side-to-side shouting and running about the ward, crawling under patients' beds and pulling off their blankets to find his sheep. Imagine the situation for a patient with a broken leg in a splint when the insane Naur-Sali violently tears off his blanket.

"Why aren't they kept separated?"

"Oh, and where should I put them?!" despairingly answers the infirmary's friendly young physician, Kirillov.

It's crowded and stuffy inside the infirmary. Patients lie in corridors due to lack of space. A casualty ward for out-patients is improvised each morning. A screen in the corridor near the outside door protects naked patients from cold and the curiosity of people continually exiting and entering.

"Imagine for yourself how enticing it is in winter, during a frost, to crowd around the entrance and look at the patients," said the doctor. Enticing enough even in springtime.

All of Korsakovsk's infirmary is depressing. Coarse bedclothes are unbelievably filthy, so patients choose to lie in their own underwear. "There's supposed to be soap to wash patients' government-issue bedclothes," shouts the doctor with frustration, "but I'll give my right arm if we've ever seen it!"

There's no ventilation. The air is close and stuffy and you're immediately sickened upon entering. For two days afterward I couldn't lose the oppressive stench that permeated my clothes during my visit.

It's impossible to speak of any kind of operating room. For minor operations, patients are taken to the military hospital. For the more serious, they're sent to Aleksandrovsk Post, which is cut off from Korsakovsk for six months out of the year. I imagined myself a patient who might need a serious operation in November: the first steamer to Aleksandrovsk, the *Iaroslavl*, would not be departing until late April of next year!

When I was in Korsakovsk infirmary's there was no... hygroscopic cotton. To dress wounds, they boiled regular cotton then left it exposed in that atmosphere to be saturated by all possible microbes and bacilli. "All we can boast of is our pharmacy," said the doctor with a sigh of relief. "Thanks to the care and insistence of the director of the medical division, Dr Poddubsky, we now have a fine selection of medicines."

Let us return, however, to the sick.

What pictures, pictures of despair, are on display in this Dantesque purgatory. Consumptives' yellow waxen faces resemble the color of the faded pillows; their eyes burn with a feverish brilliance. Here's some gnome or hideous apparition: face a skull covered with yellowed skin; a shriveled body with humerus bones, clavicles and ribs discernible; abdomen distended and impossibly bloated. He's terrible to look at. The poor man cannot sleep, pain torments him day and night—it inundates him: galloping consumption complicated by dropsy. In his eyes there is such torment, such unbelievable suffering. The poor man—a skeleton drowning in water—whispers something as we approach.

"Sooner! Sooner, I say! Give me something to end it sooner!" It's hardly possible to make out what the gasping man is mumbling.

"No, no. Think what you're saying," the doctor tries to console him. Still greater torment shows on the patient's face. He shakes is head "no."

It's hard to see a person preparing for death in general, but preparing for death here, far from his home, from everyone near and dear, here where no friendly hand will close his eyes, no relative's kiss will touch his lips—here all this is twice, ten times, harder to see.

Here's a patient, a middle-aged man with premature streaks of gray in his hair. His face is handsome, wise, intellectual. What does he suffer from? You don't need a doctor to immediately diagnose his illness from the feverish glint in his eyes, the unnaturally bright blotches on his face, and the huge drops of sweat on his lips. This is an exiled penal laborer from the *brodiagi*, the "*Nepomniashchye*,"[2] a teacher from the village of Vladimirovka.

"You were a teacher in Russia?"

"I was a teacher... Then I wasn't!" he says with a heavy sigh, sorrow crossing his face. He can say no more...

And here's a product of a *katorga* prison, a particular "Sakhalin patient." A young man, it would seem, with a healthy, sturdy constitution, but who's contracted galloping consumption due to exhaustion. Before you is a *zhigan*,[3] a type of *katorga* gambler. Gambling is his illness, a most horrible one, and the natural element he manages to exist in. His lusterless eyes watch everything with the indifferent, careless gaze of the dying and burn with feverish light, real fire, only when he talks about gambling. He's lost everything: his money, his regulation clothes. They punished him with birch rods, stuck him in an isolation cell, but still he gambled. He lost his very self, lost his labor and had to perform double *katorga*, working for both himself and the person he'd lost to. Having gambled away his bread ration for nearly the rest of the year, he's been starving for *months*, eating "from the hand" the weak broth, *balanda*, without bread. They beat him cruelly, furiously, because to gamble he'll steal anything that isn't nailed down. In the end, exhaustion led to him contracting galloping consumption.

He was in the infirmary, gambling with patients and losing his food ration, but stopped and quickly covered up the game when he saw us. Were it not for special observation over him he would gamble away even his own medicines. It seems that Sakhalin's patients are "awarded medicines" and get very little. They readily buy them from each other. The patients surrounding this wretched dying man were themselves so sick and dying they weren't averse to winning his last crust of bread.

Here are some echoes of the winter season, persons whose hands or feet have been frostbitten, some from working in the taiga, others from having recently been on the lam. They unwrap their rags—before us are hands and feet without digits covered in iodine, scabs and oozing sores. When they toss and turn their moans mix with the madmen's delirious idiotic swearing and laughter.

Here's an interesting patient: Iorkin, a former sailor and an epileptic. Lombroso[4] would undoubtedly take his photograph and add him to his collection of tattooed criminals, for Iorkin is tattooed from head to toe. A huge cross is emblazoned on his chest, his arms covered with anchors and crosses, symbols of hope and salvation, and with scriptural quotations. As is typical on Sakhalin, Iorkin's religious mania is accompanied by grandiose delusions.

"I won't be here much longer," he says, eyes alight with ecstasy. "Angels are coming to take me away."

And here's a victim suffering from his family's absence: Karpov, a Don Cossack from Novocherkassk. Today, he is somehow happy, constantly smiling, and can be talked to. He gladly speaks about one thing only—his family left behind in his homeland; about his brothers, mother, father and wife, how they live and get by. He speaks with enthusiasm, illuminated by his memories. This is a most bright moment for him. Usually, he's seriously depressed and pensive. He's a melancholic and fears attack from demons who want to draw him into immoral behavior. He's abstemious and "watches himself" on behalf of his family. But at night the demons send women to seduce him.

"There are many demons here," he cries in a frail, shrill voice, hiding under the bed and peering about. Where are they?

"There! There! There they are!"

He goes into a seizure.

Guard your pockets. Alongside the doctor and myself this whole time has been Demidov, a kleptomaniac and one of *katorga*'s most pathetic individuals. Fellow prisoners thrashed him to within an inch of his life, so the administration quarantined him. But he remained absolutely "incorrigible." Not long ago, they were giving him fifty-two birch strokes when suddenly, to everyone's astonishment, Dr Kirillov took this "incorrigible scoundrel" to the infirmary.

"Akh, so that's it!" everyone exclaimed. "He's crazy! But we've reformed him."

And here's a victim of our hospitals, a victim of our penchant for "hasty discharges." This is a *brodiaga* who is mute.

"Semen Mikhailovich! How are you?" asks the doctor.

Semen Mikhailovich smiles idiotically and gazes somewhere into a corner.

"What is this? Can he really not talk?"

"No, he suffers from a form of aphasia, and so is unable to speak and in no position to answer questions."

He only smiles foolishly, incapably, pathetically, sufferingly. In a single moment of lucidity, when the ability to speak had momentarily returned, he'd told the doctor his history. He wasn't a *brodiaga* originally. He is Semen Mikhailovich Glukharenkov, a peasant from Novgorod Province. He has family back home. He'd gone to Petersburg to earn money, was stricken with typhoid fever and ended up in hospital. The hospital discharged him too early, when he was too weak. Without a penny and with his passport having been sent to the government "to be exchanged," he had to travel on foot. Having just left city limits he "lost consciousness" and then "it happened." He was arrested, brought to court, but was mute to all questions. He spent six months in *katorga* and was later settled on Sakhalin as "Brodiaga Mute." Such was the little tale Semen Glukharenkov was able to tell the doctor in a moment of lucidity, before again losing himself in silence, before that quiet, mournful smile stole across his face.

Over all this—over the tragic silence of "Brodiaga Mute," low moans emanating from soulful depths, squabbling patients' labored breathing, the *zhigan*'s gambling stories, consumptives' asphyxiated coughs (in which you seem to hear little clumps exploding), the raving and idiotic laughter of madmen—over all this reigns the perpetually incessant cry of a maddened old soldier. There's nowhere in Korsakovsk's infirmary that this terrible cry, irritating your every nerve, cannot reach you. It poisons the final moments of those dying in the small separate ward we've entered. A man lies on a bed... a shadow, a ghost of a man... His face is white, not just pale, as if smeared with cream. His chest wheezes and whistles. He's suffocating. The doctor, explaining his illness as we approached, simply said, "Look for yourself!"

"Doctor... doctor...," says the patient, hardly breathing, his tone that of a child, helpless, pitiful and heart-rending. "Doctor... prescribe me, for God's sake, some mint... I'll improve with some mint."

"Good, good, my friend! I'll prescribe you some mint," the doctor soothed him.

"Yes-yes!... With mint... I'll... get better..."

He would die that evening.

From this small ward we walk down a narrow corridor in the direction of the insane soldier. Chains are clanking at the corridor's entrance.

"Who's that? Patients?"

"No," states a supervisor. "They're here to be certified healthy enough to receive corporal punishment."

These two patients are living out their lives in a small isolation cell here. An old penal laborer, formerly a soldier, answers the question of how many times he's been lashed and beaten in his life: "Seventy-two million, your worship!" He fancies himself a sergeant-major and a field marshal, and the whole of his life is reflected in his gloomy madness: all he does is sentence people to death or to the lash.

"That's him!" he shouts, pointing at the official and tearing his "lunatic shirt" to shreds. "He wanted to tie me up! Hang him within 24 hours! The death sentence is rescinded—sixty thousand lashes without medical assistance! You'll survive!"

Contorted on another bed sleeps a unique creature who sentences no one to death or the lash—an old truculent soldier named Piglet. He's a blind, feeble-minded old man.

"Piglet, attention!" shouts the soldier, and plucks several whiskers from Piglet's beard. Piglet yelps, wakes up, and opens his unseeing eyes. "Piglet, you wanna eat?"

Piglet doesn't answer. Having heard the doctor's voice, he's pondering something.

"Doctor, oh doctor!"

"What do you want?"

"Give me new eyes."

"Very good, I'll do that!"

"You will? Well, good." And Piglet again slips into an old man's reveries.

"You don't wanna eat, Piglet?" wails the old soldier. "It's the supervisor's presence he doesn't want! Hang him this minute! Ready the gallows! Executioner! The lash!"

We enter the women's ward. Here it's somewhat better. "These are women, after all!" explains a midwife. Recently confined women lie beside a pair of idiots smilingly discussing their suitors. The usual women's gibberish on Sakhalin. Nenila, an insane young wench who's all gussied up, approaches the doctor.

"Doctor, can you prescribe me something right now?"

"What for?"

"I'm afraid the guard could go for someone else."

"But with you all dressed up like that?"

"You're right, I'm ready for him!" Nenila laughs.

"She doesn't have a guard at all. Ravings!" the doctor quietly explains to me. "Nenilushka, you'd do better to tell the barin how you came to be here. He wants to know."

Nenila's face suddenly turns morose.

"I was tricked, oh, I was tricked! He completely tricked me, the monster, so that I went along with him! He got me involved and then, off he went. He disappeared! I should be alone?..." Nenila begins crying.

"Don't cry. Tell us what happened."

"What happened? The usual. Some merchant was sitting down, right there. Some drunk merchant. A beard on a table!" Nenila laughs. "I'm next to him, pouring him some more. 'Drink,' I says, 'you dirty so-and-so!' And my mate sneaks up behind him... Snuck up to the merchant—that drunk, stinking drunk merchant! I grab hold of his arms. My mate gets hold of his beard—pulls it back—and slits his throat! Aiee!" Nenila screams. Perhaps that was the terrible moment when she "lost the balance" of her psyche. "Blood on the wall, splashed on me, on me... The merchant made such a horrible face... Horrible..." Nenila begins to whimper and wipe away tears, then suddenly bursts out laughing. "Why am I howling like a fool? What a fool, such a fool! How ridiculous. I'm howling like a little girl and don't know why! Doctor, let me see the guard."

"Give me a small drop of wisdom," another lunatic says, approaching. This unfortunate woman was exiled to *katorga* for murdering her husband. She lost her psychic equilibrium on her wedding night.

"It happens with women... They're married off too early...," explains the doctor. "Maybe the husband's in his cups and treats her too roughly."

"We struggled!" she plaintively says. "I was taken to bed and the blood flowed. I saw him turn away from me... He turned his back, and I stabbed him."

Something in her demeanor is oppressed and full of suffering. Essentially, she has no illness. Nevertheless, what is left of her consciousness demands an answer for her depressed condition, and the wretch herself formulates explanations: first she complains of a toothache, then five minutes later she starts complaining about lumbago.

"Third day I haven't been able to straighten up! It hurts!"

"What about your teeth?"

"My teeth don't hurt. It's my back!"

"You see the cases we have to deal with," sighs the doctor.

I don't think Dr Kirillov will continue struggling with Sakhalin's many, profoundly "*katorga*," cases. Over several months he's already quite exhausted his nerves. So many have fled here, people who came with a passionate desire to bring salvation to the suffering! Kirillov's departure will be a great pity. Such persons—knowledgeable, energetic, educated, humane, honorable, with sympathetic, friendly, responsive souls—such persons Sakhalin needs.

But each year many bad persons are sent in a steamer's hold.

4

THE *KATORGA* CEMETERY

From Korsakovsk's infirmary it's not far to the cemetery. We were traveling "to the lighthouse," because the cemetery lies on a hill near Korsakovsk's lighthouse. "Your honor, see that it isn't time for me to go to the lighthouse yet," a gravely ill convict will tell the doctor attending him.

A strange procession was clambering up the hillside. Ten convicts, gripping the shaft and pushing from behind, nudged forward a telega in which lay spades and a large, awkwardly built, plain wooden coffin. Behind the tangled mass of men followed a guard sent to watch the convicts, with a revolver in his belt. "Well, well! Let's go!" the penal laborers shouted. That was it for a funeral eulogy. There's something so melancholy and heart-rending in this picture of a Sakhalin burial… That telega, the guard, those gray jackets… A lone individual who might have led to his final resting place an "unfortunate" who'd ended his days now also lies in a grave.

They buried the exile-settler. He'd murdered his cohabitant out of jealousy, then fled his house to poison himself with wolfsbane.[1] His corpse was found several days later in the taiga.

Wolfsbane is a poisonous plant growing in Korsakovsk District, in southern Sakhalin. There, the wolfsbane root is available to every penal laborer and exile-settler "for any eventuality." I was often shown this root.

"And what kind of fool keeps this trash?"

"Such is the custom… For any eventuality… It's an option, and a necessary one!" exile-settlers answered, smiling at that for which God permits no one to smile.

We continued on together, the telega crawling slowly up the hill. They brought the coffin to the first freshly dug grave and lowered it with ropes; took the spades from the telega, spit on their hands and began dumping soil onto the coffin. It fell heavily: the soil there was loamy and pebbly. Not earth, but some sort of crushed stone or brick lay piled around the freshly dug grave. Deeper and deeper the soil had sounded… A small hillock arose over the grave into which they hastily stuck an unpainted cross, slapped together out of two wooden slats and bearing no words. Some crossed themselves, others didn't. They returned to the telega.

"Now, let's go!" They stole away down the hill at a run.

"Easy, you devils!" came the panting guard's despairing voice. "Easy! Easy!…" resounded down the hill.

We were among the nameless graves.

"Can this be? Can so many really have died in the infirmary?" I looked with astonishment at the mass of freshly dug pits.

"Not quite!" answered the convict coachman, doffing his cap.

"Put on your cap, for God's sake! It doesn't matter in a cemetery."

"Quite so, your worship. The pits were dug for emergencies. There was nothing to do, the steamers weren't coming, so they sent them here to dig pits. 'Cause when it gets busy they'll need the people for work, not for pits!"

What a depressing scene! There were small hillocks on which stood some broken sticks instead of crosses. Almost no grave had a whole cross. On most there was absolutely nothing.

"Who were they?"

"Exile-settlers gone to hell. What else is there for 'em? The lazy go off to the taiga, drag themselves around here and there."

Here was a grave, covered over, as should be, by hands that were caring and possibly those of a relative. An icon had been attached to the cross. The cross was intact but the icon had been broken off, and now some exile-settler in a filthy, dark, empty hovel was praying before this icon, broken off a burial cross.

"Whoever's broke off those icons has prob'ly squandered 'em. A pair of crosses earns a few kopeks!" said my coachman, as if divining my thoughts.

Looming over a high fence, above all these small, unknown, nameless hillock graves, was a massive cast iron cross atop the tall stone vault of the merchant Timofeev.

"They murdered him!" explained the coachman.

"What for?"

"For money." Thinking for a moment, he went on. "'Twas said he had money. That's why they murdered him. He's gone…"

It would be nice to leave this cemetery, the gloomiest in all the world, and even Sakhalin itself. But there must be one "sacred grave." The grave of Naumova, a young woman, teacher and founder of Korsakovsk's shelter for exiles' children. She'd studied in Petersburg, then abandoned everything and came here, inspired by a holy idea, great sorrow and the divine wish to devote her life to serving and helping those poor, unfortunate, portentously neglected children of the criminals sent here. She had big plans. She dreamed of crafts lessons for the children, of Sunday schools for the penal laborers, of lectures and readings… She worked with all her spirit and devoted herself passionately and energetically to her affairs. She tried to do something. Korsakovsk's shelter owes its origins to her.

But the apparently weak young woman struggled against Sakhalin callousness, Sakhalin deadness, Sakhalin indifference to the suffering of one's neighbor. The young woman couldn't endure the struggles with officials who viewed her "undertakings" with hostility; she couldn't endure the trying penal atmosphere. She shot herself, leaving behind two notes. The first: "Life is too painful." In the second, she begged that all her meager pay be given to her children, to the shelter.

After this three persons arrived at once: three friends emboldened by the idea of bringing succor to the suffering. One shot herself, another went insane, the third… left to marry a former doctor's assistant who had originally been exiled. Thus ended up all three—different yet essentially the same. How hard indeed to stick with work so trying!

Korsakovsk's "intelligentsia" arranged for Naumova's solemn funeral, but thanks to Sakhalin's rumor mill and to slander they still can't understand how someone could sacrifice her life for *katorga*. The sufferer garners no mercy even in the grave.

Her grave... She had to be here somewhere... But where was she? I searched and searched but couldn't find her. "She should be there!" I was told by Mr and Mrs "Intelligent." Indeed, for hardly two years had passed since Naumova's death! Priamur's governor-general[2] had sent a lovely metallic wreath with a beautiful dedication on a copper plate for Naumova's grave. This wreath hangs... in police headquarters. "This shouldn't be. They're stealing!" But where else could they hang it? Her sacred grave is among those anonymous sinful graves because "it has to be."

5

A DAY IN PRISON

The prison "day" begins in the evening, when prisoners are given their labor assignments. So we begin our "day in prison."

Orders

The prison chancery. Typical office décor. It's dim and unkempt. Convict clerks scratch their quill-pens, writing and recopying an endless supply of Sakhalin documents: reports, memoranda, dispatches, notes, discharges, letters. Prison supervisors stand near the entrance and greet one another. The senior supervisor gives a subordinate the penal laborers' assignments for tomorrow.

"This many for unloading the steamer. This many for carpentry work. To get firewood... To the workshops... And here's that chap Iks Igrekovich Dzet, who's asked us to send people to turn over his garden."

"There aren't anymore, your honor. They've all been assigned."

"That's nothing. Send six men. List them among the carpenters. And Alfa Omegovna[1] asked to be sent a pair. We shouldn't refuse her. So what does the list look like now after all this messing around?"

"Show him the assignment list."

"Just give us a chance!"

"Well, alright, send a pair of those who were assigned to unloading..." Orders finished, the guards begin arriving.

"What do you want?"

"Your honor, Ivanov's being very rude. You give him an order and he mouths off. He cusses and embarrasses you!"

"Put him in the isolator. Three days' bread and water. And you?"

"Petrov's making a row again."

"To the isolator! Anyone else?"

"No problems," answer the others.

"Call the laborers."

A throng of penal laborers comes to the door, stops and begins greeting one another. One is in fetters.

"What do you want?"

"A result. They said report for the verdict."

"Ah! Go over to the clerk. Vasilev, read him the verdict."

The clerk stands and hastily reads, or rather mumbles, the verdict, dribbling out the words: "The Priamur Regional Court... Taking into consideration... absence without leave... extension of your term... ten more years! Are you literate?"

"Sure am!"

"Sign here." The fettered man signs his name with the same lazy, indifferent manner he listened to his extension of ten years' *katorga*, as if nothing had been said about him.

"Can I go?" he sullenly asks.

"Yes. Go."

"He'll escape again, the bastard!" remarks the warden.

Katorga's rules dictate that a "respectable" penal laborer listen to any verdict quietly, diffidently, as if it doesn't concern him. He's to show no anger. This is considered the "proper demeanor." In the case of a particularly harsh verdict, *katorga* perhaps allows one to curse the court. But *katorga* is uncharitable toward any words of self-pity, hence the "indifference" to verdicts. In actuality, they do seem troubled by overly harsh and unjustifiable extensions of sentences for "unauthorized absences." "I got ten years for seven days!" I myself watched a convict quietly listen to a verdict that extended his term by 15 years. Speaking later, without witnesses, he tearlessly said, "I'm already a ruined man! What's left for me? I'm already here forever." Such was the passion of this "rogue" who'd listened to his sentence "without batting an eye."

"There's still another verdict to read. Who's Fedor Nepomniashchy?"

"Me!" responds a half-blind little muzhik.

"You've gone to pains to hide your origins?"

"Exactly."

"Well then, listen up!"

The clerk again begins mumbling the verdict. "The Regional Court... regarding the request by Fedor Nepomniashchy... sentenced to four years for vagabondage... to acknowledge him as exile-settler so-and-so... identified by the following features... Fedor Nepomniashchy's eyes are recorded as light blue... but the exile-settler's are gray... large nose... has resolved to refuse... Did you hear? Your request's been refused."

"Turns out I wasn't recognized by a nose?" Nepomniashchy bitterly smiles. "Time to go, now that I'm not me!..."[2]

"You literate?"

"Of course I'm literate. Only, I can't sign in the evening because of night-blindness. I had to be led here."

"Alright! Sign tomorrow! Go!"

"Do I have to go back to the prison?"

"Yes."

"Ech, for God's sake!" Nepomniashchy wants to say something else but restrains himself, hopelessly waves his hand, and slowly moves blindly through the mass of penal laborers. Neither his verdict nor exclamation impresses anyone. In *katorga* it's "every man for himself."

"What do you want?" The warden turns to a group of convicts.

"Our labor terms are over."

"What? You're going into settlement? Well, chaps, so long. I wish you well. Look, behave yourselves. Don't end up here again."

"Humblest thanks!" The term-enders congratulate themselves.

"Half of them will soon be in prison again!" the warden assures me. "What do I care?"

The group breaks up. A lone fellow stands before the office building.

"I ended my term today, your worships. But they won't let me go. With an axe I could..."

"He lost his government axe," explains the senior supervisor.

"Were you drinking, chap?"

"Absolutely not. I don't drink."

"He doesn't drink!" echoes the supervisor.

"They stole my axe."

"Who stole it? Probably you know?"

The fellow scratches his head. "I really can't say who. You yourself know, your worship, what happens to those who talk."

"What a people! I'm going to report you!" the supervisor says in a fury. "They steal from each other, but say: 'Don't dare! Brother, you don't want to tell.' So they sit tight and the government axe can't be found.

"Were you given a long term?"

"Ten years!"

"Allow me to add," interjects one of the clerks, "that he's earned a little bit of money. Perhaps enough to deduct for the axe."

"That's right, there's, there's some money!" The fellow's clutching at straw like a drowning man. Hope and joy are on his face.

"Well, alright! So it shall be. Deduct the axe. Free him! Get the hell out of here!"

"Humblest thanks, your worship!"

And with such a farewell the man goes to start a new life. His place in front of the building is taken by a convict in a tattered pea-jacket and torn shirt with a battered physiognomy.

"Your worship! Show a commander's mercy! Don't let me perish!" He isn't talking, but whining.

"What's with him?"

"He got beat up again," announces the senior supervisor.

"What can I do?" The warden turns to me. "What am I to do with him? Any place I transfer him he gets beaten up. They beat him to death."

"Exactly!" adds the supervisor. "Whether sent to the isolator, which it pleased you to see, or put in the general population, it's a punishment.[3] But we didn't believe him last time and now they've thrashed him. Now I'm not going to assign him to work because they'll nail him!"

The man who's earned *katorga*'s malice is suspected of betraying two fugitives' hideout.

"What a helpful fellow he's been," the warden quietly confided to me. "Through him, I knew everything going on in the prison."

Before us stood this "helpful fellow"—beaten, helpless, despairing of his fate. *Katorga* beats him; and as for those he's assisted, what can they do with an enraged and frenzied *katorga*?

"Punish them and they'll beat him even worse! They'll finish him off!"

"Yes, finish me off, your worship," the informer miserably says. "Without fail, they'll finish me off."

"So tell me who beat you up. Who was the ringleader, at least?"

"Mercy, your worship, as if I'm bold enough to say? It'll happen! Sure enough! I won't live another day. They'll kill me."

"You see, you see! What a temper. What manners! What am I to do with you, chap?"

"Your worship!" The wretch is about to fling himself onto his knees.

"That's unnecessary, un-necessary!"

"Transfer me away from here. For example, to the taiga, or send me to the Okhotsk seacoast. I can't take these savage beatings. My little bones won't last. I can't lie or sit down. All of me's been beaten. Your worship, I lay hands on my own self!"

In his voice there's resignation and, really, a determination to do anything to please. The warden mulls it over.

"Alright! Remove him to sector two tomorrow. You'll haul timber from the taiga."

This is one of the most difficult jobs, but the wretch is as happy as if it were a holiday or a deliverance.

"Humblest thanks to you. Your wor—"

"Now what?"

"Allow me to spend tonight in the isolator, otherwise they'll beat me up again."

"Go ahead!" laughs the warden.

"Humblest thanks."

This is a man, a situation, when the isolator—*katorga*'s horror—becomes paradise.

"Is that all?"

"Yes, that's it."

"Well, now off to the prison, to roll call, to evening prayers—and sleep! Those assigned to unload the steamer can sleep late!" The warden glances at his watch. "Eleven o'clock. I want the prisoners' labor assignments ready tomorrow morning at four."

The Prison at Night

It's a cold, dark moonless night. Only the stars are shining. The fires of little lamps move here and there through the huge prison yard. It's pitch dark but you can sense the crowd's presence and breathing. We've stopped in front of some building's tall black silhouette: it's a chapel in the middle of the yard.

"Remove caps!" comes the order. "Ready with prayers. Begin."

"Christ rose from the dead…" emanates through the darkness as a hundred non-seeing men begin chanting. In the darkness the chant can be heard to the right, left, nearby and somewhere off in the distance!… As if the darkness itself has begun reciting. This is a Sunday hymn, a song of victory over death—and in such a situation! It makes a staggering impression.

The blind choir chants several more prayers, then roll call begins. Late at night there's no formal roll call, they just count people. Raising lanterns to face-level, guards pass along the rows and count the prisoners. Faces old, young, somber, tired, fierce, repulsive and commonplace emerge from the darkness for a moment, then slip into it again. At the end of each row the lantern illumines a sharply-dressed headman.

"Seventy-five?" asks the guard.

"Seventy-five!" answers the headman.

The senior guard brings the warden the total and reports that all people are accounted for.

"Off to sleep!" The throng begins to stir as if the surrounding darkness has come alive. Tramping feet, conversations, sighs and yawns are heard. Tired from their day, the convicts hurriedly disperse among the prison wards.

"Who goes there?" shouts a sentinel in front of the chains prison.[4] "Who goes there?" he desperately cries again as we come closer.

"It's the warden, why're you shouting?…"

We pass through the gate. A huge bolt thunders open and a cloud of damp, dank steam escapes from the opening door as we enter one of the chains prison's wards.

"Attention! Stand!" Drowsing fetters seem to awaken at our appearance: they begin to jingle, clang, ring and utter their own repulsive vernacular.

The feeling is hard among the sound of these fetters in the chains prison's semi-darkness. I glance at the walls. Hanging on them are some kind of broad shadows or stripes, as if a gigantic spider has covered everything with some enormous spiderweb… As if some huge bats are clinging to and hanging from the walls. They're spruce branches spread along the walls to freshen air that smells of dampness, mold and perspiration.

The prisoners are called by their surnames. They shuffle past us, fetters clinking, as huge distorted shadows move along the wall. In one of the wards are two wheelbarrow-men.[5] Both are Caucasians, put in the chains for escaping. One, a tall sturdy man with a smiling open face barely concealing the terror in his eyes, had pushed his wheelbarrow past us during roll call, chains rumbling. The other is lying in a corner.

"And what's this lying down?"

The wheelbarrow-man says something in a weak and stuttering voice.

"He's sick! Very much sick! Become weak!" explains a Tatar interpreter.[6]

During prayers he'd stood leaning against his wheelbarrow groaning, sighing, remembering some terrible phantom, his chains clinking with every move. You cannot imagine what an impression the man makes, chained to that wheelbarrow. You look at him in utter astonishment: "Why is he pushing a wheelbarrow?" You plainly see he doesn't believe in this punishment.

At the end of roll call the prisoners sing prayers. It's strange to hear: forty to fifty prisoners are in the ward but only a diminished choir of seven or eight sings. All the rest are Caucasians…[7]

I noticed they hadn't sung "Christ Has Risen" in the chains division.

"Why is that?" I asked the warden.

"They probably forgot!"

People who have actually forgotten that now is Easter week!…

Labor Assignments

Five o'clock in the morning. Just barely light. A frozen dawn. A light patina of white rime covers everything: the prison's grounds, roofs and walls. Vapor belches from opening doors. Scratching, stretching men reluctantly emerge without having had a good night's sleep; several are going through the motions of dressing in their "rags," others hastily chewing some bread. There's no sense of a fresh, cheerful workaday morning. The men arrange themselves in rows: carpenters with carpenters, laborers with laborers. Guards call out surnames from lists. "Here!... Present!..." From different ends of the yard come all tones of voice: sleepy, gloomy, sullen.

"Mohammed-Bek-Iskander-Ali-Ogly!" a guard stutteringly reads. "Argh, dammit, what a mouthful."

"Why don't you go to hell?! *Malaika*,[8] they're calling you!" Convicts nudge the Caucasian, who after three years of *katorga* has still not got used to supervisors' atrociously distorted pronunciation of his long, "Bek-family," name.[9]

Over everything reigns "the cough"—a wheezing, drawn-out, typically catarrhal cough. In a frost many are gripped by the "Gypsy sweats." Shivering, the chattering of teeth. They're hoping they won't have to wait long, when there's the shout: "Fall out!"

It wasn't very long ago that this early hour, this hour for assigning tasks, occurred simultaneously with the hour for retribution. In the middle of the courtyard they would set up the "mare"[10] and there, before all *katorga*, the executioner would punish malefactors or those who hadn't finished the previous day's assignments. *Katorga* would watch and... laugh. "The bitch!... He's screaming like a suckling pig! You don't like it!" they would laughingly respond to each of the victim's cries. It was a brutal spectacle!

Sometimes *katorga* "scrutinized" those who strove to win their comrades' esteem and enter the ranks of the "Ivans," the champions of *katorga*. An especially obstinate prisoner who'd sworn not to submit to authority would be laid on the mare, and *katorga* would curiously wait to see how he'd bear under the birch-rod blows. Clenching his teeth, sometimes until blood flowed from his lips, he would lie on the mare and groan; only savagely rolling eyes and bursting veins betrayed the horrible torment he was suffering amid his silence before *katorga*'s faces.

"Twelve! Thirteen! Fourteen!" the guard would rhythmically count.

"Don't just butter him!... Slower!... Harder!..." the impatient warden would shout, watching this silent stoic. The executioner would lash slower, the birch rod fall harder...

"Fifteen... Sixteen...," the guard would now be counting in long intervals. A moan, an involuntary cry of pain would issue from the wretch.

"He's failed! He couldn't hold out!" *Katorga* would respond in a burst of laughter.

The warden would peer down victoriously: "I broke him!"

Sometimes *katorga* would look forward to the morning regimen as simply an interesting and entertaining spectacle. "Watch, chaps, what riding tricks I'll be showing off tomorrow when they tear into me. It'll be a show!" some *zhigan* would boast after having gambled away everything including his prison clothes and rations, living off the crumbs from *katorga*'s table and, as such, playing the fool. And *katorga* would await the show.

Dying from trying to keep from laughing, it would watch the *zhigan* show off his riding tricks. But many couldn't help but burst with laughter, fall to the ground and guffaw, "I can't help it, fellas, I'm sorry."

The wretched *zhigan* would pull out the stops. He'd fall on his knees before the warden, insist that this couldn't happen and beg for mercy "for an orphan, a blessed child of the meek." He wouldn't let himself be tied to the mare, screaming even when the executioner threatened him. "Oy, little father, it hurts! Oy, mother and father, it hurts!"

"Hit him harder, the scoundrel!" the enraged warden would order.

And the *zhigan*, lying under the birch rod, would try with his funniest exclamation to wrap everything up: "Oy, my sweet grandma! My departed parents!"

Blood and flesh were made to account for those crumbs *katorga* had tossed him from its table. The punishment would end and the *zhigan* would barely, yet resolutely, with a forced, strained smile, approach his comrades.

"Alright?"

Not too long ago, screams and moans in the prison yard could be heard from your porch early on a freezing morning. But *tempora mutantur*...[11] The spirit of our great humanitarian age has manifested itself on Sakhalin, and so Korsakovsk's prison warden bitterly complained to me that he's now forbidden "to correct" criminals. Early morning punishments, lessons and spectacles are comparatively rare for *katorga*, and so the assigning of tasks proceeds and ends quietly and peacefully. Roll call is over. "Be off!" And penal laborers with axes, saws and ropes skip away from the place trying to warm themselves as they go.

6

THE CHAINS PRISON

On Sakhalin, "the chains" means the prison for the most serious criminals: officially, the "probationers' prison"; whereas the "correctionals' prison" (for the less serious or those who have completed their "probationary" term) is called the "free prison," because its inmates are allowed to go about without a convoy under just a single guard.[1]

"Our chains prison's in bad shape!" the warden forewarned me in good time. "We're building a new one, but can't finish it." To show how bad it is, the warden has led me to an uncompleted empty structure. "See this wall? Not very sturdy, is it?" The warden raps a stick against the rotten wood. "Escaping from this is nothing! Get a running start and smash your head into the wall, and you'll fly right through. The air's horrible. Winter's cold, in general it's awful."

A huge rusty bolt growls. "Attention!" orders a guard. Fetters clang, and a row of convicts appears around the sleeping platform.[2] Two convicts escaped from the chains prison the first day of Easter—despite all having given their "prisoner's word of honor"—and so now all are in lock-down as punishment.

It's damp and stuffy; the spruce hanging on the walls fails to freshen this close atmosphere. There's no ventilation whatsoever, though there is a sense of emptiness and lack of domesticity. These men have given up on everything, including themselves. There's no sign of even the slightest domesticity, of any effort to create a more tolerable existence. Even the prisoners' usual footlockers are extremely few in number. The sleeping platforms are bare, with dirty mattresses rolled up at their heads. Along these bare platforms wanders, lifting its tail, a ragged sickly cat purring and fawning over the prisoners. Prisoners love animals very much: a cat or a dog is an obligatory presence in every ward. Maybe they love animals because only they relate to them as people. In the middle of the ward is a table—though not really a table but a tall, long narrow bench. Breadcrumbs and dirty tin kettles occupy the bench.

We're looking into that ward where the two wheelbarrow-men live. "Well now, show us your instrument!" The "little wagon" squeals, chains clink, and the fettered wheelbarrow-man shows us his wheelbarrow, which weighs a full two poods and is attached to his leg-irons by a long chain. It used to be connected to the arms, but wheelbarrow-men now rarely wear manacles, except for special offences. Anywhere the prisoner goes, he pushes his wheelbarrow. He sleeps with it on a special bunk in the corner, placing it under his bed.

"How many years have you been chained to this wheelbarrow?" I ask.

"Two. But before me another wheelbarrow-man slept in this bunk for three years."

I approach the bunk. Chains have worn down the wood beside the mattress. Chains have been working on this wood for five years…

"That wood's worn out," a prisoner gloomily informs me.

This is a harsh punishment, and would be absolutely insufferable if wheelbarrow-men did not give themselves a rest now and then. It's difficult to chain a prisoner *tightly*. With a comrade's help, irons can be lubricated with grease and, though very painfully, sometimes slid off at night. Freed from them and the wheelbarrow, the prisoner can relax for several hours each month. There's even a chance for wheelbarrow-men to escape.

"Do your wheelbarrow-men work?"

"I make them. But in other prisons they refuse to work. It can't be helped. As a whole, these people are crushed."

Sullen faces circle round, eyes shimmering with hopelessness. Cold, bleak bitter gazes glow with hatred and suffering. These "probationary" people's endurance seems about to crack any moment.

One gaze is especially unforgettable. A certain Kozyrev, a Muscovite exiled by the military for disciplinary punishment, is an intellectual among the penal laborers. He has a friendly face, but such a strange, terrible gaze! A drowning man, surfacing for the last time and seeing nothing that will save him, no help anywhere, nothing except waves, surely has such a look. Hopelessly, with morbid resignation, Kozyrev looks around and silently faces the day without struggling. "Line up faster!" It's certainly difficult to meet his eyes—but to *see* as he does?

Escapees, recidivists and those under investigation are among the chains' prisoners.

"What are you in for?"

"Suspicion of murder."

"You?"

"Suspicion of theft."

"You?"

"Suspicion of murder."

"Suspicion of… suspicion of… suspicion of."

"What are you in for?"

"For murdering two people!" comes a sharp direct answer from a hard decisive voice.

"He's an exile-settler!" explains the warden. "He left *katorga* and now he's killed again."

"Who did you kill?"

"A guard and his mistress."

"What for?"

"To monkey with a beginning. She'd begun playing around with the guard. 'I'm a-gonna go live with the guard. What's there for me with you, with an exile-settler, a penal laborer?' 'You're lying,' I says, 'you won't go.' I begged, pleaded, invoked the Good Lord's name. And maybe she wouldn't have gone if the guard hadn't come along and took her. 'I'm taking her to the post,' he says. 'You're treating her badly. You beat her.' 'You lie,' I says. 'You have an Ethiopian's soul! Don't lay a finger on her. I'm not gonna let you have her. You got no right to take her from me!' 'No one asked your permission!' he says. 'Get dressed, we're leaving,' he tells her. 'Don't even look at him.' I warned him. 'Don't do it,' I says, 'or bad will come of this.' 'Ah, you, still with the threats,' he says. 'Clearly, you haven't been in the isolator for a while. I'll just say the word—and there you'll be!' He takes her and leaves…"

The exile-settler is convulsed by this one memory.

"He took her and left my head spinning. 'Vengeance,' I'm thinking. I had a little rifle, and grabbed it. They'd left along the road but I followed a path through the taiga, got near them, hid and waited. I watched them walking along and laughing. She was grinning from ear to ear with him… I finished them off. First him, then her afterward, so she could see!"

Having "finished them off," the exile-settler brutally desecrated the corpses. He literally carved them up with a knife. His cynical mockery of the bodies and the atrocity's gravity revealed a long-simmering rage.

"I myself can't remember what I did next. I was just glad he hadn't gotten her… Yes, it was serious indeed."

The exile-settler is still a young man, with a kind face. But his eyes when he speaks burn with great intensity and determination.

"You loved her, did you?"

"Certainly, I loved her. I wouldn't have killed her if I didn't love her…"

"Your worship!" an elderly fellow says to the warden while I'm speaking. "Free me from these chains! What did I do? I was absent for all of three days. Sadness overtook me, so I drank, and that's all. I gave in to a bottle of vodka and took a stroll. So why am I being held?"

"You're lying, chap. You escaped!"

"Sir, why would I escape? What for me in prison isn't good?" This "fugitive" is knocking himself out. "Be pleased to know that if everything really turns bad, I'll take the wolfsbane, and that'll really be the end. Be pleased to know there's nothing better. Wolfsbane's *katorga*'s principal remedy."

Fig. 8: Shackling a prisoner

"How long will I be here?" another morosely asks. "How long, I say!"

"Your investigation's continuing."

"Well, this is the fourth year I've been relaxing here! My patience is running thin. I'll just plead guilty…"

"Chap, it matters little if you confess. The investigation still isn't over."

"I've sat and sat for so long."

"Your worship! What's this soup they're spooning out? You can't eat it! Dirty potato! They gave us fish to break the Easter fast!…"

We begin to leave.

"Allow me to tell you…"

"Your worship, how long?… Your…"

The guard locks the door with a huge padlock. Muffled voices come from behind the door.

Korsakovsk's chains prison is one of the darkest and gloomiest on Sakhalin. Why do its inmates make not only a troubling, but a repellent, impression? Gentlemen, alongside you is human misery. But misery must be listened to with the heart. Then you will hear in this "brutality" much of human motives, in this "evil" much of suffering, in this "cynical" laughter much of despair…

We walk through the chains prison's dirty yard toward the "correctionals division."

7

THE FREE PRISON

The prisoners are at work. Only the headman and the "closet-men," that is, the ward-cleaners, the *parashechniki*—altogether, the "officials," as *katorga* jokingly calls them—remain in the prison. They sweep, scrape, scour, spiff up and whitewash everything, and fashion elaborate patterns out of fir twigs to decorate the walls. They're preparing for the commandant's visit, though of course the prison won't look the same as it does now in its typical, daily, humdrum attire.

The free prison—both Korsakovsk's and any of the others on Sakhalin—gives the impression, simply put, of a flophouse, very poor, very dirty, where the poorest urban riff-raff gather. No one there bothers with air quality, neatness or hygiene. You came, had a night's sleep—and left! "The hell with it!" Dim grimy windows let in little light. Sleeping platforms incline in two rows down the middle of each ward and also run along the walls. The filth is removable only with a knife. There's no soap that will wash it away. When the floors are mopped the floorboards are raised and the filth simply oozes under them. Such is the picture we find:

"Akh, the swine, the swine!" The warden's shaking his head as if "the swine" alone are to blame. I poke with a stick, and it sinks a foot deep into the viscous muck beneath the floorboards. It is on this virtual swamp of filth that the prison stands. People inhale this sewerage. "A very, very nasty prison!" confirms the warden. "It's just damp now. But in winter it's cold. Nasty, very, very nasty."

In almost every prison, in any ward, you will see without fail a violin. It's typically on the anteroom wall, where hangs everything the prison values most, if you please: its icon, print pictures, best linen. Next to this wall there's usually a single, comparatively clean, bed, always smartly made up with the headman's own sheets. The violin is *katorga*'s favorite instrument. I remember telling a penal laborer about that scene from *Dead House*, where Dostoevsky writes how a prisoner who's drinking rents a little fiddle and whiles away his time squeaking all day. My interlocutor seemed to like the story.

"Yes, yes, I like those who go around playing! This gentleman you're speaking of really knows what it's about."

"Yes, but you do know he was talking about an earlier time."

"That's neither here nor there. When drinking, a violin's the main thing. A happy instrument."

Pictures by the penal laborer Babaev portraying generals on galloping horses were on a wall in one of the wards.

"And where is the artist himself?"

"In a detention cell. He's in solitary."

"Really? I'll take one picture. Here's a ruble for Babaev. Get him some tea, tobacco and sugar!" I expressly gave the fellow money to help his still more suffering comrade.

"See that he gets it!"

"God bless you!"

He never got the money.

8

WORKSHOPS

Korsakovsk's workshops—the joinery, metal shop, lathe shop, cobbler's, tailor's, smithy—work well enough. Serviceable furniture made in Korsakovsk's workshops can be found in the homes of senior officials and even many homes in Vladivostok. Workshops are scattered throughout the prison yard and many craftsmen spend the night in them. The soul somehow awakens more easily when, after the "frenziedness" and stark destitution of prison, you're in a workshop. There's even a whiff of prosperity in the air here. The men get some spending money and, for a holiday, sometimes buy themselves a rest. Some have a little bed with some extra rags. Even their faces are not so *katorga*-like. The work imprints a kind of nobility and humanity upon them. The labor is compulsory, it's *barshchina*,[1] but if you want to see how a prisoner can work—work with passion and diligence and even some interest in what he's doing—then praise him.

"I say, outstanding tom-cats (prison footwear). You're clearly a good craftsman. You do quality work."

In *katorga*, a kind word is a rarity.[2] The unaccustomed kind word impresses a convict much more than the accustomed birch rod. Upon being praised, a worker's face will brighten with a smile; without fail, he'll get up from his "pile" and start boasting about his side-work.

And what painstaking, beloved work! Someone has stitched a kind of pattern all over the sole of a shoe. Not that he's paid more for this, he just loves "his" work and is trying to put the finishing touches on some jack-boot like a master jeweler cutting a rare and precious diamond. Not for nothing do people quite familiar with *katorga* say that if there could be even a little material incentive behind the labor, then *katorga* would produce fewer sluggards, gamblers and recidivists; that fewer people would ultimately end up in it. But enough "philosophy."

Before us again: a gloomy "*katorga*" picture. A young chap is hammering together a large slipshod coffin. On the floor nearby is another one, already finished.

"Are these for the recently deceased?"

"No. Word from the infirmary is there will be some soon, so we're getting ready." The chap furiously hammers in a peg. "Dammit! I was a good natural-born joiner. Worked as a craftsman at Feiner's, in Kiev, a first-class business, I'll have you know. Now I'm slapping together a coffin! Pshaw!"

"And what got you here?"

"A murder at Kiev University."

"Along with theft?"

"Along with *thefts*. Got ourselves a lot and had a fat pocket!"

"How long?"

"Life sentence."[3]

Not far off, a little old man in glasses is bending low over a pair of "tom-cats" and carefully hammering in the tacks.

"Been here long, grandpa?"

"Not long, kind sir," he cordially says. "Not long."

"And for what?"

"Murdered my old lady."

"Your wife?"

"No-o. She was my lover. We lived in harmony for ten years... And I committed such a sin!"

"How did it happen?"

"She did something stupid. We lived in Theodosia.[4] I had a reputation as a good craftsman, lived modestly, had a bit of money. But she hankered for more. 'He'll die,' she says, 'and his relatives'll get all his money! I'm gonna poison him and get that money.' She got involved with a young man: 'I'll poison him!' I could tell that was for sure. We were living like two wolves in a cage, snapping our fangs at each other. I was afraid of her—it looked like she was going to do me in; and she feared me, because she saw that I knew. What a terrible time that was, so terrible... I couldn't take it... I killed her."

What, what isn't a drama here?

9

"AID STATION"

Korsakovsk Prison's aid station has the same purpose as the infirmary and the same character as the prison. The aid station is the place where they incarcerate those who are seriously ill and need to rest. The *bogoduly*—the infirm, old or young, incapacitated by illness or injury—live here. Private beds are the aid station's only convenience. The atmosphere is as close and stuffy as in the prison. Dr Surminsky, an "old veteran of Sakhalin" the warden rapturously told me about, runs the aid station. "What a doctor, such a doctor! Then or now, he's peerless! For him, there's almost no prisoner not strong enough or unable to work. A prisoner comes to him with a complaint: 'You're lying!' he says. No one like that nowadays!"

The following may tell you about this doctor. A sailor from the *Iaroslavl* scalded his head with boiling water in the steam baths. The burn was terrible: his face and head resembled a single amorphous mass. They sent the injured man to Dr Surminsky. "Take him back to the steamer. They have their own doctor there!" So they took the wretched man to the wharf, waited a good hour until a tug arrived, then put him aboard some wildly rocking and unstable tug going to the steamer a mile out to sea…

After this, all those in *katorga* came to understand Dr Surminsky. While speaking with him I was astonished by his tender, almost loving, regard for corporal punishment. "They spatter" was all he said, as if speaking of a mignonette, and pronounced this "spatter" with such relish.

But God bless him! We'll find ourselves some better prison characters.

Here's an elderly man who is actually dressed foppishly. He purposely burned the palate of his mouth with a cigarette and irritated the wound so as to end up in the aid station.

"He doesn't want to work?"

"Exactly!" laugh the patients. "He was his ward's headman but got demoted for stealing. Now he's ashamed to face the ward. He used to have his own sleeping platform, now he's on the common one. He was a headman, a 'commander,' an 'official,' but now he's just a penal laborer." *Katorga* laughs. The poor devil's clearly suffering from wounded pride.

"What do you have to say for yourself, old fellow?"

"I'm a charity case, your worship! Just a worthless man!… I'm not needed. I live only to eat my rations!"

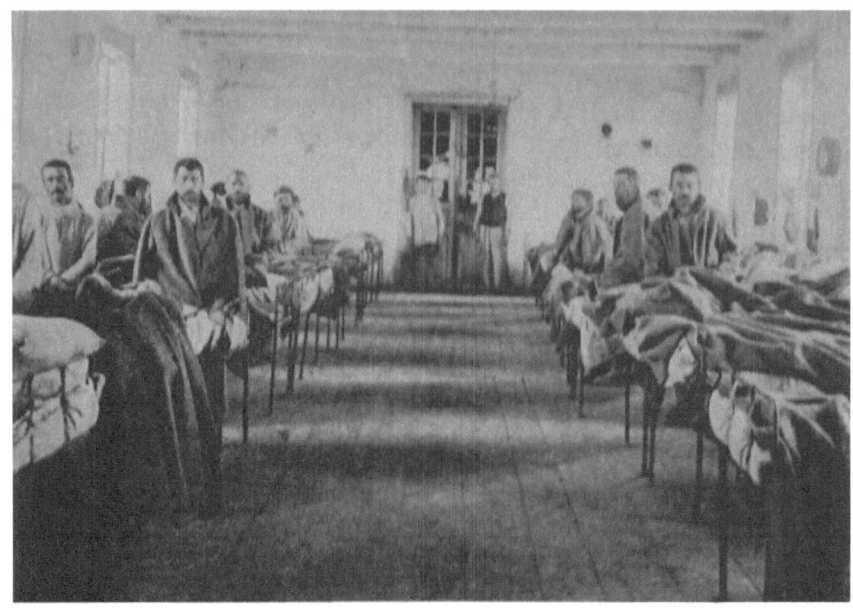

Fig. 9: Sick ward in Aleksandrovsk Post

"Do you have many years to serve?"

"Not many, because I've already served many, and had many a beating. I'm a *brodiaga*, wandered a long time through Siberia. I'd wanted to change my fate. I got caught and they beat me up—now I'm paying my dues. I can't lie down or stand up. I've already lost my innards. It's tough to be here, oh, so tough! Well, it won't be long... It won't be long..."

"Your sentence will end soon?"

"No. I'll die."

Beside him a consumptive wheezes, "If I were somewhere else I'd get better..."

"Isn't the air here terrible for him, doctor?"

"Yes... Yes... Well, what can be done?!"

10

THE WOMEN'S PRISON

It isn't large: all of one ward, with ten persons. On Sakhalin, women are forced to serve a special kind of *katorga*: they're distributed as "cohabitants" to exile-settlers. Only those under investigation are held in prison.

Upon our appearance, two get up from the sleeping platforms. One is an old Circassian and recidivist-murderer who neither speaks nor understands Russian. The other is a young woman, a peasant from Viatka Province. She ended up in *katorga* for arranging to have her child's godfather murder her husband.

"Why did you do it?"

"They gave me to him against my will. But I loved the godfather. I thought we'd go to *katorga* together. On the contrary, he went one place and me another."

Once here, she committed a crime rare for Sakhalin. With her own hands, she defended her cohabitant using a rifle. He was quarreling with some exile-settlers. Nine of them jumped him and began beating him up, so she ran to the house, grabbed the rifle and shot the first attacker she saw.

"So you really loved him, your cohabitant?"

"Certainly, I loved him. If I hadn't loved him, would I have gone to save him? They even tried to kill me... 'He's a good man,' I was thinking, 'we'll be together for ages.' But now, look what's happened..." She wipes away some tears and starts sobbing quietly.

"Nothing will happen to her," the warden assures me. "She'll be tried and sent to a remote settlement to become another exile-settler's cohabitant... Our women on Sakhalin aren't punished."

Really, from a certain point of view, this doesn't seem a punishment. But what more difficult punishment can be devised than this "assignment" to another man, this reassigning of a woman who loved so powerfully and passionately that she was prepared to sacrifice her own life? Does this not reek of something rather moldy to you? Of an obsolete time? Of serfdom, when they "gave away" others so casually, playing with their lives and hearts?

Of all the prisons I've just toured with you, this little one makes the deepest impression.

11

THE ISOLATORS

The heavy, fetid, insufferable air is damp but clear enough. Such is the general impression made by Korsakovsk's isolator cells located near the guardhouse. The most serious offenders and those under investigation are kept here.

Meet Avdeev, a youth with an unpleasant face and repellant gaze. Abnormally cynical, he gives the impression of a little wolf, cornered and vicious. As if to complete the likeness, he stands rigidly at the door's window and gnaws the wood. He's already gnawed off a fair amount, as if to sharpen his teeth. Avdeev is now around 19 years old but was already an incorrigible criminal before 15. He's sentenced to life. When he was 14 he committed that most serious of crimes: he murdered his parents.[1]

"Why did you kill them?"

"Why does anyone kill? For the money!"

His brief life is an entire novel. His illegitimate father was an officer, his mother a captured Turk. The father hitched up with her at the time of the last war[2] and brought her and their begotten child to Russia. Neither father nor mother loved this unfortunate boy. Sufficiently well-off, they nevertheless neglected him completely: Avdeev can hardly read.

"If they'd been good to me, I wouldn't have knifed them!" Avdeev calmly, cold-bloodedly and cynically says of his crime. "There was some good money—30,000. I should've gone abroad, and that have been it! But no, I started drinking. Obviously, I'm a bad seed, and so stupid!"

In *katorga*, Avdeev leaves the isolator only to lie beneath the birch rod on the mare; and he gets up from the mare only to sit in the isolator. He stubbornly refuses to work. He's tried to escape, and they've caught him. For his time away from *katorga* he's earned 500 to 600 birch strokes. And he speaks of this calmly, cold-bloodedly and cynically.

"So why do you refuse to work?"

"Ah! I don't want to, so I don't."

"But what's in store for you? You'll be ripped to shreds!"

"They don't dare rip me to shreds."

"Isn't it painful?"

"It's painful, but you have to bear it."

"Is this really better than working?"

"Of course it's better. You're flogged, and then it's over. But work is from morning to night, every day."

"Well, but is sitting in solitary really pleasant?"

"It doesn't matter! People sit!... And I'm only here talking with you because I won't work! You can give up and whine until you're dead. I won't!"

He makes a powerful impression. Personally, I think he's a "stubborn horse." A horse who, no matter how strongly pulled or whipped, refuses either to cooperate or take a step forward, even if he's being beaten. In such cases even the least experienced coachman gives the horse a little something to make it move. I think a good dose of potassium bromide would have a better effect than a birch rod on this repulsive and profoundly wretched youth, afflicted as he is by a nervous condition.

Alongside him is the worldly convict Babaev, an Armenian from Erevan Province with a sympathetic face that, when speaking, flashes an affable, ingratiating, insinuating smile. His eyes are oily, as if perpetually coated in the liquid. Voice soft and pleasant, he speaks very quietly, tenderly, unctuously.

Babaev hasn't lost his artistic streak. He loves to paint and is constantly rendering the same thing: "broad-chested" generals on "broad-chested" galloping chargers. He's covered everything in his cell with these pictures. His favorite gift is a box of paints, at which his eyes joyously sparkle...

His specialty is murdering comrades. He spots those with money in each new party of arrivals and convinces them to escape. He describes *katorga*'s horrors and how easy it is to flee; promises to get them a passport and to be a devoted comrade. It's no surprise that newcomers trust the friendly, affectionate tone of voice, the ingratiating smile, the sympathetic face. Somewhere out deep in the taiga he murders the man, takes his money and returns to the prison. He lives off this money, treating himself, buying paints and painting his favorite pictures. *Katorga* accuses him of six murders; officially, he's been charged with two. During his last escape (he's run away twice) pursuers first stumbled upon one corpse then another, and by this horrible trail came upon Babaev.

Here's this man, "sentenced to life." Investigations on Sakhalin typically stretch for several years, and so the most terrible moment for Babaev will be when the investigation ends and he's transferred from solitary confinement to the general prison.

He obsesses over and fears this moment. The prisoners are going to kill him. Oh, Lord! He prefers this pathetic despicable existence over death. Constantly thinking about the other prisoners has led him to develop a persecution complex. He never leaves the isolator, refuses even to take a walk. He's even afraid to be escorted by a soldier. "Anyone could come and murder me." And when he says this he turns pale, a spasm crosses his face, and his eyes fill with such terror that it's like he's already facing the blade. The man will probably have just such an expression when he's on the ground awaiting the fatal thrust. This obsession will probably drive him crazy… and perhaps that would be better for him. Better insanity than cognition, than constant fear and trembling.

12

"REFORMED"

"Hee-hee! Here's a man deprived of his innocence," a Sakhalin official was saying. The man involved in this strange incident was Balad-Adash, a Georgian sentenced for murder. A man of phenomenal strength, courageous, determined and proud, he was "intolerant within *katorga*." Not that he refused to work; but if he or one of his comrades wasn't assigned a job "according to the rules," he would protest and quit working. He was polite and respectful; but if cursed at, he'd turn his back and stalk off. If reprimanded "for no reason whatsoever," he'd raise an objection. Give him one word, and he'd give you ten. He was concerned with fairness and introduced it as was possible here. "It was as if he had come here to correct us, and not we him!" the official grudgingly told me.

Balad-Adash wouldn't let himself "be undone" by their boorishness.

"He puts up a fight when we drag him to the mare. 'We shall not allow ourselves to be touched by the birch rod! We'll get you somehow! Better not touch me!' he cries. What can you do with him…?!"

"Tie him up and flog him good!" interrupts someone joining the conversation.

"Thank you very much. Today you tie him up and thrash him, and tomorrow he jams a knife in your side. These Caucasians aren't to be trifled with."

Then a new warden of settlements flew in—not just arrived, but *flew* in—to Korsakovsk District. He was an energetic sort with colossal strength, severe temper and a decisive frame of mind. "How do you know they're guilty? By looking at their snouts, that's all." They turned to him "to tame" Balad-Adash, requesting he make an example of him. Everyone waited with anticipation. "What's he going to do?" Let the energetic warden himself tell us:

"I leave the chancery. I see that character standing among the prisoners. An easy pose, smiling gaze—cheeky. He sees me but doesn't doff his cap![1] And everyone, however many of those people were there, was saying, 'What, I say, is gonna happen? Who's gonna beat who?' Pride had cast its spell. I go up to him. 'I say, you so-and-so, not going to doff your cap, eh? Cap off!' And I knock him off his feet!"

Balad-Adash instantly leapt off the ground and, "possessed," got in the warden's face. "You want a fight?"

"I hit him twice more. Off his feet, he was, blood flowing."

The fight was over. Balad-Adash had been tamed.

"At the time, we thought he'd murder him. But nothing doing, as it turned out," other officials told me.

"Baladka was sobbing after that. He wouldn't speak to anyone for days. He was silent," the prisoners told me.

I saw Balad-Adash and got to know him. Balad-Adash has indeed been tamed. He can now be cursed and beaten. He turns himself over for a flogging, as many lashes as you please, and seeks this pleasure fairly often—by being a drunk, a thief, a liar, a swindler or an informer. There's no dirty trick, no foulness, this man of "lost innocence" is not capable of. He's a sluggard: all he tries to do is pile his own assignments onto others. He enjoys all *katorga*'s scorn and belongs to the *khamy*—people entirely without shame, the most despised class among even these "dregs of humanity."[2]

Among other things, I asked him about his "taming." Balad-Adash gave a little frown but then smiled broadly, as if recalling something humorous and, waving his hand, said, "I really got my snout kicked in! I sure did!"

Thus, Balad-Adash on his taming.

13

TWO ODESSANS

Odessa has provided Korsakovsk Prison two representatives, Verblinsky and Shaposhnikov. It would be difficult to find a more opposite pair: Verblinsky and Shaposhnikov, the two poles of *katorga*.

If there's been gathered for forced settlement the worst, basest, lowest riff-raff, then Verblinsky is the quintessence of *katorga*. I've come to meet Verblinsky in a detention cell, where he's being held on suspicion of murdering two Japanese during a robbery.[1] Verblinsky swears he didn't kill them. He witnessed their murder, received a share of the loot in return for his silence, but didn't kill them.

It's possible to believe him. Verblinsky would not have been capable of such a vile deed. He can knife someone who's asleep; murder someone who's been tied up; strangle a child, a sick woman or a helpless old lady. But to attack two people so as to rob them—this Verblinsky cannot do.

"Pardon me!" he heatedly protests. "How could I murder them? I was born a petty thief, I'm a natural-born pickpocket! Go anywhere in Russia and ask: Can a pickpocket murder a man? They'll laugh in your face! Why would I murder those Japanese?"

"You mean you have a 'speciality'?"

"Exactly, a speciality. Have you ever been to Odessa? Do you know Advocate ____? (Verblinsky names a once famous attorney from the south.) You could've asked him. He defended me back in '82, in Elisavetgrad, against General K's wife. I'd taken 18,000 rubles, two coonskin coats and a pearl. I paid 800 rubles for my defense. Ask him what kind of person Verblinsky is—he'll tell you! Yes, I take whatever I like from whoever I like whenever I like. Allow me to add that if I want, I'll steal from your pocket right now and you won't notice. It's been said that in Kiev during Russia's 900th anniversary there was a large theft from Prince K's home. It was my hands did that one, too!" Verblinsky's voice is proud. "And I suddenly decide to kill some Japanese! My hands would be soiled, and never in my life have I soiled them. I take what I want and I take without killing. So here I am in solitary. But I wanted to show them what Verblinsky can do, and I showed them!"

Verblinsky reported that he knew who had the pelts, the sable furs, stolen from the Japanese, but that in order to pay the ransom he needed fifty-two rubles and an "honest person" to deliver the money to the ransomer. Warden-of-settlements Mr Glinka, who's been investigating this matter, trusted Verblinsky and agreed to give him the fifty-two rubles. "Put your personal stamp on the envelope!" Glinka put his stamp on the envelope. Verblinsky added some sort of coded prisoner's mark. "Now get me an honest person who can deliver this, because I won't be able to explain it to the administration." They found him some Buriat.[2] Verblinsky spoke with him in private, gave him the address, and told him the door to knock on and what to say. "Look, don't lose this envelope!" said Verblinsky, shoving the envelope into the Buriat's chest.

"So we're leaving the detention cell," Glinka was telling me, "but I began having some doubts. 'I should seal the envelope,' I'm thinking. 'If I don't seal it, then its contents will be known and I won't get the skins.' To seal it or not? In the end, I decided to seal it."

But a piece of paper was in the envelope. Verblinsky had managed to take out the money and replace it with paper. They ran back to search him and found forty-two rubles; but ten had vanished like steam into thin air.

"I kept it for my services!" Verblinsky insolently smiled. "For the lesson! They slipped up! Ah! But I tricked them. I never needed any money, only to show you that I—in a cage, under lock and key, stuck in solitary—can suck 'em in and fool 'em. I'll do such a trick suddenly, and start carving people up!"

"Indeed, you saw them get stabbed?"

"Exactly, I saw it. I was there as the lookout. They wanted me to join in so I wouldn't report them. They finished them off in front of me."

"Were they sleeping?"

"One, that corpse they found, was sleeping. But the other, who they haven't found—he's buried in the taiga—woke up. He thrashed around a lot. They slit his throat while he was awake."

"Why haven't you revealed the murderers? Shouldn't you answer for this?"

"Mercy! You really don't know convict ways! I say anything, and they'll kill me for it."

Verblinsky is an Odessan. He owned a haberdashery in Odessa.

"It was a front, you understand," he clarifies. "I got a share of the loot in return for providing information. I'd tell them how easy it was to take some good money from houses." He doesn't say "steal." He "took" money.

"How many times have you been tried?"

"Twenty times."

"All under your real name?"

"Under various names. And what names I've had! Even here, when they caught me, they found two passports I'd laid away. 'Whatever happens,' I thought, 'I'll be able to get away.'"

This is a man who's passed through fire, water and copper pipes. He knows all Russia's prisons and jails like a first-class tourist knows Europe's hotels. And he talks about them like hotels. "It was damp there... There, it's drier. In Kharkov Central there isn't enough food and it's badly cooked. In Moscow the food's better and the living's easier. Vodka—it's expensive there but cheaper there."

Verblinsky ended up on Sakhalin because of a foul crime: he acquired through force what is usually acquired through love. He was convicted in Kiev. "Not that I liked her all that much, but she wasn't bad-looking!"

On his exterior (the typical exterior of an arch-scoundrel) and in his eyes (wily, malicious, furtive and shameless) glows the tiny soul of the wretched, the underling, the foul.

Shaposhnikov is also an Odessan. In 1887 or '88 he was convicted for his participation in a bandit gang led by the infamous Chumak. Ending up in *katorga*, Shaposhnikov immediately transformed himself. Witnessing others' suffering and misery has an effect, but Shaposhnikov has alone literally expelled the desperate cutthroat from himself so as to become a selfless defender of all the suffering and oppressed. He's transformed himself into an "advocate for *katorga*"…

After ending up on Sakhalin he, like the majority of convicts, immediately "became concerned with justice." He could not view with indifference the slightest display of unfairness. He denounced it courageously and decisively, neither stopping at nor fearing anything. They flogged him; but even while lying on the mare he would cry, "You have done wrong! We've been sent here for punishment but not for torture. We were sent here for justice. But you are committing an injustice."

"He's gotten five or six thousand birch strokes in his life. That's the kind of person he was!" the warden told me.

Then Shaposhnikov suddenly lost his mind. He began talking gibberish and trash and doing senseless things. They sent him to the infirmary, kept him there, then released him as a "mute lunatic." Since then, Shaposhnikov's been considered an "idiot." He's not punished for any of his pranks because he's regarded as insane.

But Shaposhnikov is far from being an idiot. He merely changed tactics. "I got tired of lying on the mare!" is how he explains it. He understood that the weakest goes to the wall; and he continues his former business, albeit in different form. He's still the same sincere, selfless and stalwart friend of *katorga*. As an "idiot" he's been freed from labor and obliged only to tidy up the ward. Nevertheless, he still goes to labor sites; moreover, he visits the toughest ones. When he sees that someone is exhausted, worn out or unable to cope with a particularly heavy "task," Shaposhnikov silently approaches, takes his axe and replaces him. But there's trouble if a convict—usually a newcomer—unknowingly says "Thanks!" For, in a moment, Shaposhnikov will drop the axe, spit and leave.

God knows what sustains Shaposhnikov. He's always carrying "the bread of mercy" for anyone who's gambled away his own rations. He'll feed it to a starving *zhigan*. At the same time, it is not God's will that he should receive alms. Shaposhnikov takes the bread and throws it on the floor, spits in face of the "offender" and walks away. He demands that his sacrifices be accepted with the same silence with which he gives them. He approaches, silently dispenses the bread and waits standing quietly, as if his greatest pleasure is to watch another eat. If, as rarely happens, Shaposhnikov comes into some money, he unfailingly buys something for some wretch who's been completely taken by the usurious Tatar money-lenders.

Shaposhnikov continues his objections and denunciations on behalf of *katorga* but now cloaks them in jocular form, a mask of idiocy. He exposes not the administration, but *katorga*. "Well, do you?" he shouts when *katorga* sternly and morosely stays silent to the administrator's question, "Does anyone wish to file a grievance?" "Why have you all fallen silent, you devils! You were whining and whining that the soup was bad, that the *chaldon*[3] puts rotten meat in it, that the soup's only good for washing your feet but not to feed people—and now you've fallen silent! You've even apologized to them! (He faces the officials.) They whined magnificently when you weren't here. Apparently they washed their feet in the soup and have now caught colds and lost their voices! You must answer for their silence."

Or a similar scene:

"Anyone here have a grievance to file?" asks the warden on his way to the prison.

"I have!" Shaposhnikov steps forward.

"What is it?"

"Your worship, punish these scoundrels!" shouts Shaposhnikov, indicating *katorga*. "You're showing them such magisterial mercy. Order them flogged. They're making life impossible! No peace day or night. They whine and moan! What do they moan about? 'The bread, y'see, is damp.' They're lying, the scoundrels! It's top-notch bread!" Shaposhnikov takes out a piece of really good bread that a prisoner has stashed away that day and pokes it with his finger. "It's soft bread! Outstanding! I could model a figurine from this bread! It's a wonder! But they, y'see, can't eat it. The swine!"

This "idiot" is particularly unloved by Dr Surminsky, who in turn is unloved by *katorga* because of his callousness, coldness and hostility toward prisoners. "Your worship!" Shaposhnikov turns to him on those rare occasions Surminsky visits the wards. "It pleases you to bother to appear before them like an idol! Can they stand it? They call you Doctor Water and malign you because you treat them only with water. Yet you worry over them, the scoundrels, and visit them. You should spit on them, the rogues."

"Get out of here!" hisses the doctor.

And what happens when someone protests? *Katorga* doesn't hold a grudge even against those who can't refrain from protesting—and to groan about pain is a relief.

I talked a lot with Shaposhnikov. He's still a young man, prematurely aged by his and others' sorrow and suffering. During his free time he talked often, bitterly and matter-of-factly.

"They consider me a half-wit here!" he smiled. "You do go crazy! I get up in the morning, look for my head—where's my head? No head! But my head's rolling around in the mud! Ha-ha-ha!... It's true, sometimes I lose my head.

It's really difficult not to lose it. Look at what's around: filth, sorrow, suffering, destitution, depravity, despair. That's where you lose it. It's difficult for a man not to cry. Very difficult! A fellow's drowning, but as he's drowning his noggin is telling him to strike out at anything. But he really is drowning. He's floundering about, arms busy with other things, and he can't strike out. Ha-ha-ha! It's all in his noggin, his brain-pan! A drowning fellow is called a 'scoundrel'! But he's no scoundrel, he's nothing but a drowning man. Have you ever been to Paris?"

"I have."

"Well, I was reading in some books—I don't remember whose works—that there's a building there called the 'Morgue' where they put people who've drowned in the river. Here, our barracks is the 'Morgue.' I walk in, look right, look left and see bloated drowned corpses lying on the sleeping platforms. They reek! They're rotten, and nothing resembling a human being remains. You can't believe that earlier, he had a snout! But you can tell it was a man! 'Scoundrels,' they say—but they're not scoundrels, they're drowned men. One simply sees what those who don't sleep at night see. He's himself during daytime, but at night he's thinking others' thoughts. He suffers their wounds. And do you know, barin, who doesn't sleep at night?"

"Well?"

"Me and the mouse, because death is always talking." And Shaposhnikov crows like a rooster and hops about on one leg.

Such are the strange, endlessly intriguing characters *katorga* has gathered along with Verblinsky. Unfortunately, these characters are rare, very rare. As rare as good people in the world.

14

THE MURDERERS (A MARRIED COUPLE)

"Dear, won't you have some tea? I could bring you some."

"Take a seat, sweetheart, for just a minute. You're tired."

"But what about you, dear? Seriously, I'll bring you some tea."

Such are the day-long conversations from behind the other side of the wall. My hosts, the convicted and exiled Pishchikovs, are an extremely interesting couple.

He was an Othello. Even a literary celebrity, in a certain sense. He's the protagonist of G. I. Uspensky's story "One to One."[1] He's the flogger-criminal all Russia talked about, his story an echo of the last war. Like many at the time, it was his fate to fall in love with a native Turk. Her longtime friend, he had kindly played the role of lovers' messenger, a *postillon d'amour*. He delivered messages and facilitated her intimacy with another. But little by little he and the woman drew closer because of this and got to know each other better... He fell in love with someone loved by another, and she fell in love with him. So she forgot her Turkish man, who returned to his country, married her new love, and they spent six peaceful and happy years together. He fathered four children, and she was preparing to deliver him a fifth.

Then jealousy suddenly awakened from out of the past. That Turk, her heart's fleeting guest, forgotten and disappeared over the horizon, became a specter that divided them. Her new husband's soul was torn, tormented, consumed by thoughts of her old affections for another. Horrible tormenting suspicions arose in his deranged imagination: suspicions that she loved "that man," that she was thinking about his caresses, that she'd given birth to the children—his children—while thinking of this other. This terrible psychological drama ended with a horrible verdict of "guilty." Pishchikov tied his wife to the bed and flogged her to death. Her suffering both tormented and delighted him. The torture lasted several hours... But she... She was kissing his arms. Did she love him so much she could ingratiatingly accept torture? Or was she silently forgiving him during those terrible moments—a forgiveness of his spiritual torments of which she was the unwilling culprit?... So wonders Pishchikov. He received a life sentence of *katorga*, but it was reduced by royal clemency and he now has four years left to serve.

Pishchikov's present wife is similarly a "widow through her own fault." Her trial, though not so famous, made the rounds of all the newspapers in her day. She's a former actress who with another murdered her husband, a colonel, then hid his body. The corpse was discovered, the crime revealed, and she was sent to *katorga* for a long term.

"Sharonikhye," as she's known in *katorga*, fought a not insignificant struggle that spared her the typical fate of exiled female convicts. Initially, one of Sakhalin's officials fell in love with this bold, intelligent, willful woman and chose her to be his "cook." On Sakhalin, such cooks receive a host of rights and privileges. But Sharonikhye protested immediately. "Either a 'cook' or a 'concubine' be, but 'to mix these two skills is darkness for lovers, and I'm not that type.'" She protested so loudly, energetically and stolidly that she was left alone. Then she met Pishchikov. They fell in love, and the pair of murderers married.

A pair of murderers... How strange this appellation sounds when one speaks of this sweet, infinitely kind and splendid couple living heart to heart. Their past would seem to defame them. It's impossible! Impossible that this affectionate husband—who cannot address his wife with just two words but must always add a third affectionate term—that he could be a flogger. Impossible that her perpetually active, honest hard-working hands could have been bloodied by murdering her husband!

It's hard to tear them apart: they've swum through this ocean of filth called *katorga*, swum through it and saved one another. Can reciprocal tender affection actually originate here?

He served as lighthouse warden and in the district commander's chancery. He's the commander's right hand, knowledgably carrying out all his duties outstandingly, congenially and assiduously.

As I've already said, he's a friendly and splendid husband, astonishingly gentle, even living a bit under his energetic wife's heel. Nothing of the former Othello remains in him, this Othello-*cum*-flogger.

Only once did an old wound open, a sort of jealousy. His wife has recalled it with horror ever since. He took out his razor, whetted it, locked himself in a room, then... shaved off his big bushy beard and moustache. "It was terrible to look at him! And he wouldn't come near me afterward!" explains Mrs Pishchikov. For a long time afterward he begged forgiveness and went about with a guilty look. But he wasn't jealous anymore.

As for her... There's not a moment she's unoccupied. First she's salting herring, then making flower arrangements to sell or working in her outstanding model garden or sewing clothes for Korsakovsk's "intelligentsia." And her fee is... one ruble "per fitting."

"Why so cheap?" I was astounded. "That's practically free! You should charge two at least!" She began waving her hands in alarm.

"What are you saying?! What are you saying? My husband still has four years' *katorga* left. They control him for four more years yet. If they get mad at me they'll retaliate against him. No! No! What are you saying?! What are you saying?!"

You should see how this woman speaks about her husband; hear how her voice quivers when she recalls that he still has four years' *katorga* left... In her voice there's so much love, anxiety and fear for her beloved man.

I actually got acquainted with her on the steamer. She was returning from Vladivostok, where she'd undergone a life-threatening operation. Korsakovsk's tug had barely reached the steamer when a man with an enormous beard was the first to spring onto the gangplank. It was her

Fig. 10: Group of prisoners

husband. They literally froze in each other's embrace and stood like that for several minutes. "Sweetheart!" "Dear!" could be heard through quiet sobs as tears flowed down their arms.

Do they remember their pasts? Both he and she take to drink from time to time. Perhaps it's the debt for which their consciences pay. Conscience succored by vodka...

15

GREBENIUK AND HIS HOMESTEAD

Walking through a Korsakovsk "neighborhood" your attention is invariably drawn to this little house, surprisingly neat, well constructed, even fancy: it even has a terrace. There's always someone at work in the courtyard, either an elderly woman feeding "piggies" or a tall, stooped, sickly kind of muzhik chopping, planing or sawing something. The floor, like the table, is improbably clean. Each little planed plank forms a perfect border with the cornice. I spent several pleasant hours in this domicile. Here I rested my soul from "the Sakhalin stench," Sakhalin's waywardness, the universal disaster of convict frenziedness. When you don't know where in this little spic-and-span home to put a cigarette butt, Grebeniuk goes to a carved wooden box and, not without pride, carefully extracts a faience ashtray as if it were some kind of precious stone.

"This is ours. I myself don't use it, but all the same you need it when someone visits!"

Grebeniuk extremely loves his home and his housekeeping.

"I know each little board here like I know my own patronymic," he smiles pleasantly, looking around with unfeigned affection. "I chose each from the taiga, cut it and dragged it here with my own hands. I put each in its place. I worked on my holidays and came here during lunch breaks." You can actually see that each plank is a familiar friend and how Grebeniuk, recalling each, "became human."

Grebeniuk is a jack-of-all-trades and between sunrise and sunset "doesn't rest his hands!" He's a barber, carpenter, joiner (all skills he learned while in *katorga*) and has a garden and raises "piggies."

"I also have a lot of chickens. The old woman takes care of them. And I have two pairs of sheep."

Grebeniuk is still a penal laborer. Yet for good behavior he's been allowed to live outside the prison in his own quarters. He still "fulfills duties" for the prison: he works several hours each day as a joiner, then spends the rest of his time working for himself.

"Soon my *katorga* term will end. I was sentenced to 20 years. This was shortened by clemencies, so my term will be completely over in just four months. I'll join the exile-settlers, though my house is already built."

Unlike other prisoners Grebeniuk has been given a cohabitant, regardless of the fact that he's still a penal laborer and should not be able to enjoy this particular luxury. His elderly woman came here "because of her husband," that is, because she murdered her husband. She's much older than Grebeniuk, and not pretty.

"Well, I do respect her and she respects me. We live appropriately and don't offend God!"

Their cohabitation really was established early on out of reciprocal need, rather than any other reason. Grebeniuk chose her for her diligence and housekeeping. Unlike Grebeniuk she's free from compulsory labor.

Grebeniuk was a domestic servant before coming to *katorga*.

"You were sentenced on suspicion of guilt?" I asked, using the question typical on Sakhalin. Grebeniuk was silent, pensive.

"No, sir, but you've already cut to the chase, so I'll tell you the truth. I came here for murder. We murdered the barin... I and his attendant finished him off."

"So as to rob him?"

"No. Because of his cruelty. The deceased was cruel—akh, so cruel. He gave such beatings. I was bruised from all the beatings. My insides were all knocked about, he beat me so. I was his coachman, and he had some good horses. How many times I'd fall at his feet, kissing his boots: 'Release me, barin, since I'm such a fool and cannot possibly please you.' 'I'll keep you,' he'd say, 'and the horses will keep you.' It was in my nature to groom the horses. My horses were always in good order... But how hard the deceased beat me! It's troubling to think about it now. So terrible!

"It was in '85, on September 29th, in the city of Medzhinbozh, in Podolsk Province.[1] Maybe you know it? The barin was in Kiev with his attendant, but I'd been left with the horses. The barin comes home and goes to the stable. As was his wont he said to me, 'I say, hey there, you devil!' or something similar. 'What's this you're doing?' he says to me. 'You villain. What've you been doing with the horses, eh? The horses are so thin! What've you done to them, you ignoble soul, what've you done?' But there'd been no oats for his horses. I told him this. 'Mercy, barin, the horses have been without feed and lost weight. You'll please remember I sent you a telegram about this!' 'You're lying,' he cries. 'You scoundrel! You stole the oats!' He slapped me with the back of his hand. I had a sore ear at the time and tried to block it with my hand, but he tore it away and beat me so painfully I was seeing stars. I could see I wasn't going to live by pissing myself, so I told his attendant, 'We have to kill him now, because it's either us or him and somebody's got to go.' And he told me, 'I myself wanted to talk to you about this.' So we began talking, and that same evening we finished him off."

Grebeniuk grew silent and gathered his thoughts.

"It was eleven o'clock. I was sitting in the kitchen, waiting. The attendant went to see whether he was sleeping or not. He comes back and says, 'I think he's asleep!' We drank a bottle of fruit liqueur the attendant stole that evening from supplies, took off our shoes so he couldn't hear us, and went to his room... A candle was always burning in his bedroom at night, but he was just lying there and didn't see us. His arms were folded across his chest and he was asleep. 'Let's do it,' I said. We threw ourselves on him. Tsarenko, the attendant, held him while I put a noose around his neck and punched him."

"Did he die quickly?"

"He wasn't supposed to suffer." A malicious quiver ran through Grebeniuk's voice. "He wouldn't have suffered but for a sound outside."

"What, you mean he'd woken up?"

"Exactly. He awoke just as we grabbed him. Only, he couldn't make a sound. One of his hands reached towards the wall where a revolver, sword and daggers were hanging. Tsarenko grabbed it and twisted it back. I'd already gotten the noose around his neck. He just stared at me… Then we finished him off."

Grebeniuk took a breath.

"So we finished him off. 'Now,' I said, 'we need to cover our tracks.' We dressed his body in an overcoat, shoes with galoshes, and a hat, then threw him in the river under the bridge. 'Dear fellow,' we said, 'whoever finished you off?' We went back home. 'Now,' says Tsarenko, 'let's take the money. He should have some money. What's it to him? But we need it.' I said, 'What are you, huh? What did we do this for?' 'Well,' he says, 'do as you like, but I'm taking it.' He took what money there was from behind the stove, and filled up a suitcase with new shirts and fine linen and took them to this old lady he knew. That's how we got caught… At the time, this old lady had a friend, another barin's servant. When Tsarenko brought the stolen items to her, he saw them. They found our victim the next day and people heard that Tsarenko had brought his things to this man and the widow. Word spread. Someone told the authorities and they arrested Tsarenko. He denied everything. 'I don't know anything,' he said. 'I just know that Grebeniuk strangled him under the bridge, then brought his suitcase to me and told me not to tell anyone. I was scared, so I did what he told me.' Then they arrested me. I wouldn't confess for a long time. 'Listen,'" I said, 'I don't know anything.' But then I went ahead and told them everything."

"Because your conscience bothered you?"

"Had nothing to do with my conscience! Spite got hold of me. I was sitting with Tsarenko in a dark cell in the police station. A guard was there, and although he wasn't supposed to, he's talking to Tsarenko and pitying him like he's his brother. I heard what Tsarenko told him. 'Here I am,' he says, 'innocent but sitting here because of that scoundrel.' His words pierced my heart and I shouted, 'Interrogate me now and I'll tell you all you want to know.' Then I explained how it all happened, how we strangled him, about our agreement and where Tsarenko found the money. They gave him life and me 20 years. And that's why I'm here."

"I daresay it's been difficult for you here."

"Until now, I had the strength to work. Ask anyone about me, they'll say the same thing. This is my eleventh year here and no one can say a word against me. I've never been in the isolator or under the birch rod; no guard has ever laid a hand on me. I've labored under I-don't-know-how-many wardens! There was Iartsev, God rest his soul. A cruel man, couldn't accept a prisoner who wasn't dressed in rags. But he never laid a hand on me, never gave me an unpleasant word. I labored, worked, did what I was told to do to the utmost. After dinner the others would sleep, but I'd put an axe in my belt and come here. I'd hammer here and there, climb up on my little house and work... There was no problem, and I was living well. Then my health got bad from too much strain."

Grebeniuk has a worn look and appears older than he is.

"Well, but how do you see the past?... Are you sorry you murdered him? Haven't you repented?"

"Sorry?... This is what I'll tell you, barin. You can judge me as you wish: I'm either a good or a worthless person. But I'll speak honestly to you, as if before God. Were he to rise from the grave and come here, I'd strangle him again. Were he to rise ten times, then I'd strangle him ten times! *Katorga!* They'll tell you it's hard and difficult—don't believe them, barin. They all lie, the scoundrels! They've never seen real *katorga*. I've lived here ten years. So what! I was inside for three years, and *that* was *katorga*—real *katorga*. Here, I've seen the light!"

"Stop, wait a minute! You know there've been truly terrible punishments here!"

"Yes, there have. But of course that was a different time and nothing was gained. It was all for naught. And, really, how often did it happen? Once a month... I don't know that we had any breaks all day. I didn't sleep at night, just sobbed, my eyes swollen up. But don't believe them, sir. They've never seen real sorrow. That's why they talk."

When he speaks of his sacrifices, there are in Grebeniuk's words and face so much malice and hatred for the dead man it's as if it didn't happen twelve years ago but just yesterday. Grebeniuk's guilt is quite burdensome, no doubt about it, as is his crime. And it's scandalous that "they've not made him suffer for it." But is it right that such a quiet meek man has been driven to such rage?

I asked Grebeniuk about Tsarenko: Where was he now?

"In Aleksandrovsk. They say he's just scraping by. He drinks. He's ready to kill me for betraying him. Let him!"

16

PAKLIN (FROM MY NOTEBOOK)

He's a murderer and a poet. A merciless thief and a tender father. A criminal and a man strongly contemptuous of crime. Of such contradictions is Paklin made.

He was just with me, and I'm hurrying to put down these lines so as not to lose that "criminal scent" that emanates from Paklin. An hour ago I received the following note:

> Venerable Mister Writer!
> Excuse my boldness for sending you my writings. Perhaps you will find here at least one helpful word. But if not, order your servant to toss this into the oven. I'm not a newcomer here, I know the place far and wide and would be happy to serve you in any way possible. I'm not good at writing with a pen, I cut out words like with an axe. Once again, I ask you to forgive my boldness, but I'm a Zaporozhian[1] to the core, never been a coward, and believe the saying that boldness takes the city. Still, sincerely, I ask you not to think I'm doing this with the goal of receiving treats from you. No, I would be three hundred times more grateful if you found just one word helpful. Perhaps at some point my dear relatives will glance at my stanzas, but won't know they were written by me.
> —*Timofey Paklin.*

Waiting in the kitchen for an answer was a short, stocky red-haired man. He seemed embarrassed and, though a redhead, his gray, cold, peaceful and audacious eyes were shot through with flecks of steel.

"Is it you who brought the note from Paklin?"

"That's right!" he answered with a powerful stutter.

"Why didn't Paklin himself come?"

"He didn't know whether you'd want to meet with a penal laborer."

"Tell him to come himself."

He then answered quietly: "I am Paklin."

"Why did you just tell me you weren't Paklin?" I asked.

"I didn't want to be insulted. I didn't know if you'd talk with a murderer."

"Paklin"—this isn't his real name. It's his *nom de la guerre*, under which he committed his crimes and was convicted in Rostov for murdering an archimandrite.[2] It was a brutal murder, sensational at the time. Before me stood a "celebrity," to some extent. He who calls himself Paklin is a Cossack and very proud of this. Naturally, he's one of those regarded as "congenital murderers." He loved adventure and fighting from childhood. "Nothing made me as happy as leaping onto a young unbroken steed and flying along, turning him as I would. I'd exhaust both him and myself, but my soul would feel so good." Having taught himself to read, Paklin read only books about adventure, fighting and death. "I loved to read about bandits most of all."

Paklin began his criminal career with a pair of murders. He murdered a friend "because of love." They'd fallen in love with the same girl. He was able to cover up this murder, but rumor spread through his *stanitsa*[3] and one day during a quarrel another friend said to him, "And who are you? Really, I'm nothing to you! Wouldn't you sneak from behind a corner and murder me, brother? You're a scoundrel!"

"I couldn't stand the insults," says Paklin. "That night, I saddled a horse and grabbed my guns. I killed my offender and left the *stanitsa*, not telling my family for shame."

He "took up vagabondage" and along the way acquired the name Paklin. A certain old woman took to him so as to replace the son she'd lost. He brought her to a different city and settled down with her.

"I esteemed her as my own mother. I worried over her, always gave her money so she wouldn't be in need…"

"Where is she now?"

"I don't know. At that time I had the strength… to care. But now, I have other affairs. Live as you know how. She's alive or, praise God, already dead. The bit of money we took from the house when we escaped ran dry, so I needed to steal more and more. I'd read about how richly bandits lived and I thought, 'What would it be like for me?' I was vexed: people living their happy lives while I'm living like such a dog…" At this moment Paklin looks like some Schilleresque bandit, like a Karl Moor.[4] "I never took a kopek from the poor. Indeed, it so happened I helped the poor. Never violated a beggar. But I took, as it were, quite a lot from those who violated others."

Paklin, however, doesn't try to justify himself. On the contrary, for while speaking he even refers to himself as a "scoundrel." But he talks about all this quite calmly and simply, as if about someone else.

As in most truly congenital criminals' lives, women didn't play an especially important role in Paklin's. He'd use them "for a good time," then toss them some money and move on to the next. In his day, he robbed and squandered money, traveled through various cities and marked out new victims. He ran a whole gang of thieves.

Melancholy would descend upon him from time to time. "I wanted to put a stop to it all, grab one large last sum and take off for somewhere in America." At the time, he'd lock himself away and read some popular "bandit books" from cover to cover. "I was going to be done with everything and leave for new lands to find my fortune. I'd become terribly wicked by then."

Paklin had already become notorious in Rostov Province and the Northern Caucasus. In Ekaterinograd he'd been indicted on seven counts but was exonerated of all of them. "I'll tell you the truth, my own false witnesses exonerated me. In each instance they testified I was someplace else." The police pursued Paklin. He was difficult to catch and invulnerable. People feared him. "Whenever anything happened everyone would blame me: 'It's that scoundrel's doing.' The more they talked about me the more spiteful I became: 'You say this about me, so let it be true.' I grew bitter, and the worse they talked about me the worse I became. Stealing became a pleasure."

Nighttime thefts were Paklin's specialty. "I especially liked dealing with educated persons, with merchants and clergymen. Everyone knows you can deal with them straightforwardly. No uproar, no scandal. He tells me where the money is because his life is more precious! You take the money and that's it, and before saying goodbye you even apologize for upsetting him!" Paklin said with a cold, hard ironic smile.

"But what happened if they didn't give you the money right away? Would it get brutal?"

"I had my ups and downs," he reluctantly answered.

The archimandrite of Nakhichevansk Monastery[5] proved himself to be, in Paklin's words, a "slow-witted" man.

"A friend and I called on him. We'd been watching all his comings and goings beforehand. The old man was scared, shaking. He tried to shout but my comrade grabbed him by the throat. He relaxed his grip but the old man still wanted to shout. I talked to him for almost an hour: 'You'd better not shout or report our crime, just show us where your money is…' But he wouldn't tell me. 'Kill him!' I told my friend. He drew a blade across his throat. That was it! What a gush of blood…"

Paklin looks off somewhere while saying this. His unpleasant freckle-covered face begins to blush and his lips distort into some unnatural forced smile. He starts hugging himself and stuttering more than usual. It's hard to look at him. There's a long pregnant pause.

Paklin and his accomplice were tried along with two others Paklin had fenced out of the deal and who were innocent. "I asked my defense counsel to exclude them. I didn't care, I just didn't want these innocents coming after me. He was a good fellow and tried his best."

PAKLIN (FROM MY NOTEBOOK)

During his trial Paklin spent eleven months in an isolation cell, staying there until he hallucinated. But he "didn't lose heart." When Rostov Prison's kind and humanitarian Dr K, loved by all prisoners, failed to reach an understanding with the prison administration and had to leave, Paklin gave him an icon the prisoners had ordered by subscription. "At the time all the newspapers wrote about this!"

"Just one more question, Paklin," I asked as I was leaving. "Tell me, do you believe in God?"

"In God? No. It's every man for himself."

At first glance, Paklin is holding up very well in *katorga*. He endures a most burdensome "double *katorga*," so to speak. This is as he wishes.

"He's such a half-wit!" one Korsakovsk official well familiar with Paklin's history told me. "He's a hard-working chap, exemplary. No one's ever said a bad word against him. He's also a good joiner; he taught himself while in prison and could be outstanding here, working along with the craftsmen and living high on the hog. But he 'didn't want to' and prayed to Jesus Christ to be sent to guard the Okhotsk coast. The worst cases get sent there for punishment. You don't see a living soul for half the year. You can turn into a wild man. There's no more difficult *katorga*! But he asked for it. So he lived there in solitude."

"Why did you do that?" I asked Paklin.

"I feared being hurt. Early on here, they'd punish you whether you did this or that. Well, at the time, I couldn't have withstood the slightest blow, never mind the birch rod. Because of my sin, knowing myself, I requested it. I was proud then."

"And now?"

"Now," Paklin waved his hand, "now that I've been there, if someone boxes my ears I run away without looking back! Then, I might have tried to even the score, yes, but now I think of the children. For my good behavior they've given me a cohabitant, even though I'm a penal laborer, and I have two children. They curse me, but I think about my children all the time. The more they curse me, the more I think of them!" Paklin burst out laughing. "Everything to me is like water off a duck's back. Beat me and I won't make a sound… It's the damnedest thing! I'll be in such pain but I'll just squeak a bit!"

And in that tone Paklin listened to himself in sincere amazement, as if he were surprised to find himself with normal human feelings.

I was Paklin's houseguest. His is the best home in the entire post. It's spotless, incredibly so. His wife is a beautiful young woman, a so-called "*skopets* virgin" sent to Sakhalin for having castrated nearly ten women.[6] How, how could this pair *not* have met on Sakhalin! Paklin lives with her heart to heart, as they say. He spends every spare penny on either her or the children. With a father's

Fig. 11: Bridge in the *taiga*

pride and affection he showed me his pair of chubby lads: "What little ruffians they've become!"

Elsewhere in this book, where I discuss "poet-murderers," I introduce Paklin's verses. They're not especially profound, but are interesting. He has no great understanding of versification. But there's much sadness, energy, even sentimentality in his ungrammatical lines... His notes on the savage Ainu he saw living on the Okhotsk coast reveal an ability to notice the least typical things.

Paklin's specialty is making boxes, which he does very well. I wanted to buy one from him but Paklin protested vociferously: "No, no barin, I won't allow it. You won't take it as a gift but should pay for it? Do you think I made friends with you just to sell you a box? I don't want to do that!"

"Tell me, Paklin," I asked, after he accompanied me down his porch steps. "Why did you want to meet me? Why did you write me about yourself?"

"Why?" Paklin smiled sadly. "So you could see a person who's been buried alive. See what happens underground. Does he want to be given a voice from there or not? 'Anyway,' he says, 'I'm alive'..."

17

SETTLEMENTS (THE EXILE-SETTLERS)

"Some exile-settlers have come to see you!" the flustered landlady of my apartment explained, almost in horror.

"But are they allowed to come here?"

"Listen to you! They're here! You can see them!"

I went onto the porch. A crowd of exile-settlers, at least two hundred strong, doffed their caps in unison.

"Your worship! Show a commander's mercy…"

"What do you want?"

"We need rations! There's simply no way…"

"Stop, stop, brothers! Why are you coming to me? I'm not the leadership!"

"Quite so! We know you're a writer… But if you'd be so good as to write to someone that there should be… There's no way, and we're nearly invisible from hunger! We came here from the settlements, hoped to find a little work, but all the contractors are hiring the Japanese. We get no rations and aren't allowed to go to the mainland to earn money.[1] 'Die here on Sakhalin!' So what do we do now?"

"But what about your farms?"

"What about our farms, your worship?! You sow and there's nothing. Whoever's had seeds has eaten them. They won't give us cows. Death's near!"

"Barin! Master! Yershipsulness!" An unprepossessing little muzhik elbowed his way through the crowd. This little muzhik was one of those hard-drinking craftsmen who now remind me of that song, "The Kamarinsk Muzhik": *His beard is disheveled, all ruined with damp*. His red shirt was billowing in the wind, the skirt of his little frockcoat torn and frayed. The little muzhik's shrill voice and alcoholic tears welled up from the very depths of his rent and drunken soul. For some reason, as his first duty he flung his cap on the ground with all his might.

"Master! Your highness! Allow me to explain everything to you without a hitch! Your highness! Lord benefactor! They're right about everything! As if before God, I'm saying they're right! 'Cause it's impossible! Now, for example, someone tells me, 'Moisey Levontich, it's impossible.' I tell him, 'Eat, drink and save your soul!' 'Cause I'm for everyone… Do I speak the truth or not?" He suddenly turned with bitterness upon the crowd. "Do I speak the truth or not? Why're you devils silent?"

"It's really… It's over!" The crowd answered regardlessly. "You're for this, you're for that."

"Because I'm for anyone! Myself, my blood! There goes his blood!" The little muzhik unclenched a fist holding seven kopeks. "There they go! What a pity!" Moisey Levontich beat his chest, his voice further breaking with tears. "Do I speak the truth or not? Why're you all silent? I'm for you, you devils, I'm trying to say, but you're silent!"

"It's over… It really is… Yes, you're for this, you're for that!" the crowd languidly answered again. But Moisey Levontich had flown into a rage and was hearing and listening to nothing.

"How does Moisey Levontich fare in the world?! The warden of settlements knows me personally. He visits me. 'Moisey Levontich, can you make a bust for my garden?' Of course I can, I'm a natural-born sculptor. Natural-born!" The natural-born sculptor began beating his chest again and wiping away tears. "Not just any kind, but natural-born! I'm not in Rasseya,[2] but I'm still a sculptor. 'Can you?' 'I can.' 'Here's two notes for vodka.' What a pity! What am I gonna do with 'em, these notes? If anyone has some notes—there goes the day! Do I speak the truth or not? Why, you devils…"

"Stop, listen!" I interrupted, seeing that the mellifluent "sculptor" would never end. "I can see you're a serious man. We've spoken together once before. But now you're asking me to have done with these people. Brothers, take him away." A dozen hands reached for the natural-born yet afflicted sculptor, and the puny figure disappeared into the crowd. It was a painful situation. "What can I do for you? I can't do anything."

"Exactly!" the crowd dejectedly said. "Who're you going to see, when even they can't do anything? Who *can* do anything? What can be done now?" Bitter voices all around: "It was so much better in prison!… Let's go there! And not just for show!… You have to work there, but you eat!… No work or food here. So what should we do? Only thing left is to murder and steal! So let's take to prison again. We can eat there! Better than doing nothing. Take whatever's not nailed down!"

At that moment, in reference to exile settlement, the aphorism suddenly entered my head: "*Katorga* begins when it ends." It was an aphorism that became popular everywhere on Sakhalin, even in places I never visited. "That's true. That's right. Those are the right words!" penal laborers and exile-settlers would say. "The absolute truth!" "Absolutely, completely correct! Spot on!" officials unanimously confirmed. Even those for whom it would seem to have been a troublesome comment sighed in agreement. "Write that down! Without fail, write it. It's the truth, the absolute truth. Awfully, awfully true!"

Fig. 12: A settlement

18

THE FEMALE COHABITANT[1]

Here's a fantastic picture! Where in all Russia will you see anything like it?

"God bless you, uncle!" I say.

"Deepest thanks, your worship!" the muzhik says as he's taking some piping-hot bread from the oven. Turning to his woman who's collapsed on the bed, he tells her, "You should get up. See, a barin's come!"

Reluctantly, the woman begins to rise.

"Never mind, never mind!" I say. "Lie back down, dear. Is your ladyship sick?"

"Why should I be sick?" the woman unwillingly answers, again resuming her former position. "Thank the Lord!"

"Then why are you lying down?" Something absurd is going on. Like a woman, the muzhik suddenly preoccupies himself with the cooking.

"It doesn't matter to him!" she says. "His hands won't drop the tea. He didn't buy it. Let him work!"

"This is really a disgrace!" I say. "You should get up and do some work!"

"Forget her, your worship! She's a woman!" apologizes the muzhik, clearly becoming terribly embarrassed during the course of this conversation.

"What a pain!" she says. "I worked back home and that was enough. I did housework in Russia and I'm to do still more here?! What a surprise! He might please me, but I'm not going to cringe before him. A guard already came and asked me to be his cohabitant. He's just one of many. I can have anyone I want!"

The woman is from Kostroma and strongly exaggerates the letter "o." She speaks with unusual impudence, a kind of impertinent aplomb.

"But, but, you certainly won't! How you talk!" timidly replies the exile-settler, trying to rein her in, but only for appearance's sake. "Be quiet!"

"I'll say what I want. And I'm not pleased, though now I'm completely amused. I wore an apron and did my work. Otherwise, many of you'd be without shirts. So go find another, a woman who's taken a vow of silence!"[2]

"Pshaw, you! You're a boil, woman," the muzhik confusedly smiles. "An absolute boil."

"But a boil may pop like so," she says unhesitatingly.

"That's enough out of you. Don't say a word. Why, you!"

"You're not holding a harness, so don't say 'whoa'! I'm not your horse and you're not my drayman!"

"Pshaw, you!"

"Don't spit. You're lathering. I'll see how you spit when I go live with the guard..."

"Mother, when did you come wafting in?" I turn to her, hoping to end this wild, ridiculous, scandalous scene.

"Year five."[3]

"And why did you come here?"

"Why did I come here? Why *do* women come here? Because of my husband."

"Yes, and you immediately became this muzhik's cohabitant?"

"Why 'immediately'? This is my third year and already my third family."

"What, have they all been bad? You didn't like them?"

"If they'd been good, I certainly wouldn't have left. If I left it means they were bad. Here, it's what you can get from the mate of a barefoot crew. I wanted to eat! It's no mystery. I go to the warden of settlements and say I don't want to live with him and he assigns me to another."

"But what if you're not assigned? Won't you go to prison?"

"They don't put us there. Don't worry! A sorry few sisters are here. Each year herds of murderers are driven here, but few of us sisters. Each one has the pleasure…"

It becomes absolutely unbearable to listen to this insolent, cynical chatterer, to the mockeries bursting from this sleepy indolent woman.

"You've spoiled your woman," I say, exiting the hut and approaching the exile-settler.

"All of 'em here are like that, your grace!" he apologetically answers.

"That's something amusing! I'm completely amused!" she shouts from the hut. I give the exile-settler a half-ruble.

"Deepest thanks for your mercy!" he says with unaccustomed joy.

"Wait a moment! Tell me, with a clear conscience, what you'll spend this ruble on. Will you drink it or spend it on the woman?"

For a moment, the muzhik is indecisive.

"With a clear conscience?" He begins laughing. "With a clear conscience, I'd drink the half ruble; but I'll be buying a trifle for that base woman!"

One or two days later I was passing through the same settlement. Suddenly, I heard a terrible scream. A woman's piercing voice was howling through the street.

"Good gracious, he's beating me! Mercy, he's killing me, the criminal! Oy, oy, oy! I can't take it anymore! My old bones are gone! He's killing me!"

Neighbors reluctantly spilled out of their huts and stared. "Who's screaming?" They waved their arms and turned toward a hut. "It's happening again!"

Sitting on the *zavalinka*,[4] that same sleepy indolent woman was wailing away. Nearby stood the muzhik, who was evidently talking. "The sinful man," I thought at first, believing he'd lost his patience and had "taught" his cohabitant a lesson. But as I came closer I saw something else was happening. The woman was sitting, it is true, with tousled hair, but was bawling somehow peacefully, completely indifferently, grinding her fists into utterly tearless eyes. Catching sight of me she quietened, got up and went into the hut.

"Ah, you! Boil-woman! You absolute boil!" the muzhik confusedly muttered.

"What did you do? Did you 'teach' her a lesson? Did you beat her?"

"As if!" he said despairingly. "I didn't lay a finger on her! Beat her—like hell! It was all over a little pair of boots, 'cause she wanted some boots. 'I'm off to live with the guard!' she says. Pshaw, you! So she bites me, yes, and, well, shouts—so that everyone down the whole street can hear—that I tyrannize her and that Mister Warden-of-Settlements is going to put me in my grave. But where could I get her little boots?! The slut!"

This is your characteristic Sakhalin "family."

Fig. 13: Cohabitant

19

THE MALE COHABITANT

"Barin! Sir! Your honor!" comes a shout from behind. I stop. A gasping exile-settler without a cap comes running. "I've been looking for you in all the posts!"

"What do you want?"

"You recently called on such-and-such?" He gives me the name of a certain female penal laborer whose crime has interested me.

"Yes. What of it?"

"Allow me to say she's home now." Having lowered his voice, he's now speaking in an exceedingly confidential tone. "Do you want her sent to you, or will you go yourself?" His face is animated by a complete readiness to serve.

"What are you thinking of me?"

The exile-settler's entire physiognomy grins. "You're a joker, barin. Certainly, this is what gentlemen want!"

God! Were that I was an artist, so as to sketch this very minute his base physiognomy!

"And what are you to her, that you race around arranging her affairs?"

"Me?"

"Yes, you!"

The exile-settler softly scratches the back of his head. "I'm her cohabitant!"

"Who are you?... I don't even know your name..."

"I'm Mikhaila!"

"So you... Mikhaila, this is what you do?!... To your own cohabitant, you...?"

"Mikhaila" looks at me, amazed and ironical. It's been said, *Whence come those who know no propriety?*

"Don't be alarmed," he says, laughing. "'Cause around here, it's normal. Not only are cohabitants and wives available, but so are their daughters," he concludes with absolute sincerity. "One's gotta eat, your worship. So what'll it be, your worship? Do you want her?"

It's sickening to look into this subject but the conversation is fascinating.

"Listen, you! I'll pay you the same, though not for that but for something else. Honestly tell me where your cohabitant was when I went to talk to her earlier. Here's the money."

"Deepest thanks..."

"Listen, speak honestly!"

"We always do this. Don't worry... Where was she? She'd gone off to *fart*."[1]

"This is how you both live?"

"This is how we live. But is it just us, barin? Of course, maybe you don't notice it at first. But you live your own way!" Returning quickly to his subject, he asked, "So you don't need anything?... We beg your pardon. We're deeply grateful for your generosity. Your money is *fartovye*.[2] We can gamble it, use it to drink to your health..."

After retreating a short distance he turned and shouted, "If you need something, call on Mikhaila," and gave his surname. "Always my pleasure!"

This is your no less typical Sakhalin "family."

20

THOSE WHO'VE VOLUNTARILY FOLLOWED

Here's a hut where lives a family that chose to follow its breadwinner to Sakhalin. They arrived at almost the same time: he in spring, the family in autumn, 1895. According to Sakhalin regulations he was immediately released from labor "to settle into domestic life." As with the majority of such families (if they arrive with a little money), they've managed to settle in comparatively well. They bought the hovel of an exile-settler who'd left for the mainland, started a small kitchen garden, have a cow and raise "piggies." As Sakhalinites say, this is all "thanks to You, Lord."

The hut was filthy but cozy. Children peered from behind a calico curtain enclosing a colossal bed—not Sakhalin's usual sullen, beaten gloomy children, but ones with bright flaxen hair and cheerful twinkling little eyes. Obviously, at least they were satisfied. The master of the house wasn't home, having left to haul timber from the taiga. The mistress was working at home and clearly irritated.

"Hello, mistress."

"Hello, good man. Thank you for your kind word, that kind word you've said. Usually, there aren't any other words around here besides 'rascal' and 'villain.' All day long you hear 'rascal' and 'villain.' I'd live underground so's not to hear them anymore. All the same, it's what must be. By the holy icons, I wish the earth would swallow me whole. Lord, pardon this sinner! We beseech Your mercy."

"But, auntie, are you on Sakhalin involuntarily?"

"Ah, I came here voluntarily, God forgive me! Such a distance we came. We brought such goods, and money. Later, we sold the goods. Spent what we collected and saved. Lord!" The woman began wiping away tears.

"You have to do something! Why don't you leave?"

"Where can we go? What with all eyes stabbing us with sin and shame: 'Your husband's a convict, your husband's a convict!' Where can you run from such damning eyes? My murderer wrote me again and again during the journey: 'Health's good, they give you a house, horse, cow, swine—you just have to live!' There's no one like him, that scoundrel what's damned me to tears my whole life. I'll cry forever because of that snake of a convict! Nothing he wrote was the way he knew it was. I didn't know anything when I came to this… backwoods! Neither summer nor good weather nor rain! Lord!"

"Well, on the other hand, you brightened your husband's lot. It was better for your husband that his family came! That was a blessing."

My interlocutor went into a frenzy.

"Better for him, that heartless man, that he have rotted, been stricken with palsy in *katorga* or in prison! That an asp, a killer, a fever had stricken him— that would have been better for him! Yes, and why should we now suffer for his murder, endure such torture?"

"And why was your husband sent here?"

"For what happened to a merchant. I had nothing to do with it. It was all those muzhiks. They thought they'd get some money. Well, they did—and we got time!... Because of him, because of that murderer. And me with children at hand and one sitting on my lap. Really, if I'd no children I wouldn't suffer this torment! It's worse than being some female convict, God forgive me. You're lower than any base creature!"

"Well, mother, is this... Isn't there someone below you? On the contrary..."

"But what am I higher than, in your opinion? A convict gets a food ration but I get a fig with butter. I went to the district commander for help. 'Regulations,' he says. 'You get nothing. Half a ruble for each child but nothing for you according to regulations.' A woman penal laborer gets provisions, but those who came here of themselves get nothing. Some low-life of a women, who with her lover murdered her husband, she gets a ration. I abandoned my kin and came here, and get nothing. Yes, if there were no children with me..."

"Well, what would you do if you had no children?"

"I'd be going to *fart*. Would you see me with my little murderer? I'd have become a cohabitant. In the party they had to beat the convicts away from us. The way they live now, those lovers and theirs. They don't go round like that in Rasseya, in goatskin shoes and calico and chintz dresses. A *fartuk*[1] is done up from head to toe—they shouldn't be seen. What envy!" She dries her tears. "But what have they done? They've poisoned my husband into liking that world, that one only and everything in it. But here, God forgive me, you work, struggle like a dog..."

At this moment the door opened and a young "female cohabitant," apparently a little drunk, appeared in the doorway.

"Auntie Arina, do you have some eggs? We have visitors and I want to make some chirpies."[2]

"No eggs for you. The hens don't lay for you!"

The young woman wagged her tail and scampered off.

"Sponger!" Arina yelled after her. "They come to see her, the low-life. And she wants fried eggs! How they eat on a workday! Laying down the law would bring that low-life down to earth a little, for we're living just to dig our graves. She wants to slice off a little piece because she can't cut through anything else.

That's why she chopped up her husband! But she wants 'chirpies.' Yes, that's what she wants! In winter, all the penal laborers give the girls their shirts to sew. But, y'see, she—that creature—can't sew. So she paid me and I sewed them for her. I'm worn out by my children, but sit sewing shirts while she's lying in bed chewing gingerbread. Pshaw!"

She was now in a towering rage, flying spittle revealing all her bitterness, all her resentment at her fate so different from that of the female convict. The poor woman broke down in tears.

"Well, your husband, for all that, he's good to you? He makes an effort, works for the household?

"They've made him work like a dog! But what's all his work good for?" answered the woman through her tears. "You get no rye, no oats, not a single potato. Hands raw from work… Lord, why this calamity?!" Her tears fell more bitterly still. Behind the curtain the children began to whimper. "Oh you, Devil, you won't take us!" the woman shouted and tossed a cooking fork into an earthen pot on the stove. I took my leave and departed.

This is your *katorga* "heroine."

21

THE HOMEOWNERS

Such a house could only be seen on Sakhalin. The house definitively belonged to no one. It had an owner, who'd left for the mainland. He couldn't find a buyer so he abandoned it to follow his luck. It seems choristers once lived here—now there's only "singing for night-lodging." Yet, it's not even a flophouse, for even a flophouse has an owner. You can come here whenever you want, lay down on the bare floor and sleep.

A good ten minutes were needed to hack my way to the house.

"Come in, barin! Step carefully! Nothing will happen!" the house's occupants shouted to me. The floorboards had disappeared beneath a veritable fetid quagmire: the occupants didn't like to go far. All the windows had been removed; there were no frames. And of course there was absolutely no furniture! With effort, they collectively rolled out a block of wood from somewhere for me to sit on.

THE HOMEOWNERS

Here I am sitting on a stump in an empty house, while around me stand eight "homeowners" without shoes. We're discussing their "properties." Each has a house somewhere in the settlement. A house, built "per-the-law," that gives each the right after five years to enter the peasantry and depart "for the other side," for the mainland.

"Why don't you live in your own home?" I ask at random the first occupant I see.

"It's impossible to live in it!" he smiles. "If a cock and hen were meant to be in it, your worship, then God didn't want it, because for both to be able to live together they would've had to strangle each other!" he ironically remarks on his "home."

The others smile approvingly: each has a similar home.

"So why did you build a house?"

"Why does anyone build a house on Sakhalin? Because of regulations, of course."

"But weren't you farming?"

"Your worship, what kind of farming is possible? In a word, it's Sa*kalin*! Allow me to add, your worship, that I don't know what to do with it, with the land. I've never worked it in my life."

"Then you're a craftsman of some sort?"

"Exactly, I have a craft. Only, in my opinion, my craft can't be practiced here."

"What are you?"

"A lithographer."

There really is nothing for a lithographer to do on Sakhalin, where not a single lithography stone is to be found.

"And what about you?"

"We're carpenters."

"Well, it's easy for a carpenter to find work."

"Where can you find it here?! They don't pay an exile-settler anything. I knock myself out, because there's nothing to knock together. There's work for those who go to the mainland. But, sir, understand there's no work to be found here."

"Well, and what do you do?"

"We'd be stove-setters."

It's the same song again: the exile-settler installs stoves but there's no "gentleman" to pay him anything.

"And you?"

"I worked as a trader... Allow me to say, your worship, there's absolutely no way to earn a living. There's nothing to live on. They don't give us a government ration. They discontinued them."

"It's impossible that the government doesn't give any of you money to live on!"

"Yes, of course it is… What you say is justified. There's just absolutely no way for us to live without food."

"Then why did you come here, to the post?"

"We'd hoped to find work, leave the primitive settlement and go to the post, as was possible!"

"Yes, indeed. And did you find work here?"

"No! Is there any work at all here? All those in the fishing industry are Japanese. Mr von Kramarenkov, he got assistance from the government, they gave him penal laborers who built him a whole factory—but he hires the Japanese!"

"But whatever are you doing here? Are you working at anything?"

"When jobs come along, we work. Whatever work there is."

"So, you're mooching."

"We're mooching."

"Do you steal?"

"What's there to steal here? There's all of nothing to eat!"

"Well, now that we've talked about things, what do you want from me?"

"It's just… we were talking among ourselves…"

"You're lying, brothers. I suppose you were gambling at cards? Speak— I won't tell anyone!"

The "homeowners" smile and peek at each other. "Just so, we were gambling."

Among the entire company there was all of forty-eight kopeks, which they won back and forth from each other all day long. Where had they gotten these forty-eight kopeks? Had they earned them? Possibly. Stolen them? Probably.

22

REZTSOV

"Is there, in the end, a single prosperous exile-settler who succeeds here through honest labor?" I exclaimed in despair, having surveyed the entire settlement. "And where there is neither lust nor poverty, if there is a prosperous man, he's acquired his money by smuggling vodka or through hoarding, usury, excessive greed, cruelty or the inhuman robbery of his fellow man! Is there not anyone who prospers through labor? Or is there absolutely no such person? But why can't there be? They're very few, but they can be found."

Hence, meet Reztsov, a prosperous muzhik and an extraordinary fellow. He was even a village headman at one time. No one has a bad word for him. He came to Sakhalin, to this farm, without a penny—but later, all things were possible through God. Praise be to You, God! I'm going to see this "pride of Sakhalin."

Reztsov is an exceptional joiner and a first-rate house-master. He has good gardens and fifteen head of cattle, which he raises and sells to the government. Most importantly, he's really accomplished all this through his own labor and thriftiness. Reztsov came to *katorga* seven years ago for killing a man in a fight; completed his exile-settler term; and is now a peasant…

I enter his hut—it's spotless. There's an atmosphere of prosperity.

Reztsov, still a young man, makes a strange impression. Not that it's painful. It's not. He just seems about to collapse. Such a face is shared by those who cannot sleep at night, by persons with frazzled, overstrained nerves.

"Greetings, Reztsov. I came to see how you're getting on."

"We beg your pardon, barin. We live all right. I don't offend God. There are the gardens; I have a trio of workers; there are cattle… Here, God provides and we sell everything, and I'll go to the mainland…"

"Why go to the mainland? As you say, your farm here is doing well and, praise God, you're also a joiner."

"Well, that's just it! How can one practice a trade here? Exile-settlers don't need a joiner; and in prison, they make everything for free, sir."

"But you have cattle, a farm."

"And God will stay with it, with the cattle and the farm. Only, I'll be getting out of here."

"But why, after all?"

Reztsov took a deep breath.

"Living here is terrible. We're gripped by terror and confusion. You noticed my neighbor's hut, all boarded up? A clerk lived there with his cohabitant. They had a little money… Two weeks ago, it happened. We see he's not going to work in the mornings. 'They must have moved away'—but no, he's lying dead in a pool of blood with his throat cut. The cohabitant herself arranged it. They killed him for hardly any money, for twenty kopeks split among them. Sliced him from ear to ear. They don't dare touch gentlemen, but as for their own— 'Go ahead, as much as you want.' Well, so it is with such a life! I don't know a peaceful moment… It's nighttime, the dog barks and you leap up, confusion all around, you're terrified, hands and feet go cold. 'Are they coming?' My dog somehow died, so I haven't slept for a week. I figure they must've poisoned it.

It's a telling sign. They say when the dog gets poisoned they're planning to 'come in.' It's known that I have a bit of money. How long before it happens? There's the taiga, so if the robber runs away, who's gonna find him? It hasn't happened yet, but it will! Were it not for her..." Reztsov indicates his cohabitant, who's just barely sat down at the table. A woman in the final stages of consumption, she's older than he. "If not for her, I wouldn't have stayed here one minute. When she gets a little better we'll sell everything, and if nothing happens, move to the other side. Better poverty than to live like this!"

"Your mistress is not very well!" I say to Reztsov after we've exited the hut. "You should take her to a doctor."

"She goes to the infirmary!" answers Reztsov with exasperation. "To the doctor there! The doctor can't do anything. He just tells her she's 'improving'! Bah!"

"Yes, she's unwell, very unwell."

"I'm waiting. Maybe this spring, but no later than autumn, she'll die. Then we'll get rid of everything and go to the mainland. But it wouldn't do to abandon her. Even though she's not my wife, we've spent many years together. There's been little joy and so much woe! She's already dying. I'll wait."

Does not an aridity emanate from these words? Ech, there's a phrase on Sakhalin that goes, "Only a human being is dryer than wood."

23

FREEMEN ON SAKHALIN

The Editor

If the vault of Heaven were to crash onto me, the earth to open wide beneath my feet, the sea to boil frothy white, trees begin to fly, fish to speak and birds to fling themselves into a hunt for bears, I could not be more astounded than I was at that moment. On the quay, in a short sheepskin jacket with the Order of St George medal[1] through his buttonhole and the colossal braids of the prison department on his shoulders, stood... V. N. Bestuzhev, former editor of the newspaper *Moscow Voice*[2] and many others, thunderously ordering laborers about with lightning rapidity. Imagine a Hercules, his hauberked chest covered with orders and medals—orders and medals he's bestowed on himself but has not the slightest right to. Such was this poetic individual's facade. He was directing the entire assemblage as if it was there to serve his existence only, leading and driving it with martial demeanor.

In conversation he'd often reminisced, "When in such-and-such a year I was a junior officer..." Interested friends would ask, "How did you become a junior officer when you were just a private?" "But they'd demoted me"—and despite his thoroughly spongy nature, he wasn't lying about this: he had only just succeeded in becoming a junior officer when he was suddenly demoted for various scandalous acts. He couldn't deal with subordinates without there being some disgraceful arbitrariness, verbal insults or physical violence.

After military service he got involved in everything and did nothing in moderation. He ran a huge estate, introducing the most refined, most rational agriculture—and this most rationalistic of estates went bust. Then he ran an enormous soap and candle plant where soap and candles were to have been made by special, still invisible, machinery. But no one ever saw soap or candles being made by the invisible machinery.

We find him later heading the largest publishing house in Moscow, a publishing house that simultaneously produced three daily newspapers, one weekly and one monthly journal, and a mass of *zemstvo*[3] and private publications. The publishing house went the same way as the estate and the soap plant. Also, Bestuzhev was tried by jury before Moscow's district court on charges of bigamy and acquitted, though the crime itself was acknowledged. The trial made clear that Bestuzhev had acquired his second wife, a wealthy merchant's widow, by posing as a gentleman-of-the-bedchamber and an incredibly rich man. This unfortunate woman's entire fortune was then lost at cards or squandered on various affairs. At the time, investigation of this notorious case caused a great uproar in Moscow.

To enumerate Bestuzhev's "petty affairs" would be absolutely impossible: nearly every week someone from Moscow's peace courts was investigating a "Bestuzhev matter," either because of a suit brought by him or because of accusations against him for arbitrariness, insult or violent assault. At one time Bestuzhev was the editor of *four* daily newspapers[4] and publishing three of them simultaneously!!! His literary notoriety was grandiose but short-lived. He acquired nationwide celebrity suddenly, but lost it at that very moment.

How did some descendent of the magnificent French awaken a "celebrity" one beautiful morning?

He is *bona fide*: being completely oblivious, he published Pushkin's "Queen of Spades" in his newspaper *Life*,[5] but attributed it to the nascent writer Nogtev. The editorial staff's subsequent apology and explanation added nothing to these laurels earned in a single day.

All the newspapers talked about *Life*! But this was his single moment of literary success. Bestuzhev played within journalism the role of spiritual counselor and "brother of mercy." Newspapers died in his hands. *Moscow Voice* ended its short-lived but much-suffering days in his hands. *Life* newspaper, begun by Mr Plevako[6] and ended by literary imposters, folded in his hands. The similarly founded *Bulletin of Announcements and Industry*[7] died in his hands. In his hands died, without uttering even a peep, the much-sinning *Echo*,[8] bought by Bestuzhev from the Petersburg barrister T—the infamous T who, while defending the still more infamous Luiza Filippo charged with "openly violating public morals," pulled from out of his briefcase one of her toilet accessories, shook this silky knick-knack in the air and pathetically exclaimed, "What she's been accused of doing the 'evening of the crime' is not true! As you can see, the entire matter was a result of the silk splitting in two because of the force of her can-can!"[9]

Upon conclusion of his literary activities Bestuzhev suddenly transformed into… Nizhegorod Province's superintendent of police. He was driven by a desire to participate in the then sensational Ashinov expedition to the heart of Africa.[10] Bestuzhev put together his own ensemble and astounded Moscow by parading around in an unusual Circassian coat covered in weaponry and fantastic medals. But the famous "ataman" refused to take on Bestuzhev as a Cossack officer, saying, "He's a dangerous lunatic." In a rage, the former editor and would-be officer went to the police, against whom he couldn't restrain himself. He "exceeded" his authority, managed a few "violent assaults," and we next see the former editor in the role of a constable in Tomsk. Then, we see him—more accurately, we don't see him at all. Having lost his position as constable and gotten into some "problems," he leaves Tomsk for Buenos Aires and, with an entire caravan of retainers and servants, for some reason travels around Argentina. Later, he lives in Chile, searches for his fortune in California, spends some time in a hard labor prison in San Francisco—until I finally met him on Sakhalin in the role of warden of settlements, of constructor of life for criminals doing time, of colonial propagator. Such, in a few brief lines, are the life and adventures of this landowner, factory owner, editor, policeman and globetrotter.

The first phrase with which my old friend Bestuzhev hailed me was interesting.

"You? On Sakhalin?" I had exclaimed.

"But where else did you think we'd meet?" Bestuzhev burst out laughing. "This is all right, even if I am an official." For all his shortcomings he was an honest man, managing to tell me in conversation, "Better people are needed here, but who could they send?! Who in Russia is worth anything? So they chose me. But I, truth be told, am still not one of the worst."

He'd treated Sakhalin to the same impetuosity, incoherence and lawlessness he'd subjected his entire life to. He'd established new settlements, organized workshops, built a church, school, homes for new arrivals, and done all this with naught a kopek but "with vodka." As for the overall benefit of such economic policies, I'll say more below, but for now I'll simply establish the fact that as a result of Bestuzhev's "projects," exile-settlers were completely and utterly impoverished.

A man of "dated ideas," he earned a reputation among cronies as a "severe, albeit unbegrudging, witless barin." I don't think his method of managing "trusting souls" would have allowed for the settlement of these "souls" had there been any regard for the law… When it was noticed exile-settlers were being completely ruined and Bestuzhev wasn't cut out to be the architect of a rural economy, he was made warden of Korsakovsk Prison. Finding himself in charge of people without rights or the possibility of protest, Bestuzhev revealed his vicious nature's full strength and extent, frenziedly beating, pounding and thrashing them, so that he became a rarity on Sakhalin (even the administration considered him a "nuisance") by subjecting to horrible corporal punishments people known to be sick or otherwise exempt from such punishments. God knows whether all this ugliness would have ended had Bestuzhev not been brought up on charges. Investigation revealed his unethical management of state monies. Bestuzhev was removed and ordered to stand trial.

Hoping that he'd be able to exonerate himself, he visited the governor-general in Khabarovsk, but there awaited the final blow. Bestuzhev was waiting his turn in the reception room when a specially commissioned official entered and told him, "The general said to tell you he will not meet with you… This is enough! Your case will be decided according to the law." The corpulent Bestuzhev became unsteady, his face clouded over and he collapsed foaming at the mouth. A doctor arrived. Bestuzhev was dead. He'd died from an apoplectic attack. Thus ended the days of this "free man of Sakhalin island." *Katorga* has lovingly given him its own sobriquet: "storm-chief."

"Sakhalin's Orpheus"

Korsakovsk is a herring kingdom. "The herring are running!…" This is an event for the prison, exile-settlers, entrepreneurs—for everyone. It's what they live all year for. What a fantastic picture! What a scene from a magical play! A milky river runs through the sea. The water has whitened almost a mile from shore, has become a milky color. Completely, entirely! Whale spouts sparkle; young walruses bellow; a thousand airborne seagulls wail.

And over all this rules Mr Kramarenko. "Sakhalin's Orpheus," he's exchanged his violin for herring. But the violin wasn't always Kramarenko's chosen instrument. Sometimes he played another instrument: as a clerk in an Astrakhan fish merchant's office he used to click-clack an abacus.

Kramarenko is a man of young years but "old experience." At thirty years of age he managed to become an office clerk and a virtuoso violinist, and later became a fish merchant. He's savored laurels and lives well on herring. Kramarenko was part of Astrakhan's urban estate. He was a farmer of Astrakhan herring, so to speak. But this concludes his relationship with salted fish.

Sincere, frank and creditably intelligent, he knows almost as much about herring as someone who's happened to see the fish prepared with vinegar, oil, mustard, beets, onions and potatoes. He knows that herring is a splendid accompaniment to vodka. He can swear to this. His knowledge in this area is limited. Even your most humble servant proved himself a more experienced fish merchant in comparison to this "Sakhalin Orpheus."

"Why do you salt the herring using only the dry method? That is, laying it down then pouring the salt on it?" I asked. "Why not put the fish in a brine preparation? Having tried it, the fish would be saltier and more tender."

Kramarenko looked at me wide-eyed, as if I'd just discovered America.

"Really, you know, there's an idea!!! I'll try it immediately!"

A good "idea" that has been in practice ten years already! I'd heard about this method of salting herring six years ago from Kerch fish merchants at the Nizhegorod fair.

"Did you own fish factories in Astrakhan?" I asked.

"No."

"Did you work in factories?"

"No as well. I worked as an accountant in a merchant's office. Well, but when the herring started running, a week's worth would feed you a whole year, so that was it for the accounting: they sent us all to look for workers for the factories. That's where I saw how."

And that's it. That's the whole of his schooling. The sum total of his knowledge.

Having suffered some kind of ruin back home Kramarenko, like an enterprising fellow, gave up accounting, wrapped his arm around the violin he played amateurishly well and left for Ussuri Territory,[11] which at the time was attracting many. Here, he suddenly achieved success. It's possible to say the whole territory was dancing to his violin. Kramarenko played at weddings, christenings and on estates; adorned himself in fantastic medals from exotic leaders and gave concerts as "the virtuoso to the courts of the emirs of Afghanistan, Bukhara and the Karakalpak-Kirgiz."[12] He'd readily play alike Wieniawski,[13] Berlioz,[14] the "bouncing polka," Paganini concertos,[15] and the

"Twirl" quadrille. He'd play a matchmaking ceremony like a "peasant woman wailing," thrash a folk dance out of his violin as if it were a balalaika. After all this varied artistry had sufficiently bored him and the whole region, Kramarenko went to Sakhalin "to give a concert."

On Sakhalin, he immediately fell into "fishy confusion" and even "fishy madness." "Fish—Sakhalin's greatest asset," they were shouting left and right. There were indeed fish, heaps of them, nowhere to put the fish, rivers teeming with fish, myriads of fish hugging the coastline. But how to get down to business with them, how to salt them—no one knew. They'd eaten herring but definitely didn't know how to prepare it. It was a tragic situation! Suddenly arrives the virtuoso violinist, who during the interval between a pair of dances for administrators explains, "But honestly, gentlemen, I was in Astrakhan, lived in the fishing industry, and as for salting herring, I know how." They grabbed him as if he were a godsend. Mr Kramarenko was named "technical overseer" of prison fishing industries for three years. They commissioned him to investigate fishing on Sakhalin. As a result of these investigations they managed to build an entire fish plant. The Astrakhan accountant and wedding violinist turned into a serf owner. The penal laborers assigned to him in exchange for a dirt-cheap payment to the treasury built him a plant, storage cellars and basements. True, the cellars were hardly usable: the fish rotted in them; and the basements for salting the fish leaked and the brine disappeared. But all this was not the fault of convicts assigned as temporary serfs for Kramarenko's use. It was the fault of the violinist-architect himself.

Kramarenko's initial experiences were quite pathetic. From the beginning he fell with a thud, heavily and soundly, so to speak, "into a deep place." He missed the first herring run. The second, although not missed, was used but destroyed: the brine seeped out and the fish had to be tossed back to sea. As for the third run, although the herring was at last prepared as desired, it was so bad no one wanted it.

Kramarenko is now "learning." Indeed, what is there he can't learn? Timber is free and he can get penal laborers for a penny. Kramarenko received a small yearly advance of 1000 rubles against his fish that he was obliged to spend on the prison. However, convinced that the fish merchant was benefiting personally from it, they seem to have taken away the subsidy. In Sakhalin's *Almanac* you'll find an article by Mr Kramarenko in which he quite loudly and sanctimoniously berates the "predation" of Japanese fish merchants:

> They've quite a business! Caught by the herd-full on Sakhalin, the valuable herring is cooked in cauldrons, then turned into fertilizer.

> Is this not barbarity? Is this not predation?

What does Kramarenko himself do? He catches the fish, cooks and makes it into fertilizer. That is, he's involved in the very same predation against which he so passionately and righteously cries out. All his tiny, comical "salted" fish earn not a penny, they're a simple sleight-of-hand. His principal affair—which he cannot disguise—is the fertilizer business. Having turned the herring into fertilizer he sells it to those very same Japanese. The only difference is that the treasury receives from the subsidized Kramarenko far less than it would from the Japanese lessees. This smoke-screening of the treasury is another deception. Kramarenko's industries provide nothing to the population because, as the Japanese's stooge, Kramarenko employs Japanese workers exclusively.

"Does not some more immediate larger secret explain this virtuoso's success?" you ask. It's very simple, insofar as few on Sakhalin follow their own free will. As a rarity here, each free businessman is met with open arms and receives assistance and support. The only pity is who these businessmen are…

Undoubtedly, the region has a multitude of riches, but it needs people of learning, people of aptitude, and not tight-fisted exploiters, not wedding violinists ready just to grab whatever they want, not "persons without a fixed occupation, means, or lifestyle…"[16]

But instead, the only ones who "do their thing" are either predators or those who've failed at everything in Russia. Such are those who've created the infrastructure for Sakhalin's "unfortunates"!

The "Liquor Trade"

If Sakhalin, according to a joke among local officials, is an "entirely separate and independent state," then Korsakovsk District, rendered impenetrable by the tundra and taiga cutting it off from the administrative center of Aleksandrovsk Post, represents a veritable "state within a state," a "Sakhalin on Sakhalin." Here there are unique rules, customs, laws, even a unique monetary unit. Our usual monetary symbols have been nullified in Korsakovsk. All trade, all business is conducted in liquor.

Korsakovsk District's monetary unit is a bottle of spirits, or rather, not even a bottle of spirits but a note authorizing purchase of a bottle of spirits. To understand this "devaluation" so profitable for many it's necessary to understand the conditions under which liquor is sold on Sakhalin.

The law allows spirits to be sold only from the colony's—that is, the government's—commissaries. Only persons in the "free estate," that is, officials, may purchase liquor unrestrictedly and in desired quantities. Exile-settlers are permitted to buy liquor during holidays or with notes from persons of free status. "Allow so-and-so a bottle of spirits. [Signed:] So-and-so."

A bottle of spirits in the commissaries costs one ruble twenty-five kopeks, while the market price varies from two rubles fifty kopeks to six rubles. Having obtained the necessary note, an exile-settler "buys" a bottle from the store with this money then resells it at a profit to exile-settlers and *katorga*. Or else he resells the note itself. Notes pass like assignats.[17] They're even counterfeited! Officials use these notes to purchase sables from exile-settlers (one pelt per note) and to pay for produce and labor. Essentially, in this way they get all the benefits while both giving exile-settlers merely the opportunity to trade in vodka and giving *katorga* over to drink.

Warden-of-settlements Bestuzhev, though not involving himself personally in this system, nonetheless endeavored to use the system for the purposes of state projects. He reasoned thus: "If administrators are doing this, why not the treasury? Better it go into the treasury's pocket than into administrators' pockets." He'd completely forgotten that *quod bicet bovi, non licet Iovi*.[18] Unfortunately, the inventive financier made no profit. What with the mass of notes flooding the market, their value plummeted. Here's what happened. Hard-working exile-settlers were completely ruined. Thinking they'd receive rubles for their notes, they got only pennies. Some of the most poverty-stricken exile-settlers in Korsakovsk happened to tell me about their losses in this unique financial enterprise.

I cannot begin to detail the impact of this "liquor system" on exile-settlers' morality. In Korsakovsk one buys and sells everything for alcohol, including one's cohabitant and daughters. What respect can *katorga* have for officials who purchase its labor for free, for officials who deal in liquor? And so much is said on Sakhalin about the need to maintain prestige. "*Katorga*'s becoming undisciplined! It's becoming impertinent, disobedient!" As though "prestige" were supported and maintained by certain punishments...

Birich

Birich is my next-door neighbor. He lives in the house of the penal laborer Pishchikov, who's putting me up. He's in business with one of the major fish merchants and loves terribly to talk about what great losses he incurs due to bad weather.

"Pardon me. The transports contracted from the Japanese aren't moving. Every day costs me money. The herring will be running any day now. This means thousands in losses for me! I really may lose thousands!" He loves terribly to emphasize this word "thousands."

Birich is middle-aged, small, unattractive and dresses not without a pretense toward dandyism, with a waistcoat "revealing" a chain to which could safely be attached not a watch but a dog. One gets the horrible sensation that he is not a headquarters clerk but a medic "going to the people." So it subsequently became clear.

He compulsively squeezes your hand several times when meeting and saying goodbye, as if this gives him special pleasure. When he "gets into his cups" (and this happens often with him) Birich's importunity and unusual familiarity become especially intolerable. He shows up uninvited, talks without stopping and assumes in conversation the pose of one who is more carefree than you. Strictly speaking, he doesn't even talk so much as pose, so does he sprawl in his chair and put up his feet so they're almost on the table. Then he stands up and puts his feet on the chair. "Here's someone trying so hard that his feet are higher than his head," I jokingly thought to myself. Then he slaps your knee, grabs your lapels and tosses a cigarette butt in your saucer. All of this—decidedly without any necessity—is, it simply appears, to show you at every moment that he stands on equal footing with you and can carry himself "without constraint." Such a notion entertains him, brings him inexpressible delight. When he drinks, Birich takes to cursing penal laborers especially furiously. This seems his principal occupation. Honestly, at first I thought they'd murdered this man's entire family, so profound, intransigent and furious was his hatred.

Birich visited me before I'd even managed to settle into my room. He shook my hand several times, announced he was very glad "to meet an educated man," explained right off that his wife has been to boarding school[19] and lives in the fish factory, talked about his "thousands in losses" and proclaimed himself my mentor.

"I know Sakhalin like the back of my hand. Just listen to me. I'll show you everything. You'll see such scoundrels, such rascals!"

When Birich talks about *katorga* he even forgets to add the "heretical word" normally added after almost every word, so much is he filled with hatred!

"You'll get to know them well, those rascals! You'll get to know what creatures they are! Dissolutes—it's terrible! And how! They're too soft on them! They 'pity' the scoundrels! *Pity* them! They need to be thrashed, the rascals! When Livin or the late Iartsev—God bless him—was warden, they were thrashed. When it was really *katorga*! But now, pardon me! What kind of *katorga* is it?! Is it even *katorga*? It's a mockery of the law and just a lot of nothing."

"What have you… have you somehow suffered losses because of them? Perhaps they worked for you?"

Birich became enraged.

"Me? What would I be doing with them? God have mercy on me! What can be done with these people?! I'd rather put my head in a noose! No, I use Japanese, nothing but Japanese, pardon me, for what can you do with *them*?

Last year I tried to take some exile-settlers on a sleeper car. I had a contract job on the railroad.[20] Well, things didn't go well. They were such scoundrels, such rascals…"

Etc., etc., etc. It became sickening to listen to, and necessary to get away from, Birich.

But Birich enjoyed appearing beside me everywhere and was never more than a step away. I'd be going about my business, taking a stroll, and Birich would be there like my shadow. I went to the *"katorga* theater" and Birich dogged me there, paying for a seat in the first row.

"You'll laugh! What creatures they are, eh? It's a weekday, but here they are playing at theater."

"But it's Easter now!"

"Easter is three days for penal laborers. But really, it should only be one day, as they're already allowing them such freedom. But they, the rascals, get a whole week. Eh? How does this seem to you? Is this *katorga*? They feed and drink, do nothing, aren't subjected to any punishments…"

Finally, I became suspicious of him.

"Why is it, old chap, you're always cursing *katorga*? Something's very strange…"

Birich and I had somehow ended up on the main street when we suddenly ran face-to-face into the district commander from around a corner. Birich instantly jumped away as if shocked by an electric bolt and snatched off, rather than tipped, his cap.

No! This manner of cap removal can be neither described nor portrayed. It's a product of years of *katorga* and exile-settlement and can never be lost. I can distinguish you as a penal laborer among a crowd of thousands by the way you doff your cap before authority. It didn't matter that Birich had been out of *katorga* for ten years and had regained all his "rights." The whole long history of *katorga* is contained within this greeting—so long that when encountering each other former penal laborers say, "Aha, old chap, you were in prison! They gave you thirty years!"

The district commander went on his way. Birich sensed that I had understood everything, and abashedly looked away. It was an awkward moment for me. We walked several paces in silence.

"I've had to endure much here!" Birich quietly hissed.

I stayed silent. We were quiet the rest of the way home.

In the evening, "having gotten into his cups," Birich appeared in my room and once again began savagely cursing *katorga*. Only now he added, "Are they suffering like we had to suffer? Are they living now like we had to live? And for what, I ask. Was I more of a sinner than them?!"

All the spite, all the envy of a much-suffering man toward others who had not suffered half as much—as he claimed—exploded from the core of the half-drunk Birich.

So I now learned that he had been in medicine, was sentenced for poisoning someone, served a *katorga* term then became an exile-settler, and was now not a peasant but a member of the urban estate and, by means fair or foul, had amassed his kopeks and now ran his factories like a *kulak*.[21] *Katorga* can't stand him, hates and disdains him "like a brother." Never and by no one were exile-settlers so pushed as when they worked for Birich on his railway sleeper car deliveries.

Such is Birich. This puny figure wouldn't be worth much attention, of course, were his attitude toward *katorga* not typical of that of a former penal laborer. This disgusting attitude seeps out of the muck against those still mired in the muck.

How many of these barely flush former convicts did I not see on Sakhalin? And they all spoke maliciously and hatefully about *katorga* and not otherwise. Of course, the talk among the more intelligent and educated ones was not as coarse as Birich's. But the malice came through in the tone of their voices. None of them, despite being former victims, viewed someone else's suffering with a greater humanity, saw a penal laborer as a suffering brother. No! The sufferers only embitter people! It's as though the very sight of penal laborers, their proximity, offends by making those who've surfaced from the muck recall their years of shame. "This was you," the clanking of chains tells them, and they're embittered by it. "I wore that, too!" they read in the "ace of diamonds" on the back of the prisoner's cassock.[22] In essence, all their malice, all their hatred for *katorga*, all their complaints about the "lack of discipline, the weakness of *katorga* nowadays" sing one and the same tune: "Didn't we suffer? Why are they suffering less than we did?"

From among these people so close to *katorga*, from these former penal laborers, are often selected the guards, the immediate—so to speak—command structure that plays a huge role in convicts' lives. Can you imagine how such a gentleman treats *katorga* when he gets the opportunity not only to voice, but to convey more viscerally, his malice?

24

THE *KATORGA* THEATER

Posters on all the poles throughout Korsakovsk Post announce: "With the commander's permission, there will be morning and evening performances in the Lavrov Theater during the Holy Week of Easter."

The local baker Lavrov, possessing the melancholy look of an entrepreneur, has hastily knocked together a small stage. The same fate has befallen this poor fellow as that of his Russian brethren. He's suffering the entrepreneur's fate: he's going bust. He'd relied on support from an "intelligentsia" lacking (except for cards and vodka) the requisite accouterments. Naturally, these officials haven't been attending the *katorga* theater.

The local "intelligentsia" endeavors to shun *katorga*, as shown by the following fact. The district commander complained to me that the majority of the "intelligentsia" did not wish to subscribe to the library that's been established, all because penal laborers are allowed as patrons. As if these poor people were frightened they might somehow mingle with *katorga*!...

My first visit to the theater was not a success. The "great attraction"[1] of the performance, a reading of "Notes of a Madman,"[2] could not take place due to the most unusual reason in theater history. "Just now, the actor Sokolsky has been sent to the chains prison!" they announced from the stage.

But to make up for this, the next day's performance succeeded wonderfully. The actor Sokolsky had neither been drinking nor ended up in the chains. The theater was filled because of the holiday. In the presence of a "man-of-letters," the actors tried their best. Singers sang special and unusual prison songs expressly for me. Stanzas had even been prepared to honor my arrival. *Katorga* frequently sang me the stanzas, in which the arrival of the writer and where he'd made himself known were celebrated:

> You can't pin that on me,
> For our lives are too busy
> And our future's been decreed!...

But administrators forbade the singing of the verse in good time.

Fir branches adorn the theater walls. The stage has been bordered with some mud-stained sackcloth supposed to represent a curtain. The stage floor is earthen.

It's five o'clock in the evening. The theater's full, the gallery excited: settlers with their cohabitants; exile-settlers; the "first-stringers," yellow aces on the backs of their regulation gray pea-jackets.

From behind the dirty curtain singers are drawling out a doleful, gloomy Siberian *brodiaga* song:

> Merciful little fathers,
> Merciful little mothers!
> Help us, the unfortunates,
> For much sorrow have we seen!
> Lead us, brothers and sisters, in the name of Christ.
> Anyone may come to this,
> A poor wanderer, a *brodiaga*.
> Help us, brothers and sisters: a golden crown you will receive
> In the other world.
> But today remember we are imprisoned
> Away from you, our brothers and sisters.

The song ends on a long mournful note. The curtain opens. The performance begins.

For openers, there's the skit "Again, Petr Ivanovich!"[3] From behind the dirty curtain revealing a shadow scrim appears a traditional "Petrushka." Knave, mischief-maker, naughty child and hooligan—even poor Petrushka, having ended up in *katorga*, has been "Sakhalinized." Everywhere, throughout all Rus,[4] from Arkhangel to Kerch, from Vladivostok to Petersburg, he does nothing but cheat, swindle, fight and dupe policemen. Now here he is—the parricide. This really is not the cheerful Petrushka of a free Rus but the dark hero of *katorga*.

From behind the curtain appears an old man, his father.

"Give me some money, sonny!"

"But how much do you want?" squeaks Petrushka.

"I want twenty rubles!"

"Twenty rubles! Here you go! Take it!" He smacks the old man on the head. "One... two... three... four..." counts Petrushka. The old man collapses and crawls behind the scrim. Petrushka continues beating the prostrate man.

"Now you've really killed him!" bellows the landlord's voice from behind the screen.

"'Billed' him how? I'm a down-to-earth fellow!" Petrushka quips. This elicits a burst of guffaws from the entire audience.

"Not 'billed'—*killed*!" continues the landlord. "He's dead."

"Daddy, stand up!" Petrushka pokes his father while the audience laughs relentlessly. "He's playing the fool! Get up! It's time for work!

"But really, this time I did indeed kill him!" Petrushka finally concludes, and suddenly begins howling like a village woman over the deceased. "You were my fa-a-ather! You have deserted me-e-e! Now I'm all alo-o-one, a wretched orpha-a-an!"

Delight envelops the entire audience. A groaning, a howling, arises in the theater. Feet are stamping. Feminine shrieks of laughter blend with the men's booming guffaws. It becomes nauseating...

The adventure ends when a policeman appears and Petrushka is exiled to Sakhalin. Petrushka sings:

Farewell, Odessa,
Glorious quarantine!
They're sending me to
The island Sakhalin...

"Clever!" calls out the audience.

"Brafo!" a somewhat tidy exile-settler is shouting above everyone else. He's an educated man, who during an interval loudly narrates how he was "in the Skomorokh Theater"[5] in Moscow and has seen every comedy. He's shouting "Brafo" especially to draw my attention to his sophistication.

The next performance follows with greater *fureur*. The *brodiaga* Fedorov, in a multicolored costume something like that of a harlequin's, sings verses to a tune from *Boccaccio*.[6]

You can't pin that on me...

Fedorov used to work somewhere as a theater hairdresser. He sings verily, without accompaniment, touching on the local evils of the day—the soup, which even pigs wouldn't eat; the tom-cats, which should be worn on the hands, not feet; the prison cassocks' unraveling seams and so on. His program is all crescendo. He sings without end, and after each stanza my educated spectator shouts "Brafo!" Fedorov beams, scrapes his feet, bows in all directions and clasps his hands to his heart.

The curtain is pulled back again: onstage are three stools. Having sat the evening in the chains Sokolsky, in a prison cassock, reads from "Notes of a Madman." But what's this? Here in this accursed place, among these godforsaken people, I sense something from far away...

True artistry emanates from this *katorga* stage. This *brodiaga* is clearly a lover of art and interested by it. One senses in his wordplay not only talent but a knowledge of the stage; that he's seen good performers and has successfully imitated them. He reads with passion, ardor and animation. From beneath the sea of these ruined people's gray cassocks a "living spirit" began percolating into this world...

Sokolsky has a true actor's face—nervous, lively, expressive. He's an epileptic. During a fit he bit off the end of his tongue, so that he now lisps slightly, reminding one of the late V. N. Andreev-Burlak.[7]

He preserves only a single phrase from Gogol's "Notes of a Madman": "But, you know, there's a growth beneath the Algerian dey's nose." Everything else is improvisation by a local talent, little sprinkles of digestible salt. This is Poprishchin[8]-as-penal-laborer, anticipating death as deliverance.

His monologue includes many allusions to the local prison. I know I've already mentioned its little secrets, about which of the doctors is known by such-and-such a nickname. These allusions elicit the audience's approving laughter; but true delight comes only when Sokolsky, reading nervously, passionately and clearly agitatedly, begins to shout and bang his fist on a stool. "Kill me! Better to kill me than torture me! Don't torture me!"

"Brafo him!" the educated spectator won't stop saying. Everyone in the audience is applauding—moreover, it seems, from the man loudly shouting and banging his fist on the stool than from his tone and tragic words.

"Notes of a Madman"'s gloomy impression dissipates following a skit entitled "Gray Hairs to the Beard, But a Demon to the Rib."[9] This is an improvisation; lively, pointed, rich humor; a skit about the verities of exile-settler existence. An exile-settler with a long flaxen-white beard is tending in every possible way to his cohabitant.

"Kuliasha! You should lie down! You should sit down! Don't tire your feetsies!"

Kuliasha behaves capriciously, demanding this and that, and ultimately announces that she wants to do the squatting-dance. To please her, the old man begins to walk about unsteadily. The "Kuliashas" sitting in the audience snicker. "What a reindeer!"[10] Exile-settlers just turn their heads. Penal laborers mutter some harsh words.

An old woman—the man's legal wife—suddenly appears and chases Kuliasha with a broom. Kuliasha sets the old woman down by her shoulders, and the old man and his cohabitant take leave of his wife. So ends this comedy... if not "tragedy."

Now comes the highlight of the program, the play, *Fugitive Penal Laborer*.[11] The play is a prison composition, a work of *katorga*.[12] It is a beloved militant play. Were this evening's spectacle in a *katorga* prison, then *Fugitive Penal Laborer* would be performed first. It migrates from prison to prison, from one group of convicts to the next. There's someone in every prison who knows it by heart and teaches the actors their roles.

Act one. The back of the stage is hung with some rags. To the right and left the small stage wings reveal a stove and a window, but the audience is not exacting and willingly accepts that the scene is set in a forest. The stage portrays a labor site. Three penal laborers, supposed to represent a crowd of workers, are digging in the ground. The play's hero (for some reason, the architect Vasily Ivanovich Sunin) sits off to the side, deep in thought.

A voice comes from behind the stage: "Why're you so lazy, you demons, you devils, you wood-goblins? Time to finish the job!" It's the guard's voice. A bell rings and the penal laborers begin leaving for the prison.

"We're going to gulp down some soup! Are you just going to sit there?" they say to Vasily Ivanovich.

"Clear off now, old chaps! I'll catch up with you," he answers.

Vasily Ivanovich (he's being played by that same Sokolsky, the troupe's principal actor), Vasily Ivanovich sighs deeply.

"And so it goes. Chains, labor, abuse, punishments! Nothing in life is bright, nothing is pleasing! Truly, I am a perpetual penal laborer. Should I escape? But where to? I'm surrounded by trees, the taiga! I will escape! Better to starve to death, better to die from preying beasts, than to live such a life! I'll break my chains and flee, flee..."

Vasily Ivanovich removes his chains and... at this point what is least expected occurs. Dumbfounded and startled, I look around at the audience. "What's this?" *Katorga* is bursting into Homeric laughter... They're chortling over how easy it is simply to remove one's chains.

"Farewell, chains! No one will ever wear you again! I've broken you!" says Vasily Ivanovich. "Farewell, captivity!" And he exits.

The second act is again set in the woods. Some penal laborers are sleeping, covered up in their prison cassocks. Peering around, Vasily Ivanovich approaches.

"I've escaped my pursuers! They kept after me, shooting! I escaped, but what will come of me? With what can I cover my sinful body, when even a cassock I do not have?" At this point he notices a sleeping prisoner. "He's sleeping, poor fellow, he's tuckered out and has fallen asleep on the damp ground right where he's been working... I need to take something, his cassock... from a fellow chap..." Vasily Ivanovich begins crawling on his hands and knees towards the prisoner. The audience begins snickering. "Forgive me, comrade, for stealing your very last. They'll be queuing up to question you, to hassle you! You'll have to make amends for this cassock with your own flesh and blood... But what can be done? I need to worry about myself. You'd do the same in my place." Vasily Ivanovich takes the cassock from his sleeping comrade.

From out of the audience... a Homeric guffaw. "Brafo him! Brafo!" bawls the "sophisticated" spectator in a kind of frenzy. For them, this is simply amusing. They're laughing at the "Uncle Sarai"[13] who's sleeping and doesn't know he's being robbed. For them, this is a cunning theft, nothing more.

Appearance, only appearance—no one thinks about the essence, it would seem, of such a proximate, apprehensible and touching soul.

Act three. The stage is meant to be the home of a wealthy Siberian merchant, Potap Petrovich. Vasily Ivanovich appears at his door.

"Take in a wanderer!" he shyly says from the threshold.

"Please come in, good man." The Siberian merchant ushers him in with exceptional cordiality. "Take off your things and sit down. Are you not hungry from the road?"

"Thank you for not turning up your nose at me!" answers Vasily Ivanovich. "I'll wait until you dine."

"As you please." In conversation with Vasily Ivanovich the merchant distinguishes himself by his courtesy. He questions, as they say, only after having been excused, and asks, "Where are you going, Vasily Ivanovich?"

"My path lies in all four directions," the fugitive penal laborer passionately answers. "I'm going to live not with people, but animals. I don't get along with people."

"I assume you've endured much grief, Vasily Ivanovich?"

"I cannot hide from you, Potap Petrovich. I'm a fugitive penal laborer, a chain-ganger who's escaped from prison!" He rises from the bench. "Now you'll probably drive me away? Do you disdain to sit with a *brodiaga*? Tell me, and I'll go!"

"Listen, listen to yourself, Vasily Ivanovich! I beg you not to think about this."

Vasily Ivanovich tells his story. How he was an architect, how he quarreled with his father, how during an argument his father tried to kill him.

"Then I took a gun down from the wall and…" Vasily Ivanovich grows silent.

"In that case (!),"[14] says the merchant, "I beg you, Vasily Ivanovich, to stay and live in my home. Live here as long as it pleases you."

"How can I thank you?" asks the penal laborer, much moved. At this moment the merchant's daughter arrives onstage.

"Akh!" she exclaims *sotto voce*. "Who is this unfamiliar man? Immediately upon seeing him my heart beats strongly. I love him."

An infernal, improbable guffaw by the entire audience accompanies this affectionate sally. It's really impossible to watch without laughing the convict Abramkin done up as the merchant's daughter, in a sarafan down to the knees and out to the elbows. He himself senses this is very "odd," and his own stupid, kind-hearted, brick-red physyognomy is smiling broadly. At the sight of this awkward, lanky, wonderfully ridiculous figure any gloomy melancholic would die from laughter.

Tender words spring from the actors' lips.

"Vasily Ivanovich, allow me to present my only daughter!" says the merchant. "Varenka! This is our guest, Vasily Ivanovich."

"Daddy, dinner is ready," announces Varenka, exchanging bows with the chuckling Vasily Ivanovich.

Act four.

"I should flee, flee from here!" Vasily Ivanovich is saying. "I feel my torments worsening here. I love Varenka... I, a penal laborer, a *brodiaga*, who may at any moment be captured, put in prison, given to the executioner to torture. O, what torments!" He grabs his knapsack.

"Where are you going, Vasily Ivanovich?" asks Varenka, arriving onstage.

"Forgive me, Varvara Potapovna," he bows. "I'm leaving you. I'm going to seek... not happiness, no! Happiness has not been destined for me! I'm going to seek death..."

"Why do you speak so?" Varenka interrupts. "You have seen much grief! You've never told me who you are, from where you've come. Daddy forbade me to ask you about this. Why?"

"I can tell no one!"

"No one? Not even your wife?"

"Why have you used such a word?" says Vasily Ivanovich, wiping away tears. "You're mocking a poor man."

"No, no! I said it with no intent to mock. I love you, Vasily Ivanovich. I loved you at first sight. You can tell me who you are."

"Then listen!" announces Vasily Ivanovich in despair. "Before you is a hardened criminal, a parricide! Run from me: I, a penal laborer; I, a chain-ganger. I... I... killed my own father!"

"Akh!" shrieks Varenka, and faints while the audience laughs.

"I've killed her!" the fugitive penal laborer says, wringing his hands.

"No, I'm alive!" she answers, regaining consciousness. "I beg you, don't go, wait here one minute!"

You, of course, can guess the rest.

"My daughter told me everything! She loves you and has agreed to be your wife!" says the father, entering the scene. "Vasily Ivanovich, I ask you to be her husband!"

"A new life for a hapless wretch!" With these words Vasily Ivanovich concludes the play to the audience's applause.

This is *katorga*'s favorite play. It is its creation, its reverie. The play portrays all *katorga*'s hopes and dreams. *Katorga* likes everything in it: the fortuitous escape; the fugitive convict finding happiness; the "decent people" speaking with him politely, using the formal "you" as with fellow men; that there are those in the human world who do not alienate the fallen, even ones who've

Fig. 14: A shackled prisoner

committed a very serious crime, people who see in the crime a misfortune and in the criminal a human being.

After the play—in some ways complete illusion, in others, all too real (penal laborers, fetters, prison cassocks)—we, of course, can't stay to watch the "smashing of a rock on a chest" and the program's other delights. We make for the wings. For the most original wings in the world!

25

KATORGA ACTORS

A piece of candle stuck on a bench illuminates the most original "dressing room" in the world. Hurrying to roll call, the actors are donning their prison cassocks. Those who played the chain-gangers in *Fugitive Penal Laborer* are sharing a cigarette, waiting for the entrepreneur to pay them. They've changed nothing: their costumes and chains aren't coming off. As anywhere, there's the same thespian self-conceit behind the wings.

"Thank you!" Sokolsky heartily shakes my hand when I praise his reading of "Notes of a Madman." "You've gladdened me. Still, what a theater, though it's something civilized... But I confess I was very shy to be performing in front of a writer, before a knowledgeable individual... Were you at all pleased?"

"I truly think you're very good! Were you an actor, Sokolsky?"

"An actor, no. But I did much amateur work in Sekretarevok and Nemchinovka (amateur theaters in Moscow). You know, I'm from Moscow. Are you also a Muscovite? Ah, Moscow! The Maly Theater! Mariia Nikolaevna Ermolova![1] So it was, you could jump from the 'Skvortsy' (student performances) to the Maly Theater in mid-run. You must remember that the Paradise premiered Barnay and Possart.[2] I can still see him in *Richard* as if he were before me. That monolog after he meets Elizabeth... 'That I may see my shadow!'"[3]

"Sokolsky, you devil! Go to roll call or you'll be sitting in the chains again tomorrow!" The entrepreneur's physiognomy thrusts itself from behind the curtain.

"Well... well... Excuse me. I have to go to roll call. If you would... Then again, I don't know... No, no, please excuse me!..."

"What? Do you want to call on me?"

"Y-yes..."

"Sokolsky, how can you be shy?"

"Well, good, good. Thank you. So, tomorrow, if you will..."

"Yes, but now go, you devil, or you'll end up in the chains again. They'll have to close the performance because of you."

"I'm going... I'm going... I'll see you tomorrow!" Sokolsky hurries to roll call at the prison.

"And you're an outstanding singer of couplets!" I say, turning to Fedorov, who beams.

"In a theater, you know, I feel natural... But it's said you decided to come here from Odessa. Who's playing there now?"

"The Solovtsova Troupe."[4]

"Of Nikolay Nikolaevich? Well, how is he?"

"But you know him?"

"Know him? I remember him from the Korsha.[5] I was the Korsha's hairdresser. But I don't know him! I curled Mariia Mikhailovna (Glebova)[6] several times. Roshchin-Insarov—he was a good actor.[7] I still remember him well. He plays Nekliuzhev[8] outstandingly. Ivan Platonych Kiselevsky[9] was a very serious gentleman. His wig wasn't so curly. Terrible!" Fedorov laughs at

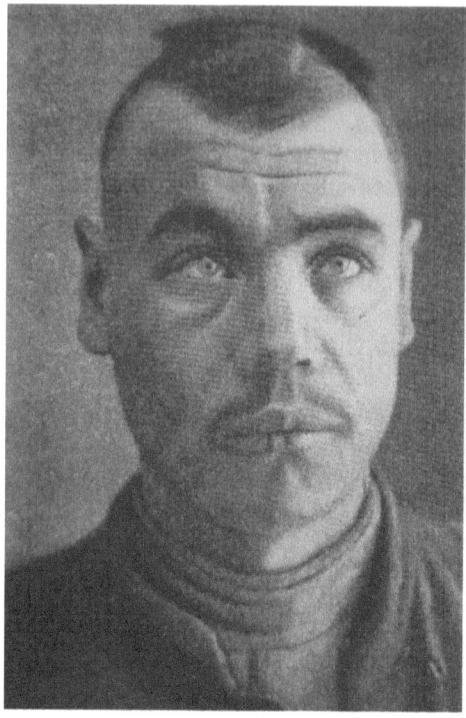

Fig. 15: Prisoner

this memory, then heaves a deep sigh. "You could hardly watch with even one eye Mr Kiselevsky in *The Old Barin*![10] Ech!"

"Abrashkin, why aren't you going to roll call?"

But Abrashkin, who played the ingénue, stands shifting from one to the other foot hoping for a compliment as well.

"Well, hello, chap, are you going to introduce yourself?" I turn to him. Abrashkin's stupid physiognomy breaks into a blissful smile.

"Your worship, I know how to shake hands, but they don't allow me to!"

"The devil's a comedian!" some penal laborers snicker. Abrashkin, his mug smiling, waves his hand.

"Just so!"

Indeed, this good-natured fellow was a murderer with a knife.

26

THE *BRODIAGA* SOKOLSKY

"Sokolsky's come to see you. He says you ordered him to come!" my landlady announced early in the morning.

"Where is he?"

"I told him to wait in the kitchen."

"Invite him in, invite him in!"

It wasn't a crime to smile at this moment; nevertheless, I tried hard to hold back a smile upon seeing the "civilian costume" Sokolsky had attired himself in to visit me: a faded red and ragged jacket, shoes full of holes, unusually narrow and short trousers fitting his legs like knickers—here was the attire of the inhabitants of Arkovo.[1]

"I came in civilian clothes because I didn't want to embarrass you with a prison cassock," he said.

"Sokolsky, don't worry about such trifles. Have a seat, we'll drink some tea!"

Conversation was at first awkward. Sokolsky sat on the edge of his chair, bashfully pulling from his pocket a white rag that took the place of a handkerchief. But little by little the conversation livened. Both of us being Muscovites, we reminisced about Moscow, the theater and the celebrities who passed through. We each forgot where we were. He proved to be a passionate admirer of Possart; I, of Barnay. We disputed, grew excited, talked ardently and loudly, so that several times the landlady glanced through the doorway with puzzlement and even fright. "What are they talking about? He's being very cheeky to the gentleman."

I recited for Sokolsky "Notes of a Madman," which I knew by heart. Writing the words down, Sokolsky laughed heartily over Poprishchin's immortal expressions. The conversation had turned to literature. Sokolsky especially loves, knows and understands Dostoevsky. He's memorized by heart all the pages of *Dead House*.

"I myself wanted to write *Notes from a Dead Island*," Sokolsky said. "It couldn't be a *Dead House*, of course. Not everyone can reach the sun! Nevertheless, I wanted to give an understanding of what contemporary *katorga* is like. I thought, 'I myself am ruined, but let me somehow make use of this.' Many of the intelligentsia are crazy about it. But they forget about it later... Here, they give up on everything... Everyone's almost about to give up... provided he hasn't smoked all his cigarettes! Here's one of mine, and it's escaped destruction. I brought it just for you. I'd be happy if you take it."

We discussed the difference between *Dead House* and contemporary *katorga*. Sokolsky spoke ardently, passionately, and got carried away like a man who bears everything on his shoulders.

"This is hardly the *Dead House*," he said, rising from his chair and gesticulating wildly. "Not even close! Oh, there was something of it here. You remember that horror, that loathing for the executioner. But here even this is nothing... Yet those divine words of Fedor Mikhailovich..."

At this moment the door opened and the warden of settlements interrupted Sokolsky in mid-phrase.

"Off to the stable, old man. I'm told my troika's arrived!"

"I'm listening, your worship!" shouted Sokolsky, and fled the room.

I grabbed my head. "Why are you doing this?"

The warden looked at me wide-eyed. "Why?"

"Yes, why don't you send somebody else?... Out of respect for me..."

He burst out laughing. "What are you doing? Do you think you're *sympathizing* with them? With murderers? Believe you me: they're murderers, murderers, murderers and nothing more! Didn't you think of what he might do to you?"

Sokolsky and I began seeing each other quite often. He willfully and happily helped me to understand *katorga*, collect its songs and compile a vocabulary of prisoners' expressions. But every time I began talking about something other than *katorga* he'd shrink away and start muttering, "No, no. Nothing about that... Not a thing about that... You're going to leave and it'll be harder for me... Let's not talk about that!"

I noticed a peculiar oddity in Sokolsky. It was as if he couldn't finish saying something... He'd arrive, sit, turn around in his chair, talk about some frivolities and leave... He appeared to have something he simply could not get off his tongue. I tried to lead him to it in the following conversation:

"Sokolsky, is there something you want to tell me? Please, be candid..."

"No, no... It's nothing, nothing... Really, it's nothing... Goodbye, goodbye!"

It was getting difficult.

"Sokolsky!" I rather forcefully began. "I'll soon be leaving Korsakovsk. You've helped me a lot with my work... You know, I'm being paid for this and consider it my duty to..."

Misery clouded Sokolsky's face. He flung me a malicious look. "Someone's coming to see you... someone's coming..." He half bit his tongue and whispered still louder. "Someone's coming... Someone's coming..." And Sokolsky fled the room.

Fig. 16: Prisoner

"My God. Why all this torture?!" I must have shouted out loud, because my landlady opened my door and asked, "Did you order tea?! Did you call?"

A little while later, I met my acquaintance Shaposhnikov "the idiot," *katorga*'s "advocate."

"Listen, Shaposhnikov. You're a friend of Sokolsky's. He clearly wants something from me…"

Shaposhnikov looked me straight in the eye and burst out laughing. "He wants to 'shoot' you, your worship. He just hasn't made up his mind!"

"To 'shoot' me? What kind of nonsense are you saying?"

"What do I mean 'to shoot'? He's going to ask for seven rubles. The Tatars have him marked. He owes seven rubles for vodka and things to the *maidanshchik*[2] and others. They know he's been coming to see your worship and they told him, 'Better ask the barin.' They promised to beat him half to death if he doesn't. But he's been choking, the rascal! Ha, ha, ha! Lately, he's running between you and the prison like a crazy fugitive. 'I'll figure it out!' he shouts. Ha, ha, ha! Thus originate *katorga*'s displays of affection!"

"Here you are, Shaposhnikov. Now go back… Don't tell him about our conversation… Say that I gave it to you, only you… Distribute it as you wish…"

Compassion flickered momentarily in Shaposhnikov's eyes, but he quickly screwed up his visage and looked at me ironically.

"Did you ever murder someone?"

"Who? Me?"

"You?"

"I've never murdered anyone."

"No one? So why did they send you to Sakhalin?" Shaposhnikov again laughed his strange laugh that gives the unfamiliar person the creeps.

27

CRIMES IN KORSAKOVSK DISTRICT

"We go into the taiga like a foot does a boot!" convicts told me. This, better than any statistics, speaks to the safety of person and property on Sakhalin. Penal laborers aren't allowed alongside a ship when steamers are being unloaded. "They'll make off with everything—that's what'll happen!"

Some exile-settlers managed to swipe some money from my landlady's kitchen table as soon as she'd turned her back. Never mind that sitting in my room was their commander, the warden of settlements.

"Your worship, forgive them!" pleaded the landlady when the offenders were caught. "Please, they weren't burning down the house."

I sympathized with her request. "Yes, leave them alone! You'll know they've burned down the house when the woman's at peace."

The warden of settlements insisted for a long time that punishment was necessary. "Impossible! They brazenly steal right under my nose. Is this what it's come to?!" But then he spat hard and waved his hand. "Then again, they're going to hell! Really, it's true. They're all starving, starving!"

Theft, robbery and brigandage are highly developed in these localities, though murder with intent to steal somewhat less so than in the other districts. I learned of four recent crimes involving murder. One exile-settler (whose funeral I described), a good, hard-working "quiet" chap, cut his cohabitant's throat out of jealousy then poisoned himself. A woman of the free estate poisoned her husband, a peasant-formerly-exiled, because he didn't want to move to the mainland, where her exile-settler "sweetheart" had already gone.

Fig. 17: Prisoner

Also, a certain exile-settler slit the throats of a cohabitant and a guard. This most recent case gives an outstanding picture of the scandalous interpersonal relationships on Sakhalin. The cohabitant was carrying on with a guard. "I'm leaving! I'm leaving!" "No, you're not!" her exile-settler cohabitant said, holding onto her. Finally, the guard showed up one day and "took" the woman from the exile-settler, directly and simply, without saying a word. He grabbed her and was bringing her to the post. "I say, things will turn out badly for you because of her!" The exile-settler overtook them on the road, murdered them and horribly violated the bodies. He literally carved them up with a knife. "He entertained his soul."[1] The fourth and final crime, whose object was theft, happened in the same post. A well-to-do clerk from among the exile-settlers was murdered. He happened to have a little bit of money, and his cohabitant arranged his murder. She won't confess, but, when I spoke to her one-on-one in the isolation cell where she's being held, she maliciously told me, "What does she see in them, these devils? Some illegal tea? She's getting by, finishing her sentence—yes, and remembering what they called 'im! Off goes our sister, an old woman without a penny to spend!..."

And after having fallen silent she added, "I didn't kill him. But even if I did, I wouldn't be sorry. Gotta think of yerself as well!"

Here are your Sakhalin "customs."

28

DEPARTURE

The steamer's ready to sail. Along the Korsakovsk wharf, crammed with sacks of flour, advances a mournful procession. On stretchers and in awkwardly fashioned chairs patients are being delivered for surgical operations in Aleksandrovsk. Suffering already, they face passage through the stormy Tatar Straits…

Is this playing itself out on the wharf a tragedy? A comedy? A tragicomedy… Agafia Zolotykh is leaving Sakhalin for home and is bidding farewell to her cohabitant, a German exile-settler. Agafia Zolotykh's story can be described with two lines from a poet:

Few of words, but a stream of woe,
A fathomless stream of woe…[1]

"Agafia Zolotykh" (this is her *brodiaga*, not her real, name[2]) ended up on Sakhalin voluntarily. Her heart's companion had been exiled to *katorga* for counterfeiting. In order to follow him to *katorga* she claimed to be a *brodiaga*. She was convicted for not revealing her origins and exiled to Sakhalin. Here, new woes awaited her. The man for whose sake she entered *katorga* died; Agafia Zolotykh revealed her true identity and asked to be returned home; but the red tape had begun—and it was just something that *had* to be done! Agafia happened to fall in with an exile-settler and went on to become his cohabitant. Little by little she became accustomed to her cohabitant, began to love him—when suddenly the decision was made to return Agafia Zolotykh to her home in Russia.

"Farewell, Karlusha!" Agafia is saying, swallowing her tears. "Don't think badly of me. Think well, or maybe nothing at all!"

"Farewell, Agashka!" answers the German, a young chap.

The tugboat casts off but returns in half an hour, disembarking onto the wharf… Agafia Zolotykh. On the steamer, Agafia Zolotykh's appearance had caused a great stir. "What 'Agafia Zolotykh'? 'Agafia Zolotykh' who? You know, we transported Agafia Zolotykh last year! We remember her well! There was even a communication about her, how when they reached Odessa Agafia Zolotykh fled the steamer and didn't wait around for the police!" They're denying that Agafia Zolotykh (who didn't want to be separated from the man she loved) ever exchanged names, and that under this name she wandered through Rus as an exiled penal laborer.[3] So now they're refusing to take Agafia Zolotykh aboard the steamer.

"This is the real Agafia Zolotykh! Everyone here knows her! There was some mistake!" prison administrators are saying.

"But what a mess! We were about to transport one Agafia Zolotykh twice!"

Agafia is returned to shore.

"Well, Karlusha, we're clearly destined to live together," says Agafia. "Let's go home!"

"And why should I go with you, Agashka?" the German straightforwardly responds. "Agashka, I've got myself another woman!" Anticipating his cohabitant's departure, the German had managed to find another, make an arrangement and come to an understanding.

Agafia shakes her head. "Karlushka, you were a villain and have remained a villain. Pah!"

"Agafia! Agafia! Where're you going? Stop!" shouts one of the "intelligentsia." "Come aboard the tug! I'll ask the captain and maybe he'll take you!"

Agafia turns on her heel. "You can all go to hell, to the Devil, to the wood-goblins!" she spitefully says, and stalks away in a frenzy.

To where? "Only the Devil knows. That's where!" as they say on Sakhalin in such instances.

Once more, in a life now ruined a third time…

However, back to the steamer.

"Everything's ready!" says… a Persian prince. An actual prince, whom letters from home unfailingly address as "His Grace." He and his brother were convicted of murdering a third brother; he served his *katorga* sentence and is now a kind of supervisor over the exiles. He's on the wharf issuing orders, speaking very strictly with penal laborers in the tone of someone who's used to being in charge.

"Alekseev, to the tugboat! Allow me, barin!" The former prince assists me down the jetty. The last barge designated for extra freight is ready to leave the steamer.

"So did they say the guards are coming?" one of the prisoners we're transporting shouts from onboard.

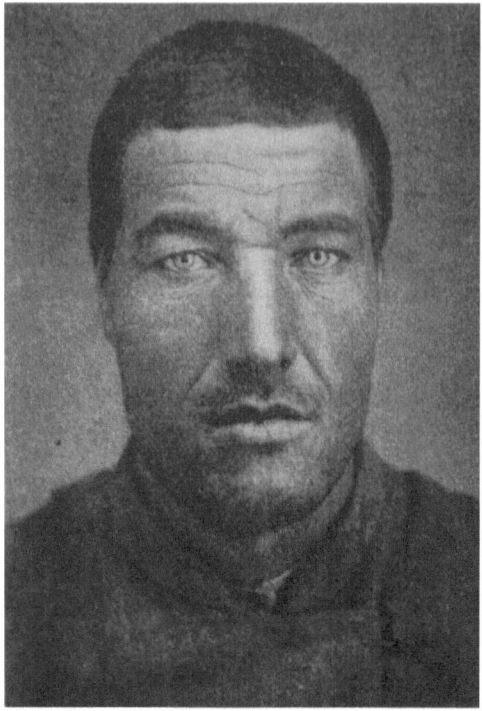

Fig. 18: Prisoner

"To hell with 'em!" an old "local" convict boastfully answers from onboard the barge.

The barge sails off. Anchor chains rumble. A telegraph sounds from the bridge. The order is given.

"Starboard turn!"

"Starboard turn!" echoes the helmsman.

"Steady as she goes!"

"Steady as she goes!"

The *Iaroslavl* gives three long whistles and slowly moves away from shore.

Farewell, Korsakovsk, so bright, so cheerful, so "not resembling *katorga*" when first seen—but with so much grief, suffering and filth languishing beneath.

The *Iaroslavl* picks up speed; the shoreline recedes into the foggy distance; and ahead lies "real *katorga*": Aleksandrovsk, where the most serious, longest-term criminals are held; Rykovsk; Onor; the taiga, tundra, mines...

"Korsakovsk—there's nothing to it! It's a paradise!" says one of the Sakhalin workers with us. "Is Korsakovsk *katorga*? Is it even Sakhalin?"

Everything I've told you is all a prelude to "real *katorga*."

29

REAL *KATORGA*

We're aboard the steamer *Iaroslavl* nearing the wharf at Aleksandrovsk Post, the island's principal administrative center, where is the largest prison, where is kept the "very pinnacle of *katorga*," that is, the longest-term and most serious convicts. The *Iaroslavl* puts in here twice a year "with a harvest of crimes and vices." Here disembarks this "harvest," here new arrivals of prisoners are unloaded, and from here they disperse to various areas.

A siren wails as the steamer cruises in to unload. It's cold and a piercing wind is blowing up a surf. A strong swell is rocking the barge that's beside the steamer. The prison department's little tugboat is puffing away. Melancholy touches my soul. Before me is a gloomy argillaceous coastline. Here and there snow has whitened the mountains, covered as if by razor stubble with prickly taiga.

"It snowed yesterday," explains one of the workers arriving for the prisoners onboard the steamer. "It just so happened there was a blizzard yesterday." Today is apparently warmer. Tomorrow there will again be a blizzard of white flies in the air. It's foggy; the wind is cutting; all this—and it's early June. This is what they call "spring" here.

To the right, breakers slash and reproach the Three Brothers, a trio of cliffs rising beside each other over the water. Protruding into the sea is the huge dark mass of Cape Jonquière,[1] with a lighthouse on its summit. In its dark hulk, as if formed by a bullet, is the black entrance to a tunnel. God knows why and for whom this tunnel is needed, or why it was necessary to bore through this huge mountain.

"Why did they do that?"

"To connect Aleksandrovsk Post with Dué."

"So people go there through the tunnel?"

"No, they go there by another road, there, over the mountains. They tow what needs transporting aboard barges. You can't go through the tunnel, it's crooked."

The tunnel was made under the direction of some gentleman who'd probably never even seen a tunnel. It's like this on Sakhalin: there were and still are mining engineers in charge of prisoners and miners, and prison wardens in charge of fishing industries—people who've never worked in these areas. And the exile-settler economy depends upon bankrupt landowners notable only for having ruined their own properties. Sakhalin is in the full meaning of

Fig. 19: Jetty, Aleksandrovsk Post

the word an assemblage of all possible unfortunates: people, to the exclusion of a few, unsuited for any kind of work; people who've been tossed overboard. As is the Sakhalin norm, the gentleman who fancied himself a builder of tunnels understood absolutely nothing about the business he'd undertaken. The tunnel was as usual dug from both ends based upon calculations that would have had the two parties meet. The men dug further and further into the mountain but failed to meet, and understandably became furious. Fortunately, a man among the penal laborers was found who understood the business, the former sapper L, whose surname resounded throughout Russia in its time and is even now not forgotten.[2] They put him in charge of the workers, and by incredible efforts the mistake was set right. A sideways corridor was dug and connected the two mismatched halves of the tunnel.

However, we return to the "unloading."

The first section's prisoners have been brought on deck. They peer closely at the gloomy shoreline. Sakhalin is making its first profound impression. The view is dumbfounding and perplexing. Roll call is taken. "Well, sit down now, boys," orders an officer. He means "sit on the barge." The prisoners, as ordered, fold their legs and… sit on the boat's deck. A joke and a sin. They manage to huddle together and get a bit of a laugh.

One after another the penal laborers walk along the gangplank onto the barge with bags over their shoulders. Because it's rocking, the prisoners go weak in the legs and don't stand but lie down beside each other. With one barge full another is brought up and loaded. The little tug, puffing and breathing heavily, drags the pitching and floundering barge toward the far distant dock. Already willfully creeping toward the steamer is another tug pulling a pair of old tubs pitching from side-to-side.

The loading is going quickly when the most difficult moment occurs. There is the depressing sight of the procession exiting the steamer's infirmary. Patients are being carried on poorly-fashioned chairs and clumsy stretchers as doctors with worried reproachful faces bustle around the procession. These are the means of conveyance for the sick.

God, what worn-out, martyred faces these patients have! One seems to be looking at me now. Head bandaged; features sharpened like those of the deceased, hardened with an expression of suffering and torment; face waxen; downcast eyes with barely a glimmer of life, like a fire burned to its coals. A barely audible groan, or rather a mournful sigh, escapes his thin white lips.

For the most part these are the seriously ill from Korsakovsk Post's infirmary, transferred here for want of an operating room in Korsakovsk. They've been waiting several months for operations usually needed immediately. There were delays because the shipping lanes had to clear. What good person will raise the issue of the need, the vital need, the scandalous need, to build Korsakovsk its own surgical facility? When will attention be given patients—racked with pain and waiting whole months for an operation—who need serious operations? How many wretched patients will escape undeserved torments and sufferings, how many lives could be spared?!

From the stern along the topsy-turvy gangplank the patients are carefully taken under the doctors' guidance to the hospital barge, though not without torment, of course. Load complete, the wretched prison tug brings us to the pier.

It feels like you're approaching an administrative center. Aleksandrovsk's quay is fully outfitted. There's a signal mast, nice little houses for those working the tugs or assigned to the chancery or post command. A little while ago, this quay was smashed to pieces, but the misfortune was set aright by that veritable benefactor in matters technical on Sakhalin, former penal laborer L. He rebuilt the quay "as it should be." On Sakhalin, it is always thus: they begin doing it any old way, then do it "for real." And why not experiment? There are many laborers, and besides, they're free.

We walk along the wooden mole to the shore. On the mole, work's in full swing. Convicts from the "free prison" haul sacks, bags and chests. Another steamer has arrived before us, bringing goods from Vladivostok. Consignees sit on their chests and look sharply around. "They won't swipe this." The beggarly prison steals what it can.

"Guard, guard," comes a piercing cry, as if there's a knife at the person's throat. "Guard, did you see where they dragged my sack?! What kind of guard are you, if they steal it and you don't see?! I'll complain to the warden."

"Where are you taking this sack?" the guard says to a convict.

"To hell with him, the scoundrel. I know it's his. I thought I had to bring it over there. Take the sack, you madman. Geez, 'no' to the lot of you—still screaming, the cursed fellow."

"Rogues."

"Put the bag down, put the bag down, I tell you," can be heard from another side.

Seeming to notice no one, a strange figure is slowly moving amid the bustling throng. He is bareheaded, in a robe of gray prison cloth down to the heels and resembling a chasuble. The wind tugs at his blond hair, his pale-blue bright eyes gaze at the sky. An expression of reverential delight is on his face as if he sees God there in the distant heavens. One hand holds a willow branch, the other seems poised for benediction. Entirely borne away by his soul, he hears nothing around him and walks straight ahead as if no one were in front of him. When he bumps into someone, he doesn't notice.

"Oo-ooh, you accursed fellow! Look where you're going."

This is the unfortunate lunatic Kazantsev, who suffers from *mania religiosa*. He goes about like this, in a long robe resembling a chasuble, head bare and arm raised in benediction, in both winter and summer. His poor relations followed him here to Sakhalin, gave him the funds of a "simple man," and now walk behind him soliciting alms for this "man of God." In his face, in his figure, in the benedictory hand, in his gait—ceremonial and measured, as if he's moving toward some great lofty goal—there's something touching, even magisterial, if you will. The connection between this man carrying his diseased soul far from this world and his vainly excited circle of paupers and wretches is a connection very strong.

At the end of the mole there's the unpleasant clanking of iron. Fettered prisoners are working here under armed guard.

"Untie your trousers," shouts a soldier standing before a tall bearded muzhik with somber eyes. "Now untie your trousers, I say."

"Untie them yourself, if you want," answers the fettered prisoner, quietly and indifferently. "Don't you push me!" he shouts when the soldier surreptitiously prods him with his rifle butt. "What're you pushin' me for, you ugly mug? I could crush you, fatso."

"There's too many to bring you all down to size. See how many of you devils are here. All you do is gobble down the government's bread. No punishment's too cruel for you cursed fellows!" swears the soldier, turning red with anger and untying the penal laborer's underclothes.

"Now that's better. Were it always like this," the convict continues in a calm voice. Calm and indifferent, this tone particularly vexes, annoys, agitates, troubles and infuriates the soldier.

"Better keep quiet. Quiet, before I knock you out."

"A lot of you tough guys here."

"Shut up," shouts the soldier, now crimson with anger and the effort to undo the pants with one hand (it's forbidden to let go of the gun with the other). "Shut up."

"Don't push," the convict shouts again, once more prodded in the side by the rifle.

A little wagon comes flying down the hill onto the mole. Chained prisoners sit on it. Barely keeping up behind it, with one arm shouldering his rifle and the other tucked in his greatcoat, comes a guard.

"Easy, you demons."

"So what, keep running."

At the entrance to the mole stand droshkies and tarantasses with penal laborers and coachmen in the seats. There's only one cabman among all Aleksandrovsk Post's exile-settlers, and he's not full-time—he can't be, because of the government. It comes down to the horses on Sakhalin. Here, indeed, is some *katorga* labor. All day long all you hear on Aleksandrovsk's main street are the sound of harness bells, all you see are the variously-named officials' madly rushing troikas. "This," you think to yourself, "is a hub of activity." Were you to ask the horses, they'd answer that administrators are a very active people.

However, a strange group of settlers who are apparently transferring is spread along a government storehouse wall. Old people, youths, women and children sit on trunks and packages with cushions and icons in their hands, with their scant, meager and pitiful goods and chattels. "Fugitives from Sakhalin," new "peasants-formerly-exiles," these are people who've completed *katorga* and exile-settlement and acquired "peasant status" and, with it, the right to depart for the mainland. It's every involuntary (and voluntary) inhabitant's cherished dream. Having sold off or else simply abandoned their huts in nearby or distant settlements, they gather here, the wished-for moment, dreamt of night and day, having arrived. The wind whistles, white granules fly and whirl about, but they sit here shivering blue with cold not knowing when they'll be offered seats on a steamer. It may be three days and no sooner before they get seats. No one has bothered to apprise them of this, no one has bothered to say when exactly it will be. And they will freeze here in the wind and cold, poorly dressed and with small children, afraid to miss "embarkation" and so remain on this accursed island.

"Sweetheart," moans a woman. "Allow me to go off somewhere. I'll just feed the baby. My wee baby at my breast. He's not moving at all."

"Food's right here. No need to go anywhere."

"It's cold, sweetheart. In cold like this nothing can breastfeed."

Such is the "wished-for day."

We approach this half-frozen group.

"Have you been sitting here long?"

"Since yesserday. We was waiting all day yesserday fer a steamer. We're freezing, but can't leave our things. Folks round here is low-lifes and they'll snatch 'em away."

"But where are you bound, the mainland?"

"Quite right, to the mainland, yer worship."

"And what will you do there, on the mainland?"

"What God permits. Whatever Vladistok (Vladivostok) allows us."

"But right now, in Vladivostok on the mainland, there's nothing for folks to do."

"All the same, we think it'll be better there. Not a thing on Sakhalin... As God wills."

"Well, do you have money for your journey?"

"We got three rubles."

"But a ticket costs more than three rubles."

"Perhaps the captain'll pity us and take a three-ruble note."

"The captain probably won't, because he has to pay a tariff."

"So we're to die here? Die on this accursed island? Just die?"

Here and there they're saying, "Give us a ticket, for Christ's sake." Beggars begging for mercy among beggars.

Off to the side, separated from the rest, an old man is sitting on a small package, weeping. He sobs like a child, tears flowing like a brook down an Asiatic face turned blue from the cold.

"What's the matter, old man?"

"No money, little father, no go home."

He's waited for this day for 23 years. Twenty-three long years. Twenty-three years of Sakhalin *katorga*. His name is Akop-Gudovich. Twenty-five years ago this small, unfortunate sobbing old man—who was then probably a dashing mountain-dweller—participated in the kidnapping of a girl, defended himself with a rifle (probably well-aimed) and ended up in *katorga*. He's dreamed of this day for twenty-three years, saving his money to leave. It seems he's collected thirty rubles but was told: "Where can you go? You need 165 rubles."

"My brothers in Erevan Province, wife left behind, and children now already big. We want die in home place," the old man bitterly sobs.

There are so many like him, having completed *katorga* and exile-settlement, dreaming of returning home, reaching the anticipated day, arriving here and hearing the words: "Show the money for your ticket first, then you can go home." They spend dozens of years on Sakhalin yearning for those near and dear—they who have already atoned for their sins but are nevertheless enduring a heavy spiritual *katorga*.

A crowd of penal laborers passes us. They're from the *Iaroslavl*. They pivot to the left along the shore, toward a large one-story building marked "Quarantine." The quarantine's courtyard is already swarming with a gray mass of prisoners. The very last barge laden with prisoners to be delivered amid this gray mass approaches the quay.

30

THE CAPITAL OF SAKHALIN

So called is Aleksandrovsk Post, where is centered the island's main administration, where is located the largest prison, where is kept the "pinnacle of *katorga*" and wherefrom originates that "real *katorga*" we will now describe.

"Is it not the truth," you hear from all the administrators, "that nothing in Aleksandrovsk reminds you of *katorga*?" I don't know another place where everything reminds you *so much* of *katorga*. Nowhere else is the sound of chains so often heard. The broad unpaved streets, little wooden houses—everything connotes an indifferent provincial settlement. You're ready to forget you're in *katorga*; but then there's the clanking of chains and a party of fettered prisoners surrounded by guards comes around the corner. This at every step. Nowhere else are the truly *katorga* conditions of Sakhalin life so repeatedly in evidence. Nowhere else does *katorga* poverty, *katorga* homelessness, so veritably strike the eye. Every twenty to thirty paces an exile-settler slowly, slavishly, ingratiatingly and submissively approaches you doffing his cap. He's a specter of poverty and typical of Sakhalin's exile-settlers: dressed in an altered prison pea-jacket; disheveled from head to toe, with neither boots nor tom-cats; anguish on his face. The Sakhalin exile-settler always begins speaking with the words "just so" and always, without fail, converses in a "roundabout way."

"Just so, your worship. Who knows how we've come to be on Sakhalin…"

"Well, say plainly what needs saying."

"Just so, how, without any guilt…"

"Just say, finally, what you need to say."

"Just so, third day no vittles... By your commander's mercy, mightn't there be..."

"Here. Here, take it and go." But then from across the street comes the same type of figure, similarly gray, similarly miserable. Gray specters of Sakhalin melancholia. And again the whiny voice, the unctuous depressing "song of the Sakhalin wretches": "Just so, as we..." Ahead are dozens, hundreds, of these gray specters singing the same doleful song.

Now and then you meet among them an especially hopeless and mournful individual. Some were exiled here because of the cholera riots.[1] They've been freed entirely from *katorga*, have transferred to the exile-settlers, but do nothing.

"Nothing to do. Soon, we'll all go back to the motherland, to Russia."

They loiter about without purpose, not yet realizing there will be no "amnesty to be sent home." Day after day these persons are becoming more hopeless and despondent as they wait to return home. These wretches believe as much in their return as they do that they've been sent here "for no reason."

"Why were you sent here?"

"Well, it was nonsense. The doctors had invented cholera. There was also news they were burying folks alive. Well, as a consequence, we didn't allow this. It was nonsense. A doctor got killed."

"Why did he get killed?"

"Well, they came down hard on him."

"And you saw how they buried people alive?"

"No. I didn't see. The people saw."

This is one of the leaders of the terrible Iuzovsky riots. A tall strapping muzhik. He was, it should be noted, terrifying during those formidable days when, crazed by the horrors around him, he brought rocks to the bazaar and shouted "Stone the doctors!" He threatened to hit over the head anyone who did not join in this terrible assault, who did not leave the bazaar "to get the doctors." He now wears the sterile look of a much-exhausted wanderer. He always walks around vainly delivering the most absurd petitions to all the officials. He gives them to everyone: the prison warden, mining engineer, land surveyor, doctors. So he walks around with papers in hand, and when he happens to see some "freeman" on the street, as he does now, he gives him a sheet.

"Show some of a commander's mercy..."

"Concerning what?"

"Concerning freedom..."

"I'm with you. But, dear man, I can't do anything."

"Lord! Who'll stand up for truth, for justice?" Despair glitters in his eyes. He's consumed by despair, lost in his belief in truth, in justice. Having called for the stoning of doctors, he is assured by his profound passion and willful spirit that he's suffering "innocently." And you will not change his mind about this. "How was it possible? How could the doctors invent cholera? Let me tell you…" And he proceeds to inform me of the news "spread by the people," about how the living, whom he didn't see but whom "the people saw," were buried.

Here's another interesting Sakhalin character. Foppishly dressed, he cuts a dashing figure and has a rogue's face that says, "at your service." He wears a fancy black jacket and trousers tucked into tall sturdy boots. With a red scarf around his neck he has the bearing of an ex-soldier. He was exiled for resisting the police. He worked as a steward in a certain Moscow restaurant with private dining rooms. What went on in these "private rooms" God only knows, but when the police showed up one night he tried to keep them from entering them. He locked the door and, when they broke it down, shot at them with a revolver. He's now out of *katorga* and has joined the exile-settlers. You see him on the street all day doing nothing. To the question as to why he's not employed, he says, "Well… I make deals…" When I needed to meet those shadiest of characters he proved an invaluable protector.

How he attached himself to me I can't explain. I hadn't even stepped onto the quay when he appeared before me, as if from out of the ground, with his constant expression: "At your service…" Before I even managed to say what I needed he flew to get it for me. I needed a horse—a horse arrived. I needed an apartment—several apartments became available. His face showed a readiness to provide another thousand services. He could get anything. There was neither good nor evil for this man, so "ready to provide" whatever and whichever pleases. I ran across him wherever I went. I'd leave the house in the morning—he'd be standing on the porch like a column. I'd return in the evening—his silhouette would appear in the dark.

"Will there be anything for tomorrow?"

"Yes, do me a favor and tell me what you want. Why have you attached yourself to me?"

"Your worship, you show a commander's mercy. Just so, and since all the gentleman administrators know you, they won't refuse you…"

"Well, about what?"

"A ticket to leave for the mainland. To a construction site." That is, the construction of the Ussuri railroad,[2] which penal laborers from Sakhalin are building. "When I was still assigned to 'labors' I found myself on the railroad. I always worked enthusiastically, meticulously. The command was satisfied with me. Your worship, with your similar approval…"

During each of our meetings there was this perpetual refrain: "Lord! I toiled. They were always satisfied. But now I'm to waste away on Sakhalin?…" I noted, however, that the most decent of exile-settlers stood somewhat aback from my cicerone, my Ussuri toiler. For example, I queried my coachman, a young man from a good exile-settler family sent here "for coining."[3]

"Listen, why does everyone shy away from that tall worker?"

"Folks don't like him," the young man reluctantly answered.

"Why?"

"Everyone knows him… In the yard there… he was the executioner…" That's why they avoid him…" This is what's called a "job" on Sakhalin. And this was the kind of jobs the Ussuri toiler was requesting.

"Tell me," I'm asking him. "Tell me straight. I know about you now. You want to work as an executioner."

"Exactly." And he looks at me with such clear bright eyes, as if this is the most respectable kind of work.

Oh, this Sakhalin street! What encounters are to be had on it!

With a cheerful happy gait Nikolka Tolstoy walks down the street, a delivery book under his arm, knocking a little iron cane along the way.

"Hello, good girl," he cheerfully hails a young exile-settler.

"Hello, uncle."

"To some, silly girl, I'm an uncle, but to your cohabitant, I'm a godfather."

Nikolka is a former executioner. He still dispenses floggings when there are no enthusiasts in prison willing to assume the role. His phrasing indicates that he flogged the woman's cohabitant when he was a penal laborer.

Nikolka was an executioner for a long time. He was "destined" to be one, for having chopped his wife's head off with an axe. "Out of jealousy," he explains with an amiable smile. He completed *katorga* and entered a settlement, but applied for something else and was last month assigned "to work" as a deliveryman for the prison chancery. He's seen me, and approaches.

"I'd like to meet you. Your worship, you show a commander's mercy. Make an appeal on my behalf. I'm suffering from a wrongful accusation. It's true, I'm not innocent. But I've suddenly gone from being an exile-settler to having to work again. All day long I run around with this book, carrying parcels. I never could've predicted such misfortune."

"Well, but carrying out floggings, was that work any easier?"

"They pay good money for that. Your worship…"

"Nikolka, is it true that when you were supposed to punish Shkolkin for killing the bandmaster's orderly, you flogged Shkolkin to death for 15 rubles?"

"He-he. Your worship, you know all about this," Nikolka merrily smiles. "Yes, indeed. You keep busy, your worship."

I need to see a Sakhalin "celebrity," the executioner Komlev. He's just left the house in which he's found temporary refuge. "Komlev! Komlev!" his mistress calls to him for me, and from behind the corner emerges Komlev, holding a child. He's leading another by the hand.

Fig. 20: Aleksandrovsk Post

Such encounters with penal laborers don't actually happen every second in Aleksandrovsk Post, encounters that nevertheless each time convey a picture of the poverty and extreme degradation of the fallen.

31

ALEKSANDROVSK POST

We're on Aleksandrovsk's main street. Were it not for pedestrians' gray cassocks or prison-issue pea-jackets, you could safely imagine yourself on some Millionaires' or Aristocrats' Street[1] in a small town in the middle of Russia's black-earth country. This is a broad street, unpaved and covered instead with planks, like a bridge. Wretched plants vegetate in the little front-yard gardens of small one-story wooden houses. There are two stone buildings on the main street: a very beautiful chapel, built to commemorate the Sovereign Emperor's deliverance from disaster at the time of his visit to Japan, when he was still the Heir Tsarevich,[2] and a building housing both a meteorological station and a school.

The main street looks gloomy. But how unusual it becomes if someone should arrive from Petersburg. It becomes unrecognizable. I have several photographs taken of it when the Main Prison Administration's director came to visit.[3] Naturally, this melancholy Sakhalin street couldn't be recognized amid the triumphal arches and flags. Naturally, the little wooden houses were unrecognizable behind the green garlands decorating them. This Sakhalin street actually had a bright appearance at the time, surprisingly dolled-up and decorative. The same was done for generally everything on Sakhalin at the time.

If you reflect, however, that in this place now occupied by a chapel, cathedral, museum, governor's mansion, meteorological station, clubhouse, offices and administrators' homes there was, just fifteen years ago, a dense impenetrable forest, then you cannot but be astonished at the Sakhalin colony's growth. Fifteen years ago an impenetrable forest; now there's a street like any other. Not in the sense of *katorga*, but in that of a typical, depressing provincial town. As I've already said, the pedestrians' clothes, indeed, the bones of a whale decorating the wooden bracings of the Sakhalin museum, curb the illusion. These are quite atypical street ornaments. The whale was beached during a storm and its bones are the museum's prized objects. "They are washed by rain, covered by dust"[4]—but they're "thinking" and "planning" of building an awning over them. "Thinking" and "planning"—Sakhalin's two most prevalent occupations.

The Sakhalin museum is a small but very interesting establishment. Everything the meager history and ethnography of this sad island can present, you will find here in several small rooms. Despondent mannequins of Sakhalin's natives—its savages—stare at you: Giliaks, Oroks, Tungus, Ainu. The stupid, congenial flat faces of Giliaks in fur-lined clothes. The screwed-up Kalmyk eyes of Tungus and Oroks stitched in furs. The intolerably reeking Ainu in their multicolored festive attire made from fish skins (this is an enigmatic tribe that is becoming extinct, a mixture of the Mongol-type with faint hints of others; strange savages with the voices of poets and kind dreamy eyes). In the museum you're shown the savages' domestic utensils and weapons and objects of their religious cult. You're shown stuffed birds, fish from Sakhalin's rivers preserved in alcohol, sections of trees, samples of Sakhalin's coal and all manner of little things, such as leftovers from the Stone Age that just barely limn the history of Sakhalin island's savages. There are two or three collections of gypsum that convicts assigned to logging brought from the taiga. They serve only to show that a talented person ended up on Sakhalin, one who in other circumstances would have become an acceptable sculptor.

"Well, where in this special Sakhalin museum is the section on *katorga*?" I asked the director.

"*Katorga* doesn't interest me." This answer is heard often on Sakhalin, containing as it does complete disdain for *katorga*, its existence and way of life. "Only purely scientific subjects interest me." As if studying "society's refuse" offers nothing of scientific interest.

The *katorga* lifestyle changes in connection to shifting views on crime and punishment. The spirit of this great humanitarian age, warm, soft and comforting as a summer breeze, is sensed here. Much that was truly terrible yesterday is today receding into the realm of an awful past. What rich informative material on *katorga*'s history might have been collected by Sakhalin's museum. I won't even mention the invaluable material for scientists, anthropologists, jurists and doctors that has been lost on Sakhalin thanks to there being not the slightest interest in *katorga*. Some time ago one of the doctors began compiling a collection of criminal types. He built a photography studio at the infirmary to shoot so called anthropological portraits. The work was going beautifully; the collection was coming along beautifully and promised to be a valuable contribution to science. Then, suddenly, this innocent occupation was for some reason found to be reprehensible. The photographs were destroyed. Why? Because of a failure to understand, because of ignorance... Valuable material for science is allowed to perish on the one hand because of ignorance, on the other because of disdain for *katorga*.

"Study what? '*Katorga*'?"

What on Sakhalin seems so absurd is serious for us.

Life for Sakhalin's administrators is depressing, dull and monotonous. Their entire daily intercourse with the world consists of telegrams from the Russian State Telegraph Agency. Telegrams are available daily except, of course, when the telegraph is down, as frequently happens and for long periods of time. Then Sakhalin's bureaucrats feel completely cut off from the world, they feel, in their own words, an oppressive, crushing painful anguish. "It's like I've been locked inside a casemate to die and no one can hear me shout, cry or moan," one of Sakhalin's ladies told me.

The telegrams—this last nerve connecting the "dead island" to the world of the living—bring administrators together at Aleksandrovsk Post's state printing office to write their messages. We'll go there, where, in fact, recognizing the familiar surroundings, the type cases, composing frames, the familiar knocking of type by the compositor's stick, the smell of printer's ink, you can in a minute forget that you're in *katorga*. We can rely upon the warmest and friendliest reception of all Sakhalin's workshops, where there's even something kindred. Journalists and typesetters, when they meet each other, are like two soldiers from the same regiment. Moreover, it's pleasing to talk in that special printer's language, so familiar and comforting for each of us, to speak in a language that's not been spoken for a long time.

"It's just like I'm in Moscow," the maker-up says to me, smiling. We turn out to be old acquaintances. He's from Moscow and used to set up at the newspaper I wrote for. He was convicted of a crime that happened behind closed doors...

Deficient in technical means, the Sakhalin printing office works well using a simple squeeze-press, managing to print the thirty-page official publication *Sakhalin Almanac*.[5] Only readers of a certain subspecies appreciate gentlemen printing-house operators.

Here's an original type among typesetters. Aged and bespectacled. A *brodiaga*. His whole life consists of matters journalistic.

"I even worked at the former *Naval Collection*,[6] of blessed memory." He says "former" as if talking about a dead relative. He speaks to me with such love for the journals.

"Do you long for journals here?"

He smiles bitterly. "It's hard. All my life has been devoted to this business. You get used to... Here, now, I find peace only in setting up telegrams. You knock 'em out just like you do the newspaper. You're just dreaming of another time—it's funny..." Tears well up in the old man's eyes as he chuckles over his reverie.

"And why are you here?"

"I'm a *brodiaga*."

"Won't you confide in me?"

"That's impossible."

What is there about this old man, finding poetry in the setting up of telegrams and speaking about a "former journal" as if about a person?

In the printing office bindery we meet an interesting personality, a recent "celebrity," in a certain sense. There was Petersburg's "murder in Apraksin Alley," a crime that drew attention for its *sang-froid*, cruelty and barbarity. A young lad murdered three women during a robbery and was sentenced to twenty years' *katorga*. Here are his strange eyes, of a completely yellow or golden color, such as only cats have. He looks at you directly, openly, piercingly—and, if it can be so expressed, you sense in these eyes no soul at all. Neither good nor evil, just absolutely nothing. Such eyes as would be met in especially vicious, cold, dispassionate thieving murderers who are typically good-looking, even attractive. You search in vain in their faces for some "mark of Cain," some "wicked" demons. Only, there's no faint glimmer of a soul in their eyes. Rather, you simply decipher in this creature's gaze a lack of humanity. The cold fixed look of a cobra. Such a look surely turns his victim's soul cold. There's neither anger, hatred nor rage in this look: with curiosity he watches the blood flow, the victim's dying spasms. With the curiosity of a cat who's just crushed a cockroach. A sense of cruelty, a sense of pity, has atrophied in these people—you read it in their eyes. As if forever blind, they have since birth lacked repugnance toward cruelty.

The bold, quick youth looks with his cat-eyes and calmly describes his murders.

"How could you do it?"

"With courage."

"Were you drunk?"

"Absolutely not. But my whole life brightened up then. I'd been working as a lackey, a waiter. I was always courageous. I courageously thought, 'If I go and murder someone, I'll get some money.'"

"Well, but now?"

"I'm learning a trade." And with love—with a love in which there's some sentimentality—he shows off a binding he's just completed, a binding lovingly made by the very hands that so calmly murdered people.

"You've made an outstanding binding, chap."

His face brightens with a wide smile of surprise. This youth, transforming from a brutal murderer into an apprentice amused with his work, produces a disarming impression, as if he's knifed three people then just sat down to play a little game.

In the same building that houses the printery there's a library. A library many "freemen" shun because penal laborers can borrow books from it. K, a young man, practically a boy, rises from behind a desk to greet us. Few in this "realm of sorrow" on Sakhalin make such a powerful impression. He looks as if he's just received some terrible news that has stupefied and utterly weighs upon him, and he speaks as if awakening from mournful thoughts that wander far, far away...

With his pale face he looks sickly. He was exiled to seventeen and a half years for murdering someone out of rage and aggravation. On Sakhalin, he's known as a meek man. It's like everything has flown out of this man and you can do what you want with the body that's left. It hasn't been easy for him on Sakhalin. He was a clerk in the mining engineer's chancery, where he clashed with the chancery manager and also a convict, a certain G who was exiled for a filthy crime. This G slandered him to the engineer, who ordered K sent to the chains for a month. The unfortunate K spent a whole month in the chains, the most terrible place in *katorga*. After his release, kind people contributed to the library he started. He makes a powerful impression, this man in whom everything seems dead.

32

SENTENCED TO PENAL LABOR...

Speaking in Sakhalin terms, in "five" (1895), 2212 people were exiled to Sakhalin; in "six," 2725. A notable fact: we annually sentence between two and three thousand to penal labor, refusing to acknowledge that it is indeed *katorga*, refusing to recognize the meaning of those sentences to an "indefinite term," to twenty, fifteen, ten, four or two years.[1]

And that is why I will first introduce you to *katorga*'s interior world, so as to familiarize you with its unique caste divisions, customs, mores, religious views, laws, crimes and punishments. I must familiarize you with those things so very "*katorga*," to which punishment people exiled to Sakhalin are subjected.

As we've already seen, all penal laborers are separated into two divisions: the probationers and the correctionals. People sentenced to no fewer than fifteen years *katorga* are assigned to the probationers. Convicts with indefinite terms are supposed to remain in the probationers for eight years; five years for those sentenced to at least twenty years' labor; and four years for those sentenced to between fifteen and twenty years' labor. The rest, usually, are now included among the correctionals.

Only the probationers' prison is a "prison" as normally understood. The probationers' or, as it's usually more simply called, the chains prison, is usually entirely separate, fenced in by a high wooden palisade. Along the walls walk guards who cannot prevent probationers from escaping in plain sight. What walls can contain, what guards can frighten, a man who has nothing left to lose but his life? And for whom death seems sweet compared with his horrible life in the chains?

The visitors' entrance to the probationers' prison is closed. As if infected with plague, probationers are completely quarantined apart from the rest of the prison; even sick probationers are held completely separately. But this, of course, does not in the least prevent correctional prisoners from penetrating the chains, bringing vodka there and joining in card games. *Katorga*'s inventiveness and resourcefulness are without limit. Like anywhere on Sakhalin, anything can be bought there and it's very expensive.

From spring to autumn, the beginning to the end of the "escape season," probationers have half their scalps shaved and are held in irons at night. Moreover, even without this damnation there's the clanking of chains permeating the Sakhalin atmosphere. As you're passing by the chains prison you can actually hear chains rumbling. Spring through autumn these half-shaven prisoners lose their human form and acquire a bestial appearance, loathsome and disgusting. This, of course, deeply torments those probationers who hadn't thought about fleeing but decided to endure patiently their heavy lot. It confronts them with dilemmas such as would probably not enter their heads in other situations.

The scheduled workday for both probationers and correctionals is supposed to be between seven and eleven hours, depending on the time of year. But this schedule is never followed. If there's a steamer—especially from the Volunteer Fleet, which absolutely cannot be delayed—convicts work "as much as possible" and even as much as impossible while being utterly enserfed to the captains. I myself witnessed how work begun at five o'clock in the morning to unload a Volunteer Fleet steamer did not end until eleven o'clock at night.

Except for Sundays and three days for fasting, probationary convicts get only fourteen days off each year. Epiphany,[2] Ascension,[3] Whitsunday and Whit Monday,[4] the Annunciation[5]—none are holidays for probationers. Nor is the law always followed. Several of the fourteen rest-days given probationers are ignored. I myself saw how convicts were turned out to unload a Volunteer Fleet steamer on a holiday during which, by law, they weren't supposed to work. They were forced to work, therefore, on a day when even the serfs of former times were free from labor.

Out of this erupts those rebellions that provoke the "compensatory measures" of suppression, measures that often result in people, regardless of innocence, becoming still more embittered and without which *katorga* is already sufficiently troubled. So it was that on a certain holiday, Korsakovsk Prison's chains convicts resolutely refused to unload a steamer.

"It's against the law!" They were given a direct promise they'd receive a workday off in exchange. "We know those promises! So many of those days have disappeared!" the chains prisoners answered, and resolutely refused to go out to work.

"This 'humanitarianism' is leading to this and that!" a warden angrily and bitterly told me regarding this. "What is this, now that we have 'humanitarianism'?! The leadership doesn't want us to flog! What, I ask you, am I supposed to do with these scoundrels?!"

But as for a penal laborer to whom I posed the question, "Why don't you want to go out to work? It'll only make it worse for you!" he answered, waving his hand, "It can't be worse than it already is. Mercy, but a holiday's given us so's we can mend and fix up what we wants. We're just about goin' around bare-assed and barefoot as it is. Everyone's reached the end of his tether. Day after day with no rest, not even a legal holiday, and we're still in irons and walking in them to work. How can it get any worse?!"

On Sakhalin, altering legal regulations is nothing for a captain favored by a warden.

"All you have to do is to go to the warden," says an agent for a certain trading firm, "and tell him to send some men. When our chartered steamer arrives, he's got an obligation!"

"But you know that according to the law today's a holiday and prisoners aren't supposed to work!"

"So what."

"But it's the law!"

"Nonsense."

If you add to this evil no nutritious food at all and clothes and footwear that give no warmth in even the slightest cold, perhaps you'll understand why these people sometimes lose their patience and the reasons for their ill-conceived escapes and the bitterness that animates *katorga*.

As circumstance allowed, I managed to visit chains prisons unaccompanied by wardens. I wanted to hear for *myself* what convicts would say. They spoke with a vulgarity we would never dream of. They're a rude people with nothing left to fear. They talked to me, risking much, if only to release their own bitter emotions; and they probably spoke because their tongues could not remain silent. Such animosity reigned in Rykovsk's chains prison that the warden hesitated to take me there.

"These are such scum, they don't deserve to be seen!" he "confided" in me.

"I've hardly come to Sakhalin to see chivalric knights!"

The chains division had been sitting "on the waste-tub"[6] for two weeks. They'd just been released for work after having been held under lock and key for two weeks, never leaving their ward except to line up morning and evening for the waste-tub in the corner. In this fetid atmosphere these men, sitting under lock and key, truly seemed like animals. I cannot deny that I was rather terrified among them. I was clearly pushing a sore spot each time I asked: "Why won't you go to work?"

"We're not going!" they shouted from all sides. "They can exterminate us all—we're not going!"

"What's the matter?" I turned to one man standing like a statue against the wall and glaring hatefully.

"And what's it to ya?" he answered in such a tone that a convict tugged me by the arm and quietly said, "Barin, move away from him!" Taking me for an administrator, they were trying to provoke me to harsh words, to rudeness, so as to vent their pent-up hatred.

Probationers are never sent to work except under a convoy of soldiers. For example, you'll often see the following scene: Probationers are jumping one after the other into a quickly moving wagon with sacks of flour. The wagon's flying along the rails and behind it runs a soldier, one hand holding a tangled greatcoat, the other a rifle, breathing heavily and bathed in sweat. The convicts won't let him in the wagon.

"No! You keep running!"

"Chaps, why're you acting like pigs?" I ask the penal laborers. "After all, he's a man just like you!"

"Ech, barin! We really want to piss him off!" answer the penal laborers.

By the same token, for example, the following scene is not so rare. As if in a frenzy, a soldier's yelling at a "chain-man" on the jetty.

"Why're you filling up your shirt with flour? Take off your shirt!"

"Take it off yourself if you want."

The guard removes the chain-man's shirt and other effects. A bunch of flour pours out. *Katorga* chuckles. While doing this, the butt of the rifle the guard has crooked under his arm somehow jabs the prisoner.

I also once saw the following scene. A probationer with a bad leg separates from his party to adjust his fetters. A guard hits him in the side with his rifle-butt.

"Hey, why did you do that?" I say. "You can see the man's injured."

The guard glances back. "Don't stick your nose where it don't belong!" There's boiling rage in his eyes.

Here are people serving a sentence of real *katorga* labor! The manservant Nikolay, a former convoy guard who murdered a convict and is now himself sentenced to *katorga*, works at the staff club in Aleksandrovsk Post.

"How's it going?" I ask.

"Indeed," he answers. "First I was a guard but now, thank God, I've landed in *katorga*."

"Why 'thank God'?"

"But why not? Only the dumbest, the morons, drag timber. Even those devils you have to watch. Any one of 'em can do you harm, 'dump' an insult on you. They do that, give you a look, so you get in their face. Look 'em in both eyes and don't run. Yes, look at 'em so they won't kill you. But touch any of 'em, and you're guilty. No, in *katorga* it's more comfortable. You don't have to watch 'em. Let 'em watch me!"

You're going on foot with a party of shackled convicts led by a convoy. What do they talk about? Without fail, about the convoy guards. They tell jokes about soldierly stupidity and dullness, laugh over the guards' appearance, then simply resort to cursing them. And *katorga* knows how to call a man names so that he keeps going from hot to cold. The guards, bitter and twisted, walk away from these hateful faces barely able to control themselves. "But you can still hear us!" gloats *katorga*. The party's quiet for a minute, then someone starts in again. "Oh, my lads, aren't these soldiers the biggest idiots—it defies comprehension!" And it starts all over. No wonder these wretched guards end up bitter. Even senior administrators complain about them. "They're worse than the convicts."

I've managed to get too close to one of the warehouses.

"Hey, you sonofabitch, what're you doing here?" shouts a guard. "Don't dare come over here, you devil!"

"What are you angry for? You shouldn't cut me like that."

"You're gettin' angry yourself! You'd better lighten up a bit," the guard says cuttingly yet again. "Don't dare mess with me! Mess with me and I'll knock you out!"

These people are really incredibly bitter. Mutual bitterness peaks whenever penal laborers escape and soldiers chase them. Bitter probationers strike a fear into wardens that they usually try to disguise with contempt: "I don't talk with such rabble. If he's a swine, I don't want to see him!"

You can imagine that what happens in probationary prisons depends entirely upon the discretion of the guards, who are often former convicts, too. For months, no administrator shows up to witness the terrible crimes that fill these prisons, to see what convicts do with and to each other. "Visiting there is dangerous!" officials explain. "You can tell everybody hates you!" This is true... Although Drs Lobas,[7] Poddubsky, Cherdyntsev and Aleksandrovsk Prison's humanitarian warden do go there. I actually believe the safest place on Sakhalin for each of these men's families would be the chains prison, particularly that section where those with indefinite sentences are held. Here, they could feel secure against the worst violations. The reason is this is a somehow different time.

For a host of reasons the probationary prison's atmosphere is that of dissatisfaction and its religion that of protest. Protest comes in all sizes and degrees. This protest is at times funny, though on Sakhalin protesting this way isn't without danger. For example, probationers won't doff their caps. At some point, I'm walking past a chain-gang. They look at me provocatively and only one ended up doffing his cap. I correspondingly did the same, and doffed my cap and bowed. In a moment the whole party doffed their caps and shouted, "Greetings, your honor!" They later exasperated me with this doffing of caps! Such is the chains prison.

By law, the prison incarcerates only the most serious criminals, from the "fifteen-yearers" to the indefinitely-sentenced penal laborers, inclusively. But upon entering the chains prison you realize that not just "humanity's monsters" surround you. No. Alongside the parricides you find here people whose only offense is that they started drinking and never showed up for roll call. Certain names among the crowd are capable of inducing terror, including the "Luganovite"[8] Poluliakhov, the "Odessovite" Tomilov and the "Muscovite" Viktorov. But you can also see the former officer K—r, kept in the chains for a month because he didn't doff his cap when meeting a mining engineer. I know of a case when an official's wife asked that a penal laborer be put in chains because… he made advances toward her maid; he paid her a call and upset her proper performance of duties. Upon this lady's request, he was temporarily transferred from the correctionals' to the probationers' division. As you can see, everything's as mixed up as a cesspool. Simply for not doffing his cap a person morally decays amid a society of professional murderers.

After completing his probationary term, a long-term penal laborer leaves the chains and transfers to the "free prison"… or, as it is called by normal people, "the correctionals' division." Short-term penal laborers, that is, those sentenced to less than fifteen years' *katorga*, enter this category directly upon arrival to Sakhalin.

Correctionals receive additional privileges. For them, ten months count as one year; they get twenty-two holidays a year; their heads aren't shaved and they aren't fettered; they go to work not under a convoy of soldiers but under the watch of a guard. They often go without any supervision at all. It is this that introduces an extremely curious phenomenon. The most difficult, veritably *katorga*, duties—for example, the cutting and extraction of timber from the taiga—are the lot of the correctionals, these less serious criminals; meanwhile, the most serious criminals in the probationers' division perform the easiest tasks. A man serving four or five years for some homicide accidentally committed during a fight is tortured from morning till night in the impenetrable taiga, while at the same time a man who premeditatedly butchered an entire family tosses himself into a wagon rolling along rails.

Excuse me! Shouldn't we be sending the probationers to the taiga? But there aren't enough guards or soldiers. Judge for yourself what such an arrangement does for *katorga*'s understanding about the fairness of punishments.

"Where's the law?!" correctionals say. "Some bastard in the chains is living like a barin, like little wagons on rails. But I'm being quiet and obedient so I can be sent without a guard and suffer in the taiga. What did I do compared to his crime?"

The correctionals' prison is the smallest of prisons. More than anything, it's a flophouse—dirty, repulsive and terrible. When, toward evening, I went for the first time to the ward where the loggers, wood-cutters and those generally assigned the most difficult jobs are incarcerated, my head began to swim and grow dull, such was the "air" inside! The prisoners had only just returned from the taiga, where they'd been working knee-deep in melting snow. Their puttees, tom-cats and pea-jackets were completely soaked. Soaked in sweat, they were lying on the sleeping platforms. I asked one to strip and was obliged to step back, so strong was the smell of the man.

"You've really sweated through everything?"

"What can you do?! I sweat. I'm bathed head to toe in it."

"Why don't you undress? Aren't you going to hang your clothes up to dry?"

"Hang 'em up?! Kuzka[9] hung his cassock and puttees over there, dozed off and had 'em stolen."

"Don't take us long!" confirmed some penal laborers, laughing.

You can imagine what happens to these people who never dry off for weeks at a time. If one wanted to clean himself, this would be impossible owing to the general condition of the sleeping platforms. They're covered with parasites. I remember I was speaking with a certain tow-haired prisoner in Onor Prison when convicts warned me, "Barin, tell him to back off. He makes people sick." Such is the fellow one lies next to on the sleeping platforms! Such is the attention paid to hygiene here! This explains penal laborers' "inexplicable" (according to prison wardens) passion for sleeping underneath the platforms: "He doesn't lie on the sleeping platforms, but crawls through the muck beneath!" But better to lie in the "muck" than next to such a fellow! Many convicts told me they couldn't even eat at first: "It made us sick. Parasites crawling everywhere… One day, you hide a little piece of bread. 'I'll return from work and have a chew,' as they say. You grab it, but they've crawled all over it… Pah!" Each time I spent several hours in the prison my clothes and underwear became filled with parasites. So that you may comprehend this terrible filth, I'll merely say that I had to throw out all the clothes I'd worn to the prison and close-crop my hair. There were no other means of "struggle"! Such are the conditions under which live men who need strength for their work.

The free prison's second function is that of a gambling den. Games last from morning to night and night to morning. At any given moment there are several dozen rubles in the bank. Games are played for money and for things: several months' bread rations, the next disbursement of government clothes. Prison moneylenders deal in and profit upon anything. Convicts gamble among themselves, and exile-settlers show up to gamble, too. Gambling are the elderly and… children. While I was in Derbinsk Prison's almshouse an exile-settler, having already gambled away his money, telega and horse, arrived to give the cashier potatoes. When I was in Rykovsk Prison a woman exile-settler came to the warden, wailing, "I sent my laddie to the prison to buy bread. But they, the monsters, lured him into the ward and won the money from him."

"Don't believe her, your worship," said *katorga* in self-defense. "She herself sent the laddie here to gamble. He comes everyday. He wins, I daresay, not a thing, but loses to the 'lurers.' Lure him, like how!"

Upon checking, this all turned out to be true…

During the course of the day, correctionals freely come and go through the prison. They're obliged only to fulfill their given "task" and to appear at evening roll call. The rest of the time they go wherever they want. Visitors may similarly freely enter and exit the prison—something which facilitates the sale of stolen goods. Several dozen exile-settlers, Tatars for the most part, always crowd around the correctionals' prison. They're all usurers and buyers of stolen goods.

The free prison's third role is to be a refuge for the homeless and even for fugitives. General Grodekov so characterized Sakhalin's free prisons during his inspection tour.[10] The prison, to do it justice, is greatly concerned with the welfare of *exile-settlers*, for—indeed—a penal laborer's future is to be an exile-settler. You always find exile-settlers eating at the free prison during dinnertime. The penal laborers don't give them bread—"because we don't have enough ourselves"—but soup, the *balanda* for which, like fodder for swine, *katorga* pays five kopeks per *vedro*[11] and gives away as asked. As such, during periods of unemployment and hunger sometimes as many as 200 exile-settlers are in the prison "eating out of one hand," as they say on Sakhalin. Arriving at the post famished, "out of their heads" and having had nowhere to rest, homeless exile-settlers from distant settlements come to the free prison to spend the night. They arrive toward evening, clamber under the sleeping platforms and sleep there till morning.

Truly, there's something deeply moving in this charity that helps the poorest of the poor. So many times did my memory of this support me in those difficult moments when my mind grew dull and *katorga*, because of its horrors, seemed nothing more than an "ensemble of scoundrels." No, even in prison, in this wicked purulent pit, *man* lives!

The free prison often serves as a den for fugitive convicts who've fled other districts. So, for example, Shirokolobov, the terror and horror of Sakhalin who'd been chained to a wheelbarrow but escaped Aleksandrovsk's chains prison; the Shirokolobov for whose capture 100 rubles was offered; the elusive Shirokolobov for whose capture an entire detachment of plain-clothes detectives was dispatched—this same Shirokolobov quietly and peacefully hid himself for an entire winter in Rykovsk Prison.

"He even received a government ration! Such was the rogue!" shouted the district's commanders and prison warden.

"But how could that happen?"

"It's very simple. We don't know his face. Who knows what he looks like? And, of course, *katorga* doesn't turn him in. So he lived there all winter. When it warmed up, he left 'to do his business.' What can you do?"

The freedoms of the free prison are generally unlimited. I wanted to track down the prisoner P, a well-known criminal, so I appealed to the warden: "He's working in the mill." I go to the mill. "Not here." "Not here" another time; "not here" a third time. I went there at six o'clock in the morning. Still "not here." But then *katorga* got to know me, and I began to benefit from their trust.

Fig. 21: Aleksandrovsk Prison

In the mill they told me, "Barin, he's never here. He's put someone else in his place. He's been paying him a ruble-and-a-half every month for the last eighteen months while he stays in the prison. He runs a business there: he's a *maidanshchik* (in charge of a dispensary and prison rations), a second-hand dealer (a junk dealer) and a 'father' (a usurer)." Out of curiosity, I watched the 'husk' (the man hired to fulfill P's labor assignment). He was a pitiful little peasant, sentenced to four years for manslaughter during a drunken bout on a patron saint's day. Every daylight hour he worked in the mill for someone else, and in the evening completed his own tasks. Only his soul kept him together in this fulfillment of a double *katorga*.

Such cases on Sakhalin are not only not rare but ordinary, commonplace and typical. A fellow gets into trouble during a drunk and ends up serving out a double *katorga*; whereas a professional criminal, one of those "most famous" murderers, strolls about, soaks *katorga* and gets rich off these wretches.

On Sakhalin, a ruble-and-a-half is worth more than fifteen rubles for us.

Such is morality in correctionals' prisons.

For good behavior over a certain period of time a prisoner can be released entirely from prison. He then transfers to the "free *katorga* command," lives not in prison but in a private apartment and performs only daily assigned "tasks."

Could you know how anyone in prison who is in the slightest bit decent aspires to this! How they all dream of breaking away from the prison's material and moral grime to settle in a free—in their "own"—apartment.

But, unfortunately, not everyone who desires this has his wish fulfilled. The warden himself cannot know each of his hundreds of prisoners, and so attestations of good behavior are made by guards who themselves are often former convicts. Recommendations for transfer to the free command are made by clerks appointed exclusively from among the penal laborers. They hold everything in their hands. Often, because of a lack of two or three rubles, a poor convict's dream of his "own" space and any hope of relief is denied…

Those who've rightly or wrongly entered the free command either get a bunk somewhere for fifty kopeks a month or live two to a shack. Every post has such a "*katorga*" village." You go there and the poverty is terrible, no one owns anything whatsoever. Nonetheless, determination glitters in the eyes of its inhabitants: "Praise the Lord we got away from that damned place!"

The Lord himself, indeed! You can't turn around in the shack. Oh, God, what has fate given these people instead! We're entering one of the mud-and-wattle huts. It's five paces square and houses two. One is a Pole. He's forty years old but looks sixty and resembles a huge stooping skeleton. His face is yellow and tight, eyes burning with a gloomy fire. He's habitually sullen, unsociable and speaks to no one. He was sentenced to twenty years for hiring someone to murder his wife. He was tormented by jealousy but too afraid to kill her himself. This tall, prematurely gray stooping man seems to have survived many a storm. His "little half"[12] is a chap from Voronezh Province exiled for violence against a young woman. "I was drunk, your honor. I was out with my gang and ran into her. Maybe I did it, maybe I didn't. I don't remember anything!" Poles apart, these two live together.

Here's another pair. A "contradictory" old muzhik—a *Sibiriak*,[13] athletic in build, habitually serious face, eyes glittering with a cold impassive brilliance. Within them, an ice-bound spirit manifests itself. With the same coldness and impassivity, surely, these eyes look back to when he, the owner of a travel inn, murdered four of his sleeping guests—three sodden merchants and their coachman—with an axe. A strong and powerful character, he was "beguiled by a demon." When a demon beguiles such a man, he goes everywhere but stays nowhere. Pity and compassion have exited his soul, for he's too strong for such "weaknesses." He exudes a truly tragic demeanor. He lives with a red-haired little muzhik, a kind-hearted creature of the world who cannot refrain from smiling even when recalling his own crime.

"'Twas in the village assembly… The muzhik wasn't one of ours, but we thrashed 'im and he died, God grant 'im eternal rest in Heaven!"

"All for nothing? Do you both get along?" I asked.

"Ain't the chap a naughty one?" said the old man regarding his "little half."

"We get by! What else can we do?!" laughed the little muzhik.

For the most part, trying to get by in a free apartment is easier than in *katorga*. Gamblers, spendthrifts, drunks, usurers—these aren't exemplars of a "freer" life in prison. This is significant when you realize that in their society a good man can decompose simply because he doesn't have the few rubles it takes to pay a guard and a clerk for an "attestation" or "recommendation."

The "chains," the "free prison" and the "free command"—all career penal laborers pass through them. This is the usual sequence. But this entire sequence is turned head-over-heels if even the most serious criminal is followed to Sakhalin by his family, and especially if he's well-versed in some trade. If he is, for example, a good cobbler, turner or wood-engraver he is already an exceptional prisoner, a *persona grata*, even a *persona gratissima*. He does not seek but is sought. In Aleksandrovsk, for example, there is the engraver Keizer. You even see regular people deferring to him. And how! He's the only engraver in the whole post; if any one of the officials needs a nice little bagatelle, he runs to him. He subtly and deftly makes those things that are sent to Khabarovsk in demonstration of Sakhalin craftsmen's prosperity and talent. "He's got it made!" I recall one of the chains prisoners telling me with an ironic smile. "Only, I tell you, he's not that good an engraver, though isn't so bad at cutting a throat. No worse than us great sinners. But he lives like a barin!" If a penal laborer's family arrives, he's released from prison, entirely freed from what would have been his assigned labors for two years, and afterward does only consignment work so that his tasks should not interfere with his establishing a household.

So it is that two criminals will not serve the same sentences for one and the same crime. The one who brings his family lives in "freedom" and does nothing for two years. The other, because he's single, sits in the chains prison, has his head shaved in summer and is shackled. A brutish killer, a professional murderer, strolls about freely and works for himself because he has a family. But a man sentenced to seventeen and a half years because, according to a sergeant-major, he was insubordinate and tore off *his own* epaulets, languishes in the chains prison. "If he'd known, he woulda got married first," laugh the convicts. All this hardly convinces *katorga* that their punishments are fair.

One shackled prisoner, in a face-to-face conversation, insisted he needed to escape. When he failed to convince me why, he emphasized, "I can't stand it!"

"Well, listen. Let's be honest. Your punishment is difficult, this is true. But, really, you earned it. You murdered five people with an axe inside thirty minutes. There has to be justice in the world!"

"Just so! But some here have chopped up not five but eight people, and they live freely, without chains, because they brought their wives with them. And so I'm sitting in the chains not because I wasted five souls but because I'm a bachelor. Take Keizer out there, he lives like a barin. But someone else, who didn't do half what he did, is sitting in the chains just because he doesn't know a trade. Where's the justice?"

What can you say to that?

We proceed, however, with the further career of a penal laborer.

Having served his "probation" in chains, having served his sentence in either the free prison or free command, the penal laborer joins the exile-settlers. He builds a "home" somewhere in the dense taiga (where it's impossible to live), a home "per-the-law" because each exile-settler, as I've already noted, has to be engaged in "domestic economy," otherwise he can't join the peasantry. After five tormenting years of near starvation, the exile-settler transfers to the "peasants-formerly-exiles" and obtains the right to leave for the mainland. A dream come true! He leaves the accursed island for Siberia, which seems a paradise to him. He's supposed to remain there twelve years, upon the expiry of which he earns the right to return home. In such a way, even the indefinitely-sentenced penal laborer, his term reduced by an amnesty or for hard work, can hope that after thirty-five or thirty-seven years he, too, may return home.

Unfortunately, such lucky ones are very few. There's no life sentence of *katorga*, but a life sentence exists. Upon entering any chains prison you can clearly read on the inmate roster the following: "Sentence: 15 years + 10 years + 20 years + 15 years." Why these terrible pluses? There are penal laborers who, in sum, have been sentenced to seventy years. As such, they will never get away from here. They have no hope whatsoever. To any discerning eye these terrible pluses on the prison door say, *Lasciate ogni speranza voi che intrate*...[14] Where do these pluses come from? They all result from escape attempts. The terms to which men are sentenced to *katorga* are not terrible; the terms which strike them with horror are those they themselves earn. Often, a man sentenced to six years will earn forty for himself. He flees, is captured, and they add to his sentence. Hope now reduced, he flees again, is again captured, and again there's an addition. Now there's no hope whatsoever. The man flees and flees, his term accumulating. The pluses grow and grow. There have even been instances when the half-dead have fled the infirmary. Through the dense undergrowth of shrubs, through the impenetrable taiga, clambering over fallen trees, the man runs, not a man but a demi-corpse, fear in his dimming eyes.

From this cursory account of that which is *katorga* you may understand, partly, what causes these people to flee, to add to their terms, to aggravate their lots. They flee the horror...

Fig. 22: A mining "cut"

33

WHO RUNS *KATORGA*?

Consider the following situation. Someone's been injured and needs a serious operation. A council meets. Occasionally, even notes are taken. For a long time, doctors deliberate and deduce what kind of operation to do, how to do it and what might be its consequences. When all have reasoned and decided they get up and leave but commission the operation itself to a guard.

"But that's impossible!"

"But that's how it's done on Sakhalin."

A man commits a crime. Two jurists, a procurator and a defense counselor consider every grain of available evidence, how he committed the crime and what his motive was. Sometimes even a psychiatric expert is called in to investigate not only the accused's health but that of all his older relatives. If the accused is found guilty, three jurists consult each other and deliberate as to the punishment and its degree. But the punishment, designed "to rehabilitate the criminal" (Sakhalin's motto!), this very revivification, is itself wholly commissioned to a guard who was formerly either a soldier or an exiled penal laborer.

To wit: Not only exiled penal laborers' fates but their pardons depend upon the guards. Pardons shorten the terms of those demonstrating good behavior. Convicts' behavior is evaluated in a punishment log. But the punishments recorded in these logs are those imposed by the guards and are never expunged by prison wardens.

"This undermines the guards' prestige in *katorga*'s eyes. How, then, can this be controlled?"

On Sakhalin, more than anywhere else, they're crazy about "prestige" and regard it as the highest distinction. Do these guards, a good half of whom consist of former penal laborers, possess the moral qualities sufficient to be entrusted with the fate of these people? In my presence, no guard squeezed a bribe out of a prisoner that I could see. That is, I never saw a prisoner hand a guard any money. But while sitting with the guards I often asked, "Where did you get this from? Where did you get that?" And often received the answer, "It was given me in the prison… One of our prisoners made it for me." Several times while I was present at prisoners' card games guards would enter. "Well, what's all this? Break it up!" a guard would say, passing between the sleeping platforms and fixedly refusing to notice the pile of cards scattered around. "Go to your own spot!" he'd say to the banker, the prison card-sharp, refusing to notice that he was burying his nose in the pack of cards he was shuffling. He must not have seen this because he didn't say anything. When I had to learn who the *maidanshchik* was in a given prison, that is, who was trading in vodka and handing out cards for gambling, I always appealed to the guards and they would unfailingly point him out. Prisoners sometimes confided in me that such-and-such a prison ringleader, a prisoner from the "Ivan" stratum,[1] was wronging them and taking their last pennies. When I pointed this out to the guards, I always got one and the same answer: "Right you are, your worship, but what can we do with him? He's a desperate man and it won't take much for him to stick a knife in your ribs. Can anything stop him? No, we'll stay quiet."

I had to find the interesting convict P. I asked in the prison chancery if he was at work in the steam mill. But however many times I went there I got the same answer: "He's not here just now. He had to leave!" Finally, the guard delivered me from this wild goose chase.

"Your worship, go to the prison. He's there. He's never in the mill."

"But he works here!"

"He's hired another prisoner to work for him. He himself spends all day in the prison. He never leaves it."

"What does he do there?"

"He's busy 'fathering'!" (A "father" in the prisoners' language is a usurer; "fathering" means usury.)

P had been convicted of robbery and murder. I got to know the fellow who performed his labor assignment for five kopeks a day, a little muzhik, as it were, sentenced for killing a man during an argument.

"It was a holiday. I was drunk, I don't remember. Maybe I did it, maybe I didn't. We was sentenced by a crowd."[2]

He has his own labor assignment that he carries out, but the rest of his time (the steam mill runs all day) he carries out another's for a five-piece a day.

"I hafta eat."

"But you're working terribly cheaply!"

"I know it's cheap. But I owe P alot. You pay for what you want!"

He owed P three rubles. P had given him a bottle of vodka he valued at three rubles, so he endured the difficult fate of double *katorga* while the murdering thief went on to clean out other convicts.

Owing partly to the instinct for self-preservation, partly to other motivations, these illiterate guards of dubious morality indulge the very worst elements of *katorga*: Ivans, *maidanshchiki*, card-sharps ("players" and "fathers"). And it may be provocatively said that only thanks to the guards are these "gentlemen of *katorga*" able to hold in such servitude the pauperized and exhausted "herd."[3]

Mr M, Sakhalin's mining engineer, would often complain to me about the interminable "rebellions" that occurred in his Vladimirsk mine.

"Were a single one of these miners to work as he should! But you go there and they're doing nothing! Same old story."

"But you have two mines where penal laborers work, the Vladimirsk and Aleksandrovsk. Aren't there any rebellions in Aleksandrovsk?"

"In Aleksandrovsk, no."

God knows penal laborers are a special sort! An absolute riddle. A riddle, however, that proved quite simple.

Several days prior to my leaving Sakhalin Mr M told me, "There's a rebellion in the Vladimirsk mine. This time it's a real rebellion. They don't want to load the steamer! I'll demand soldiers for suppression! Let them flog these sons-of-bitches."

The affair was fortunately somehow settled without floggings or suppression: the Japanese steamer *Yayama-Maru* was quickly loaded with coal and I safely disembarked from Sakhalin aboard it. En route, the fellow accompanying the load of coal boasted, "How quickly they loaded it! Eh? The steamer's chartered to the Japanese on a daily basis. I've saved some money, it was loaded so fast!"

There really was something to boast about, for the steamer had been loaded amazingly quickly.

"But how did you do it?"

"One of the fellows there, a guard, is remarkably clever and rather practical. I slipped him a red-note[4] and he made the convicts pick up the pace. They loaded during working and non-working hours. Everybody hates him, y'know. All the guards on Sakhalin hate him."

This is the reason for the Vladimirsk "rebellions."

Another guard in that same Vladimirsk mine—Kononbekov, a former penal laborer—interested me. He was a Caucasian who'd been exiled for committing a murder after losing his temper during a quarrel.

"A frivolous quarrel!" the Caucasian Kononbekov smilingly said. "But I'm hot-blooded."

On Sakhalin, he's a hero. He killed the fugitive convict Pashchenko, who was credited with thirty-two murders. His escape from the chains prison where he was chained to a wheelbarrow spread fear throughout Sakhalin. Kononbekov shot him, and you should see with what enjoyment Kononbekov tells how he killed him. How his eyes light up when he does so.

"There I was going along the mountain. I had my rifle. I was walking around—'are there fugitives or not?' I'm going along a ridge, when suddenly there's a *shu-shu-shu* in the bushes. I aimed the rifle and—bang! All I heard was a scream. A fellow ran out of the bushes, and so I thought I'd missed him. I run to the bushes, but there's another fellow twisting around. What a shot! Right in the head! Blood, blood, blood…"

The man who'd run out of the bushes was Pashchenko's mate, Shirokolobov.

"How could you… so you shot him without warning? You didn't say a word?"

"Why talk? Just shoot!"

"And you do this often?"

"I go out every day. 'Are there fugitives or not?' A fugitive—and I shoot. It's like hunting."

Kononbekov lives in a curious place with a preternaturally neat bed. Above the bed are his favorite pictures: hunting in the taiga, a lion tearing apart an antelope and a battle between the Japanese and Chinese. Bloody stains: the blood in these pictures is like that spilled by his rifle.

"Did you buy these?"

"I did. They're my favorite pictures."

"What does Kononbekov talk about with the prisoners?" I asked the guard who'd "hurried the loading" for ten rubles.

"What else does he talk about? He tells them how he's not afraid, how he 'lived by himself in the Caucasus,' killed a man or how he shot Pashchenko. There's nothing more for him to say. A shallow man!" The practical guard waved his hand.

Kononbekov has a kind of mania for murder, for blood. And under the leadership of such persons there's to be a spiritual "renewal" of exiles! *Katorga*'s fate is in their hands.

"But how do Sakhalin's officials see it?"

You first of all have to understand what nine out of ten of these officials are like. The first official I met on Sakhalin was a certain Mr B,[5] whom I'd gotten to know while in Moscow. Arriving aboard the cutter to Korsakovsk, I noticed on the jetty a man in an unlined sheepskin and a service cap who was stamping his feet and shouting the most improbably foul words at a group of penal laborers. "It looks like B! Is it really him?!" We heartily embraced.

"You? Here? On Sakhalin?"

"But where did you hope to see me?" Mr B burst out laughing.

At one point, Mr B owned a candle factory: it went bust. Then he edited three newspapers simultaneously, participated in the Ashinov expedition, worked in police stations, was convicted of bigamy and served a long sentence for assault and battery. On Sakhalin, he'd become the commander of prisons. You can imagine what a man with such morals and such an understanding of the law can do, having found himself here among that population most deprived of rights.

"Is it really you?! What're you doing here?!" Mr B said to me in a moment of candor. "Here, where it's precisely necessary *to resurrect* a man, to turn a criminal into a peaceful colonist. We need the best people. But who comes here? We're all worth the same: it's just good they've ended up here in the capacity of administrators. People like me who aren't good for anything come here! It would just be good if such people knew how to fight, like I do…" He boasted of ways "to correct" criminal natures. "They sent me a Caucasian. A contrarian, given that he said that, in his view, things 'weren't according to the law' and he was up on his hind legs. Everybody was scared of him. But without saying a word, I smashed him once in the teeth, just once…"

Such a story of "leadership" by Mr B was very sad for *katorga* and ended sadly for him: Mr B ended up in court for some "deficits" and for flogging—over a doctor's protest—an epileptic prisoner who by law was immune from corporal punishment. It's not at all surprising that the word "law," as I've just invoked it, drives such gentlemen into an absolutely incredible frenzy.

"The law…" a convict invokes.

"Ah? You're going to rebel!" an official stamps his feet.

It's not at all surprising that on Sakhalin there's no word more foul than "humanitarian." I was talking with one of Sakhalin's land surveyors about one of the doctors.

"A humanitarian fellow!" replied the surveyor.

"Here, *here*?!" I was rejoicing that there was a like-minded fellow. "Is he really an humanitarian man?!"

"It's true! A humanitarian. All he does is be humanitarian. But how can you be this way with *katorga*? On the whole, he's not a man but a good-for-nothing!"

We were speaking different languages. "A humanitarian!" The word sounds half-contemptuous, half-accusatory, insofar as the man is "allowing *katorga* to become undisciplined." And for Sakhalin's officials there's no accusation more terrible than that they're "being humanitarian." "If I'm some kind of 'humanitarian' I'll be removed!" these friendly people rationalize.

Mr B was the first official I collided with on Sakhalin. P was among the officials I collided with later before leaving Sakhalin. His wife visited me: "Try to get us on the Japanese steamer to Vladivostok."

"Why do you want to leave?"

"My husband's been fired."

"Why?"

"He did something stupid."

"What, exactly?"

"He forced a girl. Now he's under investigation."

These gentlemen's concept of morality may be further judged by the following incident. A certain official personage visiting Sakhalin was inspecting an isolation cell in Aleksandrovsk Prison.

"What are you being punished for?" he asked the man sitting in the dark isolator.

"For refusing to become the executioner."

"Really?" the personage asked the assistant commander of prisons accompanying him.

"Exactly. It's true. I ordered him to perform the duties of executioner but he disobeyed and refused."

The personage, famous in the scientific world for his enlightened and humanitarian views, was of course dumbfounded.[6]

"What? You punish a man because he's shown good intentions? He didn't want to be the executioner? Do you understand what you're doing?!"

Do they understand what they're doing!

One evening, chilled to the marrow, I returned late to my residence in Korsakovsk Post.

"A wine glass of vodka! To warm myself."

"There's no vodka!" answered my landlady, an exiled convict. "But it can be bought."

"Where can you get it now? The government store's closed."

"But perhaps there's some at…" She named an official.

"He really deals in vodka?"

"Not him but his lackey Mametka, a convict. Then again, it's all the same: Mametka sells on his behalf."

Fig. 23: A Sakhalin mine

On Sakhalin, not a single word can be believed, you have to verify everything with your own eyes. So I donned a prisoner's cassock and cap and, together with an exile-settler, my landlady's worker, went to get the vodka. We approached the official's house and the exile-settler knocked on the window in the conventional manner. The door opened and the Tatar Mametka appeared.

"Whaddya want?"

"A drop of vodka."

"And who's this?" Mametka asked, looking me up and down.

"My comrade."

Seeing through the darkness my long prisoner's cassock and pancake cap, Mametka relaxed.

"Just a minute." He brought back a bottle of vodka. "Two rubles."

The vodka turned out to be a vile-tasting watered-down liquor.

The next day I went to visit this official to ask a lot of questions about his lifestyle. I asked to see his apartment, and in the bedroom noticed an entire battery of bottles exactly like the one I'd bought the night before.

"Ah, so you live with provisions!" I smiled.

"You know it! Friends sometimes drop by. I'm ready for any event."

Within a year this official was dismissed from the service, precisely for selling vodka to exile-settlers and *katorga*. An inspection of the books for the government shops (except for these "colonization fund" shops there's nowhere to buy spirits on Sakhalin) revealed that this official had stolen so many bottles he could have poured a river!

"And have you bought many sable furs?" officials and their wives on Sakhalin would ask me. "You've bought none? That's strange!"

The purchasing of sables is especially widespread among Sakhalin officialdom. Hunting sable is nearly the only way starving exile-settlers can support themselves. Officials typically pay for sable pelts with tickets. Vodka and spirits on Sakhalin may only be purchased by persons of the free estate, that is, officials. But they may send anyone they like with a ticket, a paper note, to collect the purchase: "I request that you dispense from the stores to the bearer a bottle of vodka (or spirits) for me. [Signed] So-and-so." Such tickets may be dispensed however one wishes. Large numbers of these tickets circulate among *katorga* and exile-settlers and are perfectly acceptable as substitutes for money. The market typically values them at fifty kopeks each. The tickets can buy or, as they say on Sakhalin, "be redeemed for," a bottle of vodka. This "right" is itself bought and sold by exile-settlers and penal laborers. On Sakhalin, they're even asked for as alms: "Your worship! Do a good deed! Write me a ticket!" Officials settle accounts with exile-settlers by using tickets. The rate of exchange is one sable pelt per ticket. As such, officials get sables as virtual donations while exile-settlers sell these tickets for fifty kopeks each to whomever wants to buy vodka. No Sakhalin official acquires sables any other way.

"You know, you're really getting their sables as a gift."

"I get them as gifts, but he gets money for the ticket."

When I was still in Vladivostok I was told, "Of course, Sakhalin's craftsmen form a collective 'enterprise'! But, y'know, if he puts his mind to it, a craftsman can turn out something not half bad. Have you seen Kh's carriage? Pay attention to U's furniture. All made by Sakhalin craftsmen!"

"Ye-es! 'Twas quite a time, but short-lived!" one of the prison wardens told me apropos of this. "Craftsmen worked for us, and sometimes quite well. There were all sorts of folk among them. But then they established 'production control.' Comptrollers were sent, and they account for everything: how many working hours have been spent, how much material has been dispensed. Now, craftsmen just work for the government. Well, of course, a favorite craftsmen can still make anything to order. But now they make it to sell it—if not, then it's 'quitting time'! It's difficult."

"Well, that's good. The government shods, clothes and feeds the craftsmen who used to work for you. Were they getting anything from you?"

"Them? What for? Do you think it makes any difference to a fellow who he's working for, the government or me?"

One more thing should be added to all this. It's a very widespread custom on Sakhalin to take a woman into service. Of the 260 female penal laborers in Aleksandrovsk District in 1894, exactly half were listed as "single" and in the service of officials. Bearing this in mind, you realize that officials cannot acquire in the eyes of *katorga* that "prestige" they so worry about.

"The vicious devils!" Rykovsk's assistant prison warden had complained to me about *katorga*. "No respect whatsoever! You can imagine for yourself how they don't speak to me other than with the informal 'you'! You can listen for yourself!"

The initial inspection of any prison that I take—out of courtesy—with the warden always makes a fearful impression. Looking him in the eye, convicts there will start "to inform" you about all his scams and tricks.

"But I'm not an official! This doesn't concern me!"

"No, your worship, you listen!" And they dress down the man because of whom they all hate their lives and their fates, unashamed of the foul language they're using about him. The warden, poor fellow, just shifts from foot to foot as if standing on hot coals. "Get out of here!"

Later, he may be disappointed with these denouncers, but now, embarrassed in front of a stranger, he "takes measures to maintain prestige." But how to respond? What can he say when everything said by the convict I heard already in the home of one of his assistants, and would be hearing in each house I visited!

If this small-fry Sakhalin official contemns and hates *katorga*, then *katorga* contemns and hates him. This compels Sakhalin's officials to be on guard and to keep their distance from a *katorga* filled with hatred and contempt, and to be occupied with only economic matters such that all order—*katorga*'s entire internal structure—is left entirely in the hands of the guards, who turn out to be the actual, absolute and uncontrollable "masters of *katorga*."

Sakhalin officialdom is divided into two categories—the *Sibiriaki* or *Zabaikaltsy* (*chaldony*, as convicts call them) and those officials "shat out of Russia." The latter expression should by no means be understood as somehow insulting or abusive. "Of the imperial Russian dung"[7] is a phrase that officials thought up out of *aristocratisme*, so to speak, so as to distance themselves from penal laborers. Prisoners are "dumped" on Sakhalin, but officials are used "to fertilize"[8] Sakhalin. Therefore, when penal laborers are asked "When were you dumped here?" they say "In spring" or "In autumn of such-and-such a year." But among themselves officials say "When did you fertilize?" and answer "I fertilized in such-and-such a year." The *chaldony*, the *Zabaikaltsy* and those who began their careers on Sakhalin say of themselves that they "grew up in *katorga*." "You can't fool me, chap! I myself grew up beneath the sleeping platforms!" a *chaldon*, a prison warden, will say of himself. But the majority of them are second or third generation prison-people. Grandfather was warden of a penal labor prison, whereas the father only "wardenizes." "*Katorga* devoured my childhood! I'm a penal laborer myself! *Katorga* didn't spare me! I'm no lily-fingered barin shat out of Russia!" *chaldony* boast. Were there no formal distinction you, conversing with such a gentleman, would be unable to figure out who you were ultimately speaking to: a convict or an official. In the convicts' language they say "to nail" instead of "to kill"; "*fart*" instead of "fate"; "crook" instead of "knife"; and so on. "He just wanted to nail a beard (to deceive a victim) but got scared that he'd push a wheelbarrow (make a denunciation), and so he nailed him with a crook. Such was his *fart*!" Can you make out who's speaking—a convict or one of the *chaldon* officials? This was a story by one of the prison wardens. They use terms and concepts borrowed from *katorga*.

When these people set about making improvements to Sakhalin it is either a joke (in the form of a tunnel built by a labor party digging from both ends that ended up on different sides of the mountain) or a horror (in the form of the Onor works[9]). There could be no other result when, to build a road, they got together a bunch of *Zabaikaltsy*— people who'd never even laid eyes on a surfaced road and didn't know what it was for.

The *chaldony*, having grown up among *katorga*, are at odds with the officials "shat out of Russia" and feel perfectly comfortable on Sakhalin. They busy themselves with their homes and pretty much know how to do everything themselves. "I even have watermelons!" a *chaldon* boasts to you. "Convicts built me a greenhouse!" A *chaldon*-warden hoping to impress you with his own "activities" first of all shows off his own place, then draws your attention to other officials' homes. "I built everything myself! What palaces I've constructed! Eh? Such comforts!"

"Indeed, this all takes care of the officials. But what about *katorga*?"

"*Katorga*?! The guards deal with *katorga*! Believe me, good man, there's no one better than a guard to deal with *katorga*. No need to trouble him. I have an assortment of guards. They're all former convicts. If he's a former convict, *katorga* can't fool him."

Given such views, the arbitrariness, the complete arbitrariness on the part of the guards, goes completely unopposed by *chaldony*. Pre-reform Transbaikalia was a poor school for law and order.[10]

The officials "shat out of Russia" are, as I've already said, mostly wretches, people who've failed at everything they've tried and proven unsuitable for Russia. They threw up their hands and "escaped" to Sakhalin. For the most part, they came here having heard stories that on the frontier there is not hardship but carnival; they came dreaming of colossal "surpluses" of prison bread made by the wardens' favorites—the prison bakers; they heard about huge "estates" providing goods and supplies; and so on. Bitter disappointment awaits them. These things are all *possible*, but far from in the proportions dreamt of, because "production control" interferes and production officials poke their noses into everything.

"I ask you, what is the advantage of serving on Sakhalin or suffering this *katorga*?" these gentlemen routinely bitterly ask. "What's the advantage? Increased compensation? Produce here is twice as expensive, and for what reason? What about revenue? Why do we buy a sable with a ticket? Revenue indeed! You work and work, but they export a thousand rubles' worth of sables. Of course, there are those who sell a little vodka. They make a good profit. But you'll end up in court, and now they're stricter and stricter. Never mind what used to be. You take from penal laborers so's to pay the domestics' wages. That's no kind of profit!"

Every perquisite, of course, allowed one to live like a barin during serfdom, owning servants and workers who, "in case they displeased," could be flogged or tossed into prison. These assumptions are hard to get rid of.

Among the "unbridled" despairing population—a population that has nothing to lose—these officials feel timid. After all, hunger forces this population to be cutthroats. Murders are rampant on Sakhalin: they kill for twenty kopeks and explain that it was "for the money," such does hunger corrupt morality.

Hence there is on the one hand the swindling associated with a free and easy life and on the other the endless dread of penal laborers. Of course, all this produces very little sympathy for Sakhalin or its inhabitants among the officials shat out of Russia. The majority simply serve out their terms, measuring rather than awaiting the passage of three years' service—for only after three years can one return to Russia with one's family at government expense. Like *katorga*, officials dream only of the mainland. All of Sakhalin dreams of the mainland, cursing and swearing at "this island, were it to sink under the earth!"

And how people dream! I was staying with one official who had all of several months left in his three-year "term." On the wall above his bed hung a calendar with the day of departure highlighted. He was like a boarding-school girl awaiting the end of the school-year. Every morning he got up and happily crossed out another day.

"Ninety-two days left."

"Which day do you cross out? The current one?"

"No, the next day. So it's that much sooner. It doesn't matter—I've woken up, day's already begun, so it can be crossed out. I'm happier that there's less of the day left!"

Such can be the faint-heartedness!

Of course, you cannot demand of such people that they be interested in the life of *katorga*, that they proceed in accordance with the law or in discord with the laws guards dictate to *katorga*.

"*Katorga* and the guards can all go to hell!"

Of course, officials who end up on Sakhalin are not bad people. But it is absolutely wrong that a population deprived of "all rights" is controlled on the island by those who not only debase them but are themselves debased. Sakhalin typically has a surprisingly quick ability "to Sakhalinize" people. Prison life, birch rods and whips become somehow ordinary, but they exact a price. Much that appears terrible to another person is here taken as commonplace, routine and quotidian. "Gentlemen, where are you going?" the assistant district commander's wife, a very sweet lady, stopped me and the doctor. "Ah, they're going to flog some prisoners? Hurry up and finish that business and come back. I'll have the samovar waiting for you." Anticipating the coming spectacle had given me a fever, whereas she spoke about it as if we were going to the store to buy cigarettes. Force of habit and a lot of nothing.

It's no surprise that the salon conversations of Sakhalin's ladies are (in our view) offensive. You visit an official's spouse, and between you occurs the following exchange of opinions.

"Look at *katorga* for yourself," the lady says quite pleasantly. "You'll agree on the need for corporal punishment."

"But were you to try..."

"Ah, no! Without floggings nothing can be done with them. *Katorga*'s amazingly undisciplined. It's absolutely necessary so that anyone, for example, your friends, may order them about."

"But should 'anyone' really be able to order them about?"

"Yes, so they won't misbehave again! You simply fear for your husband. They can suddenly stick a knife into him, and what does it cost them?"

The instinct for self-preservation prevails. For the most part, these women, these officials' wives, are unsophisticated and poorly educated and we can't accurately portray their particular demands. They seem to possess the brains of a chicken.

But even sophisticated and well-educated people are "Sakhalinized" on Sakhalin. Among the Sakhalinized even are doctors, who throughout *katorga*'s history have proved a bright exception among the brutal and callous circles of authority. You're hardly pleased when, for example, you hear the following things from the lips of the *young* Dr Davydov, who's served several years on Sakhalin. I quote from his brochure, *On Shammed Illnesses and Other Means of Avoiding Labor among the Exiled Penal Laborers of Aleksandrovsk Prison*, published in 1894.[11] The illnesses Dr Davydov regards as having been "simulated" are as follows: "mental illness, bronchitis, gastroenteritis, faints, dislocations, night blindness, general indispositions." Davydov characterizes the "shamming" of prisoners with:

> Prisoners will put their feet under loaded wagons, fall under horses or stick a leg beneath a falling tree, or will *artfully* freeze themselves or parts of their bodies, working the frost-bitten parts quickly and strongly to achieve the desired degree of damage. A certain prisoner did not want to go to work, and when a guard began questioning his honesty, grabbed an axe and cut off his left forearm.

All these, in Dr Davydov's opinion, are cases of shamming by those he describes as lazy and unwilling to work. Not once does the doctor's heart and head stir with the question: "What kind of work is this that people would prefer to cut off an arm, 'artfully' freeze themselves or 'purposefully' place their feet beneath a wagon?"

Dr Davydov passionately discusses how he's dealt with such "shammers." Concerned by all the cases of mental illness that were cropping up, Dr Davydov arrived at a diagnostic method. On Sakhalin, there's a warden who offered the proverb, "It's my right to *beat* out of a prisoner the three pounds of bread he eats every day and, if necessary, more." When a mentally ill prisoner comes to Dr Davydov he threatens to send him to this warden, who's observed that "a mentally ill prisoner is just shamming." If this has no effect then Davydov, in his own words, will resort "to a large dose of *asafetida* (stinker)."[12] The patients, according to Davydov, will sometimes "declare" that they're better and request another dose. "In these cases," remarks Dr Davydov, "you're dealing either with a malingerer who'll use any trick to waste the day or a hypochondriac."

But in the young doctor's experience, the case of the following torture he subjected a certain "faker" to is even better than "any trick" he's given "as a test" to an already doped hypochondriac.

"The patient, age thirty, one leg crooked at the knee," writes Davydov, "laid in bed for two and a half years with leg muscles atrophied. When his leg was *forcefully* straightened out the muscles became animated but the patient could not stand. He was released from hospital and fell in the entryway. The patient was carried to the prison and no punishments or restrictions were allowed to be used against him." Then, "as an experiment," Davydov came up with the following option. "We explained to the patient that we would amputate his leg, and we prepared him for the operation, laid him on the table, placed in front of him all the saws and knives we had in the infirmary and applied the chloroform…"

Unnecessarily applying chloroform is a crime. Such is the level to which this young physician has been Sakhalinized that he regards as ordinary, legal and proper a crime about which he boasts as part of his "scientific" work! By his own admission this doctor subjected patients to "experiments"—a characteristic indication of how on Sakhalin even sophisticated and well educated people can be Sakhalinized.

Naturally, *katorga* cannot expect from such gentlemen protection against guards' arbitrariness!

Perhaps the single most terrible category of officials for *katorga* are the incorrigible cowards. All officials, as I've already said, "are somewhat afraid of *katorga*," and it's completely understandable that a man cannot feel himself among *katorga*. But there are people in whom this fear reaches positively Olympian heights. Because they cannot surmount their fear of *katorga*, many should not be serving on Sakhalin. Such typically produce the cruelest prison staff, for cruelty is the sister of cowardice. A former Sakhalin prison warden, a certain F who the commandant's official papers confirm was a "coward," "a timid man" and "a man who feared convicts"—this warden later painted a vivid picture of his heroic exploits on Sakhalin for the *Odessa Flyer*.[13] Prisoners who work in the mines and want to escape usually hide in the mines. You can't capture a man in a mine, and so the commandant normally limited the number of nightwatchmen he posted around shafts' entrances. Guards would be posted for several nights and then change places, but then there wouldn't be another one for ages! That's when the prisoners would leave the mines at night and take off. So F invented the following "method." When two prisoners were hiding in a mine he hid a guard in the bushes with orders to kill the fugitives as soon as they came out. The fugitives took the bait: seeing no guard, they crept out at night and the guard shot at them. One of the fugitives was killed on the spot and F ordered that the corpse not be moved: "Instead of rounding up the prisoners near the prison doors, where I normally hand out labor assignments, I ordered them to the mine so they could see their comrade's dead body and understand they could no longer escape like they used to." Ambush, murder, a bedraggled corpse—this is the cruelty made possible by cowardice, a cowardice he avenged for his shame at fearing *katorga*.

Though not distinguished by cruelty, other timid people fall under the guards' heels and become no easier for *katorga*. Such, for example, was the mining engineer M, about whom I've already spoken. By nature a very gentle and even sweet man, he was insurmountably frightened of prisoners. He emitted despairing cries such as I'd never heard when we crept into a mine and the guard disappeared for a moment behind a corner in the drift. "Guard! Guard!" wailed the poor engineer, as if convicts were already attacking him with their hacks. "Guard! Where are you! Don't dare leave me!"

"He thinks we're beasts!" convicts said. "He's afraid to come near us. There's guards all around—they could do what they want to us."

Taking advantage of his fear, guards terrified the poor engineer even more by telling stories about "uprisings" and plannings of "revolts," and the engineer unconditionally believed them and left *katorga* to their arbitrariness.

To work in his office—to work, I repeat, for a basically kind-hearted man—is considered worse than to be in *katorga*. "Watch it, or you'll end up in the chains!" Bustling about the office is a convict-clerk, a certain G, intelligent and deft but slovenly and, ultimately, a self-abasing creature. The engineer himself complained to me about G: "It's impossible to believe that this G was a man of high society not so long ago. He's a drunk, a thief—the other day he was again caught at forgery: he'd made tickets for 15 bottles of vodka."

"Why do you keep him on?"

"Who'll take him? What is there for people here?"

G well knew his commander's weak points, constantly terrified him with stories about criminal machinations, and twisted as he wished the fates of those convicts working under him in the office. For example, the former officer K, exiled for murder, was utterly stricken by his harsh insults. He was a meek and humble young man, who for no reason at all was removed from the mining engineer's office and put in the chains prison for a month. An honest man, he didn't want to join in G's scams and so G, to save himself from this "stye," tattled on him to the engineer, who believed him, and poor K ended up in the chains. I myself heard this G, with his half-drunken beat-up physiognomy, screaming at the convict, "I want you in the chains! I'll flog you to death!" And the only difference between these convicts was that he'd been exiled for a lesser crime than G's, for a crime not so foul as G's.

A Sakhalin official…

For me, having seen them all, the best of all Sakhalin officials appeared in the guise of a certain friendly warden of settlements I stayed with several days. In the capacity of warden of settlements he was obliged to look after the "construction of the exile-settler economy," but what could he do when he'd ended up serving on Sakhalin precisely because he'd "ruined the economy" of his own estate? "I don't have it in me!" he simple-mindedly confessed. A middle-aged man, he supports his family still in Russia. "As you see, I deny myself everything, even a spare cigarette! I've never been able to endure *katorga*." He's terribly homesick and curses the day he came to Sakhalin. "What a life! What do people live for!" When lying down to sleep he places two revolvers on stools on either side of the bed. On Sakhalin, "to make up the bed" means to lay out the sheets and put down the pillows, blankets and revolvers on stools next to the bed. That's how everyone sleeps, men and women.

"Why *two* revolvers?"

"Just in case. If I grab with my right, I'll shoot to my left. Two revolvers is safer. It's terrible here."

When I pointed out that under him usury was flourishing and kulaks were drinking exile-settlers' blood, he answered, "Is that so? You know, kulak-ism is to the taste of the Russian peasant. Every good homeowner becomes a kulak without fail. I even patronize the kulaks. I like them, they're good homeowners."

"But you know about the rest..."

"Akh, believe me, don't even think about the rest! They're trash, an abomination, shit—let as many good homesteads grow in this shit as possible." I drew his attention to the fact that God knows what exile-settlers and *katorga*—those left to the guards' arbitrariness—have to endure: "They're definitely suffering." And he answered, "Let 'em suffer. It's good. Suffering purifies a man. Haven't you read?..." He named a favorite publication. "No? Do so immediately. When I was coming here I bought it in Odessa and read it on the steamer. Very interesting. One criminal writes how he's in an Austrian prison and what they're doing to him. Makes your hair stand on end. But he's still grateful to his jailers and says he became better thanks to suffering. Thanks precisely to suffering!" And that's how it was! The fellow had probably read one book in his life, and this gave him the bases on which to understand the "trash."

It's not at all surprising that when I asked this nice man how I could get to the village of Khandos Two, located in his district, he answered, "Oh, it's simple. In Onor Prison they'll give you a troika, and from there it's eight versts. It'll take you half an hour!"

A kind man!

But from Onor to Khandos Two took three-and-a-half hours, not only in a troika but on horseback, and just barely through tundra and taiga. It turned out this settlement's warden had never even visited it once! Thus Sakhalinized officials "enter into an arrangement" with people they entrust "to carry out their duties and rehabilitate convicts." And if they enter into an arrangement...

In Khandos Two, forsaken among the impenetrable taiga's settlements, exile-settlers have grouped about me. They're standing and staring.

"What are you looking at?"

"Your worship, let us look at a new person. There hasn't been anyone here for two years."

A guard was the settlement's non-functioning manager, and I was staying in his hut. He went outside to set up the samovar and I talked with the female convict who had been given him as a cohabitant. She regarded me as the commandant. I was interested in a certain female convict in Khandos Two, Tatiana Erofeeva, who had been given as a cohabitant to an exile-settler. She

Fig. 24: A "wheelbarrow man"

was a real monster, thirty years old and able to become a widow thrice over on Sakhalin, where she ended up, according to her sentence, because:

1) She premeditated her stepdaughter's murder, beating her so badly that she died the following day.
2) She repeatedly stabbed needles into her stepson's eyes and poured salt in them, after which his right eye was damaged and his left eye blind.

"Does Erofeeva live here in Khandos?" I asked the guard's cohabitant.
"She does!"
"Well, what does she do? How?" (That is, How did she live? Well or poorly?) I immediately received the answer.
"No problem. She fits right in."
You'll agree this is a highly typical answer for a newly-arrived official!
Such are the morals. And such is the relationship to *katorga* established exclusively by guards' arbitrariness.

The situation for exile and *katorga* is currently under review. It's been proposed that Sakhalin *katorga* substitute for the central prisons, and the sooner the better.[14] Let punishment be strict and severe, but let it coincide with the goals prescribed by law. Let rehabilitation or even punishment not be predicated on the absolute, out-of-control arbitrariness of guards.

34

PRISON WARDENS

For the most part, a prison warden is a man who's served as either a guard or a medic. He's a complete nonentity who suddenly gets enormous power and feasts upon it. Regulations allow him to at any moment order a prisoner be given up to thirty birch strokes or up to ten of the whip. According to law, every punishment is to be logged. In fact, punishments are almost never recorded. Prisoners are flogged, and that's that. Convicts themselves say, "Don't put it in the punishment log." All sentence reductions—when a prisoner is transferred from the probationers to the correctionals, from the chains prison to the so-called free prison—are based on what's in the punishment log. To flog and record it in the journal is not one punishment but two. As such, the prison warden is completely beyond control when it comes to corporal punishment. The absence of entries in the log prevents a convict from lodging a complaint, and so the prison warden operates entirely outside the law.

Coming to light from time to time are such cases as that of the prison warden Bestuzhev, who tore up the epileptic convict Sokolsky's right not to be subjected to corporal punishment, though doctors interceded on Sokolsky's behalf.

Corporal punishment corrupts not only those who are punished, killing in prisoners the last vestiges of even a "*katorga* conscience," but also those who do the punishing. Sakhalin's atmosphere is thoroughly poisoned. Everyone regards flogging as simple, natural and normal. Even the ladies, the officials' wives who get together in the evenings, gossip about floggings and how there needs to be more of them: "Can you get by without them?"

The sight of a fellow shamefully spread out on a bench betrays something of the depraved and unruly beast residing in man. "I'm your tsar and God!"

bellows the nonentity who's originated as a guard or medic. This, as I've already said, is prison wardens' favorite saying.

Punishments are becoming a surprising humiliation.

"What does punishment mean today!" a prison warden waves his hand. "Before, when a prisoner was flogged, he had to go thank the warden."

"Why thank him?"

"For the lesson. It was the right way. He had to bow and say, 'Thank you, your worship, for giving this fool a lesson!' But this isn't done now. *Katorga*'s spoiled! All this 'humanitarianism' has come in."

There were and are those wardens who don't acknowledge prisoners not being flogged: "That's my system." Apropos of this, one of them I'll call by his *katorga* nickname, "Green Nose," has been immortalized in anecdotes. Arriving for the morning's job assignments, he'd pick out a prisoner who hadn't been flogged. "What's this, chap, not standing in formation? Forget your feet? Eh? Come here and lie down!" If the un-flogged fellow was maintaining himself "properly," was standing, so to speak, "without breathing," such that Green Nose couldn't flog for this, he'd turn around and say, "Hey, you there, Mr Quiet! Come here and lie down, chap. Executioner, give him some hot times!"

"What for, your worship?"

"Ah, you're going to back-talk now? Stretch out!"

He'd go hunting for prisoners. Along the beach in Korsakovsk District he'd spot a prisoner dawdling on a sandbar and move towards him. The prisoner, seeing Green Nose, would go further down the sandbar and the warden would follow. Finally, the prisoner would be unable to go further. Water up to his waist, he'd stop.

"What're you doing there, chap?"

"I'm catching crayfish, your worship, to cook for you."

"You're catching crayfish? That's good. But why're you running from your commander? Eh? Could it be you're not right in the head? Very well. Bring the crayfish to my kitchen, but tomorrow morning, when you come for your work assignment, you'll be treated as usual!"

The sole un-flogged convict was his personal cook, a very skilful cook, who for this reason found himself under the warden's wife's protection. The warden's wife would say, "Don't touch him!" Then she went off somewhere all day with a friend; she came back and found her husband in a state of confusion. "Did you thrash him?!" his wife asked, wringing her hands.

"I thrashed him!" Green Nose maliciously answered. "Don't be angry, darling!"

I became interested in Warden L, who'd certainly left terrible memories behind him on Sakhalin. In his day floggings took on improbable proportions.

Every morning, thirty or forty men were flogged. I asked the prisoners how this could have happened.

"He'd be ready to leave and, as it were, there'd be no problems. But then he'd get irritated. He'd look around and notice some irregularity. 'What's this, chap, how is it your jacket's torn? Huh? You tear it on purpose? On purpose?' 'Mercy, your worship, why on purpose? It got torn at work!' 'At work? But you haven't mended it? Huh? Is this how you treat government property? Like this?' 'I'd nothing to mend it with!' At this point he'd go completely crazy. 'Rip out your tendons, you bastard, and repair it! Your tendons! Tear off pieces of your skin and patch it! I'll rip your body apart so you can have a government jacket. Executioner! Lay him out! Thrash him!' And so on. The longer he went on the crazier he'd get. All you had to do was groan and he'd stamp his feet. 'They're faking, the shits. Beat them harder.' He'd order the executioner to lay out a prisoner and flog him to the limit. 'Flog him and give him no quarter, you scoundrel!'"

"He wasn't a stupid man!" his former assistant, now himself a warden, explained to me. "He knew how to control *katorga*. *Katorga* despised the executioner, and the executioner despised *katorga*. There was no coming to terms! For this reason, the executioner wouldn't just 'butter' someone."

Warden M, in charge of Korsakovsk Prison when I was there, was regarded as one of Sakhalin's harshest wardens.

"Doctor, I have a stye in my eye!" he shouted one time while getting drunk, as was his "pleasing habit." "They're promoting 'humanitarianism'! But it doesn't suit us. I'm a Razgildeevite!" he'd boast. "I remember the Razgildeev era at Kara![1] I'm a natural-born prison-worker. My father was a prison warden. I myself grew up beneath the sleeping platforms! We're not barins, so we're unsuited to humanitarianism! We like how things are!"

He'd parade about in his faded-brown official greatcoat that was perhaps twenty years old. When sober, there wasn't a smoother, more loquacious, mellifluous person than this crafty old *Sibiriak*. He called prisoners "the fraternity," "lads," "brothers," "loves," "dears" and said there could be nothing without "God's word." "Without God's word is anything really possible?!" If he was going to violate a prisoner, he'd talk to him as gently as if he were a flea.

"Come over here, love. Stretch out there, dear, you're going to get a sprinkling!"

The prisoner would fall at his feet. "Your worship, what for? Please…"

"What're ya doing, love? Dear, what're you doing?! How could I be angry with you? I'm not angry at you. Lay yourself down—down, dearie! But, for what you've just said, we're gonna add another five strokes."

"Your worship…"

"Tut-tut, dear, not very good. You're talking to the commander. Lie down! You're not listening. Another five. Lay yourself down, lad."

Seeing that the punishment would only increase, the prisoner lay down.

"That's it, brother. Better! You're with God, love. Give him a sprinkling, Medvedev. Make the flogging last. Don't hurry it, love! Make it longer and harder! Right there, just so! Better to make it last. We're not going anywhere."

And were the prisoner to wail in a voice not his own, M would tell him, "It's nothing, nothing, endure it, brother! Christ suffered and showed us the way."

Seasoned prisoners, of course, would lie down without saying a word, knowing that any appeal would simply bring additional lashes. Watching them, the warden would say, "The soul rejoices! The lads understand me with one word! I live heart to heart with these dears!"

"But didn't they ever oppose you?" I asked M, having listened to "how with God's word the father punishes his flock." He began giggling.

"Who're you? How you think! *Katorga*'s been spoiled by the new 'humanitarians.' But it wasn't so with me. His—the chap's—little soul would tremble as he'd lie down. He knew me."

Having drunk his way through the evening, he shouted, "*Katorga* needs to be held in terror! In terror! Just ask me! These 'humanitarians' only humiliate us! They're humiliating us, the bastards! They can go be humanitarians where they want, but don't butt in on *katorga*. *Katorga*'s our affair. And it's written that fear is salvation."

Rykovsk's prison warden K, a former medic, is a man of a different stamp. He loves to cut a figure and show off. He even tells cock-and-bull stories about his medical experience. How some countess, having sent her husband off to war, confided in him: "I entrust him to you! Protect him!" "Your ladyship, rest assured."

On Sakhalin, he founds settlements in bogs and names them in honor of himself. He rebuilds prisons "according to his own designs" and brags insufferably about them. "Having come from nothing," he's intoxicated by power: "When he's laid out under me, a prisoner knows every hair in my beard." He especially loves to reminisce about his time commanding Sakhalin's most notorious—but now moribund—Voevodsk Prison.

"I'd be doing the labor assignments: 'Well done, rascals! Well done, robbers!' A nice chap would answer, 'To your health, your worship!' and laugh. They'd know I was in a good mood. But if I was quiet, they were silent as the grave. I'd go about my business, not calling them rascals, and they'd say to themselves: 'Watch out!' They'd know I wasn't in a good mood. There's not a general before whom they would so tremble! I'd order a flogging, and they were so terrified you could barely hear them breathing. 'Birch rods, spades, start digging a hole!'"

"And what was this for?"

"For a grave. I was going to flog them to death. 'Medic!' I'd shout. My assistants would go quiet. Prisoners throwing themselves at my feet. The executioner's horrified I'll begin the punishment. 'Did you come just to do some buttering?' I'd shout. 'Just some buttering? I'll lay you out, too!'"

But he limited his use of corporal punishment.

"It shouldn't get that far! Prisoners get used to it and it does nothing for them. If during his life a fellow's received 3000 birch strokes, what's more to him? You could flog him every day. No, a prisoner has to *understand* his commander, that if I say 'Flog him!' it means he'll lose his hide. Ask the prisoners about me."

But there was no need to ask the prisoners, I knew the reputation K had made for himself.

"I'm not going with you to the punishment," K told me at a certain point. "If I'm at the punishment they'll end up taking the prisoner to the infirmary to die—nothing less. The prison knows that about me.

"I usually flog in my office," he said. "The mare's in the middle of the room. I start smoking a cigarette and walking around. When I come up next to the mare I shout 'Go!' But then I start doing my office work again, as if I've forgotten about him. Then I shout 'Go!' once again. I give him thirty lashes over the next few hours. He's completely worn out by the time I rip into him. He screams and groans, beseeches God and begins cursing and, in a sense, loses his mind. The office becomes like a gallows. He never forgets it."

Indeed, he never will forget. I saw people who reckoned they'd received thousands of birch strokes in their time but who couldn't compare them to the thirty they got "in the office."

"You feel every blow. He waits until the burn passes. But that's just your body, meanwhile your soul's leaking out from anticipation. You beg for death just to escape the agony."

"But this," says K, "happens to few of them. I rarely reach this point. In my opinion, there's nothing better than a dark isolator cell. It's simply—a means. It's more terrible than any flogging. As for sitting in the isolator for two weeks... Come with me, we'll take a look."

This really was something terrible. We went down a narrow corridor, along both sides of which were tiny rooms with miniature windows in the doors. The air in the corridor made my head spin. The stench was that of a kennel or a cage of wolves. Hardly had we entered the corridor than diabolic curses came at K from every cell. The men howled in fury and smashed their doors. It was reminiscent of a violent-patient ward in a madhouse.

"Open Gusev's door!" ordered K. A guard began undoing the lock. A voice filled with terror came out of the cell.

"Don't come in! Don't come near me! I'll kill you!"

Fig. 25: Dué Post

"This is the level he's sunk to!" said K, countermanding his own order. "You can see this is more effective than flogging. What's a flogging!"

It's significant that these people so renowned for their floggings unanimously say, "What's a flogging! It simply works!"

And they flog.

35

THE DEATH PENALTY

There hasn't been a single execution on Sakhalin during the four years of General Merkazin's administration.[1]

"I know this dissatisfies many!" the general told me.

But first, rather than talk about this "dissatisfaction" and the bases for his reasoning, we shared several words about how executions used to be typically carried out on Sakhalin.

The last executions took place about four years ago. Three recidivist penal laborers were executed—an old man and longtime convict laborer and a pair of young men—for committing murder during a robbery. All were put to death on the island.

Father Aleksandr, the Sakhalin cleric assigned to administer to the condemned, told me about these executions. The accused had been keeping themselves apart from one another. Father Aleksandr, on the administration's orders, came to see them three days before their executions. When the priest appeared, the condemned knew the hour of death was approaching.

"They'd grown pale, frightened, mute, unable to speak a word," recalled Father Aleksandr. "Only the old man boasted at first, laughing, scoffing at death and at his comrades... 'Well,' he says, 'what will be will be, boys, but for now, let us ponder the soul.' Well, very well. They began praying. They prayed intently, with passion and all their hearts."

"For all three days?"

"For all three days. They discussed life beyond the grave, read the lives of the saints, sang psalms and prayed together. They took walks together in the yard and wouldn't let me out of their sight. They begged me: 'Father, help us, we're terrified.' You'd run off home for half an hour, have a bite to eat, then go back to see them again. They were sleeping little and so would lose track of time whenever they awoke. I couldn't sleep while administering to them. How could I?!"

"You discussed everything with them, including religious topics?"

"Quite so! I kept up their hope: 'It's said there've been cases when pardons were announced on the scaffold.' Why should a man be deprived of hope? Without hope a man falls into despair. They tried to get everything out of me: 'When, oh when?' Well, but when they got their white linen one evening they all knew it would happen next morning. They didn't sleep that night. Only one, it seemed, dozed off for half an hour. I gave them communion that night. Morning had just broken when they were led out. I dressed in a black chasuble, and we exited."

But there was a delay. One of the persons assigned to assist in the executions was fifteen minutes late.

"Believe me," Father Aleksandr told me, "those fifteen minutes seemed longer than all three preceding days. To me! But what about to them?"

The sentences were confirmed out loud and drums beaten, but this was an unnecessary precaution. There was none of the usual foul language during the reading of the sentences.[2]

"They died astonishingly peacefully. They prostrated before the cross and gave themselves into the hands of the executioner. Only one, the youngest, Siiutin, said something: 'Were it to live, but it is necessary to die.' They mounted the scaffold and stood on the trap-door."

Only the old man who had scoffed at death fell apart. They nearly had to carry him onto the scaffold. His arms and legs were paralyzed with fear. Before his execution he requested vodka.

"Well, and did they give it to him?"

"No. Why should they? They'd already received communion at midnight, and it wasn't fitting to drink vodka at five in the morning."

The executions took a long time, during which a guard fainted. Many of the prisoners who'd come to witness the executions couldn't stand it and left.

These most recent Sakhalin executions were conducted in Aleksandrovsk Prison's yard. The terrible and dark Voevodsk Prison, located between Aleksandrovsk and Dué, was the usual site for executions before it was razed to its foundations. A gallows used to be set up in the middle of its yard. One hundred prisoners would be herded out of the prison to attend an execution; and if a prisoner from Aleksandrovsk Prison was being executed, another twenty-five men were pulled from there as well. Voevodsk Prison lay in a ravine, and from the hills surrounding it like an amphitheater you could clearly see what took place in the prison yard. In the morning, Aleksandrovsk's exile-settlers would spread out on these hills and "watch as they hanged."

This crowded amphitheater and the gallows' scaffolding together turned Voevodsk Prison into a kind of monstrous theater where horrible tragedies were performed. Many spectators told me details of those tragedies performed on Voevodsk Prison's scaffolds, but of course the most valuable, most interesting, most piercing details came from talking with the one man closer to the condemned than all other attendees, and who was present during what were truly their final minutes. This was the old Sakhalin executioner Komlev.

He had executed thirteen men on Sakhalin, ten of them in Voevodsk Prison. His first victim was the penal laborer Kucheriavsky, sentenced to death for assaulting and injuring Aleksandrovsk Prison warden Shishkov. Kucheriavsky feared execution, but not death… The night before his execution he somehow got hold of a knife and sliced an artery. Doctors were summoned and bandaged the unconscious Kucheriavsky, and brought him around about an hour later. Kucheriavsky died boldly and impertinently, tearing off the bandage that had been tied around his neck. The whole time he shouted at the prisoners that they should follow his example. The drums beat in vain: Kucheriavsky's words resounded over them. Continuing to shout, he was led in a shroud to the scaffold and made to stand on the trap-door. Komlev stood next to him and, as was usual, held him by the shoulders. Kucheriavsky continued shouting from beneath the shroud. "Don't be afraid, chaps!" His final words were, "The rope is fine and death is easy…" Komlev then waved a kerchief, assistants pulled the trap-door lever, and the execution was completed. The procedure had lasted the usual time: an hour and a half.

The condemned man is delivered in fetters. In fetters, he listens to his sentence. Then they unshackle and put the shroud on him, and loop the lard-greased noose over the shroud...

In general, the execution, having begun at five, rarely finished before half past six. Rarely can one maintain himself during this terrible hour and a half. "Some are so numbed they collapse," according to Komlev. The majority maintain strength enough only to beg the executioner: "Quicker! Pick up the pace! Not this torture, please." Most cannot hold out at this point.

The penal laborer Kinzhalov, executed for murdering the Sakhalin shopkeeper Nikitin,[3] prayed the whole time. After his sentence was recited he lost all consciousness as they were unshackling him. He had to be carried onto the scaffold. Komlev, who was holding him, says, "In my opinion, he was already dead when they put the noose on him."

According to Komlev's recollections nearly everyone turns cold and shivers during the execution, their hearts beat rapidly and they turn pale if not completely white. "You hold him by the shoulders when he stands on the trapdoor, and through his shirt you can feel his whole body is cold and shivering."

Of the thirteen executed by Komlev no one stands out like Klimenko. Klimenko's crime was as follows: He'd escaped and was captured by the guard Belov, who severely beat him during his return. Klimenko then made "a prisoner's oath" to his comrades that he'd get even with Belov. He ran off a second time and showed up at the cordon where Belov was stationed: "One picks his poison. I can't go on." Once again, Belov began leading Klimenko to prison, but along the way the prisoner killed his guard. Afterward, Klimenko delivered himself to the prison and announced his commission of the murder, told everything in detail, how and for what reason. He was sentenced to death.

Komlev had seen nothing in his time like the death of Klimenko. When he was led onto the scaffold Klimenko turned to the commandant and... thanked him for having been sentenced to death. "Because I know that I myself, your worship, am stopping this. I'm now going to be executed, and I earned it." His only request was that his wife be informed he'd accepted his execution... "And write that it was for a cause, as they say." According to Komlev, "The drum wasn't even beaten during the execution!" So quietly and peacefully did this man die.

Here you have it, how penal laborers died and what capital punishment means. Witnessing it hardly advances rehabilitation, especially for convicts driven out of prison "for attendance" or exile-settlers sitting in a quite natural amphitheater during this unnatural scene.

We now return to that discontent over the lack of executions.

The general was absolutely correct when he said many were very displeased by the lack of executions. During my visit even certain Sakhalin ladies complained, as part of their "salon" gossip, that "*katorga* lacks discipline," and argued that "the death penalty is absolutely, absolutely necessary." "If they executed one or two a year they'd get the message!" Amid these *katorga* circumstances even a lady can be Sakhalinized. But, it must be added, this redounds to the credit of Sakhalin's ladies, so much do they fear for their husbands' lives.[4] Yet, why is Sakhalin's top intelligentsia displeased?

"Forgive me, old chap," you hear at literally every turn. "But to live this way is really difficult! There's a murder every minute! Utter impunity! Really, it's just a joke to these cocks: they're simply adding on more time! A fellow's already got forty years, and he gets another fifteen. Does it matter to him, forty or fifty-five years?! No! We need to get rid of this 'humanitarianism.' The death penalty—now that's what we need!"

Having spent entire days on Sakhalin getting accustomed to a society of Komlevs, Poluliakhovs and Golden-Hands, even I lost patience with these arguments, and replied: "Better then, gentlemen, to talk of breaking people on the wheel and quartering them. This even makes sense. It hasn't been implemented, but maybe it'll help. Yet the death penalty *has* been implemented and it's solved nothing."

In actual fact! When did all these wardens' murders occur? When was Derbin killed? Selivanov? The rest? When did they try to kill Livin, Shishkov? When the death penalty was relied upon without a doubt. Has even a single official been murdered in the four years since there was an execution? No. Not a one.

"But didn't they try to murder Dr Chardyntsev? And didn't they try to kill Tymovsk District's police secretary?"[5]

Actually, both cases are under investigation. The prisoner Krikov did attack Dr Chardyntsev. Yet who came with me to meet Krikov but Dr Chardyntsev.

"Well, and now you can see the man who nearly killed me!" said the doctor as we toured the infirmary.

"What? He's really here? With you?"

"Yes. In a separate room."

"And you're not afraid of him?"

"No. Not at all. He's peaceful now. We've become great friends."

In a small private room lay the sick Krikov—pale, emaciated, worn out. Taking me for a doctor, he began in a weak and breathless voice to complain about heart palpitations and to praise his doctor.

"If not for him, I would have departed this life."

"Very serious heart ailment," the doctor whispered to me. Then we turned to discussing the recent attempt on his life. Krikov grew very agitated and grabbed his head.

"It's better you not recall, not recall this!... I don't know what happened to me then... This is what happens to me: my head spins and I can't remember what I do… It's horrible when I think of what I almost did!… And against whom?… Against the doctor!… the doctor!…" And he looked at Dr Chardyntsev with eyes full of tears, with such supplication, such gratitude that, truly, it was difficult to believe. Was it really possible that the death of this same doctor really almost came at his hands?

Krikov is not yet an old man, but is already an invalid. He can't work because of a severe heart condition. Without a doubt, he is psychologically abnormal. He always feels he's being persecuted and injured, that he's always treated with hostility. He's always disturbed by everyone and is typically unhealthily irritated. He occasionally slips straight into delirium and then, really, does not remember what he does. He'd always had most difficult relations with Dr Chardyntsev, but during one of his attacks he demanded some kind of medicine and the doctor refused.

"Aha! You want to kill me! You're keeping me in the infirmary but not treating me on purpose! That's not going to happen, I'm not turning myself over to you!" shouted Krikov and, before anyone could collect himself, he grabbed a knife from out of his boot and attacked the doctor. Fortunately, Chardyntsev was able to grab his wrist, disarm him and take him aside to a separate room and begin calming him. When Krikov came back to himself his grief, despair and shame were limitless.

He cannot recall without agitation an event that is terrible for him. As you can see, if the attempt had been premeditated this condition would be entirely impossible. I believe—and speak strictly believing this—that in all of *katorga* not one person can be found who would premeditatedly want to hurt Chardyntsev, this splendid, friendly, sympathetic humanitarian physician. He was nearly the victim of an abnormal character. What physician dealing with a mental patient is insured against this?

So this shows *katorga*'s lack of discipline?

The case of the police secretary in Tymovsk District is a case strange, mysterious and, if talking about lack of discipline, one relevant not only to *katorga*. This secretary is a young man, but he quickly mastered Sakhalin's ways.

In his chancery was a *brodiaga*-clerk, a quiet, modest, hard-working, well-bred young man named Tumanov. He'd gotten involved in some "affair" and didn't want to shame his family, so he preferred to conceal his identity and enter *katorga* under a *brodiaga*-name. On Sakhalin, they're a bit sensitive regarding verbal abuse. One day, the secretary, being for some reason in bad spirits, violently cursed Tumanov in front of everyone in the chancery, calling him a "villain" and a "scoundrel." This deeply affected Tumanov, probably especially because he'd only just gotten out of prison and almost begun feeling like a man again. He'd found a person whose fate closely mirrored his own, settling down with a certain former baroness exiled for arson, and relations between them were apparently more tender than those between a landlady and her tenant. In her words, when he came home after the scene with the secretary Tumanov "wasn't a person." He seemed crazy and walked about the room clutching his head and talking to himself. "No, no!... It's not so... I'm anything you like, but I've never been a scoundrel or a villain... No, no, this can't be left alone..."

Sakhalin's motto is "everyone for himself." Seeing that the matter might end badly, the baroness demanded Tumanov leave her home. "Do what you please, but I don't want to get mixed up in this row. That's it for me! I finished with *katorga*, then the exile-settlers and now, thank God, I'm a peasant-formerly-exiled and have a bakery and a couple cows. I'm not going to risk everything. I have a child. Leave my home immediately and forget we ever knew each other..."

"It was difficult to say this to him," she told me. "He esteemed me near to God. But you appreciate my position."

So here's Tumanov, tossed into the street having lost his head and at such a difficult moment alienated from her he "esteemed near to God," walking forward to carry out a senseless deed.

At the secretary's there is, as usual, a card game. *Shtoss*[6] is a typical way for non-exiles to kill time on Sakhalin. Suddenly, it's announced that Tumanov wants to see the secretary "about an especially important and urgent matter." The secretary enters the kitchen.

"What do you want?"

Tumanov stands before him pale as death, lips quivering. "I came to thank you for what you did today..."

The secretary is utterly certain that Tumanov has come to beg forgiveness—on Sakhalin, it's understood that those who've been abused beg forgiveness; this is possibly a remnant of those times when a convict who was flogged was absolutely obliged to thank the warden for the lesson—and so the secretary is certain that Tumanov is asking for forgiveness, and says, "Very well, very well! Come tomorrow!"

Then Tumanov takes a step forward, and with the words "this is for you from a villain and scoundrel," pulls out a revolver.

He pulled the trigger but it didn't fire. At the secretary's frightened cry the guests came running. But Tumanov was already gone, having fled the kitchen as soon as the revolver misfired. The secretary and his guests endured several unpleasant minutes. The house had numerous windows and the shutters weren't closed. Suddenly, they heard a shot outside.

At this point the story becomes shockingly strange, for their fear proved vain: a shot hadn't been fired. Fleeing the kitchen, Tumanov had either dropped or tossed the revolver. It turned out that the barrel Tumanov aimed at the secretary was never loaded! What explains this? A fortuitous oversight, or just a desire "to frighten"? If an oversight, what prevented Tumanov from firing again while the secretary stood before him grabbing the lintel and, in his own words, "was frozen in terror," being in no condition even to shout and showing no effort whatsoever to resist or disarm his enemy?

When Tumanov was captured a note was found in his pocket in which he'd written that he'd decided to "finish himself off." To all questions Tumanov only answered, "I didn't shoot. A scoundrel and a villain shot the secretary, but not Tumanov." He only asked to be transferred from Rykovsk to Aleksandrovsk. But during the transfer he began to act even stranger, and wrote notes asking to be sent for his health to… Spa, then to Biarritz.[7]

Was this a faker or an actual lunatic? When I left Sakhalin this was still unclear, as Tumanov had only just been assigned to the psychiatric ward for evaluation. But there is doubtless much strange in this affair, much that is mysterious.

The event caused great consternation among administrators. The secretary's brother, a doctor, told me, "What the hell does humanity have to do with it?! If they won't hang him, I'm ready to strangle him with my own hands." But brothers are poor judges in matters involving their brothers. Other officials are divided into two camps. One—and I'm not saying this is the best part of Sakhalin officialdom—shouts, "Hang him! Hang him as an example! *Katorga* lacks discipline. Security needs to be defended…"

"But for God's sake," I said to them, "what kind of security do you good people want to defend in such a terrible way? The security to abuse and mock penal laborers and exile-settlers? It's hardly necessary to treat a 'rehabilitating' man this way. You know that the law and government want to make Sakhalin a place for a criminal's 'rehabilitation.'"

But the answer was: "Nonsense! All this is just 'humanitarianism'!" (The most hated word on Sakhalin!) "Hang him, that's it."

Another part of officialdom—and no one is saying this is the worst part—thinks: "It's necessary for us to change much in our attitudes toward convicts." It should not be forgotten that even in this wretched, downtrodden, depressing environment people can always be found who place what's left of their honor above the pathetic residue of their bitter contemptible lives.

Be that as it may, it's a fact that my two cases of attempted murder were all that occurred during these four years since capital punishment has been out of favor, as compared to earlier, when it was in favor. All the murders of officials, all the repeated attempts like those to slice Lavin's throat or to garrote Feldman, happened when behavior was on the downturn and when an official's murder would without fail lead to capital punishment. It follows that friendly relations by penal laborers towards officials cannot be established through fear of execution. The noose, as experience has shown, is simply a rope too weak to hold officials' security up to snuff.

This touches on an exile-settler's murder of his own brother during a robbery. Actually, there are very many such cases on Sakhalin.

"Well, but in Petersburg, in Moscow, in the whole world, aren't there enough of these type murders?" the island's military governor Merkazin soundly rationalized as his basis for opposing the death penalty. "You know, this is an island completely populated by murderers, after all."

What happens on Sakhalin really does make your hair stand on end. For all our horror, it can't be understood. But it cannot be forgotten that Sakhalin is a place where everything is upside-down. In this land of wretches lost to oblivion a bottle of spirits sometimes costs ten rubles. In this land of paupers they kill a man for sixty kopeks. Exile-settlers from Valza[8] went off to hunt the fugitives Poluliakhov, Kazeev and their comrades and shot them for fear the starving men would butcher their cows. Accordingly, all "thieving murderers" are regarded with especial caution. During the perpetration of a robbery therein often lurks a vengeance very old, profound and repressed, a grudge only *katorga* can harbor.

In Mikhailovsk settlement, Aleksandrovsk District, the fugitive Shirokolobov murdered the exile-settler Potemkin's wife. This event garnered Shirokolobov the sympathy of all *katorga*.

"He did right. If not him, someone else would've done it."

"Why?"

"You don't know, barin, what a fellow this Potemkin is. He's a former *maidanshchik* and grew up like a kid into a 'father' under our roof. He drank our tears. So many folks were forever ruined because of him; so many were forced into 'marriages' (name exchanges); so many tried to run away from him and went from being short-term to indefinitely-sentenced penal laborers; so many folks were stabbed because of him!"

I happened to stop at a certain wealthy exile-settler's home that resembled an armed fortress. Along the walls, under the beds, everywhere were revolvers.

"At night, barin, we'll put a revolver on the little table near you. But stick your own under the pillow. It'll be easier to reach."

I was shocked. "What for?"

"They're getting ready to rob me. Shirokolobov's out and about. They've assigned me a guard at night. He hides in the little shed there. Let them come, let them try and rob me."

But his deathly afraid, lachrymose mistress could not resist relating to me the true reason for the imminent assault.

"My master recognized one of the fugitive murderers in Aleksandrovsk. That's why they've decided to kill us. They don't like him. He's cruel to me, that's a sin he hides! He craves money. Well, you know, this is why we live on

Sakhalin, as that's his compensation. We were released from *katorga* to exile-settlement and should gain by this. We have children, you know."

So it is in many cases, where at first only theft is suspected. Murder often happens when the intention is simply to rob. Unemployment, hunger, complete insanity are involved in those cases in which they are necessarily involved. Unfamiliarity with work, the desire not to work, prison's corruption of a man, a passion for cards—these are what push Sakhalinites to murder and rob. Among all these reasons, cardinal are the passion for cards and the impossibility of earning any money.

Nowhere, of course, are there so many "hunger murders" as on Sakhalin. A group of penal laborers told me how, having completed *katorga* "for a distant crime" and been released to exile-settlement on Sakhalin, they immediately murdered an exile-settler. At the time, they got an axe from someone "to do a little work" and went about their task.

"Stepka had to strike because he was the strongest of us all then." Stepka swung the axe. "He hit the exile-settler in the head, then himself dropped from swinging the axe."

"Why?"

"Sickly weak. Hadn't eaten anything for three days. He, that exile-settler, if he'd wanted to, could've strangled us all like kittens. We kill him, then go in the kitchen for bread. He's lying there and we're gobbling up his food. It was funny!…"

In such way they were "found out."

But the noose is bankrupt as a deterrent in the battle to choke off these murders. When did all these terrible murders, like the still memorable murder of Sakhalin shopkeeper Nikitin, happen? During the time when executions in Voevodsk Prison were in full swing and the executioner Komlev was, in his expression, "working." These cases did not, are not and will not for the time being change those many factors pushing people into crime on Sakhalin.

Do hangings "for example" generally make the terrifying impression its supporters on Sakhalin believe they do? It's necessary to tell you that owing to ignorance and complete unfamiliarity with the law very many criminals, having committed crimes, believed "the noose was their due." Having murdered the Artsimovich family of Lugansk,[9] Poluliakhov fully believed that if captured he'd be hanged immediately: "Not just anyone is a judge, you know.[10] I believed the noose couldn't be avoided." Because of this fear he murdered the little boy, Artsimovich's son. "It was a pity to kill him. He didn't lift a hand… He didn't even react to the blows I gave him as he should've… But I was thinking it wasn't another's but *my* life that was at stake, so I killed him."

Viktorov, whose murder of a young woman in Moscow caused a sensation, was also under the belief that he would be instantly hanged for it.[11] In court, he expected the death sentence. So great was his fear that he didn't realize what was being said. At the time, he believed the procurator, having produced the victim's bloodied things, was demanding Viktorov also be chopped into pieces. When it was explained he was being sentenced to *katorga*, Viktorov "was so overjoyed I didn't know whether or not to believe it." Only this horrible death penalty had compelled Viktorov to chop a murdered woman's body into pieces, to stuff it inside a suitcase and put it on a train. At the time, everyone was shocked at the criminal's cold brutality. But in essence, this "cold brutality" was nothing other than cowardice before the noose.

In the south, in Kherson, the notorious criminal Pazulsky stabbed an assistant prison warden in completely exceptional circumstances. The assistant ordered him beaten with rifle butts and Pazulsky vowed revenge. He later escaped, hid for two years, was captured and, ending up again in Kherson Prison, "kept his word." Did he know he would get the noose for this? This was his belief. But his disposition was such that he could not act otherwise. His accomplishments had won him the title in the criminal world of "a true Ivan." In this world he was feared and his orders carried out unquestioningly. As told me by the prison warden, Pazulsky prevented a prison insurrection with a single command: he gave to Iovanovich, for example, letters recommending certain privileges be extended to persons in all the prisons. I myself saw the Sakhalin prison community's incredible esteem for Pazulsky: no one dared speak to him without doffing his cap. They esteemed him because they feared him. They listened to him because they trembled before his "menace." In the case with Kherson's assistant warden, he bet the pot: he'd given his word and had to carry out his threat. He was feared because he himself feared nothing, and people of this sort have to keep their word. Otherwise, when the gilt peels off the idol the prison sees it's been bowing before a piece of wood. How they would've mocked and disdained the "cowardly" Pazulsky! As people generally will towards those who fall off a high pedestal! And Pazulsky preferred death to such a life. So he stabbed the assistant.

On Sakhalin, a certain Kapiton Zverev[12] killed Dr Zarzhevsky. This was a doctor of the old school, much loved by the wardens. The sick and weak weren't for him. When they showed up with a problem he typically wrote, "Give him fifty birch strokes." Zverev had overstrained himself with work and was in no condition to carry out his tasks and so, having already received many strokes of the "twigs," went to the doctor to request a work release. Dr Zarzhevsky gave him the usual "prescription." Then Zverev grabbed the knife he kept at hand and stabbed the doctor. This was when they were still hanging.

"But weren't you afraid they'd hang you?" I asked Zverev.

"Everyone was very surprised I escaped the noose. I thought they'd hang me."

"Then why did you do it?"

"I got sick of lying on the mare, so I decided death was better than such a life."

"So, you were ready to end your life?"

"But would he, that torturer, be torturing others? No, I'd already decided to let others live better if my life was going to end. Death's not so important."

Antonov-Baldokha, as ringleader of the once notorious "Bashi-Bazouks gang" that long terrorized Moscow, always anticipated that "when they catch me they'll hang me straightaway." His comrades said as much to him. It is only this that made him, in his expression, "work cleanly." "You take something, and strike. Because those left alive can establish your guilt and you can get the noose."

Fear of execution makes the criminal be more vicious—this is clear. Does it prevent crime? They say that in fact it does not. Criminal nature's single most important element, so to speak, shouldn't be forgotten—the criminal's extraordinary thoughtlessness. Any punishment frightens the criminal, but he always expects he'll be able to escape and won't get caught. Re-examine the majority of crimes, and what ultimately strikes you is these criminals' shocking thoughtlessness.

"Why did you kill him?"

"I heard there was money."

"Well, did you *know* how much money there was supposed to be?"

"How could I know? I didn't know. Folks said there'd be money, but there wasn't."

"Yes, indeed. But setting this aside, did you know you were risking your life with this business?"

"Certainly."

"How could you, risking your own life, not even know what you were risking it for?"

What is this if not utter thoughtlessness?

Or:

"I murdered the muzhik because he was rich. I thought, 'I'll get a couple thousand.' I was going to build a new pad; my own had fallen apart."

"Indeed. You're saying you were a poor muzhik?"

"Really poor."

"And you would build a new pad immediately? Wouldn't everyone be surprised that you had the money? Right next door, your rich neighbor is robbed and murdered. Anyone would suspect you."

"This, of course, is true. Certainly, if I'd thought this over earlier, maybe it would've been better not to kill him. But it was already lodged in my head: 'Kill, kill, I'll build a new pad, mine's already fallen apart.'"

Or:

A fellow murders, steals, then goes to his hangout and begins drinking and boasting about his money, and there he's caught, even though the man was experienced: he was a good shot, a window-crawler, a train robber, a door-lock picker, a burglar; he'd graduated through all the degrees of his craft and had performed nothing other than robbery. He certainly knew everything through and through.

"Well, why drink after you'd gotten away? Why not take off? You know, when there's a robbery the first thing police do is go to the hangout. That's where your sort is to be found."

"Certainly, that's the first thing they do."

"So, why go there?"

"I thought they'd search the train, that they'd think I was leaving the city."

Such astounding thoughtlessness compels them to escape from Sakhalin. These folks know they're heading for certain death, that before them is the icy wasteland of the Tatar Straits, but they go because "they hope." Even fear of the noose does not supersede this thoughtlessness.

From another perspective there are people who, like Pazulsky, are pushed into criminal circumstances. For them, it's better to die.

From a third perspective, a man like Zverev is pushed to such a state that death seems sanctified.

Of course, it shouldn't be forgotten that crimes on Sakhalin don't always happen because of personal initiative. Very often they happen because a sentence of *katorga* has fallen on an unlucky person, and for such a person there's no choice. Whether or not he serves his *katorga* sentence, he's expecting death…

I'm not prepared to write a tract about the death penalty in general. My task is much briefer: to say that I know about capital punishment on Sakhalin. But it is doubtless that one of the main arguments against the death penalty—the "irreversibility of the punishment" in case of judicial error—stands out nowhere as clearly as on Sakhalin. Nowhere does it so hover like a terrible specter. The judiciary commits errors everywhere, but there's hardly anywhere like Sakhalin where errors are so difficult to avoid. Consider the consequences that result in a place where you're allowed to testify without oath, where there's no threat for giving false evidence; consider the consequences in an exclusively criminal, poor and starving environment, in an environment where people sell and buy themselves for ten kopeks, where falsehood before the authorities is a custom but concealment of prisoners is the law; consider that administering justice is especially difficult given the consequences of such conditions. It's more difficult to discern the truth here than elsewhere. Nowhere is it so easy for justice, amid this utter falseness, to fall into error. Amid such conditions, the "irreversibility of the punishment" is especially terrifying.

Fig. 26: Logging crew

Capital punishment—a terrible, irremediable, possibly often mistakenly applied twenty-three-year experiment proven bankrupt as a deterrent punishment—disappeared four years ago into Sakhalin's vaults, and no one has suffered any evil whatsoever by its not reemerging.

36

EXECUTIONERS

Anytime it seems you've reached the lowest level of human degradation, you're probably mistaken. There's probably a level still lower. There's no level beneath which a person cannot sink. Bottomless is this abyss of human degradation.

—*Journal entry*

Tolstykh

"Greetings, good girl!"

"Greetings, uncle!"

"To you, silly girl, I'm an uncle, but to your cohabitant I'm a godfather!" the old Sakhalin executioner Tolstykh cheerfully jokes during his rounds.

"And why are you his godfather?"

"I flogged her cohabitant, your worship!"

"And how many folks have you flogged?"

He just chuckles. "Everyone you see around you, your worship, they were all turned over to me!"

Tolstykh is almost sixty years old but his face looks no more than forty. He's a dashing man with a moustache and always spotlessly shaven chin. He lives prosperously by Sakhalin standards, dresses foppishly in a pea-jacket, high boots and even a leather peak-cap—the epitome of Sakhalin chic. He generally "keeps to himself" and is always in a splendid mood, joking and gibing.

Tolstykh—as is clear by his strange surname—is a *Sibiriak*.[1] To the question of how he ended up in *katorga*, he answers: "'Cause o' the *wafe*!" He chopped his wife's head off with an axe.

"Why did you do that to her?"

"She was cheating, your worship."

Having landed on Sakhalin, this Siberian Othello "didn't lose his wits." He immediately drew himself up: vicious by nature, strong and cunning, he became an executioner.

Some people are born artists. They can make art out of anything. If you don't give them an instrument, they'll become virtuosos of something else. Prison wardens themselves complain, "You can't make out what a good executioner's doing, whether he's striking hard or making a show of it. It seems the blow he's striking is terrible…" Indeed, one's heart sinks as the whip[2] slices through the air… "But the whip's falling softly and painlessly. They understand what to do, the bastards. You can't control them!" Tolstykh mastered in full the wielding of the whip. And how he raked *katorga*! They would bribe him so that after a 100 lashes a man could stand up as if nothing had happened. But if they didn't pay, they wouldn't stand up. The man was cunning and resourceful and knew fully how to carry out his business "cleanly." The administration was unable to catch him and *katorga* feared him.

Feared him, but reckoned itself fortunate in those cruel days of the executioner, because it was possible to make a deal. "He knew how much to take from you!" old penal laborers clarified for me when answering the question, "How did *katorga* tolerate such a thief?"

"*Katorga* was easy for me, with none of God's wrath," says Tolstykh.

Having completed his *katorga* term, Tolstykh went to a settlement with his money and became a trader. He profiteers, cornering and reselling various used items. No one shuns him—on the contrary, they readily deal with him. "He's a clever fellow!"

When I became acquainted with Tolstykh he was going through a difficult time: he'd stabbed someone and been assigned "to work" for a month. He'd been made a deliveryman for the prison.

"I walk around day after day. My affairs are being neglected. Maybe you could take over my job for me, your worship?" asked Tolstykh. "This is hard."

"I daresay it was easier as an executioner!"

"As an executioner, certainly. I had an income."

"Would you like to be an executioner again?"

"What for? I earn a living as a trader. Being an executioner is a *katorga* affair, and now I'm an exile-settler. But sometimes I do hire myself out to do a flogging."

"How is it that you 'hire yourself out'?"

"The prison's had no executioner for the past few years. No one's wanted to do it. But the sentences were backing up and needed to be carried out. So I flogged fifty men for three silver rubles."

"But is it true what they say about you, Tolstykh, that you were paid fifteen rubles to flog the prisoner Shkolkin to death?"

He just chuckles. "That's Sa*kal*in, your worship!"

Medvedev

Medvedev, Korsakovsk Prison's executioner, is possibly the most loathsome and wretched creature on Sakhalin. His whole life is continuous fear.

Passing the prison you notice a stocky ungainly prisoner at the gate; hands like rakes; large protruding ears sticking out like burdocks; a small reddish nose. His face looks like the mug of a large bat. He won't move a step away from the gate. This is Medvedev "strolling." He continually gazes at a pocket-watch he never puts away, as if he's shackled to it!

Medvedev became an executioner "out of fear." In 1893, in Ekaterinodar, he was found guilty of murdering the owner of an inn where he worked. He'd killed him while trying to rob him. The owner, according to Medvedev, wouldn't pay the money he owed him.

"I was convicted on 'suspicion' of murder!" says Medvedev.

So this man assigned to be an executioner, who's already been found guilty, stubbornly denies he killed the innkeeper. "It's not my sin" and so on. Later, as we got to know each other better, Medvedev explained why he so insistently denies his crime.

"I was convicted without making a confession!"

"So?"

"So, they punished me. But I would say that I… They'll probably punish me further. Better stop talking."

Medvedev became an executioner out of fear of *katorga*.

"I'd heard that in *katorga* they stick people underground.³ I was so scared. That's why I volunteered to be an executioner. But I thought they'd assign me to a prison in Russia."

A pair of Caucasian bandits was scheduled for execution in the prison where Medvedev was incarcerated. There being no executioner, Medvedev volunteered. Medvedev talks about this execution with a placid vacant face, with indifference, granting only up to a point that "not everyone gets treated according to regulations."

"They shoulda given me a red shirt,⁴ but they couldn't sew, so the shirt was a lost cause. They just gave me a new cassock."

"And did you drink vodka during the execution?"

"Why, no. I was afraid I'd get tight, so I stayed sober."

"So it was of no concern? You didn't feel terrible?"

"I felt nothing. Only, when the first guy began twisting around, then it got terrible. It touched my heart." And Medvedev points to his spleen.

"Well, but was it only there that you were to carry out hangings?"

"Just so. They'd give the order, I'd do the hanging."

But Medvedev's hopes were not to be: he wasn't retained as the prison's executioner but got sent to Sakhalin.

"So, very well. You became an executioner there because you were afraid they'd put you underground in *katorga*. But why were you an executioner here as well? After all, once here you saw those were all stories and they don't put you underground."

"But I didn't have a choice by then. It was already impossible to join the other prisoners. I was an executioner, and so they would've nailed me (killed him). It was impossible for me to stop being an executioner."

Thus he remains an executioner out of fear.

Medvedev lives in horrible poverty and has no possessions whatsoever. Nothing save the mare and the whip—government implements put into his custody. Out of fear, he doesn't even take bribes. When a new party rumbles into Sakhalin there's always a group of prisoners already sentenced to the whip or birch rod and which "goes to the executioner." Not a single prisoner among those assigned "to the executioner" ever refuses him a kopek. This is an executioner's usual source of income.

But Medvedev denies this.

"It's an impossible situation. If you take money so's to flog softly, they'll boot you out of being executioner. But if you take money and begin thrashing hard, *katorga* will kill you."

The entire prison unanimously confirms that he's not on the take.

"Even if you try to bribe him, he flogs you to death!"

He sure does flog—desperately.

"So, the cur, he looks the warden in the eye. Just winks at him while he's beating you to death. He feels nothing!"

But Medvedev surely does "feel" something when he's giving a prisoner many lashes. In a single moment, this coward turns mighty. Then he beats everything out: the perpetual humiliation and mortal fear, his own poverty and fear at taking bribes. When a man he fears lies before him, Medvedev remembers all this, factoring it into the whole of his dog's life, and becomes bitterer than afraid and, later, more afraid than bitter.

Out of fear, Medvedev shuns even that certain comfort afforded an executioner. A small private room is available to the executioner, but Medvedev doesn't live in it.

"They'll knock down the door and get me at night."

He hangs out at the bakers'. Because wardens value bakers and don't flog them, the bakers don't have it in for the executioner, and so Medvedev feels safe with them. He depends on their leftovers. The bakers, of course, disdain and "heel" the dog. When a baker's drinking he'll poke fun at Medvedev and force him, for example, to sleep beneath the shop. "Or else go out in the yard!" So he lies beneath the shop like a dog. "He gets scared at night all of a sudden!"

From horror and fear Medvedev worries about what any other penal laborer dreams about: when he will complete *katorga*.

"There's something I want to ask you, your worship!" he shyly and indecisively turned to me one day, entreaty in his voice. "Ask the warden if I can still be an executioner when my term ends. How can I enter a settlement? They'll kill me, they'll kill me straight off!" He even wept, this man, whose dream is to end life as an executioner, whose fear is to enter freedom. He kneeled before me: "Ask!" and tried to kiss my hands.

Komlev

Outside the windows of Aleksandrovsk's prison chancery strolls an undersized, hollow-chested, gloomy downcast man. He walks somewhat oddly. Routinely beaten starving dogs will linger outside without taking their eyes off kitchen windows, scared of coming too close should they suddenly be scalded with boiling water. Such is Komlev, Sakhalin's oldest executioner.

He's now retired, but hails from a settlement where numerous invalids live, and he's heard that the *brodiaga* Tumanov will be hanged in Aleksandrovsk Prison for shooting at an official.

"There's no one to hang him except me." He's hanged thirteen men on Sakhalin. A specialist in these matters, he hopes "to earn three rubles."

But now, while waiting for the execution, he's hired himself out to watch the children of a female penal laborer who lives with an exile-settler. Such are Sakhalin morals.

Komlev has come to the prison to find out "not whether it'll happen, but when," and strolls outside the chancery windows because there are guards here. Komlev hates all penal laborers. He gets a beating wherever he meets them. They beat him like a dog until he falls unconscious into a ditch somewhere. Consciousness regained, he walks away. He's an unusually tough old man, fifty years old, but with a sunken chest, a body covered in scars and sometimes coughing up blood because of the beatings—but his arms are extraordinarily strong.

"Komlev"—this is his executionary pseudonym. When they beat with the thin end of the birch rods they call it "giving 'im the twigs." When they beat with the thick end, this is "giving 'im the butt-ends." From this comes the sobriquet "Komlev."[5]

Komlev was a member of Kostroma's[6] urban estate, a cleric who attended seminary school and very much loved religious texts, especially those of the Old Testament. He was sentenced to twenty years for a daylight robbery with a revolver. He fled Sakhalin in '77, but in the narrow part of the Tatar Straits, having almost reached the mainland, he was captured by a Giliak[7] and received ninety-six lashes and a twenty-year extension to his term. In those grim days there was much work for the executioner, and the executioner Tersky, another Sakhalin celebrity, needed an assistant. In the prison they cast lots to see who would be the new executioner, and the lot fell on Komlev. But Komlev still dreamed of freedom, and in '89 fled again, got captured on Sakhalin and received another fifteen years' *katorga*. "And so, a clean fifty-five years' *katorga*!" Komlev proudly says.

They also sentenced him to 45 lashes, and Tersky administered the whip to his "pupil." "Well, lie down, pupil, I'm going to show you how to flog." And he "showed" him.

In '97 Komlev told me, "I've been rotting ever since." He *was* coming apart. His body was horrible to see and it looked like red-hot seared iron. Parts had healed into white cicatrices; but in other parts there was a thin red pellicle instead of skin. "You squeeze and it leaks!" The pellicle split and out flowed some pus. On that enlightened basis his punishment had turned into something gruesome, so did the executioner desecrate the executioner.

Soon, however, Tersky was caught taking a bribe from a prisoner and they punished him without a thought. Tersky was sentenced to 200 birch strokes and Komlev got to deliver the punishment. "You taught me how to use the whip, now I'll show you how to wield the birch rod." Tersky's been rotting ever since. What he did to Komlev is a joke compared to what Komlev did to him. "According to Mosaic law, an eye for an eye and a tooth for a tooth!" adds Komlev to this story. "I knew how to flog. My body had been educated from the inside out."

The fugitive convict Gubar, sentenced to the whip for cannibalism, was, after forty-five or forty-eight of Komlev's lashes, taken to the infirmary and died three days later without ever regaining consciousness. Komlev did this after receiving a bribe from *katorga*, who detested Gubar.

The doctors assigned to executions and who attended those by Komlev say there's something incredibly strange here. It's not just Medvedev's bitterness. It is an exquisite torture. Komlev savors his power. He even dreamed up his own special costume: a red shirt, black apron and some kind of tall black hat he stitched together. After shouting "Attention!" he tarries and bides his time, as if admiring how the victim's muscles spasmodically quiver with anticipation. The doctors turn away and shout "Quicker! Quicker!" to put an end to this agony.

"But would I get beaten lightly? I had my whole life beaten out of me!" says Komlev, when asked why he deals so *cruelly* with the man laid out on the mare. Something truly horrifying emanates from this person who shows with his fingers "how many there were."

"The first was in Voevodsk... then two more in Voevodsk... Couple in Aleksandrovsk... Then another couple in Voevodsk... then one more... then three more... one more... one more... I hanged thirteen men in all."

It was horrible when he told me in minute detail how he did it; told me in monotone, as if reciting a list of the dead, saying neither "the executed" nor "the criminal" but "he" in a low voice.

"The first was Kucherovsky. He was executed in Voevodsk, in the yard, for assaulting and wounding Warden Shishkov. They ordered 100 men into the yard, and another twenty-five were herded out of Aleksandrovsk to watch. You begin nervously at first, as if you're shaking hands. I drank two glasses of vodka... It's touching and a bit pathetic when he twists and wriggles... Most terrible of all is when they're still leading him out and the priest walks ahead in his black chasuble. That's when you get nervous. In the evening, when I'd relax and 'he' would appear before me, it was especially trying."

Komlev drank heavily after this first execution. "It was terrible." But by the second he'd become inured and drank neither before nor after the execution. "All they ask is, 'Do it without torturing me.' They all turn white, give a little

Fig. 27: Komlev

shiver. You're holding him by the shoulders while he's standing on the trapdoor and you feel through his shirt how cold he is. You wave a kerchief and the assistants knock out the strut."

"And you've come here now, to do this?"

"Have to eat, don'tcha?"

"What a horrible and loathsome person," you say. But I knew the woman whose caresses he enjoyed. This woman had had a man who beat her mercilessly and took a payment of two kopeks from Komlev for her. I was interested in what Komlev would say when I told him, "Well, y'know, they really want to abolish corporal punishment soon."

"Thank God... It should end!" said Komlev, and crossed himself.

Golynsky

In 1897 Aleksandrovsk Prison (where is collected all of *katorga*'s "chiefs"— everyone most hardened and vile) was without an executioner, and not a single convict wanted to be executioner. This was the first time this had happened in the history of *katorga*. Moreover, it was impossible even to coerce those who, when given a choice, elected to remain in the isolator. But the prison could not be without an executioner and so the "whole crew" nominated Golynsky to be executioner.

"I didn't want to, but when the crew orders you, you don't say nothin'!" explains Golynsky.

"Why did you choose him?" I asked *katorga*.

"A good man. He'll handle the pain."

Golynsky is forty-seven but looks no more than thirty-five. His face is surprisingly young, simple-minded and stupid. Poor as a church mouse, walking in down-at-heel shoes, he would at first glance not make you say, "There's an executioner."

"Golynsky, how many lashes of the whip have you yourself received?"

"A hundred."

"And of the birch rod?"

"Three thousand." And he smiled almost cheerfully.

Golynsky's "suffered since childhood." He's a friendly person but hot-tempered, terrifyingly impassioned and, upon losing his temper, incredibly wicked. Like Komlev he's from the clerical class, studied in Kamenets-Podolsky Seminary,[8] and was put under police supervision for his accidental murder of a friend during a fight. "I was so furious. I cracked him square in the head and he gave up the ghost." He then served four years in the military and got tangled up in a plot with five soldiers conspiring to murder their sergeant-major ("He was cruel."). Golynsky knew about it but didn't report it and was sentenced to thirteen and a half years' *katorga*. Thanks to clemency he spent a briefer time in *katorga*, joined the exile-settlers and soon got assigned to the peasantry. Any day he would have been able to leave Sakhalin for the mainland, but: "I couldn't keep on starving. I started starving the moment I joined the exile-settlers. I'd gotten a job with the laborers, and on Sakhalin you work alot. That's how I got by, day 'n' night." This starvation ended when he and another starving exile-settler murdered a well-off Caucasian exile-settler. "Sure, I killed him. I was thin as a ghost. I swung the axe and hit him and fell along with that axe. I couldn't stand up. They had to carry me." For this murder, Golynsky received 100 lashes and a life sentence. This time he had difficulty in *katorga*. Golynsky was falsely accused of reporting a planned escape by prisoners. He was beaten so badly that "my legs have been sore ever since." But this hasn't embittered Golynsky. "Why should I be cross at 'em all? Though, I've thrashed and will forever thrash those who slandered me!" It's said that whenever he encounters these slanderers he beats them to death, and *katorga* grants this "because his hide has suffered everything—rods, whips, starvation." It was for this "compassion" they chose him to be... executioner.

I'm sitting in someone's house when Golynsky suddenly appears, his face anxious.

"Your worship, please come to the prison immediately tomorrow morning."

"What for?"

"They say there'll be a fight. But there won't be no brawl if you're there."

With a frightened face this "executioner," at pains that a brawl not happen, is having difficulty restraining a smile.

"You're really an absurd fellow, Golynsky!"

"Precisely, in my own life I'm an absurd man, your worship!"

And he sagely chuckles to himself.

37

CORPORAL PUNISHMENTS

The criminal court. Two or three persons in the gallery. Without a jury, cases unfold concerning publishers charged with defamation, innkeepers charged with violating inn regulations, *brodiagi* concealing their origins, fugitive penal laborers, etc.[1]

"Defendant Ivan Gruzdev, do you acknowledge that, having been sentenced to exile to *katorga* labor for ten years, you willfully left your place of exile and concealed your identity?"

"Quite so, your excellency, I'll admit my guilt if…"

"Are you guilty or not?"

"Absolutely, I'm guilty, your excellency."

"Mister procurator?"

"In view of the defendant's confession, I won't question the witness."

"Mister defense counselor?"

"I'm in agreement."

A two-minute speech by the procurator. What's there to say? "On the basis of articles such-and-such, such-and-such and such-and-such…" A two-minute speech by the defense counselor, "as required." What can be said? The court reads the sentence: "…to a punishment of eighty lashes…"

Observe Ivan Gruzdev presenting himself for a health certification to a doctor in a Sakhalin prison chancery.

"What's your name?"

"Ivan Gruzdev."

The doctor unfolds his "statistics sheet," looks it over and simply mutters, "God, look what they're sentencing him to over there!"

"How many?" the prison warden gazes at the statistics sheet.

"Eighty."

"Oho!"

"Eighty!" repeats the warden's assistant like an echo. "Oho!"

"Eighty!" whisper the clerks. And everyone looks at the man currently designated to receive eighty lashes. They're in shock, in horror.

The doctor goes up to him, taps his chest and listens. These are long agonizing minutes for everyone.

"Are you healthy?"

"Perfectly healthy, your worship."

"Absolutely healthy?"

"Just so, absolutely healthy, your worship."

"Hmm... Maybe you have a bad heart?"

"Not at all, your worship, nothing hurts."

"Do you even know where your heart is? You! Nothing hurts on this side? Maybe sometimes—you understand—sometimes you have an occasional cramp?"

"Absolutely not, your worship, never an occasional cramp."

The doctor raps his little hammer on the table in fury. "Look at me! Do you sometimes have a cough? A cough?"

"Not at all, your worship. I never have coughs."

The doctor is infuriated. He's almost gnashing his teeth. He looks at the prisoner with hateful eyes, his gaze clearly saying, "You must tell a lie, lie about anything, damn you!" But the prisoner doesn't understand.

"Does your head ever hurt?" the doctor nearly hisses.

"Not at all, your worship."

The doctor sits down and writes: "Defective heart." He even breaks his quill out of frustration. The warden looks over the certification document.

"Exempt from corporal punishment. Off with you!" Everyone breathes a sigh of relief and relaxes.

"That damned fellow made me work up a sweat! A sweat!" the doctor later tells me. "He was really such a numbskull, the devil! 'I'm healthy!' Damn him! But really, what can you do? Eighty lashes! You know, that's a death sentence! How is that possible? If they saw what they sentence people to."

Rykovsk Prison's executioner is Khrustsel, a stocky, well-built, unusually adroit and strong man. It's really as if he's cast from steel. Suffering glimmers in his cold, gray calm eyes when he speaks of his past misfortunes. Looking more attentively, you note his asymmetrical face—one of the indications of degeneration. He ended up in *katorga* for committing robberies as part of an armed gang somewhere around Lodz.²

"Why did you join a gang?"

"I wanted to set myself up. I thought I'd get some money, your worship. There was absolutely no land. I was swollen from hunger. Impossible to settle down."

On Sakhalin, he thought he'd somehow get settled "into a new life." He took a little of his own money, twenty rubles, and set up a *maidan* in Rykovsk Prison's chains division. He paid each prisoner in the ward fifteen kopeks a month; arranged as is usual for a pair of ward attendants to wash floors and empty waste tubs for a ruble and a half; and would open his *maidan* at dinnertime. He sold milk for five kopeks a bottle, eggs for three kopeks each, sugar for less than a kopek, white bread for six kopeks a pound, cigarettes for a kopek each, boiled pork snout for under a kopek, and matches. He was doing all right, getting by half-starved on a single prison ration and saving money and dreaming of how he'd leave for a settlement and build his own house.

"As it was, you'd lie down hungry at night. You couldn't sleep. Your belly ached from hunger. There's the locker at your head. Milk, bread, pork in it. You want some. 'No,' you think, 'I won't touch it'."

In this locker near the candles at the head of the sleeping platform Khrustsel kept everything he possessed: money and goods. Everything he needed at the time and would need in the future. As usual, the whole ward safeguarded the *maidanshchik*'s property because of the fifteen kopeks per month each chap got.

But Rykovsk's chains is the hungriest of prisons.

"Do we, your worship, let a fellow get a leg up?" says Khrustsel with rage. "A man who sets himself up is envied. There's spite… Those with nothing won't allow another anything! Out of one person's spite everyone loses."

One day upon returning to the ward Khrustsel saw his locker had been broken into: neither money nor goods were there. The chains was swaggering and smiling. "Matches burned, cigarettes smoked." The most famished *zhigany* were snoring contentedly on the sleeping platforms. "They'd gorged themselves!" The three most desperate prisoners, of the "Ivan" breed, naked from having gambled away everything, were now sitting and playing cards for money. The locker near the candles was not only broken into but had actually been covered with all sorts of filth. He went crazy and they guffawed.

"My head was spinning, I was seeing stars," says Khrustsel.

"Khrustsel was smashing his head on the sleeping platforms at the time!" relate the prisoners.

Having cried himself out, Khrustsel went to the warden and offered himself as executioner. This position was then vacant at Rykovsk Prison. The warden was a brutal man and Khrustsel immediately became his favorite. Khrustsel's flogging was unbelievable.

"I tore off their hides, that's the truth. I didn't thrash but *sliced* with the rod. I utterly hated all of them then."

But after that, Khrustsel's "heart recovered." The trio of prisoners who'd broken into the chest had been sentenced to the lash for some other reason, and it had been Khrustsel's responsibility to punish them. "There's a God in heaven!" says Khrustsel, who rejoices whenever he talks about his punishment of them. His face shines with joy at the memory. "I flogged them across the shoulder." The whip-blow "across the shoulder" is the harshest. "I myself was afraid they'd faint—that the doctors would take them away. But no, they left them. I thrashed them in full." Khrustsel's enemies were carried to the infirmary lacerated, maimed and barely alive. "That was the turning point. I flog as ordered, but not ferociously. Everyone's the same to me. I just do what the administration tells me."

Khrustsel lives in a little house. He's been given a cohabitant, a young Tatar woman. They have two children. Earnings from *katorga* have allowed him to set himself up with the necessities.

"I have a cow. Two sheep! I raise and sell swine!" Khrustsel said, showing this visitor around his homestead. He's a farmer; he has a garden. "I've planted everything." He and his Tatar woman love each other completely. Everything in their home shines like glass. But in a hallway corner, on the spotless floor, are carefully laid the official items: whip, wood soap, razor (the executioner also shaves prisoners' heads).

"Choldren, choldren, don't touch the switches! Father will be angry!" the Tatar woman shouted to a pair of splendid little children in the hallway, playing with the switches Khrustsel would that day use to administer corporal punishment. "Nofty choldren, nofty—you're terrible!" The laughing Tatarka turned to me, and there was something childish and very sweet in her laughter and mangled words. The executioner's lair, full of childish prattle, seemed in some strange way to glitter even more like glass.

"Well, I've set myself up here!" said Khrustsel.

"But *katorga* doesn't touch anything of yours? They don't wreck anything?"

"They don't dare. They know I'll kill them. If they take a sunflower seed I'll kill them." And given the way Khrustsel said this, you could believe he'd kill them. *Katorga* doesn't touch that belonging to those it believes "will kill."

Such is Khrustsel, whom it was my fate to see "at work" that evening.

"Your worship, it's impossible to find food!"

Two ragged exile-settlers—one tall as a pole, the other a stump—had begun pestering the assistant warden as soon as we dropped into the chancery that afternoon.

"Alright, chaps, alright. You'll manage!"

"Mercy, your worship. I've a household. I works all the time. How long can a fellow last on nothing? I'm losing a day. Ain't anything possible? Your worship, show a commander's mercy!" So pestered the one tall as a pole. The one who was stumpy even threw his cap on the ground: "Sakes alive! No food for the oxen but they don't allows us to leave, neither!"

"What brought you here?" I asked.

"Came to be thrashed, your worship!" answered the tall one.

"They'll be flogging us!" clarified the stumpy one.

"But for what?"

"That we don't know!"

"Administration knows!"

"For vodka!" the assistant warden explained. "They were distilling *samosiadka* (homemade vodka)."[3]

"No way was we distilling vodka!"

"Nothing to chew on—but we're going to make vodka!"

"I myself caught them caught red-handed. This one here, the tall one, came at me with an axe!"

"He's lying, your worship, don't believe him. I didn't come at him at all with an axe, but that keg did get smashed with an axe, and that's the truth. He does his harm and goes. Why'd he smash the keg? He'd no right!"

The assistant warden muttered something and stalked off. Everyone standing around was smiling.

"You put him in a bad mood, you tom-fool! Now it'll be all the worse, chap."

"He's really takin' it badly, your worship. We're missin' a day. My oxen ain't gettin' fed."

"We ain't talking against a thrashing. 'Tis the law to flog. But ain't no law says to deny a man."

I met the assistant warden in the courtyard.

"These two will be flogged today at five according to their sentences!" he explained. "What a flogging they've been sentenced to! They're just buttering them. We don't control their sentences. It happens in Russia. That doesn't matter. But here, especially, these two sons-of-bitches should be shown a thing or two."

The floggings took place around five o'clock. I arrived at the chancery with the doctor. Inside the entry hall, its wide doors opened onto the yard, were the mare and two tightly-bound fagots of birch rods over four and a half feet long.

"Doctor! Doctor!" hailed a group of prisoners who momentarily passed the open doors. Seven men were standing along the gloomy, lusterless chancery wall. The executioner was standing in the doorway with the whip. It was suffocating, depressing and terrifying.

"They're coming."

First came Ivan Vasiutin, a young lad, a *brodiaga*, "origins forgotten"—thirty birch strokes. After him came two Caucasians, then another Russian who'd fled a Siberian prison. The court had sentenced all to corporal punishment. There began the reading of the sentences, during which everyone in the chancery came to attention. Then the medical examination, having earlier been completed by the doctor, was read out. A paper was placed before the condemned.

"You literate? Sign!"

"What's that?" I asked.

"A receipt showing they've received corporal punishment."

"Whatever for?!"

"Regulations."

Both the Russians were literate and signed; all the same, Vasiutin's letters were scrawled out very unevenly. His hand wasn't shaking, though it did quiver.

For a long time the Tatars didn't understand what was being demanded of them, and this was only made clear through a prisoner-translator who talked with them a very long time, waved his hands, argued about something and finally mistakenly said, "She's illiterate, yuroship!" This took a terribly, excruciatingly long time.

"Strip!" they shouted at a Tatar. "You hear? Strip! Translator, tell him to strip! Why're you standing there like a dolt?"

The translator began talking, shouting, waving his hands and even squatted for some reason. The Caucasian looked on dully and mistrustfully, answering morosely and monosyllabically.

"Strip!" everyone shouted and showed with gestures that he should take off his shirt. At last, the Caucasian slowly undressed. The doctor approached him with his little hammer and stethoscope. Mistrust and fear glittering in the Caucasian's eyes, he backed away.

"Don't back away, you devil! Don't back away, we mean you!"

The Caucasian kept backing away.

"Translator, you dolt, why're you standing there like a post? Explain to him that I'm not going to do anything to him!"

The translator again undertook to shout, gesticulate and squat. The Caucasian listened to him doubtfully, looking askance at the doctor he'd mistaken for the executioner, hesitated, then suddenly uttered a single word. The translator clasped his hands in exasperation.

"What's he saying?"

"He asks what for is your listening tube, yuroship!"

Finally, the doctor used the stethoscope and hammer to check the Caucasian.

The tall exile-settler, Bardunov,[4] was watching all this with a smile.

"A silly folk!" he commented when his turn came. "They don't know regulations."

"Strip!"

"Don't need to, your honor. All's healthy. No need to trouble your worship."

"They're telling you to undress. Haven't you ever received corporal punishment?"

"Not in my life, your honor. First time!"

"Rub him down." A guard rubbed his body with a rag. His body reddened and welts clearly stood out—evidence of corporal punishment. "You're lying! Were you flogged?"

"I just remembered, your honor... I've had I-don't-know-how-many birches before the gentlemen wardens." It was obvious this flogged and re-flogged prisoner was playing the fool for courage.

His comrade gloomily answered, "I'm healthy. Couldn't you hurry? My oxen are still unfed. Strip again?! Here ya go. Look. Sakes alive! They flogged me. Alot. How many lashes, I've forgotten. Don't remember. Should I bother my head with that? Did they examine me? For God sakes! Can't we go first? I got a homestead."

The examinees dressed themselves, but didn't pull their trousers all the way up and kept their shirts in their hands.

"Everyone, attention now!" Khrustsel was standing next to the mare. The prisoners, waddling and muddling about in their half-raised trousers, left the hall. "Be brave, Bardunov!" someone shouted from the yard. The crowd of prisoners standing outside looked behind them. "Shut up, you scum!" Everyone stood still. I stood beside the doctor, whose face had turned blotchy.

"Vasiutin, Ivan!" The young lad approached the mare. "Off, off with the trousers!" the circle began saying. But he only turned around as if he didn't understand.

"Trousers off!" said Khrustsel, and grabbed him by the arm. "Lie down!" Vasiutin sat astride the mare, his face to the light. He was white as a sheet, eyes staring ahead unhappily. "Your head doesn't go there! That way! Lie down!" Khrustsel took him by the shoulders, turned him toward the mare and laid him down. "Move your arms! Hug the mare!" Vasiutin embraced the mare's platform.

It was shameful, unbelievably shameful, to see this half-dressed man lying on the mare. Khrustsel was looking at the assistant warden's eyes like a dog.

"Thirty strokes!"

Khrustsel grabbed a fasces of birches, held it with unusual agility, took a step back from the mare and measured the distance.

"Begin!"

Khrustsel whistled the birch rod through the air like it was a fencing rapier, then cut the air once to the right and once to the left. The whistling was harsh, depressing and repulsive.

"One!" A whistling sound, and a red stripe lay on the just-spasmed body. "Two… Three… Four… Five…" Khrustsel tossed aside the birch rod, grabbed another and switched to the other side of the mare. Another five strokes on the other side of the body. Every five strokes he quickly changed birch rods and switched from one side to the other. The whistling made my heart sink. The moments between strokes dragged out like an eternity. The assistant warden counted off. "Twenty-nine… Thirty…"

"Stop… Stop!" Vasiutin raised himself and again sat astride the mare. His eyes and face were full of tears. "It's all over! Be off!"

"Two and a half minutes!" said the doctor looking at his watch. I thought half an hour had gone by.

"Mednikov, Ivan!" Again, a man half-naked to the waist lay down on the mare.

"Khrustsel, position them." Khrustsel grabbed the Caucasians by the shoulders, nudged them toward the mare, took them by the arms and laid them down. They shuffled along heavily and stretched out their dark naked bodies. The punishment was "strictly according to sentence."

Khrustsel acknowledged with his eyes the assistant's command and grasped the whip's mid-section where the shaft meets the three tails. The punishment was to be done "with the half-whip." Khrustsel turned his whip like he was cranking a barrel-organ; the three tails slapped against the body and it reddened and swelled.

"Bardunov!"

With a very pale face he approached the mare and, trying to smile, grimaced pathetically. He began lying down on the mare.

"Trousers, trousers off!" Khrustsel stopped him.

"As the legal system requires…" A tremor seized Bardunov; he helplessly looked at everyone like a hunted rabbit and tried to smile but only grimaced.

Khrustsel pushed him lightly by the neck. "Lie down!" Bardunov began to collapse and gripped hold of the platform, seemingly so as not to cry out. Khrustsel again measured the whip along the floor. The motion was ominous. This punishment was not according to sentence but was Sakhalinistic. There was a silence, as if none in the circle were breathing. Khrustsel fixed his eyes on the assistant who stood, turned to look at me and then the doctor… and made a motion with his head. Khrustsel raised the "half-whip." It was as if a huge man sighed throughout the hall and yard. Spasms ran along Bardunov's body. God knows what kind of blow this man had anticipated and how he'd already been trembling when the comparatively light blows began falling.

"Your honor, your honor, what am I being punished for? Nothing, maybe?" said his voice, but it was somehow strange, as if not his. "Nothing, maybe?!"

The group in the yard erupted in laughter.

"He's playing the fool! He's used to it!" muttered the warden's assistant.

Bardunov got up, grabbed his trousers and, without cinching them, ran to the group of prisoners.

Seeing that this time his punishment would not be drastic his companion, Gusiatnikov,[5] the short and gloomy muzhik, was silently relieved and shuddered under each blow without making a sound. When leaving he even muttered, "Day wasted for nothing. Oxen still ain't fed!"

"That's that, I spared the bastards!" The assistant was moved by his own humanity.

Khrustsel was easily and skillfully removing the birch rods and mare.

"Aren't you going to dress?"

Vasiutin was standing like a post beside the lintel of the chancery doors, his legs bare, trousers round his ankles. He hiccupped. Huge tears ran down his cheeks. Seeing this lad was terrible and shameful. He'd been in the military, committed some crime, ran away fearing punishment, "concealed his identity" and called himself the *brodiaga* Ivan Vasiutin, origins-forgotten.[6]

"How was it you were sentenced to the birch rod?"

Brodiagi are normally sentenced to a year and a half of compulsory labor and then to a settlement. They also get the birch rod if they "obfuscate" for one reason or another and don't simply call themselves "*brodiaga*-origins-forgotten," but acquire a false name and say they're a peasant from some village when it turns out they're not. An experienced *brodiaga* does this in the hope of escaping during deportation. But why do this?

"So, you called yourself by someone else's name?"

"Yes, exactly."

"What for? Did you want to escape along the way?"

"No."

"Then why do it?"

"In prison, some fellow I didn't know showed up, said it had to be done. So I did it."

"Was this the first time you were punished?"

"The first." Tears were still running down his cheeks. He began hiccupping more strongly.

Yet, as I was leaving Bardunov, having fully recovered, was sitting at the prison gates and boasting: "For me, brothers, lying on the mare's like lying with a woman—it's all the same. That's how come I'm used to her!"

Fig. 28: Prisoner

38

KATORGA'S WAYS

"*Katorga*"—this is its official name. Unofficially, *katorga* calls itself by the sardonic name of "the mare."

"Hey, how's it going, chaps?"

"Not bad, your honor, the mare's surviving."

"Is this a laborer, too?" you ask about someone.

"He's one of ours, the mare's." The sobriquet comes from the word "mare," the bench on which prisoners are laid out for floggings.

Penal laborers, as is known, reach Sakhalin by two paths: either they "float" here by sea from Odessa or march through Siberia via Kara.[1] Corresponding to this, penal laborers are divided into the "bog-circlers" or "sea-biscuits," and the "Karaians" or "mountain-sufferers."[2] "Sea-biscuit" is a somewhat contemptuous term: "What did they see on the way? They were floating along and eating sea-biscuits. That's it!" Whereas "Karaians" is used to distinguish *katorga*'s honored and esteemed. Journeying through Siberia's transit prisons, they endured the mountains, which is why they're called "mountain-sufferers." They were in *katorga* university, so to speak, and graduated *katorga*'s highest course either in the Siberian "centrals" (the central prisons) or at Kara. They know all the customs, mores and laws. Sakhalinites generally admire the penal laborer from Siberia: penal laborers in Siberia cleave more tightly to each other and have their own ten-year labor laws—fixed and inviolable—and labor cooperatives (of which there are none on Sakhalin).[3]

Soon, however, the difference between these groups fades. The "bog-circlers" quickly get on track, assimilate *katorga*'s customs and mores and become more "devoted" than any "Karaian"—and then the words "Karaian" and "sea-biscuit" are invoked only during squabbles: "Shut up! Who're you talking to, dimwit? I, when all's said and done, am a true Karaian. But what're you? Pshaw! In a word, a sea-biscuit!"

Katorga is divided into four castes:

1) Ivans
2) Snorters[4]
3) Players[5] and
4) the luckless herd.[6]

There are in *katorga* an aristocracy and a demos; its ruling classes and subordinate masses; patricians, plebeians and slaves.

Ivans

"Ivans" are the evil, the bane, the scourge of our *katorga*—its despots, its tyrants. An Ivan is born under the birch rod, baptized by the whip and elevated by the executioner's hand to Ivan-status. He's an historical type. He arose in those terrible times, the true history of which is indelibly written in lines on the backs of the aged invalids of Derbinsk Prison's almshouse.

He arose in Kara during the "Razgildeev era," now remembered with horror.[7] At that time, in the "cut" where they extracted gold, the mare was always set up and the executioner always on duty. Birch strokes were then divided into tens and were counted on "one side" only, that is, if a man was sentenced to, say, ten strokes, the executioner gave him ten on one side, then went to the other side and administered another ten. Moreover, the second ten wasn't included in the total: two strokes counted as one. They flogged not with the birch rod but with the "butt-ends," that is, they held the rod by the thin end and struck with the thick. Blood was drawn at the first blow, rods broke, splinters pierced the body. The "tasks," that is, the daily work quotas, were difficult, and the smallest "task" left unfinished drew immediate punishment.

Back then, any violation was punished. The least impertinence, the minutest opposition by exiles to a lowly guard, occasioned brutal torture.

During those especially hard times, under the hiss of the birch rod, butt-end and lash, the "Ivan" was borne into the world. A desperate cutthroat, a long-term penal laborer with nothing to lose and nothing to hope for, he manifested protest for the whole of this beaten, worn-out, shattered *katorga*. He protested laughingly and insolently, protested against the unjust punishments, excessive "tasks," bad food and those absurd, childish little jackets issued to prisoners by way of "clothing according to legislated design." Ivan didn't pass silently before such authority but at every step protested laughingly and insolently.

Ivans were chained to the wall and the wheelbarrow, their wrists and ankles were fettered, they were flogged with the butt-end and the whip. Towards the earning of their name in *katorga*, Ivans often had to receive over 2000 lashes of the three-tailed whip—birch strokes didn't count at all. All this earned respect and conferred upon them an aureole of manliness. The administration flogged, but somewhat feared, them. These were people who any minute could stick a knife between the ribs, people who would bash in an offender's skull with their manacles.

At the time, the Ivans were something of a chivalric order. The Ivan was a man of his word and was known to do what he'd say he'd do. Pazulsky, an old Ivan once notorious in the south as an ataman of bandit gangs, gave his word in Kherson that he would stab the assistant prison warden who'd offended him. After this, Pazulsky escaped, was captured two years later, ended up in Kherson Prison and thus, after a span of two years, carried out his word and stabbed the assistant. This exacted fear and trembling before the Ivans.

These men capable of anything were doubtless a menace for wardens and guards and a terror for everyone in *katorga*. They were despots, tyrants and thieves. An Ivan straightforwardly, openly, in view of everyone, could take convicts' last most hard-earned crumbs and, then and there, spend, gamble or squander them before an owner's eyes—and suffer no protest. "What about it?! As need be, I don't begrudge my flesh and blood for you so-and-so's. I don't fear the noose, whereas you…," he'd say. Whatever Ivan did *katorga* was obliged to make up for, and often did so with its flanks. If someone else was punished for a crime committed by an Ivan, he had to stay quiet. "After all, I'm suffering for you," the Ivan would say. Ivans kept their own company, backed up each other and were *katorga*'s unfettered rulers. They ruled over life and death; were judge, jury and executioner; pronounced and directed the execution of sentences (sometimes death) that were always indisputable.

Among the innumerable terrible legends remembered by *katorga* about those times is the "execution" in Omsk Prison.[8] Two Ivans had decided to escape; then, barely a day before the planned escape, the irons on their arms and legs were unexpectedly tightly re-forged and the guard increased so that flight became impossible. Omsk Prison's Ivans secretly investigated for two months. "Who could've informed?" And, naturally, suspicion fell on a certain prisoner. While he was suspecting nothing the Ivans pronounced a sentence against him. It was death, of course, because *katorga* knows no other sentence for informing about an escape. The Ivans silently worked for two nights beneath the sleeping platform, pulling several slats from the walls. On the third night they dug a grave near their sleeping comrade, stopped up his mouth, threw him inside and buried him alive. The whole prison knew about this and was silent, not daring to breathe a word. When they opened the door for morning roll call and administrators noted the missing prisoner, they concluded he'd slipped away unnoticed and had escaped. Not until a year later, when they were rebuilding Omsk Prison, did they find behind the walls, at a depth of three-and-a-half feet, a skeleton in chains. The perpetrators remained unknown. No one reported them. No one dared report them.

Ivan is *katorga*'s evil genius. They've started so many prison riots. So many folks have paid for these riots, and how they've paid! But the Ivans always came out clean because *katorga* always covered for them. Such were the Ivans' "good old days."

Entering a prison, you can instantly tell an Ivan at first sight. Peaked cap wickedly cocked toward the ear, a shirt with a "forge" (wide-collars), an unbuttoned pea-jacket, a cassock barely resting on one shoulder; hands unfailingly in pockets; a daring, impertinent, defiant gaze; inevitably a brazen, rude and insolent tone of voice: a person quite wound up for some sort of nastiness. It's the same in all respects with these talented cutthroat long-termers, and wardens try to avoid them, typically masking their tell-tale inner fear with, "I don't even want to speak to such scoundrels. I say, I'll talk only with good people." As it were, by "not wishing to speak" to Ivans much is conceded that, of course, would never even be given to the luckless and meek herd.

Ivan is that evil, that scourge, of anyone in *katorga* who is just a bit honest, good or decent. For any thrifty prisoner, anyone enjoying the merest prosperity, they are the cruelest and foulest of enemies. Depending on the circumstances, Ivan will openly take this, swindle that or simply steal every hard-earned kopek from a prisoner.

But times are changing. Along with the arrival of better days for *katorga* come bad days for Ivans. Now that there are no more of those terrible executions the Ivans' aureole of manliness has collapsed. They are irretrievably losing all fascination for *katorga* and their terrifying tyrannical power is breathing its last. The Ivans are dying out. In a kinder, more humane regime Ivans' pernicious influence on *katorga* becomes less and less.

In Aleksandrovsk Prison, the largest on Sakhalin, where are gathered *katorga*'s "chiefs," the toughest long-term criminals, and where, moreover, corporal punishments happen by judicial sentence only, Ivans' influence is most paltry. They make no impact whatsoever. Even the herd won't tolerate them! But, all told, several years ago Aleksandrovsk Prison's Ivans did win renown throughout all Sakhalin! Ivans still obtain where wardens order corporal punishments. There, a certain aureole still encircles Ivan, though, of course, it's far from what it was during the Razgildeev era.

The Ivans' power and significance sharply declined during… the cholera disturbances.[9] In this sense "the unfortunate were helped by not being the fortunate." A spirit of fresh air was injected into this prison atmosphere, this atmosphere of blood and filth. Sakhalin's prisons filled with people brought to *katorga* only out of happenstance, people who'd committed horrors only because they were surrounded by horror and didn't understand what they were doing. They were a people benighted, ignorant and ill-fated, but not criminal.[10] These fresh, honest hardworking people did not want to obey certified murderers' laws, regulations and orders; and as there were many of them, they opposed the Ivans using that most basic of *katorga* weapons—their fists. The herd, sensing among itself a kinship of supporters and partners who'd been pauperized, burglarized and beaten by the Ivans, raised its head and enthusiastically reformed itself into a solid mass opposing the Ivans. The affair went so far that several Ivans were beaten half to death. Ivans being beaten half to death was an unprecedented occurrence in the history of *katorga*, and all this terrifically weakened Ivans' authority.

But the principal blow was the reduction in corporal punishments that caused Ivans' aureole of manliness to decline considerably. Now, an Ivan stealing a penal laborer's very last cannot say, "But don't I pay for this with my flesh and blood?"

Ivans still obtain, as I've already said, in those prisons where wardens love corporal punishment. But their power is nowhere near what it once was. Often, towards evening, you'll hear somewhere in a corner of the chains a small group of Ivans reminiscing about the good old never-to-return days when *katorga* honored Ivans; about their exploits and how they ruled *katorga*. But there's an elegiac tone to these discussions, a nostalgia for the past.

Ivan, you won't get back your earlier power and position.

The Ivans, these aristocrats of suffering, were born under the hiss of the whip, the butt-end and the birch rod and, like these, they're dying out.

Snorters

"Snorters" are *katorga*'s second caste. They would like to be Ivans but don't possess the courage. Due to their cowardice, it follows that they should be assigned to the herd, but "pride won't allow it." Snorters cannot stand that which has long ruled over them. They are those "whiners" in a village assembly. When any event occurs in the prison, any little "commotion," the snorters always clamber forward whining, shouting and bawling more than anyone, in words prepared for utterance days earlier; but when a matter comes to a "split" and officials show up, snorters silently disappear into the back row.

"What're you doing, you clumsy devil?" the prison leans upon a snorter during resolution of a split. "Were you lying, are you going back on your word?"

"But so what? Ain't I going along with everyone else? Everybody's shutting up, so I'm shutting up, too." The snorter gets dodgy as to why he's become silent when officials arrived. "Just this once let whatever happens happen—it'll sort itself out!"

The name "snorter" is a bit sarcastic. It comes from the word "to snort." This defines the snorters' profession: they "snort" at everything. There's no directive at which they won't huff about their rights. They're in eternal opposition; all they see are violations, illegalities, injustices; everything exasperates them. "They should assign a fellow a quota only if it's easy; they should send him to the isolator only if it's deserved; they shouldn't send him to the infirmary if he's completely healthy." Snorters are always crying, "It's not fair!" (behind administrators' backs, of course.)

Katorga, which simply lives and breathes dissatisfaction, likes this—and talkers always achieve success where there's much dissatisfaction. Moreover, *katorga* loves to listen if someone's speaking smoothly and well. This is an ability *katorga* highly esteems. There are many reasonably good orators among snorters. I myself listened with great interest, surprised at their instinct for the audience. What an instinct for their listeners' unhealthy and weak points, what an understanding of how to play to these points! Owing to this, snorters sometimes, when the prison's restless, acquire a certain influence over affairs. They stir things up, and not a few prison incidents, for which the poor meek herd later paid with flesh and blood, have been incited by snorters. As usual, the herd got in trouble while the snorters managed to fade into the background.

Snorters make up most of the "throats," that is, those who during arguments side with whomever pays most. They show up to defend and to accuse—sometimes to the death—for money. A fellow gets involved in some mess against a comrade, and the snorters defend him for money, orate in the prison assembly and swear it's the other prisoner who should be investigated. If anyone wants to put the screws to another he bribes the snorters. Snorters impute the fellow with some calumny, for example, that he's an informer or a denouncer; produce their own witnesses and wail about exemplary punishment. But the prison is suspicious, and the fellow who's making the charge and upon whom suspicion has just fallen now risks his life. Were snorters to have a conscience, were these wretches to have any conscience, this luckless, benighted, embittered prison would not have willy-nilly squandered so many lives.

Snorters get two big holidays a year, in spring and autumn, when the *Iaroslavl* arrives to expel onto Sakhalin a new load of "society's garbage." Then the snorters orate among the newcomers. Ingenuously taking snorters for "*katorga*'s premier personages," these lost newcomers, by virtue of inexperience and habit, even confuse them with the Ivans and hasten to curry their favor with money.

In normal times snorters live at the expense of the herd. This poor, helpless, defenseless prison mass trembles before the daring insolent snorters. "Well, so what! You can fall in love with kasha but still not get the bone!" And it pays up.

Players

In *katorga*, where everything's bought and sold and is, moreover, bought and sold very dearly, it's impossible for a fellow who has money, especially easy money, not to have influence. Without a game, a "player" simply has nothing else to do. They're all cheats; and when a player gambles with players it is, in essence, a contest in cheating. While one is unfairly shuffling the deck another is switching those cards on which a large sum's been bet. But then God graces you to notice "ah-ha, he's cheating!" and the prison beats him half to death. "You won't be doing none of your business!" If a player is an especially able cheater he acquires the esteemed title "expert."

Too many folks feed off the player because he doesn't care one way or the other. In the first place, the player never performs *katorga* labor—he hires a "husk."[11] Then, the player always has a "suborn"[12] (sometimes several) who tidies up his spot on the sleeping platform, makes up his bed, fetches him dinner and brews his tea. The player gives money to the *maidan*, which receives ten percent from the croupier and five from the punters. The "stirrup,"[13] who guards the door while the game proceeds, earns money thanks to the player and, it must be said, also takes bribes. When a novice or a newcomer shows up but the player doesn't have enough money, the "fathers" (usurers) can make loans through him so he can "set aside the bank" and gamble without risk. Ultimately, the player is a "*fartovy*" chap. He makes easy money, nothing matters to him, and so he lives without a care and gives a man a few kopeks.

The player always has a crew that's ready to support him as he wishes, in whatever he wishes, against the crowd. He can reverse a decision by the prison assembly because lots of folks are behind him. It's terrible to quarrel with him. He gives the order for a thrashing, and there's a thrashing. You need to earn his favor because if he shows forgiveness, there's forgiveness. Moreover, "little things may always fall" from him, things that among paupers play a huge role, of course.

Players are at their utmost when putting on airs and scoffing at their comrades. With some ridiculous kinds of mockery things are kept from coming to a head. I found in one of the prisons a well-known player who, as an interesting character, I'd been looking for. The poor fellow had fallen on a patch and was out of luck. Players are always dandies, but even he'd lost his glow. He was cruel, bad-tempered and perpetually sullen. He'd started losing—he'd lost a silver watch, an object of great pride. It was getting bad!

"So, chap, are you becoming a *zhigan*?"

"It's looking that way!"

Only, I came another time to the prison—"and good gracious, is that him?" I didn't recognize him at first. He was sprawled on the sleeping platforms shouting at a suborn barely able to satisfy all his whims.

"What," he shouted, "will Matvey Nikolaevich be dining on tonight?" The suborn was bearing the usual bowl of gruel. Matvey Nikolaevich half raised himself and peered at then spit into the gruel. "They feed this to dogs. Who're you giving this to, fool? Is Matvey Nikolaevich gonna eat this? What else is there to eat?"

"A little tea, Matvey Nikolaevich, if you please!"

Matvey Nikolaevich kicked some black bread off the platform. "Is there nothing for Matvey Nikolaevich to eat? No one can teach you fools! Is Matvey Nikolaevich going to eat fools' food? Let's have sausage!" The suborn gave him smoked sausage and white bread. "That's the stuff!" The suborn, snatching the piece of black bread from the floor, smiled at me idiotically.

"Funny fellows," everyone was saying. But they were sitting around hungry.

"Why are you giving him soup just so he can spit in it?" I asked the suborn. "And bread, so that he can kick it on the floor?! You know he's putting on airs with his money, while you don't have a thing to eat. Yet you'll get him sausage with white bread straightaway."

"It's impossible." The suborn was truly frightened. "God forbid I should do different. 'What're you doing?' he'd be asking. 'Don't you know who I am? Am I a prisoner or not?' 'A prisoner,' I say. 'And if I'm a prisoner, why ain't you giving me prisoner's food? Eh? Maybe I won't disdain to eat it? Why you so-and-so, don't you know that Matvey Nikolaevich is a strong and clever fellow? Give him some sausage! You little shit! Don't squander my food, give me the prison rations so's my stuff will last!' And on he goes for a whole hour! Well, I give him a ration of soup, just to keep the peace. But what's it to him—he's just showing off his power! It's the way things are! He gambled and he won!"

Once, a certain player was sent to work in the taiga. There was no way he could wriggle out of it, so he rode half a verst on horseback with a *zhigan* he'd hired and left him there. "My feet hurt," he said.

Zhigany

It is awful, however, when a player loses everything and turns into a *zhigan*. In general, in *katorga*, anyone who's poor and owns nothing is called a *zhigan*. This name is used in particular for those players who've lost absolutely everything.

This is when *katorga* turns on itself, when there are no limits, no ends to the taunts given a man who's been deprived of all his friends, admirers, defenders, hangers-on and humble servants. *Katorga* knows no mercy and shows no pity. After a *zhigan* has lost everything—money, clothes, his own labor for a year ahead, his bread ration for several months ahead—they'll gamble with him either for his spot on the sleeping platform or for his gruel. Nobody really needs either of these; they play just to humiliate him.

"The hell with you, I'm gonna soak you, dog. Three kopeks, or you sleep on the floor for three days!"

Or:

"A *trëshnitsa* (three kopeks) or you'll go hungry—one week without soup, no drinksies, no eatsies, just sit."

I went to the prison one evening after everyone had gone to bed. I look, and there's a prisoner lying on the floor in the corridor near the sleeping platform. Seeing me, he leapt up and climbed onto the platform, but his neighbor wouldn't budge.

"Stop! Where're you going? No, you lie on the floor!"

"Devil! Demon! Look, it's the barin!"

"No, you lie with the barin. Let the barin see what sort of worldly creature you are. Lie down!" The prisoner lay beneath the platform.

"'No, you lie down!'" could be heard among the laughter from all sides. "Got up for nothing. The 'barin' said you can't lie beside him! Lie down like you was lying."

"Did you gamble away your place?" I asked.

"That's it, I lost, and now this dog's lying in the shit."

"For how much did you lose your place?"

"It went for a three-girl, but I don't even have a kopek."

"Here, have three!"

"I can't! My pride's worth more than your three coins."

Clearly, the player was up against himself. There's nothing you can do with a prisoner in such cases. "You lose, you pay. A roll on the floor—now there's a game! If you don't want to pay, you'll get a real lesson!" For not paying, the prison "covers with dark," that is, beats without mercy; moreover, everyone joins in, even those who weren't involved in the game.

"That's the way it is! That's it!" the group said. "Procedure's well known! A real lesson!"

"Gonna lie down, devil?!" And the *zhigan*, to the guffaws of the entire prison, lay on the floor, on which there was more than an inch of sticky viscous filth.

The prison was bored and glad for a bit of amusement. But the truth is, this *zhigan* had come to prison for having strangled his wife out of jealousy. Sometimes there were storms in his soul. He felt love and jealousy and bitter resentment. An "Othello," if you please, in this environment!...

I entered the prison at dinnertime. Dinner was already ending. Suborns were running to the urn for hot water to make tea. Some were still finishing eating, some were putting away leftover pieces of bread for the evening, some were lying down to rest.

"We-ell, boys, time to feed the *zhigan*. What to give 'im? Or don't 'e 'ave no appekite?"

From the sleeping platforms arose a man who could easily have portrayed "Hunger." Nothing save hunger was engraved into his eyes, his pallid, bloodless, bluish face. He was a completely weakened and broken-down character. This was a *zhigan* who had gambled away his soup for two weeks. For ten days, the man hadn't seen a breadcrumb and had been living on some thin watery gruel. And how he was living!

Many actually half-rose from their places to watch. The prison eagerly anticipated the gathering amusement. This was particularly evident on one young chap's face. Evidently, the fellow was preparing something special for the *zhigan*.

The *zhigan* approached the first person sitting at the end, silently bowed and waited. With a smile he ladled him out half a spoon of soup. The *zhigan* swallowed it, bowed again and went on to the next man. This was a typical Ivan reclining in a grand pose on the sleeping platform.

"Complerments to the *zhigan*! You came 'ere to dine?"

"Certainly, Nikolay Stepanovich, if it pleases you!" answered the *zhigan* with a low bow.

"Very well!... But tells us, what would you be eating now?"

The *zhigan* tried to force a tragically funny smile and answered, "I would now be eating, Nikolay Stepanovich, gray-hens and some veal, the little hooves of a suckling pig, a tiny bit of ham, just a little touch of pork and some salted beef with horsey-radish. I do indeed think it beats spit!"

The prison chortled over his wordplay. The Ivan dipped a spoon into his soup and gave it to the *zhigan*.

"Now, lick it!" The *zhigan* opened his mouth. "Look at 'ow your jaws 'ave opened! You're gonna swallow the spoon! Ah, you're a danger with that tongue!" The *zhigan* licked off a piece of cabbage stuck to the spoon. "Lick till yer full!" The *zhigan* went on to the next man. "Stop!" shouted "Ivan." "What're you doin', ya lout? You eats and fills yerself up but don't thank yer master?"

The *zhigan* bowed again from the waist. "Your humble servant is grateful for your good deed and kindness, for your fare, yes, and for your tasks, for your kind word and for bringing me good fortune. I wishes the master many years, and still more, and still half again more and a quarter more. All the lads loves the dear master. God bless his childrens!"

"Yes-yes, you fools'll learn!" smiled "Ivan." "You even studied at the *gimnaziia*![14] Why ain't you fools learnin' there? Ya louts!"

Next was the young fellow who, judging by his face, had some special trick ready. He silently scooped up some gruel and gave it to the *zhigan*. But hardly had the *zhigan* parted his lips than the fellow shouted, "Hey! Ain't you forgot to pray to God b'fore your bread 'n' salt?"[15]

The *zhigan* crossed himself.

"Not yet! On your knees, as is proper!"

The *zhigan* went down on his knees and began to speak. What he said! Even the old counterfeiter sitting nearby couldn't suffer it, and spat, "Pshaw, you! Filthy pigs!"

The young fellow chortled deeply. "Well, now, there we are, 'atta way!" He gave him half a spoonful. "Whaddya say?"

"Glory to God, I been sated by God, no one could see me I so weren't eating but, glory to God, now I'se full, ate half-a-pood and there're seven pounds left, and we'll be eatin' 'em tomorrow," wailed the *zhigan*.

The young chap grabbed his belly. "Oy, gracious, you're killin' me! Be off!"

Next was a kind-hearted red-haired muzhik with a broad smile. "Akh, you blockhead!" he greeted the *zhigan*. "How much of me own soup you wants me to give you? What's your wish?"

"Dredge it up, little uncle!"

"Ready your soup bowl!"

The *zhigan* lifted his head and opened his mouth. The muzhik scooped up a large spoonful and carefully tipped it into the *zhigan*'s mouth. His throat spasmodically gulped it down and he went into a coughing fit, his face turning red. "Life's returning!" said the muzhik, smiling broadly. The *zhigan* carelessly cleared his throat and spat and went on to the next. This was the counterfeiter, a staid old man who lent money in the prison.

"Treat me, little uncle!"

"Get out of here, scum!" the old man answered indignantly.

"Is that all there'll be?"

"They say, 'depart without sin'..."

The *zhigan* put his hands on his hips. The whole ward focused its attention, wondering what would happen next.

"Akh, you Asmodey Asmodeevich!"[16] the *zhigan* began shaming the old man. "You're going to hoard until you're in a coffin, in a shroud, under tapers..."

"Leave, I'se tellin' you!"

"...Yes, under incense, where you belong. The end'll come for you soon, Asmodey Asmodeevich, you'll die and you won't be able to hoard no more..."

"Leave!"

"You'll vanish, old devil, die of hunger..." But at that moment Asmodey Asmodeych's suborn, returning from the kitchen with hot water, grabbed the *zhigan* by the scruff of the neck. "Let go!" shouted the *zhigan*.

"Don't be naughty!"

"Hit 'im!" howled the old usurer. The huge lanky suborn boxed the *zhigan* on the ear with all his might. "Hit 'im! Hit 'im!" shouted the old man.

"How do you like that?! How do you?!" The *zhigan* started rising from the floor, but the suborn wrenched him to the ground by his hair and grabbed his neck.

"Hit 'im! Hit 'im!" screeched the frenzied old man. *Katorga* was guffawing.

"Whatta racket!" a laughing young fellow burst out, shaking his head.

But really, the Ivan had spoken the truth: this *zhigan* had truly gone through six courses in a *gimnaziia*...

I was often inclined to ask, "Why do you beat these wretches like this?" And they always answered me with one and the same smile. "Barin, don't let yourself worry about them. They're the most useless folk. Liable to do anything!" From among them come the "husks" who work for prison moneylenders and card-sharps, and the "exchangers"[17] who have traded names with long-term penal laborers and are naturally fated to be thieves and starving murderers.

The Herd

"The herd" is the flock of Pan, *katorga*'s defeated "mob," its disfranchised plebs. It is those village peasants who came here for killing someone during a drunken holiday brawl; it is those murderers who committed their crimes out of hunger or because of extreme ignorance; it is the victims of family squabbles, ill-fated husbands incapable of arousing passionate love in their wives; it is those crushed by falling misfortune, patiently bearing their crosses, who have neither the strength nor courage nor impudence to win for themselves a position in prison. This is a people who, having been punished, may yet again turn into honest, peaceful hardworking citizens. This is why the Ivan, the snorter, the player and even the *zhigan* speak of the "herd" with nothing other than great contempt. "These prisoners ain't nothing! They just been 'taken from the plough for awhile.'"[18] Real *katorga*, "its head" (Ivans, snorters, players and *zhigany*), laugh over the herd-man. "He don't know what to do at all! Yes, what absurd folk." To be entirely candid, the herd are not considered people. "What's with this fellow? Huh? He's some kinda log. Curls up and nods off!"

These perpetually half-starved people, reminiscent of tramps, have two occupations: working and sleeping. Worn-out and poorly fed, clothed and shod, the individual performs his labors, returns and falls asleep like a log. Thus his life proceeds.

The herd is meek and therefore gets the hardest jobs. The herd is poor and therefore gets no privileges from the guards. The herd is beaten and submissive and therefore doesn't stand up to the great and terrible Ivans when they come to deal with the herd, when a scoundrel roars like thunder, "I'll tear you to pieces and let you rot—mark my words!" The herd are those who sleep without undressing, fearing their clothes will be pinched. They hide their bread in their shirts till evening but that it will be swiped, so that they're walking around with it the whole day. Returning from work to the prison, the herd's representative never knows whether his locker on the sleeping platform will be broken into or intact, whether or not his last possessions will have been pinched from it.

Ivans oppress them, snorters intimidate and clean them out, players scoff at them and starving *zhigany* rip them off. The herd trembles before each and every one. They quiver away their whole existence, because in these prisons where prisoners should be corrected and rehabilitated arbitrariness rules, Ivans are created, the strong completely rule the weak and the inveterate scoundrel is above the decent man.

39

MATVEY'S TROUBLE[1]

I was walking with the warden through the prison yard. It was almost evening and prisoners were returning from work.

"Would you like to meet a scoundrel?" said the warden, turning to a prisoner shuffling along without a cassock despite the poor weather. "Come 'ere! Where's your cassock? Gamble it away, scoundrel? I'm asking you, were you gambling?" The prisoner was silent and looked morosely off to the side. "Show me your cassock! You hear? Pull off your hide and stitch it together, you sonofabitch! I'll rip you apart! You'll rot in the isolator! Hear that? Still silent? You hear what I'm asking?"

"I heard!" the prisoner morosely answered.

"So, so, 'I heard'! And no cassock! Be off!"

Extraordinarily content with what he'd shown me, that he knew how "to pepper" a prisoner, the warden (formerly a medic commander) explained, "There's no other way with them. They'll squander and gamble away not just state property but body and soul! Really, dear chap, I know *katorga* like the back of my hand! I see through each of them from the inside-out!"

A squanderer or player *can* actually gamble away body and soul, often losing his ration for six months or a year ahead; lose not only those government clothes such as he has but those he's inherited; lose even his spot on the sleeping platform; lose his life, his future, by exchanging names with the most hardened criminal sentenced to the lash, to indefinite *katorga*, to the chains prison. This is the type that often interested me and next day, at dinnertime, I set off for the prison all alone, without the warden, and asked the prisoners to get me the prisoner in question.

"But why d'you want him, barin?" queried prisoners including those who already sympathized with and trusted me…

"I want to see an out-and-out player."

The prisoners broke out laughing. "A player! Ah, you, barin! They talk and you believe 'em. His hands have never held a card in his life! But you call him a 'player'!"

"But what about the cassock?"

"What cassock?!"

The prisoners began whispering to each other. I could hear those I knew saying, "No problem! We can do it for him!… He won't talk!… He won't tell!…"

And so I was told the story of this "gambled away" cassock.

My squanderer turned out to be the peaceful modest Matvey, an eternal toiler who never sits around doing nothing. Two days earlier, he'd been sitting on the sleeping platform sewing together something as usual, when suddenly an Ivan from another section showed up.

"Lissen, you," he turned to my Matvey. "The warden wants me for something at the chancery. But I've sold my cassock. Gimme your gov'ment issue to wear. Gimme it, y'hear? If the warden sees me without a cassock he'll stick me in the 'dryer.'"[2]

If Matvey had been told that he himself was going to the dryer, he couldn't have been as pale as he was then. If he didn't give up his cassock the Ivan would go to the dryer because of him, and for this, they "stick a man in the dark," that is, throw a cassock over his head so he can't see who's beating him and beat as only prisoners can beat: they knee him in the back without leaving a mark, though the man will remember it for the rest of his life.

The cassock was given up. The Ivan, naturally, wasn't going to the chancery and hadn't been summoned there; he simply went to another barracks and gambled away the cassock at *shtoss*. No one stood up for poor Matvey, whose last piece of property was taken and for which he'd have to answer with his back. No one stood up for him because: "You don't talk back to Ivans!"...

As they were telling me this whole story they introduced Matvey himself.

"Well, how about that cassock, chap?!"

Matvey was silent.

"Don't be scared. The barin already knows everything. Nothing bad'll happen to you!" the prisoners urged him on. But Matvey maintained the same gloomy downcast silence.

In *katorga*, you can't trust anything. You have to see for yourself. I looked at Matvey and, based on his clothes (Matvey was wearing a pea-jacket that actually lacked any holes), he had everything together, absolutely stitched together. I asked him where his spot was and went to look at his little locker. The locker was truly Matvey's: there were a needle, thread, skein, a piece of cloth ("useful for making patches"), a piece of leather (tanned and stretched just right) and a piece of string ("you can tie up what you need to"). In a word, a locker typical not of a squanderer or a player but of a modest, economical and thrifty prisoner.

"How much did the cassock go for?"

"It went for five and 60 kopeks. They tot it up before the cock crows,[3] and have had it three full days now. That means it's gone up thirty per cent."

I gave Matvey a ruble. You should have seen his face. He couldn't even rejoice he was so dumbstruck. Amazement, almost fright, was written across it. The moment he silently held money in hand all the prison chaps rushed headlong out of the ward laughing happily.

I met him several times afterward and every time, regardless of the weather, he was unfailingly in his cassock. It seems he even slept in it. Upon seeing me, he'd doff his cap and grin from ear to ear. But to my question, "Well, how's the cassock?" he'd just laugh and wave his hand. "I've landed in the kasha, as they say!"

Three days after the recoup the warden and I ran into him.

"Aha, so you've found the cassock?" the warden said. Matvey was silent. The warden was gloating. "You see, I threatened him and he found it! You just need to know how to deal with them. I, dear chap, know *katorga*! This shows that I know. They themselves don't know how much I know them, the scoundrels."

I was not about to dissuade the dear fellow. What for?

40

THE INDEFINITELY-SENTENCED PROBATIONER GLOVATSKY

He's forty-seven years old and already recognized as incapable of any kind of work. Worn-out, crippled, hollowed-out by consumption, sentenced to never leave the chains his whole life—before you may actually be the most wretched man in the world. Lying down to sleep, he doesn't know if he'll wake up the next day or if prisoners will strangle him that night. He can't part with his knife for a second. Every minute, he fears for his wretched existence. So many undeserved calamities and falsehoods have fallen upon this man's head that you actually begin to believe Glovatsky—that he came to Sakhalin "innocently."

Nikolay Glovatsky, townsman of the city of Zvenigorodok, Kiev Province, was indefinitely sentenced to *katorga* for what happened to his wife. Having completed a course in saddling at the district vocational school, Glovatsky married in 1876 and left for military service in 1877. Returning after five years, he didn't recognize his wife. During that time she'd managed to become "spoiled," given her heart to others and no longer wanted a quiet family life. But Glovatsky was still in love with her. He tracked her down on the estate of Countess Dzelinskaya, in Volynia Province,[1] thinking to kidnap her so that, away from temptation, she'd turn over a new leaf and become an honorable woman. When he arrived she fled the estate, but Glovatsky quickly caught up to her and brought her home that evening. It was a stormy and difficult night. In Glovatsky's words, his wife was in a kind of frenzy. She was screaming, "You disgust me. Understand? You disgust me! I feel nothing but loathing for you. You are a frog to me. That's how foul you are. The lash would be easier, more welcome, than to be your wife!" She praised her lovers' merits and said things that made Glovatsky's head spin. He begged and pleaded with her to come to her senses, to be reasonable; he sobbed and threatened and, finally worn out completely, dozed off toward morning.

"But I woke suddenly," relates Glovatsky, "like I'd been poked. I look—my wife's not there. I lit a lantern and left the house to find her. While I was running all over the place she was hanging in the woods near the house. She'd hanged herself." Glovatsky, in his words, forgot what he was doing out of horror. No one had seen him bring his wife back that evening, they only knew she'd run away. And so he wanted to cover up the horrible incident. "I myself don't know why I did it," he says. He took the corpse from the woods, put it in a sack, carried it through the garden and threw it in the river. The body in the sack washed ashore somewhere several days later. To all questions Glovatsky repeatedly said, "Know that I don't know, and understand that I don't understand." A tragedy was pieced together based on the noose-marks on the dead woman's neck. Glovatsky was indefinitely sentenced to *katorga* for secretly bringing his wife home, hanging her and, so as to conceal the crime, trying to sink the corpse in the river.

Let him be guilty of this. We won't believe his story. You know they all say they're suffering "innocently." The secret of her death disappeared with the late Glovatskaya and to decide who is right, justice or Glovatsky, is impossible. But there were further events, the witnesses to which remain alive.

Glovatsky came to Sakhalin in 1888. As a penal laborer with an indefinite term he was incarcerated in the then still extant and terrible Voevodsk Prison, which even wardens say was "dreadful." Over the course of three years Glovatsky received more than 500 birch strokes, all for not successfully completing assigned tasks. In vain, Glovatsky turned for relief to then physician Davydov. This typically "Sakhalinized" doctor answered him as he always answered anyone: "You want me to let you sit in a room, don't you?" Glovatsky was considered a "loafer" for appealing to the doctor and assigned an even more difficult job—dragging timber from the taiga. "They flogged me three times for the same thing: there was no way I could drag that timber, I'd lost my strength!" recalls Glovatsky, who singularly remembers the woods. Generally, in these memories of Glovatsky's, as in the memories of most convicts from the former Voevodsk Prison, nothing resonates save the hiss of the birch rods and the lash. "As it was, Feldman's[2] children would run off to him, and you'd simply pray he'd be at home. Those children (Lord, give them all that's good and all the blessings of heaven and earth), they could stop a flogging. They'd be trembling, as it were, and pale: 'Papa, don't do this, don't flog him!' So they'd shame him and then he'd wave his hands. All *katorga* prayed for them." But this was no great deliverance. "That Feldman! Startsev was then the senior guard, and as it was, until Feldman heard from his children Startsev would beat you half to death. You could barely stand on your own two feet!"

It became more and more difficult for this worn-out man to live. In '92 he completely—as they say on Sakhalin—"fell beneath the wheel of fate." "I'm walking along lost in thought. Suddenly, there's a shout. 'Ain't you gonna doff your cap?' It's Mr Dmitriev. I'd been deep in thought and hadn't noticed him sitting on his porch. 'Give 'im a hundred!'" But Glovatsky got only fifty: after the fiftieth birch stroke he was taken unconscious from the mare and lay in the aid station for two days. He'd not fully recovered when there was another flogging. They were playing cards in the prison next to Glovatsky's space and the newly installed district commander, Shilkin, suddenly showed up. The stirrups hadn't been able to give the warning and the prison was caught unawares, cards strewn all over the sleeping platforms.

"Whose spot is this?" asked the commander.

"Glovatsky's."

"A hundred!"

"But I wasn't playing…"

"A hundred!" And they "laid" a hundred on Glovatsky, who wasn't even playing cards at all. This time Glovatsky got the full hundred, but after this punishment even Sakhalin's doctor at the time placed him in the infirmary for three days and allowed him a week to recover.

"I'd just been released, was walking along barely able to move my feet, and there's a voice. Mr Shilkin's before my eyes. Well, by God, I had such a fright, like he'd risen out of the ground before me. I hadn't noticed him sitting off to the side. 'So you're still here? You gonna be rude? Still got it in your head not to bow? Fifty.' They gave it to me. I see my soul leaving my body. Death was unavoidable."

At that time, one of the Kabardans[3] in Voevodsk Prison had put together a group to escape because he was scheduled for seventy lashes. He approached people for whom death would be as it was for him—nothing. Glovatsky joined this group. Four Caucasians, Glovatsky and a penal laborer named Beilin, who would play a terrible role in Glovatsky's life, escaped. After leaving the prison Beilin separated from the group to become a lone *brodiaga*. But the five remaining fugitives knocked together a raft and set off into the Tatar Straits.

"We're sailing along. Suddenly, it gets hazy. We see a cutter. We'd been spotted and Policemaster Dombrovsky was tearing along after us. It was hopeless, and we were awaiting our fate. Waves were knocking and tossing our raft, and so the wind caught a canvas jacket that was lying on it and blew it into the water. I tried to get it with a pole but, wouldn't you know, it floated away. The cutter's approaching. 'Make way!' shouts Dombrovsky. Given our situation, we were on our knees. They take us aboard the cutter. 'Why'd you throw that fellow in the water?' asks the policemaster. 'What fellow?' 'Don't deny what I saw myself,' he says. 'That fellow flew into the water and you're the Russian who pushed him under with a pole.' 'But that was a jacket, not a man,' I say. 'Sure,' he says. 'We caught you. I saw it myself.' They were going to take us to prison. Six had escaped but they're bringing back five, 'cause there's no Beilin. 'Where's Beilin?' they ask. We swear that Beilin went off alone. They don't believe us. 'The policemaster himself saw Glovatsky push the man into the water and drown him with a pole.'"

Hence there was an investigation into Glovatsky's murder of the prisoner Beilin, who was on the lam at the time.

"I'm sitting in the chains for two years while the court's carrying out a serious investigation of my case. I'm waiting for either the gallows or the lash—and they were gonna flog me to death anyway. I'm swearing and vowing to the administration and they're laughing, saying, 'If Beilin shows up from the beyond we'll release you. There's no other way.'"

Then, all of sudden in 1894, the *Iaroslavl* delivers Beilin to Sakhalin. He'd managed to get to Russia where he'd gotten into trouble, identified himself as a *brodiaga* origins-forgotten and was now, as a *brodiaga*, arriving for a one-and-a-half year stretch in *katorga*. Glovatsky rushed to Beilin. "Tell them. You know they're going to convict me for murdering you." Beilin answered, "No. I've traded a long sentence and the lash for a one-and-a-half year term." Glovatsky turned to *katorga*. "Chaps! Stick up for me! You yourselves know this is Beilin!" But Beilin, who had a little money, had bribed the Ivans and the Ivans—those jurors, judges and executioners—made it clear: "We'll murder anyone who reports him. It's custom: a *brodiaga* can't be found guilty."

Later, seeing he would be killed either way, Glovatsky himself made it clear to the administration. "I'm accused of murdering Beilin but Beilin's alive, here. There he is!" They checked their records, questioned prisoners and correctly identified Beilin. They closed the murder case and sentenced Glovatsky to eleven years in the "first category" and sixty-five lashes. "I'd escaped for all of six days!" he says, and tears well up in his eyes at the memory of those sixty-five lashes. Beilin also received an extended term and lashes for escaping. He decided to avenge himself. "I'll give ten rubles for Glovatsky not to stay alive!" (Ten rubles on Sakhalin, where I was told the Ivan Baldonov stabbed an exile-settler for just sixty kopeks. For ten rubles, a man can be hired on Sakhalin to butcher an entire family.) For ten rubles,

Ivans were hired to lead Glovatsky to an out-of-the-way place. But for twenty kopeks, someone revealed the Ivans' plan to Glovatsky.

"What could I do? I couldn't report it to the commandant. I'd be killed either way."

Glovatsky began packing a knife and trying to stay alert. One time, towards evening, when he'd entered an out-of-the-way place, a gang of Ivans attacked him and one, Stepka Shibaev, threw a noose around his neck. However, Glovatsky managed to jam a hand into the noose and, with the other, stick a knife into Stepka's gut. The Ivans backed off. "What's the matter, you villains?" Glovatsky shouted at them. Bending over Shibaev convulsing in death pangs, he said, "Well, you bastard, look what Glovatsky's learned." A murder in prison! Officials showed up and took the dying Stepka to the infirmary and arrested Glovatsky and put him in a special cell. Meanwhile, the Ivans got together and smashed open his cell-door and beat Glovatsky half to death. They broke his arm, split his skull and "messed up his insides." Fortunately or unfortunately, guards arrived just in time and managed to pull the half-dead and unconscious Glovatsky from out of these vicious persons' hands. Glovatsky's been crippled ever since. He even has difficulty speaking, and gasps for breath.

They launched an investigation into who did it but no one knew anything.[4] Investigators interviewed the very Ivans who, of course, had assaulted Glovatsky: "Glovatsky cruelly murdered Stepka!" Glovatsky, who'd simply been defending his life, was sentenced to the "first category," to the chains prison for life and to thirty lashes. But he didn't get the lash. How could the nearly dead be lashed? The doctor pronounced him unable to withstand corporal punishment. But now, for the rest of his life in the chains, Glovatsky must day and night fear every minute because the Ivans have sentenced him to death for Beilin and Stepka.

"Here we have a sufferer indeed!" Knokht, the prison warden, was telling me.

"And what will you do?"

"What can I do? There was an investigation!"

I turned to the penal laborers. "Why have you stayed quiet?"

"What can we do? Poke our noses in, say the Ivans were hired to kill him? They'll kill us!"

Beilin is being held in the same prison. I spoke with him.

"You know that an innocent man was framed because of you. Why don't you speak up?"

"It won't do me any good. I don't care about others. Every man for himself."

Glovatsky never leaves his ward. A guard escorted him through the prison yard for my meeting with him. Otherwise, he'd have been killed.

Fig. 29: Drs R. A. Pogaevsky, L. V. Poddubsky, and N. S. Lobas (left to right)

"I always have a knife at my side. The Ivans won't forgive me Stepka. They've said they'll kill me, kill me. So I live here and wait."

I must for some reason add that this most wretched man in the world, doomed to die in the chains, pleaded when I spoke to him not for himself but on behalf of someone else, saying, "It's very hard for him."

41

KATORGA TYPES

Gray faces and cassocks. How monotonous the throng of penal laborers is! But when you know it better, enter into its existence, you will distinguish in this gray mass infinitely various types. I'm becoming familiar with the chiefs, with those who it may be said compose the "prison atmosphere," that atmosphere in which crimes are born and everyone chokes and by which, little by little, the honest and the good fall.

If you enter prison at dinnertime, what of course first draws your gaze is a small locker where there are bottles of milk and a display of boiled eggs, pieces of meat and white bread. There are also sugar and cigarettes. You may be quite assured that somewhere beneath the sleeping platforms vodka and cards have been expertly concealed. This is the *maidan*. Next to this buffet you will see, for the most part, a Tatar *maidanshchik*. Initially, in Siberian *katorga* times, *maidany* were operated exclusively by *brodiagi*. *Katorga* was richer then; the Russian people considered it a sacred duty to give to the "unfortunateers" and prisoners received loads of alms, such that a party of convicts marching through the expanse of cities and countryside would arrive in *katorga* with riches. Back then, *maidanshchiki* became rich in prison by the thousands and *brodiagi* would clean the prison out. From this stems *katorga*'s present-day hatred and disdain for *brodiagi*. This historic hatred pitted one generation against another and *katorga* still retaliates against *brodiagi* for these historic grievances. It avenges their age-old oppression, selfishness and cupidity. Financial power has now passed from *brodiagi*'s hands to those of the Tatars. The Tatars clean out poor Sakhalin *katorga* like *brodiagi* cleaned out "rich" Siberian *katorga*. This is the reason for that terrible hatred toward a Tatar that I was unable to comprehend, when in the steamer's hold prisoners almost killed this Tatar because he'd accidentally stepped on someone's foot. This ethnic hatred wears an economic lining. All of Sakhalin's wealthy—those well-to-do exile-settlers who display such haughtiness—made their fortunes for the most part in prison through the *maidan*.

"Senseless!" I reproached a penal laborer, when he told me how a certain haughty exile-settler had been knifed. "He was your mate! It was indeed difficult, he did grow rich off your blood, but then again, you murdered him!"

"It *was* difficult!" the convict actually laughed. "I've some regrets, your esteemed honor, but you should be pitying us! It was hard! While I was in prison the *maidan* owned me; so many folks was ruined 'cause of it!"

The *maidan* is the prison's snack bar, tavern, tobacco shop, gambling casino and pawnshop. The prison sells it the right to exploit, and the *maidan* is usually leased for one month or, with haggling, up to a year. The *maidanshchik* pays fifteen kopeks to every prisoner in the ward if they play only "prisoner's preference" with him, and twenty kopeks if they also play *shtoss* and "to-the-death."[1] In addition, the *maidanshchik* has to pay one ruble fifty kopeks to a pair of ward attendants, typically the most wretched *zhigany*, who are obliged to empty the waste vats, sweep or, more accurately, move from place to place the dust, and wash the prison or, more accurately, soak and smear about the viscous muck. The *maidanshchik* has to retain a stirrup, who for fifteen kopeks a day stands at the doors and calls out "Spook!" if a guard's coming, "Six!" if the commandant's coming or "Water!" if there's any danger in general. The prison in return is obliged to protect the *maidanshchik*'s interests and beat within an inch of his life anyone who, after a while, doesn't pay the *maidanshchik*. The prison pays no mind to the conditions under which a comrade owes the *maidanshchik*. The *maidanshchik* simply shouts, "Why, you so-and-so's, you'll take my money but won't deal a beating?" And the prison beats him to death. "You owe—so pay up."

The most profitable and welcome among the *maidan*'s items is vodka. Its price fluctuates depending on time and circumstance, but in the correctionals' prison the usual cost for a bottle of weakly diluted spirits ranges from one ruble to one ruble 50 kopeks. The vodka is very weak, leaving just a nasty taste in the mouth, and I witnessed Sakhalin's oldest penal laborer, Matvey Vasilevich Sokolov, the grandfather of Russian *katorga*,[2] start constant arguments over this.

"Then why give me all your money! You yourself comes to the *maidan* to drink: 'Wheresy-theresy's the vodka!' You calls on me, sends me to the kitchen so's to pour a cup. Here it is, the vodka!"

The costs of other items in the *maidan* are as follows: a bottle of milk, which at most should go for three or four kopeks, the *maidanshchiki* sell for a five-piece. Eggs, a hundred of which they get for one ruble twenty kopeks, they sell for three kopeks each. White bread, gotten for four kopeks a pound, is sold for six. Pork (there's no other meat in prison; exile-settlers don't sell beef because they need cows for homesteading), that is, boiled pork cut into three-ounce pieces, sells for five kopeks apiece, and a pound of raw pork for between twenty and twenty-five kopeks. A piece of sugar costs a kopek. A cigarette is a kopek.

This is all easy money. You can see for yourself how such prices lead to the issuance of credit! The principal means of income for *maidany*, as it is in our clubs, is cards. The *maidanshchik* receives ten percent from the croupier and five from the punter. Moreover, *maidanshchiki* engage, of course, in money-lending and in purchasing and selling stolen goods. Almost everything earned, stolen or beaten out of the prison ultimately ends up in the hands of the *maidanshchik*.

The *maidanshchik* plays a huge role during "exchanges," which in prison language are called "marriages." A marriage typically proceeds like so: If in prison there is a long-term convict wishing to exchange his name and "fate" with a short-termer, he enters into company with the Ivans and snorters, who obligatorily call for the *maidanshchik*'s participation. They find an obviously newly-arrived short-term prisoner, usually a poor one, and begin shooting for him. When you sit beside a fellow for twenty-four hours you involuntarily study his habits and character and get to know his susceptibilities and little weaknesses. So the company begins its work. The *maidanshchik* suddenly initiates an unusual friendship with the designated victim and supplies the hungry man on credit.

"Youse got nothing. Youse wary. I see youse a nice chap. Youse been taken from home, maybe given some alms, but youse gotta earn money or youse gonna steal. I trust ya. Youse an honest chap… And don't youse want a little vodka?" The *maidanshchik* gives him a cup of vodka. "Drink, drink! We'll settle up later!"

Having become tipsy, the prisoner asks for another. He becomes tipsier still. Then a neighbor "shoots" him.

"What are ya? A *fartovy* guy! Ya sit in on cards an' there'll *always* be vodka and more… See over there, that's the stuff. You'll rake in so much cash and then you'll be living, vodka or no vodka! Ya ain't timid, boss!"

"I don't have no money…"

"But just ask the *maidanshchik*. He'll take care of ya. He'll give ya a draw. Hey, uncle…" he calls to the *maidanshchik*.

"What? A little cash on the draw? Play, I'll cover youse, we'll settle up later!"

Then onto the scene arrives the "master" prepared to safely beat the simpleton, whose attention has been drawn to the few rubles they've given "to prime" him into gambling.

"Clever! Outstanding! What about him?! Go, go!" the Ivans crowding round egg him on.

"Whatta high-flyin' bird! He ain't lackin' for nothing! Should I serve up a little vodka?" proposes the *maidanshchik*.

Intoxicated from booze and success, the hero cries out, "Two rubles a trio! Six fifty-kopek pieces a pip!"

"What about him?! Wow! Go! That goes to the kitty—add it to the debt! Throw, you clumsy devil, you don't want to lose, do ya?…"

"The kitty!… The kitty!… The kitty!…"

In a word, by morning, when the hero is sleeping off his hangover, he's lost everything, even his government bread ration for a year ahead… He'll be barely visible from hunger. Then along comes the second-hand dealer.

"Rested up, dear fellow?! Off with the jacket and trousers! Remember how last night you sold 'em to me?!" The hero recalls with horror that last night it seems something of the sort did actually happen! "You mayn't remember but the prison remembers! They watched everything go!" The dealer turns to the Ivans.

"Right before our eyes!"

"Don't forget to give me your rations as well. You lost for a year ahead. Or didja forget? Those what's forget, chap, gets a drubbing. Prisoners' way—s'well known."

Then comes the *maidanshchik*.

"Youse was acting strange last night, dear fellow! Now we wants our pay. Youse ran up a tidy debt to me through the *maidan* and I paid yer losses. Lay it out! Where's the cash?"

"But you know I said last night…"

"That's a diff'rent matter, dear fellow! Last night's talk was last night. I need the money now, to pay for the goods. But if youse owes and don't pay, then we're in a jam. Chaps, what is this? A robbery?"

"Where's all the order gone in prison?" shout the snorters. "They ain't paying the *maidanshchik*! We makes a deal with the *maidanshchik* for the *maidan*, but they won't pay him! Who's gonna run the *maidan* after this? How's the prison gonna live? What's happened to our ways?"

"Let's trample him!" announce the Ivans. "In *katorga* it ain't custom that if you owes you don't pay!"

Everything that was gambled away counts as a debt. Death by starvation and the breaking of ribs lie in the future. At this moment there comes to the befuddled short-termer the "twister"-prisoner, *katorga*'s toreador.

"You want I should help you outta poverty?"

"Merciful one!"

"Lissen up and don't breathe a word. There's some long-termer looks like you. You can hire yerself out for *katorga*."

"For some twenty years? Squander a lifetime?" the prisoner, assigned to *katorga* for all of three or four years, peers in horror at the demon-tempter.

"It doesn't matter—there's no life for you. Either they'll kill you 'cause yer not paying the *maidan* or you'll kick the bucket from hunger! So you lissen up well. Yer a young fellow, don't know the ways, but I'm a twisty guy, I know all the ins-'n'-outs. And why stick around forever? We provide for first-raters. *Katorga*'ll do all it can for you! We're always springing yer kind! So many have escaped. That one, that one, that one!…" The twister spews forth imaginary names. "Ain't you lissenin'? You should lissen to others much wiser. I escape, calls myself a *brodiaga*, and if no one betrays me I gets just a year 'n' a half. It's beeyutifull! You won't be livin' the life of a husk! So, dear fellow, go to the long-termer and get down on yer knees, so's he'll trust you. There's many of us kind."

If the potential "husk" doesn't agree, the twister has only to blink. "Beat him!" screams the *maidanshchik*, and *katorga* commences to torture the incorrigible debtor. The first time they beat without crippling, kicking for the most part between the shoulder blades and certainly not in the "mug," so as "not to tear apart" the exchanger. But they warn him: "There'll be more-a that for ya, ya shithead! We'll beat ya 'til ya give every last kopek to the *maidan*!"

Ivans and snorters don't let him out of their sight, "so's he don't hang hisself."

Starving, beaten and utterly despairing, the man goes before the long-termer and says, "Agreed!"

"Remember! I didn't call on you, you yourself asked. Don't go back on your word later."

And there begins a transaction in human life. The transaction is usurious: the long-term prisoner is ostensibly paying off to the *maidanshchik* the exchanger's huge fictitious debt. But Ivans and snorters, witnessing this, add to the total so as to extract every penny they can from the wretch in this affair.

"Give him what you owes him!" wail the snorters.

"Give him what?" the prisoner who's hiring himself out makes a face. "For goodness sakes, I'm busted. The *maidan*'s been paid! The second-hand dealer has his dues! Rations for a year ahead are paid for. Give what?"

"Well, at least gimme a five-piece!" some Ivan disingenuously protests. "Don't take offense! You're a good chap, and that would be a token."

"I can't give from nothing!"

"Wanna split the payout in half?" a snorter whispers to this impoverished Ivan. "I'll stand up to speak for you, 'cause they're doing you nothing. You want me to do that?"

"Speak up!"

"A five-piece's been spit out!" the snorter commences to orate. "But it ain't sinful to hand out a red 'un. Don't begrudge this fellow, his name's really on the line. Won't be no sin to give a red note!"

"He should give a five-piece!"

"A red 'un!"

"There ain't no value to those in *katorga*!"

"It's real money, ain't no forgery."

"So you says, devil! That's a red giveaway! Let's have his name, patronymic and surname!"

"Then it's a deal! Let it go, Sidor Karpovich! That's the spirit!"

"This here marriage is a joy for you and the prison. Don't you need a little vodka from the *maidan*, Sidor Karpovich?! Let's sprinkle the young couple.³ For the love of God, let them have love and concord!" jokes *katorga*. "*Maidanshchik*, you clumsy sonofabitch, don't you know your business? Here's a wedding and you ain't serving no vodka?!"

A man has sold his life, his future, for ten rubles. The usual price of a human life in *katorga*, the usual fee for an exchange, ranges between five and twenty rubles. The snorter, per the arrangement, will himself take half of the assessed ten rubles for having "knocked up" the price, but the remaining five will be won back by the "master" or taken by the *maidanshchik* to cover the debt. "That's what they paid for you, and so what you yourself should pay! No cryin' over spilt vodka, as they say." Or they'll simply rob the drunk and sleeping man. For the prison it's neither here nor there. "Every man for himself!"

A certain tradition is then piously observed in the prison: the man who's sold his "fate" drinks until senseless, so as not to feel the pain. "Quiet your proffered soul," they say!

The short-termer trades clothes with his exchanger. If he didn't previously wear fetters, leg fetters are "fitted" onto him; his exchanger tells him his history, then he is obliged to tell him his, so as to be consistent under interrogation. Then they "adjust his characteristics." If the long-term prisoner is identifiable by certain missing teeth, then the exchanging short-termer pulls or knocks out the necessary number of teeth. If there are identifiable birthmarks, marks are burned in the corresponding places with silver nitrate. This is all done openly and in the presence of the whole ward.

"You remember everything?" they ask the exchanger.

"I remember."

"Chaps, you've seen everything?"

"Everything!" answers the prison.

They prevail upon the *maidanshchik* to serve vodka, and the "wedding" concludes. The man has sold his life, taken another's name and become a husk. The contractor is henceforth his "master." If the husk were to begin thinking of telling officials about the wedding and betrays his master, he'll be killed. *Katorga* knows no other punishment for doing so.

Here it is, morning, and there awakens, again with a hangover, a new long-term penal laborer. He is not himself. Another walks through the prison under his name while he bears the punishment for his reckless sinning. Before him is twenty years' *katorga* and, on occasion, the lash. Punishment for a crime he never committed. On his legs are fetters—another's. His crime—another's. His fate—another's. His name—another's. No, now all this is not another's, but his. "It's true!" laughs *katorga*. "A fellow 'becomes someone else.' " How should such a man feel? *Katorga*, that sage of human nature, follows him at first. "Will he hang himself?" Everything might then be found out... But later, he gets used to it... "A scurrilous fellow gets used to everything!" a certain educated penal laborer told me, tears in his eyes and recalling Dostoevsky's words.

These "weddings" thrived especially in the terrible Siberian transit prisons of old. But are they thriving now, with the existence of photographic identity cards? Here are the facts. No earlier than autumn of this year, during the disembarking of a party from the *Iaroslavl*, such an exchange was discovered. The celebrity participating in this exchange, whom I mentioned at the very beginning of my travels, was one Ivan Proidi-Svet.[4] This person has become rather mythical. Over a span of three years "*Brodiaga* Ivan Proidi-Svet" was repeatedly delivered to the steamer for transport to Sakhalin, and each time before leaving the steamer received a telegram: "Return the *brodiaga* delivered under the name 'Ivan Proidi-Svet' because he is not authentic." Who and where this Ivan Proidi-Svet is remains unknown. You'll recall that in my story about Agafia Zolotykh some other prisoner was freed instead from Sakhalin and, upon delivery to Odessa, escaped. Similarly, Moscow's once-infamous murderer "The Flea" became a quasi-mythical figure on Sakhalin. There was a Flea in every prison who always ultimately proved "not to be authentic." At one time two Fleas were on Sakhalin but neither was the authentic, elusive one whose very elusiveness had earned him the sobriquet "The Flea." Exchanges take place in Sakhalin prisons and during the transfer of parties from post to post—so how can photographs be traced when there are thousands of them? Who do you search for? Photographs are taken and stuffed into a cabinet, but the prison's convicts go on in the usual way…

I've digressed somewhat, but in speaking about *maidanshchiki* it's necessary to talk about exchanges because this type is never so clearly defined. Usurer, barkeep, casino owner—he reminds you of some huge spider sitting in the corner and sucking the blood from the criminals and wretches drawn into his web.

Are any kinds of measures taken against *maidanshchiki*? They try. The Rykovsk Prison warden proudly told me there were no more *maidanshchiki* in his prison, and minutely detailed how he'd accomplished this. This did not preclude me, when I was in the prison that same day and needed matches, from buying them at… the *maidan*.

"Asmodeys" are the "Pliushkins"[5] of *katorga*. A prisoner who hoards money and denies himself to the utmost is called an Asmodey. Probably nowhere else is this passion—miserliness—evident to such an abnormal degree. Should a prisoner in this world of squanderers develop miserliness, then it becomes truly powerful and swallows the man whole. An Asmodey will even sell the 100 grams of soap and quarter-brick of tea he gets every month.

He miserly sells half his daily bread ration and manages to wear his government-issue clothes throughout two issuance terms, though by the end of the first they're usually in tatters. An always half-starving ragamuffin even among prisoners, he must be alert every minute so as not to be robbed, and continually digs his money out and stuffs it in another place so as not to be spied upon by a dozen pairs of sharp vigilant eyes. Or else he always carries his money with him in a pouch next to his body, fearing he'll be stabbed any second.

To starve yourself, to carry on a ceaseless struggle with the inmates of *katorga*, to fear for your safety, to poison yourself and your undeniably vile existence—and for what?

I somehow found myself in the Derbinsk almshouse.

"Look, a barin, a barin!"

An old blind *brodiaga* was asleep on the platform. His cassock had slipped and on his chest, barely covered by some disgustingly filthy rags, lay a pouch of money suspended from his neck. Thus wearing his cherished pouch, he'd not slept otherwise for ten years.

"Tsk!" winked one of the old penal laborers, and softly poked the old man in the arm. The blind old man awoke like he'd received an electric shock and, not letting go of his pouch, instantly grabbed a "shiv" (prison knife) from under the pillow with his other hand. He sat on the edge of the sleeping platform staring blankly through his cataracts, cocking his head towards the sound trying to locate the danger and resembling at that moment an alert owl. When everyone's laughter spilled over him he understood that a joke had been played and began to curse furiously. And, really, it's difficult to say who was more horrible and disgusting: these depraved old alcoholic gamblers or this Asmodey, sitting here for ten years with a pouch in his hand and a knife under his pillow.

So as to increase his own wealth the Asmodey often engages in usury. There are two names for usurers in *katorga*. A Tatar usurer is called a "mother" and Russian usurers are called "fathers." The assessing of a prisoner's property is usually done "before the cock crows," that is, at night, before morning roll call. "You gamble at night," they say, during which a fair percentage of five kopeks per ruble is assessed, though the percentage is usually higher and depends upon how much money they need. There are no rules covering these unsecured loans. "However much they've agreed to, then it's settled." Loans are made in return for government items, for thievery, for murder. Paupers and players—the prison—are entirely in the hands of the mothers and fathers. A whole bunch of crimes on Sakhalin are explainable by what the mothers and fathers demand: murder or repayment.

In Aleksandrovsk's chains prison there's an interesting character named Boldanov. He was exiled for butchering an entire family. On Sakhalin, on the first day of Easter, he murdered an exile-settler for sixty kopeks.

"But how could I know how much he had," he was telling me. "I couldn't count what was in the stranger's pocket. It was a holiday, the fellow's strolling along—it's understood he should have money."

"But, to kill a man for this?"

"I was thinking I'd get back what I'd lost."

"But did a father tell you to do it?"

"A certain one of them did! If you get mixed up with them you can get anything, but it's 'goodbye life.' They takes your rations and you can't crawl out from under debt... You hands over your jacket and they takes your hide. No, everyone needs to worry about his own life. Every man for himself."

In speaking about fathers, mothers and Asmodeys it's impossible not to bring up their closest assistants, the "second-hand dealers,"[6] and their most terrible and implacable foes, the "twisters."[7] By "second-hand," the prison language means old, mostly useless, things or rags in general. When prisoners use this word to mean old clothes it is to judge their quality. The second-hand dealer is a junkman. Walking through the ward, he shouts, "Who'll sell, who'll buy?!" He buys and sells prisoners' things and makes trades; that is, for a new thing he'll give an old one along with some money.[8] Second-hand dealers work for the most part on commission for the fathers. But often, having bought stolen goods on the cheap, a dealer will begin doing business at his own risk, joining the fathers and *maidanshchiki* and acquiring enormous weight and influence. And in the presence of this sort of ill-starred prisoner passing through the ward with the traditional exclamation, "Who'll sell, who'll buy?!" you unwontedly think: "How many human lives does this fellow hold in his hands?"

We've already met the twister-prisoner when he persuaded the future husk to agree to a wedding with a long-term penal laborer and to sell his life for five or ten rubles. With fondness and a certain admiration *katorga* calls "twister" that prisoner who'll go through fire and water, copper pipes and wolves' teeth. Such a prisoner should know precisely how to fool the authorities; but he's especially renowned for dealing with Asmodeys. To win the trust of even the most dangerous Asmodey, to promise him benefits, to tempt him into some kind of deal, to swindle and wipe out or simply espy where the Asmodey stashes his money, and to steal it or "extend" it to thieves—this is the twister-prisoner's specialty. And in this speciality he approaches virtuosity, displaying at times a genius that is part pretense, cunning, wit, tenacity and treachery. "Twisting round the finger," say prisoners about a good twister and his victim. Another perennial victim of the twister happens to be "Uncle Sarai." *Katorga* uses this name for every simple-minded and gullible prisoner. "Uncle, you'd swallow a whole barn! Along with a full cart and its master!" From this comes the expression, "Uncle Sarai." ("A Kolyvansk knucklehead!"[9] *katorga* still calls such characters in its unique jargon.) But deceiving the simple-minded and gullible Uncle Sarai I'm writing about does not constitute glory for the twister. For him, there is greater glory in tricking Asmodeys. To trick an Asmodey is a fundamental pleasure for all *katorga*: enslaved, it deeply hates and despises them (but obeys and treats with respect the fathers as people of strength and power). These really are paupers, paupers to the extent that when a prisoner suddenly dies in prison, the corpse is robbed without fail and his jacket, underclothes, shoes—everything—is turned into "old clothes."

To finish with prison's esteemed personages, besides *maidanshchiki*, fathers, twisters and pecuniary second-hand dealers there remains for me to introduce you to still one more type—the "returnee."[10] So called is the penal laborer who has escaped Sakhalin, reached Russia and been "returned" under his own or a *brodiaga*-surname. The returnee is an invaluable comrade for every group of prisoners planning to escape. He knows all the ins and outs, all the taiga paths and river fords on Sakhalin. He knows "how to get through." There are favored places for escaping—"fashionable," one might say. In the past, Pogebi, that place where Sakhalin is the nearest to the mainland and the Tatar Straits only several versts wide at most, was in fashion. (Characteristically, Pogebi or "Pogibi"—from the word "to perish"[11]—is a Giliak term apparently recast by penal laborers!) Then, when checkpoints in "Pogibi" became too effective, Sartunai—a place further south on Sakhalin—became fashionable. When I was on Sakhalin everyone was trying for the mouth of the Naira, even further south.

"And why?"

"Returnees say it's possible. It's a possible place."

Shirokolobov, the terror of all Sakhalin, of both officials and prisoners, went to the Tamlovo in the extreme north to find a "new place." However, exhausted, starving and bloated from hunger, he had to give himself up to the Giliaks…

The returnee is an invaluable comrade-in-arms who can sell most needed information. In my little collection is the blood-stained *brodiaga* notebook of the notorious returnee Pashenok.[12] He was killed during a remarkably daring escape and the notebook, smeared with blood, fell out of his blouse. It is a valuable notebook. In it are noted: "the 1st stream 60 versts from 'Pogibi' is the Tengi; 2nd is the Naide; 3rd is the Tamlovo"; etc. All Sakhalin's rivers are there. Then all the settlements along the way, from Sretensk to Blagoveshchensk to Khabarovsk and through the whole of Ussuri Territory, are listed and the number of versts noted as well with surprising precision: 2,271 to 1,898.[13] Additionally, the addresses of trustworthy persons are listed:

"Ivan Vasilevich Cherkashev, shop in the new bazaar.

"Nikita Iakovlevich Turetsky, corner of Gusevskaya and Zeiskaya, his own home."

Etc.

There are protectors in all possible cities of Eastern and Western Siberia and European Russia. All the information a fugitive needs.

A returnee may furnish a fugitive with letters of recommendation. Here's a sample of such a prisoner's letter of recommendation found on a captured fugitive:

To: Iu. Gaponiko.
  My dearest comrade Iulis Ivanovich Gaponiko,[14] I humbles to asks you to take this man, as you woulds me, to Iakov.

Such letters use pseudonyms, in case of capture. Among returnees are celebrities who, in their day, have been in many prisons and exerted influence. A recommendation from such a person may be of great help in prison. There is, for example, the celebrated returnee Pazulsky. Having been arrested together with him in Odessa, the ex-banker Iovannovich obtained from him a recommendation for all Siberia, and this significantly eased the ex-banker's journey.

Returnees have a particular specialty. Finding a trusting prisoner with money, they persuade him to escape and then rob and murder him and return to prison. They'll say their comrade fell behind or that they quarreled and he went off alone, and so the returnee came back "because I was hungry." There are people who in this way have murdered up to six comrades in their time. These crimes are frequent.

One has to operate on the sly, because *katorga* kills.

With the returnees, our tour of esteemed personages ends. I'll now proceed with you to those outcasts even among a world of outcasts. To people even *katorga* despises. Here we meet first of all the "crumbers" or "piecers."[15] *Katorga* doesn't like those among it who "get ahead in the world" and become a headman, cook or baker. As well it should, for these privileged positions are impossible to reach by a clean path. To worm one's way into being a Sakhalin headman, that is, to be free from labor and become in a certain sense a commandant of penal laborers, comes only at the price of a complete renunciation of virtue, by flattering and groveling before the commandant, bribing guards, perhaps informing and denouncing. Earlier, in certain prisons, convicts were flogged not by executioners but headmen. Thus, in coming before the headman a fellow had at the same time to be ready to come before the executioner. As to the quality of rations, that is, whether or not prisoners are being served half-soaked bread by a baker holding back flour for his own use, sometimes only a "scolding" and the warden's intercession can resolve this. *Katorga* calls by the scornful names "crumbers" or "piecers" those cutting off the last "piece" and taking the last "crumbs" from prisoners.

"I'm going to crawl before the 'commandant,' too!"

"You're a prisoner and a prisoner you'll remain!"

Katorga doesn't like those who try "to raise themselves," yet despises those who debase themselves. We're already familiar with the suborn type. So called is the prisoner who finds himself another's lackey. Besides carrying out typically lackey-responsibilities he's also obliged to defend his master, to settle accounts with his own flanks and beat whomever his master tells him to. Fathers' suborns, for example, are obliged to beat up faulty debtors. But if the debtor is stronger, then the suborn suffers defeat. Of course, even *katorga* cannot but regard with contempt those who've traded away their fists and flanks.

At the next level of human degradation we meet with a very prevalent type of "piper."[16] In prison language, "to start a-piping" means to start a quarrel. Pipers are those in prison who live only to start a commotion. Tattling on and ratting out one prisoner to another, these more or less well-to-do prisoners argue among themselves so as to gain something by apparently choosing a side. All the prisons teem with these pipers. There are many such people, and not just in prison; but in *katorga*—forever embittered, terribly suspicious, distrustful of each other, hungry and nerve-wracked; in *katorga*—where for sixty kopeks they'll kill a man, where having a penny in his pocket may get a man not only beaten but murdered; in *katorga*, pipers often play a terrible role. Terrible things often come to pass "over nothing." Having beaten to death a prisoner, or at the sight of a prostrate comrade with a "mashed-up belly," *katorga* often perplexedly asks itself, "Why's all this happened? How'd it come about? How'd it start?" and the pipers prove to be the reason of all reasons, having caused a commotion to gain something. The timid beaten prisoner comes to be a hard and fast friend of the old experienced piper, because he stirs that kasha from which you might get a bone.

On an even lower level stand the "throats."[17] You know this type a bit already. Over cards, in arguments in the prisoners' meeting, they're ready to stand up for whomever will give the most. "Drowning" the truth and defending an offender means nothing to them. *Katorga* despises such people; but they often wield influence over the assembly because there are many and they always act together. "Throat" is one of the most abusive names, and so a snorter, when you call him a throat, begins climbing the wall: "I'm a snorter. I love to snort in the meeting, certainly. But, that I should hire myself out to *anyone*..." And this phrase may perchance conclude with a knife in the side, a rock or a noose from behind a corner. This of course doesn't change the fact that snorters are, for the most part, throats, but they don't like when this is said about them. *Katorga* has two nicknames for the throat. One is the witty "another's supper"; the other is the historical "Sinelnikov peon."[18] The latter comes from the time when Sinelnikov would typically pay three rubles for the capture of a *brodiaga* in Eastern Siberia.[19] Since then, *katorga* has called a "Sinelnikov peon" a man who's prepared to sell out his neighbor. It's one of the most offensive names, and if you hear two fellows in *katorga* exchanging insults—"Shut up, 'another's supper'!" "Shut up, 'Sinelnikov peon'!"—this means they've descended to the penultimate level of human degradation and are prepared to pull out their knives.

And, finally, the lowest dregs of *katorga* is before us—the *kham*. There is no further drop. "*Kham*," in essence, simply signifies in the prison language a man who is another's lover. "*Zakhamnichat*" means to take it and not give it. A man who's left without even a scrap of the semblance of the conscience of a throat, suborn or piper is called a *kham*. They befoul the prisoners' environment. The *kham* is a traitor; for lack of a bread ration, for a small respite, he'll inform on escape preparations and reveal where fugitives have hidden. This type is encouraged by the wardens, because only through them can they know what goes on in prison.

"*Kham*" is a terrible name. The man who commits himself to being one is always, if not dead, in a life that is worse than death. A search, even a surprise visit by the warden, is enough for suspicious *katorga* to see that there's "something wrong" and begin pounding to death those it considers *khamy*. It's enough to say to the lowest *zhigan*: "Seems our *kham*'s 'making waves' (informing to the commandant)," and the *kham*'s ribs will start cracking. Mostly, it's simply enough for someone "to give a *kham* a slap" for no reason, and the whole prison will attack and beat up the *kham*. He's supposed to know what he's being beaten for. To "cover with darkness" means they bury the *kham* under cassocks and pound him to a pulp, then remove the cassocks to reveal a half-dead man.

42

INITIATION INTO THE PENAL LABORERS

Everyone, of course, has heard about initiation into the penal laborers, about the brutal tortures to which the prison, bitter and dying of boredom, subjects "novitiates." Why does the prison subject novitiates to these tortures, stories of which make your hair stand on end? As I've already said, partly out of boredom, partly out of the cruelty in everything and everyone and out of a wish to vent upon someone the boiling rage that chokes a man—and partly out of practical considerations: you need to know if a man will keep from complaining to the administration even if he's subjected to horrible tortures. It is indeed necessary to know a fellow who's joining the "family." Will he always and in every way be a trustworthy comrade?

I toured all Sakhalin's prisons and can with complete confidence say that the former terrible initiatory custom for joining the penal laborers, the custom of torturing novitiates, has passed into legend and is now no more. Back then the birch rod and knout whistled here and were reflected in the prison's ways. Now, these ways have softened. "Young" *katorga* only looks surprised when you ask, "But don't you have such-and-such and such-and-such customs?" Only the old men of Derbinsk's almshouse smiled and nodded their heads, as if meeting a friendly old acquaintance, when I reminded them of stories of earlier customary tortures. "That's the way it was! Certainly." And they gladly entered into those free-ranging descriptions by which a fellow always begins reminiscing about calamities survived. But young *katorga* can't at all remember these customs: "How and who'd they benefit?"

"Benefit"—here is the alpha and omega of contemporary *katorga*'s entire worldview. There's nothing surprising in this: *katorga*'s predominant element are robber-murderers, that is, people who've committed crimes for benefit. And these people's ways, customs and laws happen to subordinate others, those penalized victims of circumstance, of family tragedies, etc.

"Benefit"—this is everything. A penal laborer who'd committed a murder on Sakhalin was telling me about his crime and recalled that after it happened someone else, a not-in-the-least-guilty exile-settler, was arrested: "But I sprung him... Because he couldn't benefit me in my affairs." But if he "could have benefited" he would have screwed the not-in-the-least-guilty fellow and all *katorga* would have understood. "A fellow has to think of his own benefit. Every man for himself."

The whole of the contemporary initiation into the penal laborers consists of the prison trying to extract from the novitiate a benefit, that is, to take advantage of his inexperience and cheat him as much as possible. For this, *katorga* has several games that can only be played with novitiates: "kerchiefs," "crucifixes," "money-purse," "thimble," "bosses" and "black-and-red." There's even something altruistic in this initiation, given that a passion for easy and certain gain, indeed, a desire to cheat one's own brother, is encouraged and taught.

Having just arrived aboard the steamer, a party is held in quarantine, subjected to medical examination and divided, without any practical benefit, into the "healthy," the "weak" and the "entirely incapable of work," before being marched off to prison. While the party is sitting in quarantine for three or four days the prison seeks to acquire varied information. Either someone's brother, an accomplice or simply an old comrade has invariably arrived with the new party and one of these, risking the isolator and birch rods, will go around the quarantine making inquiries. Risking their hides, prison "barbers"[1] run to the quarantine and sniff out who among the newly arrived prisoners has snuck in some money, who played cards or wrote letters and petitions along the way—who, in general, has any money. They suss out everyone there—how many passengers donated to Easter convict-choristers, how many successfully paid off the executioner—so that by the time the new party gets to the prison, the prison already knows the disposition of its property and on whom to focus attention.

Despite being very crowded, the prison continues receiving more people and so some have to sleep beneath the platforms. The headman assigns the novitiate the worst place, of course, hoping to squeeze money out of him for a "good spot" that costs quite dearly in prison. Famished *zhigany*, their "fur a bit overgrown," sell their last remaining possession—their spots on the sleeping platforms—and crawl under them.

The novitiate still cannot come to himself and gather his thoughts; he's confused, befuddled by his new surroundings, doesn't know how to tread, how to carry himself; he sees only one thing here, which there's no getting around, and that's that everything depends on money, that without money you disappear and that the money you'll need to get by won't be forthcoming. It's at that moment he'll be taken advantage of.

The novitiate sits on the sleeping platform and watches with fear and curiosity the men he's been condemned to live with for many—oh so many— years. Through the prison walks a true Uncle Sarai character, some scatterbrained prisoner. The knotted corner of a kerchief hangs from his jacket pocket and into this knot a coin has clearly been tied. Another prisoner, having only just given the novitiate a kind word, quietly sneaks up behind the Uncle Sarai, winks cunningly, unties the knot, takes the twenty-kopek piece and ties up in its place a single kopek. The novitiate, winked at by the "trickster,"[2] beams: "I say, well done."

"Hey, uncle!" the trickster shouts to Uncle Sarai. "Does your Freemason-self have a kopek tied up in that knot?"

"Wheresy-whatsy kopek?" Uncle Sarai stupidly asks.

"But whatsy-what's tied up in your kerchief? You idiot, you devil! Disgusting pig! Take your tied-up kopek and go."

"You're a-tellin' lies! Lyin' demon! Ain't no kopek, but a twenty-piece!" Uncle Sarai stuffs the exposed corner of his kerchief into his pocket. A crowd gathers round.

"'A twenty-piece'!" the trickster mimics. "And you can tell the diff'rence 'tween twenty-pieces and fakes? You tied up a kopek and you wants to believe it's a 'twenty-piece'!"

"Akh, you bastard!" Uncle Sarai blurts out. "You shame me in front of all the gentlemen prisoners? You wanna bet ten silver rubles it's a twenty-piece?"

"Ten?!"

"Yes-yes, ten. Cat got your tongue?!" The crowd laughs.

The trickster whispers to the novitiate, "Lissen, you, I ain't got ten rubles. Bet a red 'un and afterward just give me a silver ruble!" The novitiate waffles. "You know it's a sure thing! You saw yourself!"

"Bet!" the crowd eggs him on. But then negotiations ensue and Uncle Sarai seems to get distracted by conversation and not to be paying attention.

"He's gonna bet for me!" announces the trickster, pointing to the novitiate. "Betting a red note!"

Both lay down their ten rubles.

"Give us the kerchief! You unties it!" they pass the kerchief to the novitiate. The novitiate unties the knot and blanches: a twenty-piece!

"That's right! And you said a kopek, little fool! Don't climb into another's pocket to count the dough," says Uncle Sarai.

"But this is a swindle!" exclaims the novitiate, clutching his money.

But they'll extort the ten rubles from him or, if he doesn't give it willingly, they'll beat it out of him. "You played, you pay. 'Twas fair." Only later does he realize that the feigning Uncle Sarai and the trickster, and everyone, are a united gang of *zhigany* and players. Sleight-of-hand simply explains it: Uncle Sarai had only to untie the knot while it was in his pocket, take out the kopek and replace the twenty-piece. They especially practice this sleight-of-hand prior to meeting a new party.

But a different scene is playing itself out in another corner of the ward. "Akh, you unbaptized Tatar! Goddamned 'mother'!" a prisoner is shouting in front of several novitiates at a joker who's just taken off the crucifix that was hanging under his shirt.

"How am I a 'mother,'" the joker screams, "if I'm a Christian fellow and have a cross on my chest?"

"You don't have no cross on yer chest, you mother!"

"Oh no? Bet a five-spot."

"Lads!" the prisoner turns to the novitiates. "We'll pool together five silver pieces and snub this mother's nose!"

Everyone saw how the crucifix was torn off, and in *katorga* they so badly need the money. They quickly pool together five rubles. The polemicist undoes his shirt. On his chest is a crucifix. This all consists, of course, in the fellow having been wearing two crucifixes. The novitiates are stupefied and demand their money back. "A swindle!" But they're up against the entire prison's fists. "You played, so pay! 'Twas fair!"

We'll not dally especially long with the novitiate who keeps peering in amazement into his money purse. "How's this? There were twenty rubles here, now there's ten. They must've been stolen! Well, I'll complain!"

"Try it, you filthy informer, 'n' you'll be leavin' in a wheelbarrow!"

They've played on him the same trick swindlers often arrange in the streets of Odessa and other big cities. Along with this prisoner they'd found a purse and were just getting ready to share the spoils, when before them arose as if from the ground the purloined purse's owner.

"It's mine!"

"If it's yers, take it!"

"Stop! What happened to the two silver rubles were in it? There were two silver rubles!"

"We didn't see no silver rubles at all."

"On the contrary, you're lying! What's this? Robbery? Might you be ripping us off?"

"Them's yer ways, demon! Quit yer barking!" This prisoner turns out his pockets and holds up his change purse. Out of necessity, the novitiate does the same. The owner of the two supposedly missing rubles searches for them in the novitiate's purse, obviously doesn't find them, and hands it back.

"Clearly, someone else took 'em! Please forgive me! I now see you're honest folks!..." And off he goes to find the two missing rubles. Only then does the novitiate, having glanced in his purse, see that during its inspection ten rubles were taken from it. This is again a matter of cunning and sleight-of-hand, in that at the time someone accidentally bumps into the novitiate, starts complaining and gets him to turn around for a second.

We proceed toward a group gathered around a player. A game of "thimble" is on. There are two thimbles, under one is a little marble, under the other, nothing. When the table is occupied during dinner and the sleeping platforms in use, the game is played on a small footstool. The player moves the thimbles so fast you can't tell which is covering the marble.

"I twists and I torments," orates the player. "Bet your guess!"

"Egad, you devil, demon, goblin! At the crack of dawn, first thing in the morning, he started that game!" shout those from behind the group surrounding the player.

"And how's it your business, villain?"

"As much as it's a violation of order! That's how!..."

"But how's it you've turned out to be the 'orderer'? Who called you to establish order? Why're you such a big-wheel?"

"Don't be barking! You sold your soul to read the stars, you devil..."

"Shut up 'fore yer watermelon gets split!"

"One'll get split..."

Hands suddenly reach into boot-tops and "shivs" (knives) go into motion. Faces turn bestial as the player forgets about the game and turns to face his offender. At that moment the prisoners peep to see which thimble the bread marble is under.

"Bet, bet a red 'un!" they whisper to a moneyed novitiate near the gaming area. "Bet! Why pity him?! He beats everyone! You've got it over him! Bet, you know for certain. Right there—put the money under the card..."

"What'll it be, you demons?!" those who were complaining are challenged. "Egad, what a quarrel you've started, you devils. But what's it to you? You don't like it, so what, you'll get none of this man's fire. He's a greasy fellow, 'tis true!" The one who'd protested the game is taken away. The player, grumbling and cursing, turns back to the thimbles.

"Well, what'll it be?"

"Everything's set. The wad's under the card."

The player reaches for the thimbles.

"No, you've already moved 'em!" the crowd protests. "The playing's over. As it is, so it'll be! This is what he's betting on!"

"And maybe you looked under them, you devils?"

"Look, none of the rogues standing here saw a thing. Who coulda looked? No, it's all correct! Game's been played!"

"So how come the wad's so big?!"

"Under the card is what there is! Play by the rules! You wants to win so bad this is gettin' fishy, you son-of-a-pike! You can pay up."

"Well, as you say! All's right and I won't complain. That's it, then?"

"That's it!" underscores the novitiate.

The player lifts the thimble, the thimble is empty and he takes the wad out from under the card. Again, it's a matter of sleight-of-hand, knowing how, when the novitiate turns around during the argument, to quickly and imperceptibly switch the two thimbles.

"Deuces" and "black and red" are almost one and the same game. Players choose as they wish, deuces or other cards. Three deuces are laid face-down, two black and one red. The dealer lays them down with such amazing rapidity you can't tell when the red goes down. But during the game they distract him with some dispute or run over to say something. The dealer turns around, and that moment some prisoner peeks to see where the red card is and marks it with a pencil. "Bet on this one," they whisper to the novitiate. The dealer finishes the argument or discussion, picks up the cards again and begins sliding them from place to place. "Ready!" Wishing to immediately double his wealth, the novitiate often bets everything he has on the marked deuce. He's given that very deuce to turn over—and reveals a black card! The dealer performs this card trick after the marking has been done, replacing the red deuce with a black one marked exactly the same way. Thus, a card-sharp can only be beaten by those not averse to risk.

As evening approaches here comes the novitiate gambled into the dust, swindled, often beaten up for refusing to pay, and so he lies down on the sleeping platform, thinking, "Well, such a people!" But a neighbor consoles him. " 'Cause of this you're now a true inmate. Proper, it is. Everyone passes through the same school. That's the way." He's wiped out and, as such, initiated into the penal laborers. *Katorga* doesn't like ownership or owners, and so their money ends up wandering throughout the prison: today it goes to one, tomorrow to another…

Some of the newly initiated reflect with melancholy and horror about the coming days of hunger and sundry needs. Others sense a cruelty in their souls and are filled with the dream of how they themselves will wipe out newcomers in precisely the same way.

43

EDUCATED PERSONS IN *KATORGA*

> What terrible torture
> To endure an era without end,
> To know everything, to feel everything,
>   to see everything,
> To hate everything involuntarily,
> And to contemn everyone in the world...
> —Lermontov[1]

Have you ever looked death in the eye? If so, you'll know that "time" (this is nonsense, this notion of "time") is conditional and that in reality hours, minutes and seconds do not exist. When the trigger is cocked and ready you will think, sense and feel more than you've thought, sensed or felt for a year.

I think I'm correct to put Lermontov's verse as the epigraph to this article and to use the word "era," for a year of *katorga*... is not twelve months along with your salary every twenty days. Neither is it "four seasons," as it is for people in the world; nor 365 days, as it is for everyone. It is millions of minutes, many of which are each a long eternity. All that I would alter of Lermontov's lines are the words "in the world" so that the line reads:

To contemn everyone around us.

And how can all these Ivans, snorters, *zhigany*, Asmodeys, *khamy*, suborns and crumbers not be contemned? To contemn is to be hail-fellow-well-met with them, because this is "your society"! Because you sleep beside them on the platforms, you eat and work together—you make your life with them! Were it only "hail-fellow-well-met."

No! *Katorga* hates the "barin." *Katorga* hates the barin for his weakness, his unfamiliarity with physical labor. "How can he work in our crew? We'll have to do his job for him." *Katorga* scoffs at the barin because he shuns the mud. "No! You've found yourself here, so suffer. There's nothing to canoodle! This is how it is!" *Katorga* distrusts the barin. "He'll sell out to become a clerk!" "Barin!"—*katorga* has no worse and no more contemptuous sobriquet; and so, when I call to mind the situation for educated people in *katorga*, an entire echelon of ghosts appears before me. Forward, ghosts!

Meet the wretched *brodiaga* Sokolsky,[2] sickly, epileptic, over-stressed and worn out. I know his real name: he's from a good family and studied at university.

"God! What, what I would not do to be rid of this accursed nickname, to be able to sink to their level so as not to feel—lying on the sleeping platform—that they're scared to talk to you, that they take you for a traitor, a turncoat, a potential informer. No! Any kind of scoundrel, anyone, even a *kham* (in our *katorga* tongue) who's ready to sell himself for a fiver, can call you 'barin.' Even *he* is closer to *katorga* than you are! But what, what sacrifices have I not made for them? I drink like they do, I play cards as they do. They designated me a scribe and I got up to mischief for their sake, so they could made some money out of me. To show I didn't want any sort of privileges I joined in a swindle selling counterfeit assignats. I helped them by hiding these assignats, and when I was found out I turned in no one. *Katorga*'s threatened me for many, many years, but still I—an outcast among 'outcasts'—am a 'barin'!"

This is Sokolsky! A man with such bright eyes who performs various roles with expansive and beautiful erudition. I talked so ardently with him for an entire morning that I (but not just I! Even *he*) forgot about his prisoner's jacket…

He knows and loves his Dostoevsky. We were discussing how different present-day *katorga* is from *Dead House*; we were arguing heatedly, when all of a sudden the warden of settlements paid me a call.

"Now then, old chap, be off and tell them to change my horses!" he ordered Sokolsky.

"I'm listening, your honor!"

I felt abashed, troubled and crushed for him, and became indignant. "Why are you doing this?" I said to the warden. "After all, you see he's at my place, that he's my guest."

The warden surveyed me with astonishment.

"You absolutely sympathize with these bastards! It's nothing—he's running an errand! That's what he does!"

When Sokolsky would "run" he would run off to look for me, and I'd run off to look for him.

"Ech! These talks have only started bothering me. I'm feeling like a human being. But this won't do! I came to you as a human being but I'm leaving as…"

"Sokolsky…"

"I'm not angry at anyone. Toward you? But how could you be otherwise? Toward him? He acted mildly, didn't swear. Only, it would have been better had he smacked me in the mug at that moment than to have sent me for horses like in Dostoevsky, with a 'Be off, old chap!' "

Sokolsky retreated into himself, like a snail withdrawing into its shell when carelessly disturbed by a rough hand. We had held each other in high regard, and he'd helped me much with information about *katorga*. But now, during our long candid discussions, he wouldn't engage in a debate.

"It doesn't matter! You'll be leaving and it'll be all the harder for me."

Meet Kozyrev,[3] a wretched youth with the look of a drowning man. He nevertheless completed the *gimnaziia*'s sixth grade and is the son of well-to-do parents. His family are wealthy Moscow merchants. He was a military volunteer and ended up in *katorga* for six years and eight months for insulting his sentry commander. Now he's sitting in the chains for a cheap... forgery. He has such an honorable sympathetic face. I well know that he's always ready to share his last: he's done and does this of necessity. Moreover, his relatives haven't forgotten him. They send him a lot, comparatively.

"Then why some cheap forgery?!"

"Ech, barin!" prisoners knowing of the affair honestly told me. "It wasn't for himself! *Katorga* made him do it. *Katorga* needed this forgery. They ordered it, and here he was, a scribe, and he did it thinking he'd profit! But what did it bring him?"

His future is dark and difficult. He won't endure his additional term of *katorga*; he'll try to escape, there'll be lashes and an indefinite term, and he'll sit as a probationer in the chains prison without ever leaving. So what will become of this "other" Kozyrev? Such people perish in *katorga*; they drown leaving just bubbles on the surface. Ultimately, they perish morally, without redemption.

In the village of Rozhdestvenskoe, in Aleksandrovsk District, a certain V works as a teacher. The man attended an elite academic institution. In *katorga*, this man supposedly hired himself out for five rubles to carry out a murder. An entire investigation was needed to show he didn't commit the murder. A certain dignitary from Petersburg known personally to V arrived on Sakhalin and wanted to see him, hoping to intercede for him back in Petersburg. "Pass on my thanks," V said, "but ask him to let it be. It's too late. I'm no longer suited to be 'there.' Let me stay here."

I possess a certain denunciation I obtained as a specimen of human degradation. The denunciation is false, vile and slanderous and calumniates ten not-in-the-least guilty people—his fellow colleagues—and concludes... with a request to give away the position of scribe for five rubles a month. This denunciation was written by a former engineer now engaged in counterfeiting banknotes.

This is Valentin, the veritable Valentin you so warmly applaud at the end of act four of *Faust*.[4] How beautiful it is! It's noble! Splendid! What could be greater, more estimable, than a brother who avenges his sister's honor? This is a crime for which society *demands* a response.

You demand, and so you'll see what comes of this, for I, too, saw my Valentin "onstage"—on the sleeping platform in Onor Prison's chains division. He stood before me with a puffy debauched face, the stench of warmed-over vodka washing over me. Since entering *katorga* he's been repeatedly charged with forging and selling documents.

But you know this man... Several (rather, many) years ago, Moscow was troubled by a terrible and bloody occurrence on one of its boulevards. A young man who was strolling came upon another and, not saying a word, ended his life on the spot with a pistol shot. In court, the reason for the murder was left unclear. "Out of cruelty!" sharply answered the defendant, not wishing to make known any of the details. In public, it was said that the murderer had avenged the violation of his sister's honor, that he remained silent wishing not to proclaim the girl's disgrace, that he sent the seducer a challenge to a duel and, when this was not accepted, resorted to the pistol.

I met with him in the dimness of the chains. He'd been accused of threatening the former warden—stupid threats made while drunk. Since entering *katorga* he's been repeatedly accused of forging documents.

"How did this happen?"

"How? I handle a pen well. I studied engraving because I was bored. *Katorga* knew of my talent and demanded I make a document for a certain fugitive, with stamps according to regulations. The first time I did it out of compulsion... But later on... later on, I did it again. I made three documents in return for an old, worn-out, stolen beaver hat..."

How do these people drown? Quickly. Perpendicularly. They drop to the bottom like an axe. Given a year or two, you might at first glance not even recognize that before you is a creature upon whose chest could hang the inscription "Here at one time lived a cultured human being."

Meet the well-known Odessan, Gr—ev. In view of his perpetually beat-up, scratched and always hungover physiognomy, you would never say that before you is a man who, just two years ago, was playing a lead role in society. "Y'know, I tripped, fell and injured my face!" he says, accounting for his scratches and bruises. His is a society of specialist-thieves, of certain imprisoned card-sharps and usurers. Gazing at this man, at his now impudent, now servile manner, you suddenly say, "Yes, this is a typical flunkey, a country clerk!" Listening to his acts of vileness and filth, about his forging of notes to obtain vodka, you can't believe that this man was ever—and barely two years ago—a man of circumstances, and of very good circumstances.

And here is K—r, a former officer, wretched youth and murderer as a result of having been viciously assaulted and wounded. Friends offered what help they could during his deportation to *katorga*, but he refused them. This wretch has suffered much on Sakhalin. Fate pushed him into being a clerk in the mining engineer's chancery, where he "took on the same affairs" as the earlier mentioned G. Made uncomfortable by the presence of this pure unspoilt youth (who wasn't so facile at looking out for himself), G told stories about him to the mining engineer, claiming that K had spoken disrespectfully about him and so forth, and the mining engineer requested K be put in the chains for a month. The wretch sat among a society of recidivist-murderers, the most serious of criminals, for an entire month.

Now that he's been rescued from there he's in charge of Aleksandrovsk's library and everyone is pleased with him. He's a quiet, modest, shy youth; yet beneath this passivity lurks profound drama and aches a serious wound. "Can you make it? Will you start babbling about your memories?" He's perishing; he drinks; and you encounter him in public at those very moments, when along comes some *brodiaga*, a deserter. God knows what they're liable to say to each other, especially when drunk. What can they possibly have in common? But he lowers himself to his level.

"Surely, you must hold yourself up to the mark? And not fall, not wallow in this filth?" I posed this question to people with experience of *katorga*. "Really, shouldn't you keep aloof?"

"That's impossible in *katorga*. They'll suspect you then. 'He must be an informer, he doesn't want to be around us, he's trying to join the administration!' Moreover, they'll simply be offended. They'll ruin and poison every minute, every second, of existence. They'll cause an abomination at every turn—and there are none more inventive at abominations than *katorga*'s dregs. These scum wear you out in order to please the powerful convicts."

"Well, make them treat you with respect, with consideration."

"It's difficult. They hate and despise the 'barin' very much."

"I was rather talented!" one educated man exiled for murder was telling me. "I wrote a letter for them, a petition, which they highly valued. Without compensation, of course. I gladly shared my learning with them. *Katorga* respects knowledge very much, though these people's attitude toward knowledge is generally that of commoners, of a child who loves apples but tears down the apple tree because it's so tall. Little by little it began to dawn on me that I was facilitating their inclinations. I happened to have a run-in with some literate *brodiagi* and Ivans. For the former, I dispensed with the fees, putting together petitions free of charge. The latter couldn't bear that someone besides them was getting all the attention in prison. I put a lot of effort into avoiding a clash with them. They insulted me, called me rude names. They were even ready to assault me. They accused me of informing and succeeded insofar as *katorga* stopped trusting me. They persuaded them that the petitions I put together purposely did not say what they were telling me. And they believed this idiocy! I'll put it to you briefly—I don't know how this will end if I'm not let out of the chains prison."

Do all the educated ones really drown? Are there really none who surface? There are. L surfaced, thanks to his nationwide and tragic infamy. But he happened to serve his *katorga* sentence under absolutely extraordinary conditions that I will speak of in due time, and it is apparent to me that he surfaced with the help of a sweet, kind young woman who fell in love with him and agreed to cleave her fate to his. I saw only this one "surfaced" youth. But what did this require? An entire life! A life youthful, blossoming and beautiful. To save him, this young woman, nearly a child, with a beautiful spirit and a rare heart—this extraordinary creation who'd fallen in love with him—had to leave home and family and voluntarily go to marry him; and she suffered so much, so very much, renouncing everything and telling herself, "I will sentence myself to lifetime exile in order to save him." Heroism was needed, a self-sacrificing for this youth's salvation; in a kind of payment, a youthful, pure beautiful life was exchanged for that of a criminal. A good woman, loving to the point of self-sacrifice, can save a man, but at such a price: her innocent self sentenced to *katorga*, to that most difficult *katorga*: to witness the suffering and debasement of a loved one. Only at such a price, the price of her own life, could she save another's.

"Sakhalin demands a life for a life and concedes nothing whatsoever."

I won't touch on the notion that "much is given to him from whom much is taken." My only task is to describe what has been taken, and this is much, very much. Neither hard labor, nor bad food, nor loss of rights, nor the at times illusory and apparently meaningless nothingness is horrible. The horror is that they toss you—a person who thinks, feels, sees and understands all there is with a spiritual anguish and sorrow—onto bare sleeping platforms alongside Ivans, throats and *zhigany*. That despair that envelops you in an atmosphere of filth and blood is horrible. The fetters are not horrible! Horrible is the transformation of a man into a trickster, an informer, a maker of counterfeit assignats. Horrible is the transformation from a Valentin into a "forger of documents" in exchange for a stolen worn-out hat.

What strong individuals have perished!

44

TALMA ON SAKHALIN[1]

The following took place in Aleksandrovsk Prison's chancery in the evening, when penal laborers on work detail appear before the prison commandant with complaints and requests.

"What do you want?"

"Your worship, would it be possible if instead of a jacket I could get some heavy cloth?"

"What's your name?"

"Talma."

I stared at this huge young man with a pale puffy face, kind gentle eyes and small beard in his government-issue clothes with a prisoner's cassock slung over his shoulders.

"Impossible. Against regulations," said the prison commandant.

Talma bowed and left. I followed and for a long time watched this living enigma. He walked hunched over, his gray cassock with its ace of diamonds hanging upon his huge ungainly figure as if upon a rack. He went down the main street and turned right down narrow alleyways along one of which he'd taken an apartment.

The second time I encountered Talma was on the wharf. He was without his prisoner's cassock, in a dark suit, soft shirt and black cap. I'd arrived on a tugboat with one of the officers from the steamer *Iaroslavl*, and Talma now approached the officer. They knew each other because the *Iaroslavl* had transported Talma.

"I've come to you with a request. Here's a receipt. I've been sent red wine from Petersburg. But how can I…" (all educated and non-educated alike choke on the word "penal laborer," and so just use "worker") "…as a worker, possibly accept it? Kindly give the shipment to a restaurateur. Let him take the wine for himself. I'll give it to him. The wine is supposedly very good."

"A strange errand!" shrugged the officer after Talma left. A strange errand indeed for a man exiled to *katorga*!

Later, once we'd become familiar, Talma one day happily explained to me, "Well, I'd gotten a telegram from Petersburg!"

"That's heartening!"

"Here it is."

I well recall the telegram's contents: "So-and-so, so-and-so and so-and-so, dining in such-and-such a restaurant, remember you and drink to your health." It was signed by his friends. The telegram had brought a happy smile to Talma's always sad face and clearly raised his spirits a little. Various people in their various capacities can be encouraging!

I'd gotten to know Talma in Aleksandrovsk's hospital office, where he performed clerical work—but I should clarify a bit for the reader. *Katorga*, as it is understood by the public, practically does not exist on Sakhalin for the educated man. The educated—"gentlemen," as *katorga* calls them with hatred and contempt—neither labor in mines nor drag timber from the taiga nor lay roads through the tundra's impenetrable quagmire because Sakhalin, with its understaffed chanceries and administrations, desperately needs literate people. Any reasonably educated man having come to be on Sakhalin can instantly get a position as a clerk, teacher, meteorological station manager, statistician or anything similar. *Katorga* terms can be served out by teaching, clerking or editing in Sakhalin's print shop. At first glance, all that "*katorga*" consists of for the educated man is being turned into your average clerk.

But for the educated on Sakhalin there exists a different *katorga*. Losing all privileges of status, you are stripped of your personal dignity, and that's everything! Any "prison commander" who has originated as an expellee from the medics can at any given minute, immediately upon his wishes without court or investigation, order up to ten strokes of the whip or thirty of the birch rod. He can capriciously write "for disobedience" in the punishment log and say nothing else. He can punish you immediately upon displeasure; immediately upon a complaint from some "assistant warden," some nonentity even *katorga* contemptuously addresses with the informal "you"; immediately upon the complaint of some "guard," himself a former exiled convict. You may be serving your "clerking *katorga*" with distinction, modestly and diligently, and they'll be content with you. But should you happen to encounter on the street some petty bureaucrat who feels you doffed your cap with insufficient deference or alacrity, you're put in the chains for a month or two, and such requests by gentlemen bureaucrats are always satisfied. "I pity the man but I'm arresting him!" you often hear from the more respectable prison "commanders." "I'm arresting him because, otherwise, they'll say I'm 'spoiling' *katorga*!" On Sakhalin, it's this accusation that officialdom most fears. So here, immediately upon some petty official's foolish whim, you're shackled in the chains for a month or two, placed amid a society of humanity's utter refuse, and you need to submit to this refuse because the "prisoners' laws," as maintained and enforced in prison, create out of shackled convicts the most desperate, the dregs of the prison's dregs. A man has fallen no lower than he who is highest in the prison environment, and this is whom you must obey.

The educated live beneath an eternal Damoclean sword. This is the "sum" of their *katorga*; for years, they fearfully tremble away every waking second.

This is why you encounter such melancholy and broken persons only among educated penal laborers. Many fall into melancholia from such an existence; from out of this perpetual fear they're consumed with self-contempt and sink into despair. They begin to drink... And if you see an educated man living permanently in prison and assigned to work the same as others, it's certain that he is already a completely ruined man and has lost his human shape and form. Rarely does an educated person start off in prison, but many end up there.

Talma shared the fate of all literate people when he arrived on Sakhalin. He ended up a clerk. I became acquainted with him at the hospital office. There, under the direction of first-rate and humane people—Sakhalin's doctors—his suffering was comparatively mild. They were all pleased with such a quiet, hard-working and extremely modest young man.

Having gotten to know Talma well, I was at his place, for he'd invited me. Of course, the conversation quite often concerned his case. But what could he say that was new? He could only repeat what he'd said during legal proceedings. Letters and telegrams from Russia kept up his courage and inspired flashes of hope, but were magnesium flashes amid the impenetrable darkness, bright and instantaneous, after which the darkness seemed still darker. He himself, it seems, regarded his own case as "decided" once and for all and, when I tried to console him by saying "God provides," he only waved his hand. "It's what it is!" An interesting characteristic was that when he spoke about his case he complained neither about his suffering nor loss of rights. He didn't complain about a ruined life; but when describing how he'd been stripped of his honor, he always became greatly agitated. In connection with the latter, he kept like holy relics those newspapers in which certain journalists had protested his innocence. Clearly often read, these frayed newspapers were essential. Giving them to me to read, he said, "I know, *know*, that you will handle them carefully. Please, don't be angry with me for this request!... But still, so that something not be forgotten..." This was all that was left. It was clear that Talma knew by heart what was printed because he'd constantly reread it. His speech unerringly repeated one or another printed phrase.

With regard to the present, Talma showed me letters from his wife and letters from a certain Bitiaeva, an odd, semi-educated young woman. In letters exuding an exalted love for Talma's family, Bitiaeva wrote about Talma's wife as about a child:

> Big Sasha (Talma's wife) isn't doing well: she's always bored, melancholy and sick. But little Sasha is completely healthy. Big Sasha thinks only about joining you, and I'll go with her, to be the maid, nanny, anything!

His wife, too, informed Talma of their imminent arrival. He often said, "When my wife arrives, we're going to do such-and-such and such-and-such..." But one could hear in his tone when he said this that he himself didn't believe in her arrival. The man had believed and believed, and then despaired. But he repeated the tired phrase mechanically, out of habit. "When she arrives…"

On Sakhalin, you often hear "when the wife arrives…, when they review my case…" And people say this for years. Despite the darkness the soul must hope! It makes everything easier.

Having observed Sakhalin's ways, Talma himself, it seems, vacillated as to whether it would be good or bad if his wife came straightaway. He wrote letters telling her to think of her own health: "If you don't feel completely healthy, then don't think of traveling. It would be better to wait."

What impression did Talma make? The impression of a drowning man, drowning without a cry, without a moan, knowing he cannot anticipate help from anywhere, that it's all the same whether he shouts or not, for no one will hear. He made the same impression on others. "I'm not happy with Talma!" I was told by a doctor Talma worked under and who saw Talma everyday and, thank God, had experience with exiles. "Every day he becomes more and more apathetic. He's falling into utter hopelessness. It's not good when this manifests in prisoners. It's as though the man is waving goodbye to himself. That's when it's over."

A small—but on Sakhalin, significant—detail: when I visited Talma the first time my attention was drawn to a harmonica lying on the bed. It's no good when an educated man on Sakhalin takes up the harmonica. It means he's succumbing to extreme melancholia. It usually begins with doleful harmonica playing during long Sakhalin evenings, while a blizzard wails and beats outside the windows; then vodka turns up on the table, and then…

At the time I saw Talma, although despair had clearly enveloped him, he still hadn't completely yielded; he was hanging on and not drinking. He wasn't living alone; he'd rented two closet-sized rooms and given one to "a comrade!" as he tartly explained. By chance, I learned what sort of comrade this was—an absolute pauper, a former officer exiled for insulting his commander, "buried and forgotten." No one from Russia wrote him, no one sent him anything. He couldn't get work teaching anything or transcribing personal correspondence. He'd faced two choices: either die on the street on a convict's government ration (on which you cannot live) or request internment in the prison. Fortunately, Talma knew of his situation and took the poor man in to save him from a bitter lot. "Such a good fellow, modest, friendly, just very unlucky!" Talma explained to me. He was living completely on Talma's means.

This was the reason Talma had asked the prison commandant to give him cloth instead of a jacket—so as to outfit his "comrade." "His own is worn out. But it's time for me to be issued a new jacket. They dispense it already made, but my size is too large for my comrade, so I asked them to give me the cloth so he could sew it together at home." Talma had approached me concerning not his own affairs but to make a request on behalf of another officer, also exiled for insulting his commander and who'd only just arrived on Sakhalin. "With all your connections, you should be able to ask them to arrange something more amenable for him. He's an exceedingly good and friendly man!"

As you know, when a man's drowning he thinks only of himself. And so, gazing at this man who finds time to think of others when he himself is drowning, I unwillingly thought, "He doesn't really mean that, does he?"

Let's assume I've seen murderers who would even share their last crumbs with cats. I saw cats in the chains prisons. The people in there, each with several murders on his soul, believe "that whether it's a man or a dog that dies, it's all the same," but if one of them kills this cat, his comrades will murder him because they pity the cat. Yet, that's not love but sentimentality. I had met many a sentimental person among murderers but not a single good, genuinely good, person.

But the impression of Talma that has remained with me is namely that I saw a very good man.

45

THE CARD GAME

"And what's with him?"

"Ec-ch!... He's started gambling!" answers a staid penal laborer or exile-settler. And this "started gambling" is said in a hopeless tone, such as when commoners say, "He's started drinking!" They're saying the man's a goner.

Gambling in *katorga* is really not gambling, it's heavy drinking, a sickness. Gambling alters the entire structure, the whole life, of the prison and turns all relationships head over heels. It turns men into monsters. Thanks to gambling, hardened criminals are freed from the punishments they were sentenced to. Due to a game people change their names and suffer punishments for crimes they didn't commit. You devise perfect systems of punishment, dream (only dream) of rehabilitating criminals, but there, in prison, all your systems, plans, hopes, dreams—all this is turned head over heels thanks to the ferocious epidemic of card games in *katorga*. Epidemic, namely because you can talk about the *katorga* card game only as if about a mass illness. In essence, the old formula "sentence to *katorga* labor indefinitely" could easily be changed to "sentence to a card game indefinitely."

"*Bardadým* (king)!"

"*Shepérka* (six)!"

"Soldier (jack)!"

"Old Man Blinov (ace)!"

"Foreign figurine[1] (two)!"

"Brother's little window[2] (four)!"

"Mama! Madam! Shelikhvostka (queen)!"

"Two on the side! Clear! Figure! Deliver a bunch of money! Through the money window! *Atténdez*! No, *átténdez*!"

This is all that is heard in the ward during the dinner hour, in the evening after prisoners have returned from work, throughout the night and early into morning before work assignments. Gambling basically continues uninterrupted: when they aren't playing they're talking and thinking only about gambling.

I knew a certain penal laborer in Aleksandrovsk Prison I gave money to for gambling. He gave me no peace. He'd flit off from lunch or work, run up the back steps or stand waiting in the street. "Barin, come here! Today there'll be a good game!" At work, all he did was glance down the road: "Isn't my barin coming?" His neighbors on the sleeping platforms joked that in his sleep all he'd shout was: "*Bardadým*!... *Shepérka*! Fifty kopeks a pip!" He'd gamble, lose, be living in an ecstasy of melting and burning, this man whose eyes gleamed with a feverish flame. What he'd not do to win money gambling!

This is an illness. I've already spoken of the *zhigan* who was dying from emaciation, from galloping consumption, in Korsakovsk's infirmary. He'd lost everything down to his bread ration. For entire months he lived only on the gruel that Sakhalin's swine eat reluctantly. In the infirmary he began betting medicine. His exhausted lifeless eyes, dying from the emaciation of a man whose life they were consuming with fire, simply glittered when he spoke of gambling.

At a prison inmate's request I described the gambling in Monte Carlo. I tried to speak as picturesquely as possible, watching the impression this had on them.

"Well... well...," a voice wheezed after I'd paused at a particularly interesting point. This wheezy voice of a man sounding as if he were being strangled belonged to a prisoner who was sick and lying on the sleeping platform, who then raised himself up on an elbow. It was terrible to look at him: his face was darkened and bloodshot and his feverish eyes wide open. "Well... well...," as if he himself had been going through the game up until his fate was decided. Each one of my words, like "the number's been given" or "a trump!" elicited absolutely joyous exclamations of vexation. "Ec-ch, damn!"

They were joining in the game with all their hearts and souls. I was touching their weakest point, and they couldn't bear hearing about the game. This is their illness.

Why is this?

First, however bad, they remain their country's offspring, and if from eight in the evening until eight in the morning all of Rus plays cards, or from eight in the morning until eight in the evening thinks about cards, then what a surprise that in a little backwater on Sakhalin the same thing happens. Second, a bored prison feels the need to gamble. Third, there exists some kind of mysterious connection between criminality and a passion for cards. Passion for cards is highly developed in all the world's prisons. Maybe because they distract from nagging thoughts, card games are loved by prisoners. In Paris's Grande Roquette, *moutons* (prisoners who've been sentenced to death) play card games for diversion.[3] Similarly, for the man who's ended up on Sakhalin, there's no hope, only chance. "Here comes a chance, I'll go for it." This adds up, as I've already said, to a belief in *fart*, in fortuitous chance and the whole *fart*-cult. And the card game is merely a sacrifice to the *fart*-god: where else, if not in cards, does chance play so huge a role?! For most prisoners, there's nowhere to earn money, and so gambling provides their only hope of taking a little of the edge off their situation by allowing them to buy sugar, repair their clothes and purchase some services. And, in the end, they try to deaden their tortured consciences through this all-consuming game, this gambling, this fervor for which a man loses his head, giving himself up as if to drink in order to forget, to leave behind painful thoughts of home, freedom and the past. The most hardened criminals are, at the very least, the most typically passionate gamblers.

By this, I explain the passion of my "friend" from Aleksandrovsk Prison. He'd arrived because he murdered his wife, whom he loved very much. "I didn't kill her, I couldn't have!" he once told me in such a tone that, were some Othello to speak similarly in the final act about Desdemona's murder, the spectator's stomach would churn with pity and horror. The thought always came to me while looking at him: "Here's a man who immolates his memories in a fever." Many were the moral pangs he tried to drown in a card game!

As if that were not enough, it destroys *katorga* and exile-settlements. You're "infected," as penal laborers say, infected by cards as if by disease; and, having been infected by cards in prison, the prisoner carries this infection into a settlement. This hinders his getting better and standing on his own two feet. He gambles away all that he has and steals, murders, sells his daughter, cohabitant or wife if she's followed him into exile.

Free persons rarely appear on Sakhalin, but if one does show up, he's besieged by a throng of impoverished exile-settlers. "No vittles for three days!" So you give a man a twenty-kopek piece and he hurries to the snack bars set up in Aleksandrovsk's Market Square. You wonder, will he buy bread? No, he'll gamble. Every snack bar is simultaneously a gambling den: in a back room they're *dreaming*, and a pauper dying of starvation hopes to win and then "eat as is proper to his complete satisfaction." Passion for the game supersedes even the feeling of hunger—it is the most powerful of human emotions.

Exile-settlers on Sakhalin typically manage to say, "Barin, your worship! Give me a little note!" That is, write out for the commissary: "Issue a bottle of vodka for me. (Signed) So-and-so."

"What, you want a drink?"

"I'm dying for one!"

The man has no money and so needs a "ticket" to get a bottle of vodka. But you can be sure he'll go and bet the note on cards because these notes, as I've already mentioned, circulate like money among exile-settlers and are usually valued at fifty kopeks and accepted as stakes for gambling.

There are even whole villages occupied exclusively with gambling. Such, for example, is Arkovo village in the valley of the river of the same name along the road from Aleksandrovsk Post to the mines. "Ah, respect for the gentleman from Arkovo!" they greet the Arkovo exile-settler when he comes to the post. "Arkovo's citizenry" engage in agriculture "any old how" and do so only "to amuse themselves," for their principal source of revenue is gambling. On those days when the free laborers at the Mgachi mines get paid, you won't find a single adult exile-settler in Arkovo; children and old people will be all that's left because Arkovo's men, with their wives and cohabitants, have grabbed their samovars and cards and gone to Mgachi. They set up their samovars, doll up their wives and cohabitants in aprons and new dresses, and set them along the road to lure, treat and defeat Mgachi's common laborers on their way to shop in the post.

I was going to the Vladimir *katorga* mine once and passed a crowd of Arkovo's dwellers along the way. The women were dolled up (as "dolled up" as paupers can be), the men jabbering away with gusto and carrying samovars.

"Pleasant journey. Where are you going?"

"We're on our way to Iamam (the Vladimir mine)."

"And why?"

"The Japanese (a Japanese steamer) have arrived. It's being loaded, and they say the workers were paid early to load it faster!"

In this way Arkovo's residents go to win from penal laborers those wretched pennies they manage to earn working the coal mines. Eagle Meadow, possibly so called because of games of pitch-and-toss,[4] is near Aleksandrovsk Post and notable in its own way. It is a colossal gambling den beneath open skies.

What can you do with a man corrupted by prison and infected with a passion for cards? And how often in response to the question, "How's life?"

do you hear from those wives who've voluntarily followed their husbands—these heroic martyred wives—the hopeless, "What life?! There's no life with such a scoundrel! The whole house is empty, gambled clean away. The children can hardly be seen for hunger and I'm sent to *fart*. Everything's gone for gambling. He's a sonofabitch, in a word. A lout!"

"What did you come here for?"

"Was he just anyone? Was I coming for nothing? I came because of my feelings, but he'd already been infected in prison—grind his ashes! Had I known, I'd never have come to ruin myself."

It's the same old "Sakhalin tune."

Katorga, infected by the game, gambles with handmade cards aboard the steamer. Readers may recall that I described these cards, in the "good packs" of which the hearts and diamonds are drawn with blood. Handmade cards aren't used on Sakhalin. Here, real cards can easily be purchased in the commissaries. Prisoners can either buy them themselves or through officials' servants. Any *maidan* has as many cards as you want.

Whoever studies the reasons for Sakhalin's numerous crimes can be assured that among the thousands of reasons for them, most prominent of all is gambling, this disease of the prison, this epidemic of *katorga* ruining these wretched people's lives.

46

KATORGA'S LAWS

As with any human society, *katorga* cannot manage without its laws.

"A remarkable thing!" I once noted in conversation with a certain Sakhalin official, a member of the local "intelligentsia." "*Katorga* opposes the death penalty and corporal punishments so passionately. It's so indignant. But among themselves, they recognize just two measures: corporal punishment and the death penalty!"

My interlocutor actually bounced in his seat. He was as delighted as if I'd given him a ruble.

"That's it, that's it! You write that, write that down immediately. Towards us, they can be humane! Yet they don't practice this at all towards one of their own…"

I smiled involuntarily. "Do you really think we'd be any better as convicts?"

The poor fellow looked at me dumbfounded and, at a loss, could only answer, "This is... this is word-play on your part... This is a paradox!"

Society calculates its enemies and exiles those who in turn calculate as enemies all of society. *La guerre, comme a la guerre.*[1] For *katorga*, what convicts perpetrate against *chaldony* does not at all amount to crime. The most brutal crime calls forth no condemnation at all. Once, a man killed someone who wouldn't return his money, and *katorga* "indulged" him. "Geez, you devil, you nailed him for a pinch of tobacco." But it says this affectionately. Among *katorga* there's even a saying for the *intentional* murder of a man, that to kill a *chaldon* is only "to spill a little milk." *Katorga*'s laws envisage as crimes only those committed by penal laborers against penal laborers.

We'll look first at the laws shaping penal laborers' responsibilities. They don't have many—there are all of two. If anyone in the prison ward is scheduled for a flogging, the whole ward contributes to a pool for the executioner so he won't viciously rip him to shreds. One donates a kopek, another two, another three, according to their circumstances. Anyone who has but a penny to his name is obliged to make a donation. This is the law, from which none are exempt, for otherwise the executioner, given his demonstrable virtuosity, may cripple or even flog the man to death. Given such wardens as Feldman, who I was told loved to order floggings, the prison is frankly brought to ruin through bribing executioners, whereas executioners drink heartily and live an easy life.

The second obligation of every penal laborer is to help a fugitive. At risk to itself, the prison will hide fugitives. I witnessed the capture of an important prisoner who'd escaped from Rykovsk Prison and been discovered in that same prison's bath house. However impoverished or hungry a convict may be, he'll give his last crust of bread to a fugitive. This, too, is a law of *katorga*; and only this can explain, for example, the following strange fact: the terror and horror of all Sakhalin, Shirokolobov, having escaped from Aleksandrovsk Prison, lived all winter in Rykovsk. *Katorga* concealed and fed him, risking its hide and sharing its very last.

Non-observance of these two sacred obligations is punished with universal scorn. But on Sakhalin, universal scorn amounts to a universal beating. Such a non-observant fellow becomes a *kham*, who can and will be beaten hourly.

Katorga's civil code is brief and simple. *Katorga* allows members to conclude their own agreements as they wish, demanding simply that the agreement be piously observed. However, if an agreement is subverted it's none of *katorga*'s business. "Fell to pieces!" This is because the fathers, *maidanshchiki* and bosses—all the folks who bribe *katorga* so that *katorga* is always on their side—will take away his last from a debtor who doesn't pay and even then "clean him out like he's a rich man." Thereby they maintain credibility in their world. Often, a fellow who's been "plowed under," that is, given up his bread ration for six months or a year ahead, will from hunger purposely commit a crime so as to be sent to the isolator or the hole, where absolutely no one can take away the crust of bread he owes! Such is the origin among convicts of many crimes and offences, especially petty offences. Supposedly "nothing else explains" insubordination against authority. If instead of the isolator the only punishment is the birch rod, then a more serious crime is committed in order to end up in the "last" hole.

But there's only one solution to rid yourself completely of crippling debt, and that's to escape. Escape is the sole salvation, the only way of "changing one's fate," and *katorga* regards it with great sympathy and reverence. Once a man has escaped from prison all his responsibilities and debts amount to nothing and can never be renewed! Often, a man buried in debts flees without any hope of gaining freedom. Having wandered for two weeks half-insane from hunger, bloodied by thorns in the taiga and chilled to the marrow, he returns in rags to the same prison he fled from. He receives an extended term (a "bonus") and settles former debts with his flesh. But because of this his debts are wiped out and he is once again a credit-worthy man. This is the origin of many Sakhalin escapes, to the direct consternation of prison administrators: "What do they hope for when they flee?"

Katorga's criminal legislation is also short and simple. *Katorga* knows no such crime as "theft." In the *katorga* language only murder is called a "crime." And if, say, a fellow sentenced for armed robbery tells you, "I didn't commit any crime whatsoever!" this does not at all signify a stubborn denial. You're simply speaking two different languages: "I certainly didn't kill anyone" means there wasn't a "crime." Quite often you'll hear on Sakhalin that one has been convicted "for rioting without a crime," "for stealing without a crime," "for a gang-led armed assault without a crime."

Thievery is dismissed. Where all are lawless, lawlessness becomes the law. In case of a theft, *katorga* permits the victim to deal himself with the thief or hire people to beat up the thief. But if a thief begins stealing from one and all, then the prison will teach him a lesson on behalf of everyone, and all similar matters in the prison are resolved through communal justice. *Katorga* doesn't inform the administration; and any complaint to the administration—whether a man is innocent or guilty, it doesn't matter—ends for the complainant or informer with a savage beating by the whole prison. Neither contradiction nor deviation is tolerated regarding this matter. Everyone joins in the beating: one out of vengeance, another out of hatred, a third "to maintain order," a fourth for want of something to do (you have to amuse yourself some way). Some do it "out of propriety." You don't want to join in, but, they say, "you have to do it like everyone!"

Now we come to the gloomiest part of the *katorga* law code, for which only one word suffices—"death." These are the laws that safeguard escape. Anyone who, knowing about preparations for an escape, tells the administration about them or, knowing where a fugitive is hiding, reveals the place to officials, is subject to death. Let him transfer to another prison for safety, *katorga* will still manage to pass on knowledge of his crime and he'll be killed there all the same. If a penal laborer escapes, is captured, returned again to the same prison and calls himself a "*brodiaga*, origins-forgotten," no one knowing him has the right "to recognize" him, that is, to reveal his true name, under pain of death. Subject to this immutable law are not only penal laborers but guards, who almost never identify the *brodiagi* jailed under them. Other officials keep this law in mind, "recognizing" a returned fugitive only reluctantly. "Now just wait for the knife in your back!"

Several fugitives who'd escaped to the Japanese coast of Matsmai were delivered to Korsakovsk Post. They presented themselves as "foreigners" and muttered some cryptographic name, barely able to keep from laughing in front of convict friends and long familiar guards. But no one "recognized" them. "First time we seen 'em!" Meanwhile, the fugitives were content to play the fool and didn't reveal their names.

One official told me, "They bring a *brodiaga* to us at the post. I'm looking: 'Good gracious, he was a penal laborer who served as one of my lackeys,' and I'm thinking: 'Do I identify him or not? Do I reveal his guilt or not?' I asked to be left alone with him. He's laughing. 'Thanks, your worship,' he says. 'How's the little barin's health?' 'What are you doing,' I ask, 'thinking you're not going to reveal your true name?' 'Don't knows it!' 'You know very well that half the people here know it. They'll recognize you!' 'No one's gonna recognize me, don't youse worry!' 'You should know I'll be the first to establish your guilt. I can't *not* establish it!' 'See what'll happen if'n youse recognize me!' he says and looks at me point-blank. I argued and argued with him for two hours, showed him he couldn't hide incognito, that it'd be to his advantage to identify himself, that the punishment would be less. I managed to persuade him. 'Alright,' he says, 'I agree!' "

I remember my coachman's startled face when I told him, "I just saw (the fugitive) Shirokolobov!" The poor man actually winced. "For God's sake, barin, don't tell anyone or there'll be trouble!" But I told him I was only joking.

Hence there is without fail a universal silence concerning the fugitive that strengthens Sakhalin fugitives' hopes. Few escape with the prospect of returning to Russia, but each hopes "to change his fate," to proclaim himself a *brodiaga* while on the lam and so cut a ten- or twenty-year *katorga* sentence in half.

Katorga does not always stipulate death for a penal laborer's murder of another; but for the murder of a "comrade," it always does so without fail.

A "comrade" is not just anyone. Often, a penal laborer who's committed a murder in prison will, in answer to your question, "How could you do that to your comrade?!" perplexedly reply, "Like he was my comrade?" He'll even be mortally offended. "Would I kill a comrade for anything?" Once again, you're speaking different languages.

"Comrade" is a powerful word in *katorga*. A life and death agreement exists within the word "comrade." A comrade is chosen to commit a crime or to escape. He's not chosen for nothing, but because he well understands and is versed in extreme danger. A comrade is like a relative, the closest and dearest creature in the world. I know of a slew of cases when a comrade treated with extreme consideration another comrade sickened or wounded during an escape. Comrades are treated with love and respect, and even in letters are not addressed as anything other than "our dear comrade" or "our respected comrade." All relations towards a comrade are imbued with reverence and profound fraternal love. Killing a comrade in prison is one of the most serious crimes. Murdering in order to rob him during an escape is more serious, as *katorga* well knows.

In all Sakhalin's prisons you'll find in the "investigation" isolators the most wretched people in the world, waiting as if for execution their release from isolation. Half-mad with terror, they're verging on persecution mania. All are suspected by *katorga* of informing about a planned escape, of showing where a fugitive was hiding, of establishing a *brodiaga*'s guilt, of murdering a comrade during an escape. They have every reason to go out of their minds, these wretches, given that *katorga* says, "They won't get away from us! We're coming." It's because of this such wretches are found in *every* prison; and you see that even the law of comradeship suffers many transgressors among Sakhalin's depraved convicts.

Such are *katorga*'s civil and criminal codes. It remains only to speak about the nature of penal laborers' investigatory activities. *Katorga* has not yet evolved out of the age of torture. "To conduct a search, investigation and interrogation" is called in the *katorga* language *shmanat*, a word that should be translated into everyday language as "to torture." Dealing out communal justice, *katorga* extracts truths through brutal tortures.

Captain Morovitsky told me how, during his tenure as warden of Dué Prison, *katorga* interrogated murderers. Penal laborers would toss a pair of suspects up in the air and part ranks at the same time so that the wretches would crash to the floor. This went on for as long as the bloodied and crippled wretches didn't confess. "And this we simply call '*shmanat*'!" Ivanov, one of the penal laborers who conducted such investigations, later confirmed for me.

47

THE LANGUAGE OF *KATORGA*

Because *katorga* does many things outsiders are not to know about, a special language has been created for everyday use. Whole generations of penal laborers have devised an interesting and unique dialect often reflecting *katorga*'s worldview and history. Out of this unique dialect emerges the at once cutting yet good-natured Russian humor and that cynicism that elicits first tears, then blood.

In the *katorga* language, "to kill" is called "to stick."[1] "I got him, he's lying on the ground like he's stuck there." This shows that the origin of the phrase "to stick" is not without humor. If "to stick" means simply "to kill," then "to stick a beard" means simply "to cheat." "Be careful, he's stuck a beard, y'know!" penal laborers say. The origin of this expression possibly relates to the legendary journeys of a certain famous Siberian *brodiaga*, about whom stories live on in *katorga*'s memory. In particular, he robbed wealthy, solitary old men (Old Believers) who were salvaging their souls in the Siberian taiga.[2] He'd go robbing, so the legend goes, with just a whip. He never tied up his victim but, after thoroughly frightening him, would stick the old man's beard to a table with sealing wax so he could rummage through the hut as he wished. If the old man didn't tell him where the money was, the *brodiaga* would flog him with the whip. The blows would make the old man yelp, so that he was facing double the suffering from both the whip and the unendurable pain of his stuck beard. Having taken all he needed, the *brodiaga* would simply abandon the wretch. "Sit down, I say, you won't be giving no speech (you won't tell anyone)." This account is believable, given that it employs such original expressions as "to stick a beard" and "to glue a beard."

Katorga has two special terms for signifying how people "stick." In *katorga*, to hit a person on the head is called "to split a melon" (!);[3] but they call stabbing a knife into a person's chest "to stab the soul."[4] In the *katorga* language, the chest is called the soul. Thus Korsakovsk's executioner Medvedev, relating how he conducted hangings, told me, "As they twirled in the noose, something acted up in my soul" (and it somehow ended up in his spleen)...

On Sakhalin, various phrases are used for "to die." In Korsakovsk Post the cemetery is near the lighthouse, and when somebody dies this means they're "taken to the lighthouse." "But where's patient such-and-such?" "He went to the lighthouse, your honor!" they'll tell you in the infirmary. "Were it sooner to the lighthouse!" patients groan. In Aleksandrovsk Post the cemetery is located on a hillock where the exile-settler Rachkov sometimes pastures his cattle. So when someone dies in Aleksandrovsk Post, this means they've been "taken to Rachkov's meadow." Because Aleksandrovsk Post is the major center on the island and every penal laborer is obliged to pass through it, "Rachkov's meadow" has become generally known, and the expression "taken to Rachkov's meadow" becomes a substitute for "to die" and the threat "to send you to Rachkov" equivalent to the threat "to stick."

As for those crimes other than murder, counterfeit coins are distributed on Sakhalin. Counterfeit silver rubles are currently especially in vogue. The Japanese steamer *Yasyama-Maru*, which arrives to load coal bound for Vladivostok, anchors near Sakhalin's Vladimir mine for almost a week. The Japanese usually bring sundry items and *sake* (Japanese vodka) to sell to penal laborers at an extortionate triple the price, and they leave Sakhalin with pockets full of... false rubles. *Katorga* has re-swindled them! These counterfeit coins are made everywhere on Sakhalin and even turn up in Ussuri Territory, where they're passed off to inexperienced foreigners.

The following is typical for Sakhalin. I was asking about a certain famous woman criminal, now an exile-peasant somewhere. "Why does she go to the mainland?" "Why?! She brings over false money, most likely. She knows the business."

"Money" in the *katorga* language is called *sarga*, though this money is Japanese and "sham."[5] *Katorga* calls "sham" anything phony: money, a passport, a name. Not without humor, *katorga* calls "to make sham *sarga*" (to be engaged in producing counterfeit money) "to cook pancakes."[6] I was told an amusing incident (maybe it's just a story, but they promised and swore it was true): an administrator was interested in why such-and-such an exile-settler had become so popular. "He cooks pancakes!" said those penal laborers who like to mock administrators. The administrator understood that he was cooking pancakes for sale, as is done in the cities, and remarked, "Ah-ha, outstanding, outstanding! I'm very glad for him, let him do it! I'm very pleased by this."

Theft is, of course, the third kind of crime throughout Sakhalin. In the *katorga* language, "to steal" is called *styrit*.[7] To teach how to steal, to tell how easy it is to do, to show where the money is, is called *natyrit*. To pass on stolen goods so that none will be the wiser is called *peretyrit*. And to swindle an accomplice during the divvying up of the spoils, to conceal part of the take to your advantage, is called *ottyrit*. Neither on Sakhalin nor in the cities do we have one major theft that does not to some degree take place without *natyrshchiki* or *peretyrshchiki*, whereas the *styrshchik* himself gets nothing but trifles because the *natyrshchiki* and *peretyrshchiki*, as conveyers and marketeers of what are known to be stolen goods, "keep"[8] the lion's share. The thief is merely a common laborer working for others his whole life.

As a profession, beggary garners little for the hungry on Sakhalin. To ask for alms in the language of *katorga* is called "to shoot." This is the fine-sounding word that embarrassed me the first time I heard it; and it has played a large role in the life of penal laborer Marian Pishchatovsky. A Hercules as well as the most good-natured creature in the world (though terrible during epileptic attacks), he approached the commandant with good intentions during his visit to the prison. "Um, I'd like to shoot you…" "Take him away! To the chains!" shouted the understandably repelled commandant. Pishchatovsky sat for several months in the chains and really didn't understand what for. It never occurred to him, having lived half his life in *katorga*, that the whole world doesn't actually speak the *katorga* language! Since then, the commandant has gotten so frightened every time he's visited the prison that they take Pishchatovsky away and chain him up. Complaining to me about his misfortune, this good-natured fellow emphasized, "In my life, I've not killed a fly but that I would suffer (though he was in a penal battalion[9]). And I'm such a degenerate? Why? Because I wanted to shoot for a little sugar for my tea? I was delighted. I'm thinking, 'Here's a nice official who'll donate a little ten-piece.' I was overjoyed that he was there!"

For the words "to request" and "to go begging" *katorga* has another phrase, historically originating in Siberia—"to shoot *savateiki*." In Siberia, *savateiki* are very rich and tasty cakes baked in sour cream. A well-to-do Siberian peasant considers it a duty of conscience, a mission, a "tonic for the soul," to give a *savateika* to a *brodiaga* or fugitive convict. From this, "to shoot *savateiki*" also means in the *katorga* language to take up vagabondage. But alas! In Sakhalin *katorga*, this expression is already out of date; not only are there no *savateiki* for Sakhalin's starving—there's no bread. A Sakhalin exile-settler isn't a Siberian peasant and so if you're hungry, you don't eat. In Siberia, a peasant feeds a *brodiaga* and in return the *brodiaga* touches nothing of the peasant's. But a starving Sakhalin *brodiaga* will devour an exile-settler's fodder, cow and last horse. This is why exile-settlers hunt, capture and then murder *brodiagi*. "Here on Sakhalin, old chap, it's every man for himself!" they say on this island where, as it goes, man is wolf to man.

We now proceed to expressions designating punishment. Irony imbues them all, and this irony reminds me of that smile—crooked, quite sad, rather like a grimace—with which a man lies down on the mare. "That's how it must be." *Katorga* doesn't like the word "to hang." It calls this "to get the rope."[10] This rather instinctive fear of the terrible word is such that even an executioner, when telling you how he hanged thirteen men, somehow manages to avoid this unpleasant word, and if he does invoke it, he seems to stutter as if making confession. For precisely the same reason *katorga* dislikes the word "birch rods" and prefers the ironical term "twigs."[11] If, during a beating, birch rods are held by the thin end and struck using the thick and far more damaging end, then it's called "using the butts." *Katorga* calls whips "ladies' frocks"[12]—a phrase always said ironically. However, in general, "to receive lashes" is called "to receive awards"[13]; and to receive them to the fullest extent allowed by law means to receive "the full."[14] *Katorga* has two expressions for the word "isolator": "beehive" and "drying-room."[15] Furthermore, the latter is more often used: it's more ironic. "And where's such-and-such? I haven't seen him for three days." "He's drying out!" This means he's sitting in a dark isolator.

In order to avoid all these charms beginning with "ladies' frocks," continuing with "twigs" and ending with the "drying-room," a penal laborer has to be either especially *fartovy* or know how "to *feld*."[16] Some fellow commits twenty crimes and gets nabbed only after his twenty-first; another screws up the very first time, and so badly, that he gets twenty years. The former is reckoned to have taken fifteen people's lives, but arrives as a *brodiaga* sentenced to one-and-a-half years "for concealing his identity" and will leave and take up vagabondage again; whereas someone else—*katorga* knows who—is imprisoned and will be imprisoned for a long time for nothing. In front of everyone, one left and made do in Russia while the other, who's miles from the prison, doesn't get away: he's captured, given "awards" and saddled with an extended term.

Everything makes *katorga* believe this is blind happenstance, only happenstance and nothing more. Even for the court, given its characteristic view, this is just a game of chance. Faith in happenstance, in fate, in fortune—this is *katorga*'s basic religion. From the word "fortune" comes the word *fart*. It strictly means "luck" but, Lord, what on Sakhalin is sometimes called "luck"! In conformity with this, the words *fart* and *fartovy* hold many different meanings. "He's a *fartovy* guy!" they say of a fellow when they want to express that this man is friendly and big-hearted, a fellow ready to help a good friend without any advantage to himself. "He's a *fartovets*! A *fartovy* guy!" they enviously say about a fellow who's gotten away with all kinds of crap. But when an exile-settler says of his cohabitant, or a penal laborer says of the wife who's voluntarily followed him, that "she came for *fart*," then I'll need to explain this expression to you later.

The word *feldit* means "to deceive." But just as "stick a beard" is done against a penal laborer only, so "stick a *felda*"[17] is done against an official only. *Felda* namely signifies fraud, cunning and slyness against an official. They say the word "*felda*" is particular to Sakhalin and appeared during the time that a certain Feldman, whom I've already noted, was warden of Voevodsk Prison.

At that time, only cunning and slyness could save a penal laborer from "ladies' frocks" and "twigs," for Feldman didn't allow a prisoner to go without a thrashing. Prisoners "felded" Feldman just as Feldman, miserly adding to his wealth by feeding the prison soggy bread, "felded" the administration. The historical explanation is not without interest.

Servility and denouncing are the two most common ways of "felding." *Katorga* has two expressions for them: "to wag your rear" and "to flop beside the river."[18] In essence, "he's wagging his rear" or "he's flopping on the shoreline" means that a prisoner is cunningly avoiding the most difficult work. But in *katorga* there are only two means towards achieving this: get on someone's good side or denounce someone. Hence *katorga* says of those who fawn before administrators, "Geez, he's flopping on the shoreline like a fish in the sand. 'Don't get near him,' they say." The expression "to wag your rear" shows you what *katorga* thinks of an informer. It calls him a "little bitch"[19] because he "wags his rear" before officials, and *katorga* turns away from him as if he were a dog.

"To denounce" is called in the *katorga* language "to kick" or "push a wheelbarrow."[20] To charge a man before administrators so that he can't wriggle out of it means screwing him over completely. For this, *katorga* knows just one punishment, which it calls with prison humor "to empty like he's a rich man,"[21] that is, to beat "soundly," to beat so that the man doesn't see who's beating him, "to stick him in the dark,"[22] that is, to cover his head with a cassock. "There're two benefits!" penal laborers explain. "His head won't get busted open out of anger—he'll still be alive; and because they're 'emptying him like a rich man,' he won't squeal."

Like all worn-out, wretched and bitter people with shattered nerves, penal laborers love to harass and torment others. It's awful if *katorga*, able as it is to precisely determine persons' weaknesses, notices that a fellow is "hot-tempered" or "easily set of"[23]—that is, can easily be made angry, for then it is a cardinal pleasure for *katorga*, which is an astounding expert in this area, "to set of"[24] such a man or "get a fire"[25] from him. I could only marvel at how perfectly they knew their administrators. If only the administrators had known one-hundredth of what they knew of them! The words as spoken are, it seems, completely innocent, but you can see that they've already "set of" the warden:

"I only, in order to follow the law…"

The warden reddens. "But I'll show you the law! Deprived of all your rights, but you're gonna debate and give *me* a lesson? *He's a law expert!* Bastard, you'd do better to think about the law when you're of filching something."

"What're you saying to me?! I'm only asking for instructions…"

The warden actually jumps up and down. Were "the writer" not there…

"I'll write instructions for you! You're gonna teach me, teach *me*?!"

"Why 'teach'?! It just seems to me they should be distributing according to schedule."

"According to schedule?! *According to schedule?!*" The warden's turned completely purple.

"Calm down," I tell him. "What's the problem?! It's not worth it"

"No, not with such a knave! How he's spewing out 'according to the law, according to instructions, according to the schedule'!…"

But I can see that *katorga* is observing this scene and chuckling. The warden's "button's been pushed." In the language of *katorga*, this means to bring a man to a fury so that he's "rooting up the dirt."

"Well, why were you doing this?" I ask the penal laborer later.

"He clearly hates such important words. I don't wanna say nothing to him, but here he is not even respecting the schedule!"

"But you know that can just be torn up."

"And very easily!"

"So why are you such a cranky fellow?"

"Ech, your worship, you don't understand us. Would we be sitting here like we are if we'd happened to ask 'why'? There's just a cruelty, and it wants to ruin things."

"To set off," "to light a fire," "to push a button"—each is an expression referring to administrators, and *katorga* esteems these things. To offend, to insult one's brother for no reason at all—this, *katorga* calls "to bite."[26] It looks upon a fellow doing this as a crazed dog who bites people for no reason. It disdains and is always bothered by it. "Hey there, you're being a dog!" penal laborers will say.

When, I repeat, a person has frayed nerves, he enjoys getting on someone else's nerves. "I'm racked with pain, so let another feel it." Suffering is the poor father of sympathy. What with boredom, inactivity and a depraved majority in *katorga*, lying has become highly developed. Those who do, *katorga* calls "liars," "gossipers" and "troublemakers," but since this deficiency is universal, it's regarded amiably. *Katorga* has two terms for defining a liar in which there's more humor than spite. "As straight as an arc"[27] it says about such a fellow. Or, to characterize his stories: "Geez, is he ever painting a picture: seven versts to heaven and all through the forest!"[28] I've already said that *katorga* disdains those colleagues who crawl to the "commander," that is, the headmen, etc. They call such a person a "big wheel."[29] And for guards—truly able, if they want, to seem entirely oblivious or to catch prisoners for gambling and other prohibited activities—*katorga* has a perceptive term: "spooks."[30]

I won't introduce the whole group of lesser, common *katorga* terms. But everything has its name in *katorga*. *Katorga* is secretive and doesn't like that even its casual conversations be understood. It's as if it were demanding that a fellow involuntarily entering its midst renounce all previous things "there," in freedom, even the language he spoke. "Soup" in *katorga* is "*balanda*." One's "government bread" is a "chunk." A "spoon" is a "horse." "Vodka" is "crazy-water." A "fur coat" is a "sheep." A "knife" is a "shiv." Etc. What *katorga* calls a "passport" is very apt: "eyes." "Without 'eyes' a fellow's blind—where can he go?"

To conclude with the language of *katorga*, it remains only to speak about *katorga* curse words. "Penal laborer," "prisoner" and all the curse words of the Russian language are for *katorga* but typical conversational seasonings. Yet there is one word that causes pain. This is a vulgar commonfolk word meaning in more polite language "coquette." It is explained by *katorga*'s unique circumstances; but to indicate that a man is employed in this profession, to call him by this name, is to reach for knives. In Mikhailovskoe's investigatory prison a certain prisoner, a handsome young Caucasian, stabbed his own comrade. "What for?" "He said a certain word to me!" It wasn't necessary to ask him this "word."

48

KATORGA SONGS

It is remarkable that even the Siberian *katorga* of bygone years, gloomy and brutal, developed its own songs. But Sakhalin, never. There is the notorious:

Farewell, Odesta,[1]
Glorious (?[2]) quarantine,
They're sending me to
The island Sakhalin…

This appears to be the one and only song created by Sakhalin *katorga*, but it is sung almost never at all. Even in Siberian *katorga* there was some hint of romanticism, something that could be expressed in song. But here, there's nothing of the kind. So terribly prosaic are the surroundings, you don't express them in song. Even the coachmen—those immemorial singers and jokers—will drive a troika of small but speedy Sakhalin horses in silence without whoops or clever asides. You sit in the coach as if in a funeral hearse; and should the trace-horse begin neighing, the coachman shouts, "Quiet there, you convict!" And all those traveling fall silent once again, as if murdered. One does not sing here.

"We're bored to death!" penal laborers and exile-settlers say.

There's "No Singing" on Sakhalin, even for a free person. I remember a guard who was leaving the barracks gate one festival day. He was clearly enamored of the holiday—an accordion was in his hands and he was singing with gusto. But what passed for singing! Some kind of shout, wail or groan, as if the man were howling from a toothache in his soul. If you hadn't seen that the man was "happy" you'd have thought he was being stabbed.

Similarly, the old executioner Komlev doesn't sing when ambling within sight of the prison. Despondency hovers over him like a shadow. "Why did you come here from your settlement?" "I heard there'd be a hanging and hoped to earn three rubles. They've no one but me."

They rarely sing in prison, and not because it's against the rules. Only once did I hear singing, in Rykovsk's chains. This happened during evening. Roll call had finished and the prisoners were locked in their wards. The officials were fast asleep, the prison yard deserted and the guards curled up in their corners. The evening gloom gradually thickened until complete darkness prevailed. I was walking through the prison yard, then stopped as if rooted to the ground. "What is that—moaning? No, they're singing." Out of boredom, the chains prisoners were singing the Siberian *brodiagi*'s song "Merciful Ones"... But what singing it was! As if a funeral dirge were emanating from the chains prison. As if, having watched the twilight through barred windows, this prison was singing some kind of prayer for the dying, a death song for those buried alive inside it. It grew eerie...

The old *brodiaga* Shushakov, who lives in the village of Derbinsk, is renowned among prisoners as a singer. I tracked him down hoping "to avail myself" of him. But Shushakov wouldn't sing jail songs and spoke of them with loathing. "I won't pollute my mouth with this filth. But those I do know, I'll sing." He sang in a gentle tenor, a bit that of an old man, but still in key. Propping himself up with his arm, he sang "with sorrow" the songs of his distant homeland, perhaps remembering his house, loved ones and children. He'd fled Sakhalin "to go vagabonding" and traveled for two years, begging like Christ, so as to reach home. He spent an entire summer at home with his children, but then "got myself caught" and has been in *katorga* for sixteen years so far. He sang sad, drawn-out, melancholy songs about his village birthplace that made you want to cry. They pinched my heart. "That'll do, old man!" He waved his hand. "Ech, barin! You sing and get lost in your thoughts." This was no man, this was a "song of woe"!

Katorga has its favorite songs all the same. The people's ever-broadening literacy is evident here on Sakhalin, as if you're hearing something splash into an expanding sea. "Book songs" are very popular in *katorga*. More than anyone, it is our veritable folk poet who touches *katorga*'s soul: more than any other songs you hear "Not the Wind that Bends the Branch," "A Poor Man's Lot," "To the Poor Branch"—each a poem by Koltsov.[3]

However, once I was traveling on horseback, and there by the road digging with a hoe was an exile-settler who began pouring out "Show Me to that Abode," from Nekrasov's "Ceremonial Procession." He was singing as it's usually sung, to the tune of *Lucretia Borgia*.[4]

"Stop. What are you here for?"

"For suspicion of robbery with murder, your worship."

"How is it you're singing this song? How did you come by it?"

"'Tis nothing. Just whining!"

"But where did you learn it?"

"When we was sitting in prison. They taught it to me."

Three times I happened to hear "Vaniushka Slept Soundly," altered into the crude "Peddlars."[5] "Where did you hear it recited?" I asked the cobbler Alfimov after he sang it for me. "Not nowhere. Learned it in prison."

Of the usual folk songs only very rarely does *katorga* sing "Amid the Valley Broad," preferring as it does the *katorga* arrangement "In the Midst of Danny's Log...,"[6] a foolish and cynical song which, on the whole, the prison also rarely sings. They prefer others, even the Little Russian[7]...

The sun's a-sinking,

Evening's a-coming.

They like this for its daring refrain, which they jauntily sing to an accompaniment of wisecracks, whistles, whoops and the tapping of spoons by "the disciplinarians"—former regimental choristers.

Almost any penal laborer knows how to sing, among other frequently heard songs, the very lovely:

To the little pond went a beautiful maiden
    In the evening for her flock.
Black eyebrows, round of face
    She drove the geese home.
(Refrain.)
"Run, run, run,
"My geese, to home!

"To love just one would be enough
    "For me to be glad a century,
"But it pains my heart to live
    "Against my will in this world.
(Refrain.)

> "Don't come for me, rich man,
> "If you're not in my heart.
> "What are they to me, those palaces of yours?
> "If with my sweetheart my hut is paradise…"

Or there is a variant of the final couplet, as follows:

> "Instead of the gray-haired old man
> "I will love my dear,
> "Because my pained little heart
> "Through gold will shed tears!…"

This song is also favored because of its refrain. I remember a certain young chap—he'd been exiled for some stupid robbery—as he sang this "run, run, run, run!" He sang with all his heart. His face flushed, eyes afire, utter joy on his face, as if he were seeing before him a familiar picture of home.

Also more commonly heard is a favorite sentimental song:

> My night-time star-daughter,
> Why do you burn for half the night?
> King, king, about what do you sigh
> With the terrible words you say?
> "My sweet beauty,
> "You are my true love;
> "I give you a horse
> "With a harness, a harness of gold."
> I don't need your golden maiden,
> I don't need your fine horse—
> Give, give your horse to the princess,
> To your woman charming and dear.
> And you, beautiful maiden,
> Return my peaceful soul to me, to me…
> The king—his wife and children forsaken—
> Called out a benediction:
> "Forgive me, wife, forgive me, children!"
> Said he, almost in tears,
> "Live in friendly concord,
> "As the Lord Himself showed you,
> "Don't respond to evil with evil,
> "But respond with kindness!" said he…

This sentimental song about a king who's thrown away his kingdom because of his love for a woman is sung with great emotion. But all these songs are sung only by young convicts, and provoke indignation among the old men. "Geez, the devils! What makes them happy!" I recall one old man especially being driven to fury by the song about the young girl who "drove the geese home." The refrain "run, run" sent him into a frenzy. "I'll complain to the commandant! You're giving me no peace, you demons!" he screamed. And in *katorga*, this is an unusual threat.

"But, grandfather, why does this song bother you so much?" I asked.

"It's not something to joke about." And after a moment of silence he added, "It opens old wounds. Phooey!" God only knows what memories those well-known words "run, run"[8] reopened in this old *brodiaga*'s soul.

Few of Siberia's unique prison songs have reached Sakhalin. If in a prison there are five or six of the old, "still Siberian," *brodiagi*, they'll sit together towards evening and talk about "the good ol' Siberian life": "Mother-Siberia's crazy, the land there evil, and the folks violent!" And they'll dredge up tearful memories of their favorite *brodiaga* song, "Our Merciful Little Fathers."[9] (I covered this song in the article "*Katorga* Theater.") They sing and remember their freedom, the endless taiga, *savateiki* and the violent but kind Siberian people. But Sakhalin *katorga*, knowing nothing of either Siberia or its relationship to *katorga*, laughs at them, their memories and their songs. One (and not just one) "Sakhalinite" told me: "What a notion, that a *chaldon* (for our purposes, a "resident") might be kind to a fugitive! Not in this life, I don't think!"

There is yet another favorite Siberian song that *katorga* drags out from time to time:

> As I follow the wild winds,
> God the protector is my blanket,
> There is no arboreal shade in the tundras,
> Neither sun nor daybreak,
> And savages appear suddenly
> Like shadows along the cliffs.
> From the Angara to the mouth of the sea,
> I see savage, rocky walls,
> And savages suddenly appear
> Like shadows along the cliffs.
> Soon a horde of savages
> Will fly down the mountains toward me—
> Die with me:
> I—your brother—fear people…

When *katorga* sings this song, originating in Iakutsk District,[10] it produces a rather gloomy energy. I wished so many times to have not been able to record the reasons for these songs!

It would be interesting to know the melody to this—at one time favorite, but now moribund—*katorga* song:

> Tired he walks, and the chains rattle,
> Arms and legs are shackled.
> Quiet and sad, he gazes along
> The long, open road…
> The midday sun burns without mercy,
> He gasps with pain,
> Warm blood drips from his sores
> Gnawed at by chains…

This song is now but an echo of the abolished "way-stations."[11]

Katorga sang me a terrible song I should call a "*katorga* hymn," such is its doleful melody like the moaning of the autumn wind. *Katorga* has poured all its weary homesick soul into this tune. When you hear it, you hear the soul of *katorga*.

> Amid stone palaces you tell, you tell!
> You tell the news to stony Moscow,
> To Moscow stony, stony-white…
> You sing, sing, little lark,
> You sing, sing! You sing, sing
> Of this bitterness and captivity.
> If the news is out, then tell father
> What's become of me
> On the other side…
> I wasn't really a thief or a murderer,
> But they exiled me, a kind young man,
> To learn about *katorga*, this accursed fate—
> It's really so painfully hard
> To live on the other side!
> Ech, my sweetheart!… And you, mother!
> You forgot me as if I'd vanished.
> But there'll come a time when I'll return again
> To repay you for all misfortune and harm,
> There'll come a time, when I'll return…
> You tell about that, little lark,
> Tell the news—you tell, tell!…

They sang it to me in the prison in the evening, after roll call. They all sang. The fluid tenor of a sturdy chap, sitting on the sleeping platform and gazing somewhere up above, overpowered the choir and dolefully summoned the little lark, with his singing about injury and vengeance as if he were dreaming aloud. And from the dark corners could be heard the rending of the soul: "You tell, tell…" It was melancholy and hopeless. You might slit your throat hearing such a song.

But all these songs, originating in Siberia and brought to Sakhalin, are, as I've already said, not loved by *katorga*. They "irritate." And when it does sing, *katorga* prefers other, "happy," songs that cannot be written down. But what songs they are! No trace of cynicism… Surely, the Devil knows it well, this nonsensical collection of words whose combination produces something resembling indecent speech.

Here you have what *katorga* sings. They say that songs are the "soul of the people," and *katorga* sings songs that exude sentimentality (that surrogate of emotion which often replaces feelings and that eternally aching wound), homesickness, anger toward past grievances, a false "courage," cynicism and that *katorga* "frenziedness."

But *katorga* is more often silent.

49

KATORGA AND RELIGION

There are eleven churches on Sakhalin—but is *katorga* religious?

I recall the following scene. It was a glorious holiday. The night was clear, cold, just barely freezing. Vladivostok, its churches illuminated, glowed in the distance. To our left, the steamer *Petersburg* shone like fire. A little farther off, the giant *Ekaterinoslav* seemed a spectral ship woven of light. "Christ has risen!" could be heard wafting over the peaceful waters. The sky was fathomless and the stars burned so bright.

There was cheerful activity aboard our *Iaroslavl*. The knocking of crockery could be heard from the dining ward as preparations were being made to break the fast. Our priest was beaming, and we kissed each other warmly. We really seemed to get closer to each other, to become more brotherly. Far from home and loved ones, the feeling was special that night…

Only there, in the hold, it was quiet as a grave. The priest sprinkled holy water on the deck amid the joyful murmuring of "He has indeed risen." After coming on deck we walked past the "special sections." I glanced through a porthole at several men inside. If only someone had stood for the choristers singing and walking past, for when a clergyman was at the porthole with a cross. I especially remember the face of a certain section's headman, a "returnee." It's like I can see him now. He's watching the procession go by and—there's nothing save a wan indifference. "Geez, I say, there're so many of 'em." He didn't even cross himself when we, walking by, sang "Christ has Risen" practically to his face. Thus he met Easter—and so my heart pains me now.

"Will the father walk through the prisoners' sections?" I asked a senior officer.

I waited half an hour, and when he returned he had a rather embarrassed look. "You know, I'd hoped to ask the father to go to the special sections… I went inside, but they're all asleep."

To sleep indifferently on such a night; and this, after the transporting spiritual scenes I'd witnessed just a month earlier during confessionals. Every day during this period a man in *katorga* hardens his heart, as a certain religiously sectarian convict explained to me.

An English missionary, a member of a bible society visiting Sakhalin's prisons, was handing out prayer books to penal laborers, and it was the old convict P's turn. He politely and deferentially bowed low to the missionary and, handing back the book, stiffly and politely said to the interpreter, "Tell the gentleman he should give the book to somebody else. I don't smoke."[1]

The majority among *katorga* are atheists. And if any one penal laborer gets the notion to pray in prison this evokes universal ridicule. *Katorga* considers this a "weakness," and it despises weakness.

How have they come by this denial? They have simply used reason.

"Do you believe in God?" I asked Paklin, who murdered the archimandrite of Rostov.[2]

"No. There's just yourself," he briefly and simply answered me.

Poluliakhov, murderer of the Artsimoviches in Lugansk, regarded religious persons with great empathy. In his words, he "loved them."

"Well, what about you?" I asked.

"I agree with Darwin."

"So you've read Darwin?"

"I have since the murders." I was able to see from talking with him that he'd indeed read Darwin, but had understood him extremely peculiarly and "by his own accord."

"Where does Darwin deny the existence of God?"

"Well… life—in my view—is a struggle for survival."

"The struggle for survival," crudely understood, is feral in its entirety—this is their religion.

Several have come to denial by way of experience, so to speak. "It's all nonsense," one convict told me with a smile. "I've seen how people die…" And he had the right to say this: he—it was true—had "seen." "This most interests me. I've killed dogs for fun, and they die just like people do. No difference. Y'see, you need to get him before he gets you, so's not to suffer."

As they come to denial in *katorga*, so they come to a hatred of religion, a hatred that is expressed through disbelief. "It's not hard to get lost in such a quagmire," the Odessan murderer Shaposhnikov told me in Korsakovsk District, during one of those moments he chose to speak commonsensically and not act like an idiot.

I recall a certain penal laborer who'd been a tavern-keeper in Vologda Province. There was a fight between two customers in his establishment and he sided with one, shouting, "Give him a sound beating!" As a result, the other man was killed and he was convicted for instigating murder. Speaking about his destroyed life, about his abandoned family, about what had happened to him and what he'd lost in *katorga*, he began to tremble all over and say such things that I interrupted him. "Look at yourself! Look at yourself! At what you're saying! You fear God! You know you're a Christian." The wretch grabbed his head. "Barin, barin, I will lose my mind here."

I remember a scene that played itself out prior to a flogging. They had "designated for punishment" the indefinitely-sentenced penal laborer Fedotov, age fifty-eight. He'd been exiled to Sakhalin for robbery, had escaped, pillaged Korsakovsk District with a gang of fugitives and murdered a peasant to avoid capture. Later, he was arrested along with a certain former technical engineer in the forging of five-ruble banknotes. Most recently, he stole a little dagger from a church. "God expelled me from the Garden because I robbed him. Since then, I go without God," Fedotov explained with a sad smile. For his three crimes, Fedotov received three rounds of a 100 lashes each and was chained to a wheelbarrow for three years. Now he's developed a serious heart condition and can barely walk and hardly breathe. He periodically suffers intense vertigo and is psychologically abnormal: his suspiciousness attenuates to paranoid ravings. During paroxysms of vertigo he attacks doctors and officials with a knife. Normally, he's a very quiet, gentle and kind man, frail and exceedingly unhealthy. This time, the crime he was to be punished for related to what I've just described. I'm afraid that the doctor in Rykovsk didn't treat him "as should be." So Fedotov left without permission to Aleksandrovsk to see Dr Poddubsky,[3] whom all *katorga* unquestioningly trusts, and was sentenced to eighty lashes for escaping. Given such terrible circumstances, I'd hardly expected to meet and talk with Fedotov that evening, but he came to me with a letter.

"Who wrote this letter?"

"It's all mine."

"Why did you write a letter?"

"I didn't know if I'd be able to talk, what with all that's going on. Yes, it's hard for me to express everything—I'm choking. You can see how I'm talking."

In his letter, Fedotov "regarded it as his duty" to inform me that *katorga* viewed my inquisitiveness with great sympathy, and he asked me "not to believe just anyone" and not to fear *katorga*. "We won't hurt whoever is a human being towards us." In conclusion, he expressed the hope that my visit would prove as useful as the visit of "the gentleman Doctor Chekhov."[4]

I again encountered Fedotov that very day, under the following circumstances. No longer under investigation, Fedotov was brought to the chancery along with others "scheduled for punishment." The executioner Khrustsel, his "instruments" wrapped in clean canvas and tucked under his arm, stood humbly off to the side. Those scheduled for punishment gathered around the doors with frightened dismayed faces. I was sitting with the doctor and assistant warden at an office table.

"Fedotov!" Fedotov approached the table with a perplexed look and the unsteady gait of a sick man.

"For what reason, your worship, has it pleased you to call me?"

"But you know why you're now here. Attention, please: the sentence." And turning to me, the assistant warden began to rapidly read out the sentence. "Calling attention to… having been found guilty… eighty lashes…" The longer the assistant went on reading the indictment the more violently Fedotov's entire body shook. He stood there white as a sheet, holding his hand over his heart and confusedly muttering, "I was absent… because I went to the doctor."

After the sentence was read and we'd all sat down, he, after looking at us in startled bewilderment, stepped forward and said, "Such is God's will. For certain, I shall lose my life…" Suddenly his entire face contorted and he began choking and trembling and let out a horrible cry. He then poured out a litany of such blasphemies, such terrible curses, that to hear them was truly horrible. Reeling through the chancery, Fedotov tore his hair and clothes, beat the walls and door-jambs with his head and screamed at the top of his lungs, "Stab, strangle, beat me. Khrustsel, drink my blood… Guard, kill me…" He flung himself at the guard, tearing his shirt and baring his chest. "Kill me. Kill me." All this blasphemy poured out such as I'd never heard and, of course, would never want to hear again. It's hard to imagine that the human tongue can wrap itself around such things as this man screamed during his fit.

I was finding it hard to breathe. The doctor had gone pale and was trembling. The frightened assistant warden shouted, "Remove him! Remove him!" They grabbed Fedotov by the arms. He tried to break away and was practically dragged from the chancery. His shouting could be heard from the yard outside.

"Will they really punish him, with a heart condition?" I asked.

"Who's going to punish him? Who could possibly punish him?" the trembling doctor said.

"Then why all the formalities? What for? Why was he not put at ease immediately, told right away that the punishment he'd been summoned for wouldn't be carried out, that the reading of the sentence was only for the record? You know he's sick."

"It's against regulations," the assistant warden, a youth, muttered.

Perhaps this was one of those points at which faith gets extinguished and hatred, a certain hatred against everything, permeates the soul.

"How can I be an Orthodox Christian," I often happened to hear from penal laborers, "when I can't make holy communion at confession?" Many simply give up their faith. "It's simply driven out by force," complain both clergymen and wardens. This very deviationism normally has its source in a profound religious sentiment. "There ain't no fasting," say convicts. "You comes back from church, everyone's drinking, gambling, cursing. You cross your brow and they cackle and swear. You makes confession, comes back and begins cursing. You've so defiled yourself before communion, well, you just don't go. So you pass it by year after year." And so many truly profoundly religious people are "giving up." You talk with them, listen and marvel: "Indeed, all these people come from a 'common,' faithful and religious environment."

"Pardon me, but how can you be devoted to religion," a clergyman serving in Rykovsk settlement said to me, "when not long ago they buried bodies naked?"

"Is that so?"

"That's so. They'd put a naked body in the coffin and we'd sing over the burial. That's temptation."

"But where were the prisoner's clothes?"

"Ask around... They weren't at the funerals—only thing there was laughter."

The "illegal cohabitations" established when female convicts are distributed to exile-settlers "in the interests of colonization" have dealt a huge blow to *katorga*'s religious sentiments. These "allocations" have profaned in *katorga*'s view one of the greatest sacraments our people regard with special reverence. "Why pray here?" you quite often hear. "Why go to church here? We're living in such sin. Over there in Rasseya she lived with her husband, but here they give her to another muzhik and say, 'Live!'" Or: "The husband's in *katorga* in Korsakovsk but the wife's in Aleksandrovsk living with someone else."

I remember the "oh's" and "ah's" in Rykovsk upon the arrival of Goroshko, a husband who'd voluntarily followed his wife into *katorga*. "Well, it's a fact," a leading exile-settler shook his head, "the husband voluntarily came from Rasseya because of her; but since she's been here she's been given to three muzhiks in a row."

Marriage has lost its sacred meaning in *katorga*'s eyes: rarely, very, very rarely, do you hear someone yearningly sigh over a female cohabitant: "It'd be nice to be married. It'd be better to wed." Instead, the majority always argue as follows: "Far better not to be 'twisted round a finger.' Ain't pleasant to be handed over tied-and-bound."

"It really is difficult to maintain religious feeling among the convicts here," priests complain. A convict considers himself a "man of experience" and regards every human sentiment as alien to him. "All tenderness and sentimentality is just humanitarianism," say Sakhalin's officials.

Among penal laborers, only the correctionals' division had the final three days of Easter Week off from work. But the convicts in Dué Post had to work these three days for the private entrepreneur Maev.[5] Indifferent to everything, *katorga* hoisted its tools and went. This illegal order arrested the attention only of Dué's priest, who went directly to the workers and entered the mines on foot with crucifix in hand. This was on Easter Sunday, and *katorga* "came to its senses" and returned to the prison.

The old men of Derbinsk's prison almshouse—terrible old men; paupers who despise everything in the world save money—complained to me that they "cannot even acknowledge a priest in their eyes." For them, there is no Easter. Derbinsk's priest told me, "I went there to talk with them but they interrupted me, they won't let you go on. Here you are reading or having a conversation, but over there in a corner they're all laughing and shouting vulgar abuse at each. I ceased my activities." It seemed to me that, on the contrary, his activities needed to be strengthened; but the father only looked at me in amazement.

In Aleksandrovsk's infirmary's library I found convicts reading the following books intended for spiritual and moral instruction:

1) Sixteen copies of the brochure *How Count L. Tolstoy's Heretical Writings Are Destroying the Foundations of State and Society*.[6]
2) Twenty-one copies of the brochure *Prayers of a Slave of Alexander the Blessed* (by the poet Pushkin).[7]
3) Four copies of *Homilies Concerning Vegetarianism*.[8]
4) Fourteen copies of the brochure *Theatrical Performances During Lent*.[9]

Of course these play a huge role, these brochures about Tolstoy, whose true identity they've never suspected; about vegetarianism, which they've never heard of; and, especially, *Theatrical Performances During Lent*. At the same time that the Sakhalin library is so well armed against theatrical spectacles, it offers convicts all of five copies of the *New Testament* and only two of the *Passion of Christ*.

And that's it.

50

SECTARIANS ON SAKHALIN ISLAND

I.

When, following a murder, chains prisoners are "sitting on the waste-tub," i.e., not allowed outside, they amuse themselves with a vile and cynical parody of the religious service.

A clergyman from the Aleksandrovsk Post synod was telling me how he'd prepared for death a trio sentenced to hang. "I spent three days and nights with them, they were never out of my sight. I slept beside them. Not a half hour would go by without them saying, 'Father, get up,' so as to read the Holy Scriptures in silence. We talked all about the hereafter. This was with two of them. The third, an old man, just laughed at all this. He'd curse and say, 'It ain't bad just to sleep.' We would begin singing and he'd say, 'I'm so glad you're singing!' Thus he blasphemed and died unrepentant."

And yet, this old man was a simple Russian peasant.

"They don't believe in God!" short-timers complain in horror. "Nine out of ten are atheists!" say the better educated convicts, especially those who've lived here for a long time. But you know they're all simple Russian folk, "accustomed to God," and their piety has to erupt in a kind of protest, and it erupts starkly, passionately, heatedly and fanatically.

It has indeed erupted.

In Rykovsk and its environs there arose a sect of "Orthodoxically-believing Christians." This sect, from out of nowhere, is of purely Sakhalin origin. It arose, perhaps, as a protest specifically aimed at the atheism in *katorga*. When I was on Sakhalin two years ago these "Orthodox Christians" were suffering "persecution," but this only strengthened their sectarian belief all the more.

To my question, "What kind of sect is it?" a clergyman from the village of Derbinsk (a very unique Sakhalin priest, a Buriat who'd "raised a hue and cry") told me they were "Molokans."[1] But the sectarians told me, "Christ is a rock around Whom non-believers are smashed," as a way of saying they were not simply Molokans.

The sect is as strange as its homeland, its members as unusual as their origins. In the words of the Buriat priest, their theology is "especially inchoate" and the sect evinces no specific characteristics. He "raised a hue and cry," that is, began a to-do about the Molokans after he'd lost his way in the world. Having heard of the sectarians' existence, he tried to arrange talks with them, but the sectarian Galaktionov (who truly does know the Scriptures like a multiplication table) began "to aggressively bombard the father with falsely-interpreted texts." These talks proved so "tempting" that the priest broke them off and decided the sect he was struggling against was not only simplistic but "dangerous." Then again, this priest believes Molokanism is a dangerous sect.

These passionate sectarians have eagerly awaited "persecution" here for their putative Molokanism. Specifically, they have ardently hoped for "unjust persecution." "Let them destroy us over wrongful accusations!" They've cheerfully prepared themselves for this wrongful persecution as if for martyrdom.

The Sakhalin sect of "Orthodox Christians," to repeat once more, is a strange sect; it combines both Molokanism and Dukhoborism and includes several Flagellants.[2] Although this sect has its "Jesus Christ," it is believed to worship its leader, its "Paul the Apostle"—Galaktionov.

II.

Galaktionov walks along the road with wide easy steps, as if an iron crozier had been set in motion. A well-off exile-settler, he dresses like a cattleman in a jacket and tall jack-boots. His long blond hair falls to his shoulders; his facial hair is blond; and his deep-set eyes gaze clearly and openly. His face wears an inspired look, as if he's composing poetry at that very moment.

Galaktionov has around 200 poems. And the poems he loves to compose are *compassionate* and "perhaps to be sung." I introduce one for example:

> By some fateful mistake
> I came to be in *katorga*,
> I won't lie about
> All the punishments I've suffered:
> The rod, the lash, even the knout

Often wounded my flesh—
Is there a spirit in the world?
God has forgotten me.

His other poems are in this vein.

Galaktionov is forty years old but he's an "old sectarian" of the third, maybe fourth, generation. How his ancestors came to be in Tomsk Province,[3] he doesn't know; but in 1819, his forefathers were exiled from Tomsk "to the shores of the Enisey 400 versts from Turukhansk."[4] His parents were tried three times for Dukhoborism.

Galaktionov was born "not without purpose but for great things." For three years the prophet Grigoriushka Shvedov had been predicting his birth and declaring that he would live on in him. When death arrived, Grigoriushka gathered everyone, stood up and bowed and said, "Well, now it's goodbye to everyone!" Then he died.

"That's when I began to live," says Galaktionov.

"So, Galaktionov, do you remember Grigoriushka Shvedov's earthly existence?"

"What don't I remember?! I remember everything!" Galaktionov acknowledges that, as a child, he probably heard about the prophet from elders; but with regard to his beliefs, they're his entirely.

Recognizing since childhood that he was destined for "great things," he plunged into a study of the Scriptures, which he needed to know. "There you are, learning them like a multiplication table. At night you happen to ask, 'What equals five times five?' and you answer. Thus I know every part of the Scriptures." Sectarian passion gave Galaktionov hallucinations. During a meeting with clergymen he watched them turn into demons. This led to a verbal assault—and exile. Galaktionov had owned a squatter's plot and some small gold mines. These were taken from him and he was sent to Kamchatka. "For speaking against Orthodoxy and the Church," according to official papers, he was deprived of all rights and deported from Kamchatka for settlement on Sakhalin.

Everyone on Sakhalin immediately disliked Galaktionov. "If I'd said, 'Let's go steal,' everyone would have loved me!" Galaktionov would become so preoccupied with reading through his texts that he would drop everything and sit on his *zavalinka*. Destined since birth for "great things," he became among Sakhalin's population of the vicious and fallen an un-masker. "Before me would be a man flopping and struggling in the sand like a fish—but I'd be beating him with words, with words!" Setting out for his *zavalinka*, Galaktionov would say to himself, "I'll take a dagger and carry it on my hip. I have to kill several people today. Here and there is a man existing on nothing. But I'll murder him with words."

"I sat on a letter as upon a throne, and killed with a letter as with a sword!" says Galaktionov of himself. "I was following the man known as Saul! People were wandering in darkness but I was making the darkness still darker with my exegeses. It was as if a learned doctor came to a sick man, told him it makes no difference why he's sick or what will come of his illness and, having broken his spirit, coldly turned his back and left him in silence."

Everyone was growing more and more dissatisfied with the un-masker. At that very moment, Galaktionov heard about an inhabitant of Rykovsk, the exile-settler Tikhon Belonozhkin, who helped all and condemned no one. Tikhon Belonozhkin's attitude towards criminals was frankly astonishing. Two years earlier, the fugitive "wheelbarrow-man" Shirokolobov had been the scourge of Sakhalin. A murderous beast, he was delivered to Sakhalin from Transbaikalia chained to the mast of a steamship. When Shirokolobov escaped, all Sakhalin could only think: "I hope they kill him!" Everyone hated and feared Shirokolobov, but Tikhon Belonozhkin actually gave him refuge. Even Shirokolobov marveled: "For me?" "I condemn your actions but not you. Your actions are foolish, but who among those involved in what you do is to blame— that for us remains unknown." In Galaktionov's words, Shirokolobov horsed around in the cellar the whole night and then slept off his hangover. "He couldn't fall asleep; he was pitiful. At the time, he could say only one thing: 'I have to strike out and murder and rob right now—what else can I do?' But when morning came he hadn't touched anyone, and left bidding farewell to Tikhon as to a brother."

Tikhon Belonozhkin's attitude towards crime and criminals made a strong impression, and news about Belonozhkin reached Galaktionov at the very moment animosity against him was reaching fever pitch. "I'd begun wavering at that time. I'd sermonize but watch the village turn against me." But Galaktionov became interested in Tikhon and he went to him. "I went three times. I approached the courtyard gate but didn't enter. I'd hesitate. 'So it is,' I'd say, 'that since childhood I've studied the whole Scriptures and everything I've said has been according to the texts. What else can a clumsy muzhik teach me?' And I'd go back."

Thus he went three times.

"I met him the fourth time. Suddenly, without ever seeing him, I knew who he was. I bowed and said, 'Hello.' And he said to me, 'I've been waiting for you. We saw a bright star moving toward the sun.' 'But how many times did the star approach the sun?' I asked. 'Three times.' Then I began to tremble. 'I came to you three times,' I said. But Tikhon was laughing with joy. 'I know,' he said. Then I started telling him my doubts. I went on and on but he just looked at me and joyously laughed. 'You know everything that's written in the Scriptures about Christ,' he said. "Now what do you want?' 'I'm looking for Christ,' I said.

'Well, seek and ye shall find.' Then I fell on my knees before him: 'Mercy.' I was lying down and over me there was a sweet voice. The voice said, 'Earlier, Saul, you followed the word of death; but now, *Paul*, you will follow the word of life.'

"I began to weep, scared as a fish before the knife, but he lifted me up and kissed and kissed me. I looked in his eyes and they were like windows, as if I were gazing into a chamber, but inside there was sweetness. I saw there was sweetness in his inner chamber—and recognized my own chamber's poverty and how I'd adorned it with ornate coffins. But everyone in his chamber was alive."

By "chamber" Galaktionov means, of course, the soul.

"Seeing that everyone in his chamber was alive, but that ornate coffins were in mine, I began to cry. But he showered me with kisses. 'Do not cry! Now you're a living man.' He was saying, 'Don't cry,' but I was crying three rivers. I asked him, 'How can you tell me to be joyous when you yourself are weeping?' 'This is nothing,' he said. 'I must weep for everyone, but you are not to weep.' Right then, I understood completely."

"What did you understand?"

"Who Tikhon Belonozhkin is."

"And who is he?"

"Jesus."

"Well, listen, Galaktionov, you're a learned man, you know …"

"Wise!" Galaktionov interrupted with a smile.

"But you know that Jesus Christ lived his earthly life eighteen centuries ago."

"And he lives now."

"How so?"

"Really, when is it possible to be without Christ? Back then, Christ suffered for people's sins. But new ones have been accumulating. Who will suffer for them? Look around you. Someone kills another; the poor are reduced to poverty; human rage causes destruction. Everyone can't be guilty. Who should suffer for this?"

"And so Christ is always alive in the world?"

"Always. One must suffer so that others may go on."

"Well, why was Tikhon exiled to Sakhalin?"

"For murder!" Galaktionov unblinkingly answers. "He killed two people."

"How do you reconcile this?"

"He's from Voronezh. From the wealthy. His father's next-door tenants were enemies. It went on and got worse. One time, his father left the city and one of the neighbors thought, 'We'll make out well.' They went after Tikhon, but Tikhon grabbed a wheel-shaft and, in anger, knocked in the neighbor's head! And when the neighbor's wife turned around he knocked hers in too. Thus a never-ending spitefulness ended in murder."

"He killed them. He's a murderer!"

"It wasn't *he* who killed, it was the anger. The evil had built and built between the two families and it burst out. It was for this evil that he was transferred to *katorga*."

Galaktionov credulously put Tikhon Belonozhkin in charge of Sakhalin's "truth-believing Christians." It is he—fanatical and impassioned—who has convinced Belonozhkin of his divine mission.

The modest Tikhon would never have devised in his imagination such a name for himself. While Tikhon Belonozhkin was still living in Voronezh Province he grieved that there were no "godly ones" around him, and that others had so lost faith that "they kissed only the dead but not the living, and begged forgiveness from the dead but not the living." Swayed by Molokanism, he became a Molokan. But upon arrival to Sakhalin Tikhon Belonozhkin grew disappointed with Molokanism. "It's not all there is. It's not the truth." He began conducting quiet and modest discussions with penal laborers about what, in his opinion, should really be believed and followed. His theory of the unrealizable seems to have produced an interesting conundrum. Around him on Sakhalin, no convict is allowed to butt in when he says, "I'll judge your actions but not you." And so people who are universally recognized as "guilty"—most especially those "dear fellows"—are considered "guilty of nothing" by convicts. "That's why we love kittens!" a smiling penal laborer told me, stroking a thin and ragged kitten who was wandering along the prison's sleeping platforms. "Because everyone sees all of us as 'guilty,' but guilt means nothing to a kitten. You and I are the same to a cat."

Tikhon Belonozhkin has always undoubtedly taken advantage of *katorga*'s particular sympathies, and not just those of *katorga*. Something in this modest man makes an impression. He served his *katorga* term during the time of the warden who wouldn't acknowledge un-flogged prisoners, yet Tikhon Belonozhkin alone was excluded. "The evil would happen during inspection," convicts say, "and twenty or thirty men would get worked over. He'd look around with the eyes of a lynx. 'Who should be next?!' He'd catch sight of Tikhon but his eyes would move on. 'You who are silent! Stand at the rear of the column,' he'd say. He didn't like it when Tikhon looked at him." *Katorga* found this incomprehensible.

Certain coincidences gave *katorga* the idea that Belonozhkin was a "special" man. One evening, Belonozhkin was crying over this and that, and they were humiliating him. "Why're you sniveling? Like a woman!" "My little heart is heavy." The very next day a prisoner was flogged: he was taken off the mare half-alive and later died in the infirmary. Several similar "prophetic" instances struck fear into *katorga*, and when Belonozhkin's family came and he was released for homesteading, they gathered to talk with this "special" man and listen to his strange speech.

That's when Galaktionov became a believer. Embittered by all who'd opposed him, this un-masker had tried still harder to sermonize in a world of suffering. In the modest Tikhon, Galaktionov found safe harbor, became "enlightened" and understood that "one must make Christ veritable"—thus he "came to believe."

But instead of simply gathering for heartfelt conversation, the old law-giver proclaims that he's founded a "church." Sakhalin's society of "truly believing Christians" has twelve "apostles," and each of these "apostles" has a "prophet"—"like a pillar to a brace." Besides the "apostles" there are four "evangelists"—"the arms and legs of Christ." Those who are married, like Tikhon Belonozhkin himself, live with their wives. Those who aren't, live communally, "not according to the law but according to love, or rather, the love that is the Christian law." The men call themselves "brothers" but the women, "lovers according to the spirit." Living together, they all say, "In the name of the Father, the Son and the Holy Spirit, we thank our Father!" They bow, kiss each other and hold discussions that often touch on Sakhalin's daily evils and decide various questions—spiritual, of course, and beneficial to *katorga*. For example:

"Each person should save himself. But in a place of starvation you cannot save yourself and you will soon devour another. But this is why it is a good thing to escape from Sakhalin. A spirit may only be born on the mainland, where it may toil. But for a spirit to grow it has to be baptized with water, that is, it has to swim the Tatar Straits. The Tatar Straits is the river Jordan. A person has first 'to baptize himself with water,' and then he can go to the mainland and grow as a spirit."

They're happy to perform their rites for whoever visits. "Where there's an oven, let them be warmed." Many of them have icons hanging in their rooms. "Were that the whole house be decorated with icons! To see them always pleases a good man." But it's "necessary to believe in the spirit and not in the letter," so that "this letter not control our life."

"Join us!" Galaktionov called to me. "We've found that the letter of the law has come to us and the heavens are rejoicing."

"And what do you know of the heavens?"

"There is joy in ideas, but the heavens... Do you think highly of heaven? Man is interested in the heavens." Galaktionov very much wanted me to devote myself to Tikhon Belonozhkin. "See him for yourself! Tell him I sent you."

I found Tikhon after he'd finished work. He has a nice homestead, and had been repairing a telega.

"Greetings, Tikhon. Is it true you're the person Galaktionov says you are?"

Belonozhkin raised his head and glanced at me with his veritably "sweet," gentle and modest eyes. "You tell me."

"No. What do you call yourself?"

Tikhon gave a smile, also exceptionally "sweet." "You want that I should name myself using letters? What difference do letters make?"

I spoke for a long time with this gentle, modest and kind man. He was interested in why I'd come, and I explained as best I could that I was gathering material to write what life was like for convicts, and he said, "You're collecting oil? I understand." Bidding me farewell, he shook my hand and said, "You've put much oil in the lamp. Light it, so there'll be a flame for the people. What else is oil for?"

51

CRIMINALS AND CRIMES

I.

"Do 'they' feel repentant?" Every person in close contact with *katorga* and to whom I turned with this question always said—either from malice or genuine pity—the same thing: "No!"

"The whole time I've been here, of all the criminals I've seen—and I've seen thousands—I've met just one who truly felt complete repentance, a desire to suffer for the sin he'd committed. And he was hardly a criminal!" Dr Poddubsky, leader of the medical division, told me, and that was an old man exiled for the cholera riots.

During his medical examination the doctor had written down "enfeebled."

"Stop, uncle!" the old man interrupted him. "Don't do this! Otherwise, how will I work off my sin?"

"And what was this sin?"

"We stoned a doctor to death. We threw stones. I, too, threw a stone."

"Did you hit him?"

"This I don't know, I didn't see where my stone landed. But still, I threw it."

Nonetheless, it's risky to say they don't feel repentant. True, they never express it. A penal laborer, like many a suffering person, is above all else arrogant. Any expression of repentance, of regret about what occurred, he considers a weakness which he will therefore not permit himself, and which *katorga* will in particular never demand of him. But why not account for the views and opinions of that society among which he's come to live?

The youth Negel,[1] a killer-animal who'd committed a vile crime, was recommended to me as the most awful scoundrel in all *katorga*. But this murderer sobbed, cried like a child, when telling me one-on-one what drove him into crime; and I had to comfort him like a baby, give him water, pat him on the head and call him tender names. I recall the dumbfounded look on the face of a certain official who happened to walk in on this scene. I remember he lost his head. "What have you done to our Negel?" he immediately asked in astonishment. You should have seen Negel's face for the several seconds he remained in that office room, how he swallowed his tears and made such efforts to stifle his sobbing. "Don't mention this to anyone," he requested of me when parting. "If they know in *katorga*, they'll laugh, the bastards!" This is often the reason for that "cold and impassive attitude" toward crime. Not always is there no tragedy where there are no tragic victims.

The criminal's dark soul is not easy to look into—for what lurks in its depths? In a certain educated murderer's apartment I focused my attention on a large painting done by the homeowner that was hanging most conspicuously. The painting depicted a gloomy northern landscape with looming, sullen spruce trees. Three rocks were jumbled together beneath them. "What is this gloomy scene?" I asked. "It's a landscape chiselled into my memory! A certain tragic event happened there." It was a picture of that very place where the homeowner and his comrade killed and hacked to pieces their victim. What was this? A pretense? Or a sick desire—constant and per minute—to forever re-open a painful spiritual wound and not allow it to heal? Was this ever-conspicuous painting a pretense, or a punishment devised by the criminal for himself?

As for repentance, I don't know—but horror and despair at the crime committed live on in the criminal's soul. You can hardly believe that they regard their crimes dispassionately. Vasily Vasilev,[2] who while on the lam murdered his mate and lived off his flesh, is reputedly one of the most dispassionate and indifferent. "Just listen to how he talks! How he cut off pieces of flesh and cooked them into a soup and added fresh nettles 'for flavor.'"

"If only I weren't scared of the sea!" he exclaimed in despair, telling me about the nettles and soup of human flesh. "If I weren't scared of the sea, I'd run to the edge of the world! The sea scares me… But I'd like to go so far no one could find me! I'd even run away from myself!" Such absolute horror resounded in the voice of this terrible man before me. He went insane not long after his crime.

Don't believe the "cheerful" stories about crime. They're often just a foolish way of owning up. Of course, if "just like that" you ask as follows: "Well, hey there, chap, howdja kill 'im?" then you'll hear a story replete with braggadocio and play-acting. As for Poluliakhov,[3] murderer of the Artsimoviches in Lugansk, I'd been told he spoke about his crime unusually willingly and unusually impudently, mocking his victims by always speaking of them with "formality": "Mr Artsimovich fell right here, but Mrs Artsimovich fell there. I killed him first, then went toward Mrs Artsimovich to kill her young son. 'Madam!' I said..." Etc. I talked with Poluliakhov for two days (true, with some breaks), and my nerves couldn't hold out, so *heavy* was this man. I inquired about his entire life; tolerated all the insignificant details of his childhood and youth that were of interest and dear to him only; and went into every triviality of his life. And when, after this, he came to the story of his bestial crime, there was in his narrative neither a "mister" nor that ironic formality, neither braggadocio nor play-acting.

I will never forget that evening. We sat together, leaning closely toward one another; he spoke quietly, almost frightened that someone else was listening to this horrible tale. It was not at all easy for him to divulge his story. He even mentioned certain details with especial difficulty, ones he'd always failed to mention in his cheerful stories about the crime. Truly, such details they were! I felt like everything was swimming before my eyes and swooned at such moments. Only my unwillingness to show weakness before a convict kept me from crying out: "Water!" You see, I needed to remind myself I was there in order to study *katorga*. I remember how after one such detail I leaned back and almost collapsed into the armchair, how I drew my breath and a sigh, quickly becoming a groan, unintentionally escaped me. "There, you see, barin, even you can't listen easily," said Poluliakhov. I looked at him, and in his face there was nothing.

There are stories made cynical by candor—of consoling stories, there are none. None!

I heard many confessions—not stories but primarily confessions—wherein criminals told me everything, often answering with blushing faces the most sensitive questions I asked with difficulty. I often heard these confessions eye-to-eye, behind closed doors, usually spoken under the breath so no one could hear the "secrets of *katorga*" being told me. The criminals always tried to appear nonchalant. But all they could do was try. It didn't take a physiognomy specialist to see how their memories agitated them, and how they tried to get rid of and hide this agitation.

The criminal's usual pose when talking about the details of his crime is as follows: He sits beside you looking somewhere off in the corner and absent-mindedly playing with something in his hands. A strained, affected smile plays across his lips, his eyes alight with some unhealthy, feverish glow. The color of his face frequently changes, his cheek muscles twitch, altering and tightening the sound of his voice. After every ten minutes of his story he seems sleepy, worn-out, utterly beaten.

But I listened to the stories and met criminals compared to whom Poluliakhov was just a "beginner." Lesnikov told me how he'd butchered two families of five and six persons. Prokhorov-Mylnikov told how he'd stabbed children. I was told about graves being dug up. They passed on their impressions of people sentenced to hang, who'd stood on the trap-door and voiced their regrets only when the noose was dangling before their faces.

Talking about their crimes "among themselves" is *katorga*'s usual occupation. "It's simply horrible!" I was told by those educated people who've participated in research expeditions on the island.[4] "You'd lie down in the evening and hear what the penal laborers, my porters and guides, were saying among themselves. All you'd hear is 'I killed so-and-so; but I killed so-and-so....'"

But what else can be talked about in *katorga*? In reality, there's nothing else to say. When a new prisoner shows up no one asks him, "What are you here for?" This isn't done. Everyone respects his dignity. No one wants to reveal the "weakness" of curiosity, and so discussion of this topic builds incrementally over several days. At first the questioner himself begins to recount, "coincidentally and by happenstance," what brought him here, and during this recounting will inadvertently, even accidentally, ask, "But what brought you here?" Inevitably, in the same tone of voice, he will say, "I know you wants to tell, but you don't wants to—it ain't too inneresting." And then the newcomer's story will be heard with great interest. You need to know what a fellow's brought to the "family," what his abilities are, whether he'll be a good comrade in case of escapes or crimes.

Ivans speak of their crimes only with braggadocio, play-acting and pride. I recall, for example, Shkolkin,[5] a recidivist doing his utmost to be recognized as an Ivan. He went so far as to murder the bandmaster's orderly in broad daylight. Reckoning the bandmaster "should have money," he showed up at his apartment when he was gone, bludgeoned the orderly, dragged him into the cellar and tried to carve him up; but the thin, extremely dull kitchen knife bent and wouldn't pierce the body. So Shkolkin turned his victim face-down, half-lifted his tunic (a soldier's canvas shirt) and, after beating him to a pulp with his fists, quietly and slowly stuck the knife in to make a small incision. At that point someone heard a noise in the cellar, sensed something wasn't right and ran off to raise a hue and a cry and tell the bandmaster. The governor was passing by at that very moment, so he ordered the murderer arrested.

Shkolkin is very proud of his crime, that he was arrested by the governor himself and that, sharing the opinion of all *katorga*, he'd "expected the noose." He's proud of his diffidence.

I spoke with him on this topic several times, and each time he forgot one or another detail; but whenever he talked about the crime Shkolkin always mentioned the same unforgettable phrase: "I walked up the cellar steps with a smile." He's proud of this smile with which he walked towards a crowd of people from the cellar where he'd just tried to carve up a man.

Often, however, this braggadocio excises something else. Often, there is simply a desire to smother spiritual torments, the desire to instill oneself with "courage." A desire to suppress the horror with laughter. So it is that children afraid to be left at night in a dark room will boast of their courage by day, laughing over all the world's ghosts. "Let 'em come, let 'em!"

"I was working in the cobbler's shop," an educated criminal, a murderer, was telling me, "and a certain Smirnov, a recidivist who'd committed many crimes, a young fellow, was working there with us. It was terrible to have to listen to his stories. They were about nothing other than his murders. He remembered them with pleasure and laughter. How he scoffed at the memory of his victims! He described their death throes and pleading comically, with a cynicism that ridiculed their words and requests for mercy. Sometimes my work would simply drop from my hands!

"Just the sound of that man's voice terrified me. Yet my spot on the sleeping platform was right beside his. He slept on the end and I next to him. Once, I notice the lamp near us somehow gets knocked over and Smirnov jump up beside the platform. His face is white, like it's been smudged with chalk, and his eyes are terrified and wide open. Horror was written across his face. 'Don't come near me…,' he says, 'don't come near… I'll kill you… don't come near…' He's shaking all over, and such a voice—it was terrible to hear. I was horrified. 'Smirnov,' I say, 'what's with you? Who are you talking to?' 'He's over there,' he says, 'he's over there… covered in blood… how that blood's gushing from his throat… he's coming, he's coming… he's coming over here… Don't come near me!' He grabs hold of me and his hands are cold as ice. His teeth are chattering and I can feel the heat of his fever. 'God is with you! Who do you see?' 'Him, my last one,' he whispers. 'Just relax, let me get you some water.' 'No, no, don't leave… don't leave… Yes, that's him… him…' So we end up going to the water-basin together. He's holding onto me, looking around startled, afraid to be a foot away. I pour him some water and he comes to. He asks to lie down in my place (he was afraid to lie on the end) and I lie down beside him. 'I'm terrified,' he says. 'Then why do you laugh during the daytime?' I ask. 'Because I laugh at what's terrible. They come to me at night. I try to be courageous but they mock me.'"

Bragging about crimes—this is usually only a cry, a desperate wail, by which they attempt to muffle the voice of conscience. The criminal's soul is a sea for which there will never be a calm. Now a terrible storm suddenly erupts, now there's but a ripple on the surface. But a very large ripple is so easily mistaken for complete calm at first glance. A crime leaves an ineffaceable mark, a deep fissure in the soul. A certain penal laborer complained to me that for refusing to work, he'd been put in chains and held in seclusion for two weeks:[6]

"Who're they? Why do they want to kill us? To crush us like some insect? Indeed, can a man really be killed? I was out there, and it seemed I'd killed the man! I myself heard his bones crack when I smashed his skull with an axe. 'No,' I'm thinking, 'he won't breathe again.' I even chopped his head off. The head rolled away… But he's absolutely alive. He's living right here with me. He doesn't move a step away. They'd stuck me in the dryer.[7] They're thinking there's just one person, but he was right there with me! 'You weren't killed,' I says to him, 'otherwise you wouldn't be in the netherworld now.' They lay me down on the mare and he's standing beside the executioner baring his teeth. 'I didn't kill you, so I shouldn't be lying on the mare,' I tells him. When it's dark he goes everywhere with me. He's alive, and as long as I'm alive he'll be alive and he'll follow me to my grave beneath a nameless cross. To completely kill a man is impossible!"

II.

It remains to speak about one more type of braggadocio, very widespread, and I'll familiarize you with this type of braggadocio by using the usual spokesmen.

I'm on my way to the prison. I see a small group of prisoners has formed, and among them is some loudmouth passionately orating about something. He sees me and stops.

"Have I disturbed you? If so, I'll leave!"

The prisoners reply, "What for, barin? Disturbin' how-now?… Go on! The barin can lissen too… It's terribly innerestin'."

The speaker was relating how he'd escaped from prison, and continued slowly, coquettishly, "for effect":

"Very well!… As I was sayin', they was soundin' the alarm. All the guard, the whole comp'ny, assembled for me: 'Such-'n'-such a prisoner's escaped!' They give chase but I'm ahead of 'em. I'm runnin' in front an' they're behind me. Bayonets was glinting, bullets a-whistlin'… They's whistlin' over me head. Little by little, they stopped. They'd fired all their bullets but not a single one hit me…"

"Was they shootin' on the run?" a young chap who was being "educated" wanted to know.

"On the run."

"If they'd stopped they'd 'ave shot better."

"'Tis a pity they didn't ask you, fool!"

"Sergeant-major!" one of the listeners interrupted him. "Go on!"

"I happens, me brethren, to come to a stop. I sees I'm outta strength. 'Right here,' I'm thinkin', 'I'm gonna fall offa me feet and they're gonna git me. But there ain't no such-a man as Efim Trofimov, so me life's in me hands!' I hears them overtakin' me… Footsteps comin' closer. I look back and saw somethin' terrible: glimmerin' bayonets. The guards! But in front of me is this tree… A tall tree, almost 300 feet… I collects me strength and goes towards it. One, two and up I climb… Scramble up onto a bough and sits there. They're runnin' by underneath, outta breath, but one peels off and is barely breathin'. I grows silent, but this last of 'em sees me. 'Git down, you sonofabitch,' he shouts, 'or I'll learn ya!' 'Well,' I says, 'alright, I'll come down right away, soon as a crawfish whistles. Just wait a little while!…' A bullet coulda got me easy, but they'd fired all their bullets. And he's afraid to climb up after me 'cause I have an axe, and I'll just bash in his noggin. I hear talkin' goin' on between 'em: 'You start climbin' first!' 'No, you!' 'No, you…' And I'm sittin' there by meself not sayin' a word, havin' a grand ol' time. Only, brothers, they decide to chop down the tree, so's to knock me outta it. They starts digging up the roots with their bayonets. The whole tree's swayin' and shakin'. They're diggin' away, while I'm climbin' higher. They dig, I go higher. Once I reaches the very tip-top, I waits. The tree begins givin' way… 'Yes, again! Harder!' they're yelling, pushin' on the tree. But you can tell by their voices they can't hardly breathe for just standin' there. 'Harder still…' The tree's shakin' under me, but I'm sittin' on the tippity-top holdin' on… And as the tree's fallin', there's just a groan from the boughs and a crunchin'… When the tip-top comes crashin' to earth I hit the ground runnin'. They're at the root-end but I'm at the tippy-top, and so has a good 300 feet of *maza*[8] on 'em… Down at the tree-roots they suffered terribly, but I was sittin' comfy in me seat!"

"Fantastic!" the prisoners cheer.

But a smart-aleck who wasn't going to suffer this tall tale said, "Like they say, 'seven versts to heaven and it's all through the woods'!"[9]

"And what're you on about?" *katorga* fell upon him. "You causing a fuss, you blowing bagpipes? Don't listen and don't cause a fuss! He's an inspirer of fraternal love!"[10] *Katorga* was indignant that this "absorbing story" was interrupted.

There are many such storytellers in every prison. And what stories there are! Wild, fantastic, absurd stories about crimes that never were! You listen to yet another and marvel, "His adventures would actually fill three volumes. And what volumes they'd be! But, God knows, he's inventing such rubbish!" It's Ponson du Terrail, the *sauveur de Montpensier*[11] of *katorga*. He's not believed, but isn't listened to for the truth. *Katorga* regards him as do we our "boulevard novelists": they don't demand truth but are satisfied with clever fabrication. It's the same with them as with good storytellers, and this can hardly be called a "bragging crime." And I don't think "bragging" could make a special impression on *katorga*. Sitting beside a fellow twenty-four hours a day, studying him willy-nilly, you come to know what he's capable of and what he's not—and you'll distinguish immediately what in his stories is true and what is a boastful lie.

Katorga attributes no special value to crimes committed "in Rasseya." "We was all brave over there!" It regards with a certain respect, however, a criminal who's taken, thanks to crime, a large haul; and deeply contemns those who commit crimes for pennies. You can't surprise *katorga* with even the worst crime. You come to *katorga* to—so to speak—play among virtuosos. *Katorga*'s heroes are the recidivists, and it values only crimes and offenses committed here, on Sakhalin. Any audacious fugitive or fellow who mouths off to a warden is, in its eyes, far more a "hero" than a man who butchers an entire family in Russia. Ever since he escaped and, daringly and in full view, grabbed a guard's rifle, Poluliakhov has been esteemed by *katorga*. But only one crime grants a perpetrator indelible glory, and this is the murder of anyone from the prison administration. *Katorga* always regards such a man with esteem—that fellow who "went to the noose." You have to fear a man who fears nothing, and such a man is timidly regarded with respect. Anything less makes no impression whatsoever. "All that was is gone! Now show us who you are!" The past is dead. *Katorga* is interested only in what is "left" in a man.

Up to now we've talked only about criminals' attitudes towards the facts themselves.

"Well, what about their attitudes towards their victims?"

What do they feel towards them? Malice, rarely; disdain, often; absolute indifference, usually.

"Really now! It *is* pitiful!" a criminal usually says to you in response to the question, "Don't you pity your victims?" But better were he not to say this! He pronounces this "pitiful" as if speaking not about a life but some bauble unfortunately lost! You hear in his voice such indifference—an indifference toward everything in the world save his own person. You sense that he's saying "pitiful" simply for propriety's sake: "as it goes, that's pitiful." As such, he's humoring you!

Murderous robbers recall their victim with contempt if the wretch failed to hand over the money straightaway or put up a fight. This contempt seems to them well-deserved: had the person laid down the money his life would've gone on! One criminal was unable to recall without smiling how, when he approached her with an axe, his hapless victim cried out, "Why are you laughing? Don't you know whose home you're attacking?" "Madam!" he answered with a smile. "We don't care."

Malice towards their victims, an incalculable malice that never dies, is felt only by those criminals who've endured much before resolving to commit the crime. One penal laborer in Korsakovsk District, who murdered his "barin" because he'd horribly mistreated him, answered me with such hatred for his victim. "I'd yank him from his grave so's to strangle him again!" He was sorry that he hadn't made him "suffer before his death." I remember that a certain wife-murderer—he chopped off her head—responded to my question, "Don't you pity her?" by answering, "Were she to come back to life, I'd chop off her head again, the slut!" He said this with such hatred; though, in general, he's one of the most good-natured people in *katorga*: friendly, meek, ready to share all he's got. Clearly, the deceased did him a bad turn!

In general, those with contempt for their victims are for the most part mild, good-natured people. They're people whose patience simply snapped.

In all candor, only once did I happen to observe a truly deep regret for one's "innocent victim." This was the wretch Gorshenin, who regretted killing the engineer Korsh during a paroxysm.[12] This introduces a question that will perhaps interest you just as it has me. It's a question about hallucinations and dreams, about this "hiccup of the imagination," this "belching of the conscience." Are they pursued by their victims' ghosts, just as Shakespeare's protagonists are pursued? Or are Sakhalin's criminals made of different stuff? Though, as you know, those Shakespearean protagonists pursued by the ghosts of the murdered are not all alike. Macbeth sees the phantom Banquo in the daytime, whereas ghosts terrorize Richard III during a dream, during a terrible nightmare. But the phantom of the king and brother murdered by King Claudius appears before him neither in a dream nor while awake. I questioned all the prison doctors concerning penal laborers' hallucinations, and of all these doctors, only one Dr Lobas, a man profoundly familiar with *katorga*, was able to inform me of a particular case in which a criminal sought to pursue a ghost.

I later met with the criminal, a certain Weinstein, the recidivist on Sakhalin who murdered the mother of the earlier mentioned Negel. Some say he killed her because she declined his advances. He asserts that he killed her out of disgust. "She weren't a young woman, an' she was unfaithful to her husband. How unfaithful she was! She disgusted me, so I killed her straight outta some kinda hatred, some kinda contempt, crushed her like vermin." Her bloodstained ghost gave him no peace while he was in the isolator. He couldn't sleep at night because she'd always enter and "spatter him with blood."

I happened to hear an interesting story about hallucinations[13] from a certain exile-settler I gave a lift to from Dué Post to Aleksandrovsk Post.

"What's taking you this way?" I asked during the trip.
"I'm going to the district office to ask for a new cohabitant."
"And is your old one bad?"
"Why 'bad'? She was a good woman, but she died… Died two months ago. I can't be without a mistress in the house. Housekeeping! But they might give me someone who's worthless!" We proceeded another quarter-verst in silence. "Thank you, Lord, that she died! The Lord took her! With her gone I've peace of mind. Terrible was her suffering."
"How so?"
"She was shaking so much."
"Shaking, why?"
"Well, it'd be night. She'd start shaking at night. She tormented me—the fears! Like stewing in a fire, she was hurtin' so. She was shaking all over, and her legs and arms was like ice. 'He's coming,' she says, 'he's in the hut!' Then she'd drop off and I'm thinking she's dying right there. 'He's grabbing my legs,' she says. 'He's bending over me—he's from the grave!' 'He' kept coming after her. She'd been married and had poisoned her husband (he weren't happy 'bout that!). But he was dying in such torment that she smothered him out of fear. Such terror was in her voice. 'I must have silence, I say.' I myself almost started!… Ech, I can't recall it!… Then she exhausted herself, faded, just faded away and died. Heavenly Kingdom, may she rest in peace! That's where she no doubt is!"

A certain few complain that they see "them" in their dreams from time to time; but the majority looks at you in astonishment when you ask, "I say, do you want to see such trash in your dreams?" However, for everyone it's a case of nerves.

Ultimately, I nevertheless do not believe—do not believe because I've never seen—that a criminal is entirely at peace regarding the crime he's committed.

Perhaps their passion for cards—this gambling to which, along with similar games of chance, they give themselves over from morning to night, every spare minute and often from night to morning—perhaps this is a means by which to forget themselves and divert their minds, for the hardest criminals are also the most passionate gamblers. Each distracts and forgets himself as he may.

I witnessed how a criminal, after he'd committed a truly bestial murder,[14] sought oblivion in a game of… totalizer.[15] "You gamble and feel nothing! You forget about 'it'!" Fortunately for him, the horse-track in Moscow was open two or three times a week, and during the several weeks before his arrest this wretched and loathsome man lived in a kind of ecstasy from gambling and drink. When the corpse was discovered he was thinking of the horses: "Will she go the four versts or won't she?"

What is their attitude toward punishment? This is a far easier question to answer. They regard it very simply. They've been convicted, deprived of rights and exiled here—and so they've paid off their debts. "Ain't we been skinned alive?!"

They're told to go build "a new life." And they try to build a new life. They build a life that pleases them, not the law. They escape, proclaim themselves *brodiagi* and get a year and a half of *katorga* instead of their ten, fifteen or twenty years. This is called "changing your fate," and everyone dreams of changing his fate.

And don't believe that criminals thirst for *katorga* and endure it as recompense. Yes, it may be so—as long as they don't know what *katorga* is. While still fresh, memories are especially painful and when honest with himself, this "shaggy beast" tosses about and claws at his soul... It's then, perhaps, that they thirst for "suffering." Like people who beat their heads against walls during an unbearable toothache, so too will they try to overcome this other ache to distract their minds from this terrible improbable pain.

Over there... And here... Perchance to thirst for suffering, to enter into it, to don heavy chains, to sleep on sharp stones. But who in a kind of "atonement" wants to lie down in stinking, fetid, mucky, viscous filth?

And *katorga* is filth—a foul sucking filth.

It remains still to speak about their attitudes toward condemned innocents, towards those known to be suffering unjustly. Such are on Sakhalin, as everywhere in *katorga*, and in the prisoners' language they're said to have gone "from the plow to doing time." *Katorga* holds them in contempt. No! Not even contempt. It is a hatred, an envy of people whose souls are not in agony, and expressible only in what would be a kind of contempt. This is the hatred of the scoundrel for the honest man; the tortured envy of the filthy for the clean. And these wretches' attitude is an attitude doubly embittered. They do not trust honest people; the world of outcasts disdains and hates them... And within this hatred appears in its entirety the very suffering of the criminal soul, the agonizing pangs of conscience.

52

CRIMINALS AND JUSTICE (FROM OBSERVATIONS ON SAKHALIN[1])

> The accused don't have copies of the
> indictment: they used their copies to roll cigars.
> —*From a recent trial in Elisavetograd*

"What a district!" My hair is standing on end. "God, can these citizens really be pleading ignorance of the law?!" Even the most experienced of them, who should have known, poorly understood what happened to them in court. I'd ask them the contents of a prosecutor's speech (would they have listened to it?!) and, Lord, they spouted such rubbish. One criminal, for example, would've had me believe that the procurator, indicating some blood-stained material evidence, was demanding he be punished the same way—that is, murdered and chopped into pieces.

Most "conspicuous" offenders exaggerate the significance of their crimes and expect a death sentence. "Yet, you know that according to the law that's not going to happen!" "But how should I know?!" Though presumably nothing prevents them from looking into this matter. Uncertainty, expectation, pre-trial solitary confinement—all this shatters their nerves and produces something of a persecution complex. They all complain of "injustice." A criminal is surrounded by enemies: the investigator hates him and wants to drag him into court; the procurator lives off his hatred for him; witnesses have been bribed or coached by the police; the courts are obviously biased. Many told me they were even "underfed" before entering court. "Allow me to report to you that they wanted to suffocate me!" "How so?" "They stuck me in the isolator, so no one could see. They didn't let anyone in. They gave me the absolute worst food, it reeked—they set it near 'those places' on purpose. They hoped I'd gag."

Legends about "the olden days," about "before the reforming of the system," have been ensconced in our people's memory. Only this can explain their grossly ridiculous stories. "Originally, when the mistress[2] was arrested by the investigator, she promised to cook for him free of charge for three years. He let her go. But this caught the administration's attention and they both went to jail."

Habituation to "a system of formal evidence" has planted deep roots in the people's consciousness and perverted its notion of justice.

"They didn't judge me fairly! Didn't make sense!" a criminal often tells you.

"But you say you killed him?"

"Kill, killed, but no one saw. Weren't no witnesses, so how can they prove it? That ain't the law!"

This habituation to such a long-practiced "system of formal evidence" (?[3]) makes a person lie to the court as well as refuse to acknowledge his guilt, instead of improving his luck with a heartfelt confession.

I recall an old parricide in Dué who told me his story. It was heart-rending to listen to him: his terrible family drama, the spiritual hardship he'd had to live through and, most of all, that he, a family man, had murdered his own father. He'd gotten no leniency. But was it really impossible to find twelve jurors who wouldn't have been moved by this candid honest story, this painful tale?

"I was convicted without confessing!"

"But you didn't tell everything straightforwardly and openly. You know, your wife, son, his wife and neighbors were in court—couldn't they have backed you up?"

"Well! We knew there weren't no witnesses and so thought nothing would happen."

The peasantry—"country (the Russian) people"—make a particularly sad impression. It's not immediately possible to determine how a certain one of them has been convicted: with or without a jury.

"Twelve people were sitting opposite you in court?"

"Opposite?"

"Yes, yes—opposite! Twelve right here and two on the side. Fourteen in all."

"Who was countin'? A bunch o' folks was sitting to the right, just so. Tidy folks. Gentlepeople... Wait, wait!" He's remembering something. "That's true! They was sitting opposite, but still everyone kept coming and going. They'd come in, leave and come back again. Who was they?"

"That's it, the ones I mean! You see, they were actually your judges!"

"I say, thank you! But I was thinking, 'Oh, they're just merchants,' an' that they was takin' an interest."

Most of them can't even answer the question, "Did you have a lawyer?"

"Did you have a lawyer, an advocate?" I ask a little muzhik who's complaining he was convicted "unfairly."

"Abvakat? Nah. We wanted to get one from the tavern but he asked for too much. Didn't have enough in me pockets!"

"Wait, you know I mean, 'Was there a lawyer for you?' For free, you understand, for free? A real advocate, not someone in a tavern!"

"I wouldn't know about this."

"In front of you, in front of the bars you were behind in the court—was there anyone sitting there?"

"Indeed, someone *was* sitting there. Such a handsome gentleman. Fine figure he was. His jacket weren't buttoned. He went courageously about with his jacket flapping wide open."

The bailiff, evidently.

"Yes, but next to him? In black city clothes, with a pale silver badge right here?"

The little muzhik makes a thoughtful face—he remembers: "Curly-haired type? Not too tall?"

"Well, I really don't know how tall he was. But did 'Curly-Hair' say something?"

"Curly-Hair? Let me remember. He chattered away. Then, when the prokurter finished, he stood up. The prokurter spoke very sharp—stiffly. Asked everyone to put me underground forever—'Bury 'im,' he says."

"Very well, that was the procurator. But what about Curly-Hair?"

"He said somethin', too. Only, I confess I weren't listenin'. Meant nothin' to me."

"But that was your lawyer, your advocate!"

"I say! But I thought he was one of the masters. One of the judge's own!"

"He came to see you in prison, before you were in court?"

"Who? Curly-Hair?"

"Curly-Hair!"

"Curly-Hair weren't there. Oh, was he there or not? He *was* there!" Finally, he remembers. "That's right! He was there once. Kept askin', 'Did I have witnesses?' How could I have witnesses? We're poor people. We can't hire witnesses for nothin'!"

Is there anything more helpless?

It must be said that defense lawyers shouldn't deny their "assigned" clients due attention, for prior to court many don't even recognize their own lawyers…

53

KATORGA LABORS OF A KONOVALOVA[1]

"Is the peasant Anna Konovalova, twenty years old, guilty of arranging with others the premeditated deprivation of her husband's life by means of asphyxiation?"

"Yes, guilty."

Konovalova has been sentenced to twenty years' *katorga* labor. She's leaving for Sakhalin instead of the Island of the Cross[2] and is boarding a Volunteer Fleet steamer in Odessa's harbor.

"A first-rate woman! This'll be a good run," predicts the crew. They journey from the Black Sea to the Tropics, where the blood ignites like liquor and the women's hold turns into a floating den of iniquity. "It can't be helped!" say the captains. "Ban them or not, it doesn't matter. The bastards manage to crawl into the hold through the air vents." This is a typical phenomenon, but the female convicts don't object.

The steamer *Iaroslavl* transports female penal laborers from Aleksandrovsk Post to Korsakovsk Post. Senior officer Sh, himself a very stern man in matters of duty, kept the key to the hold and wouldn't even give it to his young assistants, and so "nothing happened" on the steamer. Here in Korsakovsk, when the female convicts were being unloaded onto the barge, they abusively screamed, "You faggots! Go to a monastery! You shipped all us women for nothing. You brought us from Odessa and coulda done whatever you wanted with us!"

The women were angry because they'd not gotten the meager earnings on which they largely depend. Crews will usually bring into the hold money as well as the vodka, cigarettes, produce, dresses and fabrics they buy in port. Young women pay; old women manage their funds. In the hold there's foul language, the selling of one's body, blood-thirsty and callous stories and an obsession with fashion. Fallen women, professional criminals, victims of circumstance, women raised in city slums, peasant women traveling to follow their husbands—all are tossed into the same purulent and disgusting heap. It's like the living have fallen into a pit of corpses.

Certain ones hold out. A famished honorable woman, abused and ridiculed, sits in a corner and unwontedly gazes with envy at how everyone around her drinks, treats herself and prances about in new dresses. The woman looks around in horror. "Where have I ended up?" A sailor appears, barely able to stand on his feet. "What do I do now?" He tells her, "Some hold out until Ceylon; but in Singapore, lo and behold, all the convict women come up on deck wearing silk dresses. They're most chic! The captains say, 'Akh, you sluts! You can strut among yourselves in the hold, but you'll march on deck dressed as prisoners.'"

So the steamer arrives in Aleksandrovsk Post, where another steamer with women's goods is already waiting. Exile-settlers, the so-called suitors, are haunting the entrances to all the administrative buildings.

"Your worship, show a commander's mercy and give me a cohabitant!"

"They *used* to give us women for that, chap! Now, they only allow you to take a wife."

"Well, allow me to take a woman as a wife. They're all single."

"Aren't you a drunk, a gambler? Why a woman for you?"

"Mercy, your worship, for setting up a home!"

The exiled women have disembarked. Those with children who've voluntarily followed their husbands are left to tremble in fear in the quarantine hut. The female convicts are sent to the women's prison.

Here on the walkway in front of the women's prison, suitors peer through windows for "cohabitants among the new mix." Female convicts survey potential male cohabitants. The women are dolled up; the suitors strut. "A piecemeal fellow, in a word!" laugh some correctionals strolling by. For the most part, all the suitors are "entirely piecemeal": a neighbor's cap, another's shoes, the jacket of a third, the woolen shirt of a fourth, the waistcoat of a fifth. Many hold the large harmonicas that epitomize exile-settler chic; several even have waistcoat chains for show; and all have gifts: spice cakes, nuts, calico-print dresses.

"Allow me to give you some nuts. What might be your name?"

"Anna Borisovna!"

"If only you'll be my cohabitant, Anna Borisovna, there won't be a day you awake or lie down without a gift. Because you've transfixed me! I'm afire."

"Alright. A little talk. Will I have to work?!"

"Not in this lifetime! Don't you know a woman don't work in the Sakhalin system? You'll be able to live at home! I'll scrub the floor so clean! Life'll be easy. You'll thank God you ended up on Sakhalin!"

"You all say that! But do you have a pocket watch? Maybe your waistcoat chain's just for show?"

"I always have me a watch. You can't hear it 'cause the cover's on it. Please! It's 11:25."

"Ah well, be off!" The suitor walks away arms akimbo. "Looks like you're walking crooked!" she yells after him.

These potential female cohabitants put on airs, scoff at and cut down the suitors. The suitors get confused and rage in their souls but show excessive courtesy.

A middle-aged muzhik from Andrey-Ivanovskoe,[3] who'd ended up in *katorga* after killing someone during a fight "at an important patronal festival,"[4] gave the commandant a note in which he pleaded: "Give me a government cow and a woman so's to establish a homestead." In the chancery office, they replied: "There aren't any cows on hand now, but you may take a woman."

He approaches the windows seriously, businesslike, and looks over the women as if looking over cattle at a fair. "We should have us a wide one, a peasant woman, 'cause if she's skinny, what can she do? Had me a skinny one, a *brodiaga*. Just chewed bread and spat up blood. Died just like that—don't even know what her real name was. Can't remember it. We needs a big-boned one, so's to work."

"Won't you come be my cohabitant?" he bows to a stout, middle-aged, pock-marked, one-eyed woman.

"And whaddya got?" the other asks, suspiciously sizing him up with a singular glance. "Maybe you got nothing to eat?"

"Why 'nothing'? Gotta horse."

"Cows?"

"No cows. Hoped for manure but didn't get it. They'll give me a woman now, but a cow won't be till spring. Go on, if you please!"

"But you got swine?"

"Pair o' swine. Six hens."

"Hens!" mimics the smart-aleck and fancy dresser with the "pocket-watch," an exile-settler from Arkovo No. 1, that most underhanded of settlements. "This devil needs a horse, not a woman! Don't go off with him, One-Eye! He'll work you to death!" He turns back to Anna Borisovna. "You'll like my ways. So, Anna Borisovna, let me ask: Does you wish to come live in merry Arkovo? You'll never sit at a table without fresh meat. You'll be munching spice cake with vodka, kerchief or not, apron or not. That Semen Ilich is a trickster. Comes for the pleasure of a lady but gives nothing for it!"

It used to be that any one of the bachelor officials from the mining administration could pay the treasury three rubles a month to have a sweet Konovalova. This has now been prohibited by the governor. Earlier, she would have simply been summoned:

"Konovalova!"

"Here."

"Get your things and come here. You've been assigned to Mikhailovskoe, to exile-settler Petr Petrov."

"I don't wanna go."

"No one's asking what you want. Grab your things and don't look a gift horse in the mouth! I don't have time for you people!"

Nowadays, if she says "I don't wanna," they tell her "As you wish!" and leave her in prison.

While female cohabitants are pairing off with suitors, a Konovalova sits alone in a large, damp, dark deserted ward. She drags herself through cheerless, gray dark days. "I wish they'd send someone to clean the floors. Maybe a spare man. That would cheer me up."

I went one day to the women's prison. There sat a German woman breast-feeding a baby. She'd lived somewhere in Revel[5] with her husband, had her own "littel shtor" but wanted to expand her options. "We had a lot of children." She torched the store and got sent to *katorga*. "All my children stayed with my husband."

Here, she lived with a cohabitant, gave birth to a child, but later got into a squabble with a guard, who complained, and they took her from her cohabitant and put her in prison. "He said I steal. I steal no-ting." With a perpetually downcast melancholy face she was wandering about the ward unable to find a place for herself and, mistaking me for an official, began to weep, "Your worship! I have not milk. Die my baby will. I lost my milk because of soup. Order them clean my floor, I want. On the way, I earned money…"

"How did you earn it?"

"Well, I…" And she so openly, simply and precisely described how she had in fact earned it, that I could not even take it in at first.

"Was this," you may ask, "a calculatedly cynical and bitter outburst?" But the German woman looked at me with such meek, kind and clear—almost childlike—eyes, that it's impossible to speak of "cynicism"! She'd only begun learning Russian in *katorga* and, as with all female convicts, called things by their names.

"I would give highest gratitude! Say I can go free for hour. One hour!"

So this Konovalova faced her long, endless days of solitude, for no one lives in the women's prison.

They brought me a Konovalova, this time an exile-settler.

"What are you in prison for?" I asked.

"I came because of my cohabitant."

"Came how?"

"I suddenly gave him what for."

"But why?"

"But what the hell did he give me? I worked, he drank!"

"Then you should have complained about him to the authorities!"

"Good heavens, why would the authorities bother over such trifles?"

"What will happen to you now?"

"Whatever! For now, they'll keep me in prison till the trial, then add more *katorga* and give me to some cohabitant again." She turned to the German woman. "And why're you sitting here?"

"I don't want to be a cohabitant."

"Fool! You're sitting in prison living on watery gruel and still won't say, 'I agree to go with a cohabitant!' Say it to a fellow! Don't be afraid!"

Whether or not she now joins a cohabitant, the woman has been given a choice: freedom or prison.

It's difficult, of course, for a Konovalova to be "obstinate." Here's one who was not. Thus we see a Konovalova who's come to an agreement with an exile-settler. She enters his dark—completely dark—hut. The "piece-meal fellow" suddenly detaches all his parts: he gives buckled boots to a neighbor, jacket to another, leather cap to a third. Before her on a bench is a frilly outfit.

"Well now, our sweet cohabitant, time for you to go out to *fart*!"

"What do you mean, '*fart*'?"

"But, to go see Mister Ivan Ivanovich. Dress yourself quick in this kerchief and apron, because Mister Ivan Ivanovich won't wait. Hurry up, or someone else'll be serving him his cohabitant. And we gots to eat."

"But this is how I should work for you?"

"This is the custom on Sakhalin. The situation. This is why we take cohabitants. But don't you worry. I'll stake your money and win such a bundle you'll go around a lady. But for now, get going."

"But you know that there, in Russia, I strangled my own husband!"

"He-he! There in Rasseya it was different! But here…! Well, strangle me! You'll have another cohabitant like me. We're all the same. That's why they're called '*katorga* labors.' Welcome to 'em!"

54

THE MOST UNFORTUNATE OF WOMEN

From the jetty to Aleksandrovsk Post is about two versts. The road leads through a copse. To the right and left of the road, beyond the ditches, stretches the coniferous taiga, hacked to pieces and quite sparse here. Snow still lies in hollows and gullies but "bear's ear" is already sprouting on tussocks and in glades. Its yellow leaf emerges curled in a tube from beneath the ground, and luxuriantly opens as if wanting to say, "Admire how beautiful I, the bear's ear, am."

"Akh, damn her," an official was saying as we were going through the copse. "Sashka-the-Bear has already been spreading herself about. Geez, her flag is flapping in the wind. Akh, what a creature! And in such cold." A dirty rag was hanging from one of the trees.

Meet Sashka-the-Bear,[1] which translates as "one who's fallen to one of the lowest levels of human degradation." Sashka-the-Bear is an Aleksandrovsk Post celebrity. She knows everyone, but her clientele consists of *katorga*'s lowest of the low: log-haulers and wood-cutters and convicts working in brick factories. Everyone despises Sashka-the-Bear. Even the lowest of Sakhalin's women speak of her with nothing other than loathing. A woman generally wins low esteem on Sakhalin; she's typically referred to by low titles. But for Sashka there exists a special nomenclature by which it's impossible to show greater contempt.

Sashka is around forty-five years old, with a flat face you can't dissemble and at one time could have been attractive, and perpetually lackluster eyes. Wind, cold and bad weather have fastened to her visage a leathery skin resembling parchment. Sashka dresses, of course, in rags.

In winter, the aging woman makes the rounds of Aleksandrovsk's neighborhood flophouses. These terrible flophouses contain former prison *maidanshchiki* and, given their décor, are indistinguishable from prisons. The same communal sleeping platforms line the walls where men, women and children sleep side-by-side. Here, too, flops the liquored-up Sashka-the-Bear until the next day.

But as soon as the cold and melancholy Sakhalin spring is in the air, Sashka relocates to the taiga near the busy road between jetty and post, and here, in the official's vivid expression, "spreads herself about" and hoists her flag—that is, hangs a rag from a tree near the road. This is a conventional sign, and you'll often witness the following scene: a convict from the free prison walking along the road as if nothing were wrong reaches the "flagged" tree, glances over his shoulder and, seeing no one, lumbers across the ditch and vanishes into the taiga.

All day long Sashka just sits in a little glade getting chilled to the marrow, waiting for callers. Passing time in the woods, Sashka goes about like a wild animal, and if she sees a freeman instead of a convict, runs from him the same way you'd flee a criminal. If Sashka happens to bump into someone face-to-face, she timidly backs away, her lackluster eyes filled with fear as if she's going to be assaulted.

Her penurious callers give Sashka two or three kopeks. So how much does Sashka earn? Twenty kopeks a day; though, in those days when, for example, miners in the nearby Aleksandrovsk mines earned a percentage on the coal mined and sold, Sashka could earn up to forty kopeks. Thus does Sashka-the-Bear, this female of the species, exist for *katorga*'s paupers.

You may think you've reached the lowest level of human degradation. No. This abyss is fathomless, and where lies the point below which a man can no longer fall is difficult to say. Even Sashka has someone she can regard with contempt. This is the *brodiaga* Matvey. Her "cohabitant." Why Sashka needs him is difficult to understand. Perhaps it is simply out of unconscious habit that she has *another*. All their interactions seem limited to reflexes.

Sashka is the *brodiaga* Matvey's means of existence.

It's evening and Sashka sits in her little glade tallying the day's earnings. Sixteen kopeks. There are still another two callers; but perhaps someone has left the shacks in the market and slowly entered a backroom speaking through his teeth, and is drinking a huge wineglass of highly diluted spirits. In the taiga the crunching of twigs can be heard. Someone's coming. The crunching comes closer and closer, the steps sharp and stealthy. Matvey appears among the trees. Sashka immediately jumps to her feet and scampers off into the taiga.

"Stop, demon!" Matvey shouts, lunging for her. He knows from her maneuver that Sashka has money, and there begins this fleeing, this hunting, this pursuit of a brutalized human for slaughter, a battle between two human creatures over who will drink a glass of vodka today. Sashka runs through the taiga, tries to hide in a thicket, circles round trees and, scratched and torn by thorns, gets hung up on a tussock. Matvey falls upon her, beats her without knocking her down and howls, "Give me the money!"

"I won't! I won't!" Sashka shouts and clutches her sixteen kopeks in her fist. Blood pours from her nose. Matvey is punching her face but Sashka won't open her hand. Matvey pulls her fingers and twists her arms until finally, unendurable pain causes Sashka's fist to open. The money is now in Matvey's hand.

Having punched her once more, an exhausted Matvey starts to recover. But Sashka suddenly leaps up and, like a dog, sinks her teeth into his arm. Matvey drags her to the ground by her hair and kicks her in the stomach with all his might. "Moan, you demon."

Sashka has collapsed as if dead. Beaten and bloodied, she comes to only because someone nudges her with his foot. "Stand up. Wipe yourself off, sinner. Mind what your mug looks like." A "caller" stands before her. Sashka begins wiping the mixture of tears, blood and mud off her face.

More than once I asked myself what this treatment was for. What was this Matvey to her? A cohabitant? A friend? A man she was used to? In a conversation with me Sashka herself pinpointed it exactly: "A steady robber."

Thus Sashka lives in the world with her "steady robber." And this, too, is called a "life"…

55

VOLUNTARY FOLLOWERS

A certain elder exile-settler told me, "On Sakhalin, the soil is soaked in blood and drenched in women's tears. Will anything grow in it after this?" In the history of Sakhalin *katorga* there are pages written in blood and tears. These pages are about those wives who've voluntarily followed their husbands to *katorga*.

The steamer carrying penal laborers is arriving at Aden.[1] Sorrow is raised from the holds: a bundle of 600 unsealed letters for home.

"I must inform you, my dear spouse," writes, after innumerable salutations, a prisoner sentenced to twelve years' labor, "that I've arrived safe to Sakhalin and from my heart wish you well. Families do very well here. To start, each soul gets fifty-five acres of land, a pair of oxen, a cow, a pair of swine, four head of sheep, six hens and fifty measures[2] of wheat for sowing and for the home. A thousand free settlers will soon arrive. So it's good here. The commandant's friendly and generous and just asked if you, my wife, will be coming soon. If you come soon, they'll release me from prison straightaway and we'll live like rich folks. But for as long as you don't come, I must languish in captivity…"

Immediately upon the steamer's arrival in Aden, a dozen men are writing to the village about how they've safely reached Sakhalin and how richly families live there. Vaska Gorely devises all this. Vaska is a "returnee." He was exiled to Sakhalin, escaped, crossed the stormy Tatar Straits on a log, grew "weak from hunger" in the taiga, reached Russia, committed a new crime and was captured. Facing him: a life sentence, being chained to a wheelbarrow, lashes. In the hold, he conducts the gambling with handmade cards; cheats at cards; provides—as an experienced fellow—advice "regarding Sa*kali*n" to noviitiates who recompense him with pennies; and saves his money so as to later get a privileged position in the chains prison and become a "father," that is, a usurer.

Each hold has a returnee, and they all tell the convicts about Sa*kali*n. They even tell something of the truth. Here's one of the injustices of Sakhalin *katorga*: Ivanov and Petrov have each committed the same crime. They've murdered together, they've robbed together. Both are sentenced to one and the same term. But Ivanov is a bachelor and sits in prison, whereas Petrov's family has followed him and so he lives freely as an exile-settler, performing only "certain" tasks and is essentially free "for homesteading." "Why am I locked up?" says the bachelor convict. "Because I killed someone? It's because I don't have a wife! If I'd a wife I'd go free!" Given this, there's the writing to wives of pure fabrication. The returnees warn them, "It's important that your wife comes soon. Soon as the wife comes, you're allowed to homestead. You won't be pining away in prison, fool!... So go on to her about how you've already arrived! Let her know about the hens, the swine and how many sheep there are! This is most important for you, *chaldony*! You *chaldony* are green!" "*Chaldon*" is a Siberian word meaning a free sedentary person. It signifies anyone who has a house and family, who has what he needs, anywhere in the world. In the way the fugitive penal laborer, the *varnak*, pronounces "*chaldon*" can be heard great hatred for even the barely well-off, that enormous contempt the homeless *brodiaga* has for all who boast of a home and family...

"Don't forget to write about the hens, the hens! She'll come right away!" mocks a returnee dictating a letter to a scribe. Every hold has its scribe who composes ungrammatical letters. In the second hold, penning letters in bold, beautiful, professional handwriting, is the *brodiaga* Mikhail Ivanov, a barber ("nicked a fellow's gullet and my business disappeared"). *Brodiaga* Ivanov writes "form letters" under the dictation of Vaska Gorely, with whom he shares his work, and each of their duplicate compositions details the charms of Sakhalin life. But in the fourth hold is a true belletrist. A well-read Pole, a joiner convicted of a foul crime against his own sister, he floridly writes, "I bow my tempestuous little head to your precious knees and kiss your sugary feet and your pale, wondrously beautiful hands." Poor, poor Matrena Nikonovna, of Tula Province, Epifansk District, Ziborovka Village! In what bewilderment she shall be when it is haltingly read out to her that her muzhik, "Stiapan,"[3] kisses her feet—"sugary," no less! So much anguish, bewildered anguish, will be on her face when they begin reading this fanciful rubbish to her.

Poor, poor illiterate Rus. So much fabrication, but also so much verifiably gripping anguish is in these letters to wives. They're full of such terrible desperate pleas: "Come here!" Certain prisoners exhort and charm. "You'll recall my vow to you in the church, and how in the prison jail you vowed you would come without fail. Don't listen to anyone: go to the city, my wife, and get yourself arrested!" They exhort and charm and use the formal "you," because a Russian likes courtesy in letters.

Others threaten. "Come here, because the administration's told us that if a wife doesn't agree to follow her husband, he can remarry." A young soldier, exiled for a crime in military service, actually sends a formal note to his wife. "If you don't come, I'll take a beauty for myself here on Sakhalin out of spite—it would be a shame to spit on you!" Certain ones threaten with a "come here." "If you don't come, then it's goodbye, Annushka. All the same, I think I'll see you. Although not soon, I'll see you. I ain't close by—but I'm coming."

Nevertheless, most exhort and request. These pining fellows entice their wives with nothing other than a "Come here!" A certain one reassures: "Only commonfolk wrongly say that monsters and an ancient king, half-fish and half-man, come out of the seas. There's nothing to this. Leave, and don't be afraid!" Another advises coming "just for your health." "You'll take baths on the steamer. The water is salty but very healthy—if a person's sick, then he can get better in this water and any illness is naturally driven out." This isn't so strange. But very many will actually try to tempt their wives with... fruit. "Oranges, which you love so much, are here as nowhere else except the Suesk (Suez), and I even bought a dozen lemons for two kopeks. Lemons as easy as that!"

Reigning over and dominating all these naïve entreaties and terrible, grasping, importunate supplications seemingly betokening death is the lie about "an easy, rich Sakhalin life." Truth be told, I would have thought this a fancy had I myself not read in prisoners' letters the following lines: "I don't know how to thank God that I've come to Sakhalin. Life here is, in a word, 'don't work: eat, drink, breathe and be happy.'" And all this, based on returnees' stories and recommendations, is written and sent to the village a month and a half before arrival to Sakhalin. And throughout the villages they read these letters. and go to the city and "get arrested" to commence a martyr's life.

What causes these women to abandon home and loved ones, "to sit in jail," to while away in transit prisons—what causes these women, whose universe ends with the neighboring village, to set off across the sea for the edge of the world, across oceans filled with monsters toward another, distant foreign land?

Love? "She's smitten!" You rarely hear this answer from "voluntary followers." More often you hear, "I say, it's no great joy to live in the village afterwards. You can't look at anyone! You can't count the insults! Anyone can shame you, anyone can slander you: '*Katorga*-woman! Your husband's a penal laborer!' I'd go anywhere to get away from here." You also often hear, "Really, what that sonofabitch wrote! Such-and-such about 'wonders'! 'Sa*kali*n, O Sa*kali*n'! I believed that snake had a conscience. He destroyed another man—but I didn't think he'd destroy his family. I trusted him. I left believing we'd really live the life... But here... he gives you 'Sa*kali*n'!" The poor woman looks around in desperation at a hut that's been slapped together, at an empty courtyard in which there's "naught a chicken," while her children whine, "Mommy! I'm hungry!" But there's not a crumb in the house.

Very many go out of a sense of duty. "Once God has brought you together there's no separating. A promise is given and there's a wedding in church—this means forever..." Very many go in hope of finding "in a new land" a new life that's peaceful, remunerative and prosperous. In the old land were sin and a brutal life. In the new land no one knows them and they know no one.

"It's just like being born again! We're gonna live." They'll give up everything for land and freedom. Everyone will work indefatigably. But once there...

"Voluntary followers" are, as I've already said, poisoned in various ways by the autumn crossing—the most difficult.[4] The steamer arrives at Sakhalin, in Aleksandrovsk Post, in our late autumn, which is Sakhalin's early winter. Here's a picture of the arrival of voluntary followers as described in a letter to me by the wife of one of Sakhalin's doctors:

> I happened to visit them (the families of voluntary followers) in the quarantine shed, where, upon arrival, they sit in this terrible place in anticipation of being claimed by their men. Many waited a very long time, until inquiries were made to locate these wretched wives' husbands. That day, Sakhalin had a powerful blizzard. It whirled and blew so you couldn't see two feet in front of you. We barely reached the shed which, as you know, is by the sea—but the sea wasn't visible; you could only hear a howl, a cry, a kind of booming. A more evil hell cannot be imagined, and many of these wives and children had nothing on but rags. People literally packed the shed. When I arrived with Dr P, everyone dashed over with questions for him: "Has my husband turned up? Where's my husband? When will he come get me?" Children wailed, "Did you find daddy? Where is he? When will he come?" But it's no great luck even when these daddies and husbands do turn up...

Those with husbands in southern Sakhalin have to wait an entire winter—a brutal, freezing Sakhalin winter—and must live in Aleksandrovsk Post on government rations that barely keep one from starving to death, until the first spring run. "But we need clothes and boots! What will my children wear?" "How will they survive?" "Yes, how will they?!" Those being asked only wave their hands.

I was walking past the depots in Aleksandrovsk Post. I see a bunch of women, and the prison's commander is distributing rations to them.

"Who are these people?"

"Voluntary followers. Tomorrow, they leave aboard the *Baikal* to Korsakovsk for their husbands."

"When did they get here?"

"They got here November last year. There're no steamer connections with Korsakovsk at that time. They winter here in Aleksandrovsk until the first spring run."

"Couldn't the steamer that brought them here have taken them to Korsakovsk first?"

"Perhaps, perhaps, but regulations require all voluntary followers be delivered to Aleksandrovsk first, and then distributed from here."

Starving and freezing because of "regulations," not understanding why they have to winter in Aleksandrovsk, these women, growling and cursing, were piling their rations in their kerchiefs and mixing everything together: groats, fish, bread. "You should be more careful, auntie!" "Mixing them makes no difference! Everything's going to the same place! We're famished. The hell with Sakhalin!" Not far away, one woman sat crying her eyes out.

"What's wrong with her?"

"Clearly, she didn't want to come here for her husband! She ruined herself over the winter!"

"Just like hunger and cold can, you can ruin yourself!"

"How can she show herself to her husband now?"

The woman was in an interesting position. "Oh, he beats me, dearies! Oh, it's the end of my little life!" the wretched woman was howling.

Next to her, another had taken up a different cause. "Why am I now on Sakhalin? I want to be in little Rasseya!"

"You yourself decided to leave!"

"But did I leave for myself? I came for all my children. I could always work as a laborer and survive on my own. But where could I go with children? I came here because of the children."

"Well, where are your children?"

"Dead. The two littlest died on the steamer, the older one died here in Aleksandrovsk Post over the winter. I'm bitter and alone, and I'm to go to my snake? They're gone because he was missing!"

I was at the unloading of the steamer *Baikal*. A woman on the wharf was pulling her hair and sobbing. Her children were crying. Next to them stood an exile-settler, beaten, disheveled, kneading the cap in his hands and repeating, "Forgive me!..." His eyes, too, were full of tears.

"Lord! Lord!" wailed the woman. "Why are You punishing me! That such a good, kind, submissive, hard-working person should be given to a bad man, a murderer! So that he can beat me to death again and cripple the children! This, from such a man! That's how he's loved me! Would that my children had a better father!"

"Forgive me... Forgive me!" repeated the exile-settler through chattering white teeth.

"Such a bitter woman!" one of the officials said to me. "There, in Russia, her bastard of a husband destroyed her life, and here she's learned the fate of falling in love with the man. She should've left him."

"So, it's impossible... That is, not to turn her over to her husband?..."

"Not possible. She came here for her husband and she has to go with her husband. Regulations!"

So after all their ordeals here they finally "go," these "voluntary followers," to the husbands they've saved from prison at the cost of their own terrible, gloomy lives. But who, instead of her "Stiapan"—her husband sentenced for killing a man during a drunken brawl—exits the prison? Out comes a *zhigan*, a gambler ready to lose both her and himself. The card game is the all-grasping, all-absorbing terror of *katorga*. I saw *zhigany* lying in hospital because of emaciation: they'd gambled away their rations and eaten nothing for weeks. I saw *zhigany* betting their medicine against other patients in the hospital. Out comes a *kham*, that most despicable creature even in *katorga*. Starved, emaciated, half-mad from the hunger of avarice, this beast will do anything for a kopek. Out comes a wretched specimen of the "herd" who's become an inveterate liar, a wily, beaten cowardly wretch. And she who is walking toward her husband Stiapan ends up living with a *zhigan*, a *kham*, a herd-man.

There are exceptions, people who manage to remain intact in prison and leave it the very same "Stiapans" who entered. One hope saves them: "The wife will come, the children will come. We'll get by." This hope preserves and saves them among the filth and horror of *katorga*.

But this is the exception. As is said here, "They're saved, but at such a price—Sa*kalin* demands a life for a life. Such is the land!" There are so many wrongful victims! So many wrongfully destroyed lives!

"She who's voluntarily followed" is assigned along with her husband to a settlement. "Not a single horse at all!" you hear from female settlers, the "voluntary followers" in Sakhalin's remote starving settlements. "They give you a hoe, but how much soil can you hoe? How can I plow a field?!"

"You should request a horse."

"They absolutely won't give us a horse. We asked and asked—we could barely get a cow on the installment plan.[5] And *brodiagi* killed that. Now we've no cow but have to pay the government each month!" This is a very common plaint. And so the meager homestead produces hardly anything, but what it does fugitives—*brodiagi*—destroy.

In the end, the female convict becomes an enviable object for "those who've voluntarily followed": "They get a ration, all of 'em. But what do we get? Don't they get a place to live? 'Walk the streets'—but I don't want to. They give her a cohabitant and if she don't like him, he's gone and they give her another!"

"*Katorga* jobs" for women amount to the sewing of linen that female convicts are obliged to do in prison. A female convict-cohabitant, especially the younger and comelier, prefer "to go strolling," and the sewing usually falls to "those who've voluntarily followed," thankful for the pennies that keep them from indigence. Here indeed is a surprising picture of *katorga*! A female convict is "strolling" but a woman who's sacrificed herself, voluntarily followed her husband, is performing her "*katorga* labors."

On the way to Korsakovsk Post I had stopped in the home of one voluntary follower and was discussing her lifestyle, when suddenly the door swung open and in flew her neighbor rustling in a new dress, a female penal laborer and cohabitant of a card-playing exile-settler—a beautiful young woman.

"Mitrevna! Do you have a little egg? I have guests again and they brought vodka and want eggies!"

Mitrevna actually turned green. "You haven't even heard of a chicken!"

"What're you snapping at, bitch?!" The cohabitant disappeared with the same rustling, slamming the door behind her.

"Leech!" Mitrevna shot after her. She wasn't a human being to this poor woman shaking with rage. "She gobbles eggies! Guzzles vodka! Strolls about! She puts on airs around her sisters! She gets a ration! That's right! And she's a convict! But ain't we convicts? She hacked her husband to pieces so's she could walk the streets?! But we're disappearing from hunger. She gets a ration, and what do we get? What do we get?!" She was howling, rattling cooking forks, thrashing about, clutching a child under her arm and continuing to work, crying with anger and speaking hatefully about the female convict—she, this "Russian woman"[6] who'd "voluntarily followed" her husband to *katorga*.

To be alive is always to fear that at any moment the loved one you came to *katorga* for could be undone by a capriciously-made complaint, and be put in fetters and sent to the chains. You curse him until out of breath for not doffing his cap to someone leaving the staff club, saying that he should that moment have stood up without his cap, trembling from impotent rage and terror, and said, "Excuse me, your worship!" You witness with every hour and minute the brutal, often foul, humiliation of your loved one.

Thank God there are on Sakhalin few women from among the intelligentsia who have voluntarily followed. In Aleksandrovsk Post you meet a miniature young woman, nearly a child, with a childlike face and girl's braids. She looks 17 years old.

"This would be one of the administrator's daughters?"

"No, this is penal laborer E's wife."[7]

Here this child is, amid *katorga*. It seems she should be living under her parents' roof. This child's life is such a tragedy it could not be endured by an experienced grown-up. Her man, still very much a youth, murdered his friend. "I did it under the influence of a cerebral inflammation!" is how he facetiously explains it. He was sentenced to twenty years' *katorga*. Theirs was a "young love" that took place while both were still in school. This child wanted to follow her wretched suitor, and so strong was the resolution leading her to become a martyr that her parents let her do it. She managed to get permission to follow her suitor aboard the same steamer that delivered him. This took a lot of work, because it wasn't "according to the rules." In Odessa, the young woman was told: "You may leave only on the next steamer. There's no way with this one." This youthful girl, straight from school, began to plead, beg and implore—and got her way. Odessa's mayor ordered her taken on the steamer. You can imagine what a journey it was. It is so difficult to be a passenger on a *katorga* transport. It's hard to travel with the shackles' incessant rumbling and clanking rising from the holds. And to listen to this terrible incessant song knowing that amid this choir *his* fetters are ringing; to walk along the deck knowing that there beneath your feet, in the hold among gray cassocks and half-shaved heads, among people who've lost their human appearance, your beloved is languishing...

"She saved me!" E told me. "I'd have perished without her. They were letting me stay in the infirmary ward so that I'd have it easier, and in Singapore a guard approached me." In Singapore, the steamer moors right alongside the dock and lowers its gangplanks. The proximity of land teases convicts. They're always entertaining notions of escape in Singapore. The guard told E:

"Listen, I left a crime behind me. As soon as the steamer gets to Vladivostok they're going to hand me over to a court, a military court that shows no mercy. My only chance is to escape. Do you want to escape with me? Here, I'll be alone in a strange land, and without knowing the language, I'm a goner. You're a man who knows the language[8] and together, we can't lose. I stand guard tonight in the infirmary—let's leave together."

"What a thirst for freedom had been awakened!" says E. "My very head was spinning. But I remembered she was there, that she'd given up her whole life for me. What was I going to do? I told the guard no."

He couldn't have escaped, of course. The British authorities would have promptly captured and returned him, and then—lashes and a life sentence to *katorga*. "I'd have perished were it not for her." The wretched E is correct. Here, in *katorga*, on Sakhalin, she saved him—but at what price?

"Sa*kalin*! You have to give a life for a life. That's the way!" So goes the convict saying. Upon arrival to Sakhalin E, as a long-termer, was transferred to the chains prison, while the young woman was taken in by Dr L's family. So began a "life" of brief distressing holidays: a half-hour meeting every Sunday in the prison. They looked forward to when E would be released from the chains. But the Sakhalin administration meddled with this. She'd received permission to follow her suitor, so, "of course, we had to get married immediately." The young woman was instructed: "Marry him immediately or leave." The wedding took place in Aleksandrovsk's cathedral. Guards from the chains division delivered the groom. Picture a marriage amid tears—a wedding during which everyone wept. "Ever since, my heart skips a beat when I think of it!" the doctor's wife told me. The young couple went from the church to Dr L's home, drank tea, and ten minutes later E was again returned to the chains. The wedding feast was over. Mrs E stayed behind and lived with Dr L's family. Like those before with her groom, the Sunday meetings in prison continued with what was now her husband.

What did this small suffering bride give up? She'd been a student at the conservatory, an outstanding student promised a bright future; and now she had to play at officials' evening soirées, play them dances, accompany their singing—all, of course, "as a courtesy." "What do you think you're doing?" Dr L's family often told her. "What are you up to? Look, you've completely exhausted yourself, you're not yourself…" "It's impossible, impossible," she'd answer, "they've sent invitations. They might take offense at me—and retaliate against *him*!" Whoever has been on Sakhalin and seen how an unfortunate woman fears for her husband deprived of his rights, will understand with what horror, surely, the poor woman's heart was obsessed by this one idea. She continued to play. The good administrators' families considered it improper to shake hands with a "convict's wife" so she, arriving in the evening to play "as a courtesy," would give a curtsey to everyone and slowly sit down at the piano to await orders. "Play!" One relentlessly cheerful figure especially pestered her—the chancery's head clerk, already mentally ill at the time and soon to be sent to a madhouse. "Listen to how you play!" he'd say with typically saturnine pomposity. "You're not playing right! Not so fast! Play slower. Now play happier! Devil knows what you're playing!" She wept and played; played hunched low over the keys so her tears wouldn't be noticed. "And still he took offense." But it was all for "him."

This went on for several months. Suddenly, a very influential person came to Sakhalin from Petersburg.[9] To honor his arrival in Aleksandrovsk, authorities staged an evening of amateur performance and a dance in the hay barn, the usual place for performances. Mrs E played in her capacity as a musician. The influential guest, before whom everyone bowed, walked around looking at those in attendance, noticed Mrs E standing beside the piano, and went straight up to her and said, "Hello, my child!" and… he kissed her hand, for he'd known her in Petersburg. Everything changed in a single moment. Officials' wives crowded round Mrs E; and after this, caps were doffed upon meeting her. Everyone gave her their uninterrupted attention and solicitude. Her husband was soon released from prison. They put him in charge of the meteorological station and even gave him a small salary. She got a job as a teacher.

They live in a small comfortable apartment near the meteorological station and school and have a child. Their apartment's adornment is a splendid piano that relatives sent from Russia. Near the piano is a portrait in a garland of spears of her great teacher, A. G. Rubinshtein.[10]

Music—it is all that beautifies her life during long, long Sakhalin winter evenings, when outside a blizzard whirls and moans and her wretched husband sits and draws or writes poems. Disciplined classical music is her only happiness, after her child—and she plays it as perhaps no one else can. Only very unfortunate persons can play very well. There is so much suffering, grief, torment and tears in her playing...

They are fortunate, if there can be fortunates on Sakhalin... But what she's been through has forever traumatized her. This trauma burns in her childlike eyes. Her entire existence is a trembling fear, a fear for him. Frivolous and still a boy, he likes a bit "to treat himself," as they say on Sakhalin, and to stroll along the street with a friend from among the officials or a visitor. One has to see her at those moments. The impact of the "influential person's" visit has certainly already weakened and there are few who like her husband. Administrators aren't pleased that an exiled convict can walk around so "freely." He bows, frivolously and insufficiently deferentially, to the small fry. Not far away are the chains and penal laborers being subjected to corporal punishment.

"I'm going with you!" says Mrs E. As if enveloped in horror, this small woman is shrinking in fear as if she were being assaulted at that very moment. He doesn't want an awkward situation in front of an outsider. She's delicate by nature, infinitely delicate, and she's scared for him. "I have to say a couple words to you!" She's trying to take him aside.

"You always have secrets. Tell me later."

This slight bruises, and she replies, "You know that I'm fightened for you! You so don't want to understand this!"

As one senior official explained to me, "He's still young, and there's no way he can understand that he's an exiled penal laborer now."

So you try to help her out, and tell him, "You know, I really should go on alone, I really need to see so-and-so."

"Outstanding, I'll go with you."

Finally, she somehow manages to take him aside, to whisper very quickly with an imploring gaze, and he, blushing slightly, says, "You know, actually, I'll come along by myself later... I have a really smooth operator here..."

Thank You, Lord!

They present a strange pair. He's capable, even talented, but rather superficially so; everything soon gets to him, everything quickly irritates him—this dilettante who considers himself a genius. He loves to strike poses, to put everything down on paper: poems, drawings, even his crimes. He regards himself as an extraordinary person passively submitting to the sacrifice he endures. She is quiet, timorous, shy, infinitely delicate and modest, as if not recognizing, in her delicacy and modesty, the great sacrifice she's making. He loves her but is sometimes capricious and domineering. She thinks only of him, looks after him as if he were grievously ill and never complains to anyone about her luck.

When she speaks about their life on Sakhalin she tries to smile happily. And this "happy smile" on a sad, pale face is like a weak ray of light in a gloomy, cloudy autumn sky… If he's involved in a conversation (and they're inseparable; this woman-child looks after him as if he were a baby), she hurriedly gazes upon him with terrified eyes as if frightenedly saying, "Can't he tell it's difficult for me?" Only once, when he was away, did she utter a reservation, which moved my heart. I'd brought her a greeting from a naval engineer (she's from a family of sailors) who knew her as a child. "Pass on my greetings. You'll see him but I… I'll certainly *never*…"

She saved her "bridegroom." But is his life worth such a sacrifice? In writing now about this martyr, I'm ashamed of my deficient prose. She warrants that mighty poem by which were portrayed "Russian Women."

"What sort of a woman is she?"
"An exiled convict's cohabitant!" the official scornfully says.
"Did he come by her here?"
"No, she came from Russia. She was his governess. G's family didn't want to come, but his governess went and filed a request and an exception was made. They've had a child here."
"How do they get on?"
"Like we get on! Pshaw, it's no kind of life."

This G held a very important position in society. He was exiled for a filthy crime. *Katorga* is a horrible thing. Like a nutcracker, it crushes a man in surprising ways. It crushes entirely this shell called "social standing" and instantly reveals either a seed or simply rot. It's hard to meet with a man who could so quickly sink to the bottom as he did. Like an axe! You wouldn't at all say that just a few years ago this drunk with a constantly bruised physiognomy was well-liked and even shone among society. It's like he's spent his whole life in arrest battalions.

Surprisingly, he "fit into place in *katorga*." He engages in petty swindling and drinks, and his favorite company is a Greek convict exiled for robbery, a specialist among the home-intrusion class. Nothing else occupies his life.

G was saved by the "cohabitant" who followed him to Sakhalin. Without her, he'd be in the chains prison and, given his ways, would have suffered everything. Thanks to her, he lives freely in his own house, drinks, works as a clerk in the mining engineer's chancery and collects petty bribes from mine laborers. But she—a cohabitant despised by all, an educated woman who arrived to spend time in a society of thugs—lives for the vodka-soaked stories of his exploits. She lives and does not complain.

"Absolutely! He beats her when he's drunk!"

"We had an educated woman, Dobrynina, who voluntarily followed her husband. She'd completed *gimnaziia*," the wife of Rykovsk village's district chief was telling me. "She died, poor thing, of nephritis. They'd been sent to a new settlement! She died there in an earthen hut. That's where the woman was taken."

Do you know what a new Sakhalin settlement is like? Surrounding it is the taiga—the coniferous, dead Sakhalin taiga. There's silence. Neither a rustle nor a peep. Only a woodpecker occasionally taps, as if nailing shut a coffin's lid. It's eerie and quiet. The wind has beaten into a plica the tops of the fir trees. Some administrator thought this would be a good place to build a settlement and gave it his name and patronymic: something like Petrovo-Ivanskoe or Afanasevo-Mikhailovskoe. Forcing its way through fallen branches and tundra, a party of exile-settlers came to this virgin wood. Few "held onto" saws because there typically weren't any. Just axes and ropes. They all came here to battle the taiga. They spent the night beneath the open sky. They chopped down trees and built huts. They somehow knocked together a small frame out of tree-trunks, covered it with soil for warmth and made a kind of roof out of branches. They'd sleep in these dark lairs and in morning issue out to uproot tree-stumps and turn the soil without a horse or plow, with just spades and hoes. Each time the hoe struck ground it turned up four inches of soil. Thus, by inches, was the taiga's soil dug up and, ever so slowly, the taiga made way for a new settlement. On Sakhalin, they say, "*Katorga* isn't in prison. *Katorga* begins with removal to settlement!" And they speak the truth.

It's hungry work. Exile-settlers come to the post for rations in two rotations. They go through the taiga with axes, usually hacking themselves a path; they cut down trees and build bridges to cross Sakhalin's swift mountain rivers. When they arrive they receive their ration, and when they return again with half a starvation allowance along the way, they eat. But wait right there. It's said that some will wrestle with the taiga for a week, living off berries and working to exhaustion, then one day gather together, filthy, sweaty, not having bathed for months, and lie around in their dark huts. Having fallen sick, they can get help from nowhere. Lying in the earthen huts' stifling atmosphere, they either recover or die.

In such a hut, in such a new settlement, lived, contracted nephritis and died the wretched Dobrynina, an educated woman who'd come to suffer *katorga* with her husband. What a life, what a death…

Thank God few educated women are among Sakhalin's "voluntary followers."

Nearby me in Odessa was such a woman who'd decided to follow her husband, exiled for killing someone during an argument. Volunteer Fleet sailors are a wonderful people, and they bustled around to make her as comfortable as possible. They gave her a cabin far from the engine where it was quieter; a chaise-lounge appeared on deck outside her cabin: "This is for you!" There was something thoughtful, touching and sad in this.

"Lord, it's like you're delivering her for execution and want to ease her final minutes!"

"But what are we delivering her to?!"

56

NATIVES OF SAKHALIN ISLAND

Two years ago a certain personage, visiting Korsakovsk Post in southern Sakhalin, absolutely had to see "a native of Sakhalin Island." A twenty-year-old chap was brought to him and the personage ceremoniously and publicly kissed this "native."

What exactly sent him into such rapture I don't know. He was kissing, I submit, not this unfortunate chap; rather, he was kissing the still more unfortunate notion of a "Sakhalin colony." Before him was a living embodiment of this notion, a free inhabitant of Sakhalin who hadn't been brought here but was born and raised here.

I saw many of these living incarnations of the colonial notion. I saw Sakhalin natives in freedom, I saw them under investigation in lock-ups, I saw them in prisons serving out criminal sentences, and I cannot say that they especially sent me into rapture.

I was tracking down the executioner Komlev, who's retired and had come to Aleksandrovsk Post "to make some easy money." Komlev is a famous Sakhalin executioner. Only two death sentences have been carried out on Sakhalin without him. He's hanged thirteen men, is a specialist in these matters and, according to his own words, "No who knows how to do this except Komlev."

Encountering an exile-settler, I asked, "Do you know where I'd find Komlev?"

"Over there, your worship, you'll see a wee hut at the end of the street. Go there. He's living with a Polish woman who's hired him to babysit her children."

"He babysits children?"

"Exactly. He'd come here to hang Tumanov…"

While I was touring *katorga* it was rumored that the *brodiaga* Tumanov would be hanged. Tumanov had fired a pistol at an official. Sakhalin insisted on a death sentence "so as to warn" *katorga*, but it didn't happen: Tumanov was sent to a mental hospital. Hearing about a death sentence, Komlev showed up in Aleksandrovsk Post to earn three rubles, for without him there was no one to do the hanging.

"He came to do a hanging but then got hired to babysit children?!"

"What else can the old cur do?!"

In the little hut a tall strapping woman was bustling around a stove. Three children were eating in a corner.

"Please sit down. Komlev's gone with the little one to 'the fund' (the government store). He'll be back soon."

"The Polish woman," a peasant from Grodno Province, was still serving her *katorga*, sentence. She'd come here (women especially don't like to betray their crimes) "for suspicion of participating in the murder of her husband."

"Suspicion fell on me because I'd been forced to marry against my will, even though another man had fallen for me. Well, they thought I'd been 'drawn' into it." In *katorga* she's learned to speak, not Russian, but the *katorga* language. "They sent me here, but how I woulda suffered in Siberia, they say. Here, I get by."

"But whose children are these? Did you bring them from Russia?"

"Why 'from Russia'? The children are from here. These two, the oldest ones, are from my first cohabitant. He was an exile-settler, then joined the peasantry and left for the mainland. But the youngest, the one Komlev's watching, is from my present cohabitant. He's a pastry cook. He'll finish his exile-settler term in a month, enter the peasantry and leave for the mainland, too."

"Well, but who's this one from?"

"This one? Who knows!"

"Hmm, but when your pastry cook leaves for the mainland, what will you and your children do?"

"They'll just give me another cohabitant."

Thus this woman—who in the past couldn't endure life with a husband she didn't love, but who now dully and apathetically moves from cohabitant to cohabitant—"serves her *katorga* sentence."

At that moment, Komlev entered the hut. In hands accustomed to lashing and hanging he carefully carried a year-old child. I postponed to another time my conversation with him. An executioner with a child in his hands…

"See me tomorrow… Only, without the child!"

What will become of these children, born of cohabitants who completed their exile-settler terms and left for the mainland, born of "who knows who" and carried in an executioner's arms?

Readers have already met "the young Zhakominikha," the charmer of Korsakovsk Post, in the feuilleton "Dark Rus."[1] Zhakominikha's father and mother were exiled convicts and she was born on Sakhalin. "On Sa*kalі*n!" as Sakhalinites say. She's never seen anything other than Sakhalin, and speaks the same language they speak in chains prisons. And when told there are other lands quite dissimilar to Sakhalin, she simply puzzledly answers, "Yes, and people there get 'framed' because of money!" The following question interests her very much: "Is it true that in Russia you don't have to doff your hat to an official?" This seems very strange to her. She knows only two sorts of people: officials and the "herd." She has two children she loves very much and tries to do everything she can for. She dresses her children like "officials' children," and everyday looks forward to being sent to *katorga*.

"You really want to be sentenced to *katorga*?!"

"Yes, indeed! They'll put me with the female cohabitants. One of the exile-settlers will choose me and the children. I'm a valuable woman." She says this in a calm businesslike tone.

Zhakominikha had been married off to a son whose parents were exiles as well. This Zhakomini[2] family had come to Sakhalin from Nikolaev[3] a long time earlier, served its *katorga* and exile-settler terms, become rich and purchased a large trading concern. The young Zhakomini lived with his wife in the Vladimirovka settlement, ran the store and hunted sable. They lived well by Sakhalin standards. But the young woman attracted the fancy of an exile-settler, a desperado from the Ivans, an "oven-fork fellow," as *katorga* calls the reckless ones, who'd completed his exile-settler term and was preparing to leave for the mainland. He told Zhakominikha about his departure the day beforehand.

"Will you take me with you?"

"I'd take you if you had some money."

Zhakominikha gave her husband strychnine that same day. Strychnine is extracted from sable and is in every trapper's home. Amazingly, the crime was discovered. Zhakominikha was giving her husband the poison at the very moment workers were coming to lunch in a neighbor's room. After Zhakomini fell on the floor the workers ran in and caught her red-handed holding a wine glass with powder residue in it. "He offed himself!" Zhakominikha suddenly declared. Then, the first thing she did was begin taking money out of a trunk.

She was utterly astounded when they brought her in for interrogation, and simply explained this as an intrigue on the part of the elder Zhakominis.

"Why should I be investigated? By what law can they keep me from going to the mainland? Is there a witness that I gave him poison?" This is *katorga*'s deeply-held belief, that if there's no eyewitness it means "you can't be convicted without confessing" and no one has the right to accuse you. And if you are accused, then it's unfair and not according to the law. "I can be suspected but not tried." An echo of old times that moves from generation to generation of penal laborers.

Still under suspicion, Zhakominikha committed a new crime—again "without witnesses." One day, Zhakomini's grave was found to have been dug up and a hole cut in the coffin lid. A gathering of Sakhalinites instantly recognized whose hand was involved. "Zhakominikha! She's always doing this! It's the first thing she does!" Zhakominikha had begun dreaming a lot about her dead husband, and if the deceased starts appearing, then you have to dig up his grave and see whether he's returned to his coffin. If he has returned, then you have to rearrange him as should be so that he stops tormenting you.

"Yes, but why are you certain that Zhakominikha did this?"

"Mercy, but she's known this remedy since infancy," answer Sakhalin's officials perfectly reasonably. "She's been among murderers since childhood!"

"My, what a woman!" I say to an exile-settler.

"Well, really, your worship, maybe in your opinion it should be otherwise. But for us Korsakovskovites, this can happen anytime. Because in every house here a mate has some wolfsbane…" Wolfsbane is a poisonous plant that grows in southern Sakhalin. "E'ryone has it!"

"What for?"

"For ourselves, in case it gets unbearable. Or for someone else, just in case. Only, she didn't use wolfsbane but trick-nine. Don't matter. That's how it is. 'Cause that's Sa*kali*n."

Viktor Negel, a young man of twenty being held for investigation in an isolator in Aleksandrovsk's chains prison, wished to see me about something. "Beware of being with Negel in private!" the prison commander warned me. For my conversations with prisoners I would arrive at the prison chancery after working hours. The prisoner would enter alone without guards, who would wait in the yard. "He'll grab something from you, jump out the window onto the street and make a run for it. There's always a bunch of exile-settlers out there, and they'll make it easy for him to escape. It's absolutely nothing for him to risk escaping. This is a fellow, my dear chap, who'll even risk his life!"

When into the chancery walked an average-sized youth, stolid and thickset, with wicked slanting eyes, Negel surely inspired no sympathy. Quite agitated by his long time in the isolator, he had an unusually openly expressive asymmetrical face, with a low narrow forehead and short, thick, fine curly hair, hard as razor stubble.

Our conversation lasted three hours, and when it ended and the prison commander came to the chancery and saw that nothing had happened, he stood rooted to the spot in amazement, so strange was the scene! Negel was wailing like a child. Utterly confused, I was consoling him, pouring him water and patting his head as if he were a little baby. "What have you done to Negel?!" was all the prison commander could find to ask.

By his own choice, Negel had told me his entire life. It was actually as horrible as his loathsome crime. His mother was murdered. Ten months later, he committed his own murder, killing the exile M's wife. The man's family had given him welcome. One day, Negel called when M wasn't home but his wife was there doing housework. "Where's Ivan Ivanych?" Negel asked. "What's it to you?!" allegedly sharply answered Mrs M. Negel grabbed an iron poker and began hitting the unfortunate woman over the head. This was really a vicious killing. Negel beat her to death, and beat her in a frenzy: her face was gone, teeth knocked down her throat. Having finished killing her he fled, washed himself and changed clothes and, after the murder had been discovered, was among the first to rush to the scene. Records show that Negel was fussing over and playing with the children of the woman he'd just barely killed (they had been at a neighbor's and weren't present during the murder). Negel more than anyone expressed sorrow, horror and indignation at the "villain," and even named a certain exile-settler as the murderer.

"What for? Why were you malicious toward him?"

"No! That's just how it's always done. Always finger another so's to avoid suspicion. It's still the custom."

Why did he so savagely murder this unfortunate woman? They say that Negel, having learned when M would be away from home, showed up with wicked intentions. Negel says that the deceased flirted with him and had given him fifty rubles at another time. When she cuttingly answered him, Negel said to her, "Why are you barking like a dog at me? You want nothing for the money except to bark? You just want to wrap me round your little finger!"

"And why not? You're still a little boy, and can be wrapped."

"I'm a *katorga*-woman's son," Negel answered her, "and you won't wrap me!"

Mrs M allegedly began laughing and Negel, losing track of himself, began beating her. He went into a frenzy and doesn't know how long he beat her—but in coming upon the body later, he gazed in amazement: "My God, what did I do to her?!"

"I didn't kill her for no reason, but for fifty rubles!"

"People may really be murdered for fifty rubles?"

Negel's face grew even darker and gloomier. "But aren't people murdered for neither this nor that? My mother was killed… For what? That guy over there, he said he killed her while he was living with her. I'll tell you straight out, he's lying! There's no way he had relations with her! He's worth all of three kopeks! Just look at him!" His own teacher, the exile-settler Weinstein, had stabbed Negel's fifty-year-old mother. They sentenced Weinstein to four years' *katorga*. This sends Negel into a rage. "Four years for my mother?! That cripple over there got *twenty years* for killing a woman! That's right! After this, it was clear there's two sides to justice!"

Negel is a native of Sakhalin. His father and mother, both exiled to *katorga* for murder, met in Ust-Kara[4] and came to Sakhalin together. He doesn't remember his father; but remembering his mother caused him to break down in tears. I was strangely moved when this foul, ruthless murderer, in tears, said, "Mama! My mama!"

"When my mother was killed I became bitter, I became another person. Ahh… it means people can be killed for neither this nor that! Very well, now we know!… Weinstein, he destroyed me. Mama left me to deal with this man. If he hadn't killed her I never would've become a penal laborer. With mama, I was completely different. But what am I now? A penal laborer. They'll sentence me to ten years. But later, if God wishes, I'll serve life."

He requested that I relate the following to the governor: "Allow me to transfer from Aleksandrovsk Prison to another. Weinstein's here, and I'm going to have to stab him."

"Why do you 'have to'?"

"I have to. I'm in the isolator now, but as soon as they let me into general, I'll find him. But I still don't want to get life. Don't allow me and him in the same prison! I won't pity him, I won't pity myself!"

"Alright! But in a different prison, will you pity whom you've killed?"

"Every hour. I so pity her it weighs on my shoulders in the isolator. Her, and her children. But the more I remember my murdered mother, my compassion for people falls away." And his slanted eyes, when he says these final words, gaze with such unmitigated evil!…

In that same Aleksandrovsk Prison I met with Abdulla-Ladin, a young Tatar, also the son of penal laborers. He was born, raised, committed a crime and is being punished, on Sakhalin. "It's even better in prison! In prison, you can eat; but in freedom, you swell up from hunger!" he laughs. His crime was truly horrible. He and two exile-settlers murdered a certain prisoner's wife, his fourteen-year-old daughter and six year-old son during a robbery. Having finished killing them, Abdulla and one of his partners murdered their third partner. "So there'd be more for us!" The unfortunate woman, who had been pregnant, was found with her stomach cut open.

"What was this for?"

"But it's simple! To see how a baby looks!" Abdulla smiles bashfully, recalling his curiosity. At *katorga*'s insistent demand, this huge Tatar with an

Fig. 30: Prisoner

idiot's face will grotesquely contort his body to show "what the baby looked like." *Katorga* roars.

"Well, though no one pities you, you should pity yourself! You know it was this that landed you in prison, in *katorga*!"

"So what? Here on Sa*kal*in everyone's been in prison." This Sakhalin native sees prison as inevitable for each and every one.

There is not a Sakhalin prison that does not have natives. Over twenty-five years ago children were born on Sakhalin, grew up amid *katorga* in an atmosphere of blood and filth and were destined from the cradle for *katorga*.

This was the greatest sin against these wretches.

Part Two

1
GOLDEN HAND

It's a Sunday evening. There's uproar and laughter around a small pristine cottage next to the Derbinsk almshouse. Carousels are crushing fallen fir-twigs, an orchestra of three violins and a make-shift clarinet squawks away, and exile-settlers are dancing the *trepak*.[1] On a small stage a wizard and magician, "origins forgotten," is chewing hot oakum and pulling a multicolored ribbon out of his nose. Corks are popping from bottles of kvas. Drunken voices resound from the kvas shop. From its windows you hear: "*Bardadym*. Dead, a ruble *maza*. *Sheperka*, a pip per bundle. Again. Again-again. A lady. Two on the side."

The owner of this Sakhalin kvas shop, as well as the gambling den, carousels, dance school, inn and *café chantant* is the "peasant-formerly-exiled" Sofia Bloeffstein. She was famous throughout Russia and most of Europe as "Golden Hand." At her trial, the table for material evidence glittered with necklaces, bracelets and rings—the evidence of her booty. "Madame witness," a court official turned to one of the plaintiffs, "do you see any of your jewelry here?" With altered countenance a lady approached this "Golkonda."[2] Her eyes burned and hands shook as she touched and handled each piece. Then, "from on high" in the dock, a voice mocked, "Madam, don't worry. No need to be so gentle: the jewelry's phony."

I remembered this event when, at six o'clock in the morning, I left to visit Golden Hand for the first time. I was looking forward to my meeting with this Mephistopheles, this "Rocambole in a skirt,"[3] this naturally gifted criminal whom neither *katorga*, nor the isolator, nor shackles, nor the hiss of bullets, nor the whistling of birch rods could subdue, a woman who, while confined in the isolator, devised and organized plans reeking of blood.

And… I was taken aback when a little old woman with a glowing wrinkled face like a baked apple, in open-work stockings, an old-fashioned housecoat and with knowingly coquettishly-curled and dyed hair, came to greet me. "Was this really her?" She was so pathetic, with "the squalid splendor of her attire and false red cheek."[4] Gray hair and yellowed cheeks would not have made the same impression. Why all this? Beside her stood a tall, healthy, solid, handsome—indeed, a truly magnificent—human specimen: her cohabitant, the exile-settler Bogdanov. Everything became clear… These crimsoned *rouées* who would play like a fresh blush of youth…

We introduced ourselves. Bloeffstein invited me to eat and we had tea and biscuits. How old she now was I could not hasten to say. I'd never seen a woman who'd been shot at and sentenced in the traditional way. It's hard to judge by her face the age of a person who's lived through such moments! She said she was thirty-five; but had she not, I would have guessed her a woman in her fifties.

On Sakhalin, a bunch of legends surrounds her. There's a persistent belief that she's not Golden Hand at all, that this is an imposter, a substitute who's undergoing her punishment while the real Golden Hand continues her elusive activities in Russia. Even officials, knowing that I'd seen and remembered a picture of Golden Hand taken during her trial, asked me after my meeting with Bloeffstein, "Well, what do you think? Is it her? Is she the one?" "Yes, what's left of her." Despite her terrible transformation she was fully recognizable, for her eyes had stayed entirely the same. Those marvelous, infinitely kind, soft, velveteen, expressive eyes. Eyes that *spoke*, so outstandingly were they able to lie.

One of the Englishmen who's toured Sakhalin has spoken with requisite delight about Golden Hand's broad erudition and "good breeding," about her knowledge of foreign languages (she speaks German).[5] But I don't think that saying *bien étage* instead of *belle étage* particularly attests to either Sofia Bloeffstein's knowledge of French or her erudition or good breeding. In a manner of speaking, this is a simple townswoman, a petty shopkeeper. For me, actually, the riddle is how Golden Hand's victims could take her for a famous actress or an aristocratic widow. Probably the answer to this turns on her very kind eyes, still so beautiful regardless of all that Sofia Bloeffstein has suffered.

But she's perpetrated as much as she's suffered. Her criminal nature hasn't given up; it stubbornly fights on and demonstrates the uselessness of stern measures in correcting criminal natures. For two years and eight months this woman was shackled with manacles. Her weak withered arms, thin as birch rods, crippled and devoid of muscles, tell you of this punishment. She can still move her right arm somewhat but has to raise her left arm by the elbow. Day or night there's no relief from the pain in her withered arm's shoulder. She can't turn from side to side or get herself out of bed. And with what terrible words Golden Hand curses her withered arm.

She was sentenced in the traditional way, and—as gentlemen witnesses usually put it—"her punishment will never be erased from participants' and spectators' memories." Everyone—from executors of the punishment to prisoners who watched—has ever since been unable to recall without smiling how "Golden Hand was thrashed." Even the never-smiling Komlev, the most terrible of Sakhalin's executioners, the terror and nemesis of all *katorga*, smiles at this memory.

"How I do remember. I gave her twenty lashes."

"She says more."

"Would've seemed more to her," smiles Komlev. "I well remember how many there were. The way I gave her twenty would've made 'em seem like 200."

She was punished in ward number nine in Aleksandrovsk's correctionals prison. Everyone attended, without exception. Those who had the sad duty of attending these terrible and disgusting rituals came as well as those for whom there was no need at all except curiosity. There were 300 men in a ward that housed 100. Correctionals stood on the sleeping platforms "to get a better view." The punishment was conducted amid convicts' cynical shouts and jokes. Every wretched shriek elicited a burst of Homeric laughter. "Komlev, give it to her! Don't just butter her." They shouted the same things they shout when one of theirs is punished. But Komlev didn't need these shouts of encouragement. An artist, virtuoso and lover of his trade, he "layered one birch rod over another" so that the blood spattered beneath the twigs.

Sofia Bloeffstein fainted halfway through the punishment. A medic brought her around with smelling salts, and the punishment continued. Bloeffstein was barely able to get up from the mare and return to her isolation cell.[6] She found no rest in solitary confinement. "Just as it seemed you'd get some peace, they called out, 'Sonka Golden Hand.' You thought, 'Are they going to do it again?' No. They wanted to take a photograph." This was done for the sake of a local photographer who's earned money selling postcards of Golden Hand. Bloeffstein was led into the prison yard and posed in a circle of "decorations." They put her next to an anvil, next to which also stood a guard and a blacksmith with a hammer, and the photographer snapped a scene of them supposedly shackling Golden Hand.

This photograph was sold by the dozens on all steamers that came to Sakhalin. "They're even sold on the foreign steamers. They're interested in her everywhere," the photographer explained, bringing me whole dozens of photographs portraying "the shackling."

"Why did you bring me so many?"

"But they're gifts for your friends. Visitors always take back dozens with them."

These are remarkable photographs. Their principal wonder is that Sofia Bloeffstein doesn't look herself, such was the impotent rage printed on her face. Like some evil, suffering, twisted demon she's clenching her teeth, as if trying with all her might to contain a tongue ready to explode with profanities. This is such a picture of human degradation! "They tortured me with these photographs," says Sofia Bloeffstein.

In part an escape specialist, she fled with her current cohabitant, Bogdanov. "But we lost our strength," says Bloeffstein with a bitter smile. "I was sick and couldn't make my way through the forest. I told Bogdanov, 'Carry me, I need to rest.' He carried me in his arms but got tired himself. He lost his strength. 'We'll sit down and rest,' he said. We sat under a tree. But a howl and the snapping of branches came through the woods. It was the posse… They were surrounding us."

The pursuers had instantly learned of Golden Hand's escape and formed a cordon and begun chasing them. One detachment drove the fugitives through the woods as the warden and thirty soldiers gathered on its edge. Suddenly, a figure in a soldier's uniform emerged from the woods. "Fire!" A thirty-rifle volley resounded, but the figure managed to drop to the ground and the thirty bullets whistled over its head. "Don't shoot! Don't shoot! I give up," rang out a desperate female voice. The "soldier" threw herself on her knees before the warden. "Don't kill me!" It was Golden Hand in disguise.

What does she do on Sakhalin?

In Aleksandrovsk, Onor or Korsakovsk, in all these places, in little villages hundreds of versts away from one another, everyone knows "Sonka-goldenhand." *Katorga* is allegedly proud of her. It doesn't like her but nevertheless respects her. The woman is a leader; she has an outstanding ability to organize plans, which has not been for nothing here. All *katorga* considers her primarily responsible for the murder of the rich shopkeeper Nikitin and the theft of 56 000 rubles from Iurkovsky. Investigation of both cases produced considerable suspicion but not a shred of evidence against Bloeffstein.

But that was earlier. "Nowadays, Sofia Ivanovna is ill and doesn't get involved in anything at all," her cohabitant Bogdanov explained. Officially, she's the proprietress of the kvas shop. She brews a splendid kvas; has built a carousel; created a four-man orchestra from among exile-settlers; found a conjuror among the *brodiagi*; and has organized presentations, dances and fêtes. Unofficially… "Even a fool knows what she does," the warden of settlements told me. "You know, all Sakhalin knows she trades in vodka. But when you carry out an inspection you find nothing but bottles of kvas." Everyone also knows full well that she buys and sells stolen goods, but neither nighttime nor daytime raids reveal where they are.

So she "fights for life," for this wretched leftover of a criminal's existence. Flopping like a fish on ice, she engages in petty criminality and dirty deals to earn a living and support her cohabitant's gambling. Her secret dream is to return to Russia, and she peppered me with questions about Odessa. "I don't think I'd recognize it now," she said. And when I told her about it, she heartily sighed, "It's like you're telling me about another world… If I could see it…"

"There's no point in Sofia Ivanovna returning to Russia now," Bogdanov characteristically snapped. "For us, there's nothing there now." This "celebrity's husband" wasn't absent for a second during my visits, and followed his cohabitant's every word as if afraid she'd say too much. His presence seemed to weigh on Bloeffstein like lead. She'd talk but be unable to get to the point.

"I have to tell you something," Bloeffstein whispered to me during one visit, at a moment when Bogdanov had conveniently gone into another room. That same day her "confidant," the long-term invalid convict K, approached me. "Sofia Ivanovna has assigned you a rendezvous," he laughed. "I'll post myself as your stirrup (I'll watch), so's Bogdanov won't catch her."

We met on the edge of the settlement. "Thank you for coming," she said. "Goodness sakes, forgive my agitation. I've wanted to speak to you, but it was impossible with him around. You saw what kind of man he is. I've met such people, and now here… He's a vulgar uneducated man—everything I earn he runs around with and loses! He beats me, the tyrant… Ah, what can I say?" Tears welled up in her eyes.

"But you should leave him!"

"I can't. You know what I'm involved in. You have to eat and drink. But really, I can't manage my affairs without a man. You know how folks are around here. And they fear him: he'll kill someone over a couple pennies. You tell me to leave him… But if you only knew…" I didn't have to ask. I knew Bogdanov was one of those guilty for the Nikitin murder and Iurkovsky robbery.

I walked along with this unfortunate woman crying as she recalled the offenses against her. Was it more an attachment to the man or an alliance with a confederate?

"You wanted to tell me something?"

She responded instantly. "Wait… Wait… Let me catch my breath… I haven't spoken of this for so long… I've been thinking, always thinking, but haven't dared speak. He forbids it… Remember how I told you I wanted to go to Russia? Perhaps you thought I'll do the same things again… But I'm old now, I don't have any more strength… I just want to see my children." While saying these words Golden Hand cried a vale of tears. "Understand that I have two daughters. I don't even know if they're alive or not. I've heard absolutely nothing from them. Maybe they're ashamed of such a mother or have forgotten me, or maybe they've died… What are they doing? All I know is they're actresses, pages in little operettas. Oh, Lord! Of course, if I'd been there my daughters would never have become actresses."

Refrain from smiling over this criminal, crying that her daughters have become actresses. See all the torment in her eyes.

"I know what goes on with these 'pages.' But I simply want to know whether or not they're alive. Track them down, find out where they are. Don't

Fig. 31: Sofia Bloeffstein

forget me here on Sakhalin. Send a telegram, simply tell me whether my children are alive or not... I don't have much longer to live, and don't want to die without knowing if my children are alive or not... Lord, to have to worry here in *katorga* without knowing... Maybe they've died... And I'll never know, I have no one to ask, no one to talk to..."

"Rocambole in a skirt" was no more. Before me was an old mother sobbing over her unfortunate children. Tears mixing with rouge flowed in muddy rivulets down her wrinkled cheeks.

O, accursed island where is so much grief!

2
POLULIAKHOV

The murder of the Artsimovich family in Lugansk was one of the most horrible crimes in recent years. Murdered during a robbery were the judge Artsimovich, his wife, their son (an eight year-old boy), a servant and the cook.

I was warned beforehand that the murderer Poluliakhov makes "a surprisingly pleasant impression"; nevertheless, I'd never experienced such a powerful shock as when I met Poluliakhov.

"They're bringing Poluliakhov from the chains!" announced the guard.

"Let him in."

I took several steps towards the door, towards the infamous murderer, and was taken aback. Appearing in the doorway was a young man of medium height betraying a natural elegance even in prison uniform, with chestnut-colored hair, a small beard and brown, remarkably handsome eyes. I'd never seen eyes softer or gentler.

"You're... Poluliakhov?" I asked with unwonted surprise.

"I am!" he answered with a bow. His voice was likewise soft, pleasant, velvety, kind and mild. It was as charming as his gaze. There was something feline to his soft elastic approach. Poluliakhov belongs to the very small number of pure-bred "natural killers" on Sakhalin. Among humans, these natural killers are jungle tigers.

I later had many long discussions with Poluliakhov and could in no way lose the friendly disposition that welled up inside me toward this man. He reminded me of an officer from Vladivostok who kept like a kitten a captured tiger cub, then bitterly sobbed when the tiger grew up and he had to shoot it.

Poluliakhov's voice bathes your soul, his eyes charm you, such is his gentility. It was often necessary to remind myself that instead of feelings, this human captive possessed only sentimentality.

But the first impression this man produces is complete trustworthiness, and it's my understanding that the unfortunate Mrs Artsimovich, when he came to her bed that night, was able to talk credulously with him with no fear for her life. "Would such a person really kill you?"

Poluliakhov is not quite thirty years old. His uncle, a wealthy old trader, raised him to believe he'd be wealthy, and always told him, "When I die, everything will be yours." Poluliakhov studied a bit in school but received his true education in a brothel.[1] Withdrawing him from school, the uncle put

Poluliakhov in his shop, so that from childhood he was involved in commerce. The clerks, so as to more easily steal, began corrupting the owner's nephew, bringing him from the age of twelve to houses of ill repute. Poluliakhov was a handsome lad, and the women fondled and caressed him. "I didn't need them, of course. But I liked it there. Every day, the clerks would tell me, 'Such-and-such sends her greetings and you've been asked to visit again.'" This flattered the boy, and he'd rob the cash register to go there. "Music, dancing, women— I loved them so much!" said Poluliakhov with a smile.

Thus were spent five years. His uncle hired a cashier to stop the clerks from stealing, but Poluliakhov seduced this young woman and she began stealing for him. "I got on her good side: 'Just take a little from the till.' And thanks to her stealing for me I'd go there, to see *them*."

Poluliakhov developed a contempt for women because of this cashier. "Because of their weakness. It's simply vile. Anything you want, they do just for a kiss. Absolute animals." Women quickly nauseated Poluliakhov. "A woman likes you to ingratiate yourself, but then she turns on you. She was the same good-for-nothing they all are, a pure bitch—you'd beat her, then pet her, and she'd fawn all over you again. I don't even consider them people." Given Poluliakhov's looks, you can assume he'd be hugely and quickly successful with women. "They disgust me, but I feel I can't live without them. I took out all my anger on them." Poluliakhov found pleasure in tyrannizing, tormenting and inflicting pain upon women who fell in love with him.

When he was eighteen, his uncle learned of his stealing, fired the cashier and banished Poluliakhov from his home. Poluliakhov set about thieving, but "was clumsy" and soon got arrested and sent to prison. For Poluliakhov, this was "like university." "I saw such people there as I never knew existed. Before, what had I been stealing that got me banished by my uncle?! Enough for bread and kvas! But there, a whole world opened up before me, so to speak. 'Steal and thrive. Life is all fun and adventure!'" Poluliakhov left prison with a wealth of knowledge and an understanding of criminal doings and from that time on, his life followed the same routine: after a successful robbery he'd go on a binge to a brothel, some ready woman would fall in love with him and he'd become her "tomcat." She'd give him every kopek, beg and steal for him. After the woman got on Poluliakhov's nerves he'd carry out another "good robbery," squander the takings at another establishment and captivate another woman.

It is further necessary to note that Poluliakhov drinks almost nothing. "So, that life made me happy. Go out with everyone, have fun and don't think about anything. It's like you're intoxicated! They're the ones drinking, but you're drunker." From time to time this intoxicating life was interrupted by imprisonment "on suspicion of robbery."

"But, Poluliakhov, had you murdered anyone at that point?"

"One time, unfortunately. It was at night. I was spotted during a robbery and they came after me. Everyone except a certain caretaker gave up the chase. I'd cross a ditch, he'd cross a ditch, I'd scale a fence, he'd scale a fence. 'You thief,' he's shouting, 'you won't get away!' Hatred possessed me. 'What a swine! He knows I didn't steal anything, so why's he still following me?' No, it was absolutely necessary to face him like a man. I had a pistol with me. I let him get closer and when he was just a foot away I turned and fired. His arms flew up and he crashed to the ground... I later read in the newspaper that an unknown criminal killed some caretaker. I learned only his name. He hadn't known me, nor I him. But he'd wanted to send me to prison, so I took his life. We both acted out of our own interests. But that's the way it is! The world's a strange place! One hunts another for nothing, one kills another for nothing! Just crazed wolves!"

His lupine life spoiled Poluliakhov.

"Get 25 000 and you can live as you want. So, I planned to open a trading office. I missed commerce."

"You must've known you'd be caught, Poluliakhov."

"Why 'caught'? You can get by with a different passport in a different city. Why do so few people in Russia live well? Those of us in prison know better!"

"Why 25 000, exactly?"

"That's what I'd decided, 25 000."

These pure-bred "natural" criminals are surprisingly auto-suggestive. For some reason, they'll seize upon a fantastic figure, for example, 25 000, and live hypnotized by it. If a lesser figure is proposed: "No! I need 25 000 to set myself up." They live and operate under the influence of a single fantastic idea. Nothing else brings them joy.

"Poluliakhov, how were you going to get this 'great sum'?"

"I didn't want to do a bunch of little jobs. I was after the money, but it wasn't as if I'd just steal whatever I found. I stole in the thousands."

"Where's it all gone?"

"I blew it in the cities."

"Why didn't you save until you had 25 000?"

"No patience. I don't have patience for anything. So, I'd decided, 'I'll get a full 25 000 and then my life will turn around completely.'"

Impatience—their characteristic trait. They're impatient in everything, even during commission of a crime. Out of impatience they commit the enormous "stupidities" (from their point of view) by which they're later apprehended. I saw this, for example, in the murder of the banker Livshits, in Odessa. The murderers were in a most favorable position. Among them was a specialist at opening safes, a celebrity among criminals renowned for his deeds in Russia, Turkey, Rumania, Greece and Egypt. These people planned a robbery only; they weren't even armed. They were going to open the safe, take the money, lock it up again and leave. A servant was collaborating with them. But the old banker was reading a book and wasn't going to fall asleep for a long time. The killers attacked, strangled and beat him, and the safe didn't even get touched because the murder so frightened the "specialist" that he ran away.

"Why would you kill an old man?" I asked the strangler, Tomilin.

"Impatience. He wouldn't fall asleep!" Tomilin answered, shrugging his shoulders.

While Poluliakhov burned with impatience and ran from city to city unable to find a place for himself ("Even in my dreams I saw myself with a different life as a trader"), he teamed up with a young woman named Pirozhkova, who'd been a domestic for the burglar Kazeev, who also did "big jobs." Poluliakhov and Pirozhkova were living in a city down south when Kazeev passed through and told them they couldn't make money there. Then, one day, Poluliakhov received a telegram from Kazeev in Lugansk: "Move here instead. There's a merchant. We can open a trading office."

A safe, which the now deceased Artsimovich suddenly ordered for some reason, was what destroyed the Artsimoviches. Purchase of this safe caused a lot of tongue-wagging in Lugansk. There was talk of an enormous inheritance the Artsimoviches were supposedly receiving. "Otherwise, why buy a safe? They've gone without a safe—now, suddenly, there's a safe!" Lugansk's residents determined the precise amount of the inheritance: 70 000. These rumors reached Kazeev, who arrived in Lugansk and began sniffing around ("What's going on here?") and immediately clicked out a telegram to Poluliakhov.

Everything favored the crime. Newcomers can quickly make themselves known in a small city, and the Artsimoviches had just fired their maid, so Poluliakhov sent Pirozhkova to them and they hired her. "Pirozhkova would have gone through fire and water for me." So Pirozhkova worked as the Artsimoviches' maid, while Poluliakhov and Kazeev lived in the city as two newly-arrived merchants preparing to open a trading office.

Was the murder planned beforehand or did robbery simply join unexpectedly with murder (as is often the case)? Poluliakhov told me, "There's no reason to lie. I immediately saw it wasn't going to work without a 'crime.' There were a lot of people in the house. Kazeev told me more than once, 'You're not leaving! We didn't come here for nothing!' And I'd reply, 'When will you find 70 000 again?!'"

Pirozhkova reported to Poluliakhov frequently. "The barin counts his money. When he goes to the safe, he closes the door behind him! I poked my nose in once, like I had a reason, and he shouted, 'Why're you loafing about here? Get out!' I saw there was a lot of money and the cook and caretaker say there's a lot. The barin always has the key. He keeps it under his pillow when he sleeps."

Pirozhkova cursed her master. "The lady's nice, but the barin ain't goin' to heaven. He curses and shouts about everything. I spend the whole day running around doing my best, but he's always shouting, always using bad words, and for no reason."

"These stories made my blood boil!" said Poluliakhov. "I myself would never use those words…" It's true, no one in prison had ever heard a profanity from Poluliakhov. "I don't like those who curse!"

I often saw this in the typical "natural" criminal. There's trouble if any one of them possesses any sort of virtue. They demand that the whole world immediately adopt this virtue—and its absence in anyone seems to them a terrible, unforgivable crime: "What kind of person is this?"

"Why is he swearing at people? The girl serves him, does his bidding, but he swears at her? He should swear at his inferior? Doesn't he regard people as people?" Poluliakhov queried everyone as to what kind of man Artsimovich was, and he heard, probably gladly, that he was a rude man. In essence, he distanced himself from Artsimovich. Perhaps Poluliakhov was frightened by his own empathy. It happened quickly: armed, he ran to their house one night intending to murder the whole family. "Yes, it was a shame. It's terrible to take others' lives. Why was I going to kill these innocent people?!" He needed to find the "guilt" in Artsimovich so as to develop a hatred toward him.

"Well, but if Pirozhkova and everyone had told you Artsimovich was a kind man, would you have killed him?"

"I don't know… Perhaps… Though maybe I wouldn't have lifted a finger…"

"Very well. Artsimovich was a rude man. But, you know, the others were good people… What about them?"

"They came afterwards… When you come to your senses… I killed him first, and then I had to kill the rest… But it had to start with him."

The day before the killing, in the evening, Poluliakhov crept to the windows of the Artsimovich house. "I got the idea of peeping through a space in the shutters to see the layout of the room." At that moment, Artsimovich came through the gate. "I hid." Catching a glimpse of a silhouette in the dark, Artsimovich shouted, "Is there a rogue loafing around here?" and said some vulgar words. Had he only known that at that moment he was two feet away from his murderer, and that this hesitant killer needed just one more inch to go the full mile.

"It was like he was punching me in the snout!" said Poluliakhov. "I even began shaking all over. You know, he didn't know who was there or why he'd come, but he was swearing at him. He wanted to be offensive. Then and there I began to hate him like a mortal enemy." Poluliakhov returned from this reconnaissance having decided to kill Artsimovich, and no later than the next day. "He meant nothing to me now."

Earlier, Pirozhkova had, with Poluliakhov and Kazeev, gotten to know the Artsimoviches' caretaker. As part of their preparations, Kazeev let drop they were planning a robbery only, but the caretaker hadn't agreed to help. This was his downfall.

"I never liked that caretaker!" said Poluliakhov. "Well, we were different people. He'd been entrusted with everything. But those serving people only do what they're told. Little folks!"

"But what about Pirozhkova?! You knew Pirozhkova was a servant, too, and that the Artsimoviches trusted her."

"Yes, Pirozhkova disgusted me. They all disgusted me… Even though she acted out of love, she was loathsome. What kind of person was she? A pet who runs after whoever it likes. She wasn't a person but a dog."

The evening of the murder, the Artsimoviches' caretaker was a guest in the home of the "newly arrived merchants," who were discussing the robbery. The caretaker "was knocking back glasses of vodka and bragging that he ran the household." The plan was simply to get him dead drunk so he'd pass out. "He was so disgusting it was painful. He guffawed and his speech was impure. He's mangling his words. A 'ho!' here and a 'ho!' there. He's bragging. Pale face with muddy eyes. Drooling, drinking and spilling vodka, tearing off pieces of sausage with his filthy hands. That's why I ended up loathing him."

It's difficult to imagine this "contempt for the people" felt by "natural" criminals, how they use it to distance themselves from a person and how little it takes for a person to disgust them.

"He's sitting there in front of me. I'm looking at him like he's some kind of reptile! So, when he tosses his head back, I couldn't help myself. I grabbed him by the throat. I strangled him because he was so loathsome."

The caretaker only "quivered a couple of times." Kazeev jumped up and actually screamed in surprise. "It's started, now let's finish it!" Poluliakhov told him. They dragged the caretaker into a shed. Poluliakhov poured a vodka for himself and Kazeev.

"I tried but couldn't drink—it reeked of the caretaker. But Kazeev, poor man, was white as a sheet, so I told him: 'Drink!' His teeth were ringing off the glass. He took a drink. I said, 'We're going,' and gave him an axe and took one for myself."

They came to the peaceful Artsimovich house. Pirozhkova was waiting at the gate. "They've gone to bed. I don't know if they're sleeping yet." She checked inside the house again, listened and came back. "Go!"

"I could hear her teeth chattering. I spun her around and gave her a kiss for courage. 'Idiot, don't be afraid!' I said. We hadn't said anything, not a word, but we all knew we were going to kill everyone." Poluliakhov went first. After him went Kazeev and after Kazeev, Pirozhkova. "You could hear Kazeev's

Fig. 32: Poluliakhov

heart pounding. It was warm in the corridor but there was a coldness tugging at our feet: we'd forgotten to close the door. Our feet and everything else were freezing. The apartment of the deceased Mister and Mistress Artsimovich was laid out like so…"

Thus Poluliakhov said "deceased," and drew on paper for me the layout of the apartment: he knew every little corner thanks to what Pirozhkova had told him.

They entered a small room off the corridor that led to the couple's separate beds. Artsimovich's bed was to the right, and his wife was sleeping with their son in a bed in a room to the left. Poluliakhov knew that Artsimovich slept with his head next to a window. "It was dark. You couldn't see anything. The only thing going around in my head was, 'Don't let anything go wrong!' My foot found the bed, and I took a swing…" The first blow struck the pillow. Artsimovich awoke and said "who" or "what"… Poluliakhov brought the axe down "on the throat" with the next swing. "I heard a snap, like I cut through it entirely." Poluliakhov stopped. There wasn't a sound. It was done.

"I went into the middle room. Listened. Mistress Artsimovich's bed was quiet. They were sleeping. The only thing I could hear sounded like a clock ticking. It was Kazeev's heart pounding. 'Stay there,' I whispered. 'You stand guard.' I found Pirozhkova's hand in the dark and it was so cold. 'Take me to the kitchen.' I went in and it was light as day in the kitchen. The moon was in the window and you could've read a book by it. I look around and see a bed and the black head of the cook on the pillow, facing the wall and somehow still sleeping. I raised the axe—and was struck by such pity. 'What for?' I'm thinking. But my hands had only just finished off the other one. There was a thud and then no more snoring. But what a moon! It was so bright… I'm watching as the black stain spreads wider and wider on the pillow… I turned around and went over to the stove." Poluliakhov tore off his bloodied top coat, wiped off his hands and ignited the coat with a candle, then went without the axe to Mistress Artsimovich's bed. "We needed her to unlock the safe. It had a combination lock."[2]

As he entered the room, Artsimovich—or "Mistress Artsimovich," as Poluliakhov always said—suddenly woke.

"Madam, don't scream!" Poluliakhov preempted her.

"Semen, is it you?" Artsimovich asked.

"No, I'm not Semen."

"Who are you? What do you want?"

"Madam, please forgive our disturbing you. We've come to avail ourselves of your wealth."

"Why did you say 'please forgive'?" I asked Poluliakhov.

"I just spoke that way. You had to be courteous. I like it when I'm treated courteously, and I myself always treat others with courtesy. Mistress Artsimovich raised herself up on the pillow: 'Do you know whose house you're in? Do you know who my husband is?' I couldn't keep from smiling right then. 'Madam,' I say, 'it doesn't matter to us!' 'But where's my husband?' she asks. 'Madam,' I say, 'don't worry about your husband. He's tied up and we've plugged his mouth. He won't be shouting, and I advise you to keep quiet as well or we'll tie you up.' 'Have you killed him?' she says. 'Not at all,' I say. 'We want your wealth, not your life. We'll take what we need and go. We won't do you any harm.' It seemed as if she'd been struck by a fever, but she looked at me and calmed down because I was smiling and looking openly at her. She was more afraid of Kazeev. 'Who's that?' she asks. 'That,' I say, 'is my comrade. Don't upset him and he won't do anything stupid to you.' The lady relaxed. 'Has Semen the caretaker put you up to this?' she asks. 'Semen,' I say, 'has nothing to do with this.' 'No,' she says, 'don't lie. I know this is a prank of Semen's.' I actually started laughing. 'Well,' I say, 'whoever's prank it is, it's all the same for you now. But if you'd be so kind as to get up, take the key and go unlock the safe.' 'I'm to go half-dressed?' she says. She'd noticed her shift had slipped off her shoulder and she was covering herself with a blanket. The lady was so calm, beautiful and stately. 'Please give me a blouse!' she says. I gave her a blouse and she put it on and buttoned it. 'Please bring the safe here,' she says, 'it's not heavy.' Then the child awoke, a boy of eight or ten. He jumped up from the bed. 'Mama,' he says, 'who's that?' But she tells him, 'Don't shout and don't be afraid, or you'll wake papa. These people are from the courthouse and we have to do this.' I'd told Kazeev to stand guard, but he was bringing in the safe. He put it next to her on the bed. 'Open it!' I said. She sat on the bed and opened it—she was so calm, just talking with me; and the boy who was looking at her was absolutely calm. 'Mama,' he says, 'I want an apple.' 'Please give him an apple,' she says. 'Get one!' I tell Kazeev. Six or seven apples with marmalade were on a plate on a little corner table. Kazeev handed it to me and I chose an apple and gave it to the boy. 'Enjoy!' I also gave him the marmalade. Mistress Artsimovich opened the safe. 'Here,' she says, 'is all our wealth.' There was all of one and a half thousand rubles in the safe and another 300 rubles in a little packet. 'But those,' she says, 'are state funds.' The only other thing was lady's jewelry—rings and earrings. 'But where's the 70 000?' I ask. She looks straight at me. 'What 70 000?' 'But the inheritance?' 'What inheritance?' I actually lost my breath. 'What they're talking about in the city?' 'Akh,' she says, 'you believed that stupid fable?' I was losing myself completely. 'Madam,' I say, 'you'd better tell the truth! Where's the money? This'll get worse!' 'Even if you kill me,' she says, 'the money won't turn up anywhere!' I was almost howling at the top of my lungs. My head was spinning. However, I see the lady's telling the truth, because with a cast-iron safe there, where else would they put the money? 'Give it to me!' I say. But she's so calm. She takes the money and gives it to me. 'I don't recommend you take this jewelry,' she says. 'You'll only get caught with it.' 'Give me everything,' I say. 'Don't worry about it!' She even began explaining how much one trinket had cost when her husband gave it to her. Her calm astonished me. My head's going round in circles—but she's relaxed! I went through the rooms again, searched one desk after another. 'That money,' I'm thinking, 'is just not here! It's time to go.' I grabbed the axe, hid it under my jacket and returned to her bed again. But she's actually smiling. 'Well,' she says, 'do you believe there's no money?' I so much didn't want to kill her, I so didn't want to… But the business was going round in my head. I was thinking that because we'd killed such an important person we'd get caught, wouldn't be forgiven, and I myself could expect nothing less than the gallows."

"One question, Poluliakhov. Did you anticipate the gallows but take the risk all the same?"

"I didn't think we'd get caught! It'd be like trying to see wind in a meadow."

How many "natural" criminals have I seen, many of whom anticipated "nothing other than the gallows," and all, when asked why they committed their crimes, only answered, "We believed we couldn't get caught. How could we be found out? Only idiots get caught!" Self-confidence and occasionally simple-mindedness are these people's outstanding features.

"I'm going through the room backwards and forwards," Poluliakhov continues his story, "and the lady's pitying me, really pitying me. She'd already astonished me with her bravery. Now she's lying down talking with Kazeev. Kazeev's hiding behind words, but she couldn't care less and keeps asking about the caretaker. 'Did he put you up to this?' I wasn't looking forward to the noose, but at the same time it seemed I couldn't kill her. But, yes, your own life is more valuable, so I went up from behind so she couldn't see me, and swung... It was over in a stroke. Then the boy jumped up from his bed. His mouth was open, arms spread out, eyes wide open. I took care of him..." Poluliakhov stopped. "Is there any more to say? It was a nasty blow..."

"As you know..."

"Well, once I'd started it was absolutely necessary... I hit him with the axe and wanted to again, but it got stuck in the boy's skull. Blood spurted onto my face. It was so hot... Like boiling water... It scorched me..."

I was having difficulty breathing. I would have shouted "Water!" if I hadn't feared showing weakness before a criminal. It felt like everything was swimming before my eyes.

"Look here, barin, you're not well...," said Poluliakhov's quiet voice. He sat in front of me white as a sheet, with strange eyes gazing somewhere in the distance; his cheeks quivered and twitched.

The two of us had talked late into the evening in the prison chancery. After Poluliakhov finished, I was shaking and staring into a dark corner.

"It was terrible!" Poluliakhov at last said after a long silence, passing a hand through his hair. "This boy's with me now in my dreams... No one's there but the boy..."

"Why was the boy murdered?"

Out of compassion.

Poluliakhov's face became gentle and meek again. "I was thinking about him when I was going through the rooms. 'Should I leave him alone or not?' I'm thinking, 'What will his life be like after what he's seen? How can he live after seeing his mother killed?' I went toward him... It was a pity... My every nerve was pulsing!" continued Poluliakhov. "I was so agitated, so agitated I forgot myself. I wanted to slaughter everyone. I jumped into the middle room and raised the axe. 'Now,' I said, 'I really should kill you two. So there'll be no witnesses. You see, I won't have destroyed all these souls for nothing. This has to be finished so no one will give anyone away, so more people won't be destroyed because of this. Hold each other and don't say a word.' I looked at Kazeev, he was whiter than a sheet, and Pirozhkova was swaying like a blade of grass. I felt sorry for her and began hugging and kissing her. Then, especially, my every nerve was pulsing. It seems I've never kissed anyone like that!"

Here the murderer is with blood-drenched face, embracing his partner in an apartment full of corpses—it would seem a monstrous fantasy were it not the monstrous truth.

"I loved her then and pitied her, pitied…"

"Well, but where's Pirozhkova now?" I asked Poluliakhov.

"Who the hell knows! Somewhere here on Sakhalin!"

"You're not interested in her?"

"Not a bit." (But Pirozhkova, out of love for Poluliakhov, didn't want to become anyone's cohabitant and has been removed to a distant settlement, to starvation, to poverty…)

That same evening, Poluliakhov, Pirozhkova and Kazeev disappeared from Lugansk and began living under false papers. The police could never have caught the murderers had Artsimovich's stepson not been involved. Determined to find his mother's and stepfather's murderers, the young man went through several southern cities and searched everywhere. In disguise, he went to a hangout and got to know its shady characters; and there, in one of Rostov's dens, he heard about some thug who'd gone on a bender, sold some valuables and, while drunk, said something about Lugansk. This thug was arrested on the young man's advice.

It was Kazeev. Kazeev had been tortured by the horrible murders and was dreaming of changing his life. He wanted "to run his own affairs" and become a detective. This dream of "running your own affairs" and becoming a detective is fairly common among professional criminals. They're often baited this way: "You're a capable chap, sensible, know all the folks—you could be our agent."

"Like a fish! The fools!" said Poluliakhov with a contemptuous smile. "They catch one fish on a hook and another goes for the same hook."

"How can they believe them?"

"What is there people won't believe? A person loses his way in the forest and sees no way out. That person will believe anyone he meets. Maybe this other person wants to lead him into a thicket and kill him—but he'll still follow him. All because there isn't a way out."

Having lost himself in his crimes, Kazeev believed he'd be pardoned and allowed to become a detective and, firmly convinced "the judges would hang them straightaway for the killings," he told where Poluliakhov and Pirozhkova would be found.

"Comrade"—among criminals both outside and inside *katorga*—is, as they say, a "great word." To give up or kill a comrade is the most serious crime there can be. On Sakhalin, I saw people who'd been languishing several years in isolation cells, awaiting with horror the "resolution of their fate" and subsequent transfer to prison, where they would be killed because they had murdered comrades while on the lam. "But you've *all* killed so *many* people!" "Doesn't matter. We killed other people. But he killed a comrade." Giving up a comrade is as serious a crime as killing him. For this, there's death.

So they went ahead and locked up Poluliakhov and Kazeev in the same ward.

"Well, Vania, what are we going to do with you now?" Poluliakhov asked him. Kazeev was silent.

"He was just shaking all over. We're sitting, silent. I'm looking straight at him and he's gazing into a corner. They brought lunch but he didn't touch it. They gave us dinner at six and he didn't touch it. Night came. I relax, lie down, but don't fall sleep. But he's sitting up. He's worn out, barely able to stay straight but too scared to lie down to sleep. If he goes to sleep, I'll kill him. It got pathetic to look at him; I felt sorry for him. I closed my eyes, pretended I'd fallen asleep and started snoring. I never snore in my sleep and don't like it when others snore—it disgusts me. But there I am seeming to snore so he'll relax. I hear him lying down and, like an axe dropped in water, he fell asleep. Next morning, I woke before him and see him sleeping like a baby. I gave him a nudge: 'Get up, Vania.' He jumped up, looked at me, eyes wide open, really surprised. He's looking around. I actually laughed. 'You're alive, alive!' I say. 'You're here, Vania. We've committed our stupidities but won't speak of that. We can't dwell on the past but must think of the future. What'll happen if we're not together? Understood? We were comrades and we'll be comrades. Understood?' He even wept.

"So I've ended up in *katorga*. If I'd killed them then in the Artsimoviches' home nothing would've happened!" exclaimed Poluliakhov. "But I felt sorry for them at the time, and that's why I'm in *katorga*."

The trial for the Artsimoviches' murder made a horrible impression. Poluliakhov conducted himself with unparalleled cynicism; in speaking about the murders, he utterly mocked his victims and boasted of his own calm and composure. "Spite possessed me: 'You're going to hang me? Well, here I am!'" Poluliakhov was expecting the death sentence the whole time. "When everyone rose and they began reading the sentence my head was bobbing. It was as if the noose was swinging in front of me, reaching for my head. However, I'm thinking 'Poluliakhov, steady now, chap. You'll be leaving this world, so let it go!' And I tried to smile."

When he was assigned "to *katorga* labors" Poluliakhov "couldn't believe my ears." "I'm looking around not understanding a thing. 'What did I hear? Am I dreaming?' I left the court like a door fallen off its hinges. My head was going round, I was gasping for breath and actually felt sick."

As the criminals were being led through the crowd outside the courthouse a shot suddenly rang out. Artsimovich's stepson had emerged from the crowd and barely missed Poluliakhov with a revolver. "At that very moment I dove into the crowd!" And the bullet flew by. "What *fart* (luck)!" Poluliakhov remarked, smiling. They arrested the shooter; but as soon as he was brought to prison Poluliakhov summoned the warden and demanded that Artsimovich's stepson be released: "I make no claims against him whatsoever."

"Why so carefree about him? Was it because you wanted to show magnanimity?"

"What 'magnanimity'?" Poluliakhov shrugged his shoulders. "I killed his mother and he wanted to kill me. I would've done the same in his place."

When Poluliakhov and Kazeev were brought to Sakhalin they were kept separate. All the prisoners said, "Poluiakhov will nail Kazeev immediately." But this precaution was unnecessary, and they've become comrades once again. "I don't have any hatred for Vania. We worked together, fell into misfortune together and had to go away together." The "comrades" were assigned to one and the same ward in Aleksandrovsk's chains prison and took places beside each other on the sleeping platform. "Vania was just a foot away from me. We shared our last crumbs."

To have someone close is a need that improbably washes away the animosity of all penal laborers. Only in such institutions as chains prisons do they so "adore" each other. It approaches the ridiculous and the poignant. On the lam, in the taiga, half dead from hunger, a convict will halve his last piece of bread to give to a comrade. He'll turn himself in to save a wounded or sick comrade. He'll carry in his arms for entire days a weakened comrade. The man barely carries a soul in his own body, but he'll carry a comrade in his arms. He'll walk several paces, collapse, rest, then pick him up and carry him again. And so on, for hundreds of versts through the impenetrable wild taiga.

"A killer of five people"—this means absolutely nothing to *katorga*. "Over there, we're all brave. It's here you reveal yourself." Murders committed "on the outside" carry no value in *katorga*. You'll never impress *katorga* by saying, "I killed such-and-such many people." Regarding this, *katorga* will only ask, "But how much did you take?" And if a fellow's "taken" little, *katorga* laughs at such a man, as it laughs at those who've murdered out of jealousy or vengeance—in general, at "the fools." "The wheel-shaft! He got into a crime without a 'purpose.'" By contrast, everyone highly values what is committed within *katorga*. A man who's talked back to a strict warden garners prestige, and is often more highly regarded by *katorga* than any famous murderer. When a Pashchenko, who's officially credited with thirty-two murders, lies down beside you on the sleeping platform, there's no boasting of killing five people!

For Poluliakhov, who had terrified the court, the situation in the *katorga* prison was most uncertain. "I killed five people. But how much I took, I was ashamed to say!" He was saved several times only by saying that he killed a judge, given that such a person… "meant I'd get the noose!" So all this inspired a certain respect: *katorga* admires those who take risks and fears only those who fear absolutely nothing.

While I was on Sakhalin Poluliakhov acquired the highest respect in the prison. An escape by him was spoken of with the greatest reverence. "Now, that's a man!" The escape was one of his most audacious, desperate and senseless acts.

Poluliakhov and Kazeev ran away with three other prisoners in broad daylight and in front of everyone. "One evening, we're lying there and I whisper to Kazeev, 'Vania, we'll get away tomorrow.' 'How?' he asks. 'Quiet,' I say. 'Be ready any minute to either get away or die together.' 'Alright!' he whispers. 'Wherever you go, I'll follow.'" Their party of five prisoners, with one convoy guard, was working at the busiest spot along the large thoroughfare just outside Aleksandrovsk Post. Time wasn't "flying by," and these chains division prisoners were not shackled. Many people, carriage-bound officials and marching soldiers, were going hither and yon along the road. Suddenly, Poluliakhov rushed the guard, knocked him off his feet, grabbed his rifle, shouted "Vania, let's go!" and ran into the woods.

Swarms of people on the road saw this and sounded the alarm. It happened only two steps away from the post, and within minutes a search party was coursing through the woods. Later, as the soldiers were going deeper into the forest, five figures appeared one after another in typical *brodiaga* fashion, the first with a rifle on his shoulder, on a bald summit nearby. It was Poluliakhov and his comrades. Officials were standing in the road but no one had a rifle at this point, and pistol fire couldn't reach them. And so, before the eyes of the commandant and all Aleksandrovsk Post, the fugitives left the hilltop and disappeared into the taiga.

All of Aleksandrovsk Post was frightened. "They managed to escape in broad daylight in front of a guard!" Resentment against the fugitives was vicious. *Brodiagi*, moreover with a loaded weapon, were terrorizing Aleksandrovsk. Going outside was awful. "Well, when they're caught they won't get off the hook."

The prison was living a fevered existence; there was not a meeting or a discussion without a "what have you heard?" For ten days, nothing was heard. The prison, which exults at any successful escape, was seized with joy. "Well, they've gotten away now! It's like trying to see wind in a meadow!" But the ones left behind also bore a malicious grudge: "Will they really get away?" Finally, it was learned that Kazeev had died at Kamyshevsk Pass. Upon discovery, his body showed wounds and massive trauma.

Poluliakhov told me how Kazeev was killed.

Kamyshevsk Pass, on the road from Aleksandrovsk Post to Derbinsk settlement, is a spot where fugitives often take refuge. When people go there they

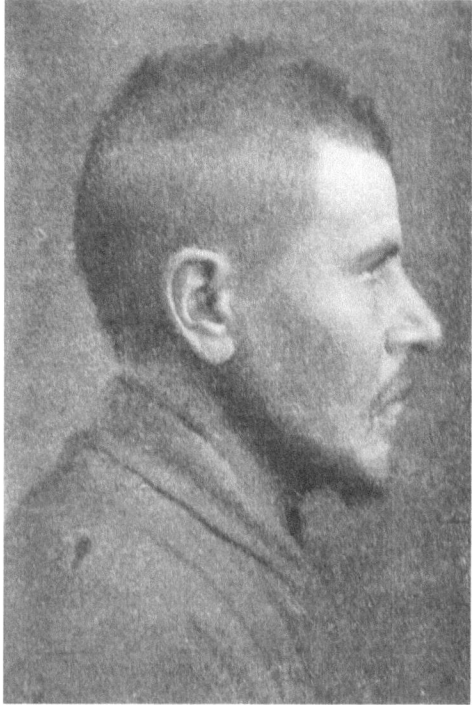

Fig. 33: Ivan Kazeev

usually carry a revolver. The road follows a narrow gully lined with undergrowth. Right and left are the terrifying slopes of huge, almost perpendicular, mountains with pine trees towering like ship masts and straight as arrows.

Along those steep cliffs, moving from tree to tree in single file, went the *brodiagi*. Kazeev was in the lead, Poluliakhov behind him. Suddenly, a shot rang out from behind bushes along the road. Running between two trees, Kazeev cried out and fell over. Poluliakhov hid behind a pine and waited second by second for another shot. But he hadn't been seen; Kazeev's tumble down the slope diverted the riflemen's attention.

"I hear voices down the mountain. I peek from behind the pine and see a glade in the bushes below. Vania's lying in this little glade floundering about, trying to get up. The men surrounded him. Vania's moaning, shouting, 'Give me some water, for Christ's sake!' And they're telling him, 'What for? You're going to die.'"

Hiding behind trees until nightfall, the four *brodiagi* got away. Rumors of them did not soon fade. They went through the taiga, traveling hungry and exhausted straight into virgin land, to tundra where no human foot had trod.

The rifle was of no use but they carried it perforce and at last, having become lost and bedraggled in the taiga and bitten bloody by insects, they came to the village of Vialza,[3] in the tundra.

"We're walking toward the village. A shepherd's grazing three cows. We go over to him and so forth. 'Anything to eat?' He gets scared; he's shaking like an aspen leaf. We say, 'Don't be afraid, we won't do anything to you. Look at us! See, you're not as scared as we are.' He got hold of himself. 'Very well,' he says, 'I drive the animals to the settlement at noon and I'll get you some bread. But wait here for me.' We gave him till noon. We're sitting, waiting. Only, we see exile-settlers with guns running out of the settlement. There are hunters and others with pitchforks and staves, shouting and waving their arms, and the shepherd's in front of them pointing at us in the bushes. Here this scurrilous soul is stirring up the whole community against us instead of bringing us bread. I'm thinking, 'That's why we had to wait and not follow him. If we'd gone with him we could've butchered a calf, cut out as much meat as we needed, and that would've been it. But I pitied the old man.' He's stirring up the exile-settlers against us. 'Starving *brodiagi* are here begging to eat!' he's saying. And if we were starving it meant we'd have to be killed, because a starving man will butcher a cow. And *brodiagi* had actually butchered one of their calves, so they were bitter toward them. 'Beat those bastards to death!' they're shouting. We began running. One of them fired and got me through the hand. It was like all my strength was lost through my fingers, and I fell." (The bullet went straight through the soft part of his left hand near the wrist bone.) "The others were lying flat on the ground. 'We surrender,' they're shouting, 'don't beat us!' However, they beat them badly. 'Don't kill our cattle!' they're screaming. They were like animals. The men hadn't done anything, but they're beating them…"

"They did so without provocation?"

"Provocation? I must say, I pity these exile-settlers. It's said they're of a different sort in Siberia. There, a *brodiaga* gladly goes to a muzhik and the Siberian muzhik always gives him bread. Because there *is* bread. But, in a word, this is Sakhalin, and there's hunger. The fellow's terrified of giving a piece of bread to his own son 'cause he himself might die. A *brodiaga* is his number-one enemy. It's the starving appealing to the starving. He dreads it. So does he have anything for poor starving me? A *brodiaga* will kill a calf straightaway out of hunger. But what's an exile-settler without a calf? He's dead! He's lost his last animal. You can buy a calf from the government but you won't have livestock. They're all going to ruin. An exile-settler over there hung himself after they killed his calf. So, they beat us and still left us hungry. I'm lying there, blood pouring out, and I'm seized by hatred *and* compassion… I'm sympathetic towards these exile-settlers, sympathetic…"

These people who murder others love terribly to summon up in themselves a sense of compassion. They like this sensation, for then they feel so good and kind and in these moments seem to think, "In essence, what a good, kind, splendid person I am! I'm so lovely!" And who doesn't want to think tenderly of himself? Who won't boast of his virtues?

"A pity!" This motif resounds constantly throughout the stories of Poluliakhov, axe-murderer of an eight-year-old child. When he says this word "pity" there is something gentle and meek in his face. He himself is moved by his own kindness.

"So, do you believe in God?" I asked Poluliakhov one day.

"No. I'm with Darwin!" he answered.

"What? You're familiar with Darwin?"

"I became familiar with him here, in prison. 'The struggle for survival,' it's called. A man eats a bird, a bird eats an insect and the insect eats something else. That's how it goes. 'The circulation of matter,' it's called. A man eats a bird not because he hates it, but because he wants to eat. And as for the bird, he's not thinking he wants to eat 'it,' he just wants to eat. The bird's not thinking about the insect, he just needs it. And that's it. Someone kidnaps a man who did nothing bad to him and goes on to take three lives. No one hated anyone, everyone just wants to eat. Everyone takes as he needs. This is called the 'struggle for survival'."

"Very well, Poluliakhov. We're existing according to Darwin. But what about the theory of adaptation? Should not man, from generation to generation, adapt himself among living people to their conditions, necessities and communal laws?"

"Adaptation?" pondered Poluliakhov. "It's impossible to adapt to everything. You can't adapt to *katorga*, for example. So I think a person adapts only to what he likes. Patience is needed for all that's left to be adapted to. But I don't have the patience. This grand 'theory of adaptation' you're talking about doesn't suit me." Thus this man qualifies "Mister Darwin" and understands him from a purely lupine perspective.

"Tell me, if you only want to talk about truth, how far America is from here," I said to Poluliakhov one day. I'd brought him a map. He looked a long time at it, measured the Pacific Ocean and Siberia according to the scale, and finally smiled.

"Well, no, it's not there! I can show you where's the water and where's the land. But which water and which land is all the same, as there's so much of it. Whatever water gets poured into its mouth, the starving earth will eat—it all goes to the devil! Go to your right you're dead, go to your left you're dead, and if you stay in one place you're dead. I have a simple story to tell. And such stories aren't terrible!" he laughed.

Of such is this man, nearly a youth, yanked from public school and conversant on Darwin; a murderer of six lives—an infinitely sympathetic man.

When Poluliakhov was being transferred from Kharkov[4] an incident took place. A female relation of the late Artsimoviches was at the railroad station. She didn't know that her relatives' murderer was among the party being moved. When the party was being led through the crowd, as is always the case, a discussion broke out as follows:

"So many doubtlessly innocent people are being sent away!"

"That young muzhik right there, for instance. I'll bet he's innocent," said the Artsimoviches' relative, turning to one of her companions. "Look at him. Now, how could a criminal have such a face?! Can we find out what he's been convicted of?"

"Tell me, please, who is that?" her companion asked the convoy officer.

"Him? That's Poluliakhov, the Artsimoviches' murderer."

The victims' relative let out a cry and fainted.

When I asked Poluliakhov about this episode he grew pensive:

"Please... Please... I'll remember... When they were driving us forward some woman shrieked and collapsed. Then I turned around and looked... Did she do that because of me? She happened to be a relative of the deceased?... Tell me, please! I wasn't paying attention... There was some crying. I thought she could've been someone's relative or...," Poluliakhov smiled, "...or she was one of my former lovers sobbing over me. I had so many in Kharkov!"

3

A FAMOUS MOSCOW MURDERER

In the Aleksandrovsk chains prison it's impossible not to be mesmerized by an emaciated, frail and sickly man with an alarmingly pained look in his eyes. He's a pitiful sight even among prisoners. A most tortured fellow.

"Who's that?"

"Viktorov."

Sakhalin administrators, all of whom *katorga* disdains, are rather proud to have "celebrities" in prison and will present to you: "A famous Moscow murderer."

Six or seven years ago all Russia was alarmed by "a mysterious murder in Moscow." In July, at the Brest-Litovsk train station, a terrible stench began coming from a basket among the unclaimed baggage. The basket was opened and, as the newspapers put it, "witnesses were presented with an utterly horrible spectacle."

Inside the oilcloth-lined basket lay pieces of a dismembered female body. Her cheeks had been cut off; the tags had been removed from her underwear. The horrible parcel had been mailed from Moscow on the 2nd of July.

All Moscow's detectives hit the streets. They searched and searched, without success. There seemed no clues whatsoever.

At that time, Moscow's chief detective was a certain Heffenbach, who'd won the renown of a Lecoq.[1] Three elements drew his attention. First of all, based upon the "wretched splendor" of the underwear found in the basket, he concluded the deceased was a prostitute. Next, his attention fell on the name—fictitious, of course—of the sender of the "baggage" and on the fictitious name of the "recipient." Both began with the letter "V." Because the person had lost his wits and was panicking, only names beginning with "V" must have instinctively entered his head, though perhaps this was light-hearted and mocking wordplay on the criminal's part. When everything's going swimmingly for a criminal, he sometimes starts boasting and, having no objection to scoring a point, likes to leave behind a calling card, a small tell-tale clue. "I say, look over here." Lastly, alongside the body in the basket was the blood-soaked wooden block the body had evidently been chopped up on. Such blocks are used to stoke the stoves of taverns and furnished rooms.

An audit was made of all the prostitutes on Moscow's books[2] and showed that one of them, who lived in Botkin House on Petrovsky Boulevard, had left for home. In fact, she'd not been around for almost a week before she allegedly left. An acquaintance of hers, Viktorov, reported that on 3 July he went to her apartment to get her things because she'd gone to her village on urgent business. Viktorov rented a furnished room on the corner of Briusov Alley and Nikitska and worked as a comptroller at the racetrack. He was found at the racetrack, taken to the police station and brought him into a room. Laid out on a table were the basket, oilcloth and bloody underwear. Catching sight of these things, Viktorov was "dumbstruck," then lost his composure, began weeping and confessed.

When Viktorov was still a boy his father shot himself in a fit of lunacy. Viktorov's sister suffered powerful bouts of hysteria. Immediately after Viktorov's arrest his brother lost his mind: he continually raved that he was drinking tea with his brother Nikolay on Sakhalin.

Viktorov had been unable to talk before age seven. And this wasn't the first time the newspapers celebrated him. He'd also become a Moscow celebrity in

1883. Thirty years old at the time, he fell into a coma that lasted twelve whole days. He was very nearly buried, and all Moscow became interested in "the living corpse of Mariinsk Hospital."

Viktorov completed only two grades at the Moscow Grammar School.[3] "I wasn't talented. The Russian language isn't easy for me!" He began drinking at twelve; became acquainted with debauchery at fifteen. At twenty, he came down with a foolish illness.[4] Viktorov's relatives are people of means. They are those who rent furnished rooms to "those ladies" in brothels. Since childhood, he's been mixed up with the demimonde. In 1881 he was sentenced to four months in a workhouse for robbery. That same year, he was implicated in the murder of the noblewoman Nakatova and her cook Pokhvisneva. "I didn't commit the murder... but I was close enough to it..." In 1883 he became a *brodiaga*. He wandered for eight years, then resumed his identity, returned to Moscow, inherited around 3000 and rented himself a furnished room.

The young woman who was murdered had lived in his aunt's brothel, then "did as she pleased and took charge of her own affairs" and moved in with him.

"Viktorov, were you her 'tomcat'?"

"Not exactly... How to put it? I didn't pay her, of course... I was her lover... But I didn't live off her money... So I took a little sometimes... All the more for the races!"

For three years he worked as tally-board comptroller at the racetrack and managed the races. "How I lived!" he says with a sad smile. "In winter I'd vegetate in a frozen apartment, so to speak... There was usually nothing to heat the furnished room with... But then summer would come and you'd jump around and spring to life. The whole summer you're living the races. You go to the racetrack with 150 or 200 rubles, go the full measure and when you'd lay it all down, you'd take 500 or 600! That's how I lived. I was on fire."[5] In Moscow, where in summer the racetrack is filled with all and everyone, there are many who "live the races all summer" but "vegetate" the rest of the year.

It is remarkable that in *katorga*, which is filled with gamblers, Viktorov does not gamble. I asked about him.

"He doesn't bet!... Some gambler!... Sometimes, when we're playing, he'll come over and put a two-piece[6] down so's to win a bit of sugar... He wins some pennies and goes away... But he does that rarely."

I asked Viktorov, "Why is this? You were such a gambler, but don't play here?"

"I'm not interested."

"But what made you gamble there?"

"I tell you, I was on fire. Because I was so close to it, I lived only for the racetrack. I was comptroller there—in the very center of it! All around me, they're laying down money, placing bets and in two minutes hundreds of tickets get thrown away. Well, I'd do it too! I couldn't stop myself. I was on fire.

I couldn't find myself for winning or losing—I was a spectacle. Tomorrow's the racetrack, and as you're trolling through the taverns you're thinking and computing; you're making your bets while you're meeting with the stable hand at "The Hunt" restaurant. You wake at the crack of dawn and gallop into the morning light. All you're thinking of is the horses; horses are running through your dreams. You don't notice the summer flying by."

Such is this afflicted man who couldn't speak before age seven, who fell into a coma, who's inherited a legacy of illness and been delivered into this world of so much grief and horror. From such conditions was born, raised and created this "famous murderer."

The hottest time for Moscow bettors is around St Peter's Day, 29 June,[7] when the "All-Russian Derby" is run. There's a general mêlée at the tally-board.

"That's when I'd get very nervous. 'Who'll take it? Who should I bet on?' Someone would say this one, another would say that one. You can't trust rumors. You grab the newspapers and they make no sense at all: they're saying different things. 'This one's not in form, that one's not ready,' they're saying. 'This one still needs work.' My head was just spinning round. You lost yourself. I had to gamble but time was running out, might you know, because I didn't have time to pay for the furnished room. I was renting two separate rooms and had remodeling expenses. But there was the Derby. You're going straight out of your mind."

The night before St Peter's Day, Nastia[8] was spending the night at Viktorov's. Around one o'clock, they were lying in bed. "Both were tipsy" and talking about the races. Viktorov asked her to pawn her things. "I have to gamble!" She reproached him that that was why she was losing all her things to him. Word followed word and Nastia slapped Viktorov. Viktorov grabbed a candelabra off the bedside table and hit her.

"She went quiet… Didn't make a sound… Gracious, I see the side of her head!… She's dead… But she suddenly wakes up and seems about to scream… I'm standing over her… She's lying there, not moving… Five minutes go by… I take her hand: it's warm… she's not getting cold… She's coming round… I'm thinking, 'You're done for!…' I was terrified…"

Viktorov grabbed a knife and slit her throat.

"I don't know why I killed her… I don't know… I just killed her out of fear; to be certain… I sit down looking at her and thinking, 'What do I do now?…' Then my eyes fall on the basket… I was supposed to send my niece some furs… I'd readied the basket, oilcloth and the camphor to sprinkle on them… Only, I hadn't sent the furs—I'd pawned them so's to gamble… I was thinking, 'I'll win the money back, get them out of hock and then mail them…'"

Viktorov suddenly got an idea what to do.

"I tip-toed barefoot into the kitchen...[9] I got a wooden block and a pail of water... I laid out the oilcloth and block like so, and got everything ready. I rolled over the deceased—and it was horrible what happened... As I raised her by the shoulders her head snapped back as if she were alive... The cut in the neck opened and blood gushed out... It was like I'd read in stories, how blood pours on the murderer as he's touching the murdered... Horrible... I threw her down... Poured out some vodka, but couldn't touch her... Poured out more vodka, then more... I got silly... I lifted her and gently put her on the floor."

In speaking of the victim, Viktorov says "the deceased" and uses formal pronouns with a kind of reverence; added to this, he fears "her," for "she" has haunted his dreams ever since. His neighbors on the sleeping platforms testify that Viktorov will suddenly jump up at night and scream at the top of his lungs. "He'll be completely white and shaking... It's all there in front of him!"

"I laid the deceased on the little block and started with her arms; I used a cleaver to cut her legs off... A sharp cleaver. I'm cutting through the flesh but can't get through the bone. I'm hitting it softly so's not to be too loud... My neighbors lived down the hall..."

This was a strange game of chance. Viktorov's neighbors were the civil servants G, a certain father and son... detectives with the Moscow police.

"I went along joint by joint so there wouldn't be any cracking... The bone separated and I cut through the tendons around the little knees... I cut off her cheeks so she couldn't be identified..."

"Were you drinking vodka at the time?"

"As if! My little arms were drenched in blood and there was no going for that. Only one thought was in my head: 'Quieter! Quieter!' Then, it felt just like something came from behind and lifted me up by my shoulders... I even felt the hands... My soul freezes... I'm on my knees and feel myself being held by the shoulders, but I'm afraid to open my eyes. There's a mirror opposite and I look in it... I was too terrified to turn around... You catch your breath, look in the mirror and no one's behind you... So I went on... I also cut off the tags from her underwear. I finished towards morning... I laid everything in the basket, doused it with camphor, wrapped it in oilcloth. I also put the block in there. I washed the cleaver in the pail, cleaned the blood that splashed on the floor—the water in the pail turned red and I went and poured it out. I come back and there's nothing save the strong smell of camphor."

At one point during our conversation Viktorov felt "unwell," and I handed him a vial of smelling spirits among those near the office window assigned for distribution to prisoners. Viktorov suddenly snapped. He jumped up white as a sheet, having lost himself, and pushed the vial away with trembling hands: "Unnecessary... unnecessary..."

"What was that? What happened?"

"Nothing... nothing... nothing..." Completely by chance, the spirits had turned out to be camphorated. I quickly closed the vial. "I can't bear the smell of that!" said Viktorov with a guilty smile, though his lips were white as his teeth chattered. Such had the camphor burned into his memory.

"I gathered up everything and dragged the basket into the next room, and the horror struck again." Viktorov was unable to sleep for two nights. Drinking "for courage," he drank "more than six liters of vodka."

"I'd drink, get drunk and eat... I ate with relish because I'd drunk so much... But then I'd become sober and that was horrible... I was afraid to go out. 'As soon as I leave,' I'm thinking, 'they'll come in and find everything...' Sitting at home was awful... I'm there alone but it seemed someone was breathing in the other room... I'd approach the door... But to go into that room and look at it was too terrible... I'm listening at the door—it's quiet... I sit down to drink more vodka... Again, there's breathing... I was terrified!..."

Finally, on the 2nd of July, he decided to leave. He hired a drayman who took him and the basket from the apartment.

"You couldn't tell anything from the basket... there was just the strong smell of camphor... When I left I opened all the windows to air the place out..."

As for posting the basket, Viktorov, after three sleepless nights, a murder and six liters of vodka, remembers it as if it were a dream.

"I remember going with the drayman into taverns four times... We drank our way through a whole bottle of vodka and so he finally got well and drunk, but I couldn't.... I'm following the dray-cart, only my legs were shaking... I'd sit down here and there in the carriage lane. We got to Smolensk Station... 'Now,' I'm thinking, 'they'll order me to open the basket...' My teeth are chattering... 'What is it?' 'Furs,' I say. 'Write down who's sending it and to whom!' they say. I nearly scribbled 'Viktorov.' 'Faster!' they say. 'What's wrong with you?' In my head I've got 'Vasilev' spinning together with 'Vladimirov,' so I scribble these names down... I get the invoice and I'm leaving, but feel like any minute they'll shout 'Stop!' from behind me. I went out to the square—my head was spinning, chest heaving—and leaned against a lamp post. It was like a weight had been lifted off my shoulders. I'm walking down the street but can't feel my own feet, I'm so happy. I got home and looked into the next room—as if there'd be someone there! I laughed at myself for such silliness and fell into bed... I didn't have a care!"

The next day, 3 July, Viktorov "formally" entered the apartment of the "deceased," said she'd received news of her mother's death and had suddenly gone to her village, and grabbed her things and took them to a pawn shop. "I couldn't throw them out, I needed the money to gamble."

The "easy life" began.

"I was a spectacle. I'd go through the taverns, get tips, check out the trial races. I'd place my bets. 'How to get money,' I'm thinking… I'd quickly blown all her money… The horses were in my head. I marveled at the time: it was as if nothing had happened. It was like a dream. Once, I asked myself, 'Was it a dream?' Only, I could still smell camphor in the rooms, as you couldn't open the windows.[10] But I wasn't too upset. Horse after horse the races went whirling round. I went first class. All the knock-out horses were running and the pay-outs were huge. You're always around the horses—when can you think of anything else?"

Suddenly, one day, Viktorov picked up a newspaper to learn about the races and read: "Terrible find in Brest-Litovsk." "Everything, everything started swimming before my eyes. The newsprint was jumping. Someone begins moaning and groaning in the next room. The smell of camphor hits my nose. Someone's coming down the corridor. My thoughts are spinning round. I'm thinking, 'What did I do?' I was struck with fear and horror… I'm waiting, can't wait, for when my neighbors come home from the investigation bureau… They came, and I summoned up my courage and went to offer them some vodka, and I ask, 'You haven't heard anything about that corpse hacked to pieces in Brest-Litovsk? I just read about it in the papers. How very horrible! What goes on these days.' 'No,' they say, 'we've heard nothing about who killed her.' My heart lightened. 'However,' they say, 'Heffenbach himself is on the case. Command's ordered him to solve this straightaway. They're sure to catch him.' My eyes bulged at these words."

Right there began the "uneasy life."

"I don't know where to hide. Anywhere I go, there's the deceased. You stay home at night, start looking around, and in she comes… Head thrown back, neck open, blood pouring out. I began spending nights in the brothels, and she'd show up there. I'm drinking and gambling. I'm drinking non-stop. If there hadn't been the racetrack I would've gone out of my mind." (True sports will hardly ever say that gambling plays such a role.) "I was all wound up for gambling, for everything. I'm spinning round and round and while the races are on, I never relax or think about anything. But when the races were over, I'd drink. I'd drink but not get drunk. And she's always there. Always. I'd run to church for the memorial ceremonies[11] and later that day, she'd appear twice. So I'm attending the ceremonies again. There were four ceremonies and I was in attendance for five days, all in different churches. You'd go, feel better, then she'd appear again. As if out of spite, all my neighbors could talk about was 'that mysterious murder.'"

The mysterious murder excited all Moscow. Detectives ran their feet off from searching; and this was the only thing the agents could talk about after coming home. "We still haven't found a thing. It's like he's gone up in smoke. We're finding nothing! Absolutely nothing!"

"I feel I'm losing my mind. I'm on fire. In the brothels at night, going to the races in the morning—the racetrack—and from the racetrack to a ceremony at church. I'm drinking in the taverns. The minute I get home at night I'm asking, 'How? What?!' I'm on fire… I go to my neighbors as if I'm expecting the death sentence right there. 'What's going on?' I ask, but I'm too scared to even look at them. But when they say 'nothing' I start floating on air. So many times I'd go to my room afterward, start laughing about something and couldn't stop. I'd bury my face in my pillow so no one could hear me shriek '*Nothing!*' I'm laughing on the outside, but inside I feel terrible. Then, suddenly, *she* would appear… I'd drink again, run home again, attend ceremonies again. I was on fire."

This being on fire ended when one day at the races Viktorov was told: "Investigators have summoned you."

"My arms and legs went numb… 'But no,' I'm thinking, 'can't be for that,' because I'd been snatching things, I'll tell you, I was robbing what I needed so's to gamble 'cause I'd gotten rid of all my own things. They brought me to the bureau and took me into a room. That half-lit room. So many folks were standing in front of the windows it blocked the sunlight. At first I couldn't make out what was on the table! But as they were leading me toward it, I screamed… The basket, the underwear, the oilcloth, the chopping block… I was hypnotized and just shouted, 'Don't make me go over there! Don't make me!' But Heffenbach's pushing me from behind. 'Go on,' he's saying, 'go on, don't be afraid. This is from Brest-Litovsk.' 'Don't make me go over there!' I'm wailing. 'I'll confess everything, just don't make me go…'"

In the detention cell Viktorov tried to hang himself from an air vent with the help of his shirt.

"She was tormenting me… The deceased… I'd open my eyes and there she'd be, sitting next to me… 'Kolia,' she'd say, 'I'll be with you wherever you go.' I couldn't stand it. And it was terrible to wait for death." Like so many, Viktorov anticipated "the noose immediately." "I'm telling you now. Have you ever been in court? The procurator was a Mr Khrulev…"

"But who defended you?"

"I don't remember. I wasn't interested. It didn't matter. But Khrulev accused me by name. So there in the middle of the table on the oilcloth was her underwear, crumpled, stuck together, blackened. Next to that was the basket itself… I felt faint when they brought these things in. It was horrible. I was in a funk in the court. I didn't realize what I was saying or what they were saying about me. But I do remember that Mr Khrulev pointed to the basket and demanded the same be done with me. Accordingly, I was to be hacked to pieces!"

The majority of these "famous murderers" believe that for them, "the noose will not be omitted for murder." And amid the fear and terror in court the majority believe the procurator is demanding the death penalty.

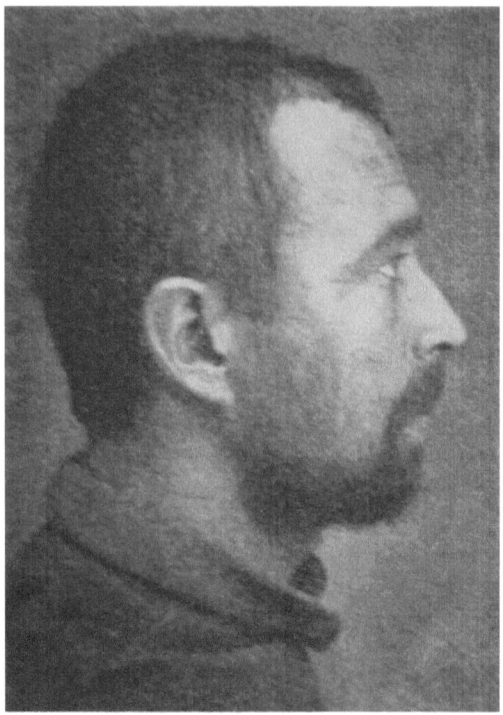

Fig. 34: Nikolay Viktorov

"I couldn't believe my ears when I was sentenced to *katorga*," Viktorov said, as have many.

In *katorga*, he complains of poor health. "The food's bad, but the main problem is the sleepless nights! I think of everything."

"What about?"

"About the past. God, it was all so stupid! Hardly believable!… But I'm also sometimes scared to go to sleep… When her spirit's being tormented… You know, that whore was a sinner… and when it's too much for her spirit…"

"What? She appears?"

"She comes to me." And this shriveled and shivering, this pitiful, frail, utterly wasted man says, raising his voice, "The main thing isn't the money… It's that I can't hold ceremonies in her memory… so she can rest in peace."

4
THE SPECIALIST

Seven years ago in Odessa a *huge* crime was committed. The old banker Livshits was found strangled in bed. Nothing was stolen; the money in a fire-proof safe in the next room had been left untouched. In the kitchen, bound head to toe with her mouth gagged, lay the suffocating cook Leia Kaminker. She said that that night some people wearing masks had forced their way into the apartment, threatened to kill her if she screamed, tied her up and gone into the bedroom. What happened there, she didn't know.

Investigations were conducted and the horrors later revealed in court. One suspect actually hanged himself in the police station. After a quite protracted, futile and error-filled investigation it was at last possible to deduce that an entire gang had gone after the banker Livshits. There was a certain Tomilin, a serial murderer, a desperate cutthroat who shot from the hip. His lover, Lutsker, was a thief by profession. There was the *brodiaga*-burglar Lvov and some widow who bought stolen goods. The cook Kaminker had been part of the gang, opening the door for the murderers and then playing her agreed-upon role in the comedy by letting herself be tied up. Only, it was strange that the murderers hadn't touched the safe. They explained that during the murder Pavlopoulos, "a specialist in safe-cracking" invited into their company, got frightened and ran off.

A search for Pavlopoulos began. It turned out that he'd since committed yet another crime. Pavlopoulos was caught burglarizing a treasury somewhere in the Crimea. Having broken into the treasury during the evening, he'd cracked the safe that night, filled his pockets with money and was waiting for his confederates to open the treasury's doors. Hearing the doors open Pavlopoulos, pockets full of money, made ready to leave. The doors opened and standing before Pavlopoulos were the police.

"One of my helpers gave me up, the bastard!" says Pavlopoulos with exasperation. He was tried, sentenced, then walked the road to Siberia. "During that time the no-goods who killed Livshits—may he rest in peace—gave me up! My career was ruined again."

"A 'career,' how so?"

"I'd prepared some 'relief work.' Everything was prearranged. I was going to go there afterward and cross the border to work as a real specialist!"

"Namely?"

"I'd open a safe!" Pavlopoulos says with a deep sigh. He has a heavy Greek accent and says, matter-of-factly, "I'd open za sef!" "Sef" actually sounds delicate when he says it, like it's a lover's name.

Pavlopoulos was removed from the road and forwarded to Odessa. Facing him in the courtroom were Kaminker—a frail, middle-aged Jewess who wept and shook the whole time—and Lvov, lanky and robust with an apathetic look, who gazed the whole time at the ceiling, wall, gallery and judge and paid not the slightest attention to what was going on, as if the case didn't concern him! Continually sobbing unrestrainedly and shouting, "I'm not guilty! I'm not guilty!" was the widow, the buyer of stolen goods who'd gone deaf in prison and was hobbling about on crutches. And there was Lutsker, who must have been very beautiful as a young Jewess, explaining to the court, "I request that you not sit me near Tomilin, or he'll kill me." A veteran familiar with the court and who'd been sentenced to *katorga*, Tomilin was there in shackles detailing the incident ever so wanly, albeit clearly and lucidly. And, terribly interested in the gallery, judge and jurors, in shackles as if already sentenced to *katorga*, was the lively, bright and middle-aged Greek, Pavlopoulos.

"Have you ever seen me before?" he asked a testifying police officer, an ace detective.

"No, I haven't met you."

"But the name 'Pan' is familiar to you?"

"Rather so!" There was even a note of respect in his voice.

"Pan" is Pavlopoulos's criminal name, his *nom de guerre*. Pavlopoulos received the name "Pan" in criminal circles for his love of the "good," free and rich life; for his drinking bouts and dandyism. "I wore a thirty-ruble blouse!" sighs Pavlopoulos on Sakhalin. "It was gossamer, not linen!" Pavlopoulos received the name "Pan" because he did only big and highly remunerative jobs. "My jobs were banks and offices. As for private individuals, you know, who are very rich, well, I'd go and practice in their homes!" As if he'd condescend to rob private parties! Pavlopoulos was absolutely uninvolved with "petty activity." He was called "Pan" especially for his exceedingly contemptuous, supercilious attitude toward all criminal brethren.[1] Pavlopoulos regarded only three or four of the people in his profession to be, like him, "worthy of respect." "There's such a one in Moscow. The rest I met abroad." The name "Pan" resounded not just throughout Russia. It was known in Rumania, Turkey, Greece and Egypt. "Throughout the East in general!" Pan explained to jurors. After the police had told the court all about Pan-Pavlopoulos, he arose from his seat, fetters clanking, and, poking his chest with his finger, said, "*I* am Pan!" The old court officers said the court had never seen a more unique defendant.

Pavlopoulos faced a witness, son of the deceased Livshits, and said, "Tell me, please, are you familiar with your deceased father's safe?"

"Yes. I now own it."

"It's such-and-such a make? Such-and-such a brand?"

"Yes."

"The lock has such-and-such a combination? It opens like this and like that?" Pavlopoulos betrayed in minutest detail all the safe's secrets.

"Yes. Yes. Yes!"

"Tell me, if you were to open the safe without a sound, how would this be done?"

"Truly… I don't know…"

"Surely, you remember. On such-and-such a side there is a pin. If you press it, the safe opens without a sound."

"On such-and-such side, you say?"

"Yes, yes. Don't fret yourself. You'll remember. Such-and-such a pin should be there."

"Yes! Absolutely correct! There is such a pin and, if pressed, the safe really does open without a sound!" remembered the witness.

"You see!" Pavlopoulos turned to the court. "I know his safe even better than he does!"

Pavlopoulos denied all involvement in the planning of the murder. "Would I really have been so stupid?!" he declaimed, passionately and persuasively. "Why would I? I have—thank God—a specialty!" Thus he said "thank God." And he so often invoked this "specialty" with such enthusiasm that the judge finally asked, "What is this 'specialty' you keep talking about?" "Opening a safe!" "Ah!" "I'm even wearing shackles because of my specialty!" Pavlopoulos said this with gusto, for Lord's sake, as if he'd received a mark of distinction. "You've heard I was known abroad for my specialty. For my specialty, I got Siberia!

"I, esteemed jurors, am, like them, a thief. But mine's a different specialty!" he clarified for the jurors. "We're split up among various specialties. One does what he can manage. Take a pickpocket: he's a pickpocket but he steals a fur coat from a ballroom's foyer. He's not performing his job. That's for 'ballroomers.'[2] Furthermore, a ballroomer doesn't go aboard trains and rob passengers. He doesn't know this business! For this, there are the 'trainsters.'[3] Everyone has his specialty. I'm a specialist at opening safes.

"I'd go and kill someone?! Me?!" he wrung his hands, and his face even radiated compassion for people able to imagine such nonsense. "Indeed, why would I? Yes, I, it so happened, was opening the safe when the owner was in the next room. But I didn't hear anyone." (Pavlopoulos, moreover, has never said "crack" a safe. He always softly says "open." "It's stupid to crack a safe, you must *open* a safe!") "I was going to open the safe, take the money and leave. I wasn't even going to awaken Livshits! And, all of a sudden, I should murder him?!"

"However," interrupted the lofty sounding chairman, "you yourself say that you had a pistol with you."

"Not just a pistol but also a dagger and brass knuckles!" Pavlopoulos passionately declared. "You yourself can judge what company I was moving in! Such a rogue's gallery! Just look at their physiognomies! Alright?" At these words, Tomilin turned and glared in utter contempt with his cold, gray impassive eyes at Pavlopoulos. "You know this rogue's gallery would kill a man for a five-piece," Pavlopoulos warmly continued. "You know they're good-for-nothings! I had watches, rings and a gold cigarette case with me. Given these, I had to carry weapons. You know, they might have killed me to get my share!"

In actuality, Livshits's murder happened as follows:

The murder wasn't planned, only the robbery was planned. The spirit behind the undertaking was the widow-jeweler, the buyer of stolen goods. She'd heard from her acquaintance Kaminker that the "master" kept all his money at home, and so she introduced her to acquaintances who occasionally sold her goods—the burglars Tomilin and Lvov. But how to open the safe? Not knowing, they would've had to bust it open and end up waking the whole building. The company then capitalized upon the arrival in Odessa of a famous "specialist in the business," and invited him to take part.

Pan entered this "good job" with typical caution. He told Kaminker to break the front door lock so he could come calling in the capacity of a locksmith. In the house in the guise of a locksmith, he studied the safe's combination configuration and details. "I only needed to study the safe once to understand it. I immediately saw it wouldn't be difficult. I had experience with that type." Pavlopoulos told the company, "It'll be an easy job!" but warned, "Just remember, no stupidity. I don't go for stupidity. Yes, keep it simple. Livshits won't hear it when I open the safe."

On Sakhalin, Tomilin told me, "That really was the arrangement. A touchy fellow, you know, a limp-wrist. In a word, Pan is garbage!"

In the evening of the appointed day Kaminker opened the door and into the kitchen came Lvov, Tomilin, Lutsker in male dress (Tomilin wouldn't let Lutsker take a step from him) and Pavlopoulos with the "necessary instruments." Livshits hadn't yet gone to bed, so the company waited in the kitchen. They were drinking vodka "for courage"—all except Pavlopoulos. He was worried they'd get him drunk and harm him.

The evil, brutal and reckless Tomilin became drunk and irritated by the delay, and Pavlopoulos began to get nervous and warned, "Just remember, no stupidity!"

"Right! As you say! We'll be quiet!"

Kaminker came over, cocked her head and said, "Seems he's gone to sleep. It's quiet." As agreed, they tied her up, put a gag in her mouth, laid her on her bed and left.

Pavlopoulos now had to open the safe. Lvov, Tomilin and Lutsker stood guard. If Livshits woke up they were to bind and gag him. He went quietly into the room containing the safe. In the next room, the old man Livshits was reading a book in a bed on which the moonlight fell. The robbers hid themselves.

So passed several minutes. Lutsker, Tomilin, Lvov and Pavlopoulos waited, not daring to breathe. The old man continued reading peacefully. "It felt like several hours passed! It was hard to breathe!" says Pavlopoulos.

Tomilin suddenly broke down. He ran to the bed, followed by Lvov. Pavlopoulos's legs gave way. The old man barely raised his head and didn't even have time to shout. Tomilin threw a noose around his neck, Lvov grabbed the other end and they pulled. Wheezing sounds, and the old man was dead.

Tomilin came back to Pavlopoulos. "I'd never seen such a face!" says Pan. He made for the door but Lvov blocked his way: "What about the safe?" Pavlopoulos pulled out his pistol: "I'll blow your head off!" The lanky fellow backed off, and Pavlopoulos was gone. "That's when we were all scared!" says Lvov.

Tomilin grew terrible and "went for the heart." Entering the kitchen, he sat on top of the bound Kaminker and, when she turned, punched her so hard in the head that she lost consciousness. Lutsker and Lvov were quaking: "We thought he'd kill everyone!" Tomilin was shouting, "roaring like a beast," cursing, swearing and swilling vodka. Lutsker begged him on her knees, "Calm down! Calm down!" He could hardly catch his breath.

Thus the murder happened.

"I got involved in such stupidity! I was connected to such scoundrels!" said Pavlopoulos on Sakhalin, beating himself about the head, genuine despair in his words. "Ah? I ended up in a murder. In a murder, when I have my own specialty!"

The jury didn't believe Pavlopoulos. He was sentenced along with Tomilin and Lvov for premeditated murder. Pavlopoulos simply shrugged his shoulders and thanked his designated attorney, the now deceased barrister Vakhovich: "Thank you for your defense. It's no fault of yours I've been found guilty. The esteemed jurymen couldn't understand us!" Such is Pan.

On Sakhalin, Pavlopoulos eluded me. You'd go to Aleksandrovsk's free prison. "Is Pavlopoulos here?" "At work. Try the steam mill." You'd go there. "Pavlopoulos's gone." I searched for him morn and night but couldn't find him anywhere.

One day, I was passing through the prison when suddenly a Caucasian exiled for several murders in his native village came running toward me—literally running. He'd complained about something, submitted a grievance, but received no answer—and was now demanding "an aynswer!" from me.

I tried in vain to tell him I wasn't an official. The Caucasian didn't want to know. "How not official? Why not official? Official beat everyone, but no official to look in legal complaint?!" His eyes glowered. "Give aynswer! Two yeers we waiting. We no want wait more."

Suddenly, someone's powerful arm grabbed the Caucasian. "Stop right there, I myself will speak to him!" Before me stood, hands on hips, a strapping young penal laborer, leather cap a-tilt, a Russian shirt with a "forge" (embroidered collar), cassock slung carelessly over one shoulder. He looked like a typical Ivan. This was the prison celebrity A, an Ivan who impressed Patrin himself.[4]

"May it please you to say who you'd be, if you're not an official?"

"But what's it to you? You know, I didn't ask who you are!"

"No, excuse me!" A blocked my path with a defiant look. "If, as it pleases you to say, you are not an official, then on what basis are you observing the prison? Eh?"

A group circled round and watched to see "how this would end." The situation was critical. Threatening to complain to the officials would mean—God forbid—losing all sympathy from the prisoners. To yield to this man would be to embarrass myself, to be ruined in the prison's eyes. To somehow degrade him, so that all this would lead to nothing; to suddenly destroy his charisma in the prison's eyes—well, for Lord's sake, how many birch strokes would this fellow take to preserve his reputation? I needed to find some way out, to make it so that he and I separated without him losing his dignity. It came into my head to bark at him as loud as I could.

"Shut up! Take off your cap! How dare you talk to me? Huh? How dare you stand before me in your cap and be cheeky, like I'm your commander? You think I'm your commander?"[5]

Everyone turned red from laughing. The Ivan (as he himself later told me) "began to lie, but when I saw I was being stupid" and had made a mistake, rejoiced at being given an out, and laughed and doffed his cap. "But you're hardly a commander, for you have our respect! Please forgive us! If you're not a commander, you're not guilty!" For everyone this was a peaceful solution and they smiled. I then saw among the crowd a face trying not to burst out laughing, black as an olive and animated with eyes of burning fire.

"What's your name?"

"Pavlopoulos."

"Ah! The renowned Pan! I bring greetings from your attorney, Mr Vakhovich!" Prior to my journey the now-deceased Vakhovich had in fact asked me to greet his unique client. Pavlopoulos beamed with happiness. All eyes now turned to him respectfully: a celebrity known by all travelers throughout Russia!

"Akh, how you've encouraged me with this! You can't present yourself this way!" Pavlopoulos then told me. "My respect had been raised 100 per cent!"

With this, our friendship began. When I'd go to Aleksandrovsk's free prison two persons always accompanied me: Pavlopoulos, who explained there was no danger in drinking vodka, playing cards, etc. around me; and A, who for a long time saw it as his duty to protect me. "Maybe some fool will treat you scandalously? You know, they're just commoners. They're prisoners, in a word."

On Sakhalin, clerks receive a pool of telegrams at the Russian Agency that they print on the local press. I would obtain the proofs and every day, Pavlopoulos would visit me to read the telegrams, for the Greco-Turkish War was on at that time. He'd set upon his nose a golden pince-nez that contrasted with his prisoner's pea-jacket, and read and shake his head. "Tsk! Tsk! Tsk! They're beating our men. They're beating the Greeks! They're beating them!" He was saddened, agitated, close to fury.

"Our ministers are good for nothing! Ministers! What they've reduced us to! What are we going to fight with now?! They've all become Deligiannises!"[6]

One day he explained, "It's because of that Deligiannis I'm in *katorga*!"

"How so?!"

"Pavlopoulos isn't my real name. I'm from Athens, and have a lawyer brother in Athens. Only I, of course, took the wrong path as a youth. I would have been a good mechanic if I'd just settled down when I came of age. I bided my time until my Greek jobs died down and, as I had a lot of money, bought some land in Greece. Then our ministers led us into these catastrophic policies. We were completely impoverished. The taxes were terrible and I couldn't cover them with my land. There were no harvests and I fell into debt. Everything was auctioned off. But I'd become accustomed to a certain lifestyle! Once again, I happened to open a safe. That's why I came here to Sakhalin, because of our ministers!"

Often, when he talked to me, his voice resonated with much heart-rending melancholy. "That's it—Sakhalin! I'm not tormented that I'm on Sakhalin! Only that I'm so far from Greece! And what's happening there now! Poor, poor Greece!" He sometimes said, "If they'd let me go, I'd volunteer! I would even die for Greece!" When he spoke of Greece, his voice resounded with such love and affection for his homeland.

Now that Pavlopoulos has served his *katorga* sentence—reduced by royal clemency—I can relate the following conversation:

"Pavlopoulos," I asked him one day, "why are you never in the mill?"

"Indeed, I am never there. I never perform *katorga*. *Katorga* labors are only for those who don't have money."

"Is that so?"

"Indeed. I hire someone else. He carries out his own tasks and mine."

"Do you pay him much?"

"A five-piece a day. It's to my advantage, for I get more."

"How do you busy yourself?"

"I deal in old clothes, loan money on interest."

"How much of a percentage do you charge?"

"As is our custom, I loan to gamblers 'before the cocks crow,' that is, before morning, for the full day. One hundred per cent a day! It's a good percentage!" he smiled.

Pan had remained an aristocrat here: a prison usurer, his was an honored and esteemed personage. Pavlopoulos, as I ascertained, was like a spider, sucking the whole prison dry. He had a bit of money, a fair bit of money. Like all penal laborers, he cherished a dream. "God provides, but I can't live that simply! As is my habit, I'll take up my specialty again." He speaks about his specialty and about safes as he does about Greece—with enthusiasm, warmth, love.

"What do you do? We've read you cracked safes."

"Opened, not 'cracked'!"

"Alright, *opened*."

"And how! You'll say that, after you've bought an explosive-proof safe and practiced on it!" Drawing and sketching, he told with extraordinary passion how to do this. "One time I was in Alexandria, in Egypt, and I'd been struggling for three months to open a Milner safe.[7] How to open it? That's quite a safe! So! It's impossible to open it by yourself. You need no less than three people! You need sixteen poods of tools alone. If you start working on it but you're not used to it, the whole house starts shaking. You can only open it from the back. Given that I've seen you many times, I can tell you're not one of those people who would own an explosive-proof safe. But if, God willing, you get one, then get yourself a Milner!" Pavlopoulos burst out laughing.

"Very well. But will you come and open it?"

"Me? Who do you take me for? I tell you this: not only am I not going to, but if I'm in that city not a single crook will go after you. They respect Pan. Pan says, 'Don't touch' and they don't touch. But you should all of a sudden think this about me? Ai-ai-ai!" He was seriously offended.

"Very well, Pavlopoulos, you're an educated man, 'with principles,' but you bear no shame, no sin, for taking people's property?"

Pavlopoulos looked at me in astonishment. "Did I ever take anything from the poor, who gained from my labor? I always helped the poor. As you know, I acted only against the wealthy."

"Indeed, *against* the wealthy!"

"So how is it their property? Believe me, you can work and earn a thousand, but others are earning a million off of you. All property is someone else's. Everyone lives through someone else's property. So I live through them because they're my 'someone else'!" he laughed. "Someone has money in an explosive-proof safe and so probably has money some other place! I don't clean the fellow out."

"Listen, Pavlopoulos," I mentioned to him one day. "You seem to like opening safes. Do you really love this work?"

"I adore it!" he answered serenely. "It's necessary to love any business. Only then does it approach art!"

Such a strange monomaniac. When I was leaving Sakhalin, Pavlopoulos came to accompany me to the wharf. He asked me to send him a history of the Greek War in the Greek language. "You travel a lot. Any time you're in Greece, pass on a son's greetings to his poor sweet homeland!" Tears were in his eyes.

"Farewell, Pavlopoulos!"

"Until tomorrow, for you!" he corrected me, winking and smiling cunningly.

5

CANNIBALS

Instances of cannibalism among fugitive penal laborers are more common than you would imagine, though only three cannibals have been officially acknowledged. Busying myself in Rykovsk's prison archive, I ran across the following document, dated 28 July 1892:

> To: His Worship Mister Warden of Rykovsk Prison, Tymovsk District
> From: Supervisor of the Central Road Murashov
>
> ### REPORT
>
> I have the honor to inform your worship of exiled penal laborer Koloskov, Pavel, who escaped between the 13th and 14th and was reported on the 15th of this July in violation of code No. 248. He was captured on the 24th of this current month; at this time there were found among his items two kettles containing a number of pieces of human flesh, roasted. Koloskov, Pavel, revealed that he had murdered an exiled penal laborer who had gone with him along the forest trail; he did not know his name but he

Fig. 35: The Onor trail

described his physique: a light-brown male, above average height, Little Russian, around 35 years old, an Orthodox believer. Records show that on that same night the exiled penal laborer Krikun-Kalenik escaped with him. I, Murashov, searched Koloskov's things and found a cassock, the deceased's dirty underwear, and roasted flesh, human, which had begun to rot from the warm temperature. The crime was committed five versts from Onor along the road leading from Khandos Two to Onor. Because of the important circumstances of the crime, I have the honor of informing your worship that convict Koloskov has been ordered held in manacles and leg irons.

This happened during the clearing of the Onor trail. This "Onor road" is memorialized in a *katorga* song composed by the "mountain-sufferers," that is, penal laborers who came to Sakhalin not by sea but overland:

When we left Tiumen[1]
It was geese we ate,
But when we came to Onor
People's what we devoured.

In one handwritten collection of verse associated with the Onor project, there is as follows:

> Many enter vagabondage
> Having been lured by their comrades.
> But when they fall asleep someone
> Strikes them with eternal sleep.
> They murder and chop up the body,
> Make a fire… and there's kebabs…
> *They don't remember him.*
> He's not the only one who's perished so.

Thus the horrible memory of the Onor project lives on in *katorga*.[2]

To whom and whence came the heroic but entirely absurd idea to cut a trail from southern Korsakovsk Post up the length of Sakhalin? The trail chanced to go through tundra and taiga undergrowth. That it is a *trail* may be judged by the fact that it took me, for example, three and a half hours to travel the eight versts from Onor to Khandos Two. It's possible to go along the trail only by horse. The horse steps carefully among the roots of unextracted tree stumps, but upon reaching a clearing, momentarily sinks up to his paunch in the thawing bog of the tundra. The work of clearing the trail lasted from early spring to the first frosts. Workers sunk tree branches and roots into the quagmire. Combined with the torture of working up to their waists in a filthy bog was the still more unendurable torture of the midges, which in summer form clouds above the tundra. Midges swarmed over workers so that they literally bled. "No exposed spot wasn't bitten!" say former laborers. "The midges were so thick they were in your mouth. You'd breathe them in and out!" People who've been in the tundra in summer will fully testify to this.

They went along this way for the whole summer, seventy-seven versts, but then this idea—to hack a trail "the entire length of Sakhalin"—was deemed completely unrealizable. The project's difficulty may be judged by the fact that of the 390 men assigned to the Onor project, only eighty returned. Of the rest, some were killed, others escaped (a portion were captured), but the majority perished in the taiga.

Workers needed almost supernatural powers to complete their assignments. Using similar powers, the local prison administration oversaw the road project; but nothing could have been realized without the presence of Senior Overseer Khanov.[3] Khanov was himself a former exiled penal laborer. It's said that he was exiled at some point for some vicious crime and served his *katorga* sentence in Kara, during the Razgildeev era that old penal laborers have ever since recalled with horror. "I'm a Razgildeevite!" Khanov said with pride. Khanov completed *katorga* and exile-settlement and, upon arriving on Sakhalin, became a supervisor. Generally, there is no crueler overseer than a former exiled penal laborer. Like any former penal laborer, Khanov hated and disdained *katorga*. Moreover, "as a convict," he knew it well and in detail.

To prevent his command of 390 convicts—watched by all of three guards—from rebelling, Khanov singled out the Ivans. *Katorga* Ivans shouldn't be confused with the "Ivan-*Nepomniashchye*," that is, the *brodiagi*. An Ivan is a long-term prisoner with nothing to lose and is the daredevil, desperado and scoundrel of *katorga*. These prisoners are usually rotten to the core—they're *katorga*'s "aristocracy." *Katorga*'s timid and beaten leftovers, contemptuously known as the "herd," regard them with fear and trembling, for they are the instigators and ringleaders of all prison disturbances. With the experienced eye of an "old Razgildeevite," Khanov familiarized himself with each new party of penal laborers and then purposefully singled out the Ivans to act as project supervisors. In this way, the Ivans were completely emancipated from labor and able to eat better, taking over distribution of prisoners' rations and acquiring the utmost opportunity to tyrannize and rob the ill-fated herd, to pound from it its last pennies, last pinches of tobacco. There'd never been a better life for the Ivans. They were on Khanov's side. And the herd—wretched, beaten and deprived of leaders—patiently bore its cross.

The old Razgildeevite employed two methods to utterly crush the herd: excessive tasks and insufficient food. Quotas were so established that everyone was always guilty of "incomplete tasks." Floggings (Khanov had the authority to flog) were by all accounts extreme. Khanov fed prisoners once a day, after work. Rations were insufficient, and what is more, the Ivans were stealing. A worn-down fellow, having finished his task, or more likely, never completing it, would, if he avoided a flogging, poke his nose into a cauldron, gobble hurriedly and, overworked and half-starved, fall asleep on the spot as if dead. How could there be protests?! So the herd lived in starvation and terror.

Having crushed the herd physically and mentally, Khanov maneuvered against the Ivans. He was able, moreover, to do this especially deftly and in penal laborer fashion. While reining some in, he at the same time granted others still greater privileges. He'd suddenly remove a certain Ivan from the supervisors and transfer him to the regular laborers, into a semi-starvation, semi-terrorizing regime. The remaining Ivans were in his hands because fewer supervisors meant larger stolen shares for each of the rest. Once among the laborers, the demoted Ivan had to submit, for by himself, what could he do when his comrades thrashed and beat him at night? "Work, you sonofabitch! No loafing!"

So, little by little, Khanov manipulated the Ivans, keeping only the most horrible of them as supervisors. But at the same time, these supervisors were as veritably devoted as dogs to Khanov. A few of them each got a big share of the spoils. The Khanov regime existed owing precisely to them, and even this convict-*cum*-overseer was not as vicious as his *katorga* supervisors. Thus practicing the dictum *divide et impera,* Khanov maintained through his devotees an iron grip over all *katorga* and did what he wanted.

Men threw themselves under falling trees in order to be maimed; others chopped off a hand (on Sakhalin there are now many of these "Onorites" with a severed left hand) only so that, being incapable of work, they'd be sent back to prison. Still others dashed headlong into the taiga to die of starvation.

Pavel Koloskov was one of the Ivans singled out by Khanov. Koloskov was initially exiled to Sakhalin for ten years for murder and robbery. He then escaped, was captured, received a flogging and was indefinitely sentenced to *katorga* with "fifteen years' probation," that is, he had to spend fifteen years in the chains prison: something utterly hopeless. In prison, he was one of the Ivans, and when he was assigned to an Onor labor gang Koloskov was immediately made a supervisor by Khanov.

"The living was good then, so to speak. You could eat your fill, there was tobacco, we even got vodka." Koloskov now recalls those days with pleasure. But they didn't last long. Khanov reined in this Ivan by the aforementioned methods. "I got angrier and angrier that I'd been transferred to the laborers. I went up to my comrades, 'What's this, chaps? What for?' They're laughing. 'As it turns out, you didn't know how to please him. Now sort yourself out as best you can. We're better off, so who cares about you? On Sakhalin it's every man for himself. But here you are whining instead of doing your job. And that's why we're here.' I was a capable fellow, but Khanov dumped and dumped on me. He'd dump such tasks on me that I lost my strength. There weren't a day I wasn't thrashed because they said I didn't finish the task. I was looking death in the face. At that point, I convinced a comrade to escape." Koloskov has been incarcerated in the Aleksandrovsk chains prison ever since.

He's still a young fellow, short-statured, broad-shouldered, verifiably "capable." His eyes gaze from under the brows of a stupid sullen face. *Katorga*, even the chains, *katorga*'s "head," dislikes and shuns him. He typically walks alone through the yard in the fenced-in chains sector, back and forth, downcast, gloomy, like a wolf tirelessly pacing its cage.

"I fled the project with a comrade!" says Koloskov.

"Did you bring provisions?"

"No! What provisions? True, when we're about to go vagabonding we always save up our food ahead of time. We dried ourselves into husks. And what drying we did! Because when you'd finished work and choked down what they gave you, it was like you never ate. That's what we were escaping!"

"You didn't even ask your comrade's name?"

"It didn't matter. We were going and going through the taiga, death coming nearer. My comrade fell down and died."

"Died on his own?"

"On his own. He'd been feeling poorly and dropped dead. It was later I lied that I'd killed him. I saw he was dead and thought I'd be next, so I gathered some brushwood. I had matches with me and lit a fire and cut several pieces from the body and cooked their edges… Only, I didn't eat the body. I did it that way on purpose. I put the pieces in a little pouch (every *brodiaga* carries a little pouch) and went on my way saying, 'Given the chance, I'll say I've eaten human flesh.' That way, I'd be arrested and put in prison. If not, I'd be sent back to the project. Because it's a terrible crime, that's why I did it. Because it's well known that such cases have happened where comrades leave work for the taiga and are killed and their flesh eaten. And so I slandered myself."

But Koloskov's not telling the whole truth.

"He's shameful!" one convict explained to me. "You're new here. But we know for certain he ate him."

I met witnesses who saw the prisoner being brought to the project with his terrible pouch. The penal laborers would have attacked and killed him if guards hadn't been defending him. *Katorga* couldn't believe such a terrible crime, and made Koloskov eat some of the cooked flesh found on him. "So you say you killed and ate him? Show your courage. Eat!" Under threat, Koloskov ate. "Good tasty meat! Better than any beef!" He even laughed. "His face showed no disgust at all," witnesses testify.

I managed to remind Koloskov of these details during our conversation. "Are they lying?"

Koloskov replied, "Whatever happened, happened!" and waved his hand.

Of the other two "Onor cannibals" only one is still alive—Vasilev. Gubar, his comrade who committed the crime with him, died, unable to withstand his punishment. His story is the same as Koloskov's. Vasilev's deceased comrade Gubar, judging by his portrait, was a dull, stupid and wicked man, one of the desperate Ivans who terrorized the prison. Khanov had at first similarly promoted him to the supervisor class, but then transferred him to the laborers and began breaking him down. Gubar couldn't stand it and persuaded Vasilev and Fedotov, a young twenty-year-old penal laborer, to escape with him. Gubar murdered Fedotov on the second day.

"I think he convinced him to escape so's to kill and eat him. He had the notion ahead of time!" says Vasilev. In Vasilev's very detailed, explicit and utterly horrible account, it is the night before the murder. "Fedotov didn't know a thing. But I had the shivers, because I'd heard that when Gubar escaped earlier from *katorga*, he killed his comrade and ate his corpse. As night fell Fedotov began snoring, but I couldn't sleep and my teeth were chattering. 'Will

Fig. 36: Vasilev

Gubar kill me?' Of course, we'd escaped with nothing, and you'll go sick in the head from what you find to eat in a forest clearing. It'll destroy your stomach. At dawn, Gubar says to me, 'Let's eat,' and nods at Fedotov. I felt a chill. 'What are you?' The other's spirit seized and terrified me. 'Well, if I refuse, then he'll persuade Fedotov, and they'll kill me.' So, I agreed. I went to get a drink from the brook. I'm looking at myself when Gubar comes over, white as a sheet. 'Eat,' he's saying, 'let's eat!' Then we went over to the body…"

Vasilev, a hearty thirty-five-year-old man, is said to be unusually physically strong. Like most very strong people he's exceptionally good-natured. I looked in amazement at this white-bearded giant with hair the color of flax and kind gentle eyes, speaking with an easy-going, rather guilty, smile. He hardly seemed a *cannibal*.

I'd been warned against meeting Vasilev. Following capture, he'd lost his mind and has ever since been disturbed and flies into a rage at any mention of the affair. But I was enormously interested in this unusual criminal. So I met with Vasilev and, having invited him to the prison chancery, which in its off-hours was reserved for my private meetings with prisoners, asked if I could be of some assistance to him. Vasilev answered, "No! In whatever way?"

He refused any offer of money. "Why for me?" He sat before me clearly confused and wringing his cap in his hands, and wanted to say something but couldn't decide what. After a very long pause, looking somewhere off to the side and smiling guiltily, he said, in his soft, kind gentle voice, "You... probably... want to know about my... case?"

"If it's too difficult for you to recall, it doesn't matter!"

"No... Yes, you're right... I know that for you, it's not out of curiosity... For you, it's out of science... Poluliakhov told me..." Poluliakhov, infamous murderer of Lugansk's Artsimovich family, is among penal laborers the best educated and most influential of their powerful authorities. He was very useful to me, and made clear to his comrades that I was neither an investigator nor an official, that there was nothing to fear from me. "Poluliakhov told me," continued Vasilev, "that you want to write how our life really is... If you need my case, please go ahead... I'm ready..."

And he told me in complete detail, blushing and paling, agonizing over the terrible memories, how they proceeded to slice off the soft parts of the corpse, cut out the liver and cook a soup in the cauldron they'd taken with them from the project. "We picked some fresh nettles and added them for flavor." According to Vasilev, he could not eat at first. "Yes, my stomach was heaving. But then Gubar sits down and digs in... And I ate."

When they were captured, Vasilev told the authorities the same thing. When he and Gubar were brought for their floggings, he dispassionately told the doctor the same, with all the details. What accounted for this dispassion? Maybe this was the dispassion of a man petrified by horror.

Katorga "pitied" Vasilev. "He's not to blame. He didn't start it. He's not that kind of man." *Katorga* hated Gubar. He was the most terrible and loathsome of the Ivans, the terror and scourge of the whole prison. Moreover, as I've already mentioned, there was the rumor that he had eaten people during earlier escapes. Everyone on Sakhalin says *katorga* collected its pennies and paid executioner Komlev fifteen rubles to flog Gubar to death.

The executioners are virtuosos in the art of wielding the lash, and not even the most experienced official's eyes can tell how hard the executioner is striking. The whole time it seems he's striking with equal ferocity, but there are hundreds of nuances within this veritable profession.

It's a fact that Vasilev and Gubar were sentenced to the same number of lashes, and Komlev punished them on one and the same day. Vasilev bore his punishment in full and remained intact. Gubar lost consciousness after the forty-eighth blow and was taken to the infirmary, where he died three days later. He'd been criss-crossed to the loins and necrosis had set in.

I asked Komlev whether it was true he'd gotten fifteen rubles to flog Gubar to death. The old executioner answered neither "yes" nor "no," just said,

Fig. 37: Gubar

"Well, I'm an impoverished fellow!" and, having grown a little quiet, invoked the prevailing excuse, "That's Sa*kal*in!"

A doctor who, as duty required, attended this horrible punishment told me about it. Komlev—this is his subsequently obtained *brodiaga*-name; he himself is from the clerical estate and at one time attended seminary school—Komlev made it appear that he was "appraising" the man. He is generally something of a "romantic," and liked to show off during an "affair." He'd show up in a red blouse, black apron and some kind of special hat he'd made. Preparing to inflict the lashes, he'd stand on tip-toes so as to seem taller. Small, veiny and muscular, with a frowning and always sullen countenance, watery gloomy eyes and inflamed eyelids, he must really have been repulsive and terrifying. "Komlev's very solemnity told us something unusual was going to happen!" the physician told me. "Before administering the first blow, he barked out his traditional 'Get ready' such that I began shaking and turned away." Komlev administered the blows unhurriedly and with "deliberation," "spaced apart" and "firmly," so that the victim thoroughly felt every blow. "Quicker! Faster!" shouted the doctor several times. Faster is not so excruciating; a benumbed man cannot entirely feel every single blow. But Komlev did not hurry... After the forty-eighth blow Gubar was "finished." "But he did withstand forty-eight of those blows!! What a warrior he was!"

"I lived in horror after that," said Vasilev.

"After the punishment?"

"No, not from the punishment but from what I'd eaten. I fell into such terror. I feared the world."

Vasilev lost his mind. Horror consumed him. He was stricken by a most energetic form of persecution mania. He couldn't sleep at night, believing he was hearing the prisoners discussing killing and eating him. When he was sent to the isolator for unruliness he ripped a plank out of the wall, and stood on the sleeping platform for twelve hours without moving, with the plank raised high above his head, shouting in a savage voice, "Don't come in! I'll kill whoever enters!" No one decided to confront this enraged Hercules, but they somehow cunningly subdued and transferred him to the infirmary. There, he refused to eat, saying the doctor wanted to poison him; and finally, on a certain terrible day, he escaped. It was indeed a terrible day: they couldn't capture Vasilev for a whole month, and it was a terrible month for the venerable physician N. S. Lobas, loved by all *katorga* for his humanitarianism. For a whole month, Vasilev was roving about somewhere, waiting for a chance to waylay and kill the physician. For a whole month, the domiciled Lobas trembled whenever he left his house. They finally captured the madman and, under Lobas's supervision, he recovered, became peaceful and now, if there's anyone Vasilev loves, it's N. S. Lobas. "Here I'd fallen into such terror I wanted to kill Nikolay Stepanovich!" said Vasilev. "This is hard for me!"

Koloskov doesn't regard it as "strange," says Vasilev, that he ate human flesh. But it is for this same reason that Vasilev experiences great renown as a "cannibal." "Now, anyone who comes here, comes to see me. They're always watching me... like I'm about to escape." Toward the end of the conversation Vasilev began getting more and more agitated. "I *should* escape. When anyone comes he looks at me and says, 'You ate a corpse?' There are so many who killed and ate during escapes. So shut up!"

Katorga says there are a few in the chains prison who, during escapes, have out of starvation eaten the flesh of murdered or otherwise dead comrades. I was shown several of those who'd confessed to *katorga* and one who, everyone pointed out, ate the flesh of a comrade who'd died from exhaustion. When I asked if what they said about him was true, he answered, "Well, if birds can eat a corpse, should a man let himself die?!"

6

THE PENAL LABORER BARONESS HEIMBRÜCK

Here is one of my most melancholy Sakhalin memories.

"The baroness? We have a baroness who bakes bread, gives lessons and sews dresses!" I was told in Rykovsk settlement. Meeting me on her hut's threshold was a tall thin woman with an intelligent, expressive gaze. How old was she? Truth is, it's difficult to fix the age of a woman in *katorga*. Sakhalin, stripping away from a person all that is good, first of all strips away youth and then health. I introduced myself.

"Baroness Heimbrück!" she answered, emphasizing the title she'd lost.

"The case of Baroness Heimbrück, accused of arson," caused a huge sensation in Petersburg. It was a "huge" and "sensational" trial. The name "Baroness Heimbrück" occupies a modest but fully distinguished place in the history of women's education in Russia. Through her initiative, the professional education of women was established in Russia: she was the first to open a women's professional school. Exceptionally well-educated, well-connected and possessing very influential relatives, yet having no means on which to live, the young woman devoted herself with enthusiasm to the notion "that woman needs to be taught how to live by her own labor. She needs to be armed for the struggle for survival." Everything was going well. The baroness worked, taught others to work and was getting by and making ends meet.

"Only, I was bored with being alone!" she recalls with a sad smile. "You're working, working, up to your neck in business, but you're still alone, so completely by yourself. There's not one kindred spirit. There are the relatives… But my relatives viewed me mistrustfully and were even shamed by my 'enterprise'…" She got to know some retired soldier. They liked each other, fell in love and a "union" was established. A "conversation" ensued. "It was terribly embarrassing! I was uncomfortable in my relatives' presence and, of course, as mistress of the school…" Marriage became necessary. Moreover, this was all he'd been thinking of, given that his affairs were complex and disordered and he had no money to pay the debts he owed someone.

"You know," he said to her one day, "we have a way out. Your furnishings are insured. If they were lost in a fire…"

"You're out of your mind!"

"No one will know. You don't even need to be there. Just agree to it. I'll do everything without you. I know a certain fellow…"

She protested. He convinced her that because "we do so little in Petersburg there'll be no risk whatsoever," that this wouldn't be the first job for the "fellow," that the "fellow" knew how to arrange things.

"You yourself will go to the theater. You won't be there." In the end, he gave her a choice. "There's no other way out, you know. Our union cannot last. This means you either agree to this arrangement or everything between us must end." Having fallen silent, he cajoled her with their love.

She agreed. "Very well. Let's do it."

One day she went to the theater, returned and found her apartment in flames.

Suspicion arose when it became clear that arson was involved. Baroness Heimbrück and her lover were arrested and put in preliminary detention. There, they somehow found a way to exchange notes. The trial before the court lasted two days. Baroness Heimbrück's acquittal was in no doubt. There was no evidence at all that she'd known about the planned arson. One day during a recess, her accomplice turned to the baroness with a question. "If they exile me, will you go with me to Siberia?" "Why not?! Of course! ("Those were the very words I used!" she says, "because I knew he was up to some mischief.") Listen, you! I'm already suffering because of your tangled affairs!" "You won't go? Very well!" He gave the court the note she'd sent him in preliminary detention: "If the investigator tells you I've confessed—don't believe it. I'll never confess, and don't you confess." There was no doubt. Both were guilty. "Bastard! Why did you do this?" she asked during the recess following the jury's verdict. "Now, at least I know you won't be with someone else. We'll go away together, and together we'll stay!" They exiled him to *katorga* in Siberia and her to Sakhalin.

In Dué Post, they were completely flummoxed: "What do we do with 'Baroness Penal Laborer'?" She didn't want to be an exile-settler's cohabitant. "I was exiled to *katorga*, but not for this!" Some of the officials tried to take her into their "service," but at the first affectionate gesture she would jump away. "You can assign me to work, but you cannot assign me to that."

There were no women's prisons. Why not *force* her to cohabitate? "She's still a baroness… somehow, it's not right." The wives of officials vainly prevailed upon them. "So what if she's a baroness? Why are you being nice to her? She's a convict! You should knock her down a peg!" These semi-literate women developed an instant hatred for the "arrogant woman," the "personage." "There goes—the 'baroness'! Oh, mother, that's no baroness!" All the same, she was the only dressmaker on Sakhalin! All the same, she was the only one who could sew a dress "as should be," "Petersburg style." She turned everyone's head, and this enraged officials' wives.

"You know, there were those among them who treated their servants comparatively civilly, but couldn't me!" recalled "Baroness Penal Laborer" with a smile. "One would call on me, and it was like being cut with a knife. At the slightest irregularity, she'd throw the dress on the floor, stomp on it and scream, 'What do you think? You're a baroness? Eh? A baroness? You're a convict! Without rights! Understand?' I'd stand there silent, smiling…" And the scornful smile she remembers this with was probably then upon Baroness Heimbrück's face. This drove officials' wives completely crazy. "So now they're running to their husbands to complain. I'm silent but they're screaming, 'You stay away from this shit!'"

So her life became complicated. Officials threw up their hands over her. "Let her live as she knows how! Or let her go to hell!" Officials' wives beseeched God. "If only a *good* dressmaker had been exiled from Russia." But for lack of one, these ever foul-mouthed women placed their orders with the baroness, paid her their improbable pennies and screamed, "Why aren't you grateful? Eh? Not enough for you? Dissatisfied? 'Cause you're a 'baroness'? Huh?" This "pious-by-her-silence" baroness was the lowest of the low in officials' wives' eyes.

"You cannot imagine what trash, what a bitch, this 'baroness' is!" one told me. "You sometimes want to pity her out of humanity; and, although she's a convict, it's a pity just the same. You want to do something for her, give her commissions so she won't go hungry. But that you'd do this—no! Arrogance! She doesn't wanna talk! As if she's under prohibition to speak a word! She doesn't wish to! She gives a look like you're doing her a favor! You know, she's a 'baroness'! What's it to her?! Such a petty little soul, the scum! She tries to wound you at every turn. You say the dress isn't right and she tells you right away, 'Excuse me, madam, that's how it's worn in Petersburg.' You know, she's from Petersburg, she's a 'baroness,' she's seen everything, knows everyone. So what am I? Well, I'm an official's wife! The wife of your commander! An honorable woman! And you're a penal laborer, an exile, a creature, an arsonist!… She doesn't understand this."

Thus went "*katorga*" for the baroness. She worked for pennies, somehow struggled, survived and… remained silent. "I thought I'd left off speaking!" the baroness recalls with a smile.

On the one hand what could penal laborers, the herd or a female cohabitant have in common with an intelligent young woman? On the other hand the officials' wives she'd served would cross the street having caught sight of her. There were the informal "you," foul language and reproaches. "So I lived between heaven and earth. The herd would reproach and mock 'the Baroness!' The local intelligentsia reproached and mocked 'the Baroness!'"

It ultimately grew unbearable and the baroness became the cohabitant of some medic exiled for murdering his wife. At least he was a man more intelligent than the rest. But she didn't do this out of love. "You know him. Can one love such a man? It was very tiresome and I grew melancholy. But he vowed and swore he'd improve himself."

Malicious delight spread throughout the community. "Eh? What? The little medic's got himself a cohabitant! There's a 'baroness' for you! A *'baroness'*! Ha-ha-ha!"

"A character utterly adrift!" the wife of one of the top officials told me with fastidious regret. "It's quite vexing that at one time she bore such a title! And she sunk so low! She got involved with a medic! Then they separated. Filth, what filth!"

I happened to learn about the medic. He is a dirty lump of fat who disgusts everyone. This fatso with a goatee sprouting round his lips—on which some kind of malignant ulcer flouted itself such as I'd not seen anywhere on Sakhalin—shies away from nothing. "Quite a specimen!" said a doctor, pointing at his face. "Have you been messing around with some young girl again?" "A specimen indeed!" leered the medic's fat face. He operates on the sly, taking advantage of exile-settlers' ignorance; steals medicine; does anything to make money whichever way, then spends it on "little tricks," "specimens" or "items" (preferably "little girls").

The debauchee-medic soon got on the educated woman's nerves. "I actually became pregnant by him!" recalls the baroness with a shiver of disgust. "Lord, what took place! What I would earn, he'd swipe to pay for young women. He began bringing them home. You kick them out of the house, come back and he's up to some nastiness again. You go into the courtyard and he's there beneath the awning. He comes home all beaten and tattered... I drove him out. He didn't go easily. He's shouting, 'This is my hut!' I didn't complain about him to the authorities. Lord! How humiliating! Everyone would laugh: 'Well, now, baroness, did you have a falling out with your medic? You should've taken the measure of him! Eh? He's an intelligent man, you know!' We separated with difficulty." The medic left; the baroness remained behind with her child.

I experienced a remarkably strange impression as a guest of this "convict-baroness," now an exile-settler. We were sitting in a small narrow room, with a neat bed covered by a quilt of gray prison cloth. A geranium sat on the window sill; beneath a lamp on a dresser was a coverlet stitched from rags. Nevertheless, the small dark room had a kind of coziness. It was clear that a person accustomed to certain comforts lived here.

While speaking with me the baroness smoked, put the butt out on the table, left it there amid a pile of ashes and spat into the middle of the floor, evincing a kind of waywardness, a Sakhalinistic frenziedness, a penal absence of womanliness. When a *katorga* laborer—her bakery assistant—entered the room, she began speaking with me in French. Her French was marvelous, beautiful and elegant. That marvelous, beautiful, elegant and literary French spoken by well educated Russians. But when we switched to Russian she spoke most unremarkably, in the "*katorga* tongue." "You have to agree I can't go to *fart*... I've worked so hard, scrabbled. I'm afraid the herd would nail me." This woman, who feverishly clings to her title of "baroness" because she quivers in terror at the title of "penal laborer," makes such a strange impression with her alternating of high French and the *katorga* jargon.

I got to know the baroness at a difficult time for her. Not long before, in the village of Rykovsk where the baroness lived at the time, a "huge event" had taken place, and the baroness was begrudging that she'd "been betrayed." It happened that a young man, the *brodiaga* Tumanov who'd been transferred to Rykovsk as a clerk in the police administration, visited and introduced himself to her as "Prince So-and-So." "He really was a prince," the baroness confirmed for me. "I don't know what caused him to renounce his name and become a *brodiaga*—he refused to say. He was educated, well-bred, intelligent— only terribly nervous, nervous to the point of illness..." He begged her leave. The baroness gave him her leave, and Tumanov began visiting her every day after working at the chancery.

God knows what took place between them but, regardless, these two people with similar upbringings and social circles were attracted to each other. They shared common views and interests and even shared "Petersburg acquaintances" in common. The baroness says she "was relaxed by these conversations! To suddenly meet here on Sakhalin a sweet, educated young man. You can only imagine!" And he told her, "You know, when I talk with you it seems there's neither *katorga* nor vagabondage, but that we're sitting together somewhere in Petersburg..."

Then, all of a sudden, Tumanov arrived one day terribly upset and beside himself. For no reason at all the official G, after having lost at cards the day before and becoming spiteful, called him a "scoundrel and blackguard."

"I can't go on like this!" said Tumanov, terribly agitated. "I have to extricate myself, because I'm a *brodiaga*! How dare they call me a 'scoundrel and blackguard'! Just because I'm in *katorga* doesn't mean I'm a scoundrel or a blackguard! I can't go on like this!"

"I'd never seen him so!" says the baroness. The young man, quick-tempered and passionate, had decided "therefore not to remain" an insult to the official... on Sakhalin... The baroness's "heart died." "I really paid because of that one. I've had enough!"

She told Tumanov, "You're planning something, you're planning to leave me. You're going to abandon me, soon you'll abandon me. I don't want to know anything, I don't want to perish..."

"So you'll follow me? Will you?"

"Leave me, if you're an honorable, decent man…"

"Very well…"

Tumanov left, but by evening all Rykovsk was in an uproar because the *brodiaga* Tumanov had tried to take the official G's life. Tumanov had showed up at another administrator's apartment where G was a voracious card-player, and requested that G be summoned to him "on an urgent matter." When G entered the kitchen Tumanov bowed and said, "I've come to thank you for endowing me with a new title. You called me a scoundrel and a blackguard." G, having entirely forgotten that morning's trifling affair (where on Sakhalin is any slighted penal laborer remembered?) and not catching the drift of the matter, replied, "Good, good. I'm not mad at you. Off you go. You'll apologize later…" "No, not later but now!" Tumanov said, leveling a revolver point-blank at G and pulling the trigger. Everyone there saw that Tumanov, eyes crazed, was pale as a corpse and barely able to stand on his feet. The revolver misfired. Tumanov fled the kitchen. He attempted to shoot himself in the temple but the revolver misfired again. Tumanov was apprehended and the situation turned rather strange, for the revolver had been loaded with all of two bullets. "Only two were needed, so I took the rest out!" explained Tumanov, who was being quite nonsensical. He was transferred to Aleksandrovsk Post and later subjected to a medical examination because he showed evidence of insanity.

But nothing was known of Tumanov's insanity at the time, and the administrative caste unanimously demanded an "exemplary punishment" for Tumanov, that is, that he be hanged as "a warning to an undisciplined *katorga*." Baroness Heimbrück begged and pleaded that nothing be done to Tumanov. "I reproach myself, myself. Maybe my words made him act so. Really, at that minute I felt completely alone! But what could I have done? The man was prepared to do God knows what—how could I talk to him? You know, I would have perished! Indeed, I would have! If I were by myself, perhaps I wouldn't have been selfish. But my child—what would become of him? Could I risk him?"

This child, from an unloved, disgusting and contemptible man, is for the baroness everything in life. She recalls her pregnancy by the medic with shuddering repellence; but she loves her child madly. Out of joy for this weak, sickly, scrofulous five year-old boy she works ceaselessly day in, day out, kneading dough, baking and setting the bread, crouching to make dresses for officials' wives for pennies, giving French lessons to a cleric's children. She loves—and cannot without tears look upon—her child. "He's been nicknamed 'the baron.' He's mocked. The officials' children push him away, so he has to play with those of the herd…" Hers is a love full of fear. "You know, he's going to grow up to be a murderer!" she says with horror. "Just imagine, given his heredity. Of course, I don't consider myself a natural criminal. How am *I* a criminal?! But look at the father. A murderer, half-crazy, a debauchee. You know, he recently lived up to his history of profligacy: I had to give my last twenty rubles to keep him out of prison. I gave it to him because my child still calls him 'papa' when he sees him, and so that he wouldn't be teased for having a 'daddy in jail'... But later on, what will become of him here on Sakhalin?! What does he see? Every day, murders, desperate starvation, floggings, *katorga*. Over there—you see their games— they're playing at 'executioners' and 'hanging' and their heroes are the executioner and long-term convict. You ask a ten-year-old boy, 'What's prison like?' 'A place where they feed you!' 'Where is it better, in prison or on the outside?' "S'well known, in prison. You die of hunger in a settlement.' You know, this all sucks away the boy's childhood. The prison for him is something ordinary, inevitable, commonplace—a career. What will become of him? The same as for the rest! A murderer. I'm raising him for *katorga*, you know, for *katorga*! To be a future murderer!... But for now, for now he's a little boy, and in him there's still nothing of this; he's a child, utterly and completely..." Before me, in tears, in a kind of hysterical fit, she kissed her boy, who'd shown up in the house crying. He'd just been driven off by the district commander's children who had been calling him "the baron."

"Mama, order them to stop calling me 'the baron'!"

Order?!

Leaving Rykovsk, I decided to ask the baroness, as she ushered me to the door after our final meeting, "Well, but that fellow... who you were convicted with... have you no news of him?"

"He's in Siberia and has finished, as have I, his term, and is now an exile-settler. He became very poor, he wrote, so I sent him money—some pennies, as it were. *Katorga* bore very heavily on the poor man. Not long ago, I received another letter. He's sick, he says, and asks me to send a little money..."

"And you...?"

"I'll send it."

I kissed her hand and left.

"Ah? Where're you coming from? From your lady-friend, the 'baroness'?" the prison warden fired at me along the way. "It's sick that she's still a man-hunter, that bitch! She got mixed up with the medic. Tumanov, I know, messed around with her. You see, I know everything, he-he! She gave her medic twenty coins, all she had, no doubt. He's fallen on misfortune, the dear fellow. She sent white bread on the sly to Tumanov in prison. Think about that! She's always sending money to her former friends. I read her mail! They all get by off her earnings. A lover of men, the bitch! She's had a trio! She's dissolute! She arrived in *katorga* dissolute; she came here as a lover!..."

7

LANDSBERG

I.

Twenty-seven years ago, a tragedy took place in Petersburg having profound significance for Sakhalin. The brilliant Guards officer and sapper Landsberg, on the eve of his marriage to a rich and distinguished woman and on the verge of a great and brilliant career, killed the money-lender Vlasov and his female domestic during a robbery. This event produced an indescribable sensation, and Landsberg's name was heard throughout Russia.[1] Still more horrible than the murder was its singularly tragic *quid pro quo*.

Landsberg was a careerist. He came from humble origins, pulled himself up by his own bootstraps and served in the Guards so as to be noticed and make a career. Vlasov, an elder bureaucrat involved in money-lending, regarded with great sympathy a petty officer trying to make his "way," and loaned him money. Vlasov had many promissory notes on Landsberg, and when his career was nearly set and Landsberg had announced his engagement to his rich and distinguished fiancée, Vlasov began to threaten him: "I have a huge 'surprise' for you for your wedding. A surprise such as you can't imagine." Landsberg feared that Vlasov would prosecute his claims, publicize his desire to marry as a means of repairing his fortunes and circumstances, and thus destroy his entire career. So he decided to get the promissory notes from Vlasov. He appeared at Vlasov's, sweet-talked the old domestic for some kvas, slit the old money-lender's throat with a razor and then, when the servant returned, finished her off and grabbed the promissory notes that were already bundled together and set on a table.

Found later among Vlasov's papers was a letter addressed to Landsberg. In this letter, Vlasov wished his protégé every happiness and as a wedding gift canceled all the promissory notes. This was the "surprise" the smiling old man had "threatened" him with. Besides this, in his will Vlasov had left Landsberg... his entire fortune. All this horror took place because Landsberg had misunderstood Vlasov, whose old-fashioned affection was expressed rather allegorically: "He-he!... I'm a 'surpriser.'" From a brilliant officer with a great career ahead of him, Landsberg fell to being a penal laborer with a shaved head and the prospect of long years in prison.

When Landsberg was arrested he was told, "In the room where you'll soon be alone there's a revolver on the table. It's loaded... That's all... Be careful."

Landsberg coldly answered, "Never mind. I'm not going to shoot myself." And he entered *katorga*.

Twenty-seven years ago, the Sakhalin colony was still forming. A smattering of *Zabaikaltsy*, ignorant and helpless, huddled together in a small ravine at Dué Post (then the only settlement on Sakhalin), a fissure between cliffs, in perhaps the most foul hole as exists on earth, and gazed at the impenetrable taiga they'd been ordered to transform into a "blossoming colony."[2] This smattering of *Zabaikaltsy* stood before Sakhalin like a child before a bristling bear. How to approach it? A colony needs a road first of all; but these people, born and raised in Transbaikalia, had never even seen surfaced roads and absolutely didn't know how "all this is done." Each of their moves quickly came to ruin. "By their own wits" they built a jetty; and the first small storm demolished the jetty. "By their own wits" they began digging a tunnel through Mt. Jonquière without any contrivance or technique save one: that a tunnel is normally dug simultaneously from both ends, and when the two parties of diggers meet in the mountain it means the tunnel is finished. People were blinded lighting fuses and crippled by clumsily prepared explosions; and both parties utterly failed to meet each other inside the mountain… They… emerged from different sides! So, setting foot in the taiga, the *Zabaikaltsy* were immediately seized with terror and taken aback. They didn't even know that you have to dig ditches for a road, and so the ditchless "roads" became mired in water and turned into bogs. At that critical moment a sapper came to Sakhalin aboard a *katorga* steamer.

On Sakhalin, everything businesslike and sensible that happened with the road and the construction of settlements was thanks to Landsberg. God knows what fate would have overtaken the Sakhalin colony had the tragic misunderstanding with the "threatening" money-lender not played out in Petersburg.

If today a prison warden, having climbed a mountain, takes from his pocket a small barometer and, with scientific gaze, begins "to determine through air pressure the mountain's altitude," it is thanks to the knowledge Landsberg brought to Sakhalin. Surrounded by scientists, it was he who brought here all knowledge needed for struggling with the impenetrable taiga. The scientists never listened to their "convict-teacher" and acted spontaneously and rashly, "on their own." The monuments to their "acting on their own" are the settlements, abandoned and sinking in their mires; the timber cuttings, tossed away as useless; the road, along which it takes three and a half hours to travel eight versts. Everything that was done "on their own" undermined and set back Landsberg's plans. The projects Landsberg undertook on Sakhalin revealed the talented man's exceptional mind and great knowledge.

Landsberg was paid special attention from the outset on Sakhalin. News of the "famous trial" had spread and the *Zabaikaltsy* could not but be interested in the "once brilliant Petersburg officer who'd moved in high society." Genteel, educated, of rarefied mind, by nature still an adroit careerist, Landsberg immediately stood out among everyone as a leader. "You know," say seamen who at the time were sailing to Sakhalin, "we'd go to Dué as usual. As usual, all the local officials would be standing there on the jetty. Immediately, at first sight, Landsberg was the most respectable. Clearly a bird in flight."

But most importantly, of course, was that he was a sapper. He built them a jetty, which was not demolished; he somehow but nevertheless corrected the ill-fated tunnel, so that they didn't have to send Petersburg a telegram about the opening of a crooked tunnel through which no one could pass, that was useless and in which only fugitives found comfort. "The tunnel was dug straight through." A road was needed, and Landsberg showed how to build it.

On Sakhalin, Landsberg immediately became the "barin," getting this nickname from *katorga*. He assigned tasks, commanded labor gangs—was, in fact, an official living outside the prison and addressed by the formal "you," a rare honor on Sakhalin. But the position Landsberg suddenly attained was a difficult one. The illiterate always hate the literate, and Sakhalin officialdom deeply resented the "exiled convict's privileged status." "It's like he's our equal."

I don't know what punishments Landsberg had to endure and which were of course awkward to raise in conversation; but he did have to live through difficult moments. Here's one instance. Sakhalin's official K especially resented Landsberg's "privileges." "I'll show him a 'privilege'!" K turned this into a crazy fixation. One time, he found Landsberg in a certain official's suite. They were sitting and talking. K could only say of this: "What? How? Sitting in the presence of authority? A penal laborer? Put him in chains! Stick him in the isolator for a week!" Landsberg sat in chains in a dark isolator for a week on bread and water; and K puffed himself up. "I showed Landsberg himself!"

At the same time, his "privileges" were indignifying *katorga*. "He was exiled same as us! Maybe even for something worse!" *Katorga* hated the "barin," the "lily-fingered," the "suck-up," the self-appointed official, and so Landsberg had to be very much on guard. At the slightest suspicion that he was "in cahoots with the administration," *katorga* would have killed him. His adroit gentility is perhaps what helped him. He could get along with all and everyone. He satisfied the administration and remained a "comrade" for *katorga*, submitting to its laws. Ability, cleverness and shrewdness had for a long time been in vogue and were useful in *katorga*'s business affairs. For example, an instance is known when Landsberg saved an official's life on Sakhalin. *Katorga* hated this official, had decided to murder him during the building of a road and told Landsberg to deliver him into an ambush. To deliver him was to risk his head; to ignore *katorga* was also to risk his head. Landsberg knew a rather clever mechanic and so, as he was delivering the official to the ambush, the equipage "suddenly" broke down and Landsberg convinced the official, "We'll be late if we leave for the site on foot. Better return to the post." The official was saved and *katorga*'s sentence wasn't carried out, for the man couldn't be delivered against his will without anyone to do it. The next day, Landsberg distributed the ringleaders to different work sites and nothing more was said about an ambush.

Having completed *katorga* and entered a settlement, Landsberg ran a shop where he sold everything: shaft-bows and harmonicas, calicoes and tar, whip-handles and candy. Somehow, you can always get these things from somewhere. Having become a petty shopkeeper, the brilliant Guards officer suddenly revealed himself a *splendid* petty shopkeeper. He ran his business outstandingly; his shop grew and grew; he established connections with trading firms. And, two years ago when I visited Karl Khristoforovich Landsberg, a steamship agency's flag was flying on a mast next to his neat and tidy little house. He's a representative for a major insurance agency, owns a transport agency and is a steamship company agent. There's still the shop—a big store!—but assistants run it, while he just supervises operations from a window.

Following a cigar, he talked to me about a coal-mining company and a company to capitalize on the fishing industry—two major enterprises he's undertaking. Landsberg has completed his terms as an exile-settler and in the peasantry. He's now a citizen of Vladivostok and travels abroad from time to time, for example, to Japan. He could, if he wished, return to Russia, but he lives on Sakhalin in a comfortable home whose windows open onto a view of the chains prison…

Landsberg married a very sweet woman, a midwife who came to Sakhalin for work. It'd be hard to find a more affectionate couple. God knows if he would've found in Russia such familial bliss as he's found on Sakhalin. It's so strange to watch these two people. It's like they're clinging to each other and saving themselves after a shipwreck.

II.

It was noisy and smoky in the wardroom of the steamer *Iaroslavl*. The steamer had arrived at night and now, early in the morning, its wardroom was full of officials who'd shown up to induct the transported prisoners. The assemblage was full of Gogolesque types! The captain met me in turn with the others, and when the time came to sit at table, a very cheerful and animated fellow said, "Karl Khristoforovich Landsberg." On his proffered hand I felt a crooked finger. This touch affected me like an electric shock, for this finger had been part of the evidence against Landsberg. He cut it when he sliced Vlasov's throat. "I'm very glad to meet you. The governor told me you'd sent him a telegram." He spoke in a very soothing voice, resonant with kindness. He's a tall, handsome imposing gentleman, mustachioed with gray streaks in his hair, though young-looking. Landsberg's now probably close to fifty but looks much younger. He retains a youthful face and the physical build of a nearly young man. He's most courteous, perhaps even too courteous—he never speaks other than with a pleasant smile. But when shaking hands our eyes met and it seemed I'd accidentally touched cold steel. Whether laughing or discussing something painful, he showed the same face. The gray bright eyes stayed the same: cold, indifferent, steely. You cannot at all dismiss the notion that Landsberg has always had these cold and impassive eyes. "Hard eyes!" unsympathetic penal laborers and exile-settlers said with hatred. "He looks at you like he's not seeing a person."

The steamer had brought candy and pastries for Landsberg's shop and Landsberg, trading pleasant jokes with the officials, very dexterously placed these light wares on the jetty as if they were gifts without recipients. This trader made such a strange impression with his beautiful, elegant movements. Having taken leave of everyone, he sat in his equipage and shouted to the coachman, "Let's go!" "Where do you want to go, barin?" the convict-coachman asked. "Home!" Landsberg exchanged one more pleasant smile with everyone and shouted to the district commandant, "I'll expect you tomorrow evening. New sheet music came with the steamer. My wife will play us the piano." The equipage sped away.

"And that coachman of his was exiled for premeditated robbery and murder!" the district commandant told me. "Among us, dear man, you'll see many surprising things."

Landsberg retains his splendid French and, like all Sakhalinites, chokes on the word "*katorga*." "When I was still… a laborer!" he reddens slightly, and looks down. We never referred to Sakhalin by name but as "this island."

Through twenty-seven years of prison and *katorga* Landsberg has borne intact his elegant drawing-room manners, but there is something of the exile-settler in the haste with which he snatches the hat from his head if he unexpectedly hears "Greetings!" This particular habit of doffing the hat is acquired only in *katorga*. You will instantly recognize the Sakhalinite out of thousands of people by his manner of hastily snatching off his hat, as if the man is frightened at what will happen if he doesn't remove it before an authority. This is something instinctive that remains with him the rest of his life. By this habit you can tell Landsberg's experience of *katorga* wasn't easy. It means there were clashes, such as they were.

For this man, whose window "opens onto a view" of the prison, any recollection of his time "as a laborer" is difficult. When he touches on this period he becomes agitated, breathes heavily and fury lines his face. And when he speaks about penal laborers you sense in his tone such disdain, such hatred. He speaks about them as if about cattle. "One shouldn't deal so with these good-for-nothings. Now they've spoiled them. They're humane towards them." And *katorga*, in its turn, disdains and hates Landsberg and tells terrible and vile rumors about him.

Officials maintain an acquaintance with him—he's one of the most interesting, wealthy and, thanks to good contacts, influential people on Sakhalin; but in conversation, they're exasperated by Landsberg. "Very well! So Landsberg's really the only fellow Sakhalin resuscitated to an honest working life. But all the same, you know, he's really impossible! Such indifference. He thinks magnificently of himself, as if not he but someone else had committed 'it'!"

But is this so? It once seemed to me there was in his words *something* of this "man of the forgotten past." All Landsberg's cozy and comfortable drawing-room walls were hung with portraits of his children, who died from diphtheria. He spoke about them. "You know, there'd never been diphtheria here, on this island... The voluntary followers brought it. All my children fell sick and died. Every one. It was a kind of punishment." Having said these words Landsberg stopped, his face turned crimson, and he lowered his head and several minutes passed in silence. These were the most difficult minutes I've ever endured in my life. "What have I forgotten?! Let's have tea!" Landsberg, rousing himself, "cheerfully" said, and we went to the dinner-table where an exile-settler footman in livery served us tea. This was the one and only time that that *something* seemed to emerge from his soul into the light of day. But Landsberg was oftentimes an insufferable interlocutor, especially when he talked about the "laborers'... lack of discipline." "God knows what goes on here on this island. Everyday there's a murderous robbery. Murder and premeditated robbery! And they still stand on ceremony with such gentlemen." Landsberg sometimes worked himself into a real apoplexy.

"Won't you be going to Russia?" I asked Landsberg.

"I want to go, I have an old mother. I want to see her once more before she dies. But to return forever—no. I'm still engaged there. I have to get something from this island. I've not remained here so many years for nothing." It's really like the fellow came here on business. He didn't do "it"—someone else did.

"This should draw your attention!" Landsberg once said to me, with anxiety such as I'd never seen. "This is what punishes your existence. Punish a man as you will, but there should be an end to it. Take away everything a man's acquired, but put a stop to this and return everything he had. Don't deprive a man of his rights for his whole life. Should a grown-up middle-aged man suffer for what a formerly young man did?!" And his voice resounded with such contempt for the "doings" of the formerly "young man." I looked

Fig. 38: K. Kh. Landsberg and his wife

in horror at the anxious Landsberg and thought, "Here, certainly, is that other who did 'it.'"

Of such is this famous man. Had not that tragic *quid pro quo* happened twenty-seven years ago, who knows what would now be of Karl Khristoforovich Landsberg? What if, on Sakhalin, the man had been able to go to the *people*?

8

THE GRANDFATHER OF RUSSIAN *KATORGA*

Sweet, kind, splendid grandfather, you now sleep in Rachkov's meadow, in Aleksandrovsk Post's convict cemetery beneath an anonymous cross. You sleep the quiet eternal sleep. What do you dream there after your much-suffering life?

Matvey Vasilevich Sokolov—"the grandfather of Russian *katorga*." There was no one in *katorga* older than he. He served "fifty years of pure *katorga*." And there was more besides. "I should have me three lives to live, brother," Matvey Vasilevich would say with a toothless smile, "for I, brother, have three life sentences." The man was thrice given a life sentence of *katorga* and three life sentences as a correctional. There was no other such person in all *katorga*.

By law, such a terrible criminal should be held his entire life in a chains prison, and it's stipulated that anywhere he goes he must be accompanied by an armed guard. But they decided to let Matvey Vasilevich Sokolov live by himself in the joinery shop without any guard. He slept on the joiner's bench winter and summer, wrapping his aged shivering body in an old wool jacket.

"I live just on vodka! You wakes in the mornin' feelin' neither yer hands nor feets, chest sunk in, no breath. You drinks a teacup of vodka—and you're a man again! I, yer worship, am a natural-born drunk."

"Matvey Vasilevich, we can't do our work 'cause you drinks the varnish!" mock the other convicts working in the joinery.

How's that? *Varnish?!*

"But I drink it when there's no vodka!" smiled grandfather. "The varnish settles and below's the sediment, but up top, 'tis pure spirit. I dilutes it with water and drinks. Pure vodka. Puts a fire in yer belly. Me hands and feets come back to me body, I comes to m'self."

Matvey Vasilevich didn't want to go to the almshouse. "Am I a beggar?! I'm a master craftsman and I'll work in the crafts shop!" Old age rendered him unable to work, so he just tinkered. But he'd been a fine joiner, a superlative one. All the prison wardens loved him for this reason. Yet, because of this, he'd catch it all the more when he escaped. When such a joiner escapes he catches hell.

At the time I knew him he was living peacefully in the shop, and everyone unfailingly referred to him as "grandfather" or by his name and patronymic and treated him with unfeigned respect, for this man had already suffered much. Everthing he knew—his craft, how to read—he'd learned in *katorga*.

He'd seen nothing in life besides *katorga*, and for him time was divided into two periods: "before the scaffolds" and "after the scaffolds." He didn't know how to measure the past otherwise. "That was still before the scaffolds!" "When they'd still not introduced the scaffolds!" "The scaffolds hadn't yet come!" That was how he measured the olden times. "It was already after the scaffolds!" "When the scaffolds had come!" That was how he determined more recent times.

He landed in *katorga* during serfdom.

"Before the scaffolds?"

"Right-o! When they still punished with the knout." This was also an "era" for him. "After there were the brandings!"—also a measurable period.

He came from a wealthy family of peasant traders that had lived according to quit-rent in Elets.[1] He was sentenced to *katorga* for killing a young woman.

"They called the girl Afimia. Afimia was beautiful, and I an outstanding lad." Matvey Vasilevich smiled, remembering his youth. "I was a stately chap and a tippler, a fool and a mischief-maker. Oo-wee! How we carried on. 'Afimia,' I'd say, 'will you marry me?' 'I will,' she'd say, because it flattered her and she fancied me and I was from a rich family. Well, we carried on. Given our situation it happened: the suitor and his love got mixed up together."

"And you loved her, grandfather?"

"I say, I so terribly loved her! Loved her so—'tis certain I was a fool. We got mixed up and had to marry. My little father and mother were on their hind legs because I had an older brother who was also married, as I'd soon be. He got mixed up with his wife and then was the first to get married. Little father and mother said, 'Naught to that! What's this? Our second son's getting married to a money-drainer! For shame! All our sons are marrying their sweethearts! Naught to that!' My family was rich and proud. 'Naught' to this and 'naught' to that. I was a scalawag, so for me it was: 'Don't you dare!' When my love saw there'd be no wedding she began to turn against me. 'I say, I need you so much it hurts!' and she began running around with others. This was to spite me. 'Let everyone see!' I says. My relatives sullied her. 'I say, she's got herself mixed up with Matvey! And now that gold-digger wants to clamber into the family!' So, I'll tell you now, that was how important your Matvey was! But I was climbing the wall, *climb*-ing the wall.

"Now, I drink," and it's because of what happened that I began to drink. It was over some greasy business. Where I'm from, boys and girls would roll around on the hills. I go to a hill and she's with someone else on a hill. It cut me, yes, it cut me! I was tipsy and I think, 'I'll kill him and nothing'll happen to me!' I was such a fool, you know! Such as could suddenly imagine, 'I'll kill a man and nothing'll happen to me!'" Matvey Vasilevich shook his head and chuckled over the young man who thought so foolishly.

"I go home, grab a rifle off the wall, go back and aim the gun like so." Matvey Vasilevich showed how he aimed the rifle. "Pow! Afimia screamed in a voice not her own and fell down. Yes, she fell down and died. I wanted to shoot him, but hit her. I couldn't see clearly for my drunken eyes. Backs turned on me. Right then, everyone renounced me. My little father and mother, the kingdom of heaven, my brothers and all my kin. My family was a proud, wealthy family and someone had suddenly shamed them all. 'Ah? A criminal!' Maybe it would've been better if they'd made an oath on their hands and knees. 'Understand,' they could've said, 'we don't want no criminal. He'll shame our whole life.' I was sentenced to ten lashes of the knout and to *katorga*. They punished me in Moscow. I only saw Moscow as they were taking me to the Horse Market.[2] As should've been, it was a good city, only it wasn't such to me then. They put me in a telega with my back to the horse and were delivering me. Folks all around! Folks *all* around! Boys running behind the telega, staring, pointing fingers. You didn't know what to look at next. Merchants coming out of their shops, watching. Money's getting thrown into the telega. My executioner went around the telega and picked it up. 'This is for you!' he says. I nodded. So I'm taken to the Market. It was market day and folks was blowing their money. Back then, there were no scaffolds. It was before the scaffolds came and they began to shame people. But then, they didn't shame you—just laid you out and jerked your clothes down. They laid me out, and how that executioner with the knout lashed my bare back! I've had many lashes, been beaten by whips, canes, birch rods and butt-ends, but there's nothing worse than the knout!"

This man, having in his time received thousands of whip, cane and birch rod lashes beyond reckoning, has for 50 years trembled at the thought of those ten lashes of the knout. That's what a punishment it was!

"I didn't think I'd survive! I'd been beat enough for a year. All the folks was tossing their money, just tossing it. I got taken from the mare to hospital, but then after a rest I got sent according to regulations along the march route to *katorga*. Gloom visited me at that point and I needed vodka. But where could I get it? The craftsmen didn't know where to get it. A comrade says to me, 'You want money? However much you wants, and more, if ya do what we does!' All I wanted was vodka. He wins me over and we make some money. They catch us and we got the cane. As the instigator, he was without a doctor's help, but I had help."

"How so, 'without a doctor's help'?"

"So it was in those days. There were two rows of soldiers with canes and they tie you to a little wagon and pull you between them, and they go *r-raz, r-raz* on your back! They pull you through till you get all you deserve. A fellow's lying there already dead, but everyone's going *r-raz, r-raz*! That's because there's no doctor to help. But if a doctor goes alongside you, there's help. He sees a fellow's about to pass out, and says, 'Stop!' Gives him smelling salts; then they go again. He takes your wrist and looks at his watch. 'He can take another hundred!' he says. But when he sees a fellow's completely gone, then everything comes to a halt and the fellow goes to hospital. The fellow lies there, recovers, and they take him again for punishment and so on until he gets everything. My comrade, bless his soul, died there immediately without a doctor's help. But they thrashed me for nigh on a full year till there was no more to give. So I lay in hospital all year. I'd fully recover and they'd go at me again."

After that, Matvey Vasilevich received lashes of the cane, whip and birch rod in incalculable quantity. "'Cause I'd always go to the grass!" he said, smiling.

"What's 'to the grass'?"

"As it was, there's nothing in winter and I'm leading a gloomy life in prison. But come spring, I'd get drawn to the grass: I'd escape. Then I'd hang around somewhere working as a laborer in summer. But come autumn and I'd start missing prison life again. I'd join my comrades. Then I'd get the lash or the cane and an extended sentence." Thus, with these absences "to the grass" Matvey Vasilevich compiled three life sentences of *katorga*.

"But didn't an imperial clemency reduce your sentence?"

"What are clemencies to me? I got three life sentences."

Everything that happened in the world simply passed this man by—this man who's known only prison, lashes and birch rods. So he lived, yearning for freedom in spring, returning to prison in autumn. "They feed you, after all!"

Except for innumerable escapes there were no other crimes for Matvey Vasilevich. He was an honest man: officials would give him money—sometimes a lot of money—to buy supplies, and he never spent a kopek on himself. "But escape, I did. Around springtime and always because of vodka! Sober—I'd do nothing; but I'd drink and the first thing I'd want to do was escape. So I'd escape, I'd drink and get caught. I'm a drunk, yer worship!"

Matvey Vasilevich quarreled with me over vodka. We had a great friendship. So many times, exhausted by Sakhalin "frenziedness," by Sakhalin "despair," I'd ask myself, "Is this the full measure of human suffering and degradation?" Afraid I was losing my wits for the horrors taking place around me, I came to this old man and nursed the spirit beneath his slurred senile talk. He'd endured and suffered everything, yet still the old man looked at everyone and recalled everything with a kind-hearted smile. So many times, gazing at this man's sweet, gentle smile, body and soul tormented for half a century, I'd ask myself, "Is this the full measure of the human spirit's blessedness, meekness and kindness?" This friendship was supported by a small service: each morning Matvey Vasilevich would meet me in the kitchen where the cook would fill his teacup with vodka—a teacup without fail, as this was his ration. One time I asked, "Has grandfather been here?" "Sure hasn't," answered the cook.

"Hasn't come for several days!" I went to see if he'd fallen ill. Matvey Vasilevich greeted me dryly and reluctantly.

"How's things with you, Matvey Vasilevich? Why are you angry with me?"

"'Tis... 'Tis nothing..."

"Tell me, what's the matter?"

"What's the matter?! If you want to help me, help an old man, then grant me a little teacup of vodka, that's what..."

It turned out that the cook, a stupid and cruel woman, had for some reason suddenly given Matvey Vasilevich rum instead of the usual "cup of vodka." "Everyone gets one shot of rum, so who're you to be such a prince?! There's many like you here who'd like to gulp down cups of vodka!"

Matvey Vasilevich refused it and left. "All my life I've drank a teacup!" And he believed this happened because I'd been intolerant of his need for vodka.

"Matvey Vasilevich, I swear to God I didn't know anything about this! Come, I'll set you up with three liters,³ you can drink whole glasses if you want. Cheers!"

"No, now that... you've offered... You've offered me a cup of vodka... and my whole life in *katorga* I've pined for it, for vodka... But you offered me vodka..." There were tears in the old man's eyes. He didn't want to look at me.

Close to death, Matvey Vasilevich arrived in the Aleksandrovsk infirmary to ask for the head physician, L. V. Poddubsky.

"I came to you to die. Attend to me in this... and close my eyes, Leonid Vasilevich!"

"That's enough out of you, old man! You'll be going to the grass again this year!"

"No, brother, I won't be going to the grass any more."

"So what ails you? Eh?"

"There's nothing ails me. I just feel death approaching. You can attend to me now, put me under your care... And *you* close my eyes, Leonid Vasilevich!"

The old man's wish was carried out. Pampered with care, he quietly and without illness passed away after lying in the infirmary for two days, as if he'd fallen asleep from senility. And during the final minutes he had "his eyes closed" by L. V. Poddubsky. So died "the grandfather of Russian *katorga*."

Once, Dr N. S. Lobas gave Matvey Vasilevich some paper and inked quills. "Grandfather, you remember so much. In your free time you should write down for yourself what you remember. Your biography."

"But indeed! With pleasure!" agreed Matvey Vasilevich, and next day brought back the paper, quills and a quarter-page's worth of handwriting.

"Here. I wrote it."

"What?"

Fig. 39: M. V. Sokolov

"The biography." He gave him the quarter-page:

The biography of exiled penal laborer Matvey Vasilevich Sokolov. Sentenced to three life-sentences of *katorga*. Completed fifty years of pure *katorga*. Received:

>The knout—ten lashes.
>The lash—so many thousands.
>The cane—so many thousands.
>The birch rod—don't remember how many.

[signed]
Exiled penal laborer Matvey Sokolov

"Is this the whole biography?"
"That's everything."

9
THE APOSTATE

Tired, beaten and worn out, I was trying to get through the taiga with my guide, the exiled penal laborer Busharov. Busharov is worth a few words, for whenever there's an argument he gets called "Cain!" He murdered his brother while robbing him; killed him in exactly the same surroundings I was now traveling in with him: a deep forest. He killed him because, like myself, his brother had money. I chose Busharov as my guide because, more than anything, he'd settled down after many escape attempts and knew Sakhalin's taiga like the back of his hand. I looked as if made of glass next to this fratricide, thief and *brodiaga*, and feared he could smash me to smithereens right there.

It was tough going. The only way to get by the tundra is to beat a path through the rising taiga with a Sakhalin horse that's grown up in the taiga. It can bound through hollows and cross enormous fallen trees. Our horses would first carefully try a spot with their hooves before stepping and struggling over tree roots and, having gotten past these, darting away, sinking and getting stuck up to their bellies in a bog. Steam poured off them. We whipped the poor exhausted animals by the minute to get them out of the quagmire. Their hind legs would only just free themselves and presto!—a little root would snap and their front legs would sink into the quagmire. Now you'd be tilting towards the head, now towards the croup, now falling over along with the horse.

"Steady on, your worship, steady on!" urged Busharov, riding ahead. "There's a guardhouse up ahead." Many had hacked this path through the taiga and were exterminated by their inhuman labors. But few now walk or ride along this path. Why would you go through the taiga? Guardhouses were added "to protect the path" because it wasn't safe, but it's said only two convict guards have been assigned to each guardhouse.

It was almost evening when we arrived at the guardhouse, where there was only an old man. The other guard had gone to the post for several days for provisions. I can't remember how I made it to a bench to lie down as if murdered. When I woke early next morning, the old man was kneeling and praying in silence to a small darkened icon hanging in the corner. He was reciting—confusedly and inarticulately—the prayers "Our Lady," "Our Father," "Heavenly Lord" and a mixed-up "Faith."

"Protective Veil of the Holy Virgin, mercy! Assumption of the Mother of God, pray and protect us for our sins! Kazan Mother of God, mercy! I pray,

Lord, for peace for (such-and-such), the servants of God! I pray, Lord, for peace and health for (such-and-such), the servants of God! I pray for me, Lord, to enter Your Kingdom!" He prostrated himself on the ground for a very long time, then rose and said, "Amen!" He crossed himself several more times and was done.

"Hello, grandfather!"

"Hello, your worship!"

Busharov was already waiting for me with a steaming cup of honeyed tea, which he always brought on excursions together with breakfast provisions: a just-opened container of… Strasbourg pâté and a tin of sardines. In the colony-fund shops (established to supply goods to penal laborers, exile-settlers and petty officials) you find nothing save Strasbourg pâté and sardines. Hence this was a perfectly reasonable arrangement. We sat ourselves down outside the guardhouse to eat the truffle and goose liver pâté with the delicious oiled sardines!

"Grandfather, have some tea with us!"

The old man hesitated and hesitated. "Thank you for the offer. I'll try some!" As I'd not asked the others to sit with me, they hadn't. I was sitting on the little stoop, the old man and Busharov some distance away. Anything else would have been "out of order!" and, clearly, the old man loved order. Having sipped his tea he poured the rest on the grass, returned the cup upright as hitherto, laid down as hitherto the nibbled lump of sugar and said, "Thank you for the fare!"

"But, grandfather, you should drink some more!"

"No, thank you." Only upon my third invitation did he say, "Well, you're really very sweet. Please pour! It's a sin, but I'll have more." The sardines made grandfather smile. "A little headless fish!" And he asked for more pâté. "Give us some more putty!" He drank the tea with avidity. "I haven't indulged myself for a long time. I haven't drank tea for nigh on half a year!" The old man was gloomy and taciturn but the food and tea were loosening his tongue.

"Do you ever go to the post, grandfather?"

"Nah. Mikhailo goes for provisions. He's younger. Why should I go? What would I do there? I haven't been for two years."

"So you live here and don't see people?"

"What sort of people are here? Sometimes a bear wanders into the guardhouse and we scare him away. Or those highwaymen…"

"*Brodiagi*, that is," explained Busharov.

"The very ones. A fellow comes, warms himself up, asks for some bread, you give it to him, he spends the night and goes on his way. But what people they are!"

"You're not afraid, grandfather?"

"Afraid of what? You should fear God, not people. I don't do anything to people and they do nothing to me. Why should I fear them?"

The old man had been loquacious and credible and so I could now pose the most ticklish question. "Grandfather, why did you end up here? On Sakhalin?"

At this point the old man was finishing his last cup of tea, eating up all his bits of bread and crossing himself three times.

"For robbing God's holy churches." I confess I'd expected anything save this.

"Is that so?"

"That's so."

"How could you do that? Were you drunk?"

"That's why I got drunk. Stone drunk. Nothing concerned me more when I was young! Everything in the church. I cleaned out thirty churches, maybe more. And in the thirty-first I displeased God and got caught."

"That's quite… You know, that's quite a crime…"

"Quite a crime?" The old man looked at me sternly and seriously. "I didn't hurt anyone. I took nothing from people. I took from God. Yes, but I took from God what He didn't need. God was giving to me, you see, but when I took what God needed, He caught up with me."

"But isn't it all the same? How can there be something God doesn't need?"

"Do you really think He needs everything in the churches? The donations? Do you think every donation pleases God? Every one?" The old man was passionate. "Another muzhik fleeced everyone in the area. He nailed poor people, took the shirts off their backs and would donate to the church and think he was holy! Does such a donation please the Lord? No, brother, you deliver to the Lord God out of righteous labors and a pure heart. For Him, *that's* a donation!"

"And how do you know what does and doesn't please God?"

"This knowledge of ours cannot be demonstrated. You'll only see its consequences. Clearly, I took nothing He needed, and God gave me what He didn't need. I had nothing my whole life. Such matters were out of my hands; but after I'd taken all of the nothing, I got caught. Clearly, I snatched what God Himself needed and so I succumbed. Clearly, it'd been a 'perfect donation' to God, made of righteous labor from one pure of heart, but I took it from God and now I'm being punished for this. 'Tis God's fair wisdom."

We fell silent.

"How did you do it? How did you break into the churches?"

"It so happened that I did break in!" the old man reluctantly said. "Only, I didn't like to do it that way. Why break into God's cathedral? It's not our right. It's terrible, and you can get caught easily. So prayer and stealth are better. After night services you stand somewhere silent, without moving, and after they lock the church you walk around. You stand silent before the patronal icons so the Lord God can enlighten you not to take what pleases

Him. You bow before the icons and take according to your spirit. And in morning, before matins, when the church is being opened and it's dark and everyone's sleepy, you slip out unnoticed."

"And you did this your whole life?"

"Thusly my entire life."

"Well, but what about that icon I see in the corner, did you take that as well?"

"The Protective Veil of the Holy Virgin? I told you I went to the post two years ago. I took it then, in the graveyard. I pried it from a cross."

"You did what? A grave, a final resting place?…"

"But what good's an icon doing there? Should it just get soaked by the rain? Tatars take pots from a stove. There was a plaque! They all had plaques! The little folk! But the icon had its place according to the grand scheme, and the scheme was observed."

"Well, but what's this old thing you've put here? You don't disturb the local churches, do you?"

"What's there to take from local churches? What kind of folk are here? Don't you know? Do the local folk think anything of God? Do they bring anything to church? Indeed, they'd rather drink vodka! God remains poor among them and because of this they go around naked! The folk! Were I never to lay eyes on them! I won't leave here for the post and go among those folk, go through that. I won't see them. Just sin there." Talking about the folk who'd forgotten God, the old apostate actually spat.

"A strange old man!" said Busharov after we left the guardhouse. "But absolutely God-fearing—a real horror! Everyone knows he's that way."

10

KATORGA'S ARISTOCRAT

"Excuse me!" the convict Pazulsky once said to me. "I can't come to the office to talk with you today. My leg hurts. Can we talk here?"

"Here? It's inconvenient. There are distractions. Too many people!"

"Them?" Pazulsky nodded his head at some inmates. "Don't let them bother you. Fellas, go to the yard, I need to talk with the barin!" And all nineteen men who shared the same ward with Pazulsky—and who at the time were sitting or lying down or playing cards—stood up and, fetters jangling, obediently exited one after the other in single file. Among them were Poluliakhov, murderer of the Artsimovich family; the Sakhalin celebrity Mitrofanov, only just captured following an unusually audacious escape; Mylnikov-Prokhorov, who slaughtered twenty people in his time; a pair from Vladivostok sentenced to death but pardoned on the scaffold just two weeks ago; Sharov, the world's biggest blockhead, who carried out an incredible escape (he avoided a guard's bullet, grabbed his rifle and fled into the taiga in broad daylight); Shkolkin, who was awaiting execution for murder; Baldanov, who stabbed an exile-settler for sixty kopeks; and others. All these people spent three hours in the yard while Pazulsky readily discoursed to me on various topics.

I was preparing to go to Rykovsk and, knowing this, Pazulsky made me an offer: "Do you want me to give you a letter of reference? There are people in the prison there who know me." He gave me several notes in which he requested I be well received and advised that I was a "safe" person and not in league with the administration. Pazulsky's reference did me a great favor and everyone followed his instructions by showing me anything I wished to see. Pazulsky's reference was sufficient to grant me the prison's full trust.

An incident during our first meeting had helped me obtain Pazulsky's favor and even gratitude. He'd asked me, "Do you speak English?" I answered yes, and suddenly Pazulsky began speaking in an unusually savage, theretofore unheard language. It could be said that, in English, "he speaks as he writes,"[1] for he is an autodidact and pronounced each letter as if he were pronouncing French. The devil knows what he was saying!

It was a critical moment, given that untutored *katorga* highly esteems any knowledge. The entire prison was gawking: "Well-well, can Pazulsky really speak English? He's not lying?" Pazulsky's pride and authority were on the line, and authority is terribly and dearly purchased. If I smirked all would be lost. "He's lying, he's boasting!" Fearing and hating Pazulsky because of this fear, *katorga* would have jeered at Pazulsky. And that would have been it.

I appealed to quick-wittedness for help. I sketched in my imagination the letters that Pazulsky had pronounced, formed words from them, guessed what he wanted to say and answered in the same barbarous tongue, pronouncing all the letters.

Thus we exchanged several phrases. You should have seen with what profound respect *katorga* listened to this conversation in an unknown language.

Later, speaking one-on-one, Pazulsky asked me, "So, I can speak English?"

"Frankly speaking, Pazulsky, you absolutely do not know how to speak English. No one could understand you."

"I myself thought this!... Yet, I've studied this damned language for so many years in prison!" Pazulsky sighed, then smiled. "Thank you for not giving me away earlier! They would've started laughing at me and I couldn't have taken that... Thanks for keeping it up." And he firmly shook my hand several times.

What does Pazulsky's charm and power over *katorga* consist of? First of all, they fear him because he himself fears nothing. He's proven this! Secondly, they're frightened of goading him lest Pazulsky were "to say what." This is very typical of Ivans, and he's a man of his word. What he says, he'll do—and he's proven this. Of such is this "man from the gallows."

Pazulsky's now an old man, sixty years old, surprisingly hail and hearty. His strength, they say, is phenomenal. His facial features are exceptionally balanced and handsome and his eyes especially notable: gray, cold, with a powerful gaze difficult to withstand. They seem used to giving orders to everyone. The red lips beneath a graying moustache twitch from time to time with a disdainful smile.

Pazulsky is a Pole. "Officially, I'm a Catholic," he says, "but it doesn't matter to me. Orthodoxy, Catholicism—I believe neither this nor that."

"Does this mean, in your opinion, Pazulsky, that there's nothing *there*?"

"Nothing!"

"And the soul?"

"What soul?! A man dies the same as a dog, it's all the same. I've seen it." And he really has seen it. "I killed a dog for fun, so's to watch it. There's no difference whatsoever. He looks at you as if to say, 'Just don't torment me. Make it quicker!' The living fear death, the dying fear pain. The body is everything. It fears pain and wants enjoyment. Life is pleasure. Only with pleasure does life begin. That's sensible. But you have to eat and drink, and for this, man won't be just a dog, pig or rat. He'll be a louse. And, heaven, what pleasures he'll have! He'll strive for pleasure. You know, a dog or a pig that you see lying and warming its side in the sun wants pleasure from life. But stick a dog in a room, give it only what it needs, and it'll start howling. It's howling for pleasure!" Such is the "philosophy" Pazulsky has devoted his intellect to.

"A fellow has money and he treats himself. He drinks fine wines, eats delicious meals, has beautiful women. 'I have money,' he says, 'and I enjoy myself through it. But you don't have money, and you don't enjoy yourself!' 'Very well, brother! If everything's about money, then I'll take your money and, through it, I'll enjoy myself. Better than me watching you!' So it is with everyone." Of such practical use is Pazulsky's "philosophy."

Pazulsky—this name is notorious in the south, southwest and in Rumania. He won't be forgotten for a long time. He was the ataman of three bandit gangs and truly "performed miracles." His specialty was robbery, robbing landlords' estates in particular. He "could never abide" murder. "It wasn't useful. I'd take what I needed: his money. But his life—what's that to me?" He holds in highest contempt homicidal robbers such as Poluliakhov. "Scum! They beat you and beat you but take nothing! What they don't need, they take; but what they do need, they can't find. Fools! These beasts grab axes when they're drunk! 'Go on, Ivashka, knock in his head! Chop him up for a week, Emel!' But why do this? Why knock in his head?!"

"Well, you know the business, Pazulsky. They say it's impossible for them without this."

"That's why they're fools! Because of this 'impossible.' Why should I deprive a man of a thing unnecessary to me—his life—when he has a thing that is necessary for me: fear."

"But if he's not afraid?"

"Well, he'll get afraid!"

Pazulsky didn't speak about his "past." This would have reeked of boasting, and Pazulsky's not one to boast. I gathered information on his past when in southern Russia. He did bring off some really big "enterprises." Having marked a landowner, Pazulsky would send to him one of his people who'd be hired as a laborer and would live there, watching and observing, so that when Pazulsky and his gang did the job he'd be very familiar with everything: the household's lifestyle, habits, layout. He'd pull the job off without a hitch, choosing the most suitable hour when no one could hinder him. Each man had his role and knew his job. Some would grab drowsy servants, others the guards. Pazulsky himself would grab the owners, never trusting them to anyone from his gang. He was afraid they might lose their tempers and kill them. He was fond of terrifying accouterments: a revolver, dagger, masks. In part, probably because you can inspire greater fear; in part, perhaps because there is in the bandit a love of the romantic and he can get enjoyment out of anything. "I needed to do all this so's to remember how nice it was later!" he noted offhandedly. His renown was so great that it's said people gave up their money at the mere mention of the name "Pazulsky." False Pazulskys even appeared in the south.

"But wasn't there a murder?" I managed to ask Pazulsky during a moment in one of our more candid conversations.

He knit his brows. "There was. That's so! A man can fall apart! You're reasoning with him, but he falls apart! Well, and… It was such rubbish, there's nothing to tell. You can't always do what you want. There are problems in every business. Remember that! Only a cow goes through life chewing its cud, belching and ruminating. But it's the opposite for a man! We aren't about that!"

The "ataman" Pazulsky's name was, of course, famous among the world of thieves and robbers. So when he landed in Kherson Prison it was no surprise that he controlled the prison, as he does on Sakhalin. The prison warden was young, new and inexperienced. But he was a kind man who treated very gently, attentively and humanely the celebrity who'd arrived in his prison. Pazulsky liked him because of this. "I started pitying him. I see the new fellow doesn't know how to control these devils, the prisoners. And I start helping him. I gave advice on how to dominate them, indeed, as it were, to shout at them. And I established order in the prison: they stood at attention. The commonfolk are cowards!" To do this, Pazulsky granted certain privileges, since he had a good position. His privileged status displeased the assistant warden, a former medic (it's surprising what a passion medics have for this position!). The assistant was jealous and began badmouthing Pazulsky to the warden. The weak-willed warden listened to his assistant. They began cutting Pazulsky down, and so Pazulsky organized a riot when they wanted to get even with the prisoners. But the riot failed and Pazulsky was arrested and dragged through the gates. The assistant then gave free rein to his nastiness. He ordered Pazulsky beaten before all the prisoners watching from the windows. For Pazulsky, this was "worse than death." He simply told the assistant, "You came to a restaurant to dine, but didn't ask the price." The half-beaten-to-death Pazulsky was put in the isolator; and when he, "beaten down" and having languished there, rejoined the general population, his first words were an oath to kill the assistant.

Pazulsky soon escaped and was at large for two years. He was captured somewhere in the Crimea and once again sent to Kherson Prison. The warden was the same, as was the assistant. The assistant had long forgotten about everything and even greeted Pazulsky amicably. "Ah! Pazulsky! God's brought you for another visit!" Pazulsky answered, "God's brought me. This is true."

One day, when an inspection of the ward was going on, Pazulsky turned to the medic-assistant, who was walking behind the warden. "Be so kind as to look at my throat, there's a pain in my neck." They went over to the window to see better. Pazulsky quickly grabbed him around the waist and slit his throat. The assistant didn't even have a chance to utter a word into Pazulsky's sleeve! He threw him on the floor and said, "Score settled!" Having said this, Pazulsky sighed with such unfeigned relief that it was as if he'd never felt satisfaction before then.

The murder of an official—"for this there's the noose," and this was why *katorga* looked with such terror at this man who, after two years, had "kept his word." Pazulsky was sentenced to be hanged. He sat in prison and waited.

"Was it terrible?"

"Tedious. 'Make it sooner!' I'm thinking, because, what was there to lose? 'I should be hanged and thrown away.'" Like the majority, like almost all "true criminals," he was superstitious even though he didn't believe in God. "In my dreams there was a tall, tall pillar. 'What's this for?' I'm thinking. 'It means I'll be hanged tomorrow!' So it was. In the evening they brought white linens, which means the execution's the next morning!" Pazulsky refused the priest; and on the scaffold he startled everyone by pushing the executioner aside. "I don't want an executioner's hands touching me, it's disgusting!" He turned facing west and donned the noose himself. Then he heard a shout: "Stop! Stop!" He'd been pardoned. "My eyes got murky. Everything was swimming, swimming," says Pazulsky.

Fig. 40: Pazulsky

The death sentence was replaced by a life sentence of *katorga*. Pazulsky was ordered to Siberia; at one of the way-stations he exchanged identities with a petty criminal he'd beat at cards and who thereon went under the name "Pazulsky," while Pazulsky managed to escape and return south. But Pazulsky's adventures and "execution" had created a sensation down south and he was recognized, captured and prosecuted. "Every dog knew me! I couldn't be mistaken. Fame ruined me!" Pazulsky was sentenced in Odessa to twelve years as a correctional, 100 lashes and three years chained to a wheelbarrow. Thus he ended up on Sakhalin.

He's in Aleksandrovsk's chains prison's worst ward. On the list of names hanging near the ward door all is made clear: "Life sentence... Life sentence... Life sentence..." And these men are morally and utterly subject to Pazulsky. A man devoid of fear and material belongings, he engages in money-lending. He's a terrible old man. He sits in his dark corner like a huge spider holding in its web nineteen frightened, pitifully squeaking fleas.

"Right here!" he once said to me, pointing to a small depression in his spot on the sleeping platform. "Do you know what this is?"

"What?"

"*This* is where *I* lie down!"

11

THE PLEBEIAN

If Pazulsky is *katorga*'s aristocrat, then Antonov, who goes by the sobriquet Baldokha,[1] is the most contemptible of its plebeians. Not that he's done anything reprehensible from *katorga*'s viewpoint, just simply "that he's quite a fellow! Neither a candle for God nor a poker for the Devil! In a word, he's a little blockhead!"

Baldokha's specialty was strangulation. He strangled in his day… "Wait! How many?" Baldokha asks himself, cracking his gnarly fingers and always losing count. "Eleven souls!" And never has he seen more than ten rubles.

Anton-Baldokha is fifty-four years old, looks less than forty, and isn't very intelligent. His physique is remarkably ungainly, his face uneven, and he makes a ridiculous sight. He was born in Moscow, in the Khitrovka.[2] He knew neither father nor mother and grew up in a flophouse. The pub was his greatest joy in life.

"What would you be doing now, Baldokha, if you were you safe in Moscow?"

"I'd be at the Little Rook! I'd be going to a pub!" Baldokha's entire face smiles. "Akh, it's a good city! So many pubs there!"

In his previous life, when he wanted to announce something unusually grand, he'd say, "I myself am asking, brothers, should we have a round?!" He speaks his own unique language, a mix of Khitrovka and *katorga*: the language of the poor and that of prisoners. A man for him is a "passenger." He doesn't ask, but "shoots according to the passenger."[3] He doesn't strangle, but "knocks in the cistern."[4] For him, a small criminal deed is a "guitar." A watch is either an "onion" or a "sunflower," depending on whether it's silver or gold. "To star-shoot a passenger during a guitar along the mill wall and pinch a sunflower—that's so good!"

"May I please shoot your esteemed honor?!" he says, asking for a ten-kopek piece.

As it happened, he "took" sunflowers and jewels but spent his entire life down at the heels. Having "taken" a nice thing, he'd go to a buyer of stolen goods and receive a well-earned 100 rubles. "A roop[5] or two!" Then he'd ruin himself and wake in the morning hungry, cold and dressed in rags yet again. He did this not so much because he'd gotten drunk but because he was unaccustomed to any kind of property; and when friends got him a top coat of blue cloth, plate-topped boots and a peaked cap "to find him some work," he instantly sold these things and resumed his previous lifestyle.

Older Muscovites still remember his notorious gang of "riotous Moscow bashi-bazouks,"[6] as they were called, who terrorized the region. The gang held Muscovites in fear and terror. In the evening, in dark alleyways, they'd grab pedestrians' fur hats, tear fur collars from their coats and take their watches. A driver would usually overtake the pedestrian in an out-of-the-way place, a pair would jump from the sleigh, rob the pedestrian, leap back into the sleigh and the driver would whip the horse and vanish into thin air. Besides these brash public robberies there were incessant murders. They strangled certain wealthy people, exclusively Old Believers.

"Why Old Believers?" I asked Baldokha, the protagonist of all these exploits.

"Oh, Old Believers? Because our informant was a porter and they were all he knew."

Baldokha was the strangling specialist in this gang of "bashi-bazouks." For the most part, he was hired for a job. He'd do a strangling and be given clothes and ten rubles.

"Why was it this way? Was it your profession?"

"Certainly, it's my profession."

"And you studied it, did you?"

"Certainly, I studied. Nothing's possible without a method."

"Where did you study?"

"But in the pub. If a drunk was slumped against the wall, I'd grab him and do him behind a cart."

"To death?"

"Why 'to death'? I don't do everyone in, only so's to keep a passenger from squealing. I wouldn't kill him, that is."

"But what about the others who wouldn't have died without you?"

"They died. Yes, it was terrible for the rest. But it meant nothing to me. I'd say, 'He can't be allowed to squeal.' Maybe you heard about the job in Orël,[7] where they picked a little gem and strangled the owner? That was my job. They took me to Orël for that reason. I was captured, in any case. They'd planned to do the job in the daytime but it happened at night. They broke into this shop, but I was standing guard behind the door in the back. Suddenly, the owner comes in. He lived next to the shop. You know how it is! There's a partition and behind the partition another apartment, and there sat the seamstresses playing songs. You could hear everything word for word. You could hear 'em breathing. They needed a hand! He'd unlocked the door and had just turned, but I got behind a machine and lay on the ground. I was hardly breathing! I'm lying on the floor and they're playing songs behind the partition. So, they couldn't hear anything!"

Baldokha was surprisingly animated while speaking of his "skill." Once, telling me how he'd carried out his work, he instantly tripped me up from behind, grabbed my waist with one arm and raised the other to my throat. I wasn't even able to blink, so completely helpless did I find myself in his hands. Baldokha had turned white as a sheet and was completely beside himself, and stood me back on my feet and jumped away. "Your worship!... Forgive me! As God's my witness, I didn't want to hurt you... On my word..." He wanted to fall to his knees. For a long time I tried to relax him.

He positively "loves his business." Indeed, this is moreover really the only business he knows; it's his only resource. After *katorga* will have wasted him, he'll have only one means to defend himself. "I'll jump from behind a machine and you won't be breathing!" Besides "his business," Baldokha can read and write. He learned in reform school. "That's what ruined me!"

It was thanks to Baldokha that the "Bazhi-bazouks" were captured. He showed up with a mate to buy timber from a lonely, elderly Old Believer woodsman. While they were talking, Baldokha strangled the old man, and then they searched the body, smashed everything in the rook, but found nothing. The next day in a pub he was reading about the murder in the newspaper: "Money, something close to 30 000, was hidden behind the deceased's boots and remained undiscovered." Baldokha burst out laughing. "Why're you laughing?" the bartender asked. "Why indeed! They killed an Old Believer in Sokolniki[8] yesterday and were fumbling everywhere for his money, but it was behind his shoes!" The "murder in Sokolniki" had created a terrible sensation in Moscow and brought the police to their knees. They learned about Baldokha's suspicious laughter from the bartender, arrested him and proved his guilt.

"But did you really go about such matters calmly?"

"But why not? Though, certainly, it was absurd, and though I always drank a glass of vodka before a job to get the blood going."

How does he endure *katorga*? I happened to ask him something about prison.

"Prison? Prison's nuthin'! Just a flophouse in the Khitrovka."

12

THE PARRICIDE

A small, exceedingly tidy little room. A bespectacled old man stands at the window mending his clothes and humming something "spiritual" to himself.

Upon entering the home of this "freeman" not living in Dué Post's prison, Dr L and I found the convict in a small, extraordinarily tidy room. He met us in the entryway, bowed especially courteously, though unlike a convict, and said, "Pardon me, Nikolay Stepanovich! Pardon me, sir!" He was familiar with Dr L, profoundly adored by all *katorga* for his friendly humanitarian attitude. We sat down and asked him to sit. "I humbly thank you, but no. Thank you." He was an unusually fine-looking old man, splendid and kind. He spoke softly, exceptionally gently, and smiled somewhat sadly, somewhat guiltily.

"Are you an exile-settler?"

"Absolutely not. I cannot join the exile-settlers. I have a life sentence. I'm actually a probationer and cannot be otherwise." Such a punishment is given for only a certain crime.

"And what did you get it for?"

"For my father. I committed parricide."

"How long have you been in *katorga*?"

"Fifteen years."

"How old are you?"

"Sixty-one."

"How old were you when you did this…?"

"I was almost fifty."

"But how old was your father?"

"My father was seventy."

A nearly fifty-year-old man who murdered his seventy-year-old father. Why this unusual geriatric tragedy?

"How could that be? Why did you do it?"

The old man looked down, grew silent, then sighed and quietly said, "It's a shame to say. But before you, Nikolay Stepanovich, I cannot remain silent. This happened long ago, when I was still young. Well, out with it! My father was a troublemaker. Mine was a great sin—but I don't repent. Judge me as you like!" He said this so gently and mildly, that he wasn't sorry he'd killed his father.

"It began a long time ago, gentlemen, after I'd gotten married. We worked the land, lived without poverty and even had hired men. I married according to my heart; and Maria gave me her heart. They called Maria 'peaceful,' and may she forever rest in peace. The house, I say, was wealthy and we began living in it. We needed nothing more and everyone in the house fell in love with Maria. This, then, should have drawn my attention.

"My father was especially interested in Maria. Among us peasants it's not good when a father-in-law is painfully kind toward his young daughter-in-law. He can't be trusted. But what did I know! I was pleased that Maria had entered my home and was loved. Only, I started to notice he was being too kind. But he was a strict old man. He controlled everyone and they didn't dare make a sound… Once, I'm lying in the hay barn sleeping, having a lazy day, when suddenly I hear Maria's voice: 'Father, can this be happening?' I could see her through a chink in the wall. Maria's going to the meadow and my father's behind her. Maria's trying to get away from him but he's following her, laughing. 'Ah-ha,' he's saying, 'I'll get you! Ah-ha, I'll get you!' Maria just ran away from him but he, the cur, was standing there following her with his eyes and chuckling to himself. 'So that's how it is!' I'm thinking. I was dazed, and lost my head then and there. I came home and told Maria to get the reins from the shed. 'You're a wolf in sheep's clothing!' I say. 'Are you playing around with my father?!' But she falls on her knees in tears. 'Leshënka,' she says, 'he doesn't mean anything. That's just the way he is.' She was saying, that is, that she was shamed by his advances. I flogged and flogged her with the reins. I went to my father. 'Father, there's this and there's that,' I say. 'You've put us off. We're going to live by ourselves. I was lying in the barn just now, and I've decided…'—I had to say 'barn' to him. The old man frowned. 'That's a bad thing,' he says, 'you lolling about in the barn deciding what to do, you puppy. The house is full as a bowl, but because you want more *I* should get lost! Geez, what you've decided! Get out of my sight, you bastard!'

"Here's what it got to: Maria comes back from the field covered in bruises. 'Who did this to you?' I ask. 'Father,' she blurts out, and begins crying. I go to my father. 'You can't do this, father!' He pulls my hair because, I say, although we were grown-ups, all us children were like wee ones before him. 'You're gonna teach me?!' he says. 'You're just a lazy-bones!' he says. 'And your Maria's the same. Kindness and affection are lost on you—so I'll prove my worth to you. You'll work for me!' But my tongue wouldn't allow me to say what bluntly needed to be said, that 'Father, you're humiliating yourself. There are others here, laborers.' Such was life.

"What is *katorga*? *Katorga*, sirs, means nothing. We beat the now deceased Maria. She was a sufferer, a martyr! My father beat her for running away from him and I beat her out of despair because it seemed she was guilty and fawning over him. So went twenty years! A life sentence!" The old man turned away, wiping his tears. His voice quivered and rose. "The Lord God punished me for Maria. I bear my cross for Maria. I've suffered and I martyr myself like she, the martyr, martyred herself. My deceased never confessed to me before her death, she was so ashamed. 'Leshënka,' she'd say, 'this is only in your mind.' She'd say, 'Leshënka, don't think this way, don't torment yourself. Father is strict, but he's just calling me to account over my work. Don't worry.' But how could I 'not worry'? I cried myself three rivers. I was beside myself. I'd beat her and she'd scream. Should the innocent suffer so much over nothing? She'd be choking on her tears and just repeating: 'Leshënka, don't torment yourself, don't think this way!'

"One winter night I'm lying down in the hut. I can hear my father's not sleeping, he's tossing and turning, huffing and puffing. He couldn't fall asleep. I'm not sleeping and Maria's not sleeping, she's shaking all over. What do I hear, but her leaving the room and my father getting up. It was like he was choking me by the neck. 'Father,' I say, 'where are you going?' 'And what's it to you?' he says. "Geez, the night-birds[1] aren't sleeping, they're hanging about! They might even burn down the hut. So I'm gonna have a look!' 'But father, I'll go with you!' 'You stay here!' he says. I went with him anyway. We'd brought our warning bell to the village, but he'd stayed home and hadn't helped. 'Go,' he'd said, 'you help. My loins hurt.' We'd left, everyone looking and laughing to themselves, because the matter was obvious…"

"Why was the affair obvious?"

"That's a sign for us peasants. When a molester gets down to business he doesn't move the bell from its spot. I came home after helping move it. 'Why didn't you move the bell, father?' I asked. 'You've simply humiliated us!' I asked him about this just once, and the old man turned dark as night. 'Don't you dare talk to me like I'm stupid,' he says. 'I'll take a stick to you, I will! I said my loins hurt.' But what loins they were! I was simply afraid nothing would keep folks from stringing him up. 'Fedulych,'[2] they'd say, 'back off, this isn't your affair.' But if we don't bury our own shit, what are we going to bury? Everybody knew our business. It was a shame. When my son Nikolushka grew up, he learned everything. He knew what the old man was! Maria had turned into an old woman. We'd worn her out. They're more beautiful in a coffin, and so he'd kept going at her. The sinning went on until the coffin was completely closed." The old man could barely hold back his tears. He remained silent for a long time before rallying himself to go on.

"The old man was powerful. He was laughing at the time. 'I should marry again,' he says, 'and soon.' Maria had died, I'd become a widower and the time had come for Nikolushka to marry. He took a bride from a good home. The young woman was modest and good. But what do you think he'd decided? Wasn't he a cur?" The old man spit with loathing. His hands shook and his head rocked.

"Wasn't he a cur? I went to town and see all the guests together, but he singles out Nastia. 'That's a clever girl for you,' he says. 'Give her to grandad!' I look and see Nastia's weeping. 'What for?' I ask. 'She's just crying!' he says. It was just too much. I see him hurrying after Nastia wherever she went. I could see he was planning to have Nastia for himself. Gentlemen, I was stricken with terror and horror. My head was spinning. 'How can it be,' I'm thinking, 'that what I feared my whole life my Nikolushka now has to suffer too? When will this end?' Later on, I see him cozying up even more to Nastiushka. So I told Nikolushka everything that happened with his mother. Nikolushka was shaking and crying. 'I'd heard rumors about our home,' he says. 'Only, I didn't believe them.' 'That's nothing to grieve over now,' I say. 'You have to look after Nastiushka!' We thought and thought: what could be done? We wanted to break away from the old man. But where do you go?!

"'Geez,' says the old man, 'what you've decided! I give you food and drink, you sponge (he says this to Nikolushka), and this is how you thank me? By taking this hard-working woman out of the home? I know all your games!' he says. 'This is what this old sod (he looks at me) is teaching you. According to you, everybody wants to be a libertine, to live it up, in your mind. Look,' he says, 'if you don't relax your games will make you fall apart before your time! But you won't get my blessing to divide your allotment. I won't break up the home as long as I live!'

"To make sure nothing happened, that nothing *could* happen, we saw we'd have to closely follow him everywhere. It was harvest time. Nastiushka was reaping all by herself along a narrow strip in a ravine. The ravine wasn't large, just a narrow gully. She was there reaping and this is what I came home to: 'Where's father?' I ask. 'He left!' they say. So my heart skipped a beat. I went to Nikolushka. 'I say, come with me right now, Nikolushka, we're going to the gully. It's not a good thing that father's left the house.' We ran to the gully and as we're running we see him fighting with Nastiushka. Her hair and blouse were tousled (it was warm, so she was wearing just one blouse and that blouse was torn). Nastiushka's defending herself but he's grabbing her. She broke away from him and started to run, but he grabbed a branch lying there on the strip's edge and went after her. 'Good,' he says, 'that's better!' We ran up then. 'Stop,' we're shouting. He saw us and began shaking and flying into a rage. 'You devils,' he shouts, 'what are you doing here?' I was seeing stars. Nastiushka was standing in her torn blouse. It was shameful! I went up to him. 'This is no good,' I say. 'Old man, I've decided this is no good!' But he says to me, 'Ah, you're gonna teach me again? All my life I've taught you, but now you're gonna teach me? Leave my home!' he says. 'Leave Nikolka here with Nastasia. But you, get out of my sight! I've fed you long enough, you sponger!' 'Old man,' I say, 'that's still not it! This isn't Maria!' And then I'm moving closer and closer and he's getting even angrier. 'Who are you,' he shouts, 'to poke me in the eye with your Maria? She slept with the whole village! Get out of here!' he shouts and waves the branch at me.

"I still don't remember how it happened. I grabbed the branch from him and hit him on the head. He knelt down but I grabbed him by the throat. I just remember that everything was shaking and that he disgusted me, like a viper. 'Old man,' I say, 'your hour's come!' 'Alësha,' he says, 'don't!' 'Old man,' I say, 'you should have thought about that earlier!' and I was squeezing his throat… I squeezed—and held tight. I squeezed till I couldn't see or understand anything. When I came to, Nikolushka was prying at my hands. 'Daddy,' he's saying, 'you've strangled Grandpa.' 'Serves him right!' I say. 'The sinner.' And that, gentlemen, is the whole affair…"

"Well, but the jury, old man, you told them everything?"

"No, what for? My conscience is clear."

"Why didn't you confess, tell everything?"

"How can I say this to you? First, I said there were no witnesses. 'It was me, just me.' Second, I was afraid to involve Nikolushka because of Nastia. They were a young couple and had lives to live, but mine was an age-old matter. And finally… it was such a shame to burden people with…"

"Well, but did your son play any part at all?"

"In this that I did? Not at all. He saw it; but I alone murdered him. There's nothing for me to hide. It doesn't matter now. I'd say so if he were involved. It doesn't matter. They've already died. Soon after I was sentenced Nikolushka died and then Nastasia after him… All of mine are dead and gone and I'm left to suffer alone!…" The old man gave a bitter and guilty smile. "I suffer and pray for Maria's soul. Perhaps it will do her well up there. What there was here!… She was an unprotesting martyr…"

13

SHKANDYBA[1]

The terminally-sentenced convict Shkandyba is sixty-four years old. He's a strapping, powerful robust old man. Shkandyba is a Sakhalin celebrity. Everyone knows him. Shkandyba's served twenty-four years of "pure *katorga*" and not once has he done any work. "So much for being sentenced as a penal 'laborer'!" he bursts out laughing. They flogged him every day for a month to make him work. All for nothing! This man has received so many lashes of the whip and birch rod!

When he, per my request, spoke with me in private, I couldn't look at his mass of scar tissue without shuddering. His whole body looked like a maple tree scarred by hot irons. "I'm a wholly ripped-apart man!" Shkandyba says of himself. "You can't stick a pin into a spot that hasn't been ripped open. Everywhere's been ripped open. May it please you to see me rub myself with some cloth? Show me where to rub." He rubs a cloth where indicated, and criss-cross stripes arise on his body—the leftovers of birch rods. "I'm a checkered man! With patterned skin. I've been thrashed all over, both sides, just like a counterfeit five-piece they use for pitch-and-toss. There's an eagle on both sides. Either way you toss it, it's always an eagle! There's an eagle on this side and an eagle on that side. So is me."

"So you were flogged on both sides?"

"Exactly. The gentleman warden was very cross with me because I didn't want to work. 'I'll show you!' he says. He thrashed and thrashed me 'til he could thrash no more. 'Turn the scoundrel on his back,' he says. That was odd! They kept going on my stomach, my chest, my legs. No one spoke out against such a beating. It was a killing! The herd started laughing when I was laid out on the mare that way. It was unusual!"

"But, all the same, you still didn't work?"

"They'd come up against a hardhead!"

Shkandyba had been a butcher by profession. He was sentenced the first time to twelve years for robbing a church and for murder. Then he escaped, was caught and finally "got the life sentence to *katorga* I deserved." He was first sent to Kara, to the gold mines. Those were terrible times. In the "cut" where the convicts worked the mare stood always ready. Each trench had its own executioner on duty all day. Shkandyba was ordered to work. He absolutely refused.

"What's this? I'm supposed to dig in the ground? I won't."

"You say you won't?"

"Just so. The earth hasn't troubled me and I won't trouble it."

Shkandyba received twenty-five lashes his first day. On his second—fifty. On his third—100; and he was taken to the infirmary barely alive. Once recovered he was brought back—and again the same: "The earth hasn't troubled me, and I won't trouble it." Again he was taken for a lashing and again brought to the infirmary. Finally, they got tired—frankly tired—of thrashing Shkandyba, and transferred him to Sakhalin.

On Sakhalin, Shkandyba immediately announced, "I won't work. And you'd better not try to make me."

"Well, we'll try a flogging!"

"With all my pleasure. It's completely within your rights. But you won't make me work."

Shkandyba went from prison to prison, warden to warden, and always boasted, "Well, my tune hasn't changed!" And each time he'd drop his arms to his sides.

K, one of the most "zealous" wardens, told me, "Yes, you can't believe what kind of man this is. I laid into him. Every day he got thirty birch strokes—and what strokes they were! It was a real serving. I go to the command station in the morning. The mare's standing there, executioner and birch rods are there. Instead of 'Hello!' my first words are, 'Shkandyba, are you going to work?' 'Certainly not!' 'Flog him!' And he goes and lies down. He really pushed it to the limit, the bastard. I'd barely arrive, not even able to ask the question, and he'd go and lie down on the mare. He didn't care!"

Another warden—also "zealous"—to whom was passed on the bloodied Shkandyba, told me, "At one point, we thought maybe he's a kind of phenomenon who can't feel pain. We sent him to a doctor for inspection. 'No,' he says, 'not true, he feels it.' This meant we were allowed to flog him."

The "spectacles" that Shkandyba provided *katorga* every morning comprised the prison's entertainment. Following him, others tried to "maintain themselves," to "show spirit" and laugh as they lay down on the mare. Moreover, *katorga* became cheeky: "What are you doing bothering me with your work? Get lost, you, go make Shkandyba work! I'm not afraid of you, you can't make me!"

Shkandyba was proving an infectious example, so they asked him to work just for "propriety's sake." "Shkandyba, you devil, just take a broom and sweep the yard! That's your whole labor!"

"I don't want to. Why should I sweep? I didn't litter and I won't sweep. If I litter, I'll take care of it for myself."

"Well, damn you, don't sweep! Just hold the broom in your hands!"

"Why would I want to hold it? It's not small, and it can rest in a corner. It won't get bored: there are other brooms there."

"Once, however, I grabbed an axe!" laughs Shkandyba.

"You wanted to work?"

"No, I needed it to chop off a guard's head. There was this guard Chizhikov and he wanted to be promoted. 'I'll make him work,' he says. 'Don't trouble yourselves. What's a flogging to him? It's a lengthy process! I'll stick a fist in his snout.' Once to my snout, twice to my snout. He's going on with his beating. 'I'll knock the spirit out of you!' he says. 'Look,' I say, 'you shouldn't go too far!' 'I'm not afraid!' he says. 'Well, but I'm afraid!' I say. I went and grabbed an axe and drove it into his neck. I wanted to cut his head clean off so no one could pretty his snout."

"And so, was he dead?"

"Unfortunately, he was still alive. His head was flopping sideways. The flesh looked like chopped beef. One more strike and he'd have been done for. But I couldn't manage such a cold deed, so I dropped the axe!" For this, Shkandyba was chained to a wall and sentenced to *katorga* for life. "I'm there, chained to the wall: 'I say, did you get what you want? Am I working?'"

Remarkable. Everyone dealt with Shkandyba, though it never occurred to anyone to examine his mental faculties. But Shkandyba's oddities, apart from his unyielding refusal to work, are numerous, such as his suddenly beginning to sing out loud, his unstoppable talking and running and jumping around like a half-wit.

"He's acting like an idiot!"

"He's feigning insanity so's not to be flogged!"

"He's impudent: 'Here, I say, everyone works, but I'll belt out a song.'"

So reasoned Sakhalin's prison administration. But when humane doctors actually appeared on Sakhalin and were prepared to defend the sick man themselves, the struggle with Shkandyba soon ended: they "didn't care" and somehow got him registered as a disabled worker. But only God knows if Shkandyba can be called insane. He's abnormal and has many oddities—but is he out of his mind?

During one of our conversations I asked Shkandyba, "You haven't said why you refuse to work"

"Well, it's not fair. There's no justice—that's why I've refused."

"Well, why is there no justice? Don't you yourself say you robbed a church and killed a man?"

"True!"

"You were sentenced to *katorga*."

"Justly so. But not to exploitation, not to death."

"Well, but to labor!"

"But I won't work. It's unfair."

"Yes, and how is it unfair?"

"It just is! Von Landsberg killed two people—but did they make him work? No, I daresay! He was commander over us. A *barin*! He was an engineer or some kind of sapper, whatever, who knew how to build a road. He didn't work, he commanded. But I should work! Why should it be that I should work? Because I killed a man? No! Because I don't know how to build a road. So I'm guilty of this? Guilty that I wasn't taught? No, brother, *katorga* is *katorga* and should be the same for everyone! But is there justice? Prisoners arrive and the literate go to the chancery as clerks and exploit their own brethren. But the illiterate go to the mountain, to the coal shafts. Why should they suffer? For being illiterate? This is what makes them guilty? Is this fair?"

Fig. 41: Prisoner

"This is why you won't work?"

"Exactly!"

"Well, but if there were 'justice' and everyone made to work alike, would you work?"

"But why not? Certainly, I'd work. Why not work? The main thing is fairness. This is why I wanted to take Chizhikov's head off. For being unfair! Flog according to the rules. Flog according to the law—flog away! They flogged me everyday and I never said a word: it was fair. Because it was the law. But punching your snout is against the law, and you can't do it. You break the law, so I'll break the law. You punch my snout, so I'll take an axe to your neck. That's what's fair. Do I contradict myself? Do yourself a favor, do what you want, only do it fairly!"

Thus has Shkandyba served his twenty-four years of "pure *katorga*," brooking nothing he considers unfair.

14

HIRED MURDERERS

They're inseparable. Wherever there's small, feeble and fidgety Karp Milovanov you'll see the silent and morose Anisim Chernyshov. They're terribly cruel to each other. Anisim is as cruel toward Karp as if he were an informer. "We ended up in *katorga* because of his tongue." Karp accuses Anisim of dirty tricks. "Don't believe anything Uncle Anisim says, brother. Believe that tongue and your tail's clean gone. 'Y'know, I say, I don't understand a thing!' Geez, and he appears all pious as well. No, brother, *you* talk with a clean conscience! But being a scoundrel is nothing for him!" Yet they are always together; sleep next to each other; and eat from the same pot. "We were sentenced together. Nothing can separate one of us from the other."

I recall meeting them on the island after they arrived with a new party of convicts. They were brought into a room for inspection and a guard ordered them to "Separate!" Both became frightened.

"Brother, Uncle Anisim's come to a turn! 'Separate!'… Why, is it absolutely necessary to separate?"

"Separate and remove your shoes completely." They quickly went into separate corners. "Go to the table!" Tall as a pole and thin as a skeleton, Anisim Chernyshov approached the table with a most miserable look. His face was knitted and he was whimpering here and there. Karp Milovanov stood in front of the table in utter dismay. His jaw hung down, fear and terror in his eyes. His legs quivered and shook. He scratched himself with shaking hands.

"Where do I lie down?" asked Milovanov.

"Why 'lie down'?"

"But, the flogging?"

"Why would you be flogged?"

"But this, I say… A flogging… Given the situation…" Everyone burst out laughing. Milovanov looked on uncomprehendingly.

"No, man, they won't be flogging you. At least not for nothing. Here, you're thrashed if you do something!"

"Thank you, your worship!" Everyone began laughing again. The relieved Milovanov himself smiled. "Did you hear, Uncle Anisim, there won't be a flogging? You hear?"

"I hear!" answered Anisim in a tone so bland it was like he was not a whit interested.

Happiness made Milovanov garrulous. He had achieved a pleasant nervous excitement and was now smiling and ready to talk non-stop.

"What were you both sentenced for?"

"For suspicion of murder!" was Milovanov's typically distinct convict answer. "It just so happened the master got killed!"

"During a robbery?"

"No! Why 'during a robbery'? God was taking care of us! We stole nothing. He just got killed."

"Why did he get killed?"

"Why are people killed? For money, of course! Such was the situation, it was over money!"

"The mistress implicated us!" Anisim morosely explained.

"Exactly. She gave us money!" underscored Karp.

"This means you were hired?"

Karp looked surprised. "What would we be hired for? We made a living as workers!"

"But how do you explain the money?"

"To show thanks, she was thanking us, as was customary. But to hire... Do they hire for such matters?" Milovanov actually began laughing.

"Did you kill him?"

"I, indeed!"

"Well, but you, Chernyshov?"

"He's not in confession!" interjected Milovanov.

"Understand that I know nothing about these matters. I ain't heard a whisper! Really, Karpushka's just spinning yarns!"

Milovanov screwed himself tight. "Geez, you, excuse me! What you're like! You won't answer and so now it's Karpushka's turn!" Milovanov winked at us and nodded at Chernyshov. "A clever muzhik, eh? The hell with your cleverness! There were a pair of souls: one runs off but the other goes to the people and comes clean! 'Weren't me, weren't me!' Well, brother, there was nowhere left to hide 'cause of your tongue. We landed in *katorga* straight off—case closed! That was it, we killed him!"

"But how did the affair happen?"

"How did it happen?! Simple and to the point? I say, because of a woman!"

"We were making a living as workers!" Anisim put in, as if these words explained everything.

"Were you earning a salary?"

Milovanov snorted. "What salary? Who'd give me and Uncle Anisim a salary?" And, in actuality, the speaker was impoverished to the point of starvation. Both were enfeebled, pitiful and weakened to such a degree that, as they say, "you'd break 'em by spittin' on 'em." Both men's heads were unusually small, like a bundle of pencils on end. Both faces were stupid and pathetic. It was as if God had "not had time to knock them together."[1]

"So we lived begging like Christ. I lived at the master's for six years but Uncle Anisim arrived after two. I say, isn't that so, Uncle Anisim?"

"I was in vernal Nikol[2] for about four years. That's true!" underscored Chernyshov.

"The master was a miller and I myself was a miller. That's why I came and settled at the mill. Now I've settled in prison."

"But where had you been?"

"Ah well, I had nowhere to go. Where was there for me to go? I'd walk on and on, then stay awhile."

"But what had you done for a profession?"

"I didn't do anything. So. I'd go and go. Where they'd hire me to work for bread and salt, I'd live. If they'd drive me away, I'd go further on. I'm a weak fellow! I was sitting down, the miller caught sight of me, and says, 'Why are you sitting there?' 'I say, for Christ's sake, won't you have mercy and hire me to work? That is, there's nowhere to find work for now! I can tinker around the house.' 'Live here!' he says. He was merciful and I began living there. Then he met Uncle Anisim and invited him in."

"Did you know each other?"

"No, why should we have?! So. I'm walking down the road and see this sickly weak fellow coming toward me. 'I say, where're you going, uncle?' 'I say, nowhere.' He didn't have shelter. 'We'll go see my master. He's a kind muzhik and maybe you can live there!' It was just one mongrel grabbing another mongrel," Milovanov began laughing to himself, "and now he's leading the other one along! The master took to Uncle Anisim. 'Go ahead and live here, tinker around over there in the mill.' So we're both living there and tinkering around! Sometimes we'd get a shirt, sometimes something else."

"Perhaps your master treated you like fools? Was he cruel?"

"What for?" Milovanov actually grew scared. "For us, he was an angel, he never called us fools! The master was most kind!"

"The muzhik was good!" Chernyshov gloomily underscored.

"A better man was impossible. That's true!"

"But he was killed! How did this happen?"

"Once again, I say, because of the mistress. The mistress arranged it. The master's wife. What a woman! She wanted everyone in wool dresses. Dress or no dress, that woman was a lump of sugar—that's just my view. Correct, Uncle Anisim?"

"She was a real woman," noted Chernyshov philosophically.

"Another such woman can't be found in the whole world! What a woman! She'll be coming here to *katorga*, you'll see. Everything's all knotted up right now.

She was a real fox. But when you run through the snow your tail leaves a trail. First, she's spinning and twisting before your eyes; next thing, she's gone! It must frankly be said the woman was a headman, a woman-king. She carried on with the barin, the landowner. She had him wrapped round her finger. She gave him a little taste and he was always in her kitchen. Well, it's a compliment to her. As would happen, her husband would leave and off she'd go to the barin. Also, as the miller-woman, she had to see him because he was the landowner. They'd drink sweetened vodka and crack nuts together. It was awful! She sent Uncle Anisim and me to the barin so many times: 'She's asking are you coming over? Her husband's going to the city.' Do I speak truly, Uncle Anisim?"

"I went to the barin's so many times. It's true!" Uncle Anisim maintained.

"Righty-o and so-so!"

"But her husband didn't know?"

"He didn't! I say, she was a woman-king. If he'd known, he wouldn't have left. He should've been more lordly toward her!" smiled Milovanov. "Her husband needed to be firm. Do I speak truly, Uncle Anisim? Why are you silent?"

"He should've taught her!"

"He certainly should've taught her! She was afraid of that. She feared it. Again and again she'd be flattering the barin in the kitchen. She fawned and fawned over him. She didn't know what to do. Then she decided!"

"Wait, wait! What about you both? You say the master was generous, but you were running between the wife and barin? You never said anything to your master?"

Milovanov looked at me in surprise. "Can anything get between a husband and wife? That was their business, a household affair. Our business was work. She told us to go. They got used to us bringing tea to the house, too. Even the dog got used to that fellow!... Then she, the mistress, made a decision. She called Uncle Anisim and me into the chamber and sat us at the table. Courteously and kindly, she says, 'You should try eating more, Uncle Karp! And you, Uncle Anisim,' she says, 'should eat more.' Akh, a clever woman! Akh, a wily one! She treated us to meat pies, vodka by the glass, and didn't take the carafe of vodka from the table. It was right and proper. 'Uncle Anisim and Uncle Karp,' she says, 'I have a deal for you. My master must be killed immediately!' My eyes popped out of my head. 'What... did you say... kill? What for?' 'Because,' she says, 'if he learns about the barin I'll lose my life, and you'll be thrown out by the scruffs of your necks. You'll die of hunger! If you help me in this,' she says, 'I won't abandon you.' And she hands us the drinking bowl.[3] 'To your health,' she says. 'And if you do everything well by me, the barin won't forget you.' So she flatters, shakes her tail and shoots. 'But, I say, if you don't agree, I'll talk about you to my husband so that he'll chase you out of the house with a stick.' She certainly was an impressive woman, and coulda done it. 'Or else I'll go to the barin when the gentleman constable's visiting him and suggest he ask for your passports,' she says. 'Perhaps you've exceeded the limits of your passports and don't have the right to live here?' Geez, the lengths she'd go. Geez! Also, no one wants to survive off lice in jail. The woman, we knew, was capable of it. She was sometimes in the constable's company and coulda convinced him! She could do what she wanted with you. She'd sized up Uncle Anisim and me. 'Geez, what an affair!' said Uncle Anisim. 'Now it's clearer to you, Uncle Karp,' he said."

"I don't know anything about these matters!" Chernyshov suddenly answered, pecking the point like a woodpecker.

"'I don't know!' But who was holding the rifle? *You* were holding it!" snapped Milovanov. "Uncle Anisim and I grieved and grieved, for we pitied the master. Well, we really didn't want to leave such a home. Where could such as us go? Who'd take us? Yes, we'd gotten accustomed to the house and it woulda been a shame to leave. A dog, I tell you, gets used to things. We grieved and grieved and went to the mistress. 'Alright, I say, we'll do it! You'll learn how later!' '*How* is not your concern,' she says. 'You just do the shooting and another will do the thinking, and I've already done that!' Indeed, she was always keeping company with the barin—a fellow with money—and the constable. They could do whatever they wanted. And they'd already decided."

"So you should have told your master what they were planning, if the 'man was an angel'!"

"I told him!" Milovanov waved his hand. "Nothing happened. He didn't pay attention. I pitied the master. He'd sat down and made himself comfortable, and I said, 'Master, I say, you keep an eye out!' He says, 'Why should I keep an eye out?' 'Just so's nothing happens, I say!' 'But for what?' he says. 'I say, you should just keep an eye out!' He says, 'You should go and get some grain from the barn, Uncle Karp, instead of chattering on about what you don't know. Really!' So he didn't pay attention. I myself told him what was being planned, but it was his affair and he did as he wished. But he also wasn't frankly telling us what was happening. That husband-and-wife business. So the man died because of himself! This happened in the afternoon. 'I'm going to the lodge to lie down,' he says. His lodge was in the woods. 'A home away from bothersome fleas!' he'd say. I prodded Uncle Anisim: 'I say, we can't let this chance slip through our fingers!' Uncle Anisim went into the chamber and came out with a gun."

"I don't know anything about this!"

"You say you didn't grab a rifle? Akh, the fellow has a clever spirit! Akh, clever! 'He's spinning a yarn,' eh?! You want to go here, there and everywhere to cover your tracks! Akh, you—forgive me gentlemen!" Milovanov vigorously shook his head disapprovingly. "Uncle Anisim and I went to the lodge. We walked up to it quietly. It was scary. What if he got up and beat us? 'Uncle

Anisim,' I say, 'look through the little door!' 'No,' he says. 'Uncle Karp, look!' Uncle Anisim's an absolutely impoverished fellow. Incompetent. He wanted to run away. 'Well, brother, not now!' I say. 'You can leave after we've gone in together!' Given the door was partly opened, I glanced inside. The master's sleeping, and how. He's snoring and drooling. He'd eaten a little and there were flies all over his mug, but they weren't bothering him a bit! I'm thinking, 'Now's the time.' So I pointed the rifle at him, but my hands are shaking like I was robbing a hen-house! The rifle's shaking and shaking. 'This ain't good,' I'm thinking. 'It'll be just like me to wake him up. Then how he'll stand up and clobber us.' He was a powerful man, so that those like us couldn't oppose him. An apple tree was growing there and I leaned against it. I'm thinking, 'Alright, I'll catch my breath.' Uncle Anisim's sitting completely on the ground, can't stand up. I caught my breath, aimed the rifle straight at his head and took aim like so... Pow-w-w!" And poor Milovanov assumed such a pose and was so pitiable, so ridiculous at that moment, that we couldn't help but start laughing. He even laughed at himself.

"Pow-w-w! The master squealed like a pig and began twisting like a fish. How he was squealing! I reloaded the rifle straightaway. Uncle Anisim grabs me by the arm and is so pale. 'Don't shoot,' he says, 'for God sakes! Let's get out of here. This is horrible.' 'No,' I say, 'we've just started! I'm not leaving yet—he's not dead.' I reloaded, aimed—and bang! Then the master stopped twisting. He's just lying there, moaning. He moaned and moaned, then died. Uncle Anisim and I clear out, go into the meadow, deep into the rye up to the edge of the woods, and dig a hole to the right of a sapling and bury the rifle."

"It was to the left of the sapling!" Uncle Anisim piped in.

"But, in fact, to the right!"

"To the left, I tell you!"

"On the contrary, to the right. There's the spot, there's the sapling and it's two steps to the..." And they began an inconclusive argument between themselves. Where was the sapling, to the right or the left? Both knew and remembered every shrub. These people knew little but what they knew, they knew thoroughly, in the same way an insect knows the very leaf he was born and lives on. Commoners have narrow horizons—a verst and a half in diameter—but inside this circle, they know every speck of dust by heart and little by little observe each throughout the course of an entire year.

"We hid the rifle in the hole," continued Milovanov after his triumphalist argument about the sapling had ended, "and we come home. 'I say, welcome us, honorable widow!' The mistress had heard everything and was sitting like canvas fixed to a bench. 'You really did away with him!' she says. 'I say, quite right. We finished him off.' She began crying. 'Akh,' she says, 'why did you do it?' 'Well, I say, you can't turn back now. You should be showing us some respect right now!' 'Please, to the table,' she says. 'Sit down.' She set down a carafe and what was left of dinner from the stove. We sit down and drink vodka."

"Did you feel you needed vodka to drink?"

"Why? No! It's just that it was there. It ended the matter. The mistress is crying. Certainly, it was a shame—her husband. 'I say, you should sit down.' We gave her some vodka. 'I say, drink with us, too. Aren't we all one? To company.' She gave us money—three paper rubles and three copper quarters—and we went to sleep because we were tuckered out. But we were arrested in the morning."

"How did that happen?"

"Some muzhik went to the cabin and saw the dead body there and raised hell. 'Whose body?' 'The miller's.' Then suspicion fell on us."

"Well, what did you do?"

"Uncle Anisim does not agree, but I can see that everyone found out because he talked. He said this and that. Couldn't he stay quiet? Certainly, they would've arrested someone else if he'd stayed quiet. But once they arrested me, as it were, the suspicion was total—silence or no. The mistress had taken a turn for the worse. She went to the barin, but the barin didn't need that filth from a jailhouse. The barin had found himself another; he had lots of women. She promised the constable three years' service in his kitchens without pay. But no, brother, you're not doing it. It turned out very badly, because I told everything. So everything became known, every word of it. They tried us. And how! They tried everyone together. They put the mistress on a bench of her own. But another barin was standing behind her. Also, you could see she'd promised to go into his kitchen without pay. Everyone's fingers were pointing at me. 'He's lying about everything!' she's saying. 'Don't believe him, mister judge!' But I stood and crossed myself. 'I'm speaking the truth,' I say. They believed me and we all went to *katorga*. Several days later I find myself in prison among a crowd of laughing prisoners. And for what?"

Thus Milovanov told how, for three rubles and seventy-five kopeks, he murdered "not the master but an angel." He tells it every time in infinitesimal detail, chuckling at the point when he comes to things that are, in his opinion, humorous, like the master "squealing like a pig." He talks about it simply, impartially, as if everything happened just so.

"How could you do this, Milovanov?" I began, in an experiment to somehow shame him.

Milovanov looked at me in surprise. "But, your worship, we really are a weak people! If I were a strong man, certainly I would've left and been able to go anywhere. But what can a weakling do? Push him this way and there he goes. In a word, I'm a weakling!"

"We found out who you were talking to, your worship!" a certain penal laborer, himself a killer of a family of six souls and another of five, scornfully noted of Milovanov. "Can he understand anything? His mind is shrunken and completely different! Nothing can make him think about how things are! So he's not even human, but some quarter of a man!"

15

THE SUICIDE

"You didn't make a copy again, you scoundrel? Again?" Warden K was screaming at the *brodiaga*-clerk Ivanov in Rykovsk's prison chancery. Before me, he loved to demonstrate his severity and notion of "controlling prisoners." "You haven't laid on the mare, reptile? I'll lay you out! Laddie, you know me! You don't know what the others demand. Under me, you'll condemn your life to the mare, you bastard! I take this sonofabitch into the chancery, but he… I'll lock you in chains… shackle you to the waste-tub. You'll be buried in shit, you vermin!"

Brodiaga Ivanov, a beardless, moustacheless youth, sat with pale face and quivering blue lips and scribbled.

"Any other way's impossible with these bastards!" K explained to me after we left the chancery. "I know how to control them! They know me and my rules. I won't say another word but what I've already said, and it'll be kept for sure."

That evening I was drinking tea with K's family, when suddenly a guard burst in: "A suicide!"

"How? What? Where?"

"A suicide in the chancery. Clerk Ivanov, the *brodiaga*, shot himself."

K and I ran to the chancery. Ivanov was already gone.

"They took him to the infirmary!"

The sentinel box beside the chancery smelled of gunpowder and blood was on the bench and floor. A revolver lay on the table.

"Whose revolver is this?"

"Mine!" one of the guards guiltily replied.

"You'll be court-martialed, you bastard! Court-martialed!" K stamped his feet. "I'm ordering you placed under investigation, now!"

"I'm sorry, I wasn't watching!…"

"Guard, you're a bastard! You put your revolver on his table!"

"I was only gone a minute, but he found the little room and—bang."
"I'll drag all of you to court, you sons-of-bitches!"
"He left a note here!" added one of the clerks.
The following was written in pencil on octavo paper:

I request that no one be found guilty in my death, it was my desire to shoot myself.

1) I fail in everything.
2) They don't understand me.
3) I request that it be written (to the address shown in Revel) that I die loving only her.
4) Do not bury my body but, if you will, cremate it. Please!
5) I request a prayer be made to Lord God, Whom I understand not with reason but believe in with all my soul.

—*Brodiaga* Ivanov

"The bastard!" concluded K. "Write a protocol."
"He'll probably survive!" announced an arriving doctor. "The bullet didn't stop the heart. He's sound!"
"The bastard's not dead?" K grew indignant. "Ah? He was playing a game! 'Take the guard's revolver!'... Chap, if you tossed your revolver to me... others would see! After all, there's folks around. Write a protocol that the revolver was secretly taken..." He busied himself with dictating the protocol.
Chancery clerks were confused and going about like lost souls. The guards swore at them: "We almost got in trouble because of you devils!"
When the doctor told him Ivanov would recover, the warden screamed, "I don't want to know about the sonofabitch!" and kept repeating, "Please give him my compliments! The bastard shoots himself!"

The doctor told me the clerks went to the infirmary every day to inquire about Ivanov. "The boy," they'd say, "is already very well."
I saw Ivanov after he'd gotten better.
"Let's drop in on him!" the doctor suggested.
"But won't I disturb him?"
"No, not at all. He'll be pleased. I told him you'd asked about him, and he said, 'Really?!' It pleased him. We'll call on him."
Ivanov was lying down, emaciated, yellow as beeswax, with white lips and deeply hollow, black-ringed eyes.
I grasped his thin, barely warm little hand. "Greetings, Ivanov! How are you? Recovered?"

THE SUICIDE

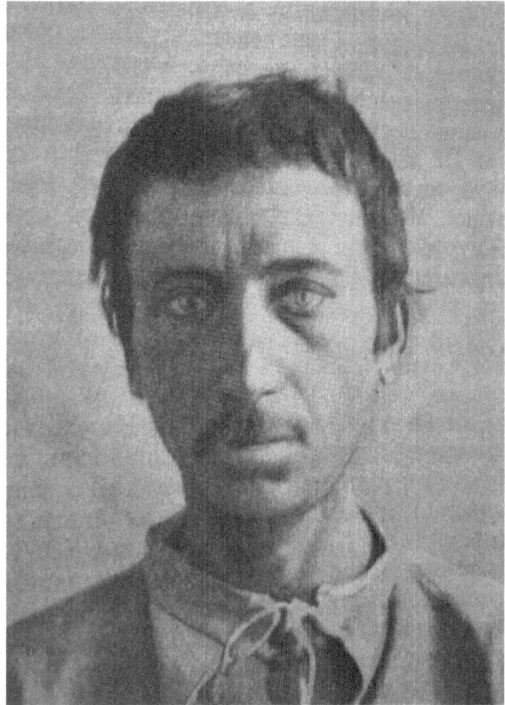

Fig. 42: Prisoner

"Thank you!" he said in a quiet voice, squeezing my hand. "Thank you very much for calling on me!..." I sat next to him. "You don't despise me, then?" he asked.

"Why? What for? God be with you!"

"But that time... in the chancery... the warden... 'Scoundrel... Sonofabitch... Vermin'... Talking about the mare... Lord, in front of a stranger!" Ivanov grew agitated.

"Don't trouble yourself, don't worry... After all, why should I despise you? I'd sooner despise him."

"Him?" Ivanov looked at me in surprise and disbelief.

"Why, of course him! He abused a defenseless man."

"Him? Him?" Ivanov repeated again and again, his face joyous, tears in his eyes. "But really... I... I wasn't thinking... I was thinking that I, that I... Such that I am... that I'm now... because of my very last words... to be sent to the mare!... Such a man that I am." He began weeping.

"Ivanov, stop. It's not good for you!" the doctor and I told him. "Don't worry yourself over trifles!..."

"Really, it's not... it's nothing... it's so... it's not from grief..." He sobbed and murmured, "But I... I... want to study a little... to read a little book... just read... I'm an educated man, after all." The poor man, he'd probably inserted "cremate" into his suicide note to show he was educated...

There lay before me a boy, a proud, tearful boy—but he was in *katorga*.

"You were with the bastard?" K shot at me in the infirmary. "Once he recovers, I'll stick him in chains for his games!"

16

THE FRENZIED

"Well, aren't they bastards? Aren't they? Eh? Well, what can you do with these folks? What can you do with them?" Rykovsk's old warden of settlements was agitatedly saying.

"Just what happened?"

"You know, two people were murdered again. Would you like to go with me to the inquest?" He gave me the details on the way.

Two "hut-sharer" exile-settlers, living together "for joint householding," that is, in a single hut, had murdered a pair of *brodiagi* who came to stay the night. They probably killed them at night as they were sleeping. Next morning, they chopped the corpses into pieces, lit the oven and were planning to roast the flesh.

"They ought to have hidden themselves, the sons-of-bitches!" the warden of settlements exasperatedly said. "But their door and windows were wide open, as if what they were doing was perfectly normal. This is really the frenzied limit! A little girl caught them red-handed. The neighbor's girl. She'd gone to their hut for some reason. She sees the hut's awash in blood, that there's some kind of pile next to the oven and they're sitting there next to the oven, cooking. Devils, no? Well, she screamed at the top of her lungs and the neighbors came! They caught them red-handed. And they don't deny it—they're talking."

In the morgue, flesh from a human chest lay on a table. Pieces of bone protruded from hands, feet and chunks of flesh that smelled like fresh beef. This beefy smell permeating the morgue as if it were a butchery was utterly horrible. A blood-smeared opened-mouthed face lay among the pieces.

"There's another head here!" announced a guard, squeamishly pointing to what seemed a sponge soaked in blood. The head was lying face down—we were seeing its back. From the doorway, children gazed in horror and amazement at the pieces of flesh.

"Akh, the bastards! The bastards!" the warden of settlements shook his head. "Write a protocol! We're going to question them." There wasn't an investigator on Sakhalin at the time, and so the officials conducting the inquiry did so most ungrammatically.

A crowd of thrill-seekers stood in front of the warden-of-settlements chancery. The two exile-settlers, middle-aged, hands tied behind them, with dull, indifferent expressions, were inside the chancery. Both were covered in blood from head to toe.

"Your worship, show a commander's mercy and let us go home!" they begged.

The warden of settlements only looked at them savagely. "What do you mean 'go home'??"

"You know—home! Really, what's all this? They bound our wrists, brought us here, rifled through our home. We have a livelihood, too, after all. There's not much there, but it's there. We've done our best and now we're being cleaned out. Let us go home."

"You're beside yourselves, is that it, you devils?"

"We're beside nothing, we're talking business! About what's there!"

"Shut up! Untie their hands, take them to the courtyard and let them at least wash their mugs. They look terrible. Wash, you devils!"

"Wash yourselves!" For the next several minutes they splashed about, so that at least their hands and faces weren't bloody.

"Write a protocol of inquiry!" the warden of settlements ordered a clerk. "Inquire, then, as to what? What's there a question about? Just write, 'They murdered them.' It's all the same, they won't wriggle out of it and nothing will be lost. The house there is being picked over, but they need to be questioned!" He turned to them. "Did you murder so as to rob them?"

"We did!" one of the exile-settlers snorted scornfully. "Robbery s'well! We took forty kopeks."

"How much money was found on them?"

"Forty-four kopeks," a guard answered.

"Because of forty kopeks you killed two souls?" the warden of settlements wrung his hands.

"But who knew how much money these souls had! These two unknowns turned up from who knows where. 'Let us spend the night,' they ask. They gave us two kopeks each. That's not a lodging rate, as we say. They're thinking, 'We're lucky,' and they came in. When we fumbled through their pockets we found a measly forty kopeks. That's the whole robbery. Listen, let us go home. Show a commander's mercy. Really, we should lose our household because of forty kopeks? You can see that everything we have is worth only ten rubles! It'll get stolen!"

"Take them to solitary confinement now!"

"Solitary confinement because of forty kopeks? Pshaw, you! Lord!" The exile-settlers were apparently being "mischievous." "Then give us back our four kopeks! They paid us for one night!"

"So they could end up in a government food ration?" other exile-settlers joked.

"Just so! Did we choose to be swollen up from starvation?!" answered one of the murderers.

Someone cursed, "Well, that's how it is!"

"Well, well, let's go to the site of the crime."

Exile-settler watchmen were standing outside the hut where the murders had been committed. But everything was already stolen. Neither a spoon nor a saucer was left in the hut. Everything had been swiped.

"Oh, you're going to get it!" the warden of settlements threatened the guards.

"Please explain what for, your worship? Mercy, can an exile-settler live on nothing? He's poor and that's that. Folks came running as soon as they could and the guards weren't posted yet. Certainly, they'll swipe any belongings they can!"

The hut was tiny, of course, without any outbuildings, crooked, askew and hastily knocked together because they hastily knock together *pro forma* the obligatory "domicile" on Sakhalin. It reeked: the floor was damp and sticky; green spots were on the bench. The blood had still not dried. The little oven around which there was still a pool of blood stood in a corner. It had a tiny opening.

"It would've taken them till evening to roast the bodies!" said the settlements' commander, looking in the oven.

"Quite right, your worship, they could only roast one arm. And that was hardly charred!" underscored a guard. "They would have been cooking all day, non-stop."

"Isn't this frenziedness, I ask you? Isn't it frenziedness?!" the warden of settlements exclaimed in horror. "Write a protocol of inspection!"

17

THE EDUCATED MAN[1]

"Excuse me! Excuse me! Sir, excuse me." Catching up to me in Derbinsk was a drunken fellow, ragged, dirty beyond belief, with a blackened eye and bruised lips. He reeked of alcohol from five paces away and was standing barring my way. "Gentleman writer, excuse me. Seeing as you're now seeking material for writing biographies of penal laborers, if you were to hear my biography it would really make you cry. Allow me to ask, do you recognize moral obligations? That's good! But since you've recognized moral obligations, you must vouchsafe me a conversation as well. Before you is a real humanitarian document, so to speak. A land surveyor. We, too, actually understand something. *Parlez vous francais? Vous*, too? I do. I went to the people when you were probably still a kid.[2] And suddenly I'm a penal laborer! Excuse me, but how is this so? Anyone can flog me. Is that fair?"

"And why did you end up here?"

"Now you're talking. You should be deeply moved by this! 'Don't kill,' they say. But what should I do if my wife, my love, my love..." He struck his chest with a fist and drunken tears fell from his eyes. "...My love, you understand. I discovered my wife with her lover in the worst crime. According to French law—'*tuez-la!*'[3]—and case closed. Excuse me, but this is promoted in the theater... by that great student of human nature, Shakespeare... and Othello, the Venetian Moor... and the whole audience applauds. But I'm sent to *katorga* for it. To *katorga*? Where's the justice, I ask you? And now, suddenly, I'm to go to the mare: 'Why are you making counterfeit money?'"

"Excuse me, but you were sent here for killing your wife or for counterfeiting?"

"Now you're talking. The wife was first, the counterfeiting came later. The counterfeiting was just out of despair. Excuse me! How could I not counterfeit? And allow me to ask you how I'm to drink vodka if I've no money? Given such a biography, should I drink vodka or not? I'd better drink some vodka soon, because my hand's coming unhinged. You understand? Unhinged! I'd like to hang a rope on a peg, but my hand's coming unhinged."

"Why do you want to hang a rope on a peg?"

"To hang myself. I need to hang myself, but my hand's coming unhinged. I tell you, I'm a *scoundrel* and I need to drink vodka now or I'll be in a white fever. Do you know what a white fever is? *Delirium tremens!* What an educated man!

Now I'm diagnosing myself, and so on. I'm self-diagnosing, yet I'm going to the mare. Perhaps the warden will tell me that there's a Buckle, that there's a civilization, that there's an England?[4] I read *A History of Civilization in England*, but I'm going to the mare. I wanted to be a Dostoevsky! To be a Dostoevsky! In *katorga*, I envisioned my mission. Ye-es! I wanted to write essays. Now everything's fallen apart. Why 'fallen apart'? Because of a humble spirit. I'd already reckoned myself an envoy from her majesty 'civilization,' and in the steamer's hold had begun writing petitions free of charge for the illiterate folk. But now they want to kill me! Because of some *brodiaga*-Ivan, a recidivist, who requested a petition to the finance minister and Petersburg's metropolitan[5] about a review of his case, and was going to pay a ruble for this petition—but I refused because it was stupid. Stupid and in bad taste. 'Akh,' they say, 'you so-and-so. You're ruining the people! You don't want to write petitions to the proper quarter? Ivan wants to correspond with the metropolitan but you don't want him to?' And now Ivan's coming down on me because I refused the service. 'Beat him! Beat him to death! He won't write a petition to the proper quarters. He's hand-in-glove with the administration. He writes letters for himself, but while we're drinking vodka and playing cards he tells the administration everything.' Suddenly, one night, they beat me black and blue, tried to kill me and tore up my writings. Then, in front of everyone in the hold, they told the officials, 'He's stealing.' And the steamer captain says, 'I'll flog you!' Excuse me! Can you imagine what I was thinking?

"There I am, sitting in a prison getting beaten black and blue, but my offender had shown up in court with rings on his fingers and his fiancée in the gallery. The ladies were fawning over him and he was playing the gallant knight. 'Nothing of the kind!' he says, for how could he admit his shady connections to a respectable woman? What a gal-*lant*! And the whole gallery's saying, 'What a gal-*lant*.' Excuse me. Now he's got his hearth, his wife and moreover, his home's inviolable. But it was all mine, mine. He violates me and it doesn't matter? He doesn't go to *katorga*, but *I* go to *katorga*? Is this justice? My wife's not a year dead and he already has a new one.

"I'm crying! I'm crying and am not ashamed! I'll write a false denunciation again and won't be ashamed. Again! 'What, gentleman warden of settlements, do you wish me to write in this false denunciation?' It's true! And I write one again for twenty kopeks. 'Do you wish me to write you a false denunciation? About whom would you like it? Twenty kopeks—and a denunciation! And you want to flog me! To flog me! If you want to flog me—you'll flog me!'" He was starting to fall apart.

"Steady, steady, God's with you! Collect yourself!"

"This upsets you? No matter. But perhaps, gentleman of free status, you've a desire to flog me! Don't you want to? I won't pester you, because I've been deprived of all my rights. But can you deprive me of my education? Can you deprive me of my intellectual soul? Will they really unstitch me? Everyone who constitutes me will be unstitched. I'll be lying on the mare with Buckle, Spencer[6] and Shakespeare, and the warden will be flogging me as well as Buckle, Spencer and Shakespeare! Buckle, too!

"Suddenly, there was the order: 'Transfer him with an ox to Derbinsk settlement.' I, with an ox?! How should I talk to an ox? As with a comrade? Certainly, he's a beast and I—certainly—am a beast! Perhaps my rights can be taken away, but not to such an extent! With an ox! And to the mare with birch rods, birch rods.

"The deceased should arise, she should see this. Akh, how she'd wring her hands! And in gloves! 'Akh, *quel horreur*, flog him like Sidorov's goat.[7] Akh, how simple!' This was her favorite word: 'Simple.' 'Akh,' she'd say, 'here's a dress. It's so *simple*.' Cheat on your husband, but he'll be flogged! Ah? What a husband! I gave her a bracelet on her saint's day." He suddenly bellowed at the top of his lungs. "Sapphires! Diamonds! Golkonda! Gorel!"[8] He burst into tears. "I gave up eating breakfast at work. Quit smoking. Saved for a whole year. Took everything apart and went to the pawnshop: 'Just don't sell them.' In winter, I went around in a high-collared jacket because I'd pawned my frock coat. For the same reason I did away with jackboots and walked through my apartments in slippers. I was indebted to the bursar. And I brought it home to her! On her saint's day! I crept on tiptoes and put it on her bedside table, opened the box and left it there. Opened the curtains so the sun could come through. A little presentation! I'm sitting, waiting. 'What'll happen?' I can't breathe. And she opened up her eyes, saw it and gasped, 'Ooh!'" He clutched his head, his face showing bitter agony.

"And it was in that bracelet that she was caught by me! Everyone in my circle had been laughing at me for so many years but I alone, the fool, had been serious. Ha-ha-ha! So there you are! I'll laugh by myself—but all of you around me will be in horror. And suddenly, I'm writing a petition about such-and-such for an illiterate exile-settler. I'm requesting the treasury provide me a cow and a woman for homesteading. Ah! A cow and a woman. A woman and a cow. I had indeed created an idol for myself. What is a woman? Heinrich Heine[9] said, 'God created her in a moment of inspiration'! But *someone* didn't have to wait for inspiration—her stockings were silk and so her lover was most pleased to kiss her feet. You really absolutely had to kiss that woman's feet! 'On your knees before her! On the floor! On the ground before her! In the dust!' But here there's a cow, and there's a woman.

"Give me twenty kopeks... What's this? A ruble? Many thanks. I understand. Truly. Everyone knows how it is, I understand. You've visited *katorga* and given him a ruble, now your conscience is clear. Give me your hand. As one educated man to another, I say, 'Thank you.' Simple and short! 'Thank you.'"

18

POET-MURDERERS
(IN THE FORM OF A PREFACE)

Lacenaire, executed in France under Napoleon III, was a most cruel murderer and a most tender poet.[1] Poetry was his favorite occupation; but his usual occupation was thievery and murder. He specialized in jewelers. Under the pretense of selling some cheap diamonds, Lacenaire would first lure the jeweler along some dark path into a rented apartment somewhere on the city limits. They would usually disagree over the terms and, when the jeweler descended the staircase, Lacenaire, following behind, would with anatomical artistry and precision thrust a sharp and slender poker into his cerebellum. With neither a cry nor a moan, the victim would fall into the arms of Lacenaire's accomplice—a fellow arisen from Parisian dregs—who would carry him downstairs and open the door.

Among the flatirons, hatchets, elegant ladies' hairpins, silk corset laces and coarse ropes in the museum of criminal implements next to Conciergerie Prison,[2] there is Lacenaire's implement, the "little cat." The "little cat" is as long and narrow as a cotter-pin, sharp as an awl or stiletto, and fitted into a small wooden handle. Lacenaire studied anatomy and himself fashioned the "little cat" for thrusting into the cerebellum. He preferred this means of killing to any other as "the most tidy." He couldn't endure "blood or any filth in general" and, while doing a killing, feared one thing only: getting dirty.

Judging by his portrait, he was an elegant gentleman with especially slender and aristocratic features, more of the Anglo-Saxon than the French type. He was blond and curly-haired with well-groomed, not overly large, side-whiskers and pale blue, impassive cold eyes. He could be taken for a medium-pedigreed lord or at least a man of society, but not a murderer at all. Newsmen of the time added that Lacenaire's hands, having served for murder, were beautiful and could compete in elegance and grooming with those of a lady.

When Lacenaire was captured, he spoke with utter detachment of the details of all his murders, even those of which he wasn't suspected, and betrayed his accomplice, even though he was not at all prompted to do so. Lacenaire had despised the "filthy creature" he'd hired for murder and decided he deserved the guillotine. A brutal tradition existed in those stern times: on the eve of execution, the condemned were made to attend a requiem mass that treated them as if dead. Encountering him in the church, Lacenaire's accomplice tried to strangle him. And on the very eve of their execution! Lacenaire squeamishly backed away. The whole time the mass was proceeding and their names were being laid to rest, Lacenaire's accomplice sobbed, collapsed and pounded his head on the floor. "The free-thinking Lacenaire," as one newsman said, "paid attention like a very well-bred foreigner attending an unfamiliar religious ceremony." Impassively, with curiosity and deference. Having gone to him for final condolences, the priest spent several hours with Lacenaire in his cell and emerged shocked and disturbed, saying, "Lacenaire will sooner turn a priest into an atheist than a priest will alter anything in Lacenaire's mind."

Within the realm of cruelty there is no limit to human inventiveness. It has devised punishments worse than death: tokens of death. As the most serious of criminals, Lacenaire would therefore be executed twice.

When they took his accomplice, half-dead from fright, to the guillotine, Lacenaire, standing on the scaffold, inched forward hoping to see how they chopped off his head. "Lacenaire, they may take this for a pose!" the priest commented. "Thank you! You're right!" Lacenaire said with a courteous bow, and backed away.

When his turn came, he calmly approached the guillotine and laid his head in the semicircular aperture. But then fortune cruelly turned her back on Lacenaire. The guillotine's blade stuck and, despite all the executioner's efforts, would not budge. So passed half a minute. Lacenaire turned to the executioner and cried, "You beast!" "At that moment," say eyewitnesses, "Lacenaire looked terrified."

Such was Lacenaire, who lived wickedly and wanted to die.

Posthumous publications of Lacenaire's poetry were terribly popular.[3] Lacenaire-the-murderer had been executed, but Lacenaire-the-poet sprang to life and became as immortal as an unsolvable riddle. It seems that among murderers, his was a cruelty distinguished by a mild, delicate and effeminate soul. His verses, superior in structure and delicate and dreamlike in content, are most similar to the verses of our Fet.[4] Shortly before his death, he turned his poetic attention to violets now growing on his burial mound...

How does one reconcile the contrast: cruelty and softness, delicacy, sentimentality?

Sentimentality—in this lies an explanation to the riddle. Even if genius and villainy are incompatible, cruelty and sentimentality get on with each other outstandingly. When people don't have butter they'll satisfy themselves with margarine, and sentimentality is the margarine of emotion. Kind people are often rough in their kindliness; but sentimental people are crueler than others. People who have cruelly and relentlessly beaten their compatriots will develop a delicate, sentimental love for a spider in a ward, for a kitten who scampers along the prison sleeping platforms; people who run about in the morning and will for no reason attack those doing nothing and say, "I'll kill you" will, later in the day, fondle the prison kitten and possibly kill the man who hits it. Were you to compare them to works by the giants of poetry, you would see that most of his verses are suffused not with powerful, deep emotion, but principally with sentimentality.

At first glance, you may not recognize that strange mixture of cruel murderer and sentimental poet that Lacenaire exemplifies. Add to this the well known psychiatric fact that a passion for assonance and rhythm is an indicator of feeblemindedness. Having fallen into feeblemindedness, the sick typically begin to speak and write so that everything's in rhythm. They write nonsensically, but at the same time their words easily fall into rhythm. For them, the words' meaning disappears and all that remains is the assonance, to which they constantly return, morning to night, for days on end. "Rhythm-makers" are a most usual phenomenon among the feeble-minded, and they speak only assonantly. This is a type of feeblemindedness.

Now, you probably won't see an unusual quantity of rhythmic verses in general—except in *katorga* in particular, where there are more of the feebleminded than there would normally be. Here, there are veritable "founts of poetry" or at least of mostly poetry.

I.

Pashchenko (this was his *brodiaga*-name) was the terror of all Sakhalin. When Pashchenko got killed, *katorga* was most pleased. Pashchenko was credited with thirty-two murders, escaped numerous times, and when it was necessary "to confirm" his guilt, prison wardens and guards in Odessa who were reporting his identifying marks to Sakhalin added, "Just don't tell Pashchenko that we've sent you this information"—or else he'd come back and kill them. Such was the terrible spell of his name.

Pashchenko found among all those in Aleksandrovsk's chains prison only one other "man of spirit," a wheelbarrow man, that is, someone sentenced like him to being chained to a wheelbarrow. This was Shirokolobov. Shirokolobov was the second terror of all Sakhalin and Eastern Siberia. Inmates backed away from him as if from a beast.

Shirokolobov had been exiled from Eastern Siberia for a series of murders. He was the son of *katorga* parents who'd been exiled for murder and were renowned among convicts. In the portrait we have of him, one sees a vacant and utterly wild look. He was caught for murdering a deacon's widow. Wanting to learn where the money was hidden, Shirokolobov had tortured his victim. He slowly sliced off pieces of her ears and nose and cut off her breasts.

They delivered Shirokolobov to Sakhalin aboard the steamer *Baikal*, strapped at his waist to the mast by metal hoops.

This was the only man Pashchenko could befriend in the prison. Smashing the prison stove to pieces, they undid their wheelbarrow chains and managed to escape together through the hole in the roof. They went to the nearest mine shaft and hid there, and forced penal laborers and exile-settlers to bring them food. They had to, otherwise Pashchenko and Shirokolobov would have gotten up to their horrible tricks.

But their residence was discovered. For some reason, a feather duster was hanging on a tree near the entrance to one of the mining galleries. This seemed strange to officials. Wasn't it a sign? A raid was organized, but the tipped-off Pashchenko and Shirokolobov left and went to the distant Vladimirsk mine and hid themselves there instead, just like so.

Towards evening one day the Caucasian Kononbekov, a former penal laborer now a guard, was going around armed with a rifle to—as he says—"hunt possible fugitives." Walking along the ridge, he heard a rustling in the bushes below. It was Pashchenko and Shirokolobov moving down the hill. Kononbekov took aim and fired into the rustling. A cry sounded from the bushes and a shadow fell. Kononbekov ran to the bushes. Pashchenko lay there gasping his final breaths. The bullet had blown the top of his head off. Pashchenko "twitched," as Kononbekov says, then died. Shirokolobov got away.

All that was found on Pashchenko was his handwritten *brodiaga*-notebook in his pocket and now soaked with blood. This booklet was later given to me.

Pashchenko had been a tall, stately, handsome muzhik, forty-five years old with a large bushy beard and impassive, cold, steady gray eyes. All that remains of this terrible man is this notebook, soaked in his blood, now lying before me. In his ungrammatical scrawl Pashchenko wrote down what he thought important and interesting, what lay on his soul—all that was most essential to him.

His *brodiaga*-diary concludes with 25 August, when Pashchenko escaped. Pashchenko crossed out the subsequent days. The last day crossed out is 30 September. He was killed on 1 October.

There follows: "March route. From Sretensk to Shilkino—97 versts, Ust-Kara—115," etc.[5]

Then there follow several addresses, such as: "Ivan Vasilevich Cherkashev, shop in the New Bazaar; Nikita Iakovlevich Turetsky, private home, corner of Gusevska and Zeiska," etc. It's not clear whether these were people he could stay with or designated places where he could "work."

At first glance the information seems strange, but in prison it is very necessary:

"Another's mind, i.e., brain, can be controlled through hypnosis."

"Solar eclipse 28 July 1896."

A list of all government ministries.

"There are 497 people (269 men, 228 women) in Russian monasteries."

"Sweden and Norway—two states under one crown. Five million residents occupy the Scandinavian peninsula. The capital of Sweden is Stockholm and the capital of Norway is Christiania."

There is a similar listing of all European states, their capitals and how many live there. Further on is information about the "Chinese faith." "According to their superstition Fvo, the Chinese god, was reborn 8000 times. Akrang-Bel is a lesser god, i.e., a minor god, of the lowest heaven. Nonsense."

This information would seem to be useless but it is necessary, absolutely essential, for the man who wants to play a "role" in prison. Prisoners, like all Russia's simple folk, highly value "precise information." Especially precise. "How many people live in Belgium?" "Five and a half million." Especially this "and a half million." This gives the information credibility. The dreamy folk, the nonutilitarian folk, "our" folk and, along with them, prisoners, especially esteem knowledge not of something worldly, ordinary or necessary, but namely a knowledge of something completely unnecessary and inessential to life. And it seems the more useless the knowledge, the more it cultivates respect. This is true wisdom.

Moving among penal laborers you come up against such questions as the following: "Your worship, how many fire-spitting mountains, that is, 'volcanoes,' are there in the world?"

"Why do you want to know?"

"I just want to know, seeing as you're a scholar."

"Oh God, I don't know."

"There are forty-eight fire-spitting mountains, that is, 'volcanoes,' in the world."

Later, one-on-one, you may say to him, "My brother, you lie about everything. Who's counted all of them?" But in front of the prison you're wary and grant him his triumph. In this reposes the prison's respect for him, and now this knowledge, when even the scholar-barin has mistaken it, earns him still greater respect. You don't throw him beneath the feet of these people who, like everyone, endure but don't love another person's superiority.

Amid all the essentials for playing a role in prison are fragments of verse. According to penal laborers, the deceased Pashchenko was very fond of poems and wrote down those that moved him. What was it like for this poetic soul to have to live inside a man who committed thirty-two murders? The murderer loved only mournful poetry. Absolutely melancholy and plaintive.

After he complains about fate, about humankind's imperfect nature:

I will hack off the wings
Of impertinent doubt,
I will commit my strength

To a secret course...
Our minds cannot step
Beyond the world's borders,
Without altering
The ancient fable.

This Faustian theme gives way to a plaint on the injustice reigning over the world:

Trifles
Amuse people,
Kings and fools
Have moved worlds.
Heavenly valleys
Awash in blood,
The rulers of heaven
Crashed into the abyss.

These utterly plaintive, circular poems affected him most of all, and he wrote them down in his notebook. Like any "true criminal," he was always complaining about everything and everyone except himself, and so the following poem especially affected him:

Again you've come, brothers and friends,
With the supplication "forgive and forget,"
And again my heart aches
From your kindness.
But where were you
When I was down and out,
When upon weak shoulders the burden
Of *katorga* labor I endured?
Where were you, when sorrows,
Like evil spasms in the dark,
Tore my heart to pieces
In the terrible, empty stillness?
Where were you, when in confusion
I set upon a new path,
When this heart needed encouragement
Like a beggar needs bread?
Where were you, when enemies
Punished me by degrees

And I, finally, lost belief
In spiritual, brotherly love?

Pashchenko so liked this poem that he wrote beneath it the letter "F"—the initial of his real, not *brodiaga*, surname.

There is only one positive poem, evincing a contempt for people, perhaps because Pashchenko found contempt pleasing:

Don't fear vital threats,
Don't unjustly strike your chest,
Don't unjustly weep tears,
For they will be arrogantly mocked.
Don't fear needs, don't fear poverty,
Don't fear your hard, sad lot;
Endure people's evil and sin.
Don't deny your wishes
Before various misfortunes,
Struggle against fate no matter what happens.
Don't lose spirit and don't cry,
For there is little sense in despondency, my friend…

Such are the verses written in this blood-soaked little notebook of a man who loved poetry and killed thirty-two people. Such verses he read and reread while resting after one murder and preparing for another.

Did he not possess a poetic soul?

II.

The poet-murderer P—v is a decadent poet. Despite this, of course, this ill-grammared man has never heard of the Decadents' existence.[6] Among the mass of poems he gave me, often strange in form, is the following simile. He writes:

When blood-crimsoned ideas
Look with green eyes
Where will you run and what will you find in your pale heart?

I became acquainted with P—v in Sakhalin's insane asylum, where he was being held. He wasn't insane in the generally accepted sense of the word. He was the way he was by nature: he was afflicted with *moral insanity*.[7] Living in freedom, he committed an uninterrupted string of crimes, always vile, foul and often revealing an astonishingly perverted nature.

P—v was almost forty years old, and the object of his hatred was the procurator who first indicted him. He cannot calmly recall this procurator and cannot forgive his expression, "a Lombroso type." But at the same time, P—v could undoubtedly have illustrated Lombroso's atlas of congenital criminals. His protruding ears lack any lobes. He has a surprisingly openly expressive asymmetrical face. The eyes are different sizes and unevenly set—one's higher, the other lower. The nose, lips—everything—seem shifted out of place. He has two completely different profiles. His upper forehead is flat and the back of his head widely overdeveloped. A clearer picture of degeneration would be impossible.

P—v is the fruit of incest. He was produced out of the union between a brother and sister. His father and mother were chronic alcoholics. The first crime he was sent to *katorga* for was his murder of a friend during an argument. On Sakhalin, besides innumerable robberies and crimes stemming from his sexual psychopathology, P—v committed a murder. He'd fallen in love with an exile-settler's daughter. But P—v's reputation on Sakhalin was terrible and repulsive. "P—v's coming!" This was a horror for exile-settlers. Foul play was predictable whenever P—v showed up in a settlement. The exile-settler, father to his beloved daughter, refused him, of course. P—v later waylaid and killed the old man.

A psychiatrist who came to Sakhalin was P—v's only salvation from the perpetual beatings and punishments he was being subjected to. The psychiatrist saw in this strange "incorrigible criminal" an unfortunate degenerate, morally and mentally ill, and brought him to that place for the "Lombroso type"—to the insane asylum. P—v, a former sailor, could have been a research specimen for Lombroso, given that he was covered in tattoos.

(I'll use this opportunity to point out what I consider to be Lombroso's mistake in talking about criminals' propensity for tattoos, for this was initially a sailors' propensity. There was a real passion for tattoos among sailors, many of whom were in the East, where the art of tattooing has continued to the present. I met many tattooed criminals on Sakhalin, and all were former sailors. Lombroso's mistake isn't at all surprising: he observed prisoners in Italian prisons, and among Italians there would be as many sailors as not. If a passion for tattoos is taken as a mark of "the criminal nature," then all countries' navies very nearly consist of only criminal natures! We return, however, to P—v.)

Of all the major and minor crimes and offenses P—v committed, he was especially enthusiastic about those he committed in the insane asylum: he wrote poetry. His muse is somber and cruel. P—v occupies himself most somberly with poesy; he writes poems incessantly and then burns or tears them into little pieces so no one can collect them.

"Why do this?"

"Because!"

"Don't you like them?"

"Certain ones I dislike. They're somehow not strongly put. I want to speak more strongly, robustly, forcefully. But the others... Who would read them? They'd laugh. Better they didn't know I wrote them." Terribly proud, P—v has a most poetical, that is, "high" opinion of his verses. And when I told him his poems could be published, he beamed and smothered me with poems. "Can I possibly recite to anyone here? *Katorga!* Are these people?!" P—v said with insouciant contempt. "But people with understanding do exist. They'll understand my ideas."

"Well, but what if they publish all about your deeds?" one of the doctors asked him.

"Let them," answered P—v, "if only they publish some of my poems."

This unknowingly decadent poet would probably be quite pleased were he to read here in print this poem which is his personal favorite:

"The Murderer"
Frenzied killer, where will you find
Rest beneath a covering of kind wings,
When you discover yourself
      Guilty of murder?
The shade of the man you killed,
The man you cheated of life,
Comes to you in a bloody, sluggish fever
      And yells: "You killed me!"
Why do you seek consolation in a church
When he who lived
Suffered ruin at your hands,
      And you murdered him?
Let the whole world, so forgiving, with cheer and
Pity for you, murderer, loom over and
Strike you, like a ricocheting bullet, with:
      "You killed him."
O, son of sin! You! Cowering and covered in blood,
Where is your conscience? Does it not exist, or is it asleep?
Run... Where to? All paths are closed to you.
      "Murderer!" it shouts.

III.

"Paklin"[8]—so indisputably does the exiled penal laborer Paklin sign his *brodiaga*-name "in the French way." Paklin likes to argue a bit, and is terribly proud.

"I've suffered so much for my pride!" he says, and has the right to say. Paklin was brought to Korsakovsk when the prison commandant there wouldn't accept prisoners not being flogged.

"I couldn't sleep, since I was obsessed by the one idea that I'd be ripped apart!" said Paklin. "If that had happened, it would have been bad for both him and me. The whip would've struck my hide just once." He became agitated, trembling at this one idea; red blotches covered his face and his eyes grew wicked.

To avoid the possibility of a flogging, Paklin volunteered for the most difficult of jobs, from which penal laborers will run as if from the plague: he volunteered to be a watchman on Patience Bay. God knows why these guardposts exist in the remote taiga, on the straits' cold stormy coast. Is it the taiga or the sea they're guarding? Life in such a guardpost is unexceptionally lonely. Even fugitives don't go there. Only the Ainu sometimes stray there, Sakhalin's disappearing savages, aboriginals dressed in sable furs in winter and with their summer dress stitched together out of fish skins. All penal laborers shun this kind of "*katorga*." They'd rather face prison and floggings. Paklin voluntarily lived amid the taiga in continual solitude for three years until they replaced the prison warden. Then he returned to the post and to people. That's how you avoid a flogging.

Paklin is a Cossack. He committed a murder during a dispute, fled and somewhere acquired the passport of a certain Paklin and began carrying out robberies. He loves very much to read, and his favorite reading "at that time" were booklets that talked about bandits. He was as fastidious about his petty thefts as he was about his murders. "Why kill? You just have to threaten. A certain educated fellow, he'll listen to words. You can explain things to him and he gets it. Better to lose your money than your life." He was lucky. Paklin always accosted "educated" people. Committing numerous thefts and robberies, always with accomplices, Paklin moved from city to city. "I'd go to a city, carouse, carry out a job, then buy my favorite books and read. I'd read from morning to night. Often, I couldn't even sleep. I'd read all night without stopping."

"And always about bandits?"

"I read only about them. They were always going round in my head. I'd put myself in their situation. I'd always put myself in their place. I'd think, 'Here's how I'd do it.'"

Paklin ended up murdering a certain cleric in the south. The victim turned out to be a person who wasn't "educated." It's necessary to emphasize Paklin's contempt and ridicule for his victim. "He suddenly says to us, 'Who will you be murdering? Who are you raising your hand to?' Pshaw! He swore he didn't have money, but he was rolling in money." Paklin redoubled his efforts. His accomplice found the money as Paklin was holding the victim and "talking" to him. "Don't shout! We're only going to take your belongings, we won't touch you." Then the accomplice smashed a chest and a table and the victim grew quiet. When the accomplice moved toward a pile of things the old man blanched so that he looked like a sheet. With a terrible look, he broke free... "My loathing was aroused. Here was a fellow truly in greed's grip. I grabbed him and slit his throat." And saying this, the red-haired, freckle-faced, stuttering Paklin smiled scornfully.

Following is what Paklin wrote in his little notebook:

I'm lying on the cliff near the lighthouse, sixty paces from the cemetery and looking at the ocean's broad surface. Everything's quiet and sadness fills my heart and languid thoughts fill my soul...
They'll come and leave me here,
My enemies, my friends!
They won't put a cross over me,
They'll bury me here so far from you.
No one from home will come
To cry with anguish
Or read my tombstone—
Neither "who he was" nor "how long he lived"...
Only a nightingale, in springtime,
Will take wing to my forgotten burial mound,
Only he will disturb my rest,
He, enraptured by beauteous spring,
Will sing, though not disturb,
The quiet dreams that fill these graves;
His song will not disturb
My buried silence...

Is not this appeal to a nightingale more objectionable than the Lacenairesque appeal to the violets growing on his burial mound? One hears in both the same sentimentality, the brute's substitute for feeling.

"I was such a scoundrel in those days!" says Paklin, speaking of the past. He uses no other word but "rotten" to describe the books he then loved. Of himself, himself then, he uses no other word but "scoundrel."

The three years he spent in solitude, in nature's midst, changed Paklin. During these three years he kept notes on the Ainu who sometimes visited him. Paklin analyzed their life, observed them and saw them all the more as enduring their poverty—that fate of the violated savage—with great humanity. "At first," he writes in his ingenuous observations, "I shared everyone's view of these Ainu: they're not people. They hunt and trap sable and that's it. But the longer I've observed them I see this is nonsense and ignorance. The Ainu are the same as people, and live very well among themselves. They're honest and friendly, only very poor. They have their God, but he's not Orthodox, and not one of them really understands Orthodoxy. But such is their faith that they, too, pray."

Now, nothing remains of Paklin's former haughtiness, arrogance or of even that *katorga* tendency toward scornful manners and pride. "Now, I'm of quieter waters, lower grasses. If offended, I endure it!" Paklin cheerfully said, and a kind, sweet smile played across his repulsive face. "At one time I couldn't stand it, yes, but now I think of the wife and child and, well, I resign myself to it." In Korsakovsk Paklin received for cohabitation a nice young woman, a "*skopets* virgin" exiled to Sakhalin. She bore him a child. Paklin has become a tender, loving husband and father, an exceptionally hard-working homeowner.

Having lived "the people's life," in his expression, Paklin began to investigate the people's troubles and needs; and in the poems he wrote and continues to write new tones can be heard. "I" began to figure more rarely and a civic motif, so to speak, can be heard in these poems.

> There is a piece of earth
> Amid blue seas,
> Inhabited by beasts and
> A haven for savages.
> Above us shines the moon and
> The sun gives warmth
> While ocean waves
> Lap the shore.
> Unlike now, there used to be
> No one here from Rus.
> By custom, we call it
> Sakhalin.
> Only the mountain summits
> Were visible,
> But now you see
> So many settlements and ports!
> Nowadays, each year,
> Upon spring's arrival,
> The steamer *Iaroslavl*
> Delivers here
> The forever condemned,
> A scurrilous folk.
> The steamer's delivering

Seven hundred people.
The captain mutters,
Without shedding a tear:
"Wait, and in autumn
I'll bring your sister."
The folk are left
To pour out their tears.
We're left onshore
And the steamer leaves.
On the jetty a convoy
Marches towards us.
The pot-bellied "Adam"[9]
Rolls around,
And following him comes
The warden on foot.
He says to the circle:
"Attention, people!
Where's the clerk?
Hurry up the roll call! Now!"
"Erofeev, Andrey,
Cheremushnikov, Vlas,
Razuvaev, Erem,
Razdevaev, Pakhom!"
So goes the roll call.
Someone steps forward
And the warden says, "Hey there, chap!
You're clearly an 'Ivan,'
You have the look of a wolf!
Are you a *brodiaga*?" "I-am-Who?"
"Speak, rascal!"
"*Who*-am-I?"[10] "You'll see, you swine!
How 'bout an executioner? Then you'll straighten up!
I'll flog you dead! Do you drink vodka?"
"I don't drink at all!"
"If you take to vagabondage here,
I'll put you in chains.
Here, everyone up to heaven high
Submits to me...
Until you know the lighthouse..."[11]
The tsar's far away!
And I can give you a hundred lashes
Without a conviction![12]

I can punish you.
You're nothing to me,
I'm your tsar, I'm your God."[13]

"For God's sake," Paklin asked me, "publish my poems. Let the groan of a man who's been buried alive go to the people."

Such is "Paklin."

IV.

I came to know the *brodiaga* Lugovskoy under very tragic circumstances. He was in the isolator in Onor prison's chains division, thinking, "Will they hang me or not?" A clerk in the prison chancery, he had the day before flown into a drunken rage, grabbed a revolver, and "vowed before his colleagues" to shoot the former prison warden who'd come to Onor for his things. Waiting for a shot through the window, they didn't sleep all night in the warden's apartment where the former warden was staying. Lugovskoy was captured towards morning. An argument ensued. The former warden, exasperated and enraged, shouted, "You're spoken of well and they don't want to kill you. But I have a wife and children. You can't just sweep this under the rug! I'm going to inform the governor. *Katorga* is so undisciplined. Let him judge you for wanting to kill me. *Katorga* must be taught a lesson!" On Sakhalin, the penalty for such actions is death. The new commander, who was less severe, urged him not to initiate a case. "This was simply a drunken boast. Keep him in the isolator and let that be all!"

The argument continued for two days. Lugovskoy knew about this, and when I comforted and reassured him, he said, with tears in his eyes and morbid anguish, "If only it would end! Sooner! Sooner from this world!"

The crime that landed Lugovskoy in *katorga* is the same crime that Valentin, in *Faust*, is applauded for attempting. He killed his sister's seducer. Having ended up among professional murderers, thieves and human beasts, Lugovskoy, in his words, "took fright" and escaped... Under the *brodiaga*-name "Lugovskoy" he was captured and "resettled into factory labor," that is, sent to *katorga* again. Here began his unmitigated downfall. Lugovskoy has a remarkable hand and, at first, *katorga* forced him to produce various needed documents. This later became his employment. "What a point I reached! I would work for a ruble, for a half-ruble!" sobbed Lugovskoy, recalling the past. "And not even a half-ruble! I'd produce a document for a torn-up old hat—that's how ruined I was!" He drank, for wine was available to everyone. "But what else could I do? I'd arrived in *katorga* with that skill." He was caught. They flogged him with birch rods and lashes.

And now this "Valentin" lay before me on the sleeping platform, a writhing, sobbing, bloated human form ravaged by alcoholism. He was squirming and sobbing, "I want to be done with this world! That's enough. There's nothing but torment for me."

The new warden entered the fray. After two days the old warden's spite, indicative of past horrors, subsided and he agreed to a "turnabout" that, in essence, involved a deal: Lugovskoy's threats were recognized as having been simply drunken boasts, and the punishment for them was reduced to a week in the isolator. It was decided not to initiate a case.

I brought Lugovskoy the good news. He couldn't believe it at first, then burst into tears. He relaxed completely and sat up on the sleeping platform smiling blissfully and becoming garrulous. He talked and talked, promised to give up drinking, discussed his poetry and said, among other things, "But I'd completely taken leave of the world. I thought I was suspended in mid-air. I even wrote poems about it."

"Even now you're writing poems, Lugovskoy?"

He gave a confused smile. "When I lose heart, it's my one consolation." While speaking about poetry he indicated his mate, also a clerk, a sober, quiet, sweet young man. "Mention my poems to Grish. He has a little notebook of them. He has it because I hid it from myself so I wouldn't tear the notebook up during a drunk. During a drunk, I'm ready to destroy, tear up or smash anything. When sober, I'm a quiet, insignificant man; but when drunk, evil possesses me."

"Well, but what kind of poems are you writing now, Lugovskoy?"

"What kind of poems do I have!" smiled Lugovskoy. "You'd just laugh. I've really not finished my education. I still need to study, but I'm in *katorga*."

"Well, read one. Why should I laugh?"

From his pocket Lugovskoy took a shred of paper he'd written a poem on with a pencil-stub. "I'd awakened in the morning. Those last memories that remained, well, I wrote about them…" And he continued:

Friends, the time has come to say goodbye
To me with the light of sunbeams
And with death soon to be reconciled
Like a stream is reconciled with the sea.
The stream that will end in that stormy sea
Fears the gray-flecked waves,
He burbles and moans in ferocious grief,
But continues sorrowfully over the pebbles.
My end is in a sea of the living,
In a backwoods far from people,
In a country severe, in an expanse
Where the trial is conducted without a judge…

POET-MURDERERS (IN THE FORM OF A PREFACE)

Anticipating the noose, a man of nothing save *katorga*, never having in his life seen a poem in print, he wrote such a poem in the isolation ward of the chains prison. In the notebook I took from his comrade to read, there lay his entire life. Everything he saw and felt had been formed into consonances inside his head, often beggarly in form but always breathing sorrow and grief.

I present a fragment of one of his "letters from beyond the grave," recounting an actual event that took place in Khabarovsk in 1887 during the execution of the penal laborer Lëgkie, who'd vengefully murdered a guard:

"The Duty Officer"
Regardless of deprivation,
Of the difficulty of heavy labors,
The villainous guard pitilessly oppresses
The people all the more.
I couldn't endure… another moment…
I found a spare hour,
And in a moment of rage
Killed the guard out of sheer frustration.
So fell the victim of my revenge,
The blow was hard and true…
When word went round,
I confessed.
And there, friends, in a dark ward
I was sitting for six months,
Languishing, as before, in black thoughts,
Unable to see God's world.
Judges called for me there,
The priest came now and then,
But as to the reward they promised—
I knew of this beforehand.
Rifle-butts banged on the floor,
And so terrifyingly they announced
The words—thus I went to confession.
The priest greeted and blessed
Me as his son
And consoled me with kind words,
Wished everything for me beyond the grave…
Then the executioner with nimble hand
Laid the noose round my neck,
And wanted to send me to my forefathers
Wearing this disgusting rope.

But then fate smiled on me,
The greased rope snapped,
And breath returned in a moment
And life crept silently back.
I was not happy that my chest swelled,
I was not happy to see the white light,
For my spirit had already wandered
Far away, to where there is no life.
I thirsted for death as for a tonic,
Searched for it as if it were my mother
So that my ordeal would soon end
Along with my life…

His notebook is full of such writings, as is his life!

"A busy man," said Lugovskoy's warden, who was terribly happy for him. "An outstanding fellow. Gentle, quiet, meek. It's just that he drinks and goes into a frenzy. He shouldn't be allowed to drink!"

V.

Nowhere are poems written as they are in Russia. Ask newspaper editors and journalists how they receive poems written, for the most part, ungrammatically and illegibly. Nowhere are there so many autodidactic poetry hacks. Autodidactic poetry hacks from among the common people regard their poems as somehow sacred. Comrades tease them, often jeeringly, but are nevertheless secretly proud of them: "Here, I say, in our cooperative, in our warehouse, in our shop, there's quite a fellow! He can write poetry!"

Sakhalin is a drop of this larger sea; a drop from this same sea. A terrible lot of poems are written on Sakhalin. In the prisons the collectors of these poems—immaculately handwritten and often with ornate illustrations drawn on the front pages—archive them as something very important, very valuable, inside penal laborers' "storages"—the little lockers sitting at their heads on the sleeping platforms and in which they also keep tea, sugar, money, tobacco, relatives' portraits and, for those who have them, letters from home.

Only after I'd earned the prison's faith and complete trust, when I'd become well known to it, did I receive such a notebook for perusal. The prison was terribly interested. "Well, what do you think?" And the prison beamed with pride upon hearing from me that "the poems are outstanding and might be published immediately." "What people we have among us!"

For the most part, the poems conformed to the style of Koltsov.[14] He is the essential Russian folk poet, whose grammar is conversational. *Katorga* sings, as songs, a bunch of Koltsov's verses. When a man wants to pour out his thoughts and feelings his soul finds Koltsov's form and spirit most suitable.

In terms of content, a lot of poems were addressed to "it": to one's distant "home," one's "friends and brothers," one's "future grave." There was a terrible bunch of complaints—about fate, people, circumstances, unfairness. There was a pile of complaints about the loss of faith, hope and love. Occasionally, there was self-flagellation. All penal laborers' conversations possess a similar content.

Sakhalin was "created" (and terrific amounts of money have been spent on this) to rehabilitate criminals. The motto of the "dead island" is: "To rehabilitate and not to destroy."

If rehabilitation and revitalization are unthinkable without repentance, then Sakhalin cannot fulfill, is unable to fulfill, its assignment, for all that happens is so terrible, repulsive and foul that the criminal only comes to pity himself in the belief that he's being punished too severely, so that to him his crimes seem small and insignificant compared to his punishments. This feeling is entirely at odds with repentance! There exists within his mind the following notion (of course, not formulated simply instantaneously): "Crime is in part a great human invention, but to this day no crime has been invented that merits the *katorga* that's on Sakhalin."

In general, I don't believe in salvation through suffering. Suffering only makes a person bitter. It's not without reason that the most brutal and inhumane guards are former penal laborers. But apart from this, what kind of result can you expect when you stick a man in a cesspit? And Sakhalin is a cesspit. A horrible and loathsome pit, where people who are resolutely alive and people who are "barely alive" fall into the same pile with those who have decomposed or are decomposing. The decomposing weigh upon them. Such a community naturally suffocates the living, and no dead man can rise.

This is why life on Sakhalin promotes only self-pity and not repentance by any means. So it is. Ask anyone who knows Sakhalin well: "Have you seen among the penal laborers any contrite ones who might see in their own guilt a prelude to punishment on Sakhalin?" They'll answer: "No."

"During my entire time I've met only one—a wizened muzhik," I was told by a certain Dr P, a keen and intelligent man who's been serving on Sakhalin for a long time and knows it extremely well. "He'd been sentenced for the cholera riots, convicted of murdering a doctor. The muzhik was weak and sick, so I wanted to put him in the infirmary. The muzhik protested. 'No, leave me... in *katorga*. I won't be alive much longer, illness will lay me out and I'll be unable to expiate my sin. And I've sinned. We killed a doctor.' 'But did *you* kill him?' 'Who knows who killed him? There was a crowd of folks there and he got killed. I cast a stone...' 'Did you hit him?' 'I don't know whether or not I hit him, I just cast a stone. I have to expiate my sin.'"

Thousands have passed through Dr P's care, but only one of those he's examined in Sakhalin *katorga* was somewhat honorable. What is more, it's possible he was innocent! All the rest have just pitied themselves. And complaints are all that can be heard in their poems.

Here's a remarkable thing: among the improbable mass of Sakhalin poems, not one is about fugitives. There's not a single *katorga* song written on this theme. There is an old, now completely forgotten, criminal song:

> The alarm sounds. Count's being taken.
> Lamtsov had decided to rove.
> With tears he bid farewell to friends,
> And soon started smashing the stove.

This song remains unique. I seem to have collected all that's been written in verse on Sakhalin, and discovered in vain that—"Nothing's been written about escape?"

Escape—the convict's secret dream, last hope, sole means of deliverance, the prison's "most blessed thing"—but not only is it not written about, it's not spoken of. In prison the liveliest, most open and candid conversation instantly turns quiet the moment you mention fugitives. Regarding this, only silence is possible. They're too sacred a thing to speak of even in poems.

VI.

Sakhalin *katorga* has its own especially epic poetry. This is the "Onor Cycle" of poems recited throughout all the prisons. It's Sakhalin's *Iliad* and hallows the Onor project—infamous, senseless, inhumanly difficult and accompanied by horrors, mass fatalities and cannibalism. The majority of such poems bear the title, "Echoes of Hell." Often clumsy in form, they are absolutely terrifying vignettes.

I present you a fragment of such an "echo," attributed to a poet who is a serial killer who served his *katorga* on the Onor project. This poem was written with his left hand: in the tundra, work was so difficult and death so unavoidable that the poem's author took an axe, put his right hand on a stump, and chopped it off so he'd become "incapable of work" and be returned to prison. Such a terrible way of avoiding work was not uncommon during the Onor clearings. Here is an excerpt from these "Echoes of Hell." This portrays the clearing of the taiga:

> There, in blood, lies the murdered body,
> Beaten to death on the spot...
> He's been treated like a chattel:
> Dragged off to the side.

No one stopped to recite prayers...
He looks at us with reproach,
And only a raven, cawing from a spruce,
Has answered the summons to a wake...

And here's another excerpt, describing cannibalism among penal laborers, cases of which were officially confirmed during the Onor project:

Many enter vagabondage
Having been lured by their comrades.
But when they fall asleep someone
Strikes them with eternal sleep.
They murder and chop up the body,
Make a fire... and there's kebabs...
They don't remember him.
He's not the only one who's perished so.

Such pictures fill all the "Echoes of Hell."

VII.

Humor is one of the special characteristics of the Russian people. Alluding to the topics of the day, humor lives on in the world of Sakhalin.

Officialdom despises *katorga*. *Katorga* similarly regards officialdom. Various "incidents" among officials provide humorous material for *katorga* poets, because the life of Sakhalin's "intelligentsia" is filled with nonsense, gossip, slander, complaints and denunciations. They're all together on a knife-edge, each prepared to drown the other in a spoonful of water. Entire stories grow out of trifles, stories involving without fail complaints and slander, often with denunciations and always with official correspondence. This correspondence is produced in the chanceries by the convict-clerks themselves. As such, *katorga* always knows everything that happens in the chanceries; knows and makes fun of it.

I present one example from the mass of humorous topical poems concerning a terrible scandal on Sakhalin. This "story" happened because of... a chicken. A hen belonging to the wife of an official joined up with a cock that belonged to a priest's wife. The official's wife and her husband saw in this an "evil design" and turned to the police for help. The police appeared in the priest's courtyard and took "the incriminating hen" to a place of permanent residence. The priest, of course, took the policemen's actions as a personal insult. Letters were written to the chancery! Complaints, official replies, whole avalanches of correspondence came falling down on Sakhalin officials' heads.

I myself heard officials debate the "chicken question" for hours with uncharacteristic passion as they predicted enormous consequences. "They don't even know if the hen is dead!"

The prison wasted no time celebrating this in verse. Here are excerpts. The official's wife complains to her spouse:

> Akh, my dear, this is awful!
> I saw the cock yesterday;
> And that hen that sang,
> You'll remember, as often as the cock,
> Has truly disappeared! But then I
> Found out that she'd gone
> Straight to the little father in sin.
> And now the priest has
> A whole bunch of chickens…

The official "turns for help to the police," who hurry "to resettle the hen in a place of residence":

> Sweat poured down their arms,
> And sand blew like a blizzard
> From under their shuffling feet…
> It was becoming quite a mess!!!

At that moment the priest comes home and…

> Barely had he entered his yard,
> When what did he see? O, shame!
> All the police had taken off their shirts,
> Thrown away their sabers,
> And were stretching their arms like rakes,
> As if they were dancing before him,
> Bending down to catch the chicken…

"So ends the story, you understand," write the chanceries.

Officials are agitated and await "the consequences from the chicken." The prison scoffs and the convict-poet reads his verses. But in the henhouse, according to the poem, the following occurs:

> At that moment the runaway,
> Sitting together with the chickens,

Said to her sister-hen:
"Why did my old mother
Bring me into the bright world?!
I can't even go out for a stroll!
What can I do?
You hardly approach a cock
And behind you, you see
All the policemen crowd!"

Thus is *katorga* amused.

19

MENTALLY ILL CRIMINALS

In Aleksandrovsk Post—Sakhalin's "capital"—you often meet on the street a tall man, handsome and heroic, a real Samson. He has curly shoulder-length hair, is always hatless and ties a silver galloon around his forehead. A similar galloon encircles his prisoner's cassock; he carries a tall crozier. He walks about talking to himself, his expression noble and inspired. It's safe to liken him to a prophet.

This is Regenov—a *brodiaga*, and a lunatic. To the question, "Who are you?" he answers, "Mankind's son." "Why so?" "My father was a serf. Everyone called him 'man,' yes, 'man.' Father was 'man,' so I'm *man*kind's son."

In the past in Aleksandrovsk Post, when Regenov couldn't do anything right and ended up under supervision in Mikhailovsk settlement's psychiatric ward, he'd occupy whole days writing a letter "to mankind."

Upon meeting me, his first question was, "Have you come from beyond the sea?"

"Yes."

"Tell me, is there mankind there?"

"There is!"

Regenov shrugged his shoulders in bewilderment. "Strange! I thought everyone had died. I write and write letters to establish the truth, but there's no answer!"

"There is no truth in the world"—this is the centerpiece of Regenov's madness. "Because of this, even the king of France became a *brodiaga*!" he explains.

"How so?"

"Just so! There's no truth anywhere, and so he became a *brodiaga*. He calls himself by another name and wanders about."

"And you know this to be true?"

"It's most true!... Tell me, is there a king in France?"

"No."

"Well, there you have it. He became a *brodiaga*. Can you really live without truth?"

Regenov has a separate room in the psychiatric ward. Sea-shells adorn window-sills on which flock pigeons he feeds with crumbs. A dog he sometimes talks to for hours lives with him in the room. "You can't talk! But mankind says you have a wonderful sense of smell, so sniff out the truth—that's more difficult!" There are two decorations on the bare walls: a violin, by which Regenov extracts harrowing sounds from his soul during occasional moments of melancholy, "so as to awaken my wayward heart"; and, in a conspicuous place of honor, there hangs a small stick with a long string. To the question, "What is this?" Regenov answers, "A whip for mankind."

Regenov is very quiet, gentle and obedient; with the doctor, he's polite, obliging and kind. But the prison command hates him, regarding him as "a receptacle of all kinds of falsehood." This is one of the phrases that instantly sends this kind and gentle man into a tempestuous fury. He stands bolt upright when he hears "I'm your God and tsar!"

It should be noted that petty Sakhalin prison administrators go into a frenzy when a penal laborer utters the word "law." Heard from the mouths of convicts, this word induces fury. "That's not according to the law!" objects a penal laborer. "I'll give you the law!" a petty Sakhalin bureaucrat, beside himself, will shout and stamp his feet. "I'll show you the 'law'!" Moreover, they add their favorite expression: "I'm your God and tsar!" I heard not only assistant prison wardens but even senior guards shout this!

Upon hearing the words "I'm your God and tsar," Regenov's eyes go bloodshot, blue veins pop out on his crimsoned face and he screams, "What? What did you say?" He becomes terrifying. He's filled with such colossal strength that God alone knows what to make of it.

Another word that sends Regenov into a frenzied state is "Suffer!" Just the memory of those who admonished him in the prisons agitates him horribly. "You eat, drink, stroll about, but you can't speak. 'Just endure it.'" While speaking of these admonishments, Regenov became excited and struck his fist on the table so forcefully that he broke the corner off. It was terrifying.

Regenov's been in prison since he was eighteen. Before that, he worked in canteens under his real name of Tolmachov. But he suddenly became convinced that "there's no truth in the world" and, "like the king of France," became a *brodiaga*. "Regenov" is his *brodiaga*-sobriquet.[1] As a *brodiaga*, he ended up in *katorga*. He'd not killed or robbed anyone. To the question, "You love the truth, so tell the truth: are there no crimes in your past?" he answers not with indignation but astonishment: "Can that really be possible? Can that really be the *truth*?"

But, truth be told, given his colossal physical strength, he's caused God knows how many uproars, led an unbelievable number of "riots" and gone berserk a countless number of times. And so this incorrigible, wild, riotous, rebel-prisoner has suffered very many punishments! Such has been his past twenty-five years. Fleeing from *katorga*, from settlement and subjugation (for escaping) to the lash and birch rod, Regenov traveled through all Siberia and reached Khabarovsk. He was sitting in a tavern in Khabarovsk, when in came a police officer. Everyone took off their hats except Regenov.

"Why aren't you doffing your hat?"

"And why should I take off my hat for you in here? Everyone's equal in a tavern. We're all drunks."

"Who are you?"

"A *brodiaga*."

"A *brodiaga*?! How dare you even talk to me! Don't you know I'm your God and tsar?!"

The officer had felt compelled to use this phrase, current not only on Sakhalin but throughout Siberia. Lord knows what Regenov did next! "I beat him up!" he succinctly explains, recalling the event. As a *brodiaga*, and for escaping, he was sentenced to six months' *katorga* with corporal punishment, to be followed by forced settlement, and was exiled to Sakhalin.

He was now, with his temper and strength, among a number of dangerous convicts on Sakhalin. He immediately escaped from prison. And when Regenov, Korobeinikov and Zavarin (all three are now in the psychiatric ward) would appear anywhere on the road, soldiers were sent after them. "Regenov, Korobeinikov and Zavarin have left Rykovsk!" This was terrifying news, and when this trio was at large, officials were wary of traveling between Aleksandrovsk and Rykovsk.

This insane character really can cause a nightmare. Several years ago, he dropped in on the quarantine building, where a party of female convicts had just been installed to await distribution as cohabitants for exile-settlers. Regenov took a fancy to one of the female prisoners and she, evidently, liked this strong handsome man. Regenov decided "to begin living according to the truth." "It's better for a man to be united." He tossed all the women and their things out of the quarantine hut, allowing just the female convict who liked him to remain, and announced, "I'll kill whoever comes near the quarantine." Guards surrounded the hut but no one entered. Regenov couldn't have been taken alive and the assailants would have suffered casualties. They decided to starve

Regenov into submission. The siege had lasted several days when the female convict, weakened by hunger, took the opportunity to leave while her lunatic mate was sleeping. Regenov then nailed shut all the quarantine's windows, broke all the benches and sleeping platforms and exited, disappointed and burning with indignation. Since then, he doesn't even want to hear about women. "Can they really live according to the truth? They're just animals!"

Regenov visited me in Aleksandrovsk Post on the very day I was leaving Sakhalin.

"I came to say goodbye. If you see mankind, say…"

"Do you have the doctor's permission, Regenov?"

"No."

"What are you doing here? They'll catch you again!"

"No, they won't!" Regenov gently smiled. "I'm not worried. I took the precaution of knocking over all the telephone poles. (A telephone line connects Mikhailovsk settlement to Aleksandrovsk Post.) I went along the road and pulled up the poles so they couldn't report that I'd left. Furthermore, I even cut the line."

Alas! The lover of truth wasn't lying. This was true.

As a result of such acts, Regenov had come to no good on Sakhalin. So it was until 1897, when there was the first visit by a psychiatrist, "not assigned by the administration," and the building of Sakhalin's first psychiatric ward. The psychiatrist, after barely examining the "incorrigible" rebel-prisoner, said, "Lord! He's really out of his mind." He assigned him to his ward, which quickly filled. In 1897 alone, in just Aleksandrovsk Post, there were seventy-three insane penal laborers.

In the psychiatric ward, Regenov soon became peaceful, gentle and amenable; and rebelled only occasionally, whenever he came in contact with prison administrators. "I now try to keep him from all contact and conflict with anyone!" the psychiatrist told me. "To this day, many refuse to acknowledge that he's insane. But he should have been sent here twenty-five years ago."

After discussing the items hanging on the wall in Regenov's room, a short near-sighted man approached me. Myopia generally produces suspiciousness. Vaguely seeing that a circle is forming, the near-sighted always keep a little "off to the side." But this man's suspiciousness was most obvious. He slowly thrust a paper into my hand, muttering, "Read and administer legal measures!" Then he withdrew.

"Pomiagshev!" the doctor quietly said to me. "It's probably a complaint against me!"

So it seemed. Taking me for the director of the medical corps, Pomiagshev described all the doctors on Sakhalin "as universally and systematically taking advantage of the sick for their own mercenary advantage."

Every time I happened to have been in the hospital, Pomiagshev would creep out of some corner and watch while I spoke with a doctor. Now, after several days, he was giving me this paper denouncing them. It was addressed to "Sakhalin's governor-general"[2] and related that I, "director of the medical corps, collude in a mercenary way with the doctors toward the goal of poorly feeding the prisoners and expropriating their money."

Pomiagshev calls himself the investigative reporter "Goriunov," and produces within the psychiatric ward a handwritten journal bearing the epigram "*Cum Deo*"[3] and entitled, "The Biographical Journal *Exploding Shells*: poems, verses, songs and caricatures compiled by self-taught investigative reporter Lavrenty Afanasevich Goriunov." In the journal, he writes, "A powerful humanity is built out of weak people." You also encounter satirical lines, such as the following:

Odessan lawyer Kupernik
Is for all Plevakos[4] a tough prick,
He loves the rich little things
Filthy little people do.
Three thousand per hour, three thousand per hour,
An extreme pity this type is so few.

But it is in the denunciations of the "miscellany" section, the journal's main section, that he relates that, "having delicate and unclear but, for me, sufficient hearing, I've heard such-and-such on a certain day." There follow accusations against doctors, administrators, guards and prisoners for all kinds of "crimes and violations." All day long, from morning to night, Pomiagshev composes these denunciations and complaints in which he asks that "such-and-such be brought to justice and sent to *katorga*."

Following is how Pomiagshev was brought to Sakhalin:

He was a citizen of one of the cities along the Volga, where he owned a shack, fell ill, and began initiating cases against everyone and writing denunciations in an effort to obtain justice. His is one of the most persistent and insufferable manias, very widespread but little recognized as an illness in everyday circles. It's the mania of frivolous litigation. Who's not heard of such an evil! Sickened by this madness for frivolous litigation, Pomiagshev naturally saw everything that happened to him as a threat and renewed his denunciations against all and everyone. He went to the extreme of deciding there was "no justice" and therefore decided to draw "the attention of the authorities" to himself. He burned down his own home so that he would be able, in court, "to describe the whole truth of my accusations and make known there is no justice." But, of course, when he began rambling and talking nonsense in court they stopped him, found him guilty of arson and sent him to Sakhalin.

From time to time he falls into a persecution mania. Terror engulfs him; everyone around him seem to be "agents of Satan" and he himself suffers under Satan's powers. At other times, by contrast, he believes he has a special mission "to establish justice" and succumbs to grandiose delusions. He composes denunciations in which he announces that "all Sakhalin authorities will assemble at six o'clock in the morning and wait until I, the investigative reporter, give the thrice-repeated signal." These "ukases" that he promulgates "by command" are, like the denunciations, highly refined insults.

It's not surprising that Pomiagshev has had a very difficult time in *katorga*. A denouncer and litigant is hated by prisoners and unsupported by the prison leadership. He's buried all and everyone under denunciations and complaints. *Katorga* beat the life out of him and prison authorities "reprimanded" him.

So it went until '97, when the psychiatrist came to Sakhalin and at last brought him to the psychiatric ward. "He is indeed sick."

"In Sakhalin's prisons few in general suffer the mania of frivolous litigation," the psychiatrist told me. But crimes committed by those "drawing attention to themselves" in order "to secure justice" are more common than is thought.

On Sakhalin, I personally saw many prisoners pestering everyone with the most absurd, baseless complaints and denunciations and spending their last pennies to pay a fellow prisoner to corroborate such a complaint. The insane make the most absurd and fantastic charges.

"This is no good!" Pomiagshev was shouting as the doctor and I entered a ward. "No good!" With an indignant gesture he pointed to a patient who, the moment he saw us, pulled a blanket over his head. "This is no good! Why's this man hiding? What's being covered up here? What's the secret? Shouldn't this attract attention? Shouldn't this be revealed? Shouldn't attention be paid to the truth here?!" And, shaking with indignation, Pomiagshev ran off, probably to compose a denunciation. The "secret" lay hiding himself beneath the blanket.

This was Iushpanich, a peasant from Viatka Province. He really is a living tragedy. He'd left home for the gold mines and on the way back was robbed. His money and passport were stolen. This had such an unfortunate effect on him that he went mad. Iushpanich believed others were trying to rob and murder him. He decided it would be better to change his name, and began using pseudonyms. He was arrested as a *brodiaga*-without-passport and exiled. He's been on Sakhalin for three years. Here, having come to trust the doctor, he revealed his true name. An investigation followed but, unfortunately, they haven't sent him home.

He's still tortured by delusions of persecution. When a new person's in the ward, he sleeps hidden beneath a blanket. "They're going to expose me again and take away my papers. It's torture." Only after long discussions with the doctor did he agree to show his face. He passionately wants to return home and falls into melancholy over this. But he'd refused to identify himself at the time of his case.

"It's taking so long! So long!"

"Perhaps you'd like to tell this gentleman about your case?" the doctor asked him.

"No! No! Better not to speak, not to get irritated." And Iushpanich dove beneath his blanket again.

"This really is a terrible case. There was no one in the court, no psychiatrist, to reach the conclusion that this *brodiaga* who was stubbornly refusing to reveal his identity was, in essence, suffering from persecution mania!" said the psychiatrist, shrugging his shoulders. "As you can see, we have too small a hospital for the insane. On Sakhalin, you find many of them in the prisons and settlements."

Following breakfast at the doctor's, I met with Z—v, a former officer. The doctor's comment that "he's a very interesting individual!" had focused my attention on him.

Z—v was exiled to *katorga* for murdering his orderly. He suspected, "through the help of hypnosis," that his wife and orderly were planning to kill him. "I could feel it!" he explained. In court, he talked about hypnosis and electricity; but it was on the way to Sakhalin, while still in the steamer, that his lunacy became definitive. He distributed handwritten postcards among the officers on the steamer: "Regarding my measure of me… 'to' + my complete mercy = transcendental certainty. Your servant, N. D. Z—v." Every day, he gave the steamer captain notes on his discoveries and inventions, along with requests that he more quickly be given a million rubles. His earlier persecution mania had turned into grandiose delusions. He didn't spend a day in prison. He was clearly insane, so they transferred him directly from the steamer to the hospital.

Now he's a quiet and safe patient, goes about freely and pesters the Sakhalin leadership, and always appears on Sundays with compliments, "as duty obliges." From time to time he falls into complete simple-mindedness. He's little interested in the past and regards hypnotism with laughter. "That's how it seemed to me!" he explained with an engaging smile. "In court I said I did 'it' under the influence of electrical currents! But that's nonsense."

He's now "the inventor of the 'Paradox' machine" and suffers from romantic delirium. He believes that all the officials' wives and daughters have fallen in love with him, that "they arrange meetings with him through secret, complex signals," but hide their feelings for fear of opprobrium. In light of this, he writes letters to each of them in turn:

Dear Ania!
Fulfilling my earlier promise, I'm giving you 175 000 rubles. Today you attracted the attention of Z—v: me, the world's Olympian-genius lover. Immediately move into my home as a lodger.

Inventor of the "Paradox" machine,
N. D. Z—v
P.S. Bring me a horse.

His "colossal success with women," which he speaks of with pleasure, forces him to pay close attention to his appearance and to painstakingly comb his red mutton-chops.

"I daresay this 'inventor' is even happy!" the psychiatrist told me. "But… whatever the case, his inventing the Paradox machine has kept him from committing murder!"

These are some of the sorry shadows among those insane criminals stuck in my mind. If these lines cause the reader to believe that a doctor should play a more conspicuous role in court, then I'll consider my task fulfilled.

20

SAKHALIN'S MONTE CARLO (THE *KATORGA* ALMSHOUSE IN DERBINSK SETTLEMENT)

Blind amputees lie in the grass in a large courtyard, warming themselves in the sun. The shivering, aged, beaten and lacerated bodies of the "tattooed ones" (with the letter "K" on the left cheek, a "T" on the forehead and an "S" on the right cheek[1]) wander around muffled in rags. A stifled drawn-out cough, old men's profanities and curses and other sounds, come from open window vents:

"*Bardadym!*"[2]
"*Sheperka!*"[3]
"Brother's little window!"[4]
"*Atanda.*"[5]

This is Sakhalin's "Monte Carlo," as it's called by officials: the *katorga* almshouse in Derbinsk settlement. It's inhabited by paupers, card-sharps and usurers. Administrators don't come here. "They can go to hell!" the warden, a sufficiently educated man, told me. "They're the dregs of Dostoevsky's *Dead House*. Let 'em sink!"

A priest tried to appeal to them but ran away. "It's impossible!" Derbinsk's Buriat priest told me. "I went to them with holy water and they welcomed me with curses, mockery and abuse. You're performing a ceremonial procession, but they're hounding you from the sleeping platforms with foul language and laughter and punning on every third word you say, laughing the whole time. 'Geez,' they shout, 'you came here to talk down your nose at us, shaggy-mane, just to keep us from gambling. Get outta here!'" And he ran out. What a disgrace.

Every Sakhalin prison is a gambling house. But Derbinsk's almshouse is famous throughout the region. Exile-settlers from distant settlements walk or ride "to gamble at the almshouse." When a healthy profit is expected, the senior usurers get together and make "a nice big pot" of 150 to 200 rubles. Senior gamblers and twisters play without risk; the punter cheats as he can.

Prison gambling is absolutely and without fail unfair. "Gambler" and "cheater" are considered synonyms. The prison doesn't consider there to be a way of gambling other than "by advantage." A game is a competition between two cheaters: the croupier attempts sleight-of-hand; the punter substitutes cards. Each keeps a steady eye on the other.

Derbinsk's almshouse produces huge losers. Before my eyes, an exile-settler who'd come to play lost everything: his house, telega, the clothes on his back. He got some rags in an "exchange," and left a pauper.

The filth and stink in the wards, where forty or fifty old men live together, is inconceivable. The old men complain, "They took away the soap we're supposed to have. They don't wash our bedclothes!" The bedclothes have never been cleaned and are unraveling at the seams. Prisoners wear them until they're sallow-colored rags literally falling off the body. The sleeping platforms on which the dirty, sick men lie are saturated with filth. Insects teem among piles of rags.

Inside this stinking ward they're playing *shtoss* on the *maidanshchik*'s platform. Old men stand against the walls surrounding the gamblers. The whole ward is interested in the game. The *maidanshchik* gets ten per cent from the bank for his cards and five per cent on every ruble the punters bet. In return, he pays each man in the ward twenty kopeks a month, hires a pair of cleaners to tidy up the ward at the cost of one ruble fifty kopeks a month, and pays a stirrup fifteen kopeks a day. The stirrup stands near the door and, if there's some danger, shouts, "Water!"; but if administrators are coming, "Six!" But administrators never come to Derbinsk's almshouse and so the stirrup, strictly speaking, does nothing. But such is the arrangement. "When they play, he stands at the door"; moreover, "you have to give a poor old man something to do."

The stirrup knew I was neither "water" nor "six" and so he let me in.

"Are they gambling?"

"Passionately!"

All the "fathers," the almshouse's usurers, were sitting cross-legged facing each other on the Tatar *maidanshchik*'s platform and following the croupier's and punter's every move. The game was high stakes, "one-on-one," because the smaller bettors had dropped out.

The *brodiaga* Ivan-Proidi-Svet[6] was dealing the cards. An old penal laborer with scars on his cheeks and forehead where he'd excised his "tattooed letters," he had tattooed on himself: "Almshouse's number one mark!" Evidently a warrior at one time, he was now enough of a cripple to be sitting usually in the sunlight, warming his old "broken" bones. A wreck, you'd think. But, for cards, he's reborn. For cards, he becomes "strong" and sharp-sighted. His hands were not shaking at all but were a machine; his twitches had turned imperceptible. He dealt firmly, without haste, laying down card after card with a distinct slap. He was dealing onto a small clear space on the *maidanshchik*'s sleeping platform, and was doing so silently and automatically, like a machine. "Win!... Lose!..." shouted the old men lining the walls. He didn't touch the money. The money was taken or paid out by the old fathers. His only concern was dealing.

The exile-settler, having just lost his horse, steadied himself. Blood rushed to his face, then he blanched but his lips turned red. He took a card from the stack, placed it under his money, and looked at it only when the "chance cards" were revealed. He was keeping his cards close to his face so they couldn't be seen. But surrounding him there was a "telegraph." Old men were looking at the cards and signaling what he had. Someone would wrinkle his nose or eyes or look into his beard. Proidi-Svet would look around, read the signs and learn what cards the exile-settler had. The exile-settler would glance from time to time at the old men like an angry wolf. It was terrible. He gambled with a knife in his boot top so that if need be, he could "stick" someone. The old men also had knives—one, in his shoe; another, at his side—just in case anything happened. There's no other way to gamble in prison.

Having revealed the chance cards, Proidi-Svet stopped and waited.

"Go on!" said the exile-settler.

Proidi-Svet laid down another pair and waited.

"Go on!"

Proidi-Svet didn't move.

"Three on the side!" the exile-settler maliciously said.

Proidi-Svet laid down a seven.

"Not that!"

Proidi-Svet laid down an eight.

"Go on!"

Proidi-Svet slapped down the winning six.

The exile-settler spitefully threw his crumpled card on the floor, shifted from one foot to the other, blanched, blushed, spit into his hands, shuffled the cards, took a card from the middle of the deck, split the deck and announced to Proidi-Svet, "Bet's under the card!" Proidi-Svet revealed the chance cards…

The game proceeded very quietly, almost silently, as the man lost everything he owned. Brief interruptions would occur as the exile-settler traded away his telega, his broken silver watch, his pea-jacket, cap, trousers and waistcoat, his shoes. The exile-settler spat unprintable words at the fathers, who spat unprintable words at the exile-settler. His possessions garnered him almost nothing.

"Don't put me in a coffin, you bastards!"

"Shut up, or don't come to us!"

"Here's a burial shroud for you, you sons-of-bitches! Take it!" They'd hand him the money.

All this time Proidi-Svet sat quietly, impassively, as if oblivious to what was happening around him. A complete machine, he'd been turned off. "Proidi-Svet—deal!" The machine started up again.

"Clear the cards!" shouted the exile-settler for the last time.

Proidi-Svet revealed a winning ace.

"That's it!" said the fathers with one voice. The old men began to wander off. "Easy come, easy go!"

The exile-settler went silently into a corner and silently took off everything down to and including his wool-knit shirt and undershirt. When he took of his boot and his knife fell on the floor, it was instantly snatched away.

The exile-settler donned some rags resembling a chasuble, pulled a ratty prisoner's cap onto his head and silently exited, walking unsteadily. Passing through the courtyard, he greedily gulped in the fresh clean air. His legs quivered like he was drunk. Leaving the gate, he turned and stepped forward, hardly knowing where he was going or why, his gait appearing more and more unsteady. A woman exile-settler approaching from the opposite direction came up alongside him, but then, frightened, she jumped away and for a long time watched the man's jerky, unsteady walk.

In the almshouse courtyard the fathers settled themselves into his telega and drove off to sell his horse.

When there's no extra money around, the old men play among themselves, gambling away their last pennies for one another's rags. What strange and terrible figures there are among these people, from whom all life has been torn by birch rods, lashes, prisons, *katorga*, escapes and man-hunts.

Fig. 43: Residents of Derbinsk almshouse

Take the old blind *brodiaga*... Boris Godunov.

"Why are you 'Boris Godunov'?"

"Well, that's what a certain warden named me when I was still young. There happened to be two *brodiagi* named Boris in prison. 'Well,' he says, 'in that case you'll be Boris Godunov.' So's to distinguish me."

"And who was this 'Boris Godunov' you're named after?"

"Damned if I know!"

Boris Godunov "will tell no one" why he was first exiled to *katorga*. Once on the lam in Siberia, however, he became known as "the people hunter." He robbed and murdered religious pilgrims. The old man loves to recall that time, and when he does his lips spread into a broad, sensuous smile. "Many of those pilgrims would go along the highway. That's how I made my living. You get to a spot and set a trap, sit behind a bush and wait. Along comes a pilgrim hoping to be nice, then another just the same, but now it's gonna be different..." The old man laughs. "You jump out of the bushes and go for the throat. You use a feather (a knife) or you throttle her or smash her skull. Done. You go through her things. Pilgrims travel with a bit of money that their parents in the village give them to buy icon-candles. You take a loaf of bread from her sack, settle down and have a meal."

"And where would all this happen—on the road?"

"Not on the road. In the bushes. You just grab them on the road. But then you drag them by their feet into the taiga. You can't leave the pilgrim nearby—she'll start stinking and they'll find the evidence. A rumor will get about that in such-and-such a place there's a killer, and they'll be afraid to go there. I'd do this in spring, but they wouldn't find the body till autumn, and so the women were still going there on their pilgrimages."

"And in summer?"

"In summer you wander about 'cause you got the pilgrims' money. But in winter you live with workers or else go and get yourself captured so's to sit in prison as a *brodiaga*. But in spring you head for the bushes again… I went blind 'cause of the dark and stink in the 'slator (the isolator)."

Though blind, he's still an old card player. He loans money and is one of the most pitiless of the fathers. He maltreats the old man beside him, through whom he plays cards.

"I daresay, don't they cheat old man Godunov?" I asked him.

"Hardly, it's probably he who defrauds them! He knows every card by touch."

Alongside him is the bane of the entire almshouse—Marian Pishchatovsky. Pishchatovsky is all of forty-five years old, a stocky, high cheek-boned, barrel-chested, *bona fide* Hercules. Government-issue underwear is always tight on him and his enormous muscles discernable through his sleeves. He is fantastically strong. Quiet and gentle as a sheep, he is an epileptic, however, and everyone flees in terror when he's seized by an attack.

It's owing to his illness that he's in *katorga*. In Pishchatovsky's words, he never "remembers anything" after his head goes into a spin. After being conscripted into military service he became terribly homesick, and it was then that his "incident took place." At some point ("I can't remember how") he beat up a junior officer. Once in *katorga*, he assaulted a convoy guard here. The guard thrust a bayonet into his stomach. Pishchatovsky has a long terrible scar on his abdomen, and the doctor can't imagine how he survived. Pishchatovsky bent the rifle. "I was terrifically strong in those days!" he says. It's been terrible for Pishchatovsky in *katorga*. During his paroxysms he destroys everything around him and the prisoners ("there's only one way to deal with me," he says) gang up on Pishchatovsky and beat him nearly to death, until he can no longer stand. In this way *katorga* prevents Pishchatovsky from perpetrating a tragicomic incident.

An official once visited the prison where he was being held. When Pishchatovsky is in a sensible state of mind, he is, as I've said, quiet and gentle as a sheep and ingenuous as a child. He is astonishingly honest, can't figure out the prison's money-lending tricks, and therefore utterly penniless. So a naïve idea popped into Pishchatovsky's head: "I'll ask this nice fellow for some tea and sugar." He approached the official, bowed and announced, "I'd really like 'to shoot' you…" It goes without saying that the response to Pishchatovsky was, "Take him to the chains! Put him in irons!" Pishchatovsky uncomprehendingly replied, "Why's he saying this?" The point is, in the prisoners' language "to shoot" means to ask a favor.

Pishchatovsky has remained astonished by this event up to now.

"Well, he thought you wanted to kill him."

"Why did he think I wanted to kill him if I said 'to shoot'? If we mean 'to kill' we say 'to nail.'"

They stuck Pishchatovsky in manacles and leg irons and threw him in a dark isolation cell. He suffered an attack in there and the doctors protested, "Why is he being chained and held in the isolator? He's an epileptic!" They transferred Pishchatovsky to the almshouse. He's now afraid to talk about his attacks. "It'll happen again!" According to residents, none of them can sleep because he savagely screams and curses all night. His face is kind and sad and he has a clever tongue. He wears an expression as if afraid something terrible will suddenly happen to him. He'll be on the verge of terror, when suddenly, "He beats us all up again!" say the old men.

"Everyone runs from me as if from the plague!" Marian almost tearfully complained. "But I'm really gentle. What do I do to anyone? I'm meek."

The unfortunate Pishchatovsky is clearly overburdened and tormented by this universal alienation.

The most interesting of the almshouse's residents, or *bogoduly*, as they're called on Sakhalin, are, of course, the tattooed ones.

Few exist. They're specters from the bad old days. *Katorga*'s ancient past. Back when they were still tattooing, the executioner would use a special instrument to make small incisions on the cheeks and forehead—"K," "T," "S"—and would rub black dye into the cuts. Scabs would initially form but then, after the scabs fell off, there'd be black letters. Over time, the black letters would turn blue; and it really is terrible to see these letters on men's faces. On some men scars have replaced letters because they've been excised or seared off with red-hot irons.

"Was this something they did to escapees?"

"No. Why 'to escapees'? They did it to themselves. Scars on the cheeks and forehead mean they cut their brands out. Whether they cut them out or seared them off with irons, they're gone. But so what?! You still have the same pattern! They're terrible to look at, simply not human."

Their histories are surprisingly monotonous.

Take Kazimir Krupov, a seventy-year-old man. During Nicholas I's reign[7] he was exiled for ten years for murder. He was to be in Kara for ten years but couldn't stand it and escaped. He was captured and had his sentence extended to fifteen years. Reflecting that "you come to ruin anyway," he fled again after two years. He was captured and sentenced to *katorga* indefinitely. "It was indeed indefinite. Forty-five years—now isn't that some term?"

Here's a complete wreck: Matvey Kirdeiko, a citizen of Vilna, eighty-three years old. He entered *katorga* in 1858 sentenced to twelve years for robbery and murder. Then, after two or three years, he escaped from Kara, received an extended sentence, escaped again and received another extended term. Finally, he was sentenced indefinitely.

"But how many times did you escape, grandfather?"

"Five times, maybe more. Who can remember now? I've forgotten everything. It's neither here nor there. I only know I'm sentenced indefinitely."

Here's Vraltsev, a seventy-year-old man, a peasant from Saratov Province. He came to *katorga* on a fifteen-year term, has served thirty years, but is still indefinitely sentenced, also because he escaped. "I was treated very badly, so I escaped," he said. "Now that they've put me in the almshouse they don't bother me. Indeed, no one bothers with me any more. I was bothered and bothered, then got thrown away."

Such are all their histories. Originally sentenced to comparatively brief terms, they nonetheless escaped and "pluses were added." In the entryway to a Sakhalin prison ward it's not uncommon to see on the prisoners' roster: "So-and-so 6 years + 10 + 15 + 15 + 20..." There are convicts serving "terms" of over ninety years who were originally sentenced to six or eight, that is, for comparatively minor crimes. Exact sentences of six, seven or eight years' *katorga* are given for designated crimes. But then, amid the insufferable conditions, people recoil from the horror and short-term penal laborers are transformed into indefinitely-sentenced convicts.

Cripples and amputees—this is *katorga*'s new living history. It's a history of excessive labors and punishments. Take this man who froze both feet in the taiga while on the lam, so that they had to be amputated. He lost a hand the same way.

"What were you doing in the taiga in winter?"

"Your worship, there weren't a life in the prisons!"

The difficulties convicts face when on the lam go without saying; but what should be said about prison life if people flee from it to the taiga during winter?

At logging sites in the taiga there would be numerous "icicles."[8] "You know our clothes. What kind of clothes are they? Are they at all warm? They send you into the taiga to haul logs and you freeze." After which, hands and feet are amputated. Many, of course, maimed themselves.

"What's this here? Was this a frozen foot that was amputated, too?"

"No, I did that myself. A tree was falling and I stuck my foot under it. It got smashed to pieces and they cut it off."

Or:

"I cut my own hand off. Put my right hand on a tree stump, chopped it off with my left."

"But why? What for?"

"To get out of tasks and punishments."

Sakhalin officials explain this away as convict "laziness." But people will hardly deprive themselves of a hand or a foot out of laziness. Anyway, laziness has never been heard of anywhere in *katorga*. "They give you a task you can't complete, then flog you, assign you to a punishment regime and lower your bread ration. Next day, you're even weaker and again they flog you and lower your ration. You become completely weak and can't fulfill any task. They flog and flog you—a starving man. You get desperate and either stick your foot under a wagon wheel or a falling tree or chop off your hand."

This is where the history of corporal punishment in *katorga* was written.

"When I broke the Easter fast Warden L beat me all night through to morning. 'Here's your meal to break the fast,' he says. Over yonder they're singing 'Christ Has Risen,' whereas I'm on the mare getting thrashed."

Is it any wonder that the people on Sakhalin, as all the clerics complain, give up on religion?

"They gave me thirty-five birch strokes over the course of a day!"

"How so?"

"Just so. They flogged me in the chancery. The warden's sitting there doing paperwork. But I'm lying on the mare and the executioner's going at me. Warden's writing away, then says 'Go!' There's the birch rod, then he starts writing again. I went home at dinnertime and all I could do was lie down. That's how the whole day had gone."

Warden K, who'd perpetrated this punishment, himself told me why this happened. "That's my system. It's simple: he's flogged and sent away. They know their place. If you're lying down for a whole day, you'll suffer!"

Isn't this torture? In which law is anything similar described?

"They thrashed me for two months, first on all my limbs, then on my knees and elbows. I couldn't lie down, I had to stand. For a whole month after the thrashings I was pulling splinters outta me. I was rotting. And I'm still rotting!"

They do indeed rot.

"Such were the punishments. In Aleksandrovsk Prison, when they were carrying out a flogging in a neighboring ward, one of the prisoners got up from under the sleeping platform and slit his own throat out of terror. Fellow lost his mind. That's how horrible it was."

This is also a fact. But the old men, hearing these stories more often than *katorga*'s younger generation, simply laugh. "So it was! Such was *katorga*! At Kara they had the Ragildeev era and here they thrashed us. They shredded the flesh!" They show their old scars and they truly are ripped-up pieces of flesh. "But that's *katorga*!" And the ancient men talk about *katorga*'s terrible initiation ceremonies from olden days.

In this horrible, fetid almshouse where everyone breathes with terror, they don't sleep except with knives under their pillows or the piles of rags that serve as pillows. They steal as well as fear. The old men always rob each other at night.

"Hang a few! They need to hang them!" complain the usurers, the fathers. "There ain't a single night you can sleep through peacefully. All the old men are talking among themselves, all saying, 'Get 'im once he falls asleep.'"

If some old man's died in the ward, the rest will descend upon and strip him of everything, leaving behind a stark naked corpse. This is typical. The old men who've stripped many a deceased complain, "You can't find any money on most of 'em!"

"I've stripped some twenty dead men!" one old man complained to me. "As if I got anything! They hide it, the devils! I've always kept myself near where the fathers are in the ward. So many times I bought myself a spot on the sleeping platforms in those wards. I spent all my money. All you're thinking is, 'Who here is gonna die and how're we gonna make use of him?' A fellow's about to give up the ghost and you're waiting, not sleeping all night. He gets quiet during the night and you gets near him—but no, he's still breathing. 'What're you expecting, Afanasich?' he says. This gets a laugh from the others. From not sleeping at night, everyone's just tired of him. You're getting more worried by the day that he might get taken to the aid station. But we don't tell anyone about them, because it's better for us if they die in the ward. Finally, the man dies. As he's coming to his end, nigh on everyone in the ward's up all night. We jump on him and find twenty rubles, no more, beneath his pile of rags. And that's all there is on those who own hundreds. They hide it, the living devils! So he dies, but no one can find the money."

The old men leave on the sly, to find a place in a field to hide their money where no one can see it. But when I was there in summer, one of the old fathers had been blathering away in the almshouse. Someone followed when he went to hide his money, and the next time the old man returned he found an empty hole. He couldn't stand it and hanged himself, perhaps several months before a death that would have come anyway.

So live these people, unless they're put in the "aid station" before ending up in a graveyard. The aid station is nothing like the infirmary. Not one bit. There are few doctors on Sakhalin, and so those from a neighboring settlement have to visit Derbinsk's almshouse. Usually a so-called "bandager,"[9] a former penal laborer barely trained in medicine, is in charge of the aid station.

Derbinsk's almshouse's aid station is a place of horrors, death rattles and depravity. It's a small room where twenty patients lay, eking out their final hours. Here among the men were two old women: Afimia and the one-eyed "Aniutka." Every day in the aid station Afimia and her "master," a blind paralytic, would hurl abuse at each other.

"There's no peace from them!" complained old men enduring their final moments.

"But you're dying, you old devils!" shouted the blind paralytic. "You're just wasting bunk space, you bastards! Die now. Only the living thinks about living." Both his legs had been amputated and he was fumbling and flailing about with his hands. "Afimia! Afimia! Where are you?"

"I'm here. What's with you? Eh? Go to hell!"

"Don't you dare leave. Where are you? Have you gone over to Levonty again?" On the verge of tears, the old man was venting his fears. "Akh, my eyes can't see! If I could see, I'd thrash some of you! Akh, you thieves! She's in cahoots with you all!"

"It's because of her I'm lying in the aid station!" he complained to me about Afimia. "Such a despicable old woman! She's not supposed to leave me for a minute. She costs me a ruble a week. I pay her a ruble and every day she drinks tea with me, always eats a white bun and drinks milk! But never so much as a 'thank you'! She's always running off to Levonty. He's surely dying, the cur, but is always hankering after another's woman. Afimia-a-a-a!..."

"I'm here. Don't scream like you're being slaughtered!"

The bandager happily houses the old man, a father wealthy by *katorga* standards, who pays him by the fifty-kopeck piece for the Hoffman drops[10] the bandager gives him for "greater stimulation."

Fifty-eight year-old Afimia competes against the one-eyed, fifty-six year-old "Aniutka." Aniutka is blind in one eye. The other eye is jaundiced and she purposely irritates it so she can stay in the aid station. The bandager lets her stay in the aid station because he enjoys her favors.

"I'll tell the doctor here how you poisoned your eye!" Afimia taunts her.

"Why should I go getting blind?" snaps Aniutka. "Look, I haven't told how you tear open your knee so's it won't heal!"

Aniutka, like Afimia, specializes in bartering her old body.

What horrible, loathsome, foul agedness! Derbinsk's almshouse is like shit piled up in the sun—and these disgusting, terrible, pitiful, wretched people have suffered so much.

THE END

NOTES

Introduction

1 As qualified by the following exceptions: *The Way of the Cross*, trans. Stephen Graham (New York: Putnam, 1916); *Judas Iscariot and Other Stories*, trans. Guido Bruno (New York: Guido Bruno, 1919); "Three Chinese Tales," trans. John Dewey, in *Beyond the Looking-Glas* (Moskva: Glas, 1997), 167–82; "Ivanov Pavel," trans. James von Geldern and Louise McReynolds, in *Entertaining Tsarist Russia: Tales: Tales, Songs, Plays, Movies, Jokes, Ads, and Images from Russian Urban Life, 1779–1917*, ed. idem (Bloomington: Indiana University Press, 1998), 250–59. The only full-length study of Doroshevich's life and career is S. V. Bukchin, *Sud'ba fel'etonista: Zhizn' i tvorchestvo Vlasa Doroshevicha* (Minsk: Nauka i tekhnika, 1975). For brief treatments in English, see Louise McReynolds, "V. M. Doroshevich: The Newspaper Journalist and the Development of Public Opinion in Civil Society," in *Between Tsar and People: Educated Society and the Quest for Public Identity in Late Imperial Russia*, eds. Edith W. Clowes, et al. (Princeton: Princeton University Press, 1991), 233–47; Charles A. Ruud, *Russian Entrepreneur: Publisher Ivan Sytin of Moscow, 1851–1934* (Montreal: McGill-Queen's University Press, 1990), 59–64 et passim.
2 Equivalent to a college-preparatory private school.
3 See S. V. Bukchin, ed., *Teatral'naia kritika Vlasa Doroshevicha: Vospominaniia memuary* (Minsk: Kharvest, 2004).
4 McReynolds, "V. M. Doroshevich," 234.
5 Ruud, *Russian Entrepreneur*, 59.
6 Frederick W. Skinner, "Odessa and the Problem of Urban Modernization," in *The City in Late Imperial Russia*, ed. Michael F. Hamm (Bloomington: Indiana University Press, 1986), 211. See also Roshanna P. Sylvester, *Tales of Old Odessa: Crime and Civility in a City of Thieves* (DeKalb: Northern Illinois University Press, 2005); Patricia Herlihy, *Odessa: A History, 1794–1914* (Cambridge: Harvard University Press, 1986).
7 Ruud, *Russian Entrepreneur*, 60.
8 Ibid., 64; McReynolds, "V. M. Doroshevich," 239.
9 *Russkii biograficheskii slovar' v dvadtsati tomakh* (Moskva: Terra-knizhnyi klub, 1999) 6: 362–64.
10 See Maikl Dzhekobson and Lidiia Dzhekobson [Michael and Lidia Jakobson], *Prestuplenie i nakazanie v russkom peseinom fol'klore (do 1917 goda)* (Moskva: SGU, 2006).
11 Andrew A. Gentes, "The Institution of Russia's Sakhalin Policy, from 1868 to 1875," *Journal of Asian History* 36, no. 1 (2002): 1–31; idem, "Sakhalin's Women: The Convergence of Sexuality and Penology in Late Imperial Russia," *Ab Imperio*, no. 2 (2003): 115–38; idem, "No Kind of Liberal: Alexander II and the Sakhalin Penal Colony," *Jahrbücher für Geschichte Osteuropas* 54, no. 3 (2006): 321–44.

12 A reference to the Great Reforms which began in the late 1850s and abolished serfdom in 1861.
13 *Zapiski iz mertvogo doma*, often inaccurately translated as *Notes from the House of the Dead*.
14 See Recommended Readings at the end of this book.
15 This census has now been published. See A. I. Kostanov, ed., *"Byt' mozhet, prigodiatsia i moi tsifry." Materialty Sakhalinskoi perepisi A. P. Chekhova. 1890 god* (Iuzhno-Sakhalinsk: Rubezh, 2005).
16 V. M. Doroshevich, *Vospominaniia*, ed. and intro. S. V. Bukchin (Moskva: Novoe Literaturnoe Obozrenie, 2008), 563. This eulogy first appeared in *Russkoe slovo* (3 July 1904).
17 Bukchin, *Sud'ba fel'etonista*, 76.
18 V. M. Doroshevich, *Kak ia popal na Sakhalin* (Moskva: Tipografiia T-va I. D. Sytina, 1905), 14.
19 E.g., letter to brother Mikhail, 30 January-22 February 1854, Omsk, translated in *Fyodor Dostoevsky: Complete Letters, Volume One: 1832–1859*, ed. and trans. David Lowe and Ronald Meyer (Ann Arbor: Ardis, 1988), 188.
20 Doroshevich, *Kak ia popal*, 26.
21 Quoted in Bukchin, *Sud'ba fel'etonista*, 77.
22 Governor-general from 1893 to 1898.
23 Doroshevich, *Kak ia popal*, 43.
24 Ibid., 44.
25 Ibid., 45.
26 Ibid., 51.
27 Ibid., 55.
28 Ibid., 79.
29 Ibid., 141–42.
30 Ibid., 129.
31 Brian Reeve, "Introduction," in Anton Chekhov, *A Journey to Sakhalin*, trans. Reeve (Cambridge, Eng.: Ian Faulkner Publishing, 1993), 27–28.
32 Cathy A. Frierson, *Peasant Icons: Representations of Rural People in Late 19th Century Russia* (New York, Oxford: Oxford University Press, 1993).
33 John Reed, *Ten Days That Shook the World* (Hammondsworth: Penguin, 1977); Hunter S. Thompson, *Hell's Angels* (London: Penguin, 1999).
34 The original title simply lists what is described in this feuilleton.
35 A. P. Salomon, "O. Sakhalin," *Tiuremnyi vestnik*, no. 1 (1901): 20–53; no. 2 (1901): 68–80.
36 N. Novombergskii, *Ostrov Sakhalin s prilozheniem avtobiografii i portreta ubiitsy Feodora Shirokolobova* (S.-Peterburg: Tipografiia Doma Prizreniia Maloletnykh Bednykh, 1903).

Part One

1. Portraits of Sakhalin

1 Named after Jean François de Galaup, comte de La Pérouse (1741–88?), a French naval officer and explorer.
2 *Mertvyi ostrov*—an allusion to Fedor Dostoevskii's autobiographical *Zapiski iz mertvogo doma*, which is typically translated as "Notes from the House of the Dead." However, this distorts the original Russian, which adverbilizes the "house," not its inhabitants, as "dead." Neither Dostoevskii nor Doroshevich considered the inhabitants of these respective places to be "dead," as (in Doroshevich's case) the following pages make clear.

NOTES 457

3 Japanese Principality of Matsmai, today called Hokkaido.
4 After completing their sentences convicts could join the peasant estate.
5 See Book Two, "Poluliakhov."

2. First Impressions

1 This refers to the governance of Russia before the Great Reforms of the 1860s that abolished serfdom and instituted other changes.
2 "Little Club" or "Little Numbskull."
3 *Platessa luscus.*

3. The Infirmary

1 Chorea, a disease of the nervous system causing involuntary muscle spasms.
2 *Brodiagi* were vagabonds, often fugitive criminals, who made up a distinct subculture in tsarist Russia and especially Siberia. They often adopted the pseudonym *Nepomniashchii* ("Origins-Forgotten") to disguise their identities.
3 Prison slang, from *zhiganut'* (to lash).
4 Cesare Lombroso (1835–1909), influential criminologist who believed that criminal natures were identifiable by physical characteristics.

4. The *Katorga* Cemetery

1 *Borets*, in Russian slang—a plant belonging to the genus *Aconitum*.
2 Sakhalin was administered as part of the huge Priamur (Amur River) Territory.

5. A Day in Prison

1 Like Dzet, presumably a wealthy (in this case female) merchant or settler whose name is almost certainly the pseudonym of a former *brodiaga*.
2 This pseudonymous penal laborer had been trying to claim the identity of someone registered in the exile-settler category who had probably died or escaped.
3 This often happens; informers are subjected to punishment "as a blind" so that the informer appears to be in the supervisor's disfavor. Often, informers suspected by other convicts even ask to be subjected to corporal punishment, "but that they'll be murdered." [D.]
4 *Kandal'naia tiur'ma.* Prisoners here had their ankles (and sometimes wrists) shackled.
5 *Tachechniki*—prisoners chained to wheelbarrows for punishment.
6 In tsarist Russia Moslems and Central Asians were collectively referred to as "Tatars."
7 Meaning they did not know either the Russian language or Orthodox prayers.
8 The title of all young Caucasians. The old are called *Babai*. [D.]
9 Bek is a common surname, from the Iranian word for "master."
10 *Kobyla*—euphemism for the executioner's bench.
11 "Times change."

6. The Chains Prison

1 *Katorga* had two categories of prisoners: *ispytuemye* (probationers) and *ispravliaiushchikhsia* (correctionals).
2 *Nara*—a plank shelf running along the walls and sometimes down the middle of a ward where prisoners slept and spent much of their time. Even if there were upper and lower rows of *nary*, wards were often so crowded that some prisoners ended up sleeping beneath them.

8. Workshops

1 The corvée imposed during serfdom.
2 I recall meeting a slightly tipsy exile-settler in Aleksandrovsk Post, who greeted me: "Christ has risen, barin!"
"He has indeed!"
The exile-settler doffed his cap, bowed at the waist—no, lower than the waist, so that his hands nearly touched the ground.
"Your most humble servant thanks you."
"What are you thanking me for, you strange man?"
"For a kind response. Yours was an exceedingly kind response." [D.]
3 *Bez sroka*, which literally meant "without a term (limit)." In actuality, this sentence signified twenty years.
4 Town in the Crimea.

11. The Isolators

1 The murder happened in Voronezh. [D.]
2 Russo-Turkish War of 1877–78.

12. "Reformed"

1 Balad-Adash knew he'd been sent "to tame" him. [D.]
2 *Khamy* were prisoners' subordinate sexual partners—"bitches" in modern American prison slang.

13. Two Odessans

1 Small numbers of Japanese seasonal fishermen and their families lived on Sakhalin.
2 The Buriats are an indigenous people of central Siberia.
3 *Chaldon* is *katorga*'s term for a prison warden. [D. In fact, "*chaldon*" carried several different meanings, as Doroshevich's later use of the word demonstrates.]

14. The Murderers (A Married Couple)

1 "Odin na odin," by Gleb Ivanovich Uspenskii (1840–1902).

15. Grebeniuk and His Homestead

1 In what is today southern Ukraine.

16. Paklin (From My Notebook)

1 The Zaporozhians were a Cossack host.
2 A senior cleric in the Orthodox hierarchy.
3 Cossack village.
4 The protagonist of Friedrich von Schiller's (1759–1805) play, *The Robbers* (1781).
5 This monastery seems to have been located in present-day Azerbaijan.
6 The *skoptsy* were a (in certain cases self-)castrating Old Believer sect often punished by the government with exile. Female *skoptsy* were castrated by having their breasts and/or *labia pudendi* excised. Doroshevich includes the following note about "*skopets* virgins" (*bogoroditsy*): "Such young women are not castrated; they have only the responsibility of attracting others to the sect."

17. Settlements (The Exile-Settlers)

1 Japanese were employed by the local fisheries. The reference to the mainland means the opportunity to work on the Trans-Siberian railroad, to which thousands of Sakhalin convicts were assigned.
2 Mispronunciation of *Rossiia* (Russia).

18. The Female Cohabitant

1 [*Sozhitel'nitsa*.] So-called are those *katorga* women distributed among exile-settlers "for the purpose of jointly conducting agriculture." That was the previous official term for it. Now, even officially—for example, in the *Sakhalin Yearbook* [*Sakhalinskaia kalendar'*]—it's called "illegal cohabitation," which is much closer to the truth. [D.]
2 The woman sarcastically uses the word *molchal'nitsa*, usually used to refer to a piously religious woman.
3 In '95. Women typically arrive in autumn. [D.]
4 Mound of earth surrounding a peasant hut and used for weather protection and sitting on.

19. The Male Cohabitant

1 *Fart* comes from the word *fortuna* and generally means "good luck" in prison dialect. A *fartovyi* is someone who's lucky. For women, "to go off to *fart*" has particular significance. [D.]
2 "Fortunate."

20. Those Who've Voluntarily Followed

1 A Sakhalin prostitute.
2 A "chirpy" [*vereshchaga*] is a fried egg. [D.]

23. Freemen on Sakhalin

1. *Georgii.* The Order of St George was established in Russia in 1769 to reward distinguished military service. As of 1856 there were four grades, the two highest represented by gold crosses, the two lowest by silver crosses.
2. *Golos Moskvy.* Vladimir Nikolaevich Bestuzhev was in actuality not officially the editor of *Moscow Voice* and the other newspapers Doroshevich credits to him; but he did play this role in practice.
3. *Zemstva* (pl.) were local ruling councils established after 1861.
4. Of which only three were based in Moscow, the other in St Petersburg. [D.]
5. "Pikovaia dama" in *Zhizn'*.
6. Fedor Nikiforovich Plevako (1842–1908), famous Petersburg lawyer and speaker on legal affairs.
7. *Vestnik ob''iavlenii i promyshlennosti.*
8. *Ekho.*
9. Filippo was a popular singer on the Petersburg stage. The date of her trial is unknown.
10. Having concocted a plan to turn Abyssinia into a Russian colony, the adventurer Nikolai Ivanovich Ashinov (who styled himself a "free Cossack") led an expedition to the region in 1889 that was ridiculed by the press. Arrested that same year by French authorities in western Africa, he was remanded to Russian police.
11. Between Khabarovsk and Vladivostok.
12. *Kirgiz-kolpakskii.* A reference to ancestors of the Karakalpak of modern Uzbekistan.
13. Henryk (Henri) Wieniawski (1835–80), celebrated Polish violinist.
14. Hector Louis Berlioz (1803–69), French Romantic composer.
15. Niccolò Paganini (1782–1840), Italian violinist and composer.
16. An ironic use of the legal terminology defining *brodiagi*.
17. Tsarist paper money.
18. "What is allowed the ox is not allowed Jupiter."
19. She is the daughter of a certain woman of the intelligentsia sentenced for arson. After schooling, she arrived to join her mother on Sakhalin and here become such a good "match"… [D.]
20. Convict laborers from Sakhalin were used to build the Trans-Siberian railroad.
21. "Tight-fisted peasant."
22. A prisoner's cassock bore a black diamond on the back.

24. The *Katorga* Theater

1. D. writes this in English.
2. "Zapiski sumasshedshego," by Nikolai Gogol (1809–52).
3. "Opiat' Petr Ivanovich!"
4. Archaic name for Russia, commonly used by tsarist-era writers for rhetorical purposes.
5. The Skomorokh Theater was a puppet theater with a long tradition in Russian performance art.
6. An 1879 comic opera by Franz von Suppe (1819–95).
7. Vasilii Nikolaevich Andreev-Burlak (1843–88), popular stage actor.
8. Fictional diarist of "Notes of a Madman."
9. "Sedina—v borodu, a bes—v rebro."
10. *Kakaia maral'!* Probably a metonym for the reindeer's antlers and, *mutatis mutandis*, identifying the old man as a "cuckold."

11 *Beglyi katorzhnik.*
12 It may actually have been composed by Ivan Osipov (1718–75), a robber in the Volga region who went by the pseudonym "Van´ka Kain," gained renown as a folklorist, and was eventually sentenced to death by Catherine the Great.
13 So prisoners call a "duffer," a "scatterbrain." [D. *Sarai* is Tatar for "shed."]
14 Doroshevich seems to be indicating with this exclamation mark his surprise at the irony of this line.

25. *Katorga* Actors

1 Mariia Nikolaevna Ermolova (1853–1928), popular dramatic actress with the Malyi Theater.
2 Liudvig Barnai (Ludwig Barnay) (1842–1924), German actor; Ernst Possart (1841–1921), German actor and producer.
3 The reference is slightly mistaken: Richard delivers this line after meeting with Anne, not Elizabeth. See the final line of Act I, Scene 3 of Shakespeare's *Richard III*.
4 From Kiev's Solovtsova Theater, founded in 1891 by Nikolai Nikolaevich Solovtsov (1857–1902) and others in the Dramatic Actors' Company (*Tovarichestvo dramaticheskikh artistov*).
5 Korsha Theater in Moscow, founded in 1882 by F. A. Korsh.
6 Famous actress, married to N. N. Solovtsov.
7 Nikolai Petrovich Roshchin-Insarov (1861–99), actor with both the Korsha and Solovtsova theaters.
8 Character in the comedy *Our Friend Nekliuzhev* (*Nash drug Nekliuzhev*), by Aleksandr Ivanovich Pal´m (1822–85), published in *The Word* (*Slovo*) in 1879.
9 Ivan Platonych Kiselevskii (1839–98), famous dramatic actor.
10 *Staryi barin*, another comedy by Pal´m, published in *Notes of the Fatherland* (*Otechestvennye zapiski*) in 1873.

26. The *Brodiaga* Sokolsky

1 A disreputable settlement on the island.
2 The *maidanshchik* ran the *maidan*, a combination black market and gambling concession.

27. Crimes in Korsakovsk District

1 We've already encountered the crime of this unfortunate "hero" in the "Chains Prison." [D. Note that Doroshevich has altered the story somewhat.]

28. Departure

1 From the poem, "Orina, mat´ soldatskaia" ("Orina, a Soldier's Mother"), by Nikolai Aleksandrovich Nekrasov (1821–77).
2 Zolotykh means "Of the Golden (Ones)."
3 Thus you can see that regardless of photographic identity cards, "exchanges" continue to the present day. [D.]

29. Real *Katorga*

1 In Russian, *Zhonkver*. Named—probably during La Perouse's 1787 exploration of the island—after Jacques-Pierre de Taffanel de la Jonquière (1685–1752), French admiral and governor of New France.
2 This is the exiled Guards officer, K. Kh. Landsberg, discussed in Book Two.

30. The Capital of Sakhalin

1 A reference to events associated with the 1887 miners' strike and riots in the town of Iuzovskii in the Donbass (see below).
2 The Trans-Siberian railroad's easternmost section connecting Vladivostok to Khabarovsk.
3 For counterfeiting. [D.]

31. Aleksandrovsk Post

1 Common street names in imperial Russia.
2 There was an attempted assassination of tsarevich Nicholas Aleksandrovich during his visit to Japan in 1891.
3 Director of the Main Prison Administration (*Glavnoe tiuremnoe upravlenie*) Mikhail N. Galkin-Vraskoi toured the island in 1894.
4 Quoting Vladimir A. Giliarovskii (1855–1935), writer and journalist. The line is from Giliarovskii's major work, *Moskva i moskvichi* (*Moscow and Muscovites*), a section of which was first published in 1873, though Doroshevich is probably quoting the 1881 edition.
5 *Sakhalinskii kalendar'*.
6 *Morskoi sbornik*.

32. Sentenced to Penal Labor...

1 These were all the possible *katorga* terms.
2 *Kreshchenie* (Christ's manifestation before the Magi), celebrated on 19 January.
3 *Voznesenie Gospodne* (Christ's ascendance to heaven), celebrated on the fortieth day after Easter.
4 *Troitsin i Dukhov dni* (commemorating the Holy Spirit's descent), celebrated beginning the fiftieth day after Easter.
5 *Blagoveshchenie* (marking the angel Gabriel's announcement to the Virgin Mary), celebrated on 7 April.
6 *Na parashe*. The *parasha* was a large tub used for human waste in Russian prisons. The word is etymologically (and disgustingly) related to that meaning "to steam" or "to stew."
7 Nikolai Stepanovich Lobas (1858–?) wrote about his experiences on Sakhalin. See Lobas, *Katorga i poselenie na o-ve Sakhaline* [*Penal Labor and Settlement on Sakhalin Island*] (Pavlograd: V. S. Lobas, 1903); and *Murderers (certain psycho-physical traits of criminals)* [*Ubitsy (nekotorye cherty psikhofiziki prestupnikov)*] (Moskva: Sytin, 1913).
8 Luga is a city near Petersburg.
9 "Vermin"—undoubtedly a nickname.

10 Nikolai Ivanovich Grodekov (1843–1913), governor-general from 1898 to 1902 of Priamur Territory (including Sakhalin).
11 Approximately 21 pints or 12 liters.
12 *Polovinshchik.*
13 Siberian-born ethnic Russian.
14 "Abandon all hope ye who enter…"

33. Who Runs *Katorga?*

1 Prison society's top caste, detailed below.
2 Doroshevich is pinpointing here the muzhik's ignorance of trial by jury.
3 *Shpanka*, convict society's "commoners," detailed below.
4 *Krasen'kaia*—a red-colored ten-ruble banknote.
5 The picaresque Bestuzhev, already introduced.
6 This is probably a reference to Dmitrii Andreevich Dril' (1846–1910), a justice ministry official and polymath with advanced degrees in medicine and law, training in psychoneurology and finance, and an active interest in children's welfare, who inspected Sakhalin in 1896. Dril' represented Russia at several international congresses on penology; and in addition to his travels to Siberia and Sakhalin visited French prisons on New Caledonia, leading to his 1899 book comparing France's and Russia's exile systems.
7 *Rossiiskogo navoza.*
8 *Navozit'.*
9 Described below.
10 Before 1861, regional governors ruled Transbaikalia and other Siberian territories as virtual satrapies.
11 *O pritvornykh zabolevaniiakh i drugikh sposobakh ukloneniia ot rabot sredi ssyl'no-katorzhnykh Aleksandrovskoi tiur'my.*
12 Odiferous resin produced by an herb of the same name.
13 *Odesskii listok*, the newspaper Doroshevich was working for while on Sakhalin. The warden in question here is A. S. Fel'dman, who sued Doroshevich for libel.
14 During the 1870s a series of central prisons was created throughout Russia for those sentenced to *katorga*. Even at that time they were considered temporary. As the Sakhalin penal colony developed, many of these prisons' inmates were transferred to the island. However, some facilities remained open until the end of the tsarist era.

34. Prison Wardens

1 Ivan Evgrafovich Razgil'deev was the notorious commandant of the Kara Valley *katorga* mines in Transbaikalia between 1849 and 1852. During his tenure a typhus epidemic reportedly claimed the lives of 1000 penal laborers.

35. The Death Penalty

1 Vladimir Dmitrievich Merkazin, military governor of Sakhalin, 1894–98.
2 Drums were used to drown out cursing and shouting by the condemned.

3 It's said his murder was wholly planned by the celebrated "Golden Hand," who came under investigation afterward but was freed for lack of evidence. [D. See below.]
4 This off-beat sentence suggests a sop to the censor.
5 Both incidents in Ryl'sk village. [D.]
6 A popular game of chance.
7 In Belgium and France, respectively.
8 A settlement on the Val'ze River near Aleksandrovsk.
9 This apparently refers to the town of Luga, near Petersburg.
10 He murdered a judge and his family, as described in Book Two.
11 This is Nikolai Viktorov, described in Book Two in "A Famous Moscow Murderer."
12 Roughly, "Captain-of-the-Beasts."

36. Executioners

1 "Tolstykh" translates as "Of the-Fat-Ones," meaning he was a member of Sakhalin's elite.
2 *Plet'*—a short, three-tailed, knotted leather whip which could, if intended, be fatal.
3 There was an historical basis to this rumor. Prior to the eighteenth century, Russian prisoners were sometimes held in earthen cells called "tombs."
4 Common attire for particularly audacious criminals and convicts.
5 The word for "butt" is *komel'*.
6 A city on the Volga River northwest of Moscow.
7 Giliaks worked as bounty hunters.
8 Kamenets-Podol'skii was an ancient city founded in what was originally Lithuania-Poland.

37. Corporal Punishments

1 By noting that these trials took place without juries, Doroshevich is suggesting they ignored judicial procedures introduced in 1864.
2 In Poland.
3 Variant of *samosidka*. This moonshine liquor, more commonly known as *samogon*, was a popular black market product in Siberia and the Russian Far East, where it was peddled by Russian peasants and Chinese itinerants.
4 A pun-filled name, to wit: *bard* ("bard"), *barda* ("distillery waste"); *bardak* ("brothel," "chaos").
5 From *gusiatnik* (goose-run).
6 "Vasiutin" might be roughly translated as "Your Shelter."

38. *Katorga's* Ways

1 The Kara Valley near the Shilka River in eastern Transbaikalia, where a number of *katorga* prisons were located.
2 In order: *krugobolotintsy, galetniki, karintsy, terpigortsy*.
3 Having left Sakhalin, I read in Vladivostok newspapers that the former footpath through the transit prisons had been replaced by rail transport in those places where the railroad has already been built; I read this and was heartily glad for the ill-fated "mountain-sufferers." So many folks have said thanks for this easement of the difficult journey. So much superfluous unnecessary suffering has been eliminated, so many of

the horrors that have occurred in these "transit prisons" are now passing into the realm of legend. So many folks will literally be saved. You will see what these transit prisons were and the commanding role they played in the lives of many penal laborers from my following essays. [D.]
4 *Khrapy*; *khrapa*, sing.
5 *Igroki*; *igrok*, sing.
6 *Shpanka*—a word typically referring to sheep or cattle.
7 Razgil´deev was then commandant of Kara *katorga*. This was around the time of *Dead House*. [D.]
8 Omsk was the capital of Western Siberia. Dostoevskii served his *katorga* sentence in the fortress there, as described in *Notes from a Dead House*.
9 Associated with the 1892 famine.
10 All those exiled for disorderly behavior who were pardoned and, instead of *katorga*, assigned to a settlement. [D.]
11 *Sukharnik*.
12 *Podduvala*.
13 *Stremshchik*.
14 Tsarist Russian equivalent of grammar or high school.
15 Russians traditionally offer bread and salt to visitors and guests.
16 Slang for a miser. See below.
17 *Smenshchiki*.
18 Those "taken away from the plough," as they say, are deemed completely innocent. But this is a term of contempt which *katorga* applies to all the herd. [D.]

39. Matvey's Trouble

1 A "Matvei" is what they call a thrifty muzhik in *katorga*. Neither a penal laborer nor a drunk nor a thief nor a profligate, he is, for the most part, a quiet, gentle, friendly and meek fellow. [D.]
2 The isolator. [D.]
3 They tot it up before dawn. [D.]

40. The Indefinitely-Sentenced Probationer Glovatsky

1 In western imperial Russia. Today part of Ukraine.
2 Voevodsk's warden, A. S. Fel´dman.
3 A tribal people of the Caucasus.
4 Two investigators were assigned to Sakhalin's peace courts only recently. [D. In 1864 so-called peace courts (*mirovye sud´i*) were established to hear criminal cases in rural districts.]

41. *Katorga* Types

1 "Prisoner's preference" (*arestantskii preferans*) and "to-the-death" (*v konchinku*) were, like *shtoss*, games of chance.
2 He's been in *katorga* for fifty years: three "life sentences." [D. Sokolov is described in Book Two.]
3 Russian newlyweds are traditionally sprinkled with vodka during wedding receptions.

4 Actually, Ivan Proidi-Svet (whose name means "Ivan-Walks-the-World") has heretofore not been mentioned, but will be encountered in Book Two.
5 Pliushkin—a character in Gogol's *Dead Souls* and shorthand for "a collector of useless things."
6 *Barakhol'shchiki*.
7 *Kruchie*.
8 Even in modern-day Russia, the notion of dealing in second-hand items is somewhat unfamiliar. Hence Doroshevich's protracted explanation.
9 *Tuis kolyvanskii*. Kolyvansk District was a mining region in Siberia's Altai Mountains. Literally, a *tuis* (var., *tues*) was a container of any size made out of birch bark.
10 *Obratnik*.
11 *Pogibnut'*—usually in reference to a shipwreck.
12 *Katorga* credited him with 32 murders. [D.]
13 This refers to these towns' nautical distances from St Petersburg.
14 Prisoners are always very polite in letters to each other. [D.]
15 *Krokhobory, kusochniki*.
16 *Volynshchik*.
17 *Gloty*.
18 *Sinel'nikovskii zakup*.
19 Nikolai Petrovich Sinel'nikov (1805–1892), governor-general of Eastern Siberia from 1871 to 1873.

42. Initiation into the Penal Laborers

1 That is, those who "shaved off" information.
2 *Lovkach*.

43. Educated Persons in *Katorga*

1 From Mikhail Iur'evich Lermontov's (1814–41) long poem, *Demon* (*The Demon*, 1841).
2 In Korsakovsk Post. [D.]
3 In Korsakovsk's chains prison. [D.]
4 Doroshevich is probably referring to *Faust et Marguerite*, an adaptation of Goethe's poem/play by composer Charles-Francois Gounod (1818–93) and librettist Jules Barbier (1825–1901), that premiered in Paris in 1859 and later formed part of the Bolshoi Theater's repertoire. At the conclusion of act four Valentin is stabbed in the heart after confronting Faust for seducing his sister Marguerite.

44. Talma on Sakhalin

1 In 1895 Aleksandr L. Tal'ma was convicted by the Penza circuit court of murdering his grandmother and her housemaid during a robbery and sentenced to fifteen years' *katorga*. After Doroshevich met with him on Sakhalin, he advocated his innocence in several articles he wrote for *Rossiia* in 1899–1901. The popular support generated by this publicity helped to free Tal'ma and led to the conviction of another man.

45. The Card Game

1 *Zamorskaia figura.*
2 *Bratskoe okoshko.*
3 Built in 1837, La Grande Roquette was one of Paris's largest prisons. *Moutons* was actually French slang for "prison informants," though this might be the reason Doroshevich identifies them as being "sentenced to death."
4 *Orlovo pole* (Eagle Meadow) is etymologically related to *orlianka* (pitch-and-toss).

46. *Katorga's* Laws

1 "Do what you have to do."

47. The Language of *Katorga*

1 *Prishit'.*
2 Originating during the seventeenth-century schism within the Russian Church, Old Believers often sought isolation in Siberia.
3 *Raskolot' arbuz.*
4 *Udarit' v dushu.*
5 *Lipovaia.*
6 *Pech' bliny.*
7 This and the following variations are corruptions of *stianut'* (to pinch).
8 *Ottyrivaiut.*
9 Which suggests he was a violent offender.
10 *Zasluzhit' verevku.*
11 *Lozy.*
12 *Manty.*
13 *Poluchit' nagradnye.*
14 *Poluchit' polniak.*
15 *Pchel'nik, sushilka.*
16 *Fel'dit'* (see below).
17 *Berut na fel'du.*
18 *Bit' khvostom, udarit' plesom.*
19 *Suchka.*
20 *Liagnut'... svezti tachku.*
21 *Nalit' kak bogatomu.*
22 *Nakryt' temnuiu.*
23 *Spidchidarnyi, skipidarnyi.*
24 *Zaskipidarit'.*
25 *Ognia dobyt'.*
26 *Ukusit'.*
27 *Priamoi, kak duga.*
28 *Sem' verst do nebes, i vse lesom!*
29 *Shishka.*
30 *Dukhi.*

48. *Katorga* Songs

1. An intentional mispelling of "Odessa."
2. Doroshevich's question mark.
3. "To ne veter vetku klonit," "Doliu bedniaka," "Vetku bednuiu." Aleksandr Vasil'evich Kol'tsov (1809–42) wrote about village life.
4. "Ukazhi mne takuiu obitel'," from "Paradnyi pod''ezd," by N. A. Nekrasov. *Lucretia Borgia* was an 1833 opera by Italian composer Gaitano Donizetti (1797–1848).
5. "*Khorosho bylo Vaniushke spat'*,"... "*Korobeiniki.*"
6. "*Sredi Danily brevna*" puns on "*Sredi doliny rovnyia.*"
7. I.e., Ukrainian.
8. Thus do they gather together geese in the village. [D.]
9. "Miloserdnye nashi batiushki."
10. Tsarist Siberia's northeasternmost region.
11. *Etapy* (way-stations) characterized the overland march route into Siberia prior to the 1880s, after which marching was largely replaced by rail and barge travel. However, Doroshevich was mistaken to imply that all stations had been abolished.

49. *Katorga* and Religion

1. I.e., "I don't need the paper for rolling cigarettes." [D.]
2. City northwest of Moscow.
3. Leonid Vasil'evich Poddubskii, director of Sakhalin's medical division, senior physician of Aleskandrovsk Post's hospital and also director of the meteorological station.
4. A reference to Anton Chekhov's 1890 visit.
5. At the "Sakhalin" company of coal mines, Maev's contract provides that he pay penal laborers an insignificant amount to work in the mines, but in essence this is serf labor: he can, as he pleases, send a worker either to the mines or to his own household as a cook or a driver. [D.]
6. *O tom, chto ereucheniia grafa L. Tolstogo razruchaiut osnovy obshchestvennago i gosudarstvennago poriadka*. The church excommunicated Lev Tolstoi in 1901.
7. *O pominovenii raba Bozhiia Aleksandra*. Pushkin's book celebrating the religiosity of Tsar Alexander I.
8. *Poucheniia o vegetarianstve.*
9. *O teatral'nykh zrelishchakh Velikim postom.*

50. Sectarians on Sakhalin Island

1. The Molokans were a pacifist Old Believer sect that permitted the drinking of milk during Lent (*moloko* = "milk").
2. The Dukhobors ("Spirit-Wrestlers") are another Old Believer sect, as were the Flagellants (*Khlysty*).
3. In Western Siberia.
4. Turukhansk was the name of both a city and territory in northern Enisei Province, in Eastern Siberia, where sectarians were often exiled.

51. Criminals and Crimes

1 In Aleksandrovsk Prison. [D.]
2 A report on this case of cannibalism was published by Doctor N. P. Lobas in the journal, *Physician* [*Vrach*], no. 37 (1895). [D.]
3 In Aleksandrovsk Prison. [D.]
4 Several men exiled for political crimes to Sakhalin, such as Bronislaw Pilsudski (1866–1918) and Lev Sternberg (1861–1927), participated in or even led scientific expeditions there.
5 In Aleksandrovsk Prison. [D.]
6 In Rykovsk Prison. [D.]
7 Isolator. [D.]
8 A gambling expression meaning "forward progress." [D.]
9 A prisoners' saying for a fellow who never says a true word. [D.]
10 "An inspirer of fraternal love" signifies a prisoner of hideous appearance. "To blow bagpipes" means "to start some trouble." [D.]
11 Pierre Alexis Ponson du Terrail (1829–71), prolific French novelist whose titles include *La Duchesse de Montpensier*.
12 In Tiflis. [D.]
13 In addition to the murder of an intellectual who will be discussed later. [D.]
14 Viktorov, after killing his lover in Moscow, mutilated and dismembered the corpse beyond recognition and mailed it by train. [D.]
15 A type of horse-race betting scheme.

52. Criminals and Justice (From Observations on Sakhalin)

1 This parenthetical subtitle may have been added to mollify the censor.
2 This refers to a mistress who hired this story-telling worker to commit a murder. [D.]
3 Doroshevich's question mark.

53. *Katorga* Labors of a Konovalova

1 In 1899 the Petersburg circuit court tried the peasant Anna Konovalova and several others in the murder of her husband three years earlier. Two persons were sentenced to ten years' *katorga* but Konovalova was exonerated of being an active participant. The prosecutor then asked for a retrial, during which Konovalova was found guilty only of not reporting the crime and sentenced to just three months in jail. Given this, it appears that Doroshevich has merely expropriated her name for use in this feuilleton, but did not mean to refer to the woman just described. Indeed, he uses it to refer to "another Konovalova" as well. It is worth noting that "*konovalova*" was a pejorative term for a female Gypsy or other supposed social parasite.
2 *Krestovskii ostrov*, located in St Petersburg's Neva River delta.
3 A Sakhalin settlement.
4 *Khramovyi prazdnik*—celebration held to honor the naming of a church.
5 After 1917, "Tallinn," capital of present-day Estonia.

54. The Most Unfortunate of Women

1 *Sashka Medvedeva*. Derived from the word for "bear" (*medved*), "Medvedev" is a common Russian surname; however, because Doroshevich intends both a pun and to emphasize Sashka's ferality, I've chosen the present translation.

55. Voluntary Followers

1 A city on the coast of modern-day Yemen, ruled as a British colony from 1839 to 1967.
2 Meaning 50 poods.
3 A corruption of "Stepan."
4 Voluntary followers (*dobrovol'nye*) were transported to Sakhalin twice a year, in spring and autumn, separately from male convicts.
5 The Sakhalin administration offered a small number of cattle for purchase on an installment plan.
6 An ironic reference to N. N. Nekrasov's poem, "Russkie zhenshchiny" ("Russian Women"), about the Decembrists' wives who followed them into exile.
7 This was O. M. Ellinskaia, wife of Boris I. Ellinskii, a member of the People's Will who arrived on Sakhalin in 1894. He had been sentenced the previous year to 20 years' *katorga* for murdering a police informant.
8 At the time, Singapore was a British colony.
9 This may refer to the 1897 visit by A. P. Salomon, director of the Main Prison Administration between 1896 and 1900, who disapproved of the penal colony.
10 Anton Grigor'evich Rubinshtein (1829–94), pianist and composer who founded the Russian Musical Society in 1859 and, in 1862, the country's first musical conservatory, in Petersburg.

56. Natives of Sakhalin Island

1 *Temnaia Rus'*. This points to an editorial mistake, since this feuilleton does not, in fact, appear in the collection translated here.
2 I've chosen to retain this russified form of the Italian surname "Giacomini" because of Doroshevich's use of the diminutive "Zhakominikha."
3 On the Black Sea, near Odessa.
4 Main prison of the *katorga* administration located in the Kara Valley, Transbaikalia.

Part Two
1. Golden Hand

1 Russian folk-dance.
2 A wealthy trading state in sixteenth- and seventeenth-century India.
3 A reference to the adventurous hero of a cycle by Ponson du Terrail entitled *Les Exploits de Rocambole ou les drames de Paris*, published between 1859 and 1884.
4 Doroshevich here juxtaposes two lines from N. N. Nekrasov's 1859 poem, "Ubogaia i nariadniaia" ("Squalid and Splendid").

NOTES   471

5 A reference to Harry De Windt and his book, *The New Siberia* (London: Chapman and Hall, 1896), in which he describes his 1894 visit to Sakhalin.
6 Corporal punishment of women is now against the law. This was one of the last instances. [D.]

2. Poluliakhov

1 *Publichnyi dom*, a sort of men's club where sex was just one of many services provided.
2 This detail contradicts Doroshevich's previous comment that Artsimovich slept with the key under his pillow.
3 Apparently a variation on "Val′ze," a settlement at the confluence of the Val′ze and Poronai rivers.
4 There was a large transfer prison in Khar′kov, in Ukraine.

3. A Famous Moscow Murderer

1 In his popular stories, Émile Gaboriau (1832–73) based the character Lecoq upon Parisian criminal-*cum*-spy François Vidocq (1775–1857).
2 Prostitution was legal and officials maintained registers of prostitutes.
3 *Moskovskoe Meshchanskoe uchilishche*.
4 Probably syphilis.
5 *V polugare*. *Polugar* was a burn-processed form of diluted vodka.
6 *Semitka*, which despite its root (*sem′*=seven) designated a two-kopek coin due to the fact that an originally seven-kopek coin was devalued 3.5 times by the currency reductions of 1838.
7 Technically, 29 June was the Feast Day marking the end of the week-long fast of Sts Peter and Paul. Today, this holiday is celebrated on 12 July in accordance with the Gregorian calendar.
8 Another mistake from the original publication, as this is the first mention of Viktorov's victim's name.
9 Many Russian boarding houses had common kitchens.
10 A contradiction of the previous detail that Viktorov opened the windows after removing the body.
11 *Panikhida* (sing.)—an extended series of rites to honor the deceased.

4. The Specialist

1 *Pan* is Polish for "gentleman" and "landowner." But there's also an allusion here to the wanton Greek god Pan.
2 *Paradniki*.
3 *Poezdoshniki*.
4 Prison warden Patrin was at that time the terror of all *katorga*. He killed a prisoner not long ago. [D.]
5 An Ivan can be nothing but rude toward a commander. [D.]
6 A reference to Greek statesman Theodoros Deligiannis (1820–1905).
7 Milner safes are world-renowned. Englishman Thomas Milner founded his safe company in 1830 and invented an explosive-proof safe in 1854.

5. Cannibals

1 In Western Siberia, where parties were organized for the march into exile.
2 The Onor project began in spring 1891 under orders from Sakhalin's commander, General V. O. Kononovich, and commander of Tymovsk District, A. M. Butakov.
3 V. I. Khanov actually had 450 prisoners under his control and who began dying immediately. The Sakhalin administration began an investigation in 1892 and Khanov and an assistant were accused of torturing and murdering prisoners. Despite making national headlines, the investigation dragged on until 1900, when it was closed by Sakhalin's military governor M. N. Liapunov on the grounds that the accusations could not be corroborated.

7. Landsberg

1 Karl Khristoforovich Landsberg, an ensign in the Sapper Battalion of the Life Guards, was sentenced to fifteen years' *katorga* in 1880 for robbing and murdering the elderly court counselor E. A. Vlasov and his cook Semenidova. Famous legal reformer and journalist Anatolii Fedorovich Koni (1844–1927) chaired the trial and later wrote about the case. See A. F. Koni, *Na zhiznennom puti*, 5 vols. (S.-Peterburg/Leningrad, 1912–29) 1: 266–84.
2 A euphemism commonly used to describe Russia's Siberian colonies.

8. The Grandfather of Russian *Katorga*

1 Near Tambov in central European Russia.
2 Floggings were often done in a market square.
3 *Chetvert'* (a fourth).

10. *Katorga's* Aristocrat

1 A common aphorism in Russian.

11. The Plebeian

1 "Little Blockhead."
2 Market district known for its squalor and criminality.
3 "Po passazhiru streliaet."
4 "Baku zakolachivaet."
5 "Ruble."
6 Bashi-bazouks were irregular troops of the Ottoman sultan. The word means "damaged head" in Turkish.
7 City south of Moscow.
8 Northeastern district of Moscow.

12. The Parricide

1 Slang for "robbers."
2 The storyteller's patronymic.

13. Shkandyba

1 Deformed.

14. Hired Murderers

1 Line from scene four of the 1824 play *Gore ot uma* (*Woe from Wit*), by Aleksandr Sergeevich Griboedov (1795–1829).
2 This could refer to any one of a number of towns in Imperial Russia.
3 *Poiasochka*.

17. The Educated Man

1 This both homages and parodies Dostoevskii's *Notes from the Underground*.
2 A reference to the "Going to the People" movement of 1874.
3 "Kill her!"
4 A reference to Henry T. Buckle (1821–62), who wrote *A History of Civilization in England* (1857).
5 High church cleric.
6 Herbert Spencer (1820–1903), British philosopher and author of *A System of Synthetic Philosophy* (1862–93).
7 A cryptic peasant saying.
8 See earlier note on Golkonda. As for "Gorel," this may refer to the city of Gorel'de, in what is today Turkistan.
9 Johann Heinrich Heine (1787–1856), Jewish-German poet whose lyrics inspired such composers as Felix Mendelssohn and Franz Schubert.

18. Poet-Murderers (In the Form of a Preface)

1 Pierre-François Lacenaire (1803–36) was a published poet and a murderer. However, Doroshevich is mistaken in claiming that his execution took place under Napoleon III: France was still being ruled by King Louis-Philippe in 1836. Lacenaire's case inspired Dostoevskii to write *Crime and Punishment*.
2 Paris's first prison, established in 1391.
3 In addition to poetry, Lacenaire wrote his memoirs and about his criminal case. His works have been reprinted as recently as 2004.
4 Afanasii Afanas'evich Fet (1820–92), poet of naturalist and spiritual tendencies.
5 These are locations east of Lake Baikal through which exiles were transported to the Pacific coast and on to Sakhalin.
6 Group of mainly French writers and artists who promoted the Symbolist movement during the late nineteenth century.
7 Written in English.
8 Written in Latin letters.
9 Prisoners' nickname for one of the officials. [D.]
10 This is the manner typical of *brodiagi* who don't answer questions about their status. [D.]
11 In Korsakovsk Post there is a cemetery near the lighthouse. [D.]

12 At his own discretion, the district commander has the right to give up to 100 birch strokes or thirty of the whip without evidence or a court order. [D.]
13 Sakhalin officials' favorite saying, very much hated by convicts. [D.]
14 See Book One, "*Katorga* Songs," note 3.

19. Mentally Ill Criminals

1 Probably derived from *regent* (regent).
2 Sakhalin actually had no governor-general.
3 "With God."
4 See Book One, "Freemen on Sakhalin," note 6.

20. Sakhalin's Monte Carlo (The *Katorga* Almshouse in Derbinsk Settlement)

1 "Criminal exiled to penal labor." K = *katorgu* (to penal labor); T = *tat'* (criminal); S = *soslannyi* (exiled). Doroshevich describes below how these tattoos were made.
2 A king. [D.]
3 A six. [D.]
4 [*Bratskoe okoshko.*] A deuce. [D.]
5 *Attendéz.* [D.]
6 See Book One, "*Katorga* Types."
7 1825–55.
8 Frozen corpses.
9 *Pereviazchik.*
10 A tincture of ether (popularly known as "sweet vitriol") invented by German physician Friedrich Hoffman (1660–1742).

BIBLIOGRAPHY

In English

Adams, Bruce F. *The Politics of Punishment: Prison Reform in Russia, 1863–1917*. DeKalb: Northern Illinois University Press, 1996.
Brooks, Jeffrey. *When Russia Learned to Read: Literacy and Popular Literature, 1861–1917*. Princeton: Princeton University Press, 1985.
Chekhov, Anton. *A Journey to Sakhalin*. Trans. Brian Reeve. Cambridge, Eng.: Ian Faulkner Publishing, 1993.
Idem. *The Island: A Journey to Sakhalin*. Trans. Luba and Michael Terpak. Westport, Conn.: Greenwood Press, 1977.
Chisholm, W. C. "Saghalien, the Isle of the Russian Banished." *Chamber's Journal* 8 (April 1905): 301–4.
Daly, Jonathan W. "Criminal Punishment and Europeanization in Late Imperial Russia." *Jahrbücher für Geschichte Osteuropas* 47 (2000): 341–62.
De Windt, Harry. "The Island of Sakhalin." *Fortnightly Review* 61 (January–June 1897): 711–5.
Idem. *The New Siberia*. London: Chapman and Hall, 1896.
Doroshevich, V. M. "Ivanov Pavel." Trans. James von Geldern and Louise McReynolds. *Entertaining Tsarist Russia: Tales: Tales, Songs, Plays, Movies, Jokes, Ads, and Images from Russian Urban Life, 1779–1917*. Eds. von Geldern and McReynolds. Bloomington: Indiana University Press, 1998. Pp. 250–9.
Idem. *Judas Iscariot and Other Stories*. Trans. Guido Bruno. New York: Guido Bruno, 1919.
Idem. "Three Chinese Tales." Trans. John Dewey. *Beyond the Looking-Glas*. Moscow: Glas, 1997. Pp. 167–82.
Idem. *The Way of the Cross*. Trans. Stephen Graham. New York: Putnam, 1916.
Dostoyevsky, Fyodor. *The House of the Dead*. Trans. David McDuff. New York: Penguin, 1985.
Eklof, Ben. *Russian Peasant Schools: Officialdom, Village Culture, and Popular Pedagogy, 1861–1914*. Berkeley: University of California Press, 1986.
Gentes, Andrew A. *Exile to Siberia, 1590–1822*. Basingstoke: Palgrave-Macmillan, 2008.
Idem. "No Kind of Liberal: Alexander II and the Sakhalin Penal Colony." *Jahrbücher für Geschichte Osteuropas* 54, no. 3 (2006): 321–44.
Idem. "Vagabondage and Siberia: Disciplinary Modernism in Tsarist Russia." *Cast Out: Vagrancy and Homelessness in Global and Historical Perspective*. Eds. A. L. Beier and Paul Ocobock. Athens: Ohio University Press, 2008. Pp. 184–208.
Idem. "The Institution of Russia's Sakhalin Policy, from 1868 to 1875." *Journal of Asian History* 36, no. 1 (2002): 1–31.
Idem. "*Katorga*: Penal Labor and Tsarist Siberia." *The Siberian Saga: A History of Russia's Wild East*. Ed. Eva-Maria Stolberg. Frankfurt am Main: Peter Lang, 2005. Pp. 73–85.

Idem. "Sakhalin's Women: The Convergence of Sexuality and Penology in Late Imperial Russia." *Ab Imperio*, no. 2 (2003): 115–38.
Hawes, Charles H. *In the Uttermost East*. New York: Arno Press and The New York Times, 1970.
Holmgren, Beth. *Rewriting Capitalism: Literature and the Market in Late Tsarist Russia and the Kingdom of Poland*. Pittsburgh: University of Pittsburgh Press, 1998.
Howard, Benjamin. *Prisoners of Russia: A Personal Study of Convict Life in Sakhalin and Siberia*. New York: D. Appleton and Co., 1902.
Kennan, George. *Siberia and the Exile System*. 2 vols. New York: The Century Co., 1891.
Lombroso, Cesare. *Criminal Man*. Trans. Mary Gibson and Nicole Hahn Rafter. Durham: Duke University Press, 2006.
McReynolds, Louise. *The News under Russia's Old Regime: The Development of a Mass-Circulation Press*. Princeton: Princeton University Press, 1991.
Idem. "V. M. Doroshevich: The Newspaper Journalist and the Development of Public Opinion in Civil Society." *Between Tsar and People: Educated Society and the Quest for Public Identity in Late Imperial Russia*. Eds. Edith W. Clowes, et al. Princeton: Princeton University Press, 1991. Pp. 233–47.
Ruud, Charles A. *Russian Entrepreneur: Publisher Ivan Sytin of Moscow, 1851–1934*. Montreal: McGill-Queen's University Press, 1990.
Steinberg, Mark D. *Moral Communities: The Culture of Class Relations in the Russian Printing Industry, 1867–1907*. Berkeley: University of California press, 1992.
Stephan, John. *Sakhalin: A History*. Oxford: Clarendon Press, 1971.
Idem. *The Russian Far East: A History*. Stanford: University Press, 1994.
Wood, Alan. "Administrative Exile and the Criminals' Commune in Siberia." *Land Commune and Peasant Community in Russia: Communal Forms in Imperial and Early Soviet Society*. Ed. Roger Bartlett. New York: St. Martin's Press, 1990. Pp. 395–414.
Idem. "Crime and Punishment in the House of the Dead." *Civil Rights in Imperial Russia*. Eds. Olga Crisp and Linda Edmondson. Oxford: Clarendon Press, 1989. Pp. 215–33.
Idem. "Sex and Violence in Siberia: Aspects of the Tsarist Exile System." *Siberia: Two Historical Perspectives* [with John Massey Stewart]. London: The Great Britain-USSR Association and The School of Slavonic and East European Studies, 1984. Pp. 23–42.

In Russian

Bukchin, S. V. *Sud'ba fel'etonista: Zhizn' i tvorchestvo Vlasa Doroshevicha*. Minsk: Nauka i tekhnika, 1975.
Chekhov, A. P. *Ostrov Sakhalin*. Moskva: Kukushka, 2004.
Dril', D. A. *Ssylka i katorga v Rossii (Iz lichnykh nabliudenii vo vremia poezdki v Priamurskii krai i Sibir')*. S.-Peterburg: Tipografiia Pravitel'stvuiushchago Senata, 1898.
Doroshevich, V. M. *Kak ia popal na Sakhalin*. Moskva: Tipografiia T-va I. D. Sytina, 1905.
Idem. *Sakhalin (Katorga)*. 2 vols. Moskva: I. D. Sytin, 1903.
Idem. *Teatral'naia kritika Vlasa Doroshevicha: Vospominaniia memuary*. Ed. S. V. Bukchin. Minsk: Kharvest, 2004.
Idem. *Vospominaniia*. Ed. and intro. S. V. Bukchin. Moskva: Novoe Literaturnoe Obozrenie, 2008.
Dzhekobson, Maikl, and Lidiia Dzhekobson [Michael and Lidia Jakobson]. *Prestuplenie i nakazanie v russkom peseinom fol'klore (do 1917 goda)*. Moskva: SGU, 2006.

Fel'dstein, G. S. *Ssylka: eia genezisa, znacheniia, istorii i sovremennogo sostoianiia*. Moskva: T-vo skoropechatni A. A. Levenson, 1893.

Foinitskii, I. Ia. *Uchenie o nakazanii v sviazi s tiur'movedeniem*. S.-Peterburg: Tipografiia Ministerstva putei soobshcheniia (A. Benke), 1889.

Iadrintsev, N. M. *Sibir' kak koloniia: k iubileiu trekhsotletiia. Sovremennoe polozhenie Sibiri. Eia nuzhdy i potrebnosti. Eia proshloe i budushchee*. Sanktpeterburg: Tipografiia M. M. Stasiulevicha, 1882.

Idem. *Russkaia obshchina v tiur'me i ssylke*. S.-Peterburg: Tipografiia A. Morigerovskago, 1872.

Iakubovich, P. F. *V mire otverzhennykh: zapiski byvshago katorzhnika*. 2 vols. Moskva and Leningrad: Khudozhestvennaia literature, 1964.

Ishchenko, Marina Ivanovna. "Formirovanie postoiannogo russkogo naseleniia Sakhalina (konets XIX—nachalo XX v.)." *Sovetskaia etnografiia*, no. 3 (1991): 102–11.

Kostanov, A. I. (ed.). *"Byt' mozhet, prigodiatsia i moi tsifry." Materialty Sakhalinskoi perepisi A. P. Chekhova. 1890 god*. Iuzhno-Sakhalinsk: Rubezh, 2005.

Idem. *Gubernatory Sakhalina*. Iuzhno-Sakhalinsk: Arkhivnyi otdel administratsii Sakhalinskoi oblasti, 2000.

Idem. *Osvoenie Sakhalina russkimi liudmi*. Iuzhno-Sakhalinsk: Dal'nevostochnoe knizhnoe izdatel'stvo Sakhalinskoe otdelenie, 1991.

Lobas, N. S. *Katorga i poselenie na o-ve Sakhaline*. Pavlograd: V. S. Lobas, 1903.

Idem. *Ubiitsy (Nekotorye cherty psikhofiziki prestupnikov)*. Moskva: SGA, 2008.

Maksimov, S. *Sibir' i katorga*. 3 vols. S.-Peterburg: Tipografiia A. Transhelia, 1871.

Miroliubov, I. P. *Vosem' let na Sakhaline*. S-Peterburg: Tipografiia A. S. Suvorina, 1901.

Novombergskii, N. *Ostrov Sakhalin s prilozheniem avtobiografii i portreta ubiitsy Feodora Shirokolobova*. S.-Peterburg: Tipografiia Doma Prizreniia Maloletnykh Bednykh, 1903.

Panov, A. A. *Sakhalin kak koloniia: Ocherki kolonizatsii i sovremennago polozheniia Sakhalina*. Moskva: I. D. Sytin, 1905.

Poliakov, I. S. *Puteshestvie na ostrov Sakhalin v 1881–1882 gg*. S.-Peterburg: Tipografiia A.S. Suvorina, 1883.

Salomon, A. P. "O. Sakhalin." *Tiuremnyi vestnik*, no. 1 (1901): 20–53; no. 2 (1901): 68–80.

GLOSSARY

Barin—master, lord
Brodiaga—vagabond
Chaldon—variously meaning prison warden, Siberian-born Russian, settled resident
Droshky—anglicization of *drozhki*, a carriage
Katorga—penal labor (and see Introduction)
Pood—anglicization of *pud*, unit of measure equal to 16.38 kg. or 36 lb.
Taiga—forest
Tarantass—anglicization of *tarantas*, a springless carriage
Telega—wagon
Tundra—permafrost
Verst—anglicization of *versta*, unit of measure equal to 1.06 km or 0.66 mi

www.ingramcontent.com/pod-product-compliance
Lightning Source LLC
Chambersburg PA
CBHW030103010526
44116CB00005B/72